MICROPROCESSOR INTERFACING

Written by: Professor Andrew C. Staugaard, Jr.
Computer Science Dept.
The School of the Ozarks

Book 2

Model EB-6402
HEATH COMPANY
BENTON HARBOR, MICHIGAN 49022
595-2944-05

ISBN 0-87119-077-X

Unit 7

THE 6809 ADVANCED MICROPROCESSOR

CONTENTS

INTRODUCTION

Up to this point, your microprocessor software knowledge has been limited essentially to the 6800 instruction set and its addressing modes. Devices that are upward compatible with the 6800, like the 6801, enhance the 6800 software capabilities, but do not drastically improve its efficiency.

As personal and small business computers became popular, a need for a high performance 8-bit microprocessor quickly became a reality. Such a device must be capable of efficiently implementing high level computer languages like BASIC, PASCAL, COBOL, and FORTRAN. In addition, earlier processors, like the 6800, are incapable of efficiently providing high resolution color graphics–a very desirable feature in small systems.

Thus, this unit is designed to acquaint you with the 6809 advanced microprocessor. As you will soon discover, the 6809 was designed to meet all the requirements of a high performance 8-bit microprocessor. You will study the 6809 instruction set and its very powerful addressing modes. Then, you will be introduced to the I/O lines of both the 6809 and its sister, the 6809E.

UNIT OBJECTIVES

When you complete this unit, you should be able to:

1. Describe the internal CPU register structure of the 6809.
2. Define position independence.
3. List the four instruction categories of the 6809 instruction set.
4. Describe the operations of the major 6809 instructions.
5. List the eight fundamental addressing modes of the 6809.
6. Interpret 6809 instruction source code.
7. Write 6809 instruction source code, given a software task.
8. Determine post byte values required for various 6809 operations.
9. State the basic functions of the 6809 and 6809E I/O lines.
10. Describe the differences between the 6809 and 6809E.
11. State the basic functions of three new support devices designed for the 6809 and 6809E.

THE 6809 REGISTER STRUCTURE AND INSTRUCTION SET

Before we begin a detailed discussion, we will take a general look at the 6809. First, the 6809 is a **high performance 8-bit microprocessor.** It does not contain internal hardware features like the 6801 or 6805 and, therefore, cannot be classified as a microcomputer by itself. Thus, the 6809 requires external RAM, ROM, and I/O support before it can function as a microcomputer.

As we mentioned in Unit 6, the 6809 was designed primarily for the microcomputer systems market. It contains an enhanced 6800 CPU register structure, instruction set, and several new addressing modes. These enhancements make the 6809 a very efficient device for implementing higher level program languages such as **BASIC, PASCAL, FORTRAN,** and **COBOL.**

Many people say that the 6809 is a "souped-up" 6800. This is true to some extent. Before the 6809 was developed, a survey of 6800 users was conducted; and many of their suggestions were incorporated into the design of the 6809. As far as computing power is concerned, you might say that comparing the 6809 to the 6800 is like comparing the power of an eight-cylinder automobile engine to a four-cylinder engine. The 6809 is compared to several popular 8-bit microprocessors in Figure 7-1.

Performance Criteria	MC6809	Z-80A	MC6800	8085
Number of Instructions	1.0*	1.56	1.72	2.30
Number of Bytes	1.0	1.31	1.58	1.80
Number of Microseconds	1.0	1.80	2.40	2.20
	(2 MHz)	(4 MHz)	(2 MHz)	(5 MHz)

*Normalized to 1.00 for the MC6809 — poorer performance has higher numbers.

Figure 7-1

Comparing the 6809 to several popular 8-bit microprocessors. (Data supplied by Motorola, Inc.)

A major result of the 6800 user survey mentioned above was that many small systems designers wanted an 8-bit device that approached the performance of a 16-bit device. They did not want to convert to a 16-bit design if such an 8-bit device were available. This makes sense because many existing 8-bit system designs could be easily upgraded to use a high performance 8-bit MPU like the 6809. However, a new system designed around a 16-bit MPU would require new support devices, peripherals, production fixtures, test fixtures, etc. This is a major reason why many of the newer personal and small business computing systems are using a high performance 8-bit microprocessor like the 6809, rather than a 16-bit microprocessor. Again, **the application dictates.** For comparison, a performance scale of several popular 8-bit and 16-bit microprocessors is provided in Figure 7-2. Note that the 6809 approaches the performance of many 16-bit devices.

Now, let's see what makes the 6809 a very high performance device. In this section, we will discuss the 6809 register structure and instruction set. Although the 6809 is not directly compatible with the 6800, you will find your knowledge of the 6800 to be very helpful in understanding the subsequent material.

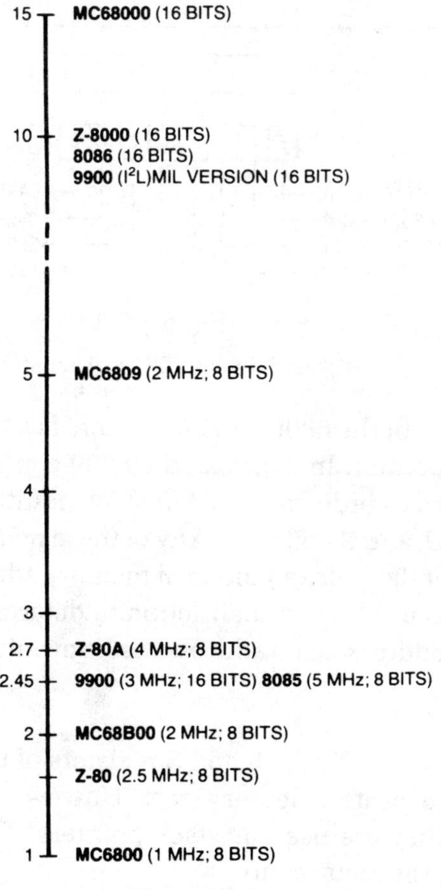

Figure 7-2

Relative performance of several popular 8- and 16-bit microprocessors. (Data supplied by Motorola, Inc.)

The 6809 Register Structure

The internal CPU register structure of the 6809 is shown in Figure 7-3. You will note that the accumulator structure of the 6809 is identical to that of the 6801. There are two 8-bit accumulators, A and B, and a 16-bit accumulator D. Accumulator A forms the high byte of D, and accumulator B forms the low byte of D.

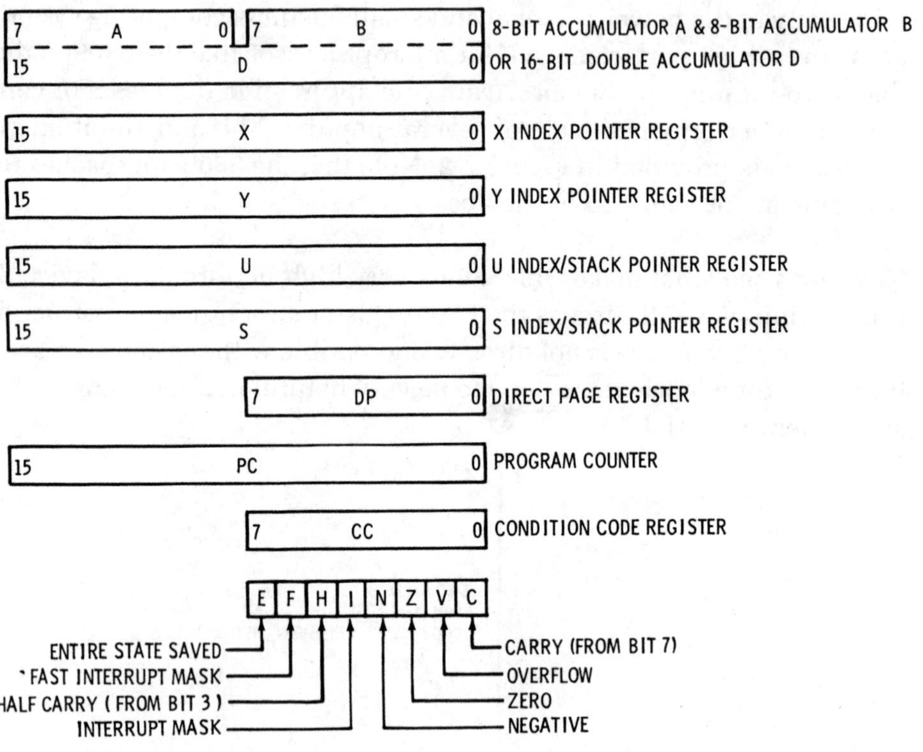

Figure 7-3

The internal 6809 CPU register structure.

Recall that, in the 6800 and 6801, there is a 16-bit index register and a 16-bit stack pointer. In contrast, the 6809 contains four 16-bit registers that can be used as index registers **or** stack pointers. These registers are called the **X, Y, U,** and **S** registers. Any of these registers can be used as a **pointer** register for the indexed mode of memory addressing. A pointer register is one that is used by an instruction to determine an **effective address.** An effective address is the address that is eventually accessed by the instruction.

In addition, the X, Y, U, and S registers of the 6809 can be used as stack pointers to locate a memory stack. However, there are some differences in the way they are used as stack pointers. These differences will be discussed in the next section.

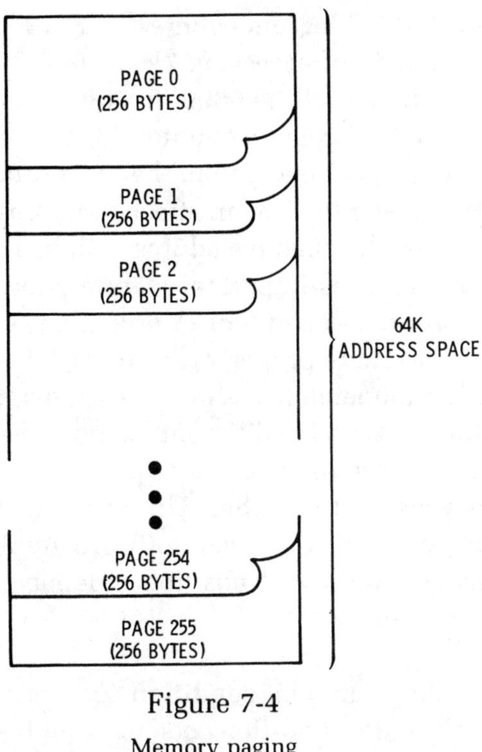

Figure 7-4
Memory paging

The 6809 contains an 8-bit register called the **direct page,** or **DP,** register. The direct page register is used for the direct mode of memory addressing. It is used to form the high byte of the effective address when direct addressing is specified.

Like the 6800, the 6809 is capable of addressing a 64K address space. You can break this space up into 256 **pages,** with each page containing 256 bytes as illustrated in Figure 7-4. The first page, labeled page 0, contains the first 256 bytes of the address map. The second page, labeled page 1, contains the second 256 bytes of the address map, and so on, until the last page, labeled page 255, contains the last 256 bytes of the address map. In higher level programming, it is often convenient to locate various subroutines and interrupt service routines on separate memory pages. With the 6809, the direct page register is used to define the page and, thus, locate a subroutine or service routine during the direct mode of addressing. Recall that, with the 6800, you can only access the first 256 addresses, or page 0, using direct addressing. However, with the 6809, you can use the direct page register with direct addressing to access any 256 byte block of addresses within the entire 64K address space. You will see how the direct page register is used with direct addressing in the next section.

The 6809 contains a 16-bit **program counter,** or **PC.** Thus, as mentioned above, the 6809 is capable of accessing 2^{16}, or 64K, addresses. On the surface, you might assume that the 6809 program counter performs the same functions as the 6800 program counter. This assumption is almost true, with one very important exception: the 6809 program counter can be used as a pointer register to form an effective address for many of the 6809 instructions. Thus, the effective address can be **relative** to the program counter's contents. This important feature allows 6809 programs to be completely **position independent**. A program is said to be position independent if it will execute properly, regardless of where it is located in memory. Position independence allows programs to be executed on different systems that might have different memory maps. A completely position-independent program doesn't require any alterations when transferred from one system to another. This is a very important feature, especially for high level standardized software implementation. The next section discusses more about position independent programming with the program counter.

Finally, the 6809 contains an 8-bit **condition code register,** or **CCR**. The 6809 uses all eight bits of its condition code register. Recall that the 6800 and 6801 only use the first six bits of their CCR, with the two most significant bits permanently set to 1's.

The first six bits of the 6809 CCR are identical to those of the 6800, and perform the same functions. The last two bits of the 6809 CCR are called the **Fast Interrupt Mask,** or **F-flag,** and the **Entire State Saved,** or **E-flag,** respectively.

The F-flag is used in the same way as the I-flag to mask out a new interrupt called the **fast interrupt request**, or **FIRQ.** Recall that, with the 6800, a standard interrupt request, or $\overline{\text{IRQ}}$, will cause all of the internal 6800 register contents to be stacked. With the 6809 $\overline{\text{FIRQ}}$, only the program counter and condition code register contents are stacked. This allows for a faster interrupt response when it is known that the existing accumulator and index register data does not need to be saved.

The E-flag is used by the 6809 to determine how much unstacking is required during a return from interrupt operation. When the E-flag is set, the 6809 knows that all of its internal register contents were stacked during the interrupt and that all the registers must be unstacked. When the E-flag is cleared, the 6809 knows that only the program counter and condition code register contents were stacked during the interrupt and that only these two registers must be unstacked. Thus, the E-flag is **automatically** set during a standard interrupt, and **automatically** cleared during a fast interrupt. We will say more about these two CCR bits when we discuss the 6809 interrupts later in this unit.

The 6809 Instruction Set

The 6809 instruction set contains 59 fundamental instructions. These fundamental instructions are used with 19 addressing modes to allow the 6809 to perform over 1400 unique operations. In the remaining parts of this section, we will introduce you to the 6809 instruction set. Then, in the next section, you will see how these instructions are used with different addressing modes to make the 6809 a very efficient software device.

The 59 fundamental instructions of the 6809 instruction set can be categorized as follows:

- Data Movement Instructions
- Arithmetic and Logic Instructions
- Test and Branch Instructions
- Miscellaneous Instructions

With your knowledge of the 6800 instruction set, many of the 6809 instruction operations will be familiar to you. We will, therefore, emphasize those instructions that are "new" and need some explanation.

Data Movement Instructions

The data movement instructions are listed in Figure 7-5. Note that you can load and store any of the 6809 accumulators, and index registers. However, when loading or storing one of the 6809 16-bit registers, you must remember that two bytes are required. For example, the instruction LDX $$ 0100 will load the index register with the contents of memory locations 0100_{16} and 0101_{16}. The contents of memory location 0100_{16} are loaded into the high byte of X, or X_H. The contents of memory location 0101_{16} are loaded into the low byte of X, or X_L.

Mnemonic		Operation
LD	LDA	Load A
	LDB	Load B
	LDD	Load D
	LDS	Load S
	LDU	Load U
	LDX	Load X
	LDY	Load Y
ST	STA	Store A
	STB	Store B
	STD	Store D
	STS	Store S
	STU	Store U
	STX	Store X
	STY	Store Y
TFR	R1, R2	Transfer R1 to R2
EXG	R1, R2	Exchange R1 with R2
LEA	LEAS	Load effective address into S
	LEAU	Load effective address into U
	LEAX	Load effective address into X
	LEAY	Load effective address into Y
PSH	PSHS	Push onto S-stack
	PSHU	Push onto U-stack
PUL	PULS	Pull from S-stack
	PULU	Pull from U-stack

Figure 7-5

The 6809 data movement instructions

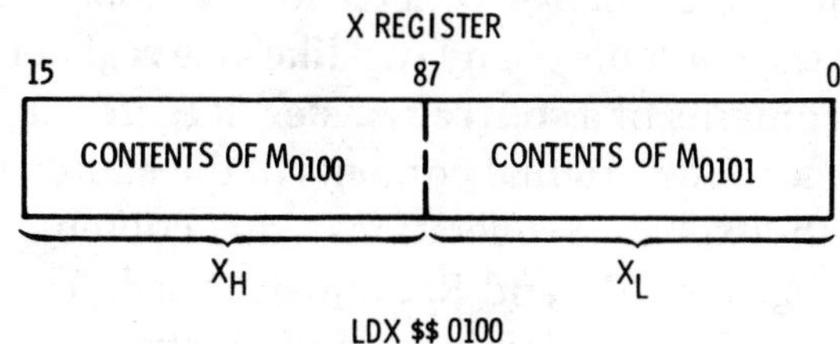

Figure 7-6
Example of a 16-bit load operation

As another example, the instruction STY $$ FC00 will store the contents of Y into memory locations $FC00_{16}$ and $FC01_{16}$. The high byte of Y, or Y_H, is stored in memory location $FC00_{16}$, and the low byte of Y, or Y_L, is stored in memory location $FC01_{16}$. The results of these two example operations are illustrated in Figures 7-6 and 7-7. Note that the instruction only specifies the effective address of the high memory byte. The low memory byte is always the next consecutive memory location, and is accessed automatically by the 6809. With these two examples, the remaining 6809 load and store operations should be self explanatory.

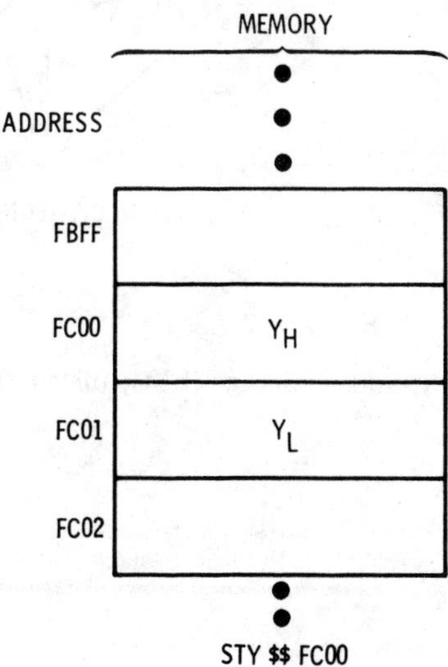

Figure 7-7
Example of a 16-bit store operation

The 6809 transfer, or TFR, and exchange, or EXG, instructions allow you to transfer and exchange the contents of any two **like size registers.** With transfer operations, the contents of a **source register, R1,** are transferred to a **destination register, R2.** The original contents of the source register remain unchanged. With exchange operations, the contents of the source and destination registers, R1 and R2, are swapped. The source and destination registers are specified as part of the instruction, as you will see in the next section.

The various transfer and exchange possibilities are illustrated in Figure 7-8. One important requirement is that you can only transfer and exchange between registers of the same size. Thus, you cannot, for example, exchange the contents of A and X.

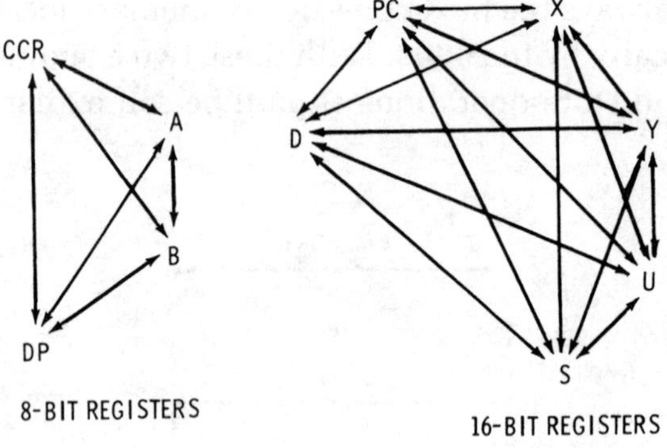

Figure 7-8

The 6809 transfer (TFR) and exchange (EXG) instruction options

The 6809 load effective address, or LEA, instructions are used to load the specified pointer register with the effective address which results from the instruction address calculation. For example, suppose the **effective address** determined from an LEAS instruction is $50FF_{16}$. Then, S is loaded with the value $50FF_{16}$ rather than the data located at location $50FF_{16}$. You must use an **LDS** instruction if you want to load S with the data located at the effective address $50FF_{16}$. This will be much clearer when we discuss addressing modes in the next section and you observe some specific program examples.

The 6809 push, or PSH, and pull, or PUL, instructions are used to push and pull internal register data to and from a memory stack defined by the S or U registers. A stack defined by the S register is called a **hardware stack.** A stack defined by the U register is called a **user stack.** A stack defined by the S register is called a hardware stack because the 6809 automatically uses the S-stack during subroutines and interrupts. The U-stack is never used automatically by the 6809 and is always available to the user. With the PSH and PUL instructions, any or all of the internal 6809 register data may be pushed or pulled onto the S- or U-stacks. This will be demonstrated in the next section.

Arithmetic and Logic Instructions

The 6809 arithmetic and logic instructions are listed in Figure 7-9. With your knowledge of the 6800 and 6801, all of these instructions should be familiar to you with the exception of the SEX instruction.

The mnemonic SEX stands for **sign extend.** This is a 1-byte instruction that allows you to convert an 8-bit signed value in accumulator B to a 16-bit signed value in accumulator D. Thus, the SEX instruction **extends** the **sign** of a value from bit 7 of B to bit 15 of D.

Mnemonic		Operation
AND	ANDA	AND with A
	ANDB	AND with B
	ANDCC	AND condition code register
ASL	ASLA	Arithmetic shift left A
	ASLB	Arithmetic shift left B
	ASL	Arithmetic shift left memory
ASR	ASRA	Arithmetic shift right A
	ASRB	Arithmetic shift right B
	ASR	Arithmetic shift right memory
COM	COMA	Ones complement A
	COMB	Ones complement B
	COM	Ones complement memory
EOR	EORA	Exclusive OR A
	EORB	Exclusive OR B
LSL	LSLA	Logic shift left A
	LSLB	Logic shift left B
	LSL	Logic shift left memory
LSR	LSRA	Logic shift right A
	LSRB	Logic shift right B
	LSR	Logic shift right memory
OR	ORA	OR memory with A
	ORB	OR memory with B
	ORCC	OR condition code register
ROL	ROLA	Rotate left A
	ROLB	Rotate left B
	ROL	Rotate left memory
ROR	RORA	Rotate right A
	RORB	Rotate right B
	ROR	Rotate right memory
ABX		Add B to X (unsigned)
ADC	ADCA	Add to A with carry
	ADCB	Add to B with carry
ADD	ADDA	Add to A
	ADDB	Add to B
	ADDD	Add to D

Figure 7-9

The 6809 arithmetic and logic instructions.

Mnemonic		Operation
CLR	CLRA	Clear A
	CLRB	Clear B
	CLR	Clear memory
DAA		Decimal adjust A
DEC	DECA	Decrement A
	DECB	Decrement B
	DEC	Decrement memory
INC	INCA	Increment A
	INCB	Increment B
	INC	Increment memory
MUL		Multiply A times B (unsigned)
NEG	NEGA	Negate A (twos complement)
	NEGB	Negate B (twos complement)
	NEG	Negate memory (twos complement)
SBC	SBCA	Subtract from A with borrow
	SBCB	Subtract from B with borrow
SEX		Sign extend B into A
SUB	SUBA	Subtract from A
	SUBB	Subtract from B
	SUBD	Subtract from D

Figure 7-9

The 6809 arithmetic and logic instructions

Test and Branch Instructions

The 6809 test and branch instructions are listed in Figure 7-10. The test instructions include a bit test, or BIT, byte test, or TST, and compare, or CMP. These test operations are identical to those of the 6800. However, you will note that with the CMP instruction, you can compare data to A, B, D, X, Y, S, and U. Of course, when comparing to a 16-bit register, two data bytes must be specified.

All the conditional and unconditional 6800 and 6801 branch options are available to the 6809. However, for each branch option, the 6809 includes a **long branch** instruction.

Recall that, with the 6800 and 6801, you are limited to a branching range of -128_{10} to $+127_{10}$ locations from the program counter contents. This is because the signed relative address offset in the branch instruction is only one byte. To branch beyond this range, you must branch to a branch. However, the 6809 includes a **long branch** instruction for each branch option. The 6809 long branch instructions use two relative address offset bytes. Using the long branch instructions, the 6809 has a branching range of $-32{,}768_{10}$ to $+32{,}767_{10}$ locations. Thus, for each branching option, the 6809 includes a short branch and a long branch. The long branch mnemonic is preceded by an "L" in Figure 7-10.

Mnemonic		Operation
BIT	BITA BITB	Bit test A Bit test B
CMP	CMPA CMPB CMPD CMPS CMPU CMPX CMPY	Compare with A Compare with B Compare with D Compare with S Compare with U Compare with X Compare with Y
TST	TSTA TSTB TST	Test A Test B Test Memory
BCS	BCS LBCS	Branch if the carry (C) flag is set
BEQ	BEQ LBEQ	Branch if the register contents are equal to the memory contents (Z flag set)
BGE	BGE LBGE	Branch if the *signed* register contents are *greater* than or *equal* to the *signed* memory contents
BGT	BGT LBGT	Branch if the *signed* register contents are *greater* than the *signed* memory contents
BHI	BHI LBHI	Branch if the *unsigned* register contents are *higher* than the *unsigned* memory contents
BHS	BHS LBHS	Branch if the *unsigned* register contents are higher than or the *same* as the *unsigned* memory contents
BLE	BLE LBLE	Branch if the *signed* register contents are *less* than or *equal* to the *signed* memory contents
BLO	BLO LBLO	Branch if the *unsigned* register contents are lower than the *unsigned* memory contents
BLS	BLS LBLS	Branch if the *unsigned* register contents are *lower* than or the *same* as the *unsigned* memory contents
BLT	BLT LBLT	Branch if the *signed* register contents are *less* than the signed memory contents
BMI	BMI LBMI	Branch if minus (N flag set)
BNE	BNE LBNE	Branch if the register contents are *not* equal to the memory contents (Z flag cleared)
BPL	BPL LBPL	Branch if plus (N flag cleared)
BRA	BRA LBRA	Branch always (unconditional)
BRN	BRN LBRN	Branch never
BSR	BSR LBSR	Branch to subroutine
BVC	BVC LVBC	Branch if the overflow (V) flag is cleared
BVS	BVS LBVS	Branch if the overflow (V) flag is set

Figure 7-10

The 6809 test and branch instructions

Miscellaneous Instructions

The remaining 6809 instructions that do not fit conveniently into any of the previous categories are called miscellaneous instructions. They are listed in Figure 7-11. The three new instructions of interest here are the CWAI, SWI, and SYNC instructions.

Mnemonic		Operation
CWAI		AND CC, then wait for interrupt
JMP		Jump
JSR		Jump to subroutine
NOP		No operation
RTI		Return from interrupt
RTS		Return from subroutine
SWI	SWI1	Software interrupt 1
	SWI2	Software interrupt 2
	SWI3	Software interrupt 3
SYNC		Synchronize to interrupt

Figure 7-11

The 6809 miscellaneous instructions

The 6809 CWAI instruction takes the place of the 6800 WAI instruction. The CWAI instruction is a 2-byte instruction that contains an immediate data byte as shown in Figure 7-12. Before putting the 6809 in a wait-for-interrupt state, the CWAI instruction ANDs its immediate data byte with the condition code register. This allows you to set or clear the various CCR flag bits prior to the wait state. For example, suppose you wish to clear the I-flag prior to the wait state so that an interrupt request will be acknowledged. This can be accomplished by using the hex value EF_{16} as the immediate data byte in the CWAI instruction. Recall that the I-flag is in the bit 4 position of the CCR. Thus, ANDing the value EF_{16}, or $1110\ 1111_2$, with the CCR will clear the I-flag and leave the remaining CCR flag bits unchanged. Such an operation is often desirable before entering the wait-for-interrupt state.

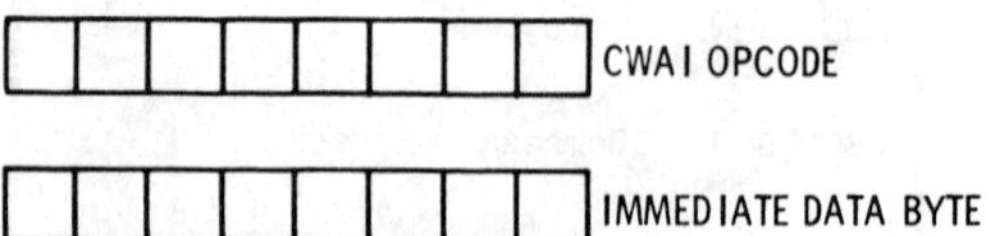

Figure 7-12

The CWAI instruction format

The 6809 instruction set includes three software interrupts: SWI1, SWI2, and SWI3. Recall that the 6800 instruction set has only one software interrupt. With the 6800, many system ROM monitor software packages use the single software interrupt for single stepping routines, breakpoint routines, etc. This makes the SWI instruction unavailable to the user. With the three software interrupts of the 6809, it is very unlikely that a system monitor will use all three. It is hoped that at least one SWI will be left available to the user.

The 6809 SYNC instruction is used to synchronize the system software with an expected external hardware event. The instruction mnemonic **SYNC** stands for **synchronize-to-interrupt** and will be discussed in more detail when we look at the 6809 interrupts.

A summary of the instruction operations for each 6809 instruction set category is provided in Figure 7-13.

On the surface, it might look as though the 6809 instruction set is not as powerful as the 6800 instruction set. However, the power of the 6809, and any processor for that matter, is found in its addressing modes. The 6809 addressing modes are the topic of our next discussion.

6809 Data Movement Instructions

- Load and Store A, B, D, X, Y, U, and S
- Transfer and Exchange Between A, B, DP and CC, and Between D, X, Y, U, S, and PC
- Push and Pull Onto S Or U One Or More Of A, B, X, Y, U, S, DP, CC and PC
- Load Effective Address Into X, Y, U and S

6809 Arithmetic Instructions

- Add and Subtract Memory Into A, B and D
- Add and Subtract Memory With Carry Into A and B
- Add 8-Bit Immediate Data To A, B, X, Y, U and S
- Add 16-Bit Immediate Data To D, X, Y, U and S
- Add A, B and D To X, Y, U and S
- Increment and Decrement Memory, A, B, D, X, Y, U and S
- Multiply A Times B

6809 Logic Instructions

- AND, OR and EOR Memory Into A and B
- Shift And Rotate Memory, A and B
- Complement, Negate and Clear Memory, A and B
- AND and OR Immediate Data Into CC

6809 Test and Branch Instructions

- Arithmetic Compare Memory With A, B, D, X, Y, U and S
- Logical Compare Memory With A and B
- Test For Zero and Minus On Memory, A and B
- Short Branch (14 Conditions)
- Long Branch (14 Conditions)

6809 Miscellaneous Instructions

- Jump and Jump To Subroutine (Extended, Indexed and Indexed Indirect Addressing)
- Branch And Branch To Subroutine (8-Bit, 16-Bit PC-Relative and PC-Relative Indirect Addressing)
- Return From Subroutine and Interrupts
- Three Software Interrupts
- Interrupt Synchronization Instructions
  - Wait For Interrupt
  - Sync — Next Interrupt Causes Execution To Continue

Figure 7-13

A 6809 instruction operation summary

Self-Test Review

1. Describe the internal CPU register structure of the 6809.

2. What is a pointer register?

3. What is an effective address?

4. How does the 6809 provide memory paging?

5. Define position independence.

6. What two 6809 condition code register flags are not available in the 6800?

7. What is the function of the two CCR flags in question #6?

8. List the four instruction categories of the 6809 instruction set.

9. Describe what will happen when the 6809 encounters a STU $$ A1BF instruction.

10. How is register data swapped within the 6809?

11. What is the purpose of the 6809 LEA instructions? ____________

12. Which of the 6809 registers are used as stack pointers for the 6809 PSH and PUL instructions? ____________

13. What is the function of the 6809 SEX instruction? ____________

14. What is a long branch instruction? ____________

15. Suppose you wish to clear the F-flag of the CCR prior to a wait-for-interrupt state. What immediate data byte is required in the CWAI instruction? ____________

Answers

1. The 6809 contains the following internal CPU registers:

   8-bit Registers
   Accumulator A
   Accumulator B
   Direct Page Register
   Condition Code Register

   16-bit Registers
   Accumulator D, made up of A and B
   X index pointer register
   Y index pointer register
   S index/stack pointer register
   U index/stack pointer register
   Program Counter

2. A pointer register is a register that is used by an instruction to determine the effective address for that instruction.

3. An effective address is the address that is eventually accessed by the instruction.

4. The 6809 provides memory paging by dividing the external 64K address space into 256 pages of 256 bytes per page. The direct page register is used to point to a particular page during the direct addressing mode.

5. Position independence is that quality of a program that allows it to execute properly, regardless of where it is located in memory. Instructions which use position independent code form the effective address relative to the program counter's contents.

6. The two 6809 condition code register flags that are not available in the 6800 are the **Fast Interrupt Mask,** or **F-flag**, and the **Entire State Saved,** or **E-flag.**

7. The function of the F-flag is to mask-out the 6809 fast interrupt request, or $\overline{\text{FIRQ}}$.

   The function of the E-flag is to tell the 6809 the amount of unstacking that is required during a return-from-interrupt operation.

8. The four instruction categories of the 6809 instruction set are:

- Data movement
- Arithmetic and logic
- Test and branch
- Miscellaneous

9. When the 6809 encounters an STU $$ A1BF instruction, it will store the contents of the U register into memory locations A1BF and A1CO. The high byte of U, or U_H, is stored in memory location A1BF. The low byte of U, or U_L, is stored in memory location A1CO.

10. Register data is swapped in the 6809 using the exchange, or EXG, instruction.

11. The purpose of the 6809 LEA instructions is to load the specified pointer register with the effective address, rather than the data located at the effective address.

12. The S and U registers are used as stack pointers for the 6809 PSH and PUL instructions.

13. The function of the 6809 SEX instruction is to convert an 8-bit signed value in B to a 16-bit signed value in D.

14. A long branch instruction uses two relative offset bytes, and provides a branching range of $-32{,}768_{10}$ to $+32{,}767_{10}$ locations.

15. To clear the F-flag prior to a wait-for-interrupt state, you must provide an immediate data byte of BF_{16} in the CWAI instruction. This results from the F-flag being in bit position 6 and assumes that all other CCR flags are left unchanged.

THE 6809 ADDRESSING MODES

You are now familiar with the 59 fundamental instructions that comprise the 6809 instruction set. Recall that the 6800 instruction set contains 72 fundamental instructions. This does not mean that the 6800 is a more powerful processor than the 6809! What makes the 6809 such a powerful software device? The 6809 addressing modes. It is not merely the number of fundamental instructions that make one processor more powerful than another. More important, it is the various ways in which these fundamental instructions can be used to access memory.

The 6809 instruction set uses eight fundamental addressing modes. Variations of the eight fundamental addressing modes provide 19 unique ways of addressing memory. Therefore, the 6809 is capable of performing over 1400 unique operations. In contrast, the 72 instructions of the 6800 operate using six addressing modes. The 6800 is, therefore, only capable of performing approximately 200 unique operations.

The eight fundamental addressing modes of the 6809 are: **inherent, immediate, direct, extended, register, indexed, indirect,** and **relative.** With your knowledge of the 6800, you should recognize six of these.

The eight fundamental addressing modes of the 6809 will be discussed in this section. It is very important that you make a sincere effort to understand this material. You will discover that the "key" to understanding the 6809 is a firm knowledge of its addressing modes. In addition, the 6809 addressing modes are also common to other high performance microprocessors. A good knowledge of this material will help you understand other existing and future high performance devices.

Inherent and Immediate Addressing

These two 6809 addressing modes are identical to those of the 6800. Instructions using inherent addressing are usually one byte instructions, such as INCA, DECB, LSRA, etc. The addressing is inherent, or implied in the instruction.

Instructions using immediate addressing can be two, three, or four bytes long with the 6809: a 1- or 2-byte opcode, followed by a 1- or 2-byte operand. Recall that, with immediate addressing, the instruction operand follows the opcode in the instruction statement as shown in Figure 7-14. However, with the 6809, several of the instruction opcodes are two bytes. For example, the compare to accumulator D, or CMPD, instruction has an op-code of $10A3_{16}$. Now, if you want to compare an immediate value to D, you must supply a 2-byte operand in addition to the opcode, since accumulator D is a 16-bit register. Thus, any CMPD immediate instruction must be four bytes long. If you were to compare the value $FFFF_{16}$ to accumulator D, the required code must be:

Source Code	Object Code
CMPD #	10
	A3
FF	FF
FF	FF

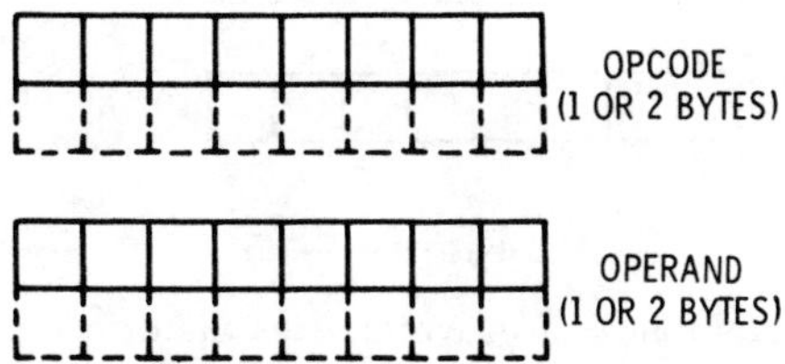

Figure 7-14

Format of a 6809 instruction which uses the immediate addressing mode

Consider the CWAI instruction as another example of immediate addressing. The 6809 CWAI instruction opcode is 3C. However, this must be followed by an immediate operand byte. The operand byte that follows the 3C opcode is the value that will be ANDed with the condition code register. To clear the I-flag, the required code must be:

Source Code	Object Code
CWAI	3C
EF	EF

Direct Addressing

Direct addressing with the 6809 is similar to that of the 6800. The only difference is the involvement of the 6809 direct page register.

Instructions using direct addressing are two or three bytes long: a 1- or 2-byte opcode, followed by a 1-byte address. The 6809 direct addressing mode format is shown in Figure 7-15.

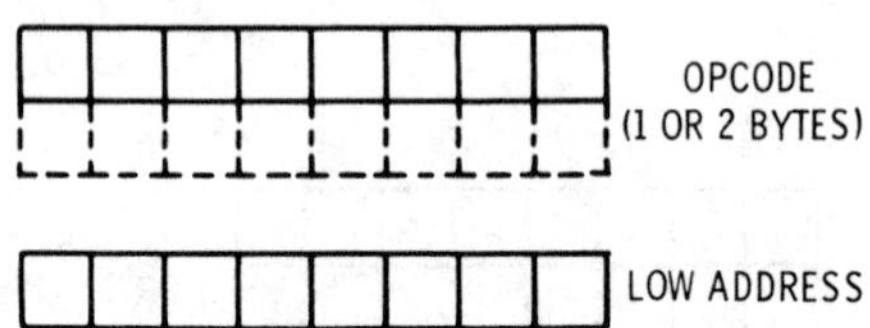

Figure 7-15
Format of a 6809 instruction which uses the direct addressing mode

When the 6809 encounters a direct address instruction, it uses the contents of the direct page register to provide the high address byte. The low address byte is provided by the instruction. For example, suppose the direct page register contains the hex value 02 (page 2). What will happen when the 6809 encounters the instruction LDA $ FF? Since the direct page register provides the high address byte, accumulator A will be loaded with the contents of memory location $02FF_{16}$. By changing the direct page register contents, you can change the effective address of the above instruction, or any instruction using direct addressing. This is why it is very important to keep track of the direct page register's value when programming the 6809.

Another way to view the direct page register's involvement in direct addressing is illustrated by Figure 7-16. Note that the address generation circuitry of the 6809 will generate the logic for the lower eight 6809 address lines as a result of the instruction. The logic for the upper eight 6809 address lines is generated by the direct page register during the execution of the direct addressing instruction.

As you will discover later, the 6809 direct page register is automatically cleared during a reset operation. Thus, after $\overline{\text{RESET}}$, the direct page register points to page 0. Direct addressing with page 0 is identical to 6800 direct addressing.

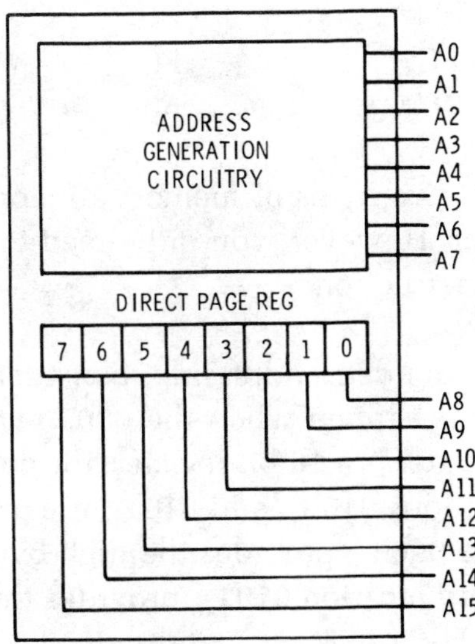

Figure 7-16
6809 direct address generation

Extended Addressing

Extended addressing with the 6809 is identical to that of the 6800. The instruction opcode is followed by a 2-byte address as shown in Figure 7-17. However, because some of the 6809 instructions use 2-byte opcodes, the extended addressing instruction can be three or four bytes long.

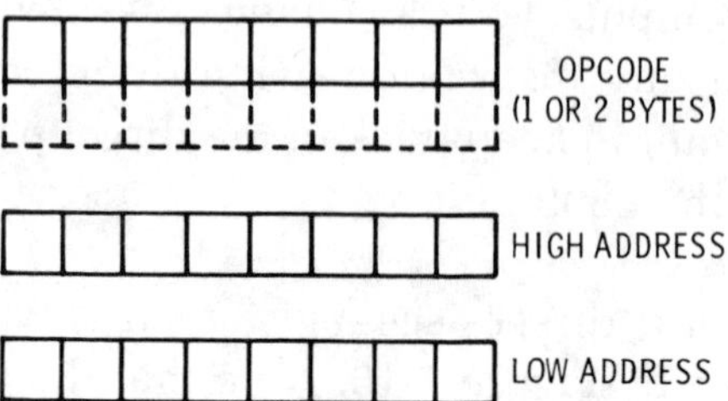

Figure 7-17

Format of a 6809 instruction which uses the extended addressing mode

As an example of extended addressing, suppose you wish to store the contents of the Y register at memory locations FC50:FC51. The STY instruction has an opcode of $10BF_{16}$. The required code must therefore be:

Source Code	Object Code
STY $$	10
	BF
FC	FC
50	50

Recall that you must use two bytes of memory to store the Y register, since it is a 16-bit register. However, you only need to specify the first memory address in the instruction.

As another example of extended addressing, consider the instruction CMPU $$ 0100. What will happen when the 6809 encounters this instruction? Since the U register is a 16-bit register, the contents of the two consecutive memory locations 0100_{16} and 0101_{16} are compared to the U register. Memory location 0100_{16} provides the high byte of the value to be compared to U. Memory location 0101_{16} provides the low byte of the value to be compared to U.

Register Addressing

A new addressing mode available to the 6809 is register addressing. An instruction using this form of addressing is always two bytes long: the instruction opcode followed by a **post byte**. The 6809 instruction format for register addressing is shown in Figure 7-18. With register addressing, the instruction post byte is used to define the registers that are to be used in the instruction operation.

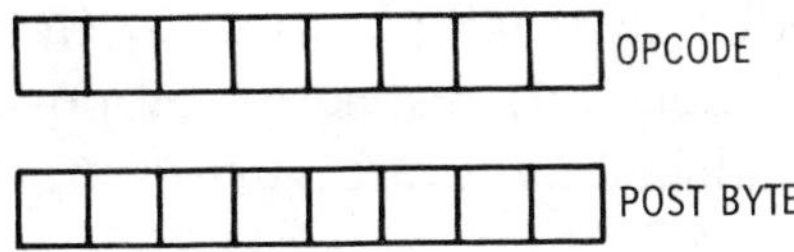

Figure 7-18

Format of a 6809 instruction which uses the register addressing mode

Only four 6809 instructions use register addressing. They are the transfer (TFR), exchange (EXG), push (PSH), and pull (PUL) instructions. With the TFR and EXG instructions, the post byte defines the source (R1) and destination (R2) registers involved in the instruction transfer or exchange. The post byte codes for the TFR and EXG instructions are given in Figure 7-19. Notice that the upper four bits of the post byte define the source register and the lower four bits define the destination register.

For example, a post byte of 1000 1011_2, or $8B_{16}$, is required with a TFR instruction to transfer the contents of accumulator A to the direct page register. This same post byte will swap the contents of accumulator A and the direct page register when used with an EXG instruction.

POST BYTE

7	6	5	4	3	2	1	0
SOURCE (R1)				DESTINATION (R2)			

Register	Code
D	0000
X	0001
Y	0010
U	0011
S	0100
PC	0101
A	1000
B	1001
CCR	1010
DP	1011

Figure 7-19

Post byte codes for the 6809 TFR and EXG instructions

What post byte is required to exchange the contents of X and Y? From Figure 7-19, you see that a post byte of $0001\ 0010_2$, or 12_{16}, is required. Can this post byte be used with a TFR instruction to transfer Y to X? No, since this post byte defines X as the source register and Y as the destination register. However, you could use this post byte with a TFR instruction to transfer X to Y.

The PSH and PUL instructions use the post byte to define the registers that are to be pushed to, or pulled from a memory stack. The post byte codes for the PSH and PUL instructions are given in Figure 7-20. A register will be pushed or pulled if its respective bit position is set (logic 1). The push/pull order is also shown in Figure 7-20.

As an example, consider the instruction PSHU A5. What will happen when the 6809 encounters this instruction? The PSHU instruction causes 6809 registers to be pushed onto a memory stack defined by the U register. The post byte defines the registers that are to be pushed. In this example, the post byte is $A5_{16}$, or $1010\ 0101_2$. From Figure 7-20 you can determine that the PC, Y, B, and the CCR are pushed onto the U-stack. The PC is pushed first, followed by Y, B, and the CCR.

As another example, consider the instruction PULS 58. What will happen when the 6809 encounters this instruction? The PULS instruction causes information to be pulled from the S-stack and placed in the 6809 registers. The post byte defines the registers that are to be pulled. In this example, the post byte is 58_{16}, or $0101\ 1000_2$. From Figure 7-20 you can determine that the U, X, and DP registers are pulled from the S-stack. The DP register is pulled first, followed by the X and U registers.

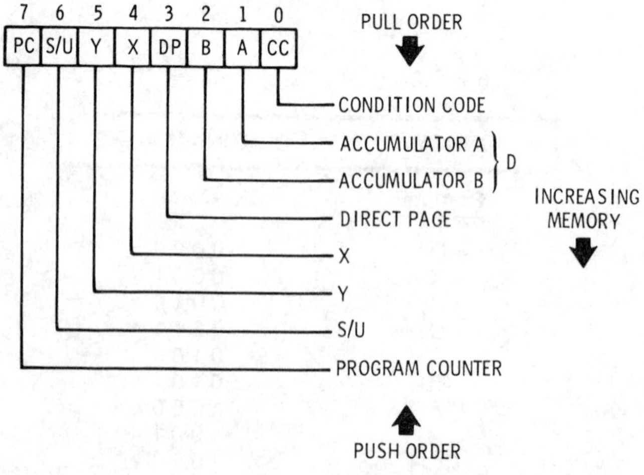

Figure 7-20

Post byte format for the 6809 PSH and PUL instructions

Note that since we are using the S-stack, bit position 6 of the post byte applies to the U register. However, if we were using the U-stack, bit position 6 would apply to the S register.

There is one other point that we need to make about the S-and U-stacks. Recall that, with the 6800, the stack pointer always points to the **next available** location on a memory stack. This is not true of the 6809 stack pointers. The 6809 stack pointers always point to the **top** of their respective memory stack. The top of the stack is the last position in the stack. This difference is illustrated in Figure 7-21.

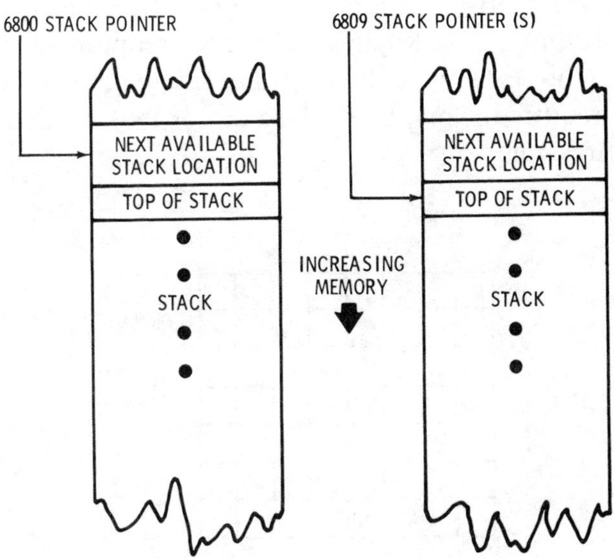

Figure 7-21

The 6809 stack pointers versus the 6800 stack pointer

Indexed Addressing

The real power of the 6809 comes from its indexed addressing capabilities. Recall that, with the 6800, indexed addressing was primarily used when working with tables and strings of memory data. An instruction using indexed addressing forms the effective address by adding the contents of the index register to the index offset byte provided in the instruction. The 6800 index register can be incremented and decremented to permit sequential access to memory data. With the 6809, the indexed addressing mode has been greatly enhanced by the addition of more index registers and several different indexing modes.

The 6809 registers that can be used for indexed addressing are the X, Y, S, and U registers. We will refer to these as **pointer** registers. The different indexing modes available to the 6809 are **constant offset indexed, accumulator offset indexed,** and **auto increment/decrement indexed** addressing.

The general instruction format for 6809 indexed addressing is shown in Figure 7-22. Note that an indexed addressing instruction can be from two bytes to five bytes in length, depending on the form of indexing used. As before, the instruction opcode is one or two bytes, depending on the instruction. Then, the opcode is **always** followed by a **post byte.** With indexed addressing, the post byte defines the type of indexing to be used: constant offset, accumulator offset, or auto increment/decrement. In addition, the post byte specifies which pointer register is to be used: X, Y, S, or U. The post byte is then followed by one or two offset bytes when required. Now, let's take a closer look at each form of 6809 indexed addressing.

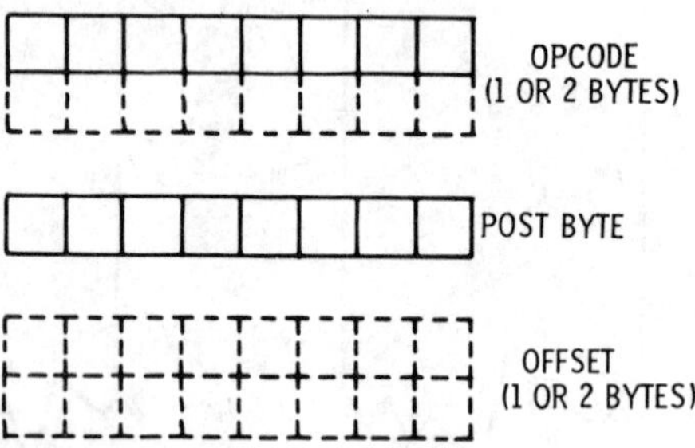

Figure 7-22

General format of a 6809 instruction which uses the indexed addressing mode

CONSTANT OFFSET INDEXED ADDRESSING

There are four types of constant offset indexed addressing available to the 6809. They are: **zero offset indexed, 5-bit offset indexed, 8-bit offset indexed,** and **16-bit offset indexed.** With any of these, the offset is always added to the specified pointer register to determine the effective address.

With zero offset indexed addressing, the offset is always zero. Therefore, the effective address is always the contents of the specified pointer register. The symbol used along with the instruction mnemonic to specify this indexed mode is "**,R**", where R is the specified pointer register. For example, the instruction STA , Y will store the contents of accumulator A at an address specified by the Y register. In other words, the Y register **points** directly to the address where A is to be stored.

No instruction offset bytes are required with zero offset indexed addressing. The instruction will consist of the opcode byte(s) followed by the post byte.

With 5-bit, 8-bit, and 16-bit constant offset indexed addressing, the effective address is formed by adding the given offset value to the specified pointer register. The symbol used along with the instruction mnemonic to specify these indexed modes is "n,R". With this symbol, n is the offset value, and R is the specified pointer register. The effective address is therefore n + R.

As an example of a 5-bit constant offset operation, consider the instruction LDX 3,S. With this instruction, the high byte of the X register, or X_H, is loaded with the contents of address 3 + S. The low byte of the X register, or X_L, is loaded with the contents of address 3 + S + 1. Note, since X is a 16-bit register, two consecutive memory addresses must be accessed for the LDX operation.

When using a 5-bit constant offset, **no** offset byte is required in the instruction listing. The 5-bit offset value is included as part of the post byte. You will see how this is done shortly, when we discuss the post byte in more detail.

As an example of an 8-bit constant offset operation, consider the instruction LDA 5B,X. Here, accumulator A is loaded with the contents of address $5B_{16}+X$. As another example, the instruction STA 5B,X will store accumulator A at address $5B_{16}+X$.

When using an 8-bit constant offset, one offset byte must follow the post byte in the instruction listing. The offset byte, not the post byte, contains the 8-bit offset value.

As an example of a 16-bit constant offset operation, consider the instruction CMPA 10A5,U. With this instruction, the contents of address $10A5_{16}+U$ are compared to accumulator A. As another example, the instruction STD FC05,X will store the high byte of accumulator D at address $FC05_{16}+X$ and the low byte of accumulator D at address $FC05_{16}+X+1$.

When using a 16-bit offset, two offset bytes must follow the post byte in the instruction listing. The first offset byte contains the high offset value. The second offset byte contains the low offset value. The 6809 instruction formats for the various forms of constant offset indexed addressing are summarized in Figure 7-23.

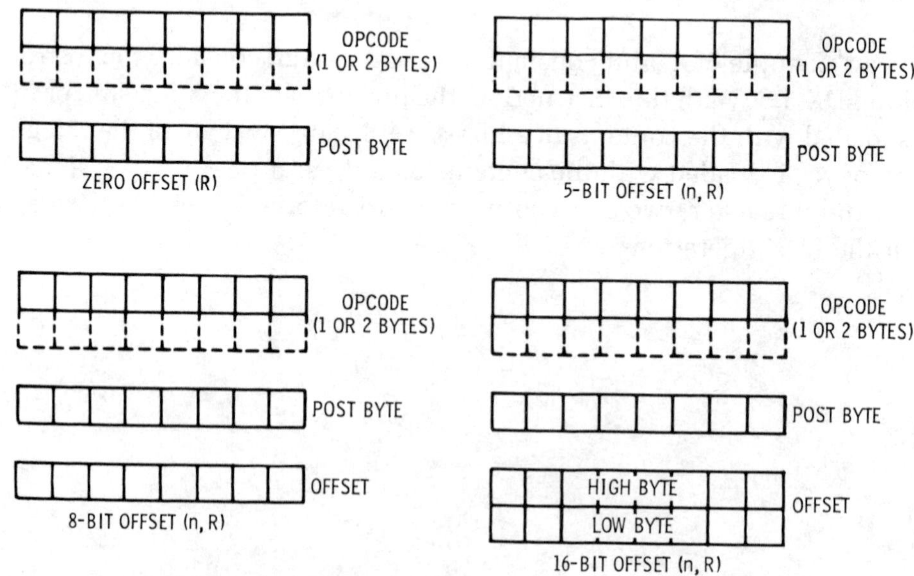

Figure 7-23
Instruction format summary of the 6809 constant offset indexed addressing modes

It should be pointed out that the offset values are signed. The most significant offset bit, therefore, determines the sign of the offset. If the most significant offset bit is a logic 0, the offset is positive. Conversely, if the most significant offset bit is a logic 1, the offset is negative.

ACCUMULATOR OFFSET INDEX ADDRESSING

Accumulator offset indexed addressing is similar to constant offset indexed addressing. The difference is that the offset is always the contents of one of the 6809 accumulators (A, B, or D). Thus, the effective address is formed by adding the contents of the specified accumulator to the specified pointer register. For example, the instruction LDA B,X will load accumulator A with the contents of address B + X. As another example, the instruction STY D,U will store the contents of the Y register. The high byte of the Y register, or Y_H, is stored at address D + U. The low byte of the Y register, or Y_L, is stored at address D + U + 1. The advantage of using an accumulator offset is that, results of operations which are generated in the accumulators can be used directly for memory addressing, without an intermediate store operation.

The instruction format for accumulator offset indexed addressing is shown in Figure 7-24. Note that no offset bytes are required since the post byte is used to specify the accumulator that is to be used in the operation.

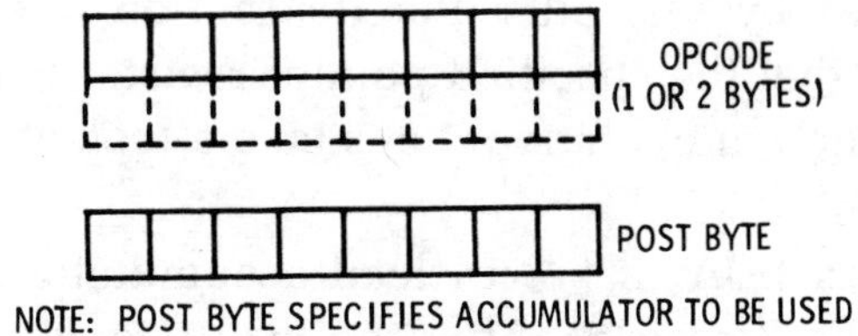

Figure 7-24
Format of a 6809 instruction which uses the accumulator offset indexed addressing mode

AUTO INCREMENT/DECREMENT INDEXED ADDRESSING

The 6809 auto increment/decrement indexed addressing mode provides a convenient method for stepping through memory data tables. In the auto increment mode, the specified pointer register is incremented by one or two **after** the instruction operation. In the auto decrement mode, the specified pointer register is decremented by one or two **before** the instruction operation. The instruction format for the auto increment/decrement mode is shown in Figure 7-25. No offset bytes are required since the post byte specifies auto increment or decrement by one or two.

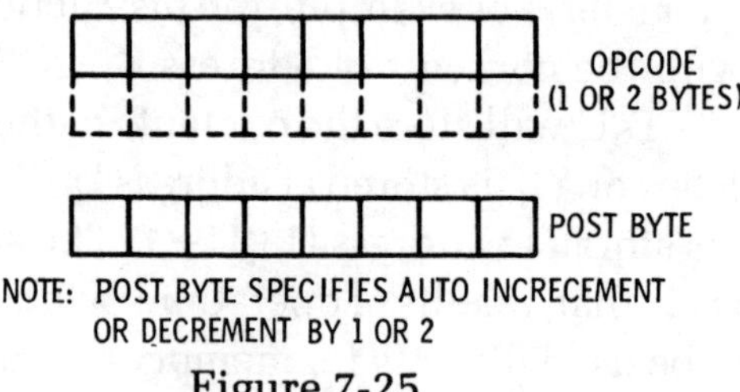

Figure 7-25

Format of a 6809 instruction which uses the auto increment/decrement indexed addressing mode

The operation symbols for the auto increment mode are "**,R+**" and "**,R++**". The symbol ,R+ means that the specified pointer register (R) is incremented by **one** after the instruction operation. The symbol ,R++ means that the specified pointer register is incremented by **two** after the instruction operation. Let's take a look at some examples.

The instruction LDA ,X+ will load accumulator A from the address specified by the X register. After the load operation takes place, the X register is automatically incremented by one. The instruction LDD ,X++ will load accumulator D with the contents of the two consecutive addresses; X and X + 1. After the load operation, the X register is automatically incremented by two.

The operation symbols for the automatic decrement mode are "**,-R**" and "**,--R**". The symbol ,-R means that the specified pointer register (R) is decremented by **one** before the instruction operation. The symbol ,--R means that the specified pointer register is decremented by **two** before the instruction operation. For example, the instruction STA ,-Y will decrement Y by one, then store the contents of accumulator A at the address specified by Y. The instruction STD ,--Y will decrement Y by two, then store the contents of accumulator D at the two consecutive addresses Y and Y+1.

Note that you will normally use auto increment/decrement by one when loading or storing an 8-bit register. However, auto increment/decrement by two is normally used when loading or storing a 16-bit register.

Recall that, with the 6800, you must insert an increment or decrement instruction in your program when stepping through memory data tables. However, with the 6809, this is not necessary since the incrementing and decrementing is automatic.

With the auto increment/decrement addressing modes, you can use the X and Y registers as stack pointers. For example, a STA ,-X instruction will push accumulator A onto a stack defined by the X register. Conversely, a LDA ,X+ instruction will pull accumulator A from a stack defined by the X register. Similar instructions can push/pull data onto a stack defined by the Y register. The X and Y registers can, therefore, be used as stack pointers when additional memory stacks must be provided for the system program. Now, let's look at several simple 6809 instruction sequences that used indexed addressing.

The 6809 instruction set does not include any instructions that allow you to add directly to the pointer registers. However, using index addressing and the load effective address, or LEA, instruction, you can add directly to any of the pointer registers. For example, the single instruction LEAY A5,Y will add the 8-bit offset $A5_{16}$ to Y and then load the sum back into Y. Recall that the LEA instruction loads the specified register with the effective address rather than the data at that address. Thus, that effective address value $A5_{16}+Y$ is loaded into Y, rather than the data at address $A5_{16}+Y$.

The instruction LEAX D,X will add the contents of D to the contents of X and load the sum back in X. How about the instruction LEAY A,S? This instruction will add A to S then transfer the sum to Y. It should be noted that the original contents of both A and S remain unchanged.

Write an instruction sequence to push the contents of the direct page, or DP, register onto a stack defined by the X register. The following instruction sequence will perform the given task:

```
TFR DP, A
STA ,-X
```

You must first transfer the DP register to one of the accumulators, since there is no 6809 instruction that will store the direct page register directly. Then, the accumulator is pushed onto the X-stack using the auto decrement by one store instruction.

Write an instruction sequence that will unstack the direct page register from the X-stack. The following instruction sequence will do the job:

```
LDA ,X+
TFR A,DP
```

Here, the process is just reversed from the previous stacking example.

Write an instruction sequence that will move a data table from memory locations 5000_{16}-$50FF_{16}$ to memory locations 8000_{16}-$80FF_{16}$. The following instruction sequence will perform the given task:

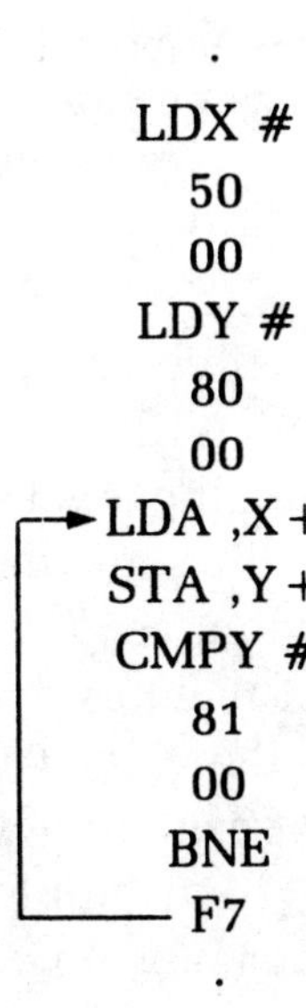

Note how the X and Y registers are used as pointer registers and automatically incremented by the LDA and STA instructions.

You should now begin to see the power and versatility that indexed addressing adds to the 6809 instruction set. However, there are still two more important addressing modes to discuss before our addressing mode discussion is complete.

Indirect Addressing

Indirect addressing means that the effective address for an instruction operation is contained at the location specified by the operation. This differs from other forms of addressing in that the effective address is not obtained **directly** from the instruction. Rather, it is obtained indirectly by way of an intermediate address, sometimes called an **absolute address.** Any of the indexed addressing modes previously discussed can use indirect addressing. We will use a bracket, or "[ ]", around the indexed mode symbol to denote indirect addressing.

For example, consider the instruction LDA [7C,X]. Without the brackets in the above instruction, accumulator A would be loaded with the contents of address $7C_{16}+X$. However, the brackets denote indirect addressing and create a whole new meaning for the instruction. With indirect addressing in the above instruction, accumulator A is loaded with the contents of the address found at memory locations 7C+X : 7C+X+1. Suppose the X register contains the value 0100_{16} prior to the execution of the LDA [7C,X] instruction. A segment of memory containing this instruction is shown in Figure 7-26 for example purposes. The address obtained from the instruction, or absolute address, is $7C_{16}+X$, or $7C_{16}+0100_{16}$, which equals $017C_{16}$. At this address you find the value FC_{16}. At the next consecutive address, $017D_{16}$, you find the value 00_{16}. Consequently, the effective address is $FC00_{16}$. Thus, accumulator A is loaded with the contents of address $FC00_{16}$ which, in this example, is the value AA_{16}.

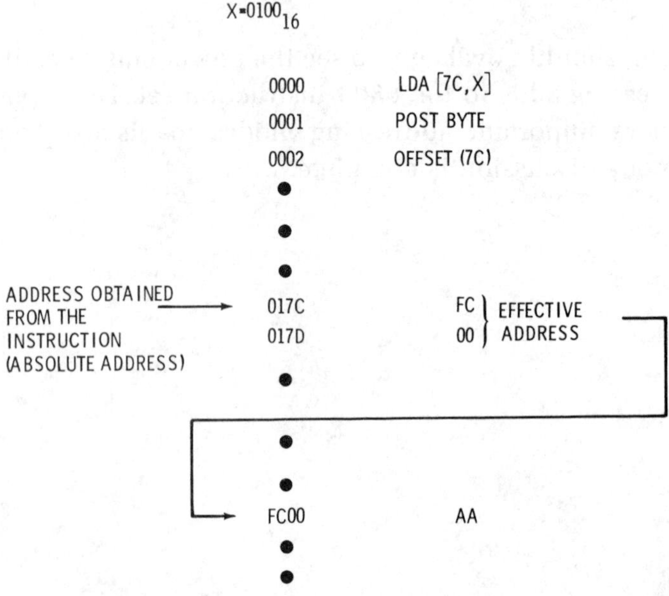

Figure 7-26

An example of an indirect load operation

Next, consider the segment of memory shown in Figure 7-27. What will happen when the STD instruction is executed? The STD instruction will store the contents of accumulator D at two consecutive memory locations. The question is, where? The address obtained from the instruction is A+Y, or using the values shown in Figure 7-27, $A+Y=05_{16}+0200_{16}=0205_{16}$. At address 0205_{16}, you find the value 01_{16}. At address 0206_{16}, you find the value 55_{16}. The effective address is, therefore, 0155_{16}. Consequently, the high byte of D is stored at address 0155_{16}, and the low byte of D is stored at address 0156_{16}.

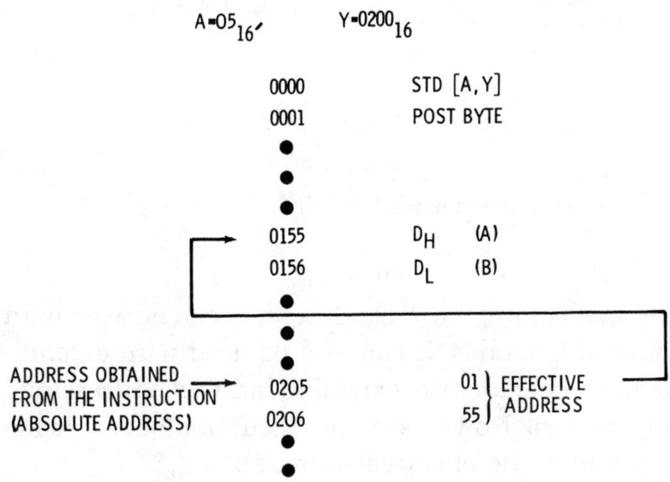

Figure 7-27
An example of an indirect store operation

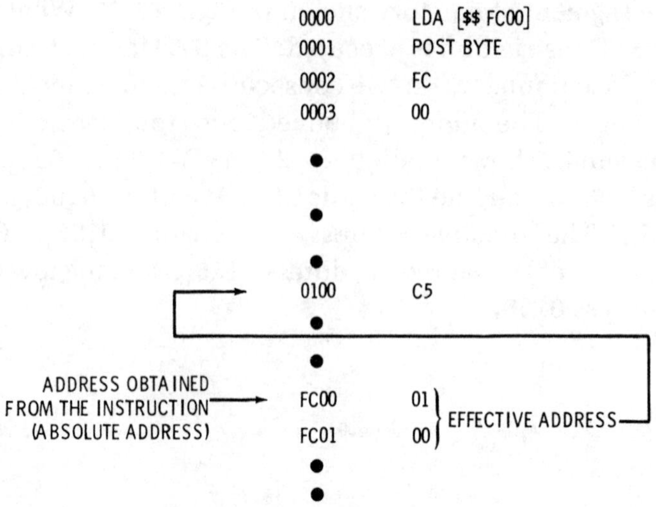

Figure 7-28

An example of extended indirect addressing

As we mentioned before, indirect addressing can be used with any of the indexed addressing modes. It can also be used with extended addressing. For example, consider the **extended indirect addressing** instruction shown in Figure 7-28. Do you see how accumulator A is loaded with the value $C5_{16}$, found at the effective address 0100_{16}?

As you will discover shortly, the post byte is used to specify indirect addressing in both the indexed and extended addressing modes.

Relative Addressing

As with the 6800, the 6809 uses relative addressing for its branch instructions. Recall that the branch destination is formed by adding a relative offset provided in the branch instruction to the program counter's contents.

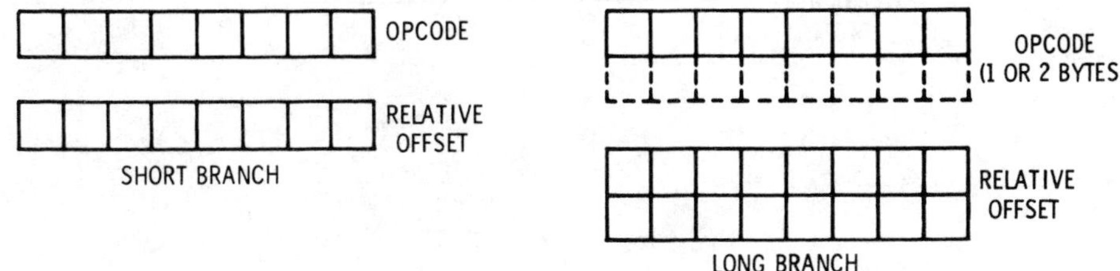

Figure 7-29
Instruction formats for the 6809 short and long branch instructions.

The instruction format for 6809 branches is shown in Figure 7-29. Short branch instructions use one relative offset byte and long branch instructions use two offset bytes. The example program listed in Figure 7-30 illustrates a short BRA instruction. Notice that there is no difference between this and a similar 6800 BRA operation.

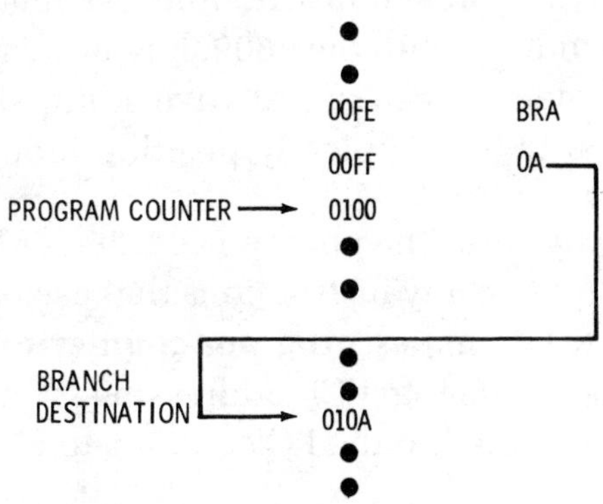

Figure 7-30
Execution of a 6809 short branch instruction

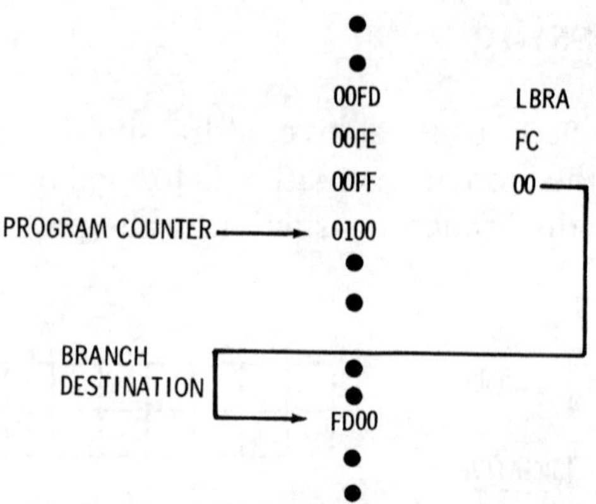

Figure 7-31

Execution of a 6809 long branch instruction

The program listed in Figure 7-31 illustrates a long BRA, or LBRA, instruction. Note the advantage of the long branch is that the branching range is increased with the use of a two-byte offset. However, the long branch instruction requires at least three bytes and in many cases four bytes, since many of the 6809 long branch instruction use two opcode bytes.

Earlier, we stated that an extreme advantage of relative addressing is position independence. Recall that, with position independent code, a program will execute properly regardless of where it is placed in memory. With the 6800, only the branch instructions use relative addressing and are position independent. With the 6809, however, any instructions that are used to access memory can use relative addressing. Thus, 6809 programs can be written to be completely position independent.

Relative addressing always uses the program counter, or PC, as a pointer register. Thus, we will refer to any instructions that use relative addressing (except branch instructions) as **program counter relative,** or **PCR,** instructions. The symbol to denote PCR addressing is "**n,PCR**" where n is the offset value that is added to the PC contents to form the effective address.

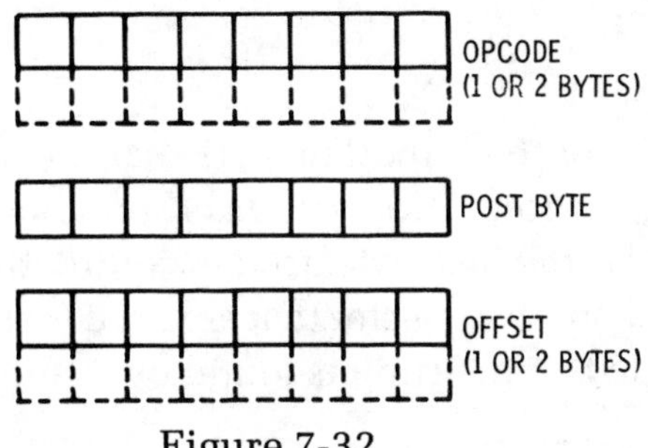

Figure 7-32

Format of a 6809 instruction which uses the program counter relative addressing mode.

Consider the instruction LDA B5,PCR. This instruction will load accumulator A with the contents of address $B5_{16}$+PC. In the same way, the instruction STX 0100,PCR will store X at two consecutive addresses: 0100_{16}+PC:0100_{16}+PC+1. As you can see, the program counter is being used as a pointer register. Therefore, the instruction operation is always **relative** to the program counter's contents. Program counter relative addressing uses an instruction format as shown in Figure 7-32. Note that a post byte is required with one or two offset bytes.

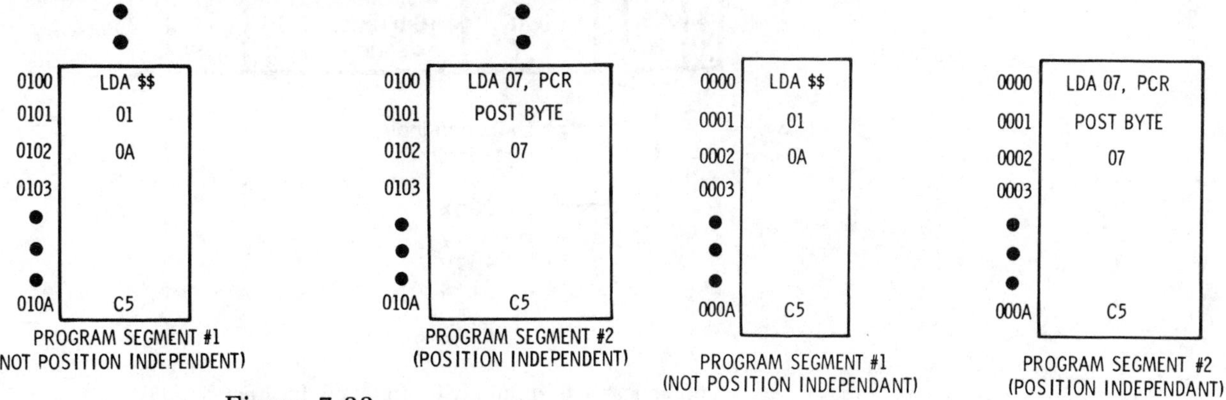

Figure 7-33

Position independent code versus non-position independent code

Figure 7-34

Position independent code versus non-position independent code

To drive home the very important concept of position independence, let's examine the two LDA operations in Figure 7-33. Here, program segment #1 uses extended addressing to load accumulator A. Program segment #2 uses program counter relative addressing to load accumulator A. Both programs will load accumulator A with the value $C5_{16}$, located at address $010A_{16}$. Now, suppose you move program segment #1 and program segment #2 to a different area of memory as shown in Figure 7-34. Note that program segment #2 will still execute properly and load accumulator A with the value $C5_{16}$. However, program segment #1 will load accumulator A with the contents of address $010A_{16}$, whatever that may be. To make program #1 execute properly, you must change the LDA instruction to LDA $$ 000A. Program #2 does not require any changes.

The Post Byte

You are now aware of the important role that the post byte plays for indexed addressing, indirect addressing and program counter relative addressing. But, how is the post byte used to control the selection of the addressing mode and pointer register that are used for the instruction operation? The answer to this question is found by examining Figure 7-35.

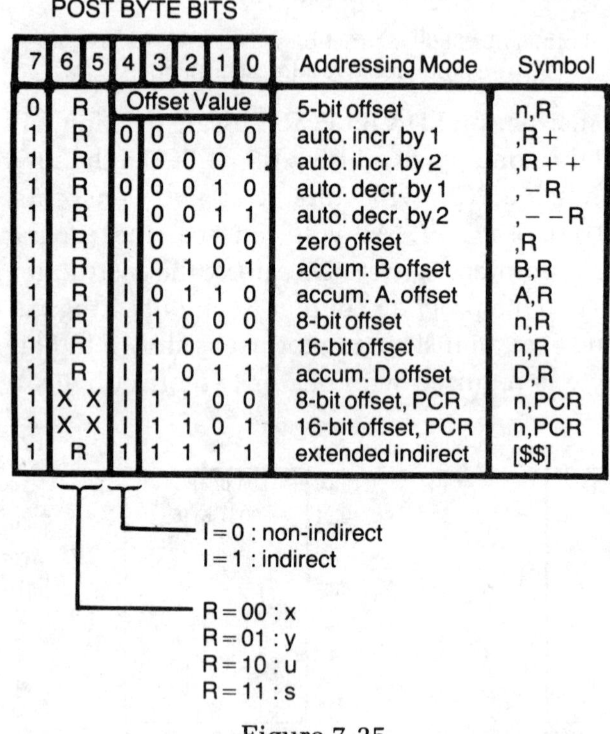

POST BYTE BITS

7	6	5	4	3	2	1	0	Addressing Mode	Symbol
0	R		Offset Value					5-bit offset	n,R
1	R		0	0	0	0	0	auto. incr. by 1	,R+
1	R		I	0	0	0	1	auto. incr. by 2	,R++
1	R		0	0	0	1	0	auto. decr. by 1	,−R
1	R		I	0	0	1	1	auto. decr. by 2	,−−R
1	R		I	0	1	0	0	zero offset	,R
1	R		I	0	1	0	1	accum. B offset	B,R
1	R		I	0	1	1	0	accum. A. offset	A,R
1	R		I	1	0	0	0	8-bit offset	n,R
1	R		I	1	0	0	1	16-bit offset	n,R
1	R		I	1	0	1	1	accum. D offset	D,R
1	X	X	I	1	1	0	0	8-bit offset, PCR	n,PCR
1	X	X	I	1	1	0	1	16-bit offset, PCR	n,PCR
1	R		1	1	1	1	1	extended indirect	[$$]

Figure 7-35

6809 post byte summary for indexed, indirect, and PC relative addressing

The post byte codes in Figure 7-35 can be summarized as follows:

- Bits 0 through 3 specify the addressing mode to be used. Except that, in the 5-bit constant offset mode, bits 0 through 4 contain the 5-bit offset value.
- Bit 4 is used to specify indirect or non-indirect addressing with the above exception. When set, indirect addressing is specified.
- Bits 5 and 6 are used to specify the pointer register for any of the indexed addressing modes.
- Bit 7 is used to specify the 5-bit constant offset mode. When cleared, the 5-bit offset value must be placed in bits 0 through 4. This bit must be set for all other addressing modes.

To see how a post byte value is determined, consider the instruction LEAY A,X. Recall that this instruction will add the contents of accumulator A to X, and save the sum in Y. The question is: What post byte value is required with the LEAY instruction opcode to perform this operation? By examining the instruction, you determine that accumulator A offset indexed addressing is the addressing mode being used. Consequently, from Figure 7-35, you find that bits 0 through 3 of the post byte must be 0110. Bit 4 of the post byte must be cleared, or 0, since indirect addressing is not required. The pointer register is the X register and, therefore, bits 5 and 6 of the post byte must be 00. Finally, bit 7 of the post byte must be set, or 1, since a 5-bit offset is not being used. Thus, the required post byte is $1000\ 0110_2$, or 86_{16}.

Self-Test Review

16. List the eight fundamental addressing modes of the 6809. ________

17. Suppose the 6809 direct page register contains the value $C5_{16}$. What happens when the 6809 encounters a LDA $ 10 instruction? ________

18. Suppose the 6809 is reset and the instruction in question #17 is executed. Is there any difference in the instruction execution? If so, what is the difference? ________

19. Which 6809 instructions use register addressing? ________

20. What is the proper source (mnemonic) code to transfer the contents of the U register to the S register? ________

21. What post byte is required to perform the transfer operation in question #20? ________

22. What post byte is required with the PSHU instruction to push the D, X, and S registers onto the U stack?

23. Suppose the U register contains the value 0100_{16} prior to executing the instruction in question #22. At what address will the PSHU instruction begin pushing?

24. List the three basic forms of indexed addressing available to the 6809.

25. Write an instruction that will store the contents of accumulator D at two consecutive addresses specified by the X register and a constant offset of $A7_{16}$.

26. What instruction post byte value is required to perform the operation in question #25?

27. Write an instruction to add the value 05_{16} to the U register.

28. What instruction post byte value is required to perform the operation in question #27?

29. Write an instruction to add accumulator A to Y and save the result in X.

30. What instruction post byte value is required to perform the operation in question #29? ______________________________

31. Write an instruction to push accumulator D onto a stack defined by the Y register. ______________________________

32. What instruction post byte value is required to perform the operation in question #31? ______________________________

33. How does indirect addressing differ from non-indirect addressing? ______________________________

34. Write an instruction to load accumulator A indirectly using the S register as a pointer register and a constant offset of $B5_{16}$. ______________________________

35. What instruction post byte value is required to perform the operation in question #34? ______________________________

36. Interpret the instruction STA 10,PCR. ______________________________

37. What is the advantage of writing programs using relative addressing? ______________________________

Answers

16. The eight fundamental addressing modes of the 6809 are: **inherent, immediate, direct, extended, register, indexed, indirect,** and **relative.**

17. If the direct page register contains the value $C5_{16}$, the LDA $ 10 instruction will load accumulator A with the contents of address $C510_{16}$.

18. Yes, the reset operation clears the direct page register. Consequently, accumulator A is loaded with the contents of address 0010_{16}.

19. There are four 6809 instructions that use register addressing. They are the **transfer** (TFR), **exchange** (EXG), **push** (PSH), and **pull** (PUL) instructions.

20. The source code required to transfer the contents of the U register to the S register is TFR U,S.

21. From Figure 7-19, the post byte required to perform the transfer operation in question #20 is $\mathbf{34_{16}}$.

22. From Figure 7-20, the post byte required to push the D, X, and S registers on the U stack is 56_{16}.

23. With the 6809, the stack pointers point to the top of the stack. Thus, if the U register contains the value 0100_{16} prior to executing the PSHU instruction, the instruction will begin pushing data at address 0100_{16}-1, or $00FF_{16}$.

24. The three basic forms of indexed addressing available to the 6809 are: **constant offset indexed, accumulator offset indexed,** and **auto increment/decrement indexed.**

25. The required instruction is STD A7,X.

26. From Figure 7-35, the instruction post byte value to perform the STD A7,X operation is $\mathbf{1000\ 1000_2}$, or $\mathbf{88_{16}}$.

27. The single instruction **LEAU 05,U** will add the value 05_{16} to the U register.

28. From Figure 7-35, the instruction post byte required for the LEAU 05,U instruction is 0100 0101_2, or 45_{16}. Note that you can use the 5-bit constant offset addressing mode. The constant offset, 05_{16}, is therefore included as part of the post byte in bits 0 through 4.

29. The single instruction **LEAX A,Y** will add A to Y and save the result in X.

30. From Figure 7-35, the instruction post byte value required for the LEAX A,Y instruction is 1010 0110_2, or $A6_{16}$.

31. The instruction STD ,--Y will push accumulator D onto a stack defined by the Y register.

32. From Figure 7-35, the instruction post byte required for the STD ,--Y instruction is 1010 0011_2, or $A3_{16}$.

33. With indirect addressing, the effective address is not obtained directly from the instruction. Rather, the effective address for the operation is contained at the location specified by the operation. This intermediate address location is called the absolute address.

34. The instruction LDA [B5,S] will load accumulator A indirectly using the S register as a pointer register and a constant offset of $B5_{16}$.

35. From Figure 7-35, the instruction post byte value required for the LDA [B5,S] instruction is 1111 1000_2, or $F8_{16}$. Notice that bit 4 is set to specify indirect addressing.

36. The instruction STA 10,PCR will store accumulator A at an address determined by adding the value 10_{16} to the contents of the program counter.

37. Position independence.

THE 6809 INTERFACE LINES

You should now be familiar with the internal structure and software capabilities of the 6809. To complete our discussion of the 6809, we need to take a look at its I/O lines. Again, you will find your knowledge of the 6800 very beneficial here, since interfacing with the 6809 is very similar to that of the 6800.

We will begin this section by describing each of the 6809 interface lines. Then, we will take a look at a sister chip to the 6809, the 6809E. Finally, you will see how the power of the 6809 and 6809E can be extended with several new interface devices.

Data, Address, and Timing Signals

A pin assignment diagram of the 6809 is provided in Figure 7-36. You should recognize most of the 6809 interface lines, since many of its I/O features are similar to those of other 6800 family processors.

Like the 6800, the 6809 is a 40-pin NMOS device. It operates on a single +5V power supply. You can tell that it is an 8-bit processor, because it has eight bi-directional data lines, D0 through D7.

How many addresses can be accessed directly with the 6809? You can determine this by counting the number of address lines in Figure 7-36. You will note that there are 16 address lines, A0 through A15. Consequently, the 6809 is capable of directly accessing a 2^{16}, or 64K, address space.

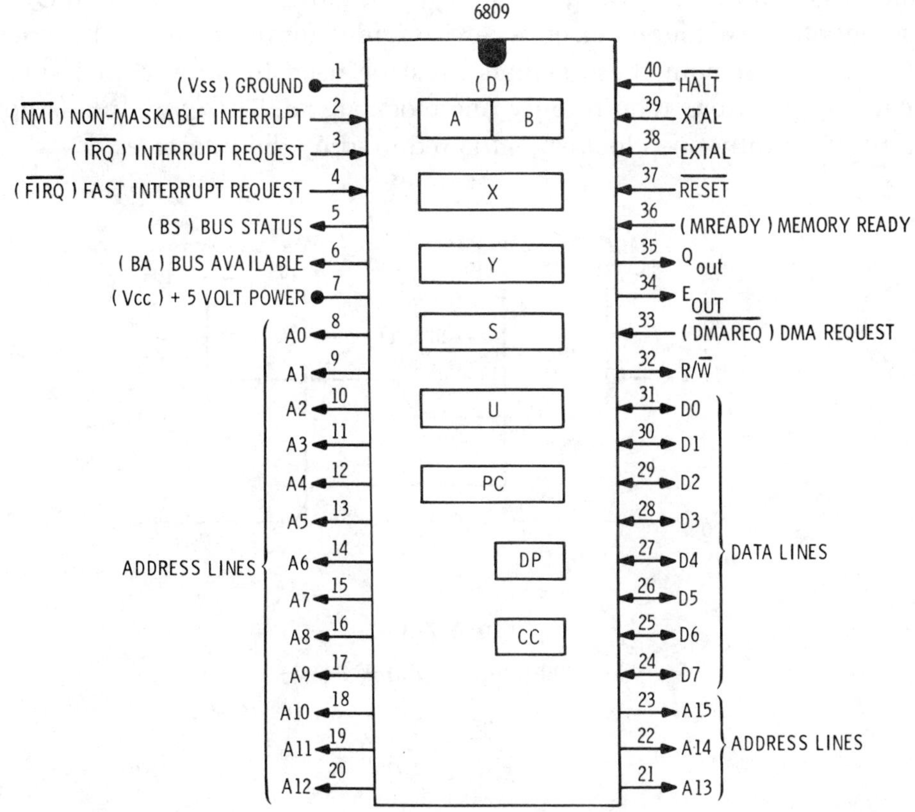

Figure 7-36
The 6809 I/O lines

Timing for the 6809 is provided by an **internal** clock that operates in the same way as the 6801, 6802, 6803, and 6808 internal clocks. A crystal is connected across the 6809 XTAL and EXTAL lines. The internal clock circuit divides the crystal frequency by four to establish the internal clock frequency. An external clocking source can also be used to drive the 6809. The external signal is applied to the EXTAL line and the XTAL line must be grounded.

The maximum operating frequency for the standard 6809 is 1 MHz. However, the 6809 is also available in a 1.5 MHz version and 2 MHz version. These devices are called the 68A09 and 68B09 respectively.

Timing for interfacing is provided by two separate output lines labeled E_{OUT} and Q_{OUT}. The E_{OUT} line is similar to the Ø2 clock line of the 6800. The Q_{OUT} line is the same frequency as E_{OUT}, but leads E_{OUT} by 90°, or ¼ cycle as shown in Figure 7-37. Address information is valid when Q_{OUT} goes high, and data is valid when Q_{OUT} goes low. Since E_{OUT}, and Q_{OUT} are out of phase, four clock edges are provided for interfacing. This does not mean that both these signals must be used for interfacing, since many applications require only one clock signal. The Q_{OUT} line is not used when only one clock signal is required by the interface.

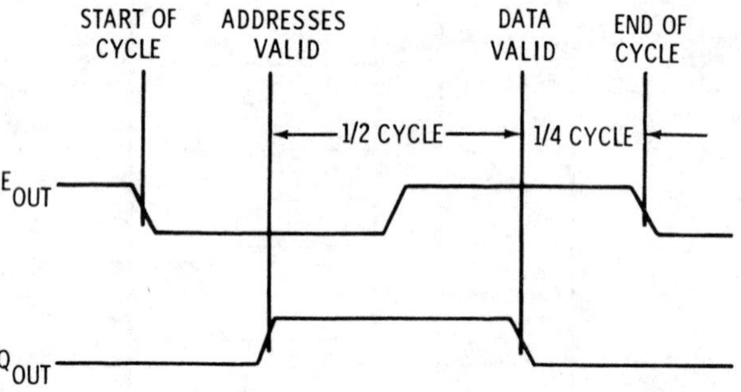

Figure 7-37

The 6809 interface timing signals

Control Lines

The 6809 control lines include the memory ready line, interrupt lines, and halt line. Each of these lines provide a means for external control of the 6809 processor.

The **memory ready**, or **MREADY**, line is used to stretch the E_{OUT} and Q_{OUT} clock signals for interfacing with slow memories. This line is used exactly like the 6802 and 6808 memory ready lines to stretch the data valid portion of the clock signals to a maxmimum of 10 MPU cycles. The effect of an active memory ready line on the E_{OUT} and Q_{OUT} signals is illustrated in Figure 7-38.

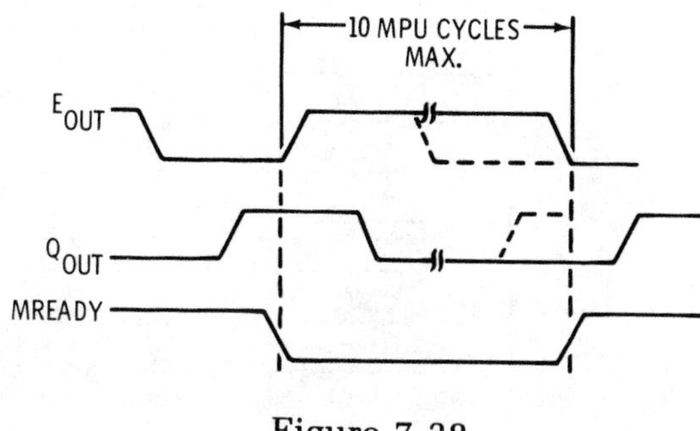

Figure 7-38

Stretching E_{OUT} and Q_{OUT} with the MREADY line

The 6809 hardware interrupts include $\overline{\text{RESET}}$, $\overline{\text{NMI}}$, $\overline{\text{IRQ}}$, and $\overline{\text{FIRQ}}$. You are familiar with the first three of these as a result of your 6800 knowledge. The sequence of events for the 6809 $\overline{\text{RESET}}$, $\overline{\text{NMI}}$, and $\overline{\text{IRQ}}$ interrupts is almost the same as that for the 6800. However, there are some minor differences.

The 6809 **$\overline{\text{RESET}}$** interrupt clears the direct page register and sets the F-flag in the condition code register. These operations do not take place with a 6800 $\overline{\text{RESET}}$ since the 6800 does not contain a direct page register or F-flag.

The 6809 **non-maskable interrupt,** or $\overline{\text{NMI}}$, sets the E-, F-, and I-flags of the condition code register. The E-flag is set to indicate that the **entire** 6809 internal register **states** are **saved**. Recall that the E-flag is the entire state saved flag. During the $\overline{\text{NMI}}$ sequence, the 6809 automatically stacks its register contents on the S-stack in the order shown in Figure 7-39. In addition to setting the E-flag, the F-, and I-flags are set by the $\overline{\text{NMI}}$ sequence, to prevent $\overline{\text{FIRQ}}$ or $\overline{\text{IRQ}}$ interrupts from interrupting the $\overline{\text{NMI}}$ interrupt.

The 6809 **interrupt request,** or $\overline{\textbf{IRQ}}$, also stacks the internal register contents on the S-stack as shown in Figure 7-39. Consequently, the $\overline{\text{IRQ}}$ sequence sets the E-flag of the condition code register. However, the $\overline{\text{IRQ}}$ sequence does not set the F-flag. A fast interrupt request, or $\overline{\text{FIRQ}}$, can, therefore, interrupt the $\overline{\text{IRQ}}$ sequence.

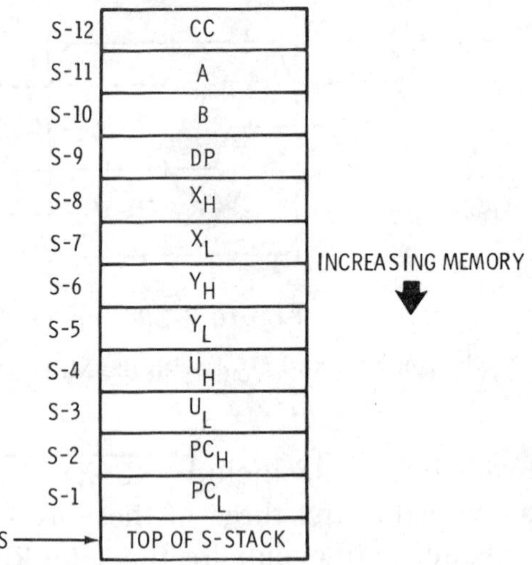

Figure 7-39

The 6809 register stacking order on the S-stack during the $\overline{\text{NMI}}$, SWI, and $\overline{\text{IRQ}}$ interrupt sequences.

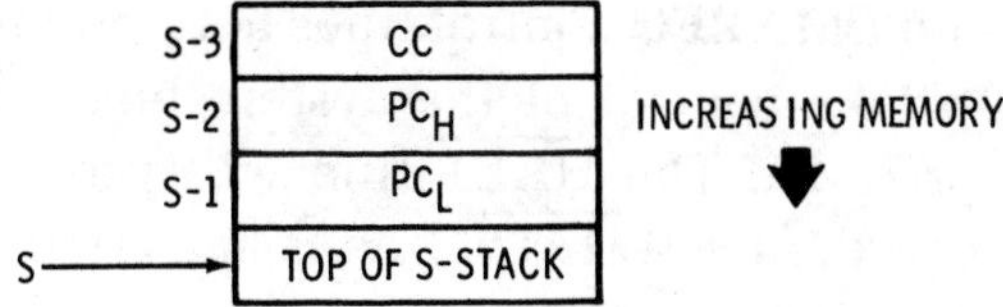

Figure 7-40

The 6809 register stacking order on the S-stack during the $\overline{\text{FIRQ}}$ interrupt sequence.

The **fast interrupt request,** or $\overline{\textbf{FIRQ}}$, is new and unique to the 6809. This interrupt is used for fast response times when it is known that all the internal register data does not have to be saved on the stack during the interrupt. The $\overline{\text{FIRQ}}$ sequence only stacks the program counter and condition code register as shown in Figure 7-40. Consequently, the $\overline{\text{FIRQ}}$ sequence clears the E-flag of the condition code register before the stacking operation. In addition, the $\overline{\text{FIRQ}}$ sequence sets both the F-flags and I-flags of the condition code register to prevent another $\overline{\text{FIRQ}}$ or $\overline{\text{IRQ}}$ interrupt from interrupting the sequence.

All of the 6809 interrupts are **vectored** interrupts. This means that each interrupt has an interrupt vector located at a designated memory location. Recall that the vector directs the processor to the first instruction in the respective interrupt service routine. The 6809 interrupt vector assignments are given in Figure 7-41. The interrupt vectors are usually stored in ROM at the addresses shown.

Interrupt Description	Vector Location	
	MS Byte	LS Byte
Reset ($\overline{\text{RESET}}$)	FFFE	FFFF
Non-Maskable Interrupt ($\overline{\text{NMI}}$)	FFFC	FFFD
Software Interrupt (SWI)	FFFA	FFFB
Interrupt Request ($\overline{\text{IRQ}}$)	FFF8	FFF9
Fast Interrupt Request ($\overline{\text{FIRQ}}$)	FFF6	FFF7
Software Interrupt 2 (SWI2)	FFF4	FFF5
Software Interrupt 3 (SWI3)	FFF2	FFF3
Reserved	FFF0	FFF1

Figure 7-41

The 6809 interrupt vector assignments

The 6809 **$\overline{\text{HALT}}$** and **$\overline{\text{DMAREQ}}$** control lines both provide a means for an external device to take control of the system bus structure for direct memory access, or DMA. The $\overline{\text{HALT}}$ line will provide for **halt mode DMA.** That is, when the 6809 $\overline{\text{HALT}}$ line is activated, or low, the 6809 will tri-state itself from the external data and address buses as long as the $\overline{\text{HALT}}$ line is held low. All the internal 6809 register data is retained.

The **$\overline{\text{DMAREQ}}$** line will provide a means for **cycle stealing DMA.** Recall that cycle stealing DMA is normally used for dynamic memory refresh. When the $\overline{\text{DMAREQ}}$ line is activated, or low, the 6809 will tri-state itself from the external data and address buses for up to fifteen MPU cycles. After the fifteenth MPU cycle, the 6809 will **steal** one cycle to refresh its internal registers. The 6809 will again tri-state itself if the $\overline{\text{DMAREQ}}$ remains active.

Status Lines

The 6809 status lines include the read/write, or R/$\overline{\text{W}}$ line; bus status, or BS line; and bus available, or BA, line.

You already know that the R/$\overline{\text{W}}$ line indicates the direction of data transfer on the data bus lines. It must be used when interfacing with any read/write device.

The 6809 **BA** and **BS** lines are used together to communicate the status of the MPU to peripheral devices. The four MPU states indicated by the BA and BS lines are shown in Figure 7-42.

BA	BS	6809 STATE
0	0	NORMAL RUNNING
0	1	INTERRUPT ACKNOWLEDGE
1	0	SYNC ACKNOWLEDGE
1	1	HALT/BUS GRANT

Figure 7-42
The 6809 MPU states indicated by its bus available (BA), and bus status (BS) lines.

The first MPU state, **normal running,** should need no explanation. The next state is called the **interrupt acknowledge state.** This state tells peripheral devices that the 6809 has accepted an interrupt. Thus, a peripheral device has an indication of when its interrupt has been accepted.

The third MPU state is called the **sync acknowledge state.** Recall that the 6809 instruction set includes a **SYNC** instruction. In the first section of this unit, we said that the SYNC instruction is used to synchronize the system software to an external hardware event, such as an interrupt. Here's how it works. When the SYNC instruction is executed, the 6809 waits for an interrupt. This is called the **syncing state,** and is indicated by the BA and BS line status as shown in Figure 7-42. If an interrupt request ($\overline{\text{IRQ}}$ or $\overline{\text{FIRQ}}$) occurs during the syncing state and it is **not masked,** the 6809 will break the syncing state and execute the respective interrupt service routine. However, if an interrupt request occurs during the syncing state and **is masked,** the 6809 will execute the next sequential instruction after the SYNC instruction.

The next instruction might begin a data transfer operation which is different from the normal interrupt service routine. Time is saved, since no interrupt stacking or vectoring is involved. Thus, the SYNC instruction allows you to schedule some interrupts and synchronize them with the system software.

The fourth MPU state is called the **halt/bus grant state.** This state provides external devices with an indication that the 6809 has tri-stated itself from the external address and data buses. This will normally take place as a result of a DMA operation.

The 6809E

The 6809E is a sister chip to the 6809. Its internal CPU register structure and instruction set are indentical to the 6809. However, its I/O lines are slightly different, as you can see from the 6809E pin assignment diagram in Figure 7-43. The 6809 XTAL, EXTAL, MREADY, Q_{OUT}, E_{OUT}, and $\overline{DMAREQ}$ lines are gone. In place of these 6809 lines, the 6809E has substituted the TSC, LIC, AVMA, E_{IN}, Q_{IN}, and BUSY lines. Let's take a brief look at the functions of these new lines.

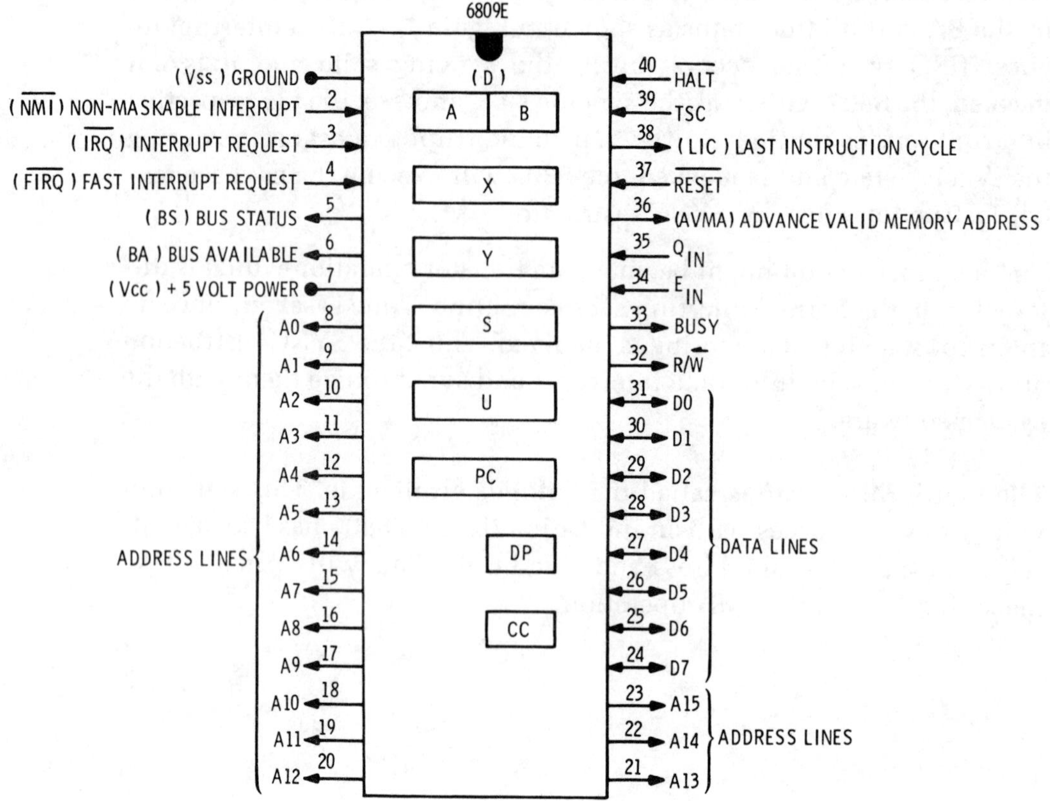

Figure 7-43
The 6809E I/O lines

First of all, the 6809E does not contain an internal clock. This explains why the 6809E does not have the XTAL and EXTAL lines. **You** must supply the E and Q clock signals at the E_{IN} and Q_{IN} lines of the 6809E respectively. The E_{IN} and Q_{IN} clock signals must be 90° out of phase as shown previously in Figure 7-37. The frequency you supply drives the internal 6809E circuits directly and is not divided by four. You must also use one or more of these clock signals when interfacing the 6809E to peripheral devices. The standard 6809E operates at a maximum frequency of 1 MHz. However, like the 6809, the 6809E is available in a 1.5 MHz version and a 2.0 MHz version. These devices are called the 68A09E, and 68B09E respectively.

The 6809E **TSC** line stands for **three state control.** This line replaces the $\overline{\text{DMAREQ}}$ line of the 6809 and is used for the same purpose. When the TSC line is active (high), the 6809E tri-states its address and data buses. Thus, the TSC line can be used for DMA purposes.

The 6809E provides three additional status lines called **last instruction cycle**, or **LIC**; **advance valid memory address**, or **AVMA**; and **BUSY**. All three of these lines were included to facilitate multiprocessor interfacing with the 6809E. It is anticipated that the 6809E will be used in larger and more complex systems involving many different processors. Such systems are called **multiprocessor systems**. In a multiprocessor system, several processors usually share the same address and data bus structure. When this is the case, **bus arbitration logic** is required to act as a traffic cop and direct the usage of the common bus structure. Many times, the bus arbitration logic is another processor, dedicated to the arbitration task. In any event, the multiprocessor system arbitration task is simplified when the system processors communicate status information in advance to the bus arbitrator.

The 6809E last instruction cycle, or LIC, line is an output status line that goes high during the last MPU cycle of every instruction. Such a signal can provide the bus arbitration logic in a multiprocessor system with a head start in the arbitration process. Its like putting on your right turn signal so the traffic cop knows you intend to make a right turn.

The advanced valid memory address, or AVMA, line also provides some advance notice to the bus arbitration logic. This output line goes high when the 6809E is about to use the address and data bus structure. An advance notice of one bus cycle is provided. Thus, if the address and data buses are being multiplexed, as in hidden memory refresh, other devices using the data and address buses are given advance notice that the 6809E is about to use the bus structure.

Finally, the BUSY line does just what it says: it tells the bus arbitrator and other processors in the system that the 6809E is "busy" using the bus structure. In a multiprocessor system, MPU busy lines are used by the bus arbitrator to make sure that only one processor is using the bus structure at any given time.

6809/6809E Support Devices

Both the 6809 and 6809E are directly compatible with all of the 6800 family of peripheral devices. You will use a 6821 PIA for parallel interfacing. For serial interfacing, you will use a 6850 ACIA. Other 6800 family peripheral devices which are directly compatible with the 6809 and 6809E include the 6840 PTM, 6843 FDC, 6844 DMAC, 6845 CRTC, 6847 VDG, 6860 MODEM, and 6883 SAM. Interfacing these devices to the 6809 or 6809E is almost identical to 6800 interfacing. In most cases, you simply substitute the 6809 E clock line in place of the 6800 Ø2 clock line.

Several new peripheral devices have been developed specifically for the 6809 and 6809E. To date, these devices include the **6829 memory management unit, 6839 floating-point ROM,** and **6842 serial DMA processor.** Let's take a brief look at the capabilities of each device.

The 6809/6809E has often been referred to as "a 500 horsepower engine with a 5-gallon gas tank". This is because the high performance MPU is only capable of addressing 64K bytes directly. In an effort to provide a bigger "gas tank" for the 6809/6809E, the **6829 memory management unit,** or **MMU**, was developed. The 6829 MMU expands the address space of the 6809/6809E from 64K bytes to a maximum of 2M bytes. The address bus expansion is accomplished as shown in Figure 7-44. Note that the 6829 MMU combines the lower eleven address lines of the 6809/6809E (A0-A10) with ten of its own (P11-P20) to form a 21-line address bus (PA0-PA20). The 6829 MMU produces its eleven address lines (P11-P20) using the upper five address lines of the 6809/6809E (A11-A15). This is accomplished internally using several programmable **task** registers. The 2M byte address space is conveniently mapped by the 6829 MMU into 1024 pages of 2K bytes each.

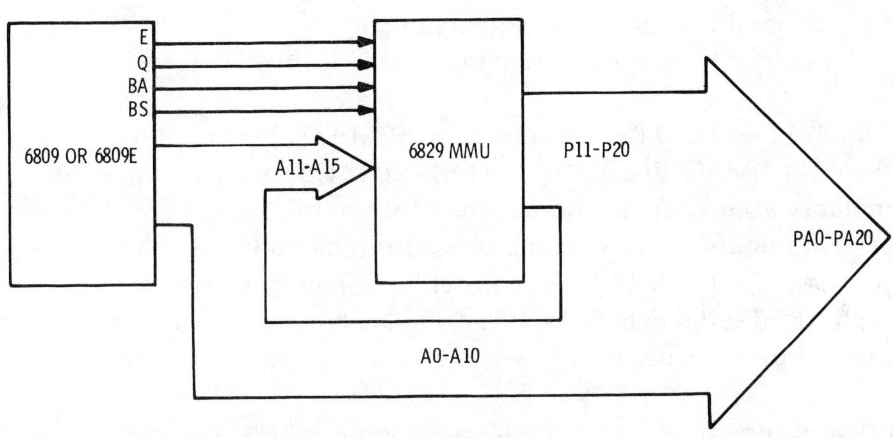

Figure 7-44
Address bus expansion of the 6809/6809E using the 6829 Memory Management Unit, or MMU.

The **6839 floating point ROM** was developed to facilitate the use of high level languages, like BASIC, PASCAL, and FORTRAN in 6809/6809E systems. The 6839 provides completely position independent 6809 code to implement both single and double precision floating point arithmetic. The following floating point operations are provided by the 6839:

Add
Subtract
Multiply
Divide
Square Root
Integer Value
Absolute Value
Negate
Compare
Integer/Floating Point Conversions
Binary Floating Point/Decimal String Conversions

The **6842 serial DMA processor,** or **SDMA,** is the serial counterpart of the 6844 DMAC. Recall that the 6844 DMAC provides for parallel direct memory access. In multiprocessor systems, high speed serial **data links** are commonly used as communication channels between the system processors. The 6842 SDMA provides direct memory access for such high speed serial data links. It is capable of providing serial data transfer rates of up to 4 megabaud.

If you desire more information on these peripheral devices, we suggest you consult the respective data sheets.

Self-Test Review

38. Describe the difference between the 6809 E_{OUT} and Q_{OUT} lines. ___

___

39. List the four hardware interrupts of the 6809. ___

___

40. What are the two major differences between the $\overline{IRQ}$ and $\overline{FIRQ}$ interrupts? ____________________

41. Which 6809 interrupt sequences **do not** set the E-flag of the condition code register? ____________________

42. How can direct memory access be provided with the 6809 control lines? ____________________

43. What four MPU states are indicated by the 6809 BA and BS status lines? ____________________

44. When is the sync state acknowledged? ____________________

45. Is there any difference between the internal **chip** structure of the 6809 and 6809E? If so, what is the difference? ____________________

46. What additional status lines are provided with the 6809E? ____________________

47. Where are these additional 6809E status lines used? ____________________

48. What is bus arbitration logic? ____________________

49. What three new support devices have been developed specifically for the 6809 and 6809E? ____________________

50. What is the function of the 6829 MMU? ____________________

Answers

38. The 6809 E_{OUT} and Q_{OUT} lines are both output clock lines used for interfacing. They are the same frequency; however, Q_{OUT} leads E_{OUT} by ¼ cycle, or 90°.

39. The four hardware interrupts of the 6809 are: **$\overline{\textbf{RESET}}$, $\overline{\textbf{NMI}}$, $\overline{\textbf{IRQ}}$,** and **$\overline{\textbf{FIRQ}}$**.

40. The two major differences between the $\overline{\text{IRQ}}$ and $\overline{\text{FIRQ}}$ interrupts are:

    1. The $\overline{\text{IRQ}}$ sequence stacks all the 6809 registers on the S-stack. The $\overline{\text{FIRQ}}$ sequence only stacks the program counter and condition code register on the S-stack.

    2. The $\overline{\text{IRQ}}$ sequence sets the E-flag of the condition code register. The $\overline{\text{FIRQ}}$ sequence sets both the I-flag and F-flag of the condition code register. The $\overline{\text{FIRQ}}$ interrupt therefore has a higher priority than the $\overline{\text{IRQ}}$ interrupt.

41. The **$\overline{\textbf{RESET}}$** and **$\overline{\textbf{FIRQ}}$** interrupt sequences do not set the E-flag of the condition code register.

42. Direct memory access can be provided with the 6809 in two ways:

    A. Halt mode DMA can be provided using the 6809 $\overline{\text{HALT}}$ line.

    B. Cycle stealing DMA can be provided using the 6809 $\overline{\text{DMAREQ}}$ line.

43. The four MPU states indicated by the 6809 BA and BS status lines are: **normal running, interrupt acknowledge, sync acknowledge,** and **halt/bus grant**.

44. The sync state is acknowledged when the 6809 executes a SYNC instruction.

45. Yes, the 6809 chip contains an internal clock circuit and the 6809E does not.

46. The additional status lines provided with the 6809E are the **last instruction cycle,** or **LIC,** line; the **advanced valid memory address,** or **AVMA** line; and the **BUSY** line.

47. The additional 6809E status lines are normally used in multiprocessor systems for bus arbitration.

48. Bus arbitration logic is usually a dedicated processor in a multiprocessor system. It is used as a traffic cop to direct the usage of the common bus structure.

49. The three new support devices developed for the 6809 and 6809E are the: **6829 memory management unit, 6839 floating point ROM,** and **6842 serial direct memory access processor.**

50. The function of the 6829 MMU is to expand the address space of the 6809/6809E from 64K bytes to 2M bytes.

Unit 8

THE 68000 — PART 1

CONTENTS

INTRODUCTION

You are now about to begin the final leg of your journey through this comprehensive course. The next three units are devoted to one of the most advanced microprocessor devices currently available, the 16-bit 68000. The intent of these three units is to acquaint you with the basic features and capabilities of the 68000. As you will soon discover, the 68000 is a very sophisticated device. Consequently, if you ever program or interface the 68000, you will need to consult the 68000 data sheet and application notes to obtain the specifics not provided in this course.

This unit, Part 1, will acquaint you with the functional I/O features and software capabilities of the 68000. You will want to pay particular attention to the 68000 addressing modes. The next unit, Part 2, discusses the 68000 I/O lines and exception processing using its supervisor mode of operation. Finally, in Unit 10, or Part 3, you will learn how to interface the 68000 to memory and peripheral devices.

UNIT OBJECTIVES

When you complete this unit, you should be able to:

1. Explain how the 68000 provides a 16 megabyte address space.

2. List the four functional bus categories of the 68000 I/O lines.

3. Explain how 68000 data is organized in memory.

4. Describe the internal CPU register structure of the 68000.

5. State the difference between the 68000 user and supervisor modes.

6. Define each of the following 68000 addressing modes:
   - implied addressing
   - immediate addressing
   - absolute addressing
   - register direct addressing
   - register indirect addressing
   - program counter relative addressing

7. List the five instruction categories of the 68000 instruction set.

8. Describe the operation of the various 68000 MOVE instructions.

9. State the arithmetic and logic capabilities of the 68000.

10. Interpret 68000 instruction operation symbols.

11. Explain the function of the 68000 program control instructions.

12. Write a 68000 program to move a block of data within memory.

AN INTRODUCTORY LOOK AT THE 68000

The microprocessor/microcomputer world has been in a state of rapid deployment ever since the introduction of the first microprocessor back in 1971. The chart in Figure 8-1 gives you an idea of how one manufacturer's product line has evolved through the years. Note that the trend is towards increased circuit complexity which results in higher device performance. When will it all stop? Who knows? Dr. Gordon Moore, co-developer of the integrated circuit and head of the Intel Corporation, predicted in 1965 that "circuit complexity", and therefore capability, "will double each year." Dr. Moore's prediction has been accurate to date and should hold for the foreseeable future.

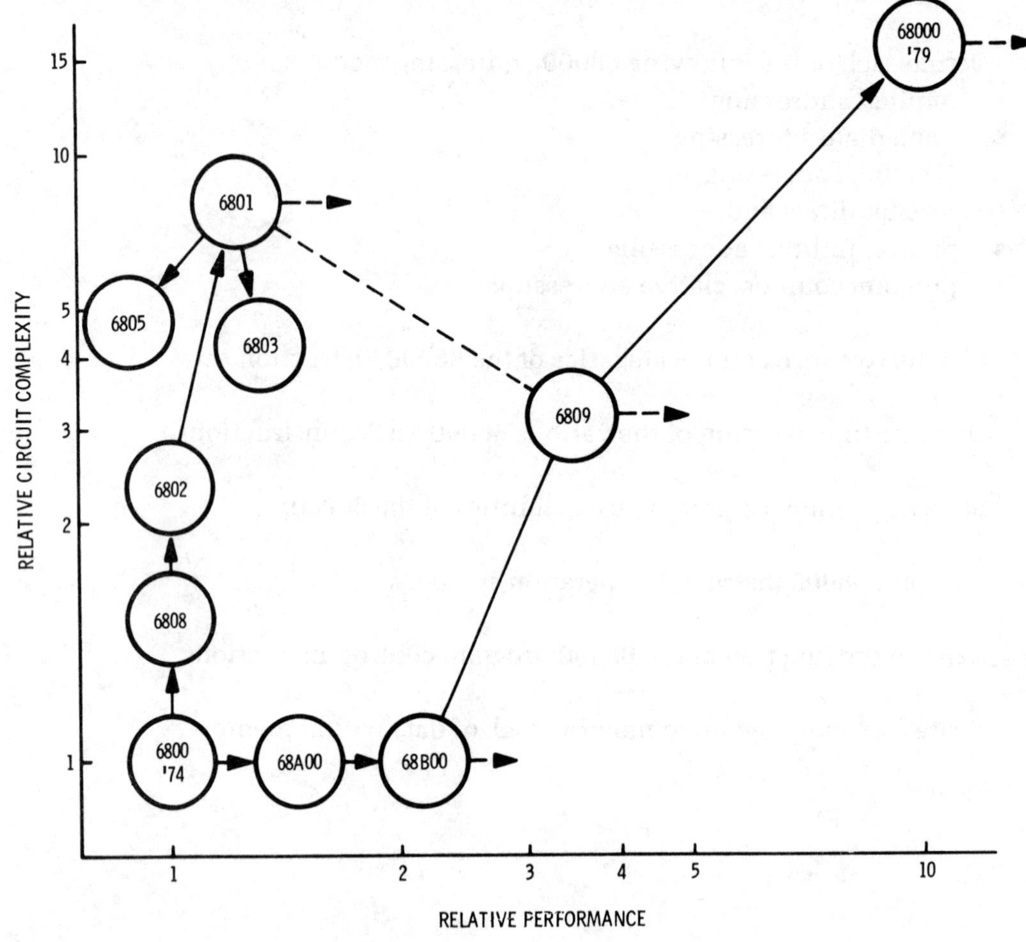

Figure 8-1

Evolution path to the 68000.

In most cases, the applications world has not kept up with the introduction of new and more powerful devices. Thus, introduction of new devices has slowed down, not because of technology restrictions, but because applications, and therefore demand, need to catch-up. The future will indeed be a period of applications technology using the devices available today.

In this course we have followed the development path of the Motorola family of microprocessors and microcomputers. To complete our journey, we must look at one more device, the 68000. This section will provide you with a general overview of the 68000 in preparation for detailed discussions provided in the subsequent material.

Functional I/O

A functional I/O diagram of the 68000 microprocessor is shown in Figure 8-2. In general, the 68000 is a 64-pin device. You will note that it operates on a single +5V power supply and is clocked at 4, 6, 8, or 10 MHz, depending on the particular device ordered. The clock signal must be generated externally and applied to the 68000 clock input line. The 68000 does not contain any internal hardware features like the 6801 and 6805.

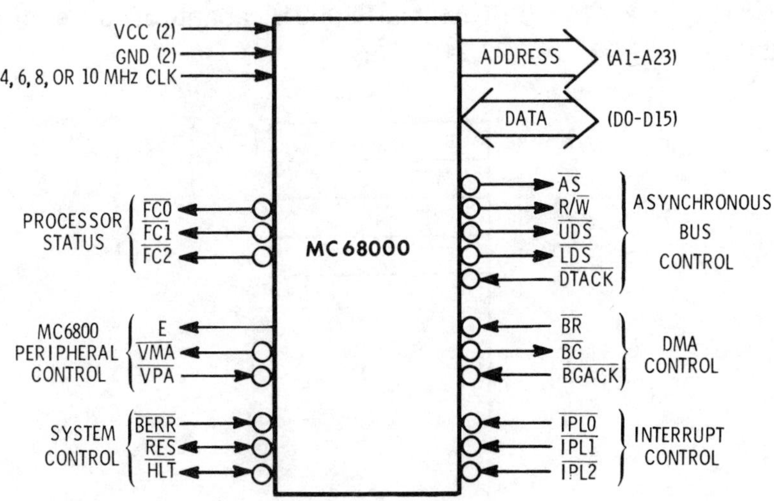

Figure 8-2

Functional I/O diagram of the 68000.

The 68000 is manufactured using **HMOS** technology. Recall that HMOS is a special high density version of NMOS. The acronym HMOS stands for **high density, short channel MOS**. With HMOS technology, twice as many components can be integrated as with standard NMOS technology. Coincidently, the 68000 has approximately 68,000 transistors integrated into one chip. In addition, HMOS technology provides higher speeds and lower power dissipation than standard NMOS.

The 68000 is a **16-bit** processor since its data bus has 16 data lines labeled D0-D15. Thus, data is transferred between the 68000 and memory or peripheral devices 16 bits at a time. However, as you will see later, you can also transfer data one byte at a time by dividing the 16 data lines into two bytes: a low order data byte consisting of data lines D0-D7, and a high order data byte consisting of data lines D8-D15. This allows you to interface the 68000 to 8-bit memory and peripheral devices.

The 68000 address bus has 23 address lines, labeled A1-A23, as shown in Figure 8-2. You would therefore calculate that the 68000 is capable of providing 2^{23}, or 8,388,608 unique addresses; right? Well, almost. Actually, the 68000 provides 16,777,216 unique addresses by using an even and odd address strobe such that there are 8,388,608 even addresses and 8,388,608 odd addresses. Therefore, we say the 68000 is capable of addressing a 16 **megabyte**, or **16M byte**, address space. Here, **M** stands for the decimal value **1,048,576**. In computer jargon, M = K×K = 1024 × 1024 = 1,048,576. Thus, the 68000 is capable of addressing a 16M, or 16 × 1,048,576 = 16,777,216 bytes.

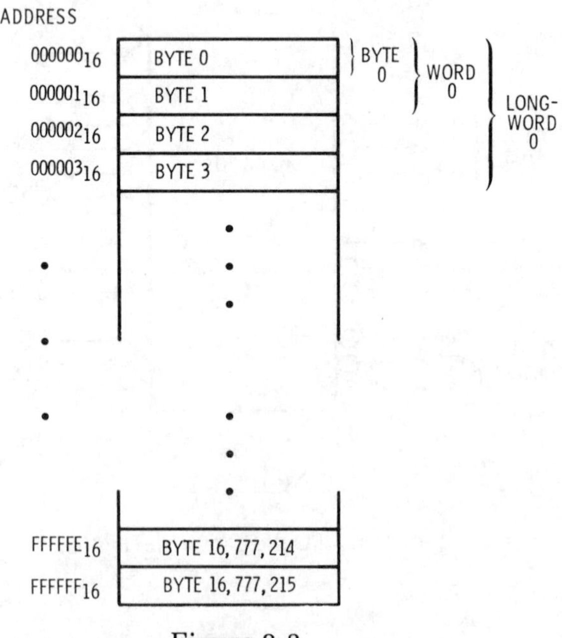

Figure 8-3

Memory organization for the 68000.

Memory interfaced to the 68000 is **byte-size** memory, as shown in Figure 8-3. However, the 68000 can operate with **byte size data**, or 8-bits; **word size data**, or 16-bits; and **long-word data**, or 32 bits. A 16-bit word must therefore use two address locations and a 32-bit long-word must use four address locations. Consequently, the 16 megabyte address space provides an **8 megaword** or **4 megalong-word** space. Words and long-words must always begin at an **even address**, the high word byte is first and the low word byte is last. Memory data organization for the 68000 is illustrated in Figure 8-4. When the 68000 accesses a 16-bit data word in memory with its 16 data lines, it will access an even and odd address simultaneously. The even addresses are interfaced to data lines D8-D15 and the odd addresses are interfaced to data lines D0-D7. You will see how this is accomplished when we discuss memory interfacing in Unit 10.

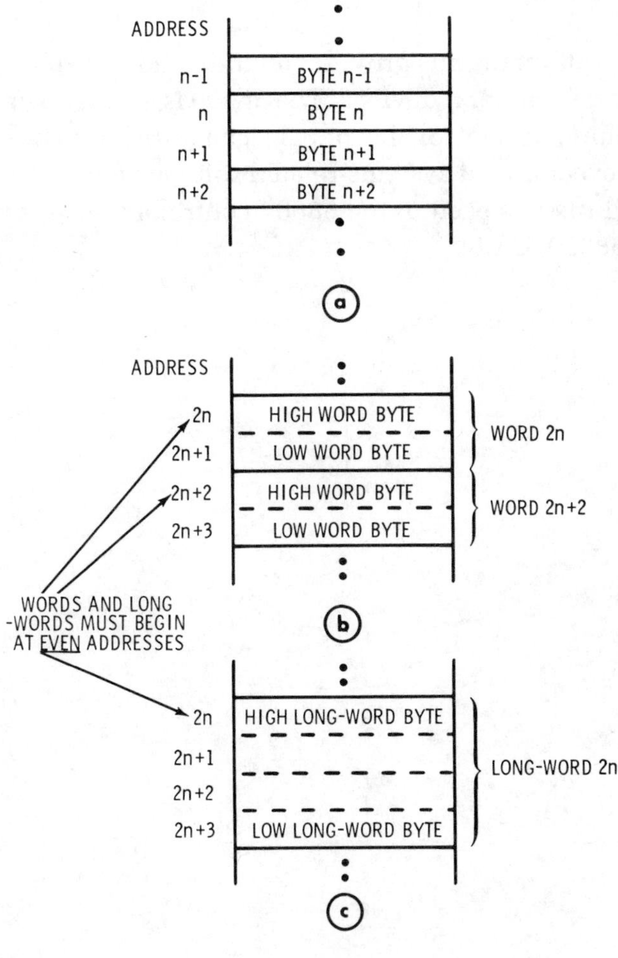

Figure 8-4

Byte size, or 8-bit, **a** ; word size, or 16-bit, **b** ; and long-word size, or 32-bit, **c** data in memory.

The control bus of the 68000 can be divided into five functional categories, as follows:

- Asynchronous bus control
- DMA control
- Interrupt control
- System control
- 6800 peripheral control

These control features allow the 68000 to be used in a wide range of systems applications. For example, the interrupt control lines provide for seven levels of vectored interrupts that can use up to 192 unique interrupt service routines stored in memory. The 6800 peripheral control lines allow you to easily interface the 68000 with the entire family of 6800 peripheral support devices.

Finally, the 68000 status bus provides an indication of MPU status to external logic and peripheral devices. The 68000 is a systems-oriented processor. Therefore, its control and status signals are specifically designed for optimum execution of systems-related software and hardware operations. We will discuss each of the 68000 control and status bus lines in Part 2 of the 68000, Unit 9.

Inside the 68000

Now that you are acquainted with the external properties of the 68000, let's take a look at its internal register structure. The 68000 CPU register structure is shown in Figure 8-5. This structure consists of eight data registers, nine address registers, a program counter, and a status register.

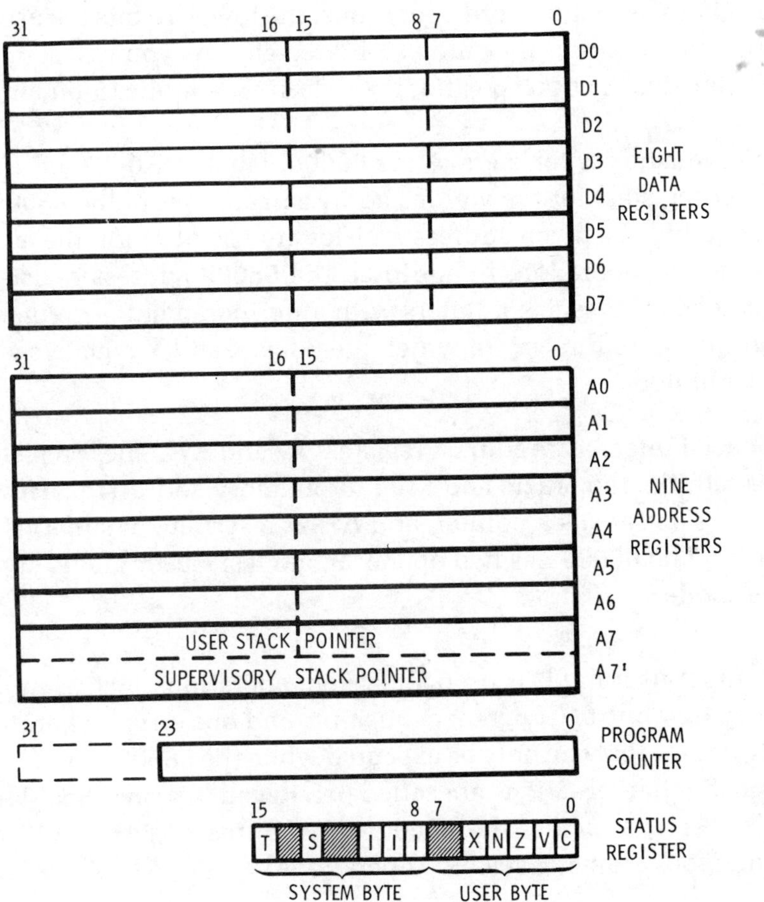

Figure 8-5

The 68000 CPU register structure.

The 68000 uses a register architecture, rather than an accumulator architecture as you have seen in the past with other 6800 family processors. A register architecture allows for greater programming flexibility and provides more efficient execution of high level software.

The eight data registers of the 68000, labeled D0-D7, are used for byte, word, and long-word operations. Note that each data register is 32 bits long. For byte operations, only the lower eight bits of the respective data register are used. For word operations, the lower 16 bits are used. A long-word operation uses the entire 32-bit register. As you will soon discover, the 68000 instruction specifies the data size — 8-bit, 16-bit, or 32-bit.

The nine address registers of the 68000, labeled A0-A7 and A7′, act as pointer registers for the various addressing modes of the 68000. The 32-bit contents of a given address register are used to form the effective address for an operation. In addition, the 68000 address registers can be used as memory stack pointers with auto increment/decrement addressing, similar to the way in which the 6809 X and Y registers are used as stack pointers.

Of special interest are address registers A7 and A7′. These registers can be accessed like the others and used for memory addressing. However, A7 serves as a user stack pointer, and A7′ as a system, or supervisory, stack pointer. The 68000 has two operating modes: a **user mode**, and a **supervisor mode**.

The supervisor mode is used for system operations such as interrupt servicing, I/O control, program debugging, and bus errors. There are several instructions that can only be executed when the 68000 is in its supervisor mode. Such instructions are called **privileged instructions**. When it is in the supervisor mode, the 68000 uses address register A7′ as a stack pointer for automatic stacking operations.

The user mode is for "normal" program execution. Privileged instructions cannot be executed in this mode. In the user mode, the 68000 uses address register A7 as a stack pointer for automatic stacking operations.

It should be emphasized that the contents of address register A7 and A7′ can be different, depending upon the mode of operation (user or supervisor). You can, therefore, view the 68000 as having nine unique address registers: A0-A6, A7, and A7′. However, only eight address registers are accessable in any given mode. You cannot access the supervisory stack pointer, or A7′, in the user mode; and you cannot access the user stack pointer, or A7, in the supervisor mode.

The 68000 program counter, or PC, is 24 bits long and, therefore, can address 2^{24}, or 16M bytes of data. The PC is used to access the address space and is also used to form effective addresses in the program counter relative addressing mode. Note from Figure 8-5 that the PC is actually 32 bits long. However, present versions of the 68000 only use the first 24 bits of the PC. Future enhancements of the 68000 might use all 32 bits of the PC and, thus, provide for a 2^{32}, or 4,294,967,296 byte address space — over **4 billion** bytes!

The 68000 status register is two bytes long, or 16-bits as shown in Figure 8-6. The lower status register byte is called the **user byte**, and the upper status register byte is called the **system byte**.

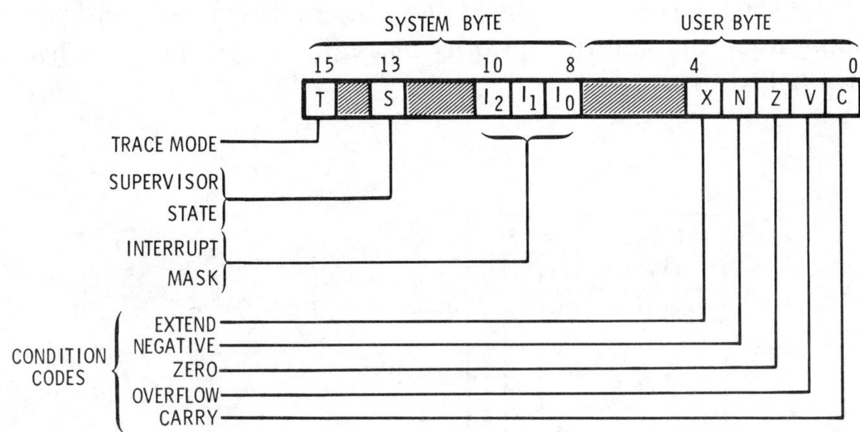

Figure 8-6

The 68000 status register.

When you are operating in the user mode, you can only access the user byte portion of the status register. The user status byte consists of five condition code flags: C, V, Z, N, and X. You are familiar with the function of the C-, V-, Z-, and N-flags from your previous 6800 family experience. The X-flag is new and requires some explanation.

The letter X stands for **extend**. This flag bit is used in multiprecision arithmetic operations. Recall that in multiprecision operations, two or more data words are used to represent a given quantity. When you are performing multiprecision arithmetic operations with the 68000, the X-flag is used as a carry flag during the operation. You can, therefore, say that the 68000 extend, or X, flag is a multiprecision carry flag. Operations which affect this flag include add, subtract, negate, rotate, and shift.

The system status byte can only be accessed and altered in the supervisor mode. This status byte contains system-related status and control information. It has three interrupt mask bits, a user/supervisor mode select bit, and a trace mode select bit.

The three interrupt mask bits (**I_2, I_1, and I_0**) are used to define which interrupt levels will be masked and which will not be masked. We will refer to the contents of these three bits as the **interrupt priority mask**. Recall that the 68000 uses seven interrupt levels. These interrupt levels are labeled 1 through 7 and are prioritized as shown in Figure 8-7. Note that level 7 is the highest priority and level 1 is the lowest priority. The level of a given interrupt is determined from the logic present on the three interrupt control lines of the 68000. This will be discussed later. In any event, given an interrupt level, it is either accepted (not masked) or ignored (masked), depending upon the interrupt priority mask in the system status byte as shown in Figure 8-7.

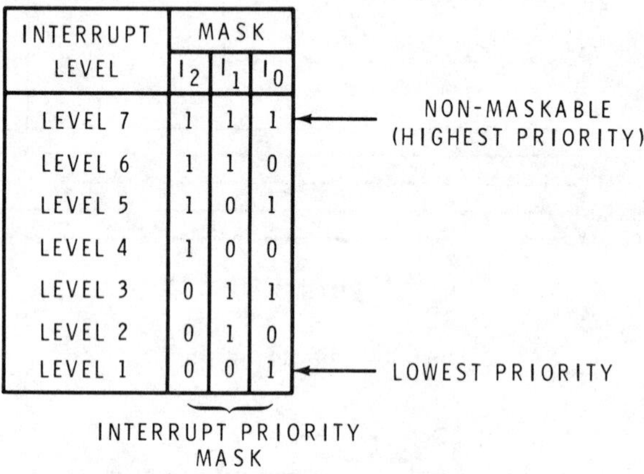

Figure 8-7

Interrupt priority mask definitions.

For example, suppose the interrupt priority mask is 101. Then, using Figure 8-7, you can determine that interrupt levels 6 and 7 are not masked and will be accepted when present at the 68000 interrupt control lines. However, interrupt levels 1 through 5 are masked and will be ignored by the 68000. In summary, an interrupt level above the interrupt priority mask is accepted, and an interrupt level at or below the interrupt priority mask is ignored. Note from Figure 8-7 that interrupt level 7 is a special case and can never be masked. Therefore, **level 7 is always a non-maskable interrupt level**.

The user/supervisor mode select bit, or **S-bit**, of the status register is used to select between the user or supervisor operating modes of the 68000. When set, the 68000 is placed in its supervisor mode. When cleared, the 68000 is placed in its user mode.

The trace mode select bit, or **T-bit**, allows you to single-step your program for debugging purposes. When the T-bit is set, the 68000 will execute only one instruction at a time. After each instruction is executed, the 68000 will vector to a debugging routine that you have placed in another part of memory. Such a routine might display the internal 68000 register contents. After the debugging routine is completed, the 68000 will return to execute the next instruction, and so on, as long as the T-bit is set. Continuous program execution is provided when the T-bit is cleared. The details of the trace mode are discussed in Unit 9.

You know that the 68000 is a 16-bit microprocessor because it has 16 data lines. However, note that its internal register structure is essentially a 32-bit structure. This allows the 68000 to execute "number crunching" operations very efficiently. In addition, we suspect that some future version of the 68000 might be made into a 32-bit microprocessor with the addition of 16 more data lines. Only time will tell; however, remember that the internal ingredients are already there and future enhancements are sure to come.

Self-Test Review

1. What is HMOS technology, and how does it differ from NMOS technology? ______

2. How does the 68000 provide a 16M byte address space? ______

3. Define word and long-word, as applied to 68000 data. ______

4. What are the four major bus categories of the 68000 I/O lines? ______

5. List the five functional categories of the 68000 control bus. ______

6. What type of internal architecture is used by the 68000, and what are the main advantages of this architecture? ______

7. List the internal 68000 registers and indicate the size of each register. ________________________

8. What are the user and supervisor operating modes of the 68000, and how do these modes affect the use of address registers A7 and A7′?

9. What are the two functional parts of the 68000 status register?

10. What is the purpose of the X-flag in the 68000 user status byte?

11. Suppose the 68000 system status byte contains an interrupt priority mask of 100. Which interrupt levels are masked and which are not masked?

12. What is the function of the T-bit in the 68000 system status byte?

Answers

1. HMOS is a special high density version of NMOS. The acronym HMOS stands for high density, short channel MOS. HMOS is twice as dense, faster, and dissipates less power than NMOS.

2. The 68000 provides a 16M byte address space by using its 23 address lines in conjunction with even and odd address strobes. Thus, there are 8M even addresses and 8M odd addresses that provide a total address space of 16M bytes.

3. A 68000 data word consists of 16-bits.
   A 68000 data long-word consists of two words, or 32-bits.

4. The four major bus categories of the 68000 I/O lines are the **data** bus, **address** bus, **control** bus, and **status** bus.

5. The five functional categories of the 68000 control bus are:

   - Asynchronous bus control
   - DMA control
   - Interrupt control
   - System control
   - 6800 peripheral control

6. The 68000 uses a **register architecture**. The main advantages of a register architecture are programming flexibility and more efficient execution of high level software.

7. The 68000 contains the following internal registers:

   - Eight 32-bit data registers (D0-D7)
   - Nine 32-bit address registers (A0-A7, and A7′)
   - One 24-bit program counter (PC)
   - One 16-bit status register

8. The 68000 user mode is for normal program execution. When it is in this mode, the 68000 uses address register A7 as a stack pointer for automatic stacking operations.

   The 68000 supervisor mode is used for system operations such as interrupt servicing, I/O control, and program debugging. In this mode, the 68000 uses address register A7′ as a stack pointer for automatic stacking operations.

9. The two functional parts of the 68000 status register are the **user status byte** and **system status byte**.

10. The X-flag is used to indicate a carry which is generated during a multiprecision arithmetic operation. Operations which affect this flag include add, subtract, negate, rotate, and shift.

11. With an interrupt priority mask of 100, interrupt levels 1 through 4 are masked and interrupt levels 5, 6, and 7 are not masked.

12. The function of the T-bit in the system status byte is to put the 68000 in its trace mode. The trace mode allows you to single-step a program by executing one instruction at a time for debugging purposes.

THE 68000 ADDRESSING MODES

As you discovered with the 6809, the real power of a processor is found in its addressing modes. The 68000 is no exception. The 68000 uses six fundamental addressing modes. Variations of these six fundamental addressing modes provide 14 unique ways of addressing memory and the internal registers of the 68000. These 14 addressing modes are used with 56 fundamental instructions to provide over 1000 unique operations for the 68000.

The six fundamental addressing modes of the 68000 are: **implied, immediate, absolute, register direct, register indirect,** and **program counter relative** addressing. In this section, we will discuss each of these fundamental addressing modes in detail. Then, in the next section, we will apply these addressing modes in our discussion of the 68000 instruction set. You will find that your 6809 addressing mode knowledge will be very beneficial in understanding the subsequent material.

Implied and Immediate Addressing

You are familiar with implied, or inherent, addressing from your previous 6800 family knowledge. With this form of addressing, the operation and the registers to be used in the operation are implicit, or understood, within the context of the instruction. For example, the return from subroutine, or RTS, instruction implicitly refers to the stack pointer and program counter. Recall that the RTS instruction causes the program counter to be pulled from the stack. No additional instruction information needs to be supplied with the implied RTS instruction since the operation is understood by the processor.

With immediate addressing, the operand to be used during the operation is contained in the instruction. With the 68000, the operand can be a byte, word, or long word. The formats for a 68000 immediate addressing instruction are shown in Figure 8-8.

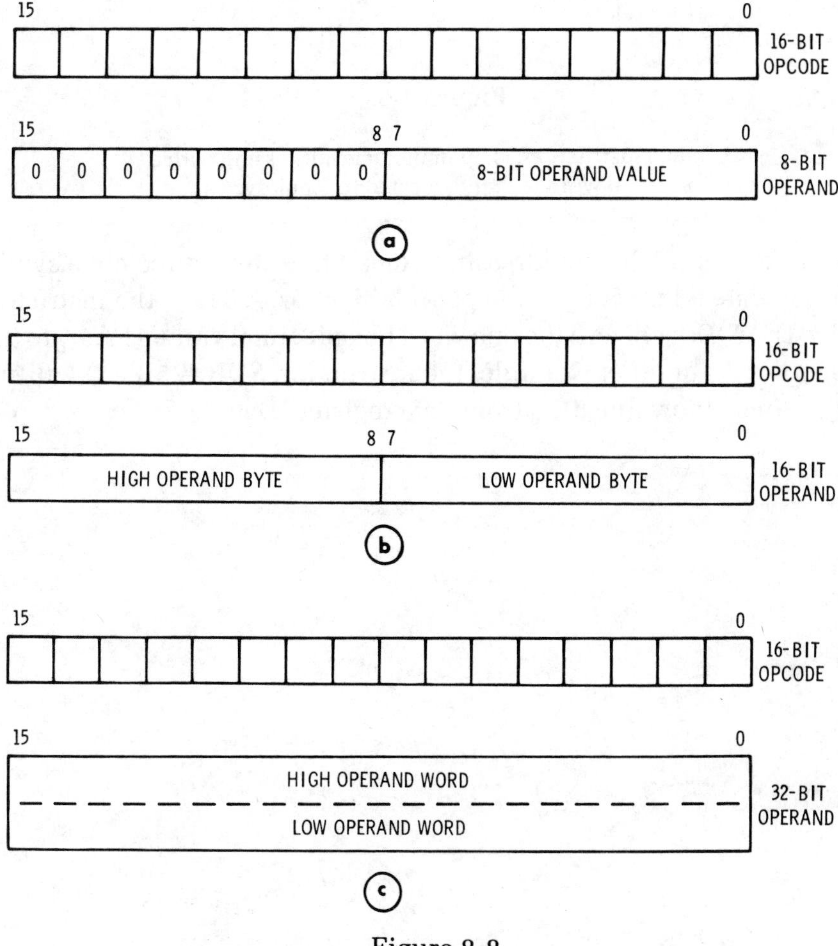

Figure 8-8

Formats for a 68000 instruction using immediate addressing with an 8-bit operand **a**, 16-bit operand **b**, and 32-bit operand **c**.

Note from Figure 8-8 that, since the 68000 is a 16-bit processor, the length of a line entry in the instruction statement is one word, or 16 bits. However, recall that the 68000 uses byte-size memory. Therefore, the instruction will occupy twice as many memory locations as there are words within the instruction statement. For example, an instruction using immediate addressing with a one word operand will occupy four consecutive memory locations as shown in Figure 8-9. We will continue to show 68000 instruction format statements in 16-bit lengths as in Figure 8-8, keeping in mind that the instruction format changes as shown in Figure 8-9 when it is contained in memory.

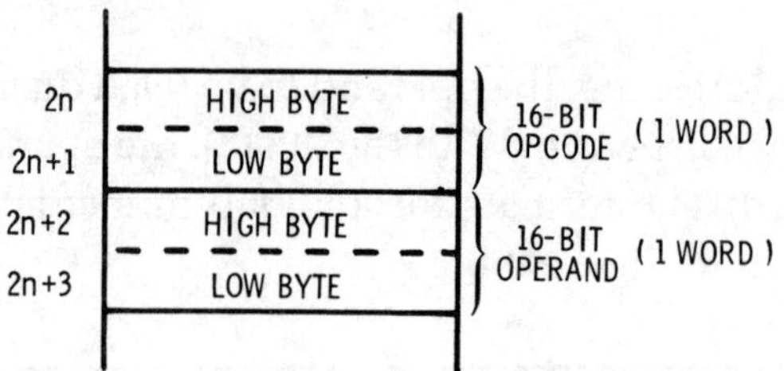

Figure 8-9

A 68000 instruction using immediate addressing with a one-word operand, located in memory.

Now back to immediate addressing. Recall that the source code symbol for immediate addressing is the pounds sign, or #. Thus, the instruction ADD # 1FA5, D0 will add the one word hexadecimal value $1FA5_{16}$ to data register D0. As another example, the instruction SUB # 5B, D7 will subtract the one byte value $5B_{16}$ from data register D7.

There is another form of immediate addressing available to the 68000, called **quick immediate addressing**. With quick immediate addressing, the immediate operand is part of the instruction opcode as shown in Figure 8-10. Obviously, an instruction using quick immediate addressing will execute faster than one with standard immediate addressing since fewer instruction words are required. The operand must be an unsigned value from 0 to 7, and is inserted in bits 9, 10, and 11 of the instruction opcode. Thus, the instruction ADDQ # 1, A0 will increment address register A0 by one. The "Q #" in the above instruction denotes quick immediate addressing. In the same way, the instruction SUBQ # 1, D5 will decrement data register D5 by one. As you will see later, the 68000 uses quick immediate addressing in place of special increment and decrement instructions.

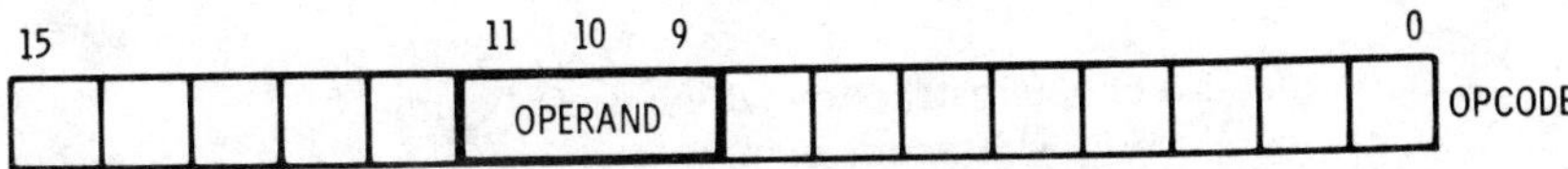

Figure 8-10

Format of a 68000 instruction which uses quick immediate addressing.

Absolute Addressing

Absolute addressing with the 68000 is similar to direct and extended addressing with the 6800. The address of the operand, or effective address, follows the instruction opcode. There are two forms of absolute addressing available to the 68000: **absolute short addressing** and **absolute long addressing**.

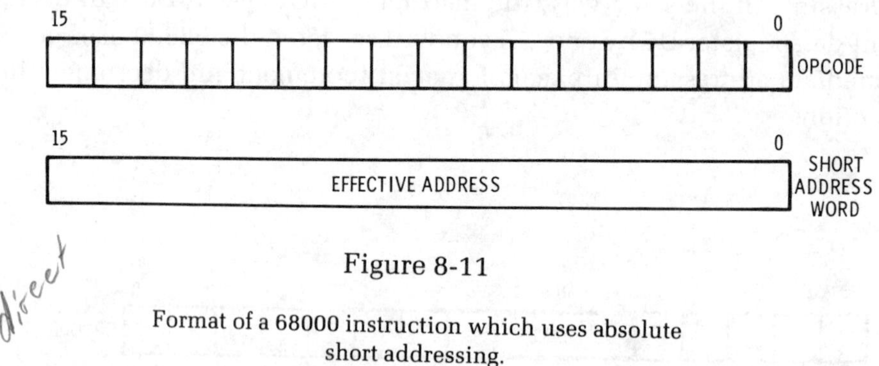

Figure 8-11

Format of a 68000 instruction which uses absolute short addressing.

With absolute short addressing, one address word follows the instruction opcode as shown in Figure 8-11. The instruction address word points to the address at which the operand is to be found as shown in Figure 8-12. In other words, the instruction address word is the effective address for the operation. Short absolute addressing with the 68000 is similar to direct addressing with the 6800 and has its limitations. The short address word in the 68000 instruction can range from 0000_{16} to $FFFF_{16}$. However, memory addresses range from 000000_{16} to $FFFFFF_{16}$. To compensate, the 68000 automatically extends the sign of the short address word as follows:

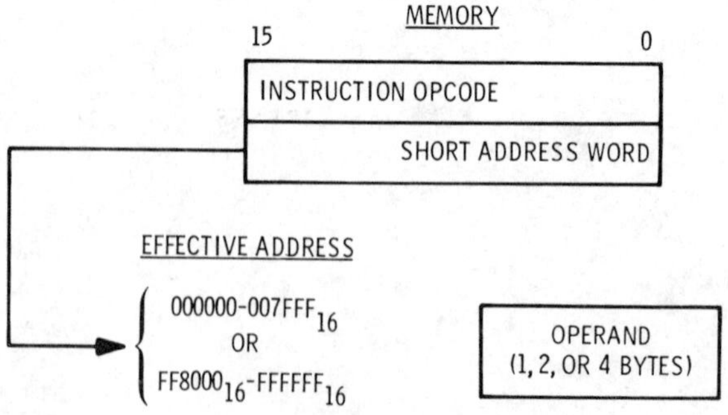

Figure 8-12

With absolute short addressing, the sign-extended address word in the instruction points to the operand in memory.

- Short addresses between 0000_{16} and $7FFF_{16}$ will point to memory locations 000000_{16} through $007FFF_{16}$, respectively.

- Short addresses between 8000_{16} and $FFFF_{16}$ will point to memory locations $FF8000_{16}$ through $FFFFFF_{16}$, respectively.

Consequently, the 68000 can only address the lowest 32K bytes of memory or the highest 32K bytes of memory using absolute short addressing.

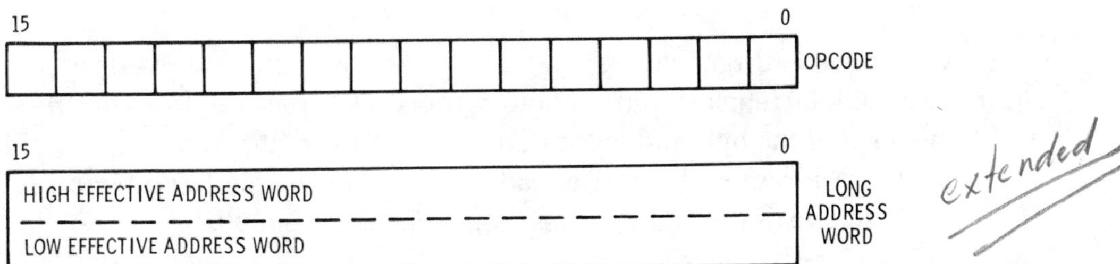

Figure 8-13

Format of a 68000 instruction which uses absolute long addressing.

With absolute long addressing, two address words, which are equivalent to one long address word, follow the instruction opcode as shown in Figure 8-13. The high address word is first, followed by the low address word. The long address word in the instruction is the effective address of the operand as illustrated in Figure 8-14. Long absolute addressing with the 68000 is like extended addressing with the 6800 since you can access the entire address space. Note that the long address word in the instruction can range from 000000_{16} to $FFFFFF_{16}$, or the entire 16M byte address space of the 68000.

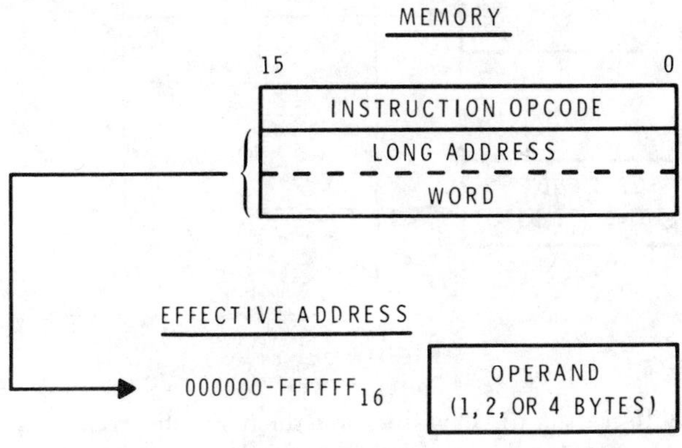

Figure 8-14

With absolute long addressing, the long address word in the instruction points to the operand in memory.

Finally, with absolute addressing and the addressing modes that follow, the effective address will be the address of an operand which can be 8, 16, or 32 bits in length. Recall that the instruction opcode specifies the data length. When the data is 16 or 32 bits in length, the effective address must always be an **even** address. If it is not, the 68000 will automatically jump to an error routine called a **trap**. Traps will be discussed in the next unit.

Register Direct Addressing

With register direct addressing, the operand is contained in one of the internal 68000 registers rather than memory. Data register direct addressing means that the operand is located in one of the eight data registers of the 68000. Address register direct addressing means that the operand is located in one of the eight address registers of the 68000.

Instructions which use register direct addressing are only one word, or 16 bits long. The 16-bit instruction opcode specifies the internal register that contains the operand. Both data and address register direct addressing are illustrated in Figure 8-15. Notice from Figure 8-15 that the symbols Dn and An are used to indicate a 68000 data register and address register, respectively. We will use these symbols whenever no particular data or address register is specified.

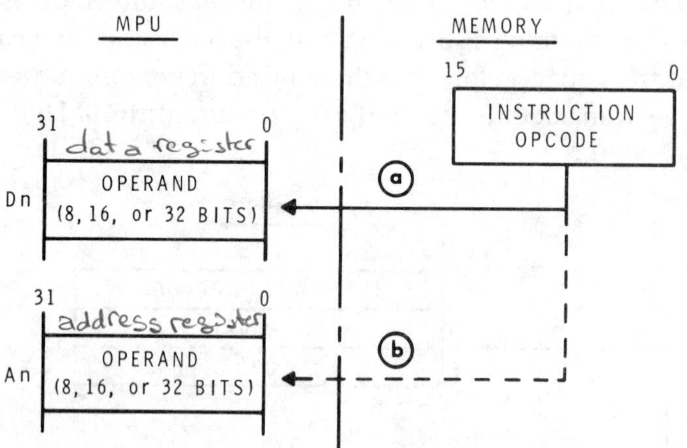

Figure 8-15

With register direct addressing, the instruction opcode points to the data register **a** , or address register **b** that contains the operand.

Register Indirect Addressing

In general, instructions which use register indirect addressing form the effective address of the operand using the contents of one of the 68000 address registers. Register indirect addressing with the 68000 is similar to indexed addressing with the 6809. There are five different variations of this addressing mode as follows:

- Address register indirect
- Address register indirect with postincrement
- Address register indirect with predecrement
- Address register indirect with offset
- Address register indirect with offset and index

ADDRESS REGISTER INDIRECT

The term "indirect" in this addressing mode means that one of the 68000 address registers **indirectly** accesses an operand located in memory. The contents of the address register specified by the instruction is the effective memory address of the operand as illustrated in Figure 8-16. In other words, the specified address register points to the operand in memory. Instructions using this addressing mode are one word in length. The instruction opcode specifies the address register to be used in the operation.

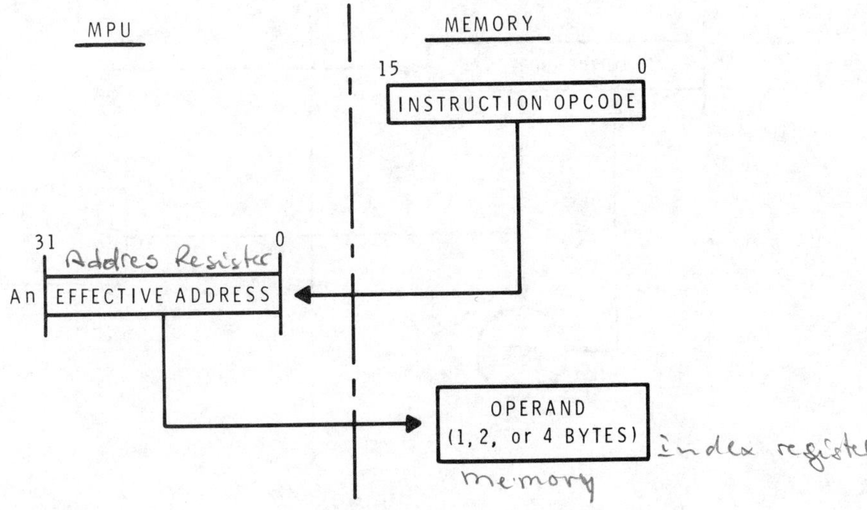

Figure 8-16

With address register indirect addressing, the address register specified by the instruction contains the effective address which points to the operand in memory.

ADDRESS REGISTER INDIRECT WITH POSTINCREMENT

This addressing mode is very similar to the 6809 auto increment addressing mode. The effective address of the operand is contained in the specified address register as before. However, **after** the instruction operation is performed, the respective address register is automatically incremented by 1, 2, or 4. The amount of incrementing depends on the size of the operand. An 8-bit operand will cause the respective address register to be incremented by 1, a 16-bit operand causes incrementing by 2, and a 32-bit operand causes incrementing by 4. The postincrement addressing mode is illustrated in Figure 8-17. Recall that both the operand size and address register to be used are specified by the instruction opcode. Consequently, instructions using this addressing mode are only one word in length.

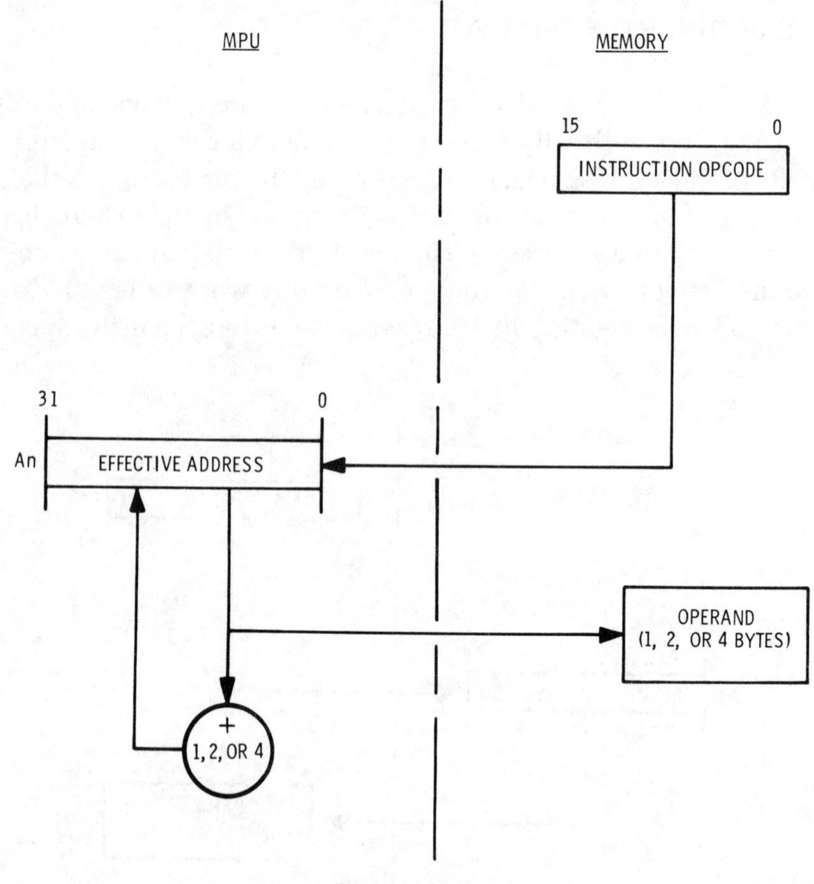

Figure 8-17

With address register indirect/postincrement addressing, the specified address register contains the effective address which points to the operand in memory. Then, after the instruction operation is performed, the respective address register is incremented by 1, 2, or 4, depending on the size of the operand.

ADDRESS REGISTER INDIRECT WITH PREDECREMENT

This addressing mode is identical to the previous mode, except that the specified address register is decremented by 1, 2, or 4 **before** the instruction operation is performed. The amount of decrementing again depends on the size of the operand. The predecrement addressing mode is illustrated in Figure 8-18.

Recall that with the 6809 auto increment/decrement addressing modes you could use the X and Y registers as stack pointers. Now, with the 68000 postdecrement and preincrement addressing modes, you can use any of the 68000 address registers as stack pointers. Data that is 8, 16, or 32 bits long can be pushed onto a stack using predecrement addressing, and data can be pulled from a stack using postincrement addressing. Any of the 68000 address registers can be used as stack pointers during the push/pull operations. Consequently, you can create up to eight user stacks with the 68000.

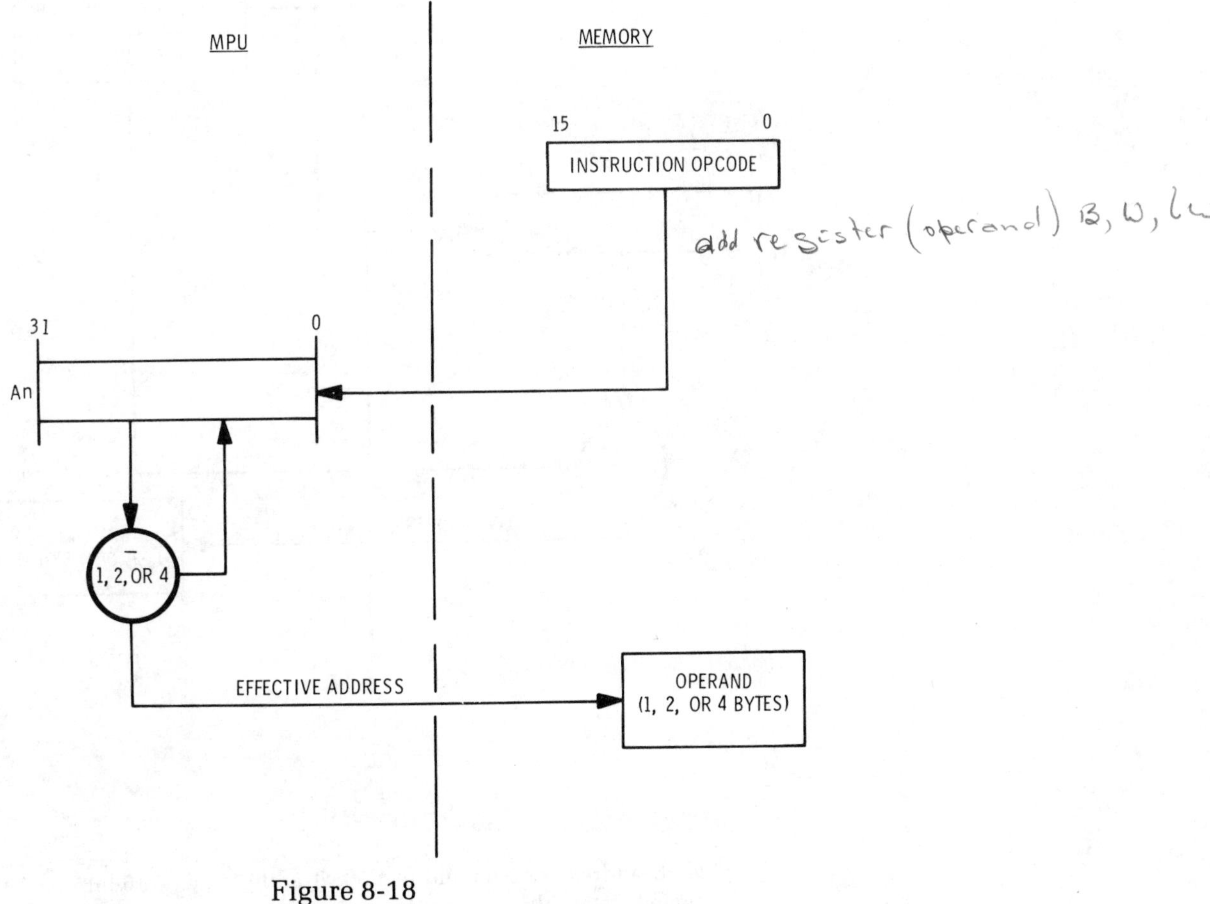

Figure 8-18

With address register indirect/predecrement addressing, the specified address register is decremented by 1, 2, or 4 before the instruction operation is performed. The decremented address register then contains the effective address which points to the operand in memory.

ADDRESS REGISTER INDIRECT WITH OFFSET

This form of addressing is very similar to indexed addressing with the 6800, except that one of the 68000 address registers is used as the pointer register. In this mode of addressing, a 16-bit signed offset value is added to the contents of the specified 68000 address register to form the effective address of the operand. The 16-bit signed offset value follows the opcode in the instruction statement. Address register indirect with offset addressing is illustrated in Figure 8-19.

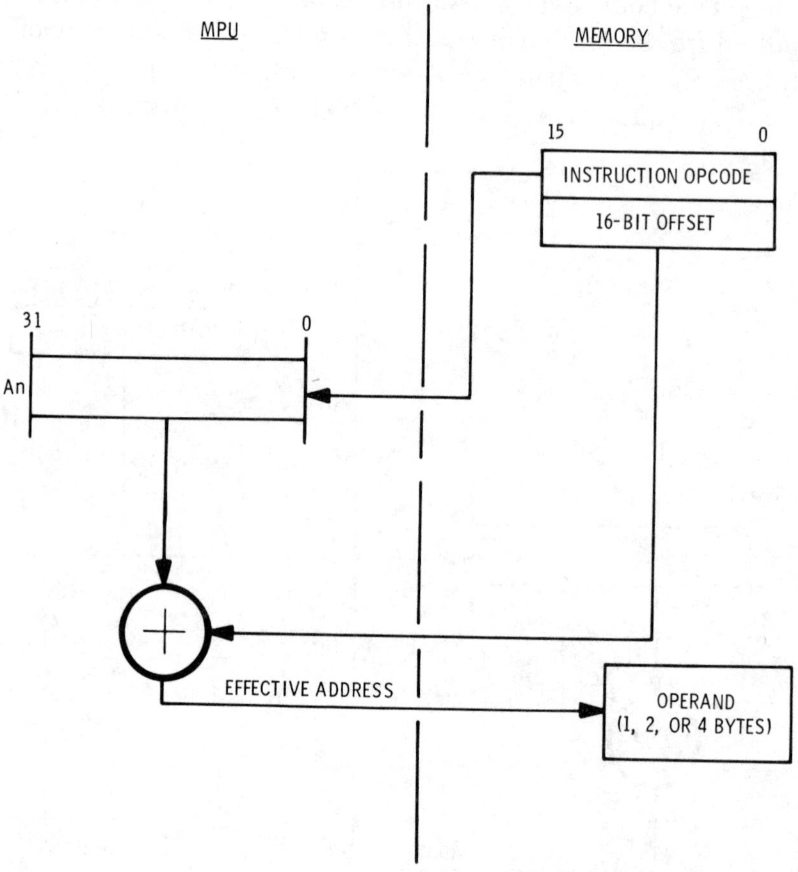

Figure 8-19

With address register indirect/offset addressing, a 16-bit signed offset value is added to the specified address register to form the effective address of the operand.

ADDRESS REGISTER INDIRECT WITH OFFSET AND INDEX

With this mode of addressing, the 68000 forms the effective address of the operand by adding an 8-bit signed offset and the contents of an index register to the specified address register. The "index" register used in this operation can be any of the 68000 data or address registers. The process is illustrated in Figure 8-20. The instruction opcode specifies the base address register to be used and the size of the operand. The word that follows the instruction opcode is divided into an index byte and an offset byte. The index byte is the high byte and specifies which one of the 68000 data or address registers is to be used as the index register in the effective address calculation. The offset byte is the low byte and contains the 8-bit signed offset value to be used in the effective address calculation.

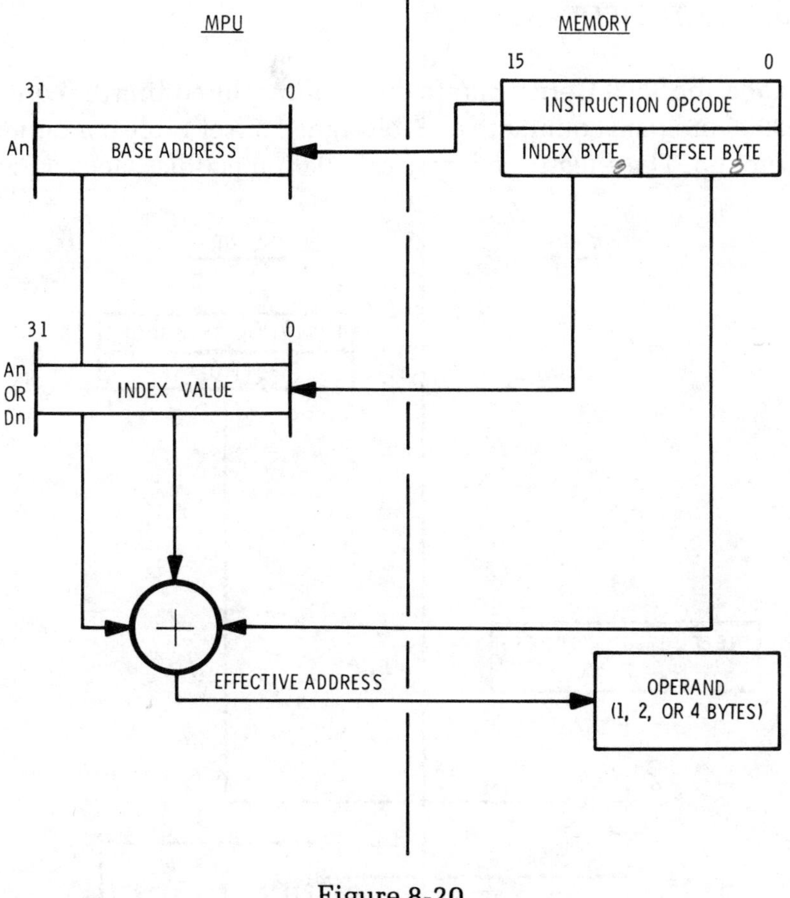

Figure 8-20

With address register indirect/offset and index addressing, the effective address of the operand is formed by adding an 8-bit signed offset and the contents of an index register to the specified address register.

Program Counter Relative Addressing

Like the 6809, the 68000 branch instructions use relative addressing to determine branch destinations. Both short and long branches can be performed with the 68000. Short branches use an 8-bit relative offset, and long branches use a 16-bit relative offset. The relative offset is added to the program counter contents to determine the branch destination address. The 68000 branch instruction will be discussed in the next section.

Also like the 6809, you can write 68000 programs with complete position independence by using the program counter to access data in memory. This is called program counter, or PC, relative addressing. There are two types: PC relative with offset, and PC relative with offset and index.

PC RELATIVE WITH OFFSET

In this mode, the 68000 forms the effective address by adding the contents of the 68000 program counter to a 16-bit signed offset value contained in the instruction. The effective address calculation is illustrated in Figure 8-21.

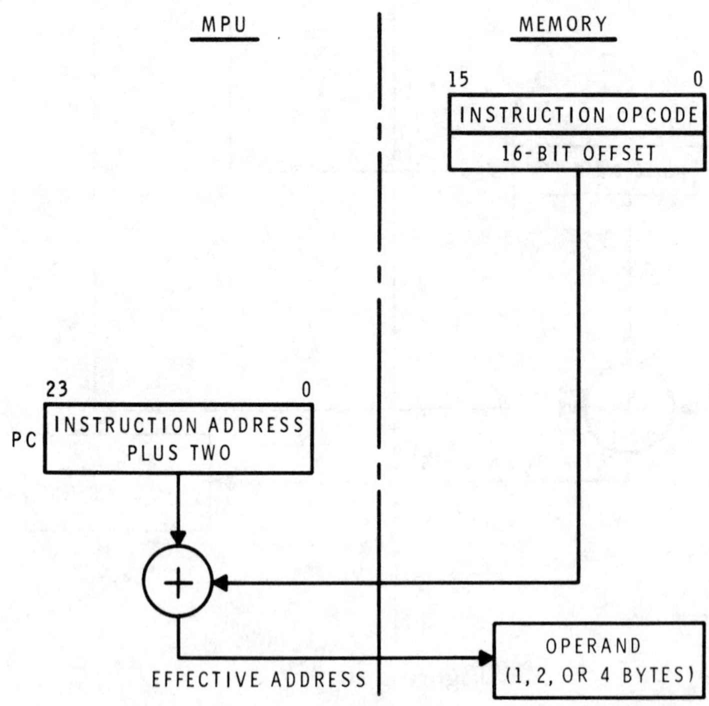

Figure 8-21

With PC relative addressing, the effective address of the operand is formed by adding the program counter contents to a 16-bit signed offset value contained in the instruction.

PC RELATIVE WITH OFFSET AND INDEX

With this mode of addressing, the 68000 forms the effective address by adding an 8-bit signed offset and the contents of an index register to the program counter. The "index" register can be any of the 68000 data or address registers. Note from Figure 8-22 that the word that follows the instruction opcode is divided into two bytes: an index byte and an offset byte. As before, the index byte specifies the 68000 data or address register to be used in the effective address calculation. The offset byte contains the 8-bit signed offset value to be used in the effective address calculation.

Before leaving PC relative addressing, we must make one more very important point. With the 68000, the program counter always points to the **current instruction address plus two**. For example, if a branch instruction is located at address $0B5000_{16}$, then the program counter contains the value $0B5002_{16}$. This value would then be used to calculate the branch destination. The same is true of any instruction that uses PC relative addressing.

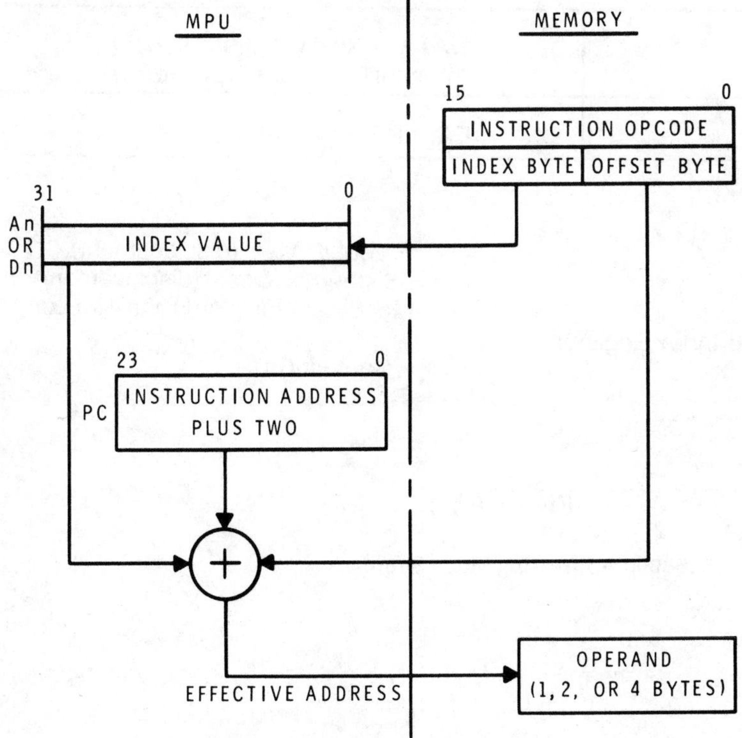

Figure 8-22

With PC relative/index addressing, the effective address of the operand is formed by adding an 8-bit signed offset and the contents of an index register (An or Dn) to the program counter contents.

A summary of the 68000 addressing modes is provided in Figure 8-23. Before taking the self-test review and going on, you should review the figures provided in this section, since they illustrate all of the 68000 addressing modes.

Mode	Effective Address Generation
Register Direct Addressing	
Data Register Direct	EA = Dn
Address Register Direct	EA = An
Absolute Addressing	
Absolute Short	EA = (Next Word)
Absolute Long	EA = (Next Two Words)
Program Counter Relative Addressing	
Relative With Offset	EA = (PC) + d_{16}
Relative With Index and Offset	EA = (PC) + (Xn) + d_8
Register Indirect Addressing	
Register Indirect	EA = (An)
Postincrement Register Indirect	EA = (An), An ← An + N
Predecrement Register Indirect	An ← An − N, EA = (An)
Register Indirect With Offset	EA = (An) + d_{16}
Indexed Register Indirect With Offset	EA = (An) + (Xn) + d_8
Immediate Data Addressing	
Immediate	DATA = Next Word(s)
Quick Immediate	Inherent Data in the Opcode
Implied Addressing	
Implied Register	EA = SR, USP, SP, PC

NOTES:
EA = Effective Address
An = Address Register
Dn = Data Register
Xn = Address or Data Register used as Index Register
SR = Status Register
PC = Program Counter
SP = Supervisor Stack Pointer (A7′)
USP = User Stack Pointer (A7)

d_8 = Eight-bit Offset (displacement)
d_{16} = Sixteen-bit Offset (displacement)
N = 1 for Byte, 2 for Words and 4 for Long Words

( ) = Contents of
← = Replaces

Figure 8-23

68000 Addressing Mode Summary.

Self-Test Review

13. What are the six fundamental addressing modes of the 68000? ____

14. What is implicit with implied addressing? ____

15. What is the size of an operand in a 68000 operation, and where is the operand size specified? ____

16. Explain the difference between immediate and quick immediate addressing. ____

17. What areas of the 68000 address space can be accessed using absolute short addressing? ____

18. What areas of the 68000 address space can be accessed using absolute long addressing? ____

19. Define register direct addressing. ____

20. Define address register indirect addressing. ____________________

____

21. What 68000 addressing mode would be used to push a 16-bit value onto a memory stack defined by address register A5? ____________________

____

____

22. How is the effective address formed using address register indirect with offset addressing? ____________________

____

23. How is the effective address formed using PC relative with offset and index addressing? ____________________

____

24. A 68000 instruction which uses PC relative with offset addressing is located at hex address $30A500_{16}$. The 16-bit offset value contained in the instruction is $1A50_{16}$. What is the address of the operand, or effective address? ____________________

Answers

13. The six fundamental addressing modes of the 68000 are: **implied, immediate, absolute, register direct, register indirect,** and **program counter relative** addressing.

14. With implied addressing, the operation and the registers to be used in the operation are implicit, or understood, by the processor.

15. An operand in a 68000 operation can be 8, 16, or 32 bits long. The size of the operand is specified in the instruction opcode.

16. With immediate addressing, the operand is an 8-, 16-, or 32-bit value that appears in the instruction statement in addition to the instruction opcode. With quick immediate addressing, the operand is a value between 0 and 7 which is located within the instruction opcode. Instructions using quick immediate addressing will execute faster than those using immediate addressing.

17. Only the lowest 32K bytes and highest 32K bytes of the 68000 address space can be accessed when you are using absolute short addressing.

18. The entire 16M byte address space of the 68000 can be accessed when you are using absolute long addressing.

19. Register direct addressing means that the operand is contained in one of the internal 68000 data or address registers.

20. Address register indirect addressing means that one of the 68000 address registers contains the address of the operand, or the effective address.

21. You must use address register indirect with predecrement by 2 to push a 16-bit value onto a memory stack defined by address register A5.

22. Using address register indirect with offset addressing, the 68000 forms the effective address by adding the contents of the specified address register to a 16-bit signed offset contained in the instruction statement.

23. Using PC relative with offset and index addressing, the 68000 forms the effective address by adding an 8-bit signed offset and the contents of an index register to the program counter. The index register can be any of the 68000 data or address registers.

24. It is given that a 68000 instruction which uses PC relative with offset addressing is located at address $30A500_{16}$. If the offset value is $1A50_{16}$, then the effective address must be $30A500_{16} + 2_{16} + 1A50_{16} = 30BF52_{16}$. Note, with the 68000, you must add 2 to the instruction address to obtain the PC contents.

THE 68000 INSTRUCTION SET

As we stated earlier, the 68000 uses 56 fundamental instructions with the addressing modes discussed in the last section to provide over 1000 unique operations. The 56 fundamental instructions of the 68000 can be categorized as follows:

- Data Movement Instructions
- Arithmetic and Logic Instructions
- Bit Manipulation Instructions
- Program Control Instructions
- System Control Instructions

In this section, we will acquaint you with each of the above instruction categories. Many of the 68000 instructions will be familiar to you because of your 6800, 6801, 6809, etc. instruction set knowlege. We will therefore concentrate our discussion on those instructions which are "new" and unique to the 68000.

Data Movement Instructions

The 68000 data movement instructions are listed in Figure 8-24 along with their respective operations. You should be surprised to see that there are no load or store instructions for the 68000. Instead, the 68000 uses a variety of MOVE instructions to transfer data between its internal registers and memory. These MOVE instructions are very flexible since they can be used with most of the addressing modes discussed in the last section.

Instruction	Operation	Operand Size	Operation Symbol
EXG	Exchange Registers	32	Rx↔Ry
LEA	Load Effective Address	32	EA→An
LINK	Link and Allocate	—	See Text
MOVE	Move Data from Source to Destination	8, 16, 32	(EA)s→(EA)d
MOVEA	Move Address	16, 32	(EA)s→An
MOVEM	Move Multiple Registers	16, 32	(EA)→An, Dn An, Dn→EA
MOVEP	Move Peripheral Data	16, 32	(EA)→Dn Dn→EA
MOVEQ	Move Quick	8	#xxx→Dn
PEA	Push Effective Address	32	EA→SP@–
SWAP	Swap Register Halves	32	Dn[31:16]↔Dn[15:0]
UNLK	Unlink	—	See Text

Symbols:
- s = source
- d = destination
- [ ] = bit numbers
- EA = effective address

Figure 8-24

The 68000 data movement instructions.

The basic 68000 MOVE instruction is used to transfer data between two data registers, from memory to a data register, and from a data register to memory. In addition, the MOVE instruction is used to move data between two memory locations. These various move operations are illustrated in Figure 8-25. The general source code format for the MOVE instruction is:

MOVE <source>, <destination>

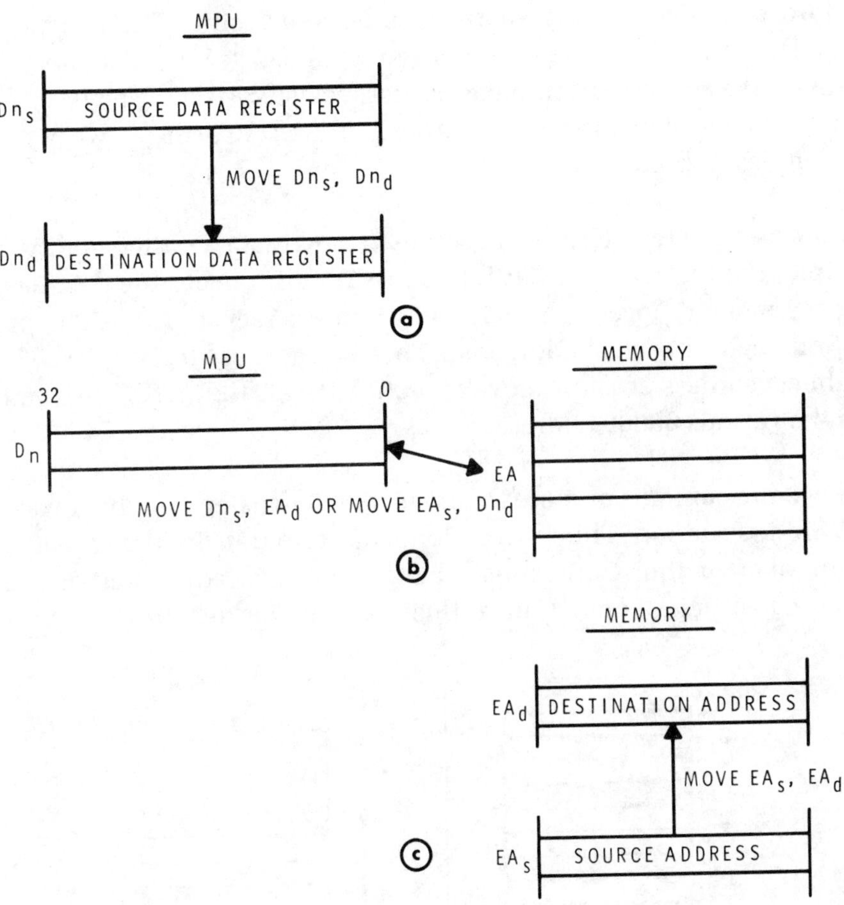

Figure 8-25

The 68000 MOVE instruction is used to move data between data registers **a** , to or from memory **b** , and within memory **c**.

Now, let's look at some examples. The instruction MOVE D0, D5 will move the contents of data register D0 to data register D5. When it is used in this manner, the 68000 MOVE instruction is similar to the 6809 transfer, or TFR, instruction. As another example, the instruction MOVE # F7A5 , D3 will "load" the value $F7A5_{16}$ into data register D3. Here, the MOVE instruction acts as the load, or LD, instruction that you are familiar with from other 6800 family processors. To provide a 68000 "store" operation, you must also use the MOVE instruction. The instruction MOVE D1, $5F00 will store the contents of data register D1 to memory, beginning at address $005F00_{16}$ using short absolute addressing. The instruction MOVE D1, (A0) will store the contents of data register D1 to memory, beginning at the address specified by address register A0 using register indirect addressing. Note that the parenthesis around A0 in the above instruction denotes indirect addressing.

You can also use the MOVE instruction to move data within memory. For example, the instruction MOVE (A3), (A5) will transfer the data beginning at a memory location specified by address register A3 to a memory location beginning at an address specified by address register A5. There are almost endless possible move operations using the MOVE instruction with the various 68000 address modes.

To move the contents of more than one 68000 register, you must use the MOVEM instruction. This instruction is used to transfer the contents of any number of the 68000 internal registers to or from memory. The MOVEM instruction operation is illustrated in Figure 8-26.

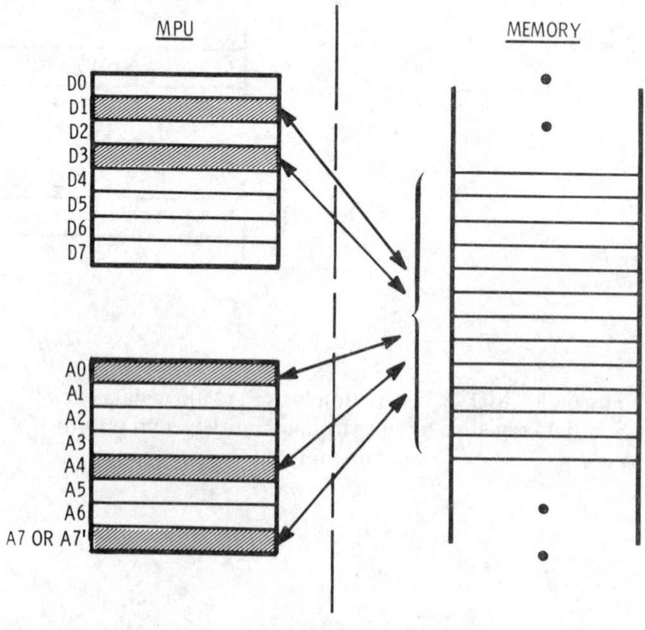

Figure 8-26

The 68000 MOVEM instruction is used to move the contents of several registers to or from memory.

As an example, consider the instruction MOVEM D0/D1/A0/A1 , $4F50. This instruction will move the contents of D0, D1, A0, and A1 into memory beginning at address $004F50_{16}$. Conversely, the instruction MOVEM $4F50, D0/D1/A0/A1 will move the contents of memory beginning at address $004F50_{16}$ into registers D0, D1, A0, and A1. As with all 68000 instructions, the instruction opcode must specify the data size (8-, 16-, or 32-bit) of the information to be moved.

The MOVEQ, or move quick, instruction is used to load byte-size, or 8-bit, data into any of the 68000 data registers. For example, the instruction MOVEQ #C7,D0 will load data register D0 with the value $C7_{16}$. The data is sign extended when loaded into the respective data register. Thus, data register D0 actually contains the value $FFFFFFC7_{16}$ after the above instruction is executed. Recall that the 68000 data and address registers are 32 bits long. In this example, the remaining 24 data register bits are filled-in with all 1's or F's, since the immediate data value, $C7_{16}$, is negative. The MOVEQ instructions are only one word long, since the 8-bit signed value is part of the instruction opcode. This allows for faster execution of an 8-bit data load operation.

The instruction MOVEP, or move peripheral data, is used to transfer data between the 68000 data registers and 8-bit peripheral devices. Recall that the 68000 address map is divided into odd and even addresses. As you will discover in Unit 10, data lines D0-D7 are interfaced with odd addresses and data lines D8-D15 are interfaced to even addresses. When you are interfacing 8-bit peripherals to the 68000, you must interface them to consecutive odd **or** even addresses so that data transfers can take place on data lines D0-D7 **or** D8-D15, respectively. The MOVEP instruction will transfer the contents of any 68000 data register to consecutive odd or even addresses, so that either the low order data bus (D0-D7) or high order data bus (D8-D15) is used for 8-bit data transfers. The MOVEP instruction opcode specifies odd or even addresses and how much of the data register is to be transferred. More will be said about the MOVEP instruction in Unit 10, when we discuss how to interface 8-bit peripheral devices to the 68000.

Several of the 68000 data movement instructions provide a means of moving address information rather than data information. These are the MOVEA, LEA, and PEA instructions.

The MOVEA, or move address, instruction is used like the MOVE instruction, except that you are transferring address information from the source to the destination. Therefore, the destination is always one of the 68000 address registers. For example, the instruction MOVEA #07F3, A5 will load address register A5 with the immediate value $07F3_{16}$. The instruction MOVEA (A0), A1 will load the contents of memory, beginning at an address specified by address register A0, into address register A1.

The LEA, or load effective address, instruction will load the respective address register with the effective address rather than the data at that address. This is similar to the 6809 LEA instruction. In the above example, the contents of address register A0 is the effective address for the operation. Thus, the instruction LEA (A0), A1 will load address register A1 with the contents of address register A0. Note the difference between the MOVEA (A0), A1 and LEA (A0), A1 instructions.

The PEA, or push effective address, instruction is similar to the LEA instruction. However, the effective address is pushed onto the stack rather than loaded into an address register. For example, the instruction PEA (A0) will push the contents of address register A0 onto the user or system stack, depending on the 68000 operating mode. The instruction PEA −5, A0 will subtract 5_{16} from address register A0 then push the result onto the stack.

Two relatively simple, but powerful, data movement instructions are the EXG and SWAP instructions. The EXG, or exchange, instruction is used to exchange the contents of any two data or address registers. In addition, you can exchange the contents of a data register and an address register. These three possible exchange operations are illustrated in Figure 8-27 with the following exchange operation examples:

EXG D1, D4
EXG A3, A7
EXG D2, A5

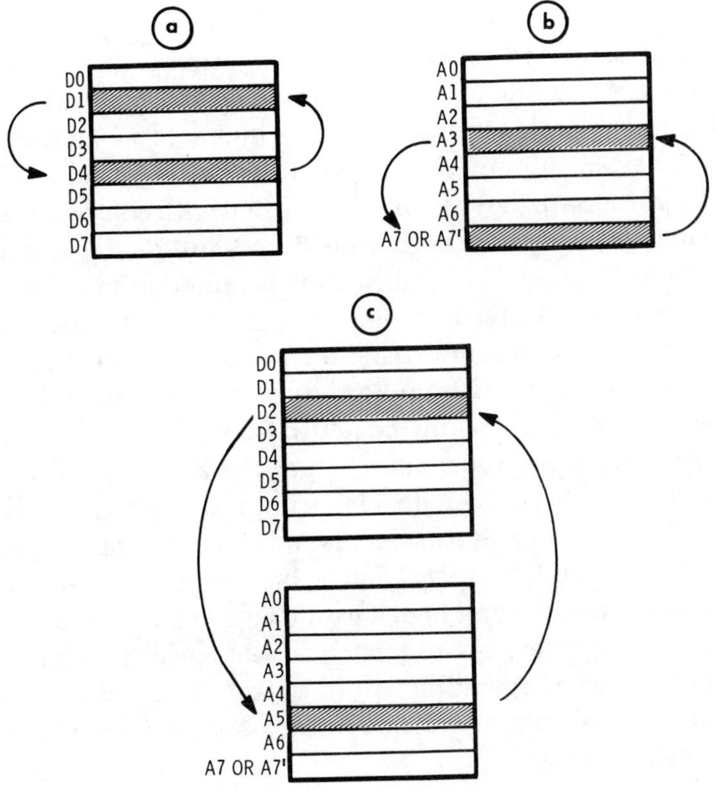

Figure 8-27

The EXG instruction is used to exchange the contents of two data registers **a** , two address registers **b** , or a data and an address register **c**.

All EXG operations exchange the entire 32 bits of the respective registers. The SWAP instruction is used to exchange the two 16-bit halves of a data register as illustrated in Figure 8-28. For example, the instruction SWAP D5 will exchange the two 16-bit halves of data register D5.

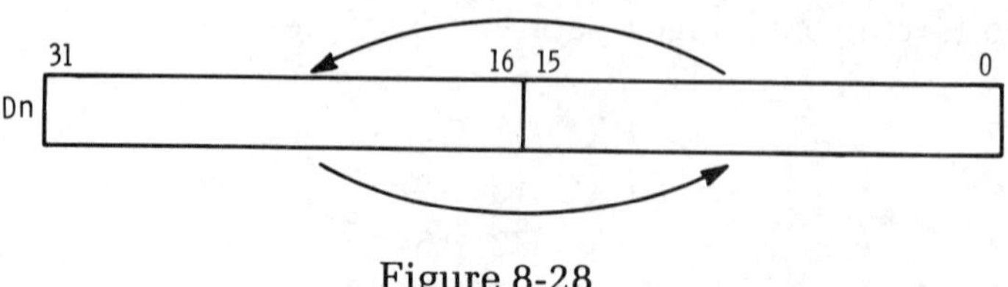

Figure 8-28

The SWAP instruction is used to exchange the two 16-bit halves of any data register.

The 68000 LINK and UNLK instructions provide an interesting feature when you are working with stacks during nested subroutines. Recall that a subroutine is nested if it is called by a higher level subroutine. In other words, a nested subroutine is a subroutine within a subroutine. As subroutines are nested, the system stack is filled with consecutive subroutine data, since each nested subroutine simply builds the system stack. As subroutines are un-nested, information is pulled from the stack to restore the processor to its presubroutine state. During a subroutine, it is often necessary to stack current register data prior to the next subroutine call. When you are returning from a subroutine, you must remember to unstack any register data before the return is executed, or else the processor will not return to the proper point in the program. As you can imagine, the stack can get quite messy with a large number of nested subroutines. It's like putting your scratch pad calculations for 100 calculus problems on a single sheet of scratch paper. Then trying to figure out later which calculations go with which problem. It would be much easier and reduce errors if you used a separate piece of scratch paper for each problem. The same is true of subroutines operating within a stack. You can reduce errors and retain individual subroutine data if you assign the nested subroutines to separate stack areas.

The LINK and UNLK instructions take advantage of the large 68000 address space by allowing you to set up separate stack areas for individual nested subroutines. The LINK instruction is typically used at the beginning of a nested subroutine. This instruction displaces the stack pointer with a 16-bit signed offset to create a separate scratch-pad stack for that subroutine. The 16-bit signed offset displacement value follows the instruction opcode in the LINK instruction statement. The UNLK instruction is then used at the end of the subroutine to restore the stack pointer just prior to returning to a higher level subroutine.

Arithmetic and Logic Instructions

The 68000 arithmetic and logic instructions are listed in Figure 8-29 and Figure 8-30, respectively. The 68000 arithmetic instructions provide the four basic arithmetic operations of add, subtract, multiply, and divide. In addition, related operations such as clear, compare, negate, sign extend, and test are also included.

Instruction	Operation	Operand Size	Operation Symbol
ADD	Add	8, 16, 32	Dn + (EA) → Dn (EA) + Dn → EA
ADDQ	Add Quick	8, 16, 32	(EA) + #xxx → EA
ADDA	Add Address	16, 32	An + (EA) → An
ADDX	Add with Extend	8, 16, 32 16, 32	Dx + Dy + X → Dx *
CLR	Clear a Data Register or Memory	8, 16, 32	0 → EA
CMP	Compare	8, 16, 32	Dn – (EA)
CMPI	Compare Immediate	8, 16, 32	(EA) – #xxx
CMPM	Compare Memory	8, 16, 32	+ (Ax) – + (Ay)
CMPA	Compare Address	16, 32	An – (EA)
DIVS	Signed Divide	32 ÷ 16	Dn/(EA) → Dn
DIVU	Unsigned Divide	32 ÷ 16	Dn/(EA) → Dn
EXT	Sign Extend	8 → 16 16 → 32	$(Dn)_8 \rightarrow Dn_{16}$ $(Dn)_{16} \rightarrow Dn_{32}$
MULS	Signed Multiply	16 * 16 → 32	Dn * (EA) → Dn
MULU	Unsigned Multiply	16 * 16 → 32	Dn * (EA) → Dn
NEG	Negate	8, 16, 32	0 – (EA) → EA
NEGX	Negate with Extend	8, 16, 32	0 – (EA) – X – EA
SUB	Subtract	8, 16, 32	Dn – (EA) → Dn (EA) – Dn → EA
SUBQ	Subtract Quick	8, 16, 32	(EA) – #xxx → EA
SUBA	Subtract Address	16, 32	An – (EA) → An
SUBX	Subtract with Extend	8, 16, 32	Dx – Dy – X → Dx *
TAS	Test and Set	8	(EA) – 0, 1 → EA[7]
TST	Test	8, 16, 32	(EA) – 0
ABCD	Add BCD with Extend	8	$Dx_{10} + Dy_{10} + X \rightarrow Dx$ *
SBCD	Subtract BCD with Extend	8	$Dx_{10} - Dy_{10} - X \rightarrow Dx$ *
NBCD	Negate BCD with Extend	8	$0 - (EA)_{10} - X \rightarrow EA$

Symbols:

EA = effective address

[ ] = bit number

* = may also be performed directly on memory data

Figure 8-29

The 68000 arithmetic instructions.

Instruction	Operation	Operand Size	Operation Symbol
AND	Logical AND	8, 16, 32	$Dn \wedge (EA) \rightarrow Dn$ $(EA) \wedge Dn \rightarrow EA$ $(EA) \wedge \#xxx \rightarrow EA$
OR	Logical OR	8, 16, 32	$Dn \vee (EA) \rightarrow Dn$ $(EA) \vee Dn \rightarrow EA$ $(EA) \vee \#xxx \rightarrow EA$
EOR	Logic XOR	8, 16, 32	$(EA) \oplus Dy \rightarrow EA$ $(EA) \oplus \#xxx \rightarrow EA$
NOT	1's Complement	8, 16, 32	$\sim(EA) \rightarrow EA$
ASL	Arithmetic Shift Left	8, 16, 32	
ASR	Arithmetic Shift Right	8, 16, 32	
LSL	Logic Shift Left	8, 16, 32	
LSR	Logic Shift Right	8, 16, 32	
ROL	Rotate Left	8, 16, 32	
ROR	Rotate Right	8, 16, 32	
ROXL	Rotate Left with Extend	8, 16, 32	
ROXR	Rotate Right with Extend	8, 16, 32	

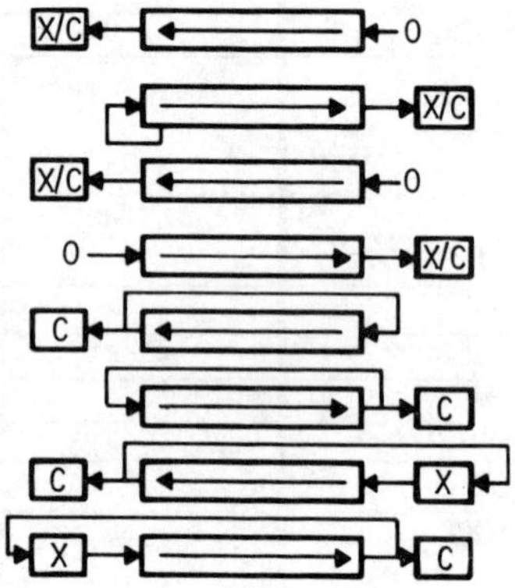

Symbols:

$\wedge$ = AND
$\vee$ = OR
$\oplus$ = XOR
$\sim$ = invert

Figure 8-30

The 68000 logic instructions.

The ADD and SUB instructions allow you to add to or subtract from a data register, address register, or the contents of an effective address. The operand size can be 8, 16, or 32 bits. Look at the operation symbols for the ADD and SUB instructions in Figure 8-29. These symbols summarize the various add and subtract options available to the 68000. Notice that the ADDX and SUBX instructions are similar to ADD and SUB. However, they allow for multiprecision arithmetic since the X-flag of the status register is part of the arithmetic operation.

The 68000 EXT, or extend, instruction is similar to the 6809 SEX instruction since it allows you to extend the sign of a data register value. You can extend the sign of an 8-bit value to a 16-bit value, or a 16-bit value to a 32-bit value.

The MULS, or signed multiply, instruction will multiply two 16-bit values and produce a 32-bit signed result. Note from the operation symbol in Figure 8-29 that the operation multiplies a 16-bit data register value times a 16-bit operand value located at the effective address. The 32-bit product is placed back in the respective data register. The MULU, or unsigned multiply, instruction performs the same operation as the signed multiply, except that the 68000 treats the operands as unsigned values. Unsigned multiply operations are used for multiprecision arithmetic.

The power of the 68000 instruction set is evident from its two divide instructions. Up to this point, you have not seen a divide instruction for any of the 6800 family processors. Special algorithms must be written to provide the divide operation for these processors. This is no easy task. With the 68000, one instruction performs the divide operation. The DIVS, or signed divide, instruction divides a 32-bit data register value by a 16-bit operand value located at the effective address. The signed quotient is placed back in the respective data register. The DIVU, or unsigned divide, instruction performs the same operation as the signed divide, except that the operand values are treated as unsigned numbers for multiprecision operations.

The 68000 is capable of performing arithmetic operations directly on BCD values. Add, subtract, and negate operations are performed on 8-bit, or two BCD digits, using the ABCD, SBCD, and NBCD instructions, respectively.

You should be familiar with the remaining 68000 arithmetic and logic instructions as a result of your 6800 family instruction set knowledge. However, we should mention a few items to finish-up this discussion. The TAS, or test and set, instruction is used like the TST instruction to test for a zero value. However, only 8-bit values can be tested and after the test, bit 7 of the value is set. Such an operation is typically used to allocate memory to different processors in multiprocessing systems. Finally, note that you can perform the 68000 shift and rotate operations using either the C-flag or X-flag of the status register.

Now review the operation symbols for the instructions listed in Figures 8-29 and 8-30. These symbols summarize the arithmetic logic capabilities of the 68000.

Bit Manipulation Instructions

The 68000 bit manipulation instructions are listed in Figure 8-31. Recall that the 6805 instruction set includes several bit manipulation instructions. These instructions allow you to set, clear, and check the status of a single bit. Single bit operations are common in dedicated control applications. The inclusion of bit manipulation instructions in the 68000 instruction set should give you some indication of the broad application range of the 68000, from single bit operations to 32-bit operations.

Instruction	Operation	Operand Size	Operation Symbol
BTST	Bit Test	8, 32	t bit of (EA) → Z
BSET	Bit Test and Set	8, 32	t bit of (EA) → Z 1 → bit of EA
BCLR	Bit Test and Clear	8, 32	t bit of (EA) → Z 0 → bit of EA
BCHG	Bit Test and Change	8, 32	t bit of (EA) → Z ~ bit of (EA) → bit of EA

Symbols:
t = test
~ = invert
Z = Z-flag of the status register

Figure 8-31

The 68000 bit manipulation instructions.

Briefly, the four 68000 bit manipulation instructions allow you to test the status of any bit within a data register, or a single memory location. With BTST, or bit test, the specified bit is tested and the Z-flag of the status register is set accordingly. If the bit tested is a logic zero, the Z-flag is set. Conversely, if the bit tested is a logic one, the Z-flag is cleared. By using a subsequent branch operation, you can alter the program execution based on the status of a single bit.

The BSET, or bit test and set, instruction tests the specified bit, affecting the Z-flag accordingly. Then the bit that was tested is set. Likewise, the BCLR, or bit test and clear, instruction tests the specified bit and subsequently clears that bit.

The BCHG, or bit test and change, instruction tests the specified bit, affecting the Z-flag accordingly. Then the bit status is reversed (1 ⟶ 0, or 0 ⟶ 1).

We should emphasize that these instructions can be used on any of the 32 bits within a data register, or any of eight bits within a memory address location. The bit number to be tested is specified in the instruction statement.

Program Control Instructions

Instructions which alter program execution are called **program control** instructions. Program control instructions include branch instructions, jump instructions, and return instructions. These instructions are not new to you, they are simply being classified under a new category. The 68000 program control instructions are listed in Figure 8-32.

Instruction	Operation
Conditional	
B_{CC}	Branch conditionally (14 conditions) 8- and 16-bit displacement
DB_{CC}	Test condition, decrement and branch. 16-bit displacement
S_{CC}	Set byte conditionally (16 conditions)
Unconditional	
BRA	Branch always 8- and 16-bit displacement
BSR	Branch to subroutine 8- and 16-bit displacement
JMP	Jump
JSR	Jump to subroutine
Returns	
RTR	Return and restore condition codes
RTS	Return from subroutine

Figure 8-32

The 68000 program control instructions.

The three conditional program control operations are Bcc, DBcc, and Scc. The suffix "cc" in each of the above operations means that the operation depends on one of the test conditions listed in Figure 8-33. For example, Bcc becomes BEQ for the "equal to" condition.

"cc" Suffix	**Condition**	**Test**
CC	Carry Clear	C=0
CS	Carry Set	C=1
EQ	Equal	Z=1
NE	Not Equal	Z=0
MI	Minus	N=1
PL	Plus	N=0
GT	Greater Than	Z∧(N⊕V)=0
LT	Less Than	N⊕V=1
GE	Greater Than or Equal	N⊕V=0
LE	Less Than or Equal	Z∨(N⊕V)=1
HI	Higher Than	C∧Z=0
LS	Lower Than or Same	C∧Z=1
VS	Overflow	V=1
VC	No Overflow	V=0
T	Always True	For DB_{CC} and S_{CC} only
F	Always False	

Symbols:
∧ = AND
V = OR
⊕ = XOR

Figure 8-33

Test conditions for the 68000 Bcc, DBcc, and Scc instructions.

The Bcc operation is the conditional branch operation that you are familiar with for other 6800 family processors. All of the familiar 6800 branch conditions are provided with the 68000 Bcc operation (Refer to Figure 8-33). As we mentioned in the last section, the 68000 is capable of both short and long branches for each branch condition. With short branches, an 8-bit signed offset is added to the program counter to form the destination address if the condition is met, or true. With long branches, the signed offset is 16 bits. Thus, the 68000 has a branching range of -128_{10} to $+127_{10}$ with short branch instructions, and a range of $-32{,}768_{10}$ to $+32{,}767$ with long branch instructions.

The instruction format for a conditional branch, or Bcc, instruction is shown in Figure 8-34. Notice that the desired branch condition test code is placed in bits 8 through 11 of the Bcc instruction opcode. If an 8-bit offset is used, it is placed in bits 0 through 7 of the instruction opcode. However, if a 16-bit offset is used, it must follow the Bcc instruction opcode. When a 16-bit offset is used, bits 0 through 7 of the opcode must be cleared, or contain all 0's.

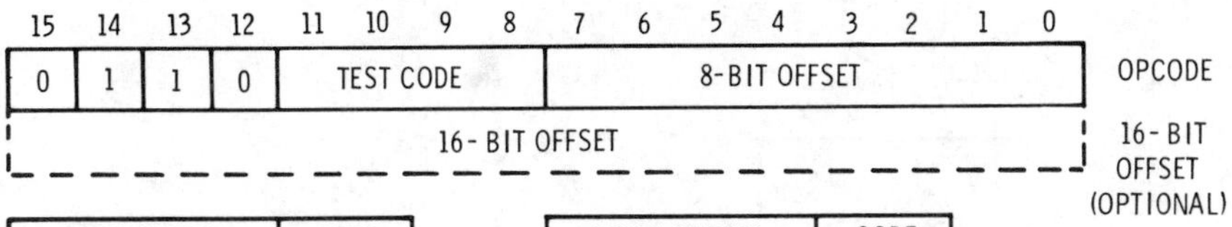

15	14	13	12	11 10 9 8	7 6 5 4 3 2 1 0	
0	1	1	0	TEST CODE	8-BIT OFFSET	OPCODE
16-BIT OFFSET						16-BIT OFFSET (OPTIONAL)

"CC" SUFFIX	CODE
CC	0100
CS	0101
EQ	0111
NE	0110
MI	1011
PL	1010
GT	1110

"CC" SUFFIX	CODE
LT	1101
GE	1100
LE	1111
HI	0010
LS	0011
VS	1001
VC	1000

Figure 8-34

The 68000 conditional branch, or Bcc, instruction format.

The decrement/conditional branch, or DBcc, operation provides the 68000 with a new and unique conditional branching capability. Many times, conditional branches are used to execute a loop a given number of times. To do this, you will typically initialize a software counter for the number of times the loop is to be executed. Each time the loop is executed, the counter is decremented by one. When the counter reaches zero, the program breaks out of the looping routine. The amount of looping is controlled with a conditional branch instruction and a decrement instruction. With the 68000, the DBcc instruction combines the conditional branch and decrementing operations for executing loops into one instruction. When DBcc is executed, the specified branch condition is tested. If the condition is met, or true, the branch does not take place and the next sequential instruction in the program is executed. If the branch condition is not met, or false, a 68000 data register is decremented by 1 and the branch takes place, only if the decremented data register does not equal −1. If the branch condition is false and the decremented data register equals −1, the next sequential instruction in the program is executed. The flowchart in Figure 8-35 summarizes the DBcc operation.

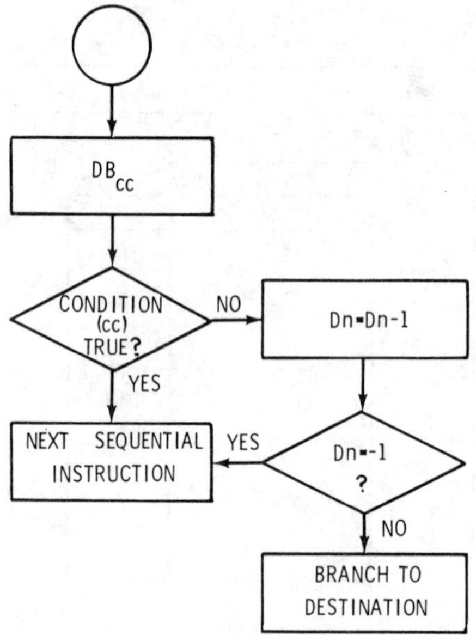

Figure 8-35

Execution of the DBcc instruction.

Aside from the automatic decrementing feature of the DBcc instruction, it is different from a standard branch, or Bcc, instruction since it branches when the condition is false. The standard Bcc instruction branches when the condition is true. You will discover another difference between DBcc and Bcc by looking at the DBcc instruction format in Figure 8-36. Notice that only 16-bit offsets are allowed. The 16-bit offset must follow the instruction opcode. The DBcc instruction opcode contains the branch condition test code in bits 8 through 11. The 68000 data register number (0-7) to be decremented is contained in bits 0 through 2 of the opcode.

15	14	13	12	11	10	9	8	7	6	5	4	3	2	1	0	
0	1	0	1	TEST CODE				1	1	0	0	1	DATA REG. NUMBER			OPCODE
16-BIT OFFSET																16-BIT OFFSET

"CC" SUFFIX	CODE
CC	0100
CS	0101
EQ	0111
NE	0110
MI	1011
PL	1010
GT	1110
LT	1101

"CC" SUFFIX	CODE
GE	1100
LE	1111
HI	0010
LS	0011
VS	1001
VC	1000
T	0000
F	0001

Figure 8-36

The 68000 decrement/conditional branch, or DBcc, instruction format.

Another difference between DBcc and Bcc is that the DBcc instruction can use the always true, or **T**, and always false, or **F**, branch test conditions. The always true condition, or DBT, instruction will never branch since the test is "always true." Consequently, the DBT instruction is similar to the 6801 and 6809 branch never, or BRN, instruction. It can be used as a two-word, no-operation instruction. You can also hide, or bury, another instruction in the 16-bit offset position of the DBT instruction statement.

The always false condition, or DBF, instruction will always branch unless the specified data register equals −1. This instruction provides you with an easy method of moving blocks of data within memory. For example, suppose a data table is located at addresses 040000_{16} through 050000_{16}. You wish to move this table to addresses $0A0000_{16}$ through $0B0000_{16}$. The program in Figure 8-37 will accomplish this task. The program first loads address register A1 with the old beginning table address, and address register A2 with the new beginning table address. We will use data register D6 as our counter. Therefore, data register D6 is loaded with a value equal to the table length minus 1. This value is required because the counter is decremented to −1 before the loop is broken. The MOVE (A1)+, (A2)+ instruction then uses register indirect addressing with postincrement to move the data table. Since the DBF condition test is always false, the MOVE (A1)+, (A2)+ instruction will be executed repeatedly until data register D6 is decremented down to −1. Of course the DBF instruction opcode must specify the always false, or F, branch condition, and that data register D6 is to be decremented. The DBF 16-bit offset must be the correct value to cause the program to branch back to the MOVE (A1)+, (A2)+ instruction each time the loop is executed.

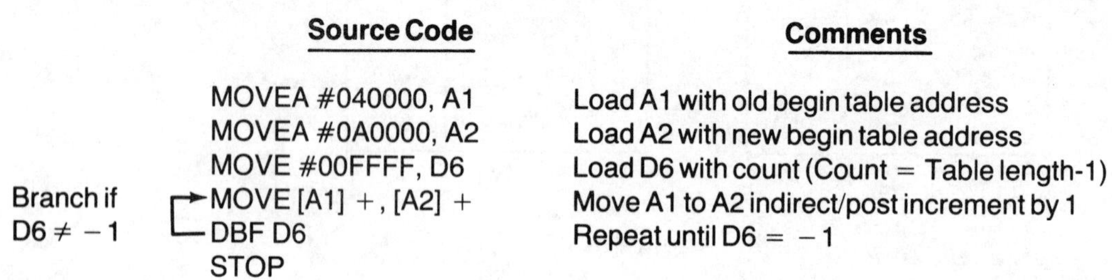

Figure 8-37

The DBF instruction can be used to move blocks of data within memory.

The set according to condition, or Scc, operation provides another unique feature for the 68000. The Scc instruction is used to test for any of the conditions listed in Figure 8-33. If the condition being tested is true, the effective address location is set to all 1's. If the condition being tested is false, the effective address location is cleared to all zeros. The Scc instruction operation is summarized by the flow chart in Figure 8-38. The Scc instruction can use the addressing modes discussed in the last unit to form the effective address to be set or cleared. It is important to note that this is **not** a branching operation like Bcc and DBcc. An effective address location is simply set or cleared depending upon the condition test. The next sequential program instruction is always executed after the Scc operation is performed. The Scc instruction can be used to test for a current condition during the execution of a program. Then, later on, you can check to see if the condition was true or false by reading the effective address location.

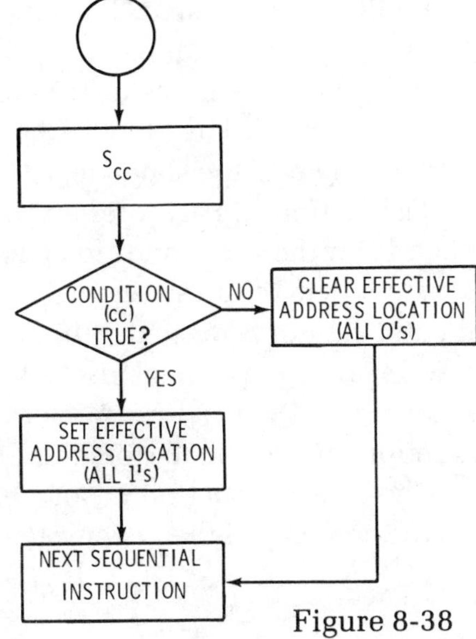

Figure 8-38

Execution of the Scc instruction.

There are no additional surprises in the 68000 program control instructions listed in Figure 8-32 except for the RTR, or return and restore condition codes instruction. Recall that you must use an RTS instruction at the end of a subroutine to return to the main program. The RTS instruction simply pulls the old program counter value from the stack so that execution of the main program picks up where it left off. However, many times it is desirable to save the condition code status flags on the stack during a subroutine. You can do this with a MOVE instruction at the beginning of the subroutine. You could restore the condition codes at the end of the subroutine with another MOVE instruction followed by the RTS instruction. However, there is an easier way. The 68000 will restore the condition codes and return execution to the main program with one instruction, RTR.

System Control Instructions

The 68000 system control instructions are listed in Figure 8-39. Notice that these instructions are divided into three instruction subcategories: privileged, trap generating, and status register instructions. As you are aware, privileged instructions can only be executed in the supervisor mode. Trap generating instructions can be executed in the user mode, but they are used with exception processing. We will, therefore, defer our discussion of these two instruction subcategories until the next unit, when we discuss the 68000 supervisor mode and exception processing.

The status register instructions allow you to change and store the contents of the 68000 status register. Four of these instructions can be used to change the contents of the user status byte. You can AND immediate (ANDI), OR immediate (ORI), or exclusive OR immediate (EORI) to the user status byte of the status register. In each of these operations, you must provide an immediate data byte in the instruction which will affect the user condition codes as desired. The MOVE EA to CCR instruction is used to load the user status byte of the status register with a value from memory. The "CCR" designation in each of the status register instructions in Figure 8-39 stands for the **user** condition codes. Any time an instruction affects the system byte of the status register, it is considered a privileged instruction and cannot be executed in the user mode. Notice from Figure 8-39 that when a system control instruction affects the entire status register, it is considered a privileged instruction. Finally, the MOVE SR to EA instruction allows you to store the contents of the entire status register in memory. This instruction is not considered privileged since it does not affect the contents of the system status byte of the status register.

Instruction	Operation
Privileged	
RESET	Reset external devices
RTE	Return from exception
STOP	Stop program execution
ORI to SR	Logical OR to status register
MOVE USP	Move user stack pointer
ANDI to SR	Logical AND to status register
EORI to SR	Logical EOR to status register
MOVE EA to SR	Load new status register
Trap Generating	
TRAP	Trap
TRAPV	Trap on overflow
CHK	Check register against bounds
Status Register	
ANDI to CCR	Logical AND to condition codes
EORI to CCR	Logical EOR to condition codes
MOVE EA to CCR	Load new condition codes
ORI to CCR	Logical OR to condition codes
MOVE SR to EA	Store status register

Figure 8-39

The 68000 system control instructions.

Self-Test Review

25. List the five instruction categories of the 68000 instruction set.____

26. What 68000 instruction is used to load and store information? ____

27. Briefly describe the operation of each of the following MOVE instructions:

    MOVE ____
    MOVEM ____
    MOVEQ ____
    MOVEP ____
    MOVEA ____

28. What will happen when the 68000 executes the instruction MOVE (A4), (A2)? ____

29. Write a 68000 instruction(s) that will transfer the contents of data registers D5, D6, D7 and address registers A2, A3, A4 to memory, beginning at an address specified by address register A7.

30. What will data register D5 contain after the execution of the instruction MOVEQ #A5, D5? ____

31. What will happen when the 68000 executes the instruction SWAP D7? ____

32. Which 68000 instructions can be used to create separate memory stack areas for nested subroutine data?____

33. Are there any basic differences between the arithmetic capabilities of the 6809 instruction set and the 68000 instruction set? If so, what are the basic differences? ______

34. Provide the 68000 instructions that go with the following operation symbols:

$Rx \longleftrightarrow Ry$ ______
$Dn/(EA) \longrightarrow Dn$ ______
$(Dn)_{16} \longrightarrow Dn_{32}$ ______
$(EA) - 0, 1 \longrightarrow EA\ [7]$ ______

35. How is the 68000 instruction set like the 6805 instruction set? ______

36. What is a program control instruction? ______

37. What are the three conditional program control operations used by the 68000? ______

38. Provide the hexadecimal opcode for a branch if equal, or BEQ, instruction using an 8-bit offset of $5B_{16}$. ______

39. What is the function of the DBcc instruction? ______

40. What are the major differences between the Bcc instruction and DBcc instruction? ______

41. What is the difference between the 68000 RTS and RTR instructions? ______

Answers

25. The five instruction categories of the 68000 instruction set are:

    - Data movement
    - Arithmetic and logic
    - Bit manipulation
    - Program control
    - System control

26. The 68000 MOVE instruction is used to load and store information.

27. MOVE is used to transfer data between the 68000 data registers and memory. In addition, this instruction is used to transfer data between two data registers or two memory locations.

    MOVEM is used to transfer the contents of any number of 68000 internal registers to or from memory.

    MOVEQ is used to load byte-size data into any of the 68000 data registers.

    MOVEP is used to transfer data between the 68000 data registers and 8-bit peripheral devices.

    MOVEA is used to transfer address information between the 68000 address registers and memory.

28. The instruction MOVE (A4), (A2) will cause memory data stored at an address specified by address register A4 to be moved to an address specified by address register A2.

29. The instruction MOVEM D5/D6/D7/A2/A3/A4, (A7) will perform the given operation.

30. Data register D5 will contain the value $FFFFFFA5_{16}$ after execution of the instruction MOVEQ #A5, D5, since the immediate data value, $A5_{16}$, is negative.

31. The instruction SWAP D7 will cause the two 16-bit halves of data register D7 to be exchanged.

32. The 68000 LINK and UNLK instructions can be used to create separate memory stack areas for nested subroutine data.

33. Yes, the 68000 instruction set includes divide instructions and the 6809 instruction set does not include any divide instructions. In addition, the 68000 instruction set is capable of performing arithmetic operations directly on BCD values and the 6809 does not have this direct capability.

34. The following 68000 instructions go with the given operation symbols:

$Rx \longleftrightarrow Ry$: EXG
$Dn/(EA) \longrightarrow Dn$: DIVS or DIVU
$(Dn)_{16} \longrightarrow Dn_{32}$: EXT
$(EA) - 0, 1 \longrightarrow EA\ [7]$: TAS

35. Both the 68000 and 6805 instruction sets contain bit manipulation instructions.

36. A program control instruction is an instruction which is used to alter the program execution.

37. The three conditional program control operations used by the 68000 are: conditional branch, or Bcc; decrement/conditional branch, or DBcc; and set according to condition, or Scc.

38. The opcode for a BEQ instruction using an 8-bit offset of $5B_{16}$ would be $0110\ 0111\ 0101\ 1011_2$, or $675B_{16}$. (Ref. Figure 8-34).

39. The DBcc instruction is used to conditionally execute a software loop a given number of times.

40. The major differences between the Bcc instruction and DBcc instruction are as follows:

- Bcc branches when the condition test is true and DBcc branches when the condition test is false.
- DBcc causes a specified data register to be decremented each time it is executed.
- Only 16-bit offsets are allowed with the DBcc instruction. The Bcc instruction can use either an 8-bit or 16-bit offset.
- The DBcc instruction can use the always true, or T, and always false, or F, branch test conditions and the Bcc instruction cannot.

41. The 68000 RTR instruction causes both the program counter and condition codes to be pulled from the stack during a return-from-subroutine operation. The RTS instruction only pulls the program counter from the stack during a return-from-subroutine operation.

Unit 9

THE 68000 — PART 2

CONTENTS

INTRODUCTION

In the last unit, you were introduced to the functional I/O capabilities of the 68000. In this unit, we will expand on that introduction and acquaint you with each of the 68000 I/O lines in preparation for 68000 interfacing, which is covered in the next unit.

In addition to a discussion of the 68000 I/O lines, we will discuss a very important feature of the 68000 called **exception processing**. Exception processing allows the 68000 to execute interrupt service routines, error checking routines, single-stepping routines, and special exception instructions. You will want to pay particular attention to this material, since the 68000 derives much of its power from its exception processing capabilities.

UNIT OBJECTIVES

When you complete this unit, you should be able to:

1. Describe the function of each of the 68000 I/O lines.

2. Explain the difference between asynchronous and synchronous bus control.

3. List the 68000 asynchronous and synchronous bus control lines.

4. Explain how the 68000 provides both asynchronous and synchronous bus control.

5. Describe the DMA sequence provided by the 68000 DMA control lines.

6. State the five status indications provided by the 68000 function code lines.

7. List the three processing states of the 68000.

8. Define exception processing.

9. Describe how exceptions can be generated internally and externally.

10. List the five 68000 instructions that can be used to generate an exception.

11. List the major steps in the general exception processing sequence.

12. Calculate a user interrupt vector address, given a user interrupt vector number.

THE 68000 INTERFACE LINES

You should now be familiar with the internal structure and software capabilities of the 68000. Before you can use the 68000 in a system, you must be familiar with its interface, or I/O lines. The I/O lines of any microprocessor can be grouped into four functional categories as follows:

- power and clock
- data and address
- control
- status

From our introductory discussion in the last unit, you are already familiar with the 68000 power, clock, data, and address lines. In this section, we intend to acquaint you with the 68000 control and status lines. You will find that a sound understanding of these two I/O line categories is essential when interfacing to the 68000.

Control Lines

The 68000 interface lines are shown in Figure 9-1. Recall from the last unit that the 68000 control lines are divided into five functional categories: asynchronous bus control, DMA control, interrupt control, system control, and 6800 peripheral control. We will examine each one of these control line categories in detail.

ASYNCHRONOUS BUS CONTROL

Some background information on asynchronous bus control versus synchronous bus control is appropriate at this time. Your interfacing experiences with the 6800 family processors up to this point have involved **synchronous bus control**, meaning that bus control is synchronized, or clocked, using a common system clock signal. In the case of the 6800 family, the common clock signal is the ø2 or E clock signal, depending on the particular 6800 family processor being used. With synchronous bus control, all data transfers within the system are controlled by the common clock. Thus, all read and write operations must take place within the confines of the common clock cycle. Recall that this creates a problem, especially when interfacing with slow peripheral devices, such as slow memories. To interface slow devices to a synchronous system, the clock cycle must be stretched to accomodate the device. This problem does not exist with asynchronous bus control.

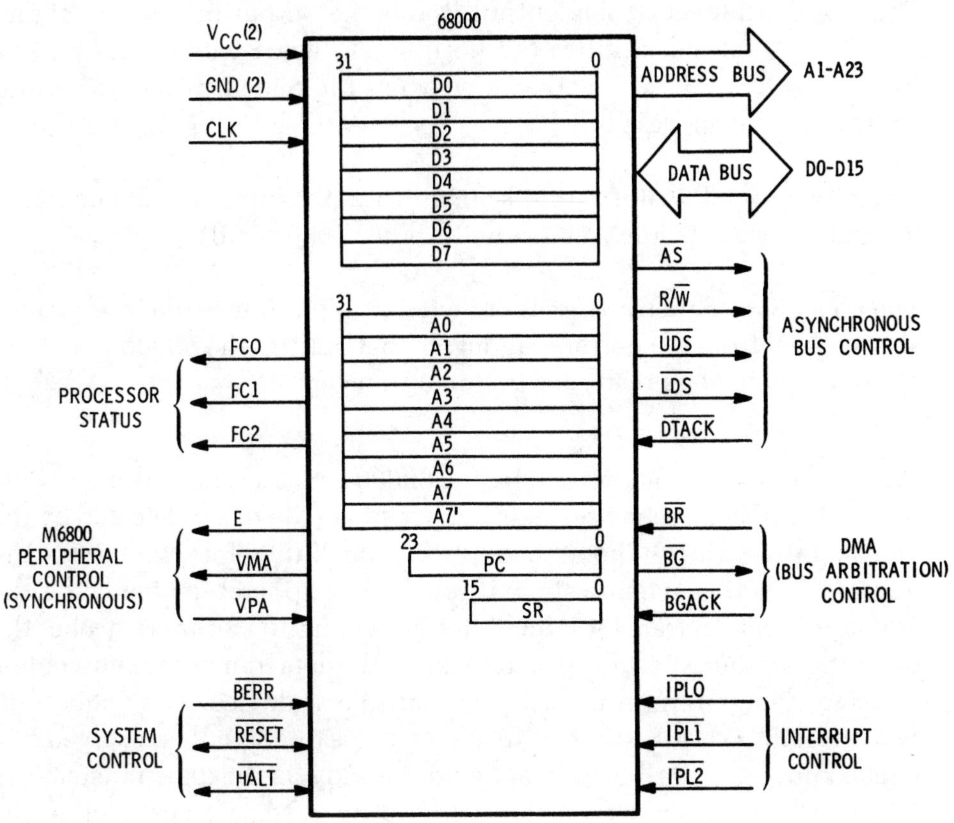

Figure 9-1
The 68000 I/O lines.

Asynchronous bus control does not depend on a common clock signal. Instead, a handshake procedure is used between the processor and its peripheral devices to synchronize the data transfer. Two handshake signals are normally used for this purpose.

1. An output signal from the processor that notifies the peripheral device when data is to be transferred.

2. An input signal generated by the peripheral device that notifies the processor that the peripheral device is ready for the data transfer.

With this type of bus control, you can interface to any type of peripheral device, regardless of that device's speed. You will soon discover that both synchronous and asynchronous bus control can be provided by the 68000.

From Figure 9-1, you can see that the 68000 provides five asynchronous bus control lines labeled $\overline{AS}$, $R/\overline{W}$, $\overline{UDS}$, $\overline{LDS}$, and $\overline{DTACK}$. The first four of these lines are output control lines, and the last, $\overline{DTACK}$, is an input control line as indicated by the arrows in Figure 9-1.

The $\overline{\text{AS}}$, or **address strobe**, output line is the output handshake signal from the 68000 that notifies the peripheral device when data is to be transferred. This line is active low when the 68000 provides a valid address on the address bus.

The **R/$\overline{\text{W}}$,** or **read/write**, output line indicates the direction of data transfer on the data bus, the same as with other 6800 family processors.

The **$\overline{\text{DTACK}}$,** or **data transfer acknowledge**, input line is the input handshake signal from the peripheral device that notifies the 68000 when the peripheral device is ready for the data transfer.

When data is to be read or written, the 68000 activates the address strobe, or $\overline{\text{AS}}$. At the same time, the required peripheral device is selected by the 68000 address lines. The address strobe must, therefore, be part of the address decoding scheme since it tells the peripheral device when the 68000 is ready to transfer data. After activating the address strobe, the 68000 enters the wait state until it receives the data transfer acknowledge, or $\overline{\text{DTACK}}$, signal from the selected peripheral device. The 68000 will wait until the $\overline{\text{DTACK}}$ signal is received. Once this signal is received, the 68000 knows that the peripheral device is ready for the data transfer. The 68000 then reads or writes the data via its 16 data lines. Notice the asynchronous bus control provided between the 68000 and a peripheral device using the $\overline{\text{AS}}$ and $\overline{\text{DTACK}}$ control lines.

So, what is the purpose of the $\overline{\text{UDS}}$ and $\overline{\text{LDS}}$ output asynchronous control lines? Recall that the 68000 address space is divided into even and odd addresses. Also, data lines D8-D15 provide data transfer between the 68000 and the even addresses, and data lines D0-D7 provide data transfer between the 68000 and the odd addresses. The **upper data strobe**, or **$\overline{\text{UDS}}$**, is active when data is to be transferred to and from the even addresses on the upper data lines, or D8-D15. The **lower data strobe**, or **$\overline{\text{LDS}}$**, is active when data is to be transferred to and from the odd addresses on the lower data lines, D0-D7. To transfer 16-bit data, both $\overline{\text{UDS}}$ and $\overline{\text{LDS}}$ are activated so that 16-bits of data are transferred simultaneously on data lines D0-D15.

The address interface circuit in Figure 9-2 shows how even and odd addresses are interfaced to the 68000. With this method of interfacing, byte-size data can be transferred by activating either the lower data strobe ($\overline{\text{LDS}}$), or upper data strobe ($\overline{\text{UDS}}$). Thus, byte-size data is transferred from consecutive odd addresses or consecutive even addresses. This allows 8-bit memory and peripheral devices to be interfaced to the 68000. On the

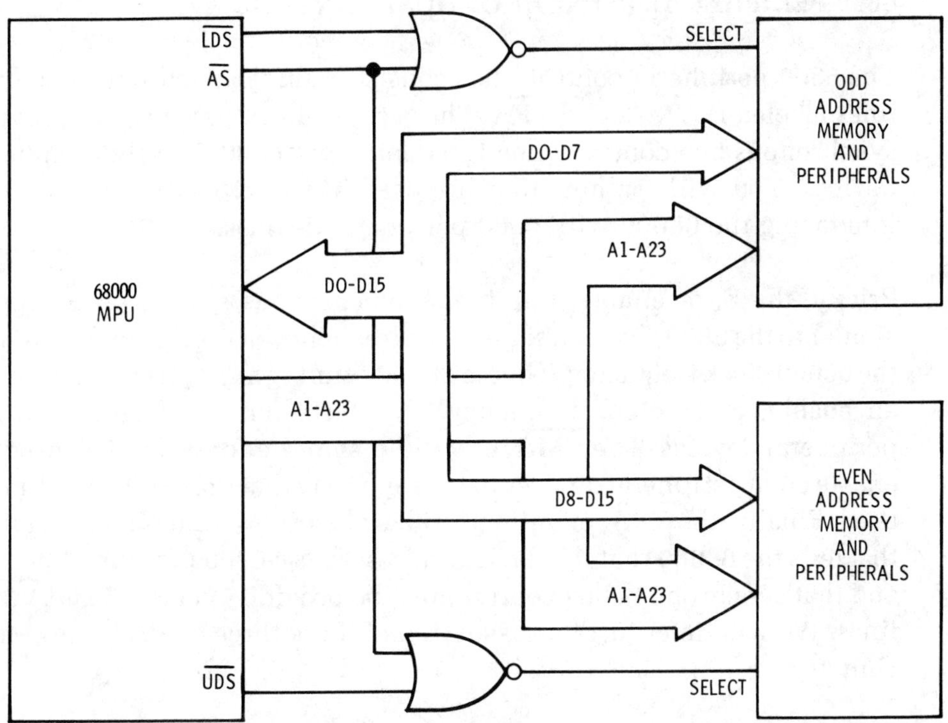

Figure 9-2
Even/Odd address interfacing to the 68000.

other hand, 16-bit data can be transferred by activating both the lower data strobe, or $\overline{LDS}$, and upper data strobe, or $\overline{UDS}$, simultaneously. The table in Figure 9-3 summarizes the data transfer options available to the 68000 using this even/odd address interfacing scheme.

$\overline{LDS}$	$\overline{UDS}$	R/$\overline{W}$	DO-D7	D8-D15
1	1	X		
0	0	1	WORD READ	
0	1	1	LOW BYTE READ	
1	0	1		HIGH BYTE READ
0	0	0	WORD WRITE	
0	1	0	LOW BYTE WRITE	
1	0	0		HIGH BYTE WRITE

X = DON'T CARE

(shaded) = INACTIVE OR TRI-STATED

Figure 9-3
Data transfer options using the 68000 $\overline{LDS}$, $\overline{UDS}$, and R/$\overline{W}$ control lines.

6800 PERIPHERAL (SYNCHRONOUS) CONTROL

The 6800 peripheral control lines consist of three synchronous control lines labeled E, $\overline{\text{VMA}}$, and $\overline{\text{VPA}}$. These control lines are used to provide synchronous bus control when interfacing with 6800 family peripheral devices. You will see how they are used in Unit 10, when we discuss interfacing the 68000 with 6800 peripheral devices.

Briefly, the **E**, or **enable**, line is the synchronous system clock signal similar to the 6800 Ø2 clock signal. The frequency of the E signal is 10% of the 68000 clock frequency. Thus, a 68000 running at 10 MHz will provide an enable, or E, clock frequency of 1 MHz for interfacing to 6800 peripheral devices. The **$\overline{\text{VMA}}$**, or **valid memory address,** line is used to enable 6800 peripheral devices in the same way that the 6800 $\overline{\text{VMA}}$ line is used. Finally, the **$\overline{\text{VPA}}$**, or **valid peripheral address**, line is an input line that tells the 68000 that the device addressed is a 6800 peripheral device and that synchronous bus control must be provided via the E and $\overline{\text{VMA}}$ lines. We will defer further discussion of these three control lines until Unit 10.

INTERRUPT CONTROL

There are three interrupt control lines for the 68000 labeled $\overline{\text{IPL0}}$, $\overline{\text{IPL1}}$, and $\overline{\text{IPL2}}$ in Figure 9-1. These three lines provide the priority level of the device requesting an interrupt. Recall that there are seven interrupt priority levels. The logic at these three input lines determines the interrupt level as shown in Figure 9-4. A given interrupt level is either masked or not masked, depending on the interrupt priority mask in the 68000 status register. We will discuss what happens when the 68000 accepts an interrupt in the next section.

$\overline{\text{IPL2}}$	$\overline{\text{IPL1}}$	$\overline{\text{IPL0}}$	INTERRUPT LEVEL
0	0	0	LEVEL 7
0	0	1	LEVEL 6
0	1	0	LEVEL 5
0	1	1	LEVEL 4
1	0	0	LEVEL 3
1	0	1	LEVEL 2
1	1	0	LEVEL 1
1	1	1	NO INTERRUPT

Figure 9-4
Interrupt level definitions for the 68000 interrupt control lines.

DMA CONTROL

The DMA control lines are used to provide external devices with direct access to the system address and data bus lines. In larger systems and multiprocessor applications, the 68000 DMA control lines are used by external bus arbitration logic to control access to the system bus structure. The DMA control lines are, therefore, sometimes called **bus arbitration control** lines.

The three DMA control lines are labeled $\overline{BR}$, $\overline{BG}$, and $\overline{BGACK}$ in Figure 9-1. The $\overline{BR}$, or **bus request**, line is an input line that is used by external devices to gain control of the bus structure. This line tells the 68000 that it must relinquish the address and data busses.

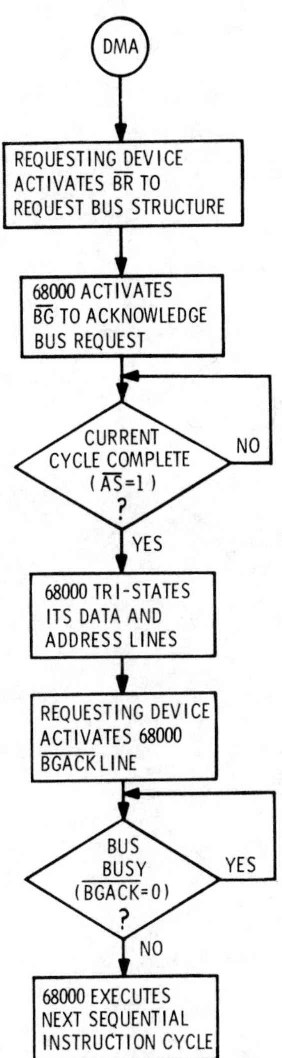

Figure 9-5
Summary of the 68000 DMA control sequence.

One clock period after receiving a bus request, the 68000 will activate its $\overline{BG}$, or **bus grant,** output line to acknowledge the bus request input. However, the 68000 will not give up the bus structure until it has completed its current instruction cycle. Therefore, an active bus grant output line does not necessarily mean that the requesting device can take control of the bus structure. The requesting device must monitor the 68000 address strobe, or $\overline{AS}$, line to determine when the 68000 has completed its current instruction cycle. When the 68000 address strobe, or $\overline{AS}$, line goes high, the 68000 will tri-state its data and address lines from the bus structure and, thus, allow the requesting device to take control.

When the bus requesting device takes control of the bus structure, it must activate the 68000 **$\overline{BGACK}$,** or **bus grant acknowledge**, line. This input line tells the 68000 and other DMA devices that the bus structure is unavailable. In effect, the $\overline{BGACK}$ line is a **bus busy** input line for the 68000. The 68000 will remain in a tri-state condition until its $\overline{BGACK}$ input line is deactivated, or returned high. Other DMA devices can also monitor the $\overline{BGACK}$ line to determine the bus busy status. The flowchart in Figure 9-5 summarizes the 68000 DMA control sequence just described.

It should be emphasized that the 68000 will relinquish the system bus structure whenever it receives a bus request via its $\overline{BR}$ input line. Consequently, the 68000 considers itself the lowest priority device on the bus structure. With several DMA devices using the bus structure, bus arbitration logic must be used to control and prioritize the bus requests.

SYSTEM CONTROL

From Figure 9-1, you see that there are three system control lines labeled BERR, HALT, and RESET. These three system control lines are separate, yet interrelated. They are called system control lines since they are used to control system related functions.

The **BERR,** or **bus error**, line is an input line that is used to notify the 68000 that there is a problem with the instruction cycle currently being executed. With asynchronous bus control, this condition might exist if a peripheral device fails to respond with a DTACK signal during a data transfer. An external timer can be used to assert the bus error signal if a peripheral device doesn't respond with the DTACK signal within a given time period. When the 68000 receives a bus error, or BERR, signal it has two options:

1. To rerun the instruction cycle that created the bus error.

2. To execute an error service routine similar to the way in which it executes an interrupt service routine.

The first option is exercised if the 68000 receives a **HALT** signal along with the BERR signal. When this happens, the 68000 will complete its current instruction cycle, then place itself in a high impedance state. The 68000 will then repeat the instruction cycle that was being executed when the bus error was received as soon as both the BERR and HALT signals are removed, or returned high. The cycle can be repeated continually if both BERR and HALT are activated/deactivated repeatedly.

The second option is used if the BERR signal is received alone, without HALT. Here, the 68000 will vector to a bus error service routine that you have placed in memory. The vectoring procedure used by the 68000 will be discussed in the next section. If two consecutive bus errors are received via the BERR input line (without HALT), the 68000 will automatically enter a **halt** state until it is reset. This is called a **double-bus error**.

You have just seen how the 68000 **HALT** line is used with the BERR line. When the HALT line is used by itself, it can be used to single-step instruction **cycles** or provide direct memory access. This feature is similar to the HALT feature provided with other 6800 family processors. When HALT is active (low), the 68000 will finish its current instruction cycle and enter a high impedance state until the HALT line is returned high. By continually activating/deactivating the HALT line, you can execute one instruction cycle at a time for debugging purposes. However, since most instructions are made up of many instruction cycles, you would not normally use the $\overline{\text{HALT}}$ feature to single-step complete instructions. Instead, you would use the T-bit, or trace mode, feature of the 68000 to single-step the entire instruction.

You can also use the $\overline{\text{HALT}}$ line to provide for halt-mode DMA as with other 6800 family processors. However, as you are aware, the 68000 has separate DMA control lines for this purpose. You will, therefore, **not** normally use the $\overline{\text{HALT}}$ line for DMA.

You will note from Figure 9-1 that $\overline{\text{HALT}}$ is also an output line. This is a feature unique to the 68000. The 68000 will activate its $\overline{\text{HALT}}$ line when it enters a halt state as a result of a **catastrophic failure**. A catastrophic failure is defined as any bus or internal error that causes the 68000 to automatically enter its halt state. A double bus error is an example of a catastrophic failure. When this happens, the 68000 enters a high impedance state until it is reset. The $\overline{\text{HALT}}$ output signal therefore tells external devices that a catastrophic failure has occurred.

The 68000 **$\overline{\text{RESET}}$**, line is also a bidirectional line as shown in Figure 9-1. The $\overline{\text{RESET}}$ line is used as an input line to reset, or initialize, the 68000 in the same way as other 6800 family processors are reset. However, to reset the 68000, both the $\overline{\text{RESET}}$ line and $\overline{\text{HALT}}$ line must be activated simultaneously. When the 68000 $\overline{\text{RESET}}$ and $\overline{\text{HALT}}$ inputs are both active (low), the 68000 vectors to a reset service routine that you have placed in memory. The vectoring process will be discussed in the next section. It is important to note that you cannot properly reset the 68000 without applying an active low signal to both the $\overline{\text{RESET}}$ and $\overline{\text{HALT}}$ input lines.

The 68000 $\overline{\text{RESET}}$ line can also be used as an output line to reset external devices. There is a system control instruction called **RESET**. When the RESET instruction is executed, the 68000 provides a low output signal on its $\overline{\text{RESET}}$ line for 124 clock pulses. The execution of the RESET instruction does not affect any of the internal 68000 data, address, or status registers. Consequently, you can insert a RESET instruction anywhere in your program when it is necessary to reset an external device. The RESET instruction acts as a no-operation, or NOP, instruction as far as the program execution is concerned. An application might be to reinitialize a PIA, ACIA, PTM, or some other external device during the execution of your 68000 program. As you are aware, the initialization routine for an external device is simplified if the device is reset prior to its configuration.

The table in Figure 9-6 summarizes the input and output features of the 68000 system control lines.

INPUT			
$\overline{BERR}$	$\overline{HALT}$	$\overline{RESET}$	OPERATION
0	0	1	REPEAT CYCLE
0	1	1	BUS ERROR ROUTINE
1	0	0	SYSTEM RESET
1	0	1	HALT AND TRI-STATE

OUTPUT		
$\overline{HALT}$	$\overline{RESET}$	OPERATION
0	X	CATASTROPHIC FAILURE
1	0	SOFTWARE RESET OF EXTERNAL DEVICES

Figure 9-6
Input control operations
a. and output control operations
b. provided by the 68000 system control lines.

Status Lines

There are three output status lines provided by the 68000. These lines are called **function code** lines and are labeled **FC0, FC1,** and **FC2** in Figure 9-1. Like the 6809 status lines, the logic on the 68000 function code output lines provides an indication of current processor status as shown in Figure 9-7. Notice that the function code lines are used to indicate user mode operation, supervisor mode operation, and to acknowledge the acceptance of an interrupt. In addition, by monitoring these lines, an external device can determine if the 68000 is accessing memory data or is executing a program instruction in either the user or supervisor modes. In Unit 10, you will see how the 68000 function code status lines are used to partition memory into four functional regions: user data memory, user program memory, supervisor data memory, and supervisor program memory. Each memory partition can provide up to 16 megabytes and, thus, the 68000 can be made to directly address up to 64 megabytes of memory! However, we will not discuss this application until Unit 10.

FC2	FC1	FC0	OPERATION
0	0	0	▨
0	0	1	USER DATA ACCESS
0	1	0	USER PROGRAM ACCESS
0	1	1	▨
1	0	0	▨
1	0	1	SUPERVISOR DATA ACCESS
1	1	0	SUPERVISOR PROGRAM ACCESS
1	1	1	INTERRUPT ACKNOWLEDGE

▨ = CURRENTLY UNDEFINED

Figure 9-7
Operation status indications provide by the 68000 function code lines.

Self-Test Review

1. Explain the difference between asynchronous and synchronous bus control.

2. What is the main advantage of asynchronous bus control over synchronous bus control?

3. List the 68000 asynchronous and synchronous bus control lines.

4. Explain how the 68000 $\overline{AS}$ and $\overline{DTACK}$ lines are used to provide asynchronous bus control.

5. Which 68000 data strobe(s) is activated when data is to be transferred to or from an even address?

6. Which 68000 data strobe(s) is activated when 16-bit data is to be transferred to or from memory?

7. What is the function of the 68000 valid peripheral address, or $\overline{VPA}$, line?

8. Briefly describe the DMA sequence provided by the 68000 DMA control lines for direct memory access operations. ______

9. List the three system control lines of the 68000. ______

10. How can the 68000 be made to rerun an instruction cycle? ______

11. How can external devices be reset during the execution of a 68000 program? ______

12. What are the five status indications provided by the 68000 function code lines? ______

Answers

1. With synchronous bus control, data transfers between the MPU and peripheral devices are clocked, using a common system clock signal. The read and write operations must take place within the confines of the common clock cycle.

   With asynchronous bus control, a handshake procedure is used to transfer data between the MPU and peripheral devices. Asynchronous bus control does not depend on a common system clock signal.

2. The main advantage of asynchronous bus control is that any peripheral device, regardless of that device's speed, can be interfaced to the MPU.

3. The 68000 asynchronous bus control lines are:

   - Address Strobe, or $\overline{AS}$
   - Read/Write, or $R/\overline{W}$
   - Upper Data Strobe, or $\overline{UDS}$
   - Lower Data Strobe, or $\overline{LDS}$
   - Data Transfer Acknowledge, or $\overline{DTACK}$

   The 68000 synchronous bus control lines are:

   - Enable, or E
   - Valid Memory Address, or $\overline{VMA}$
   - Valid Peripheral Address, or $\overline{VPA}$

4. When data is to be read or written the 68000 activates its address strobe, or $\overline{AS}$, line. After activating the address strobe line, the 68000 enters a wait state until it receives the data transfer acknowledge, or $\overline{DTACK}$, signal from the selected peripheral device. Once $\overline{DTACK}$ is received, the 68000 reads or writes the data via its 16 data lines.

5. The 68000 upper data strobe, or $\overline{UDS}$, is activated when data is to be transferred to or from an even address.

6. The 68000 activates both the upper and lower data strobes ($\overline{UDS}$ and $\overline{LDS}$) when it transfers 16-bit data to or from memory.

7. The function of the 68000 valid peripheral address, or $\overline{VPA}$, line is to indicate to the 68000 that a 6800 peripheral device has been addressed, and that synchronous bus control must be provided via the E and $\overline{VMA}$ lines.

8. Refer to Figure 9-5. Briefly, the DMA sequence is as follows:

    - The bus requesting device activates the 68000 bus request, or $\overline{BR}$ line.

    - The 68000 acknowledges the bus request by activating its bus grant, or $\overline{BG}$, line.

    - The bus requesting device monitors the 68000 address strobe, or $\overline{AS}$, line.

    - When the 68000 $\overline{AS}$ line goes high, the bus requesting device activates the 68000 bus grant acknowledge, or $\overline{BGACK}$, line and takes control of the system bus structure.

    - The 6800 remains off the bus until its $\overline{BGACK}$ line is deactivated.

9. The three system control lines of the 68000 are:

    - Bus Error, or $\overline{BERR}$
    - Halt, or $\overline{HALT}$
    - Reset, or $\overline{RESET}$

10. The 68000 can be made to rerun an instruction cycle by activating then deactivating its $\overline{BERR}$ and $\overline{HALT}$ lines simultaneously.

11. External devices can be reset during the execution of a 68000 program by inserting a RESET instruction in the program.

12. The five status indications provided by the 68000 function code lines are:

    - User data memory access
    - User program memory access
    - Supervisor data memory access
    - Supervisor program memory access
    - Interrupt acknowledge

PROCESSING STATES AND EXCEPTION PROCESSING

The 68000 always operates in one of three processing states: **normal, halted,** or **exception**. When the 68000 is fetching and executing instructions stored in memory, we say it is in its normal processing state. A special case of the normal processing state is when the 68000 executes a **STOP** instruction. Even though this instruction stops the program execution, the processor is still considered to be in its normal processing state.

The 68000 can also be placed in a halted state. In this state, the processor discontinues program execution and tri-states itself from the data and address bus structure. The halted state can result from an active $\overline{\text{HALT}}$ input, bus request, or catastrophic failure.

The exception processing state occurs when the 68000 is forced to deviate from its normal processing state. The term "exception" is used since operations in this state are exceptional to the normal processing state. Interrupt handling is an example of exception processing. With the 68000, other exception processing operations include trap operations, trace operations, and error operations. These operations are all called **exceptions**.

In this section, we will concentrate on the exception processing state of the 68000, since you are already familiar with the normal and halted states. We will begin with a discussion of the 68000 supervisor mode and how it relates to exception processing. Then, we will acquaint you with the different exception processing operations performed by the 68000.

Supervisor Mode and Privileged Instructions

Recall that the 68000 has two operating modes: user and supervisor. The normal processing state uses the user and supervisor modes. The exception processing state uses the supervisor mode exclusively. The S-bit of the status register determines the operating mode. If the S-bit is set, the 68000 is in its supervisor mode. If the S-bit is cleared, the 68000 is placed in its user mode.

When the 68000 is externally reset, it automatically enters the supervisor mode. The 68000 then remains in the supervisor mode until a privileged instruction is executed that will clear the S-bit of the status register. Recall that privileged instructions can only be executed in the supervisor mode. The 68000 privileged instructions are listed again in Figure 9-8. The instructions that can be used to clear the S-bit and enter the user mode are indicated with an asterisk (*) in Figure 9-8.

PRIVILEGED INSTRUCTION	OPERATION
RESET	RESET EXTERNAL DEVICES
RTE *	RETURN FROM EXCEPTION
STOP	STOP PROGRAM EXECUTION
ORI TO SR *	OR IMMEDIATE TO STATUS REG.
ANDI TO SR *	AND IMMEDIATE TO STATUS REG.
EORI TO SR *	XOR IMMEDIATE TO STATUS REG.
MOVE EA TO SR *	LOAD-NEW STATUS REG.
MOVE USP	MOVE USER STACK POINTER

* = INSTRUCTIONS USED TO TRANSFER OPERATION FROM SUPERVISOR TO USER MODE

Figure 9-8
The 68000 privileged instructions.

The **RTE**, or **return from exception**, instruction is an implied instruction that can be used to enter the user mode. This instruction is similar to the return from interrupt, or RTI, instruction with which you are familiar from other 6800 family processors. Other priviledged instructions that can be used to enter the user mode are **MOVE EA to SR**, or **load-new status register; ANDI to SR**, or **AND immediate to status register; ORI to SR**, or **OR immediate to status register;** and **EORI to SR, or exclusive-OR immediate to status register**. Each one of these instructions is capable of clearing the S-bit of the status register and, thus, place the 68000 in its user mode.

The remaining privileged instructions listed in Figure 9-8 cannot be used to enter the user mode. However, they are still considered privileged since they can only be executed in the supervisor mode. You are already familiar with the RESET instruction. This instruction is used to reset external devices. The **STOP** instruction is used to stop the program execution similar to the 6800 family WAI instruction. However, STOP also loads an immediate data value into the status register. The immediate data value can be used to change the user condition codes and interrupt priority mask. However, it cannot be used to clear the S-bit and enter the user mode. The **MOVE USP**, or **move user stack pointer**, instruction allows you to transfer the user stack pointer to or from a specified address register in the supervisor mode.

To summarize, an external reset will place the 68000 in its supervisor mode. You will normally execute a program in this mode to initialize the various registers of the 68000 as desired. Then, you must use a privileged instruction to clear the S-bit of the status register and enter the user mode for normal processing.

Now, you might be wondering how you can get back to the supervisor mode from the user mode. You **cannot** simply set the S-bit of the status register. Any instruction that affects the S-bit is privileged and cannot be executed in the user mode. The only way that you can get back to the supervisor mode is with an **exception**. Exceptions and exception processing are the topics of our next discussion.

Exceptions

As we stated earlier, an exception is an event that forces the 68000 to deviate from its normal processing state. The exception causes the 68000 to vector to a routine in memory that is written to service the exception. This is called an **exception service routine**. As you will see shortly, the exception vectoring process is very much like the interrupt vectoring process of other 6800 family processors. There are two general categories of exceptions: **internally generated exceptions** and **externally generated exceptions**.

INTERNALLY GENERATED EXCEPTIONS

Internally generated exceptions occur as the result of one of the following conditions:

- Internally detected errors
- Special instructions
- Instruction tracing

Internally detected errors that generate an exception include address errors, privilege instruction violations, illegal opcodes, and unimplemented opcodes. The 68000 will generate an **address error exception** whenever a program attempts to access a word or long-word at an odd address. Recall that words and long-words must begin at even memory addresses. A **privilege instruction exception** is generated whenever you attempt to execute a privileged instruction in the user mode. Privileged instructions must always be executed in the supervisor mode. An **illegal instruction opcode exception** is generated if the instruction opcode is not defined as part of the 68000 instruction set. All of the above errors are detected internally and each will cause the 68000 to vector to a separate exception service routine in memory. The service routine would be written to analyze and correct the error, or generate an error message.

An **unimplemented opcode exception** is generated if the first four bits of the opcode are 1010 or 1111. None of the 68000 instruction opcodes begin with these bit patterns. As you will see shortly, both of these beginning instruction bit patterns cause the 68000 to vector to an unimplemented opcode exception service routine in memory. Thus, you can define your own instruction operations using these unimplemented codes and exception vectoring.

EXCEPTION INSTRUCTIONS	OPERATION
TRAP	UNCONDITIONAL TRAP
TRAPV	TRAP ON OVERFLOW
CHK	CHECK REGISTER AGAINST BOUNDS
DIVS	SIGNED DIVIDE
DIVU	UNSIGNED DIVIDE

Figure 9-9
The 68000 exception generating instructions.

The five instructions listed in Figure 9-9 can generate an exception. These are called **exception instructions**. The **TRAP** instruction always generates an exception. The TRAP instruction opcode must include a vector number that points to one of sixteen possible TRAP exception vectors. Thus, the TRAP instruction is like a multilevel software interrupt, with sixteen possible software interrupt levels.

The **TRAPV**, or **TRAP if overflow**, instruction generates an exception only if the 2's complement overflow, or V-, flag of the status register is set. The associated exception service routine can be used to correct the 2's complement overflow condition.

The **CHK**, or **check register against bounds**, instruction will generate an exception if a specified data register value is less than zero, **or** greater than the contents of an effective address specified by the instruction. This instruction is helpful when creating data arrays in memory.

The **DIVS** and **DIVU**, or divide, instructions will generate an exception if you attempt to divide by zero. The divide by zero exception service routine would obviously be written to display an error message.

Finally, if the trace, or T-, bit of the status register is set, a **trace exception** is generated after each instruction execution. Recall that the trace feature allows you to single-step your program, instruction-by-instruction, for debugging purposes. After each instruction execution, the trace exception service routine would be executed as long as the T-bit of the status register remains set. The trace exception service routine might be written to display the internal register contents of the 68000.

EXTERNALLY GENERATED EXCEPTIONS

There are three ways that an exception can be generated by an external event. First, an exception can be generated as the result of a **bus error**. Recall that a bus error results when the 68000 $\overline{\text{BERR}}$ input line is activated. If $\overline{\text{HALT}}$ is activated with $\overline{\text{BERR}}$, the instruction cycle that created the bus error is repeated. If $\overline{\text{BERR}}$ is activated without $\overline{\text{HALT}}$, a bus error exception is generated.

The second way an external exception can be generated is with the 68000 interrupt request lines ($\overline{\text{IPL0}}$, $\overline{\text{IPL1}}$, $\overline{\text{IPL2}}$). An interrupt exception is generated when the interrupt logic level on these three lines is greater than the value of the interrupt priority mask in the status register. As you will soon discover, 199 unique interrupt vectors are possible for the seven interrupt levels of the 68000.

The third way an external exception can be generated is by providing an external $\overline{\text{RESET}}$ to the 68000. The $\overline{\text{RESET}}$ exception service routine is used to initialize the system and recover from catastrophic failures.

The table in Figure 9-10 summarizes the internally and externally generated exceptions just discussed. In addition, the exceptions are listed in order of their priority. Notice that $\overline{\text{RESET}}$ is the highest priority exception and divide by zero is the lowest priority exception. Also notice that some exceptions will cause the current instruction to be aborted and others will not be executed until the current instruction has been completed.

Now let's see exactly how the different 68000 exceptions are executed, or processed.

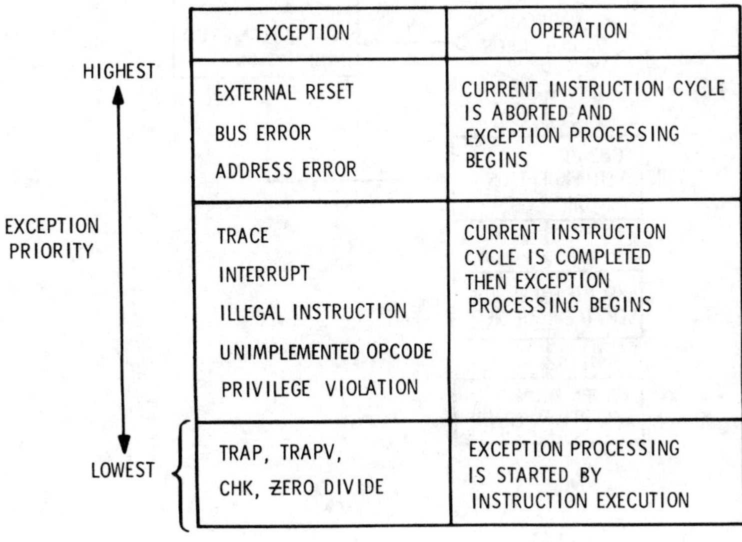

EXCEPTION	OPERATION
EXTERNAL RESET BUS ERROR ADDRESS ERROR	CURRENT INSTRUCTION CYCLE IS ABORTED AND EXCEPTION PROCESSING BEGINS
TRACE INTERRUPT ILLEGAL INSTRUCTION UNIMPLEMENTED OPCODE PRIVILEGE VIOLATION	CURRENT INSTRUCTION CYCLE IS COMPLETED THEN EXCEPTION PROCESSING BEGINS
TRAP, TRAPV, CHK, ZERO DIVIDE	EXCEPTION PROCESSING IS STARTED BY INSTRUCTION EXECUTION

Figure 9-10
A prioritized summary of the 68000 internally generated and externally generated exceptions.

Exception Processing Sequence

When an exception occurs, the 68000 automatically enters the supervisor mode and begins processing the exception. This is referred to as **exception processing**. The flowchart in Figure 9-11 summarizes the general sequence of events performed during exception processing. This sequence is the same for all 68000 exceptions except $\overline{\text{RESET}}$, which we will discuss separately.

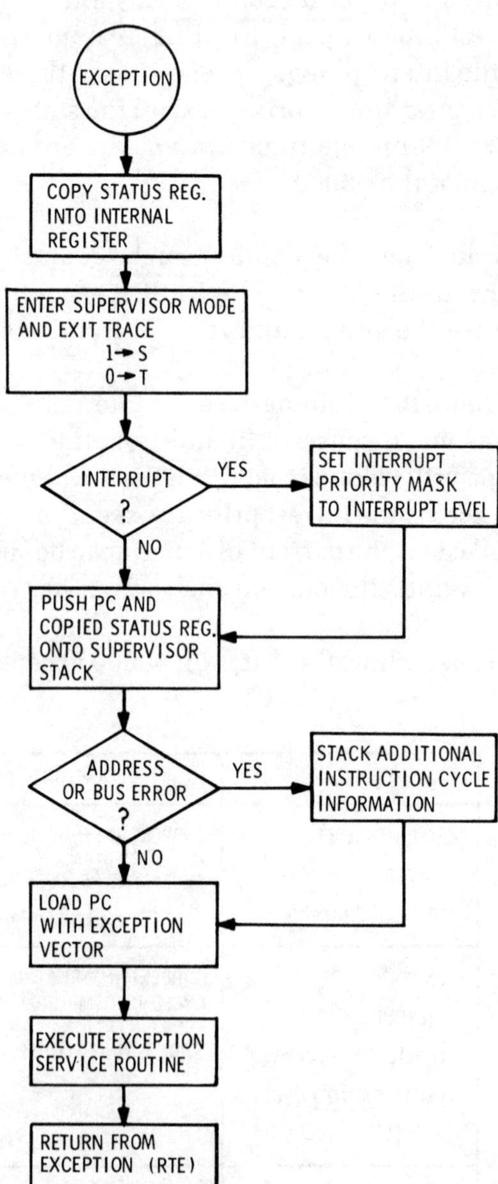

Figure 9-11
General sequence of events performed during an exception (not $\overline{\text{RESET}}$).

Once the exception is detected, the 68000 status register is copied in an internal register. You cannot access this internal register. The 68000 temporarily stores the current status register contents in this unaccessible internal register until it is pushed onto the stack. Next, the 68000 automatically enters the supervisor mode by setting the S-bit of the status register. Notice also that the T-bit is cleared so that tracing does not affect the exception sequence. If you are executing a trace exception, the T-bit status will be restored at the end of the exception so that the tracing mode can be continued for the next user instruction. If the exception is an interrupt, the interrupt priority mask in the status register is set to the interrupt level that generated the exception. This prevents lower level interrupts from interrupting the exception sequence. Next, the program counter and **copied** status register are pushed onto the supervisor stack. If the exception is due to an address or bus error, additional instruction cycle information is pushed onto the stack to aid in analyzing the source of the error. Finally, the program counter is loaded with the respective exception vector and the exception service routine is executed.

You must provide a return from exception, or RTE, instruction at the end of the exception service routine to return the processor to its pre-exception status. The RTE instruction pulls the program counter and copied status register from the stack. The S-bit of the copied status register will always return the processor to the mode it was in prior to the exception.

The exception processing sequence for the externally generated $\overline{\text{RESET}}$ exception is shown in Figure 9-12. Notice that nothing is stacked during this exception since it is assumed that the system is to be initialized. However, the supervisor stack pointer is loaded with the contents of addresses 000000 through 000003. This allows you to automatically initialize the supervisor stack pointer each time the $\overline{\text{RESET}}$ exception is executed. In addition, the interrupt priority mask is set (all 1's) so that no other interrupts can interrupt the $\overline{\text{RESET}}$ exception. The $\overline{\text{RESET}}$ exception vector is located in addresses 000004 through 000007. Consequently, the program counter, or PC, is loaded with the contents of these addresses to begin the execution of the $\overline{\text{RESET}}$ exception service routine.

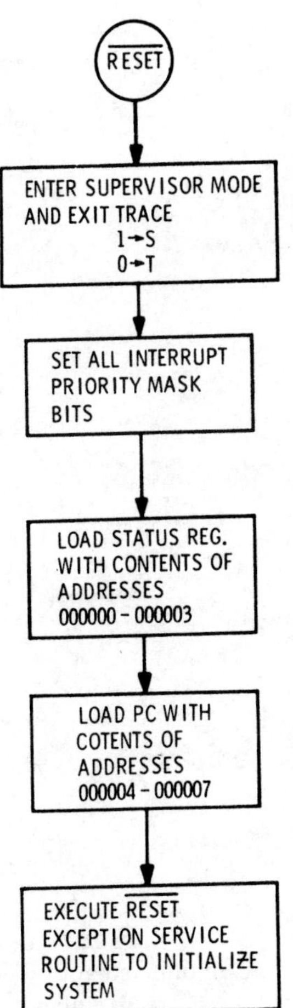

Figure 9-12
The 68000 external reset exception processing sequence.

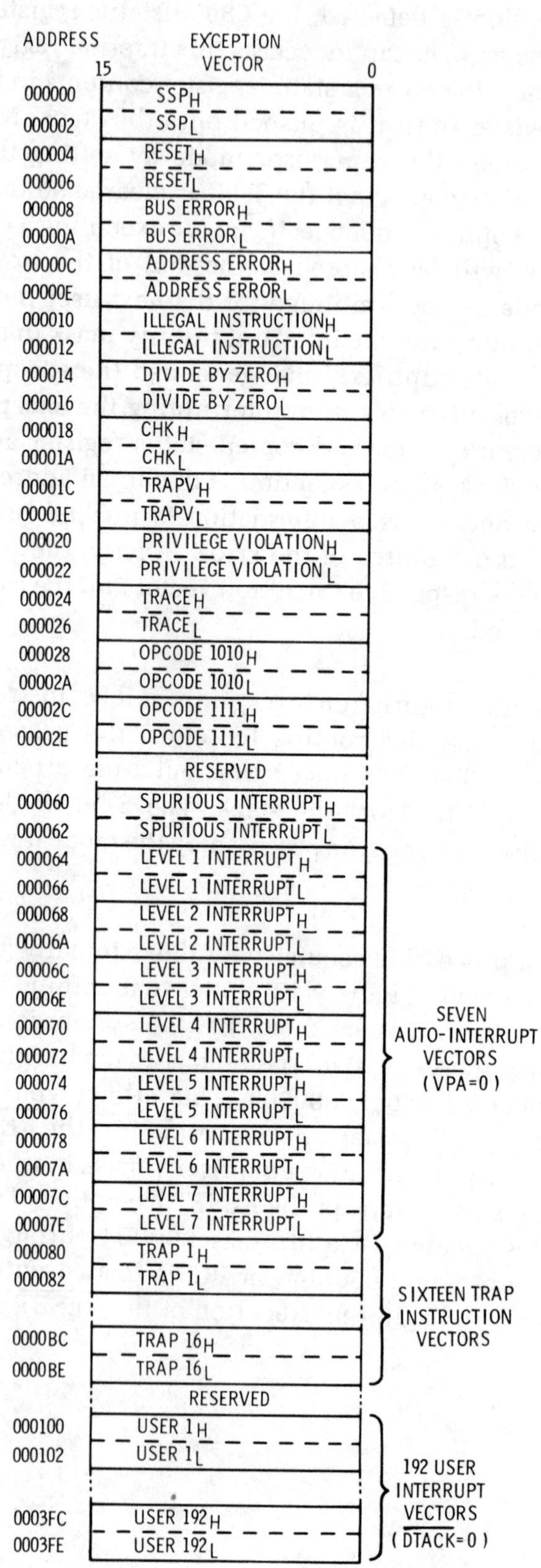

Figure 9-13
The 68000 exception vector address map.

Exception Vectoring

To complete our discussion of exception processing, we must discuss exception vectoring. Like interrupt vectoring for the 6800 family, exception vectoring is used to access the exception service routine for the 68000. The exception vector address map for the 68000 is shown in Figure 9-13. You will note that the 68000 exception vectors are located at memory addresses 000000_{16} through $0003FF_{16}$, comprising the first 1024, or 1K bytes of memory. Consequently, these memory addresses will normally be assigned to ROM in a 68000 system. Each vector in Figure 9-13 is 32 bits long, or two words, since the vector value is fetched and loaded into the 32-bit program counter during exception processing. With present versions of the 68000, the upper eight bits of the program counter are not used.

The vector words are located at even addresses. For example, the high RESET vector word, or $RESET_H$, is located at address 000004_{16} and the low RESET vector word, or $RESET_L$, is located at address 000006_{16}. When the RESET exception is processed, the program counter is loaded with the contents of memory addresses 000004_{16} through 000007_{16} as illustrated in Figure 9-14. The RESET exception service routine will then be executed beginning at the address contained in the program counter. You might also note from Figure 9-13 that memory addresses 000000_{16} through 000003_{16} contain the 32-bit value to be loaded into the system stack pointer, or SSP, during RESET exception processing.

There are 255 unique exception vectors; however, present versions of the 68000 only require the use of 227 vectors. The unused vector locations are reserved by Motorola for future enhancements of the 68000. You will note from Figure 9-13 that there is a 32-bit exception vector for each exception that we have discussed in this section.

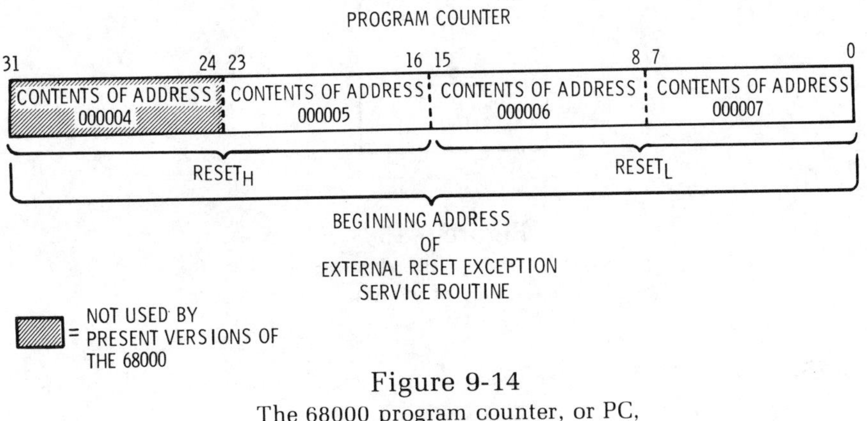

Figure 9-14
The 68000 program counter, or PC, containing the 68000 $\overline{\text{RESET}}$ exception vector.

Of special interest are the 68000 interrupt exception vectors. These consist of a **spurious interrupt vector, seven auto-interrupt vectors,** and **192 user interrupt vectors**. When an interrupt exception is processed, the exception vector is determined by one of three 68000 control lines as illustrated by the flowchart in Figure 9-15. After the interrupt level is accepted, the 68000 sets all of its function code output status lines. This is the interrupt acknowledge state and tells the interrupting device that its interrupt has been accepted. The 68000 then waits for a response from the interrupting device.

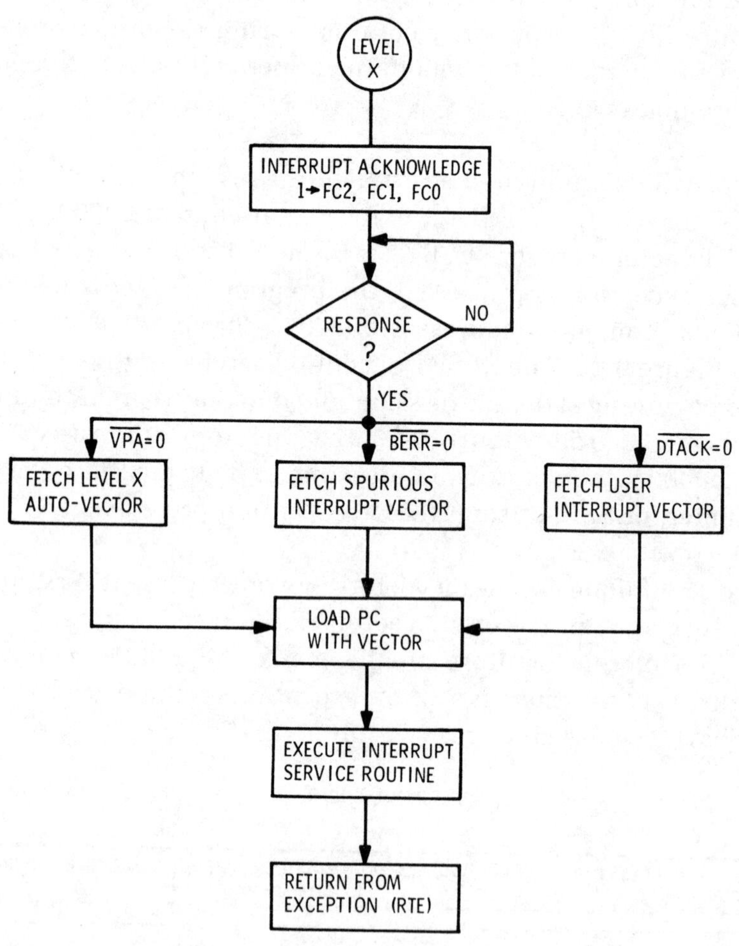

Figure 9-15
Interrupt exception processing sequence of events.

If the interrupting device responds by activating the 68000 valid peripheral address, or $\overline{VPA}$, input line, the 68000 accesses one of the seven auto-interrupt vectors shown in Figure 9-13. The vector that is accessed depends on the interrupt input level. For example, if interrupt level 3 is being processed, the level 3 auto-vector located at addresses $00006C_{16}$ through $00006F_{16}$ is fetched and loaded into the program counter.

If the interrupting device responds by activating the 68000 data transfer acknowledge, or $\overline{DTACK}$, input line, one of the 192 user-defined interrupt vectors is accessed. When the interrupting device activates $\overline{DTACK}$, it must supply an 8-bit **vector number** on data lines D0-D7. The vector number should be a value between 40_{16} and FF_{16}. The 68000 then uses this vector number to form the user vector address as shown in Figure 9-16.

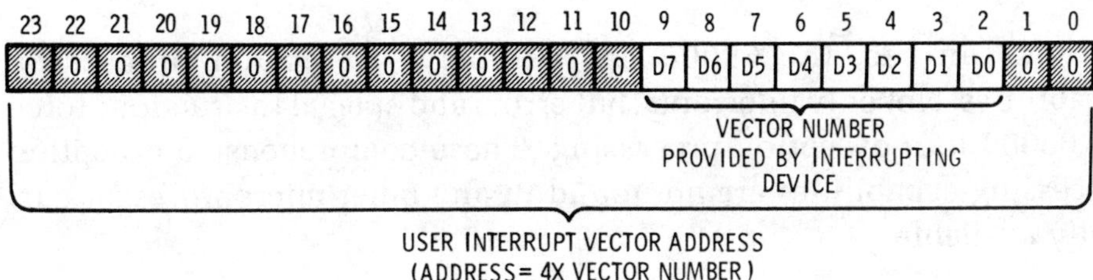

Figure 9-16
User interrupt vector address determination.

Notice that the vector number is shifted left by two bit positions, and located in bits A2 through A9 of the vector address. All other vector address bits are cleared. In effect, shifting a value left by two bit positions, multiplies that value by four. Consequently, you can say that the 68000 multiplies the vector number by four to obtain the vecotr address. For example, if the interrupting device activates $\overline{DTACK}$ and provides a vector number of 77_{16}, the vector address is $4 \times 77_{16} = 0001DC_{16}$. You might note that vector numbers below 40_{16} can be used, but the vector address which results will access a vector which is already defined for a non-interrupt exception. Thus, user-defined vectors allow the interrupting device to select up to 256 unique interrupt service routines. However, you should only use the 192 vectors allocated to the user-defined interrupts. The vector, and consequently the routine, selected will depend on the nature of the interrupt.

Peripheral devices that have been specifically designed to interface with the 68000 have the capability to supply vector numbers and thus provide user-defined vectoring. When you interface peripheral devices to the 68000 that do not have this capability, you must use auto-vectoring, by activating the 68000 $\overline{VPA}$ line. Such is the case when interfacing 6800 family peripheral devices to the 68000.

There is one other interrupt vectoring possibility that we have not discussed. This is the spurious interrupt vector, which is automatically accessed when the interrupting device activates the 68000 bus error, or $\overline{BERR}$, input line. When $\overline{BERR}$ is activated instead of $\overline{DTACK}$ or $\overline{VPA}$, the 68000 assumes that the interrupt request was **spurious** or **inadvertent**, possibly caused by "glitches" on the interrupt request lines. In this case, the spurious interrupt vector is fetched from memory locations 000060_{16} through 000063_{16}. The spurious interrupt service routine might simply be an RTE instruction to return the processor to its pre-interrupt state.

As you can see, the 68000 has extensive exception processing capabilities. Not only interrupts, but errors and special instructions force the 68000 into exception processing. These comprehensive exception processing capabilities are not found in any other microprocessor currently available.

Self-Test Review

13. What are the three processing states of the 68000?

14. Define exception processing.

15. How must the 68000 enter the supervisor mode when operating in the user mode?

16. List the privileged instructions of the 68000 and indicate which ones can be used to enter the user mode from the supervisor mode.

17. What are the two major exception categories of the 68000?

18. What three conditions will cause an internally generated exception?

19. Provide at least two internally detected errors that will generate an exception.

20. What is an unimplemented opcode exception?

21. List the five 68000 instructions that can be used to generate an exception.

22. What are the three ways that an exception can be generated as the result of an external event?

23. List the major steps in the general exception processing sequence.

24. Where are the 68000 exception vectors located in memory?

25. What are the three different classifications of interrupt exception vectors?

26. An interrupting device supplies a vector number of FF_{16}. What is the address of the user interrupt vector?

Answers

13. The three processing states of the 68000 are **normal, halted**, and **exception**.

14. Exception processing is the processing of an exception. It occurs when the 68000 is forced to deviate from its normal processing state as the result of an exception. When an exception occurs, the 68000 will automatically vector to an exception service routine in memory.

15. The 68000 can only make a transition from the user mode to the supervisor mode with an exception.

16. The privileged instructions of the 68000 are: **RESET, RTE, STOP, ANDI to SR, ORI to SR, EORI to SR, MOVE EA to SR,** and **MOVE USP.** All of these except RESET, STOP, and MOVE USP can be used to clear the S-bit of the status register and, thus, enter the user mode.

17. The two major exception categories of the 68000 are **internally generated exceptions** and **externally generated exceptions**.

18. The three conditions that will cause an internally generated exception are **internally detected errors, special instructions,** and **instruction tracing.**

19. Internally detected errors that generate an exception include **address errors, privilege instruction violations, illegal opcodes,** and **unimplemented opcodes.**

20. An unimplemented opcode exception is an exception that is generated if the first four bits of the instruction opcode are 1010 or 1111. You can use this exception to create your own 68000 instructions.

21. The five 68000 instructions that can be used to generate an exception are: **TRAP, TRAPV, CHK, DIVS,** and **DIVU**.

22. External exceptions can be generated as the result of a **bus error, interrupt request,** and an **external $\overline{\text{RESET}}$.**

23. The major steps in the general exception processing sequence are: (Refer to Figure 9-11).

    - Copy the status register.
    - Enter the supervisor mode.
    - Clear the T-bit.
    - If the exception is an interrupt, set the interrupt priority mask to the interrupt level that generated the exception.
    - Push the program counter and copied stack pointer onto the supervisor stack.
    - If the exception is due to an address or bus error, push additional instruction cycle information onto the supervisor stack.
    - Load the program counter with the respective exception vector and execute the exception service routine.
    - Return to program (RTE).

24. The 68000 exception vectors are located at memory addresses 000000_{16} through $0003FF_{16}$.

25. The three classifications of interrupt exception vectors are: **spurious interrupt, auto-interrupt,** and **user interrupt** vectors.

26. If an interrupting device supplies a vector number of FF_{16}, the address of the user interrupt vector is $4 \times FF_{16}$, or $0003FC_{16}$.

Unit 10

THE 68000 — PART 3

CONTENTS

INTRODUCTION

You have now been acquainted with the software and hardware features of the 68000. In this last unit, you will learn how to interface 6800 peripheral devices to the 68000 to produce a workable microcomputer system. You will also be introduced to several new peripheral devices and systems designed to support the 68000. Finally, you will see how the capabilities of the 68000 can be efficiently utilized in a multiprocessor industrial data acquisition system. This will be done in an effort to stimulate your thinking for other possible applications of the 68000.

UNIT OBJECTIVES

When you complete this unit, you should be able to:

1. Explain how the 68000 address space can be expanded from 16M bytes to 64M bytes.

2. State the four functional address partitions that can be decoded with the 68000 function code lines.

3. Explain how two PIAs can be used to provide 16-bit I/O ports for the 68000.

4. Explain why synchronous interfacing is generally slower than asynchronous interfacing.

5. Describe an asynchronous interface circuit that can be used to interface synchronous devices to the 68000.

6. Describe the features of the 68120 and 68121 IPCs.

7. State the difference between a board level design module and a microcomputer development system.

8. Develop a functional diagram of an industrial data acquisition system which uses the 68000.

9. Suggest possible applications for the 68000.

INTERFACING TO 6800 PERIPHERAL DEVICES

The 68000 is supported by all of the 6800 family peripheral devices listed in Figure 10-1. You are now familiar with most of these devices, and understand how to interface them to the various 6800 family processors. In this section, we will show you how to interface several of the more popular 6800 peripheral devices to the 68000. You will see how these devices are used to transfer 8-bit data to and from the 68000. In addition, you will see how 16-bit parallel data transfer can be accomplished using two 6821 PIAs.

As you are now aware, the 68000 can interface to peripheral devices using synchronous or asynchronous bus control. Although the 6800 peripheral devices are synchronous, they can also be interfaced to the 68000 using asynchronous bus control. We have, therefore, divided this section into two parts: synchronous interfacing and asynchronous interfacing.

68000 SUPPORT DEVICES
MC6821 Peripheral Interface Adapter MC6840 Programmable Timer Module MC6843 Floppy Disk Controller MC6845 CRT Controller MC6849 Dual Density Floppy Disk Controller MC6850 Asynchronous Communication Interface Adapter MC6852 Synchronous Serial Data Adapter MC6854 Advanced Data Link Controller MC68488 General Purpose Interface Adapter (IEEE 488) MC6847 Video Display Generator MC6860 Digital MODEM MC6846 ROM-I/O-Timer

Figure 10-1
The 6800 family peripheral devices that support the 68000.

Synchronous Interfacing

Before we discuss interfacing specific peripheral devices, let's review how memory is interfaced to the 68000. Recall from Unit 9 that memory is interfaced to the 68000 using an odd/even address scheme as shown in Figure 10-2. The odd memory addresses are interfaced to data lines D0-D7 and the even memory addresses are interfaced to data lines D8-D15. The 68000 lower data strobe, or $\overline{\text{LDS}}$, and upper data strobe, or $\overline{\text{UDS}}$, control lines are used to access the odd and even addresses, respectively.

Since the 68000 uses memory mapped I/O, any 8-bit peripheral device will interface to the 68000 using the odd/even address scheme. Thus, a given 8-bit peripheral device will be assigned to consecutive odd addresses or consecutive even addresses. A single device is used to transfer 8-bit data to and from the 68000 on data lines D0-D7 **or** D8-D15. Two devices are activated simultaneously to transfer 16-bit data to and from the 68000 on data lines D0-D15.

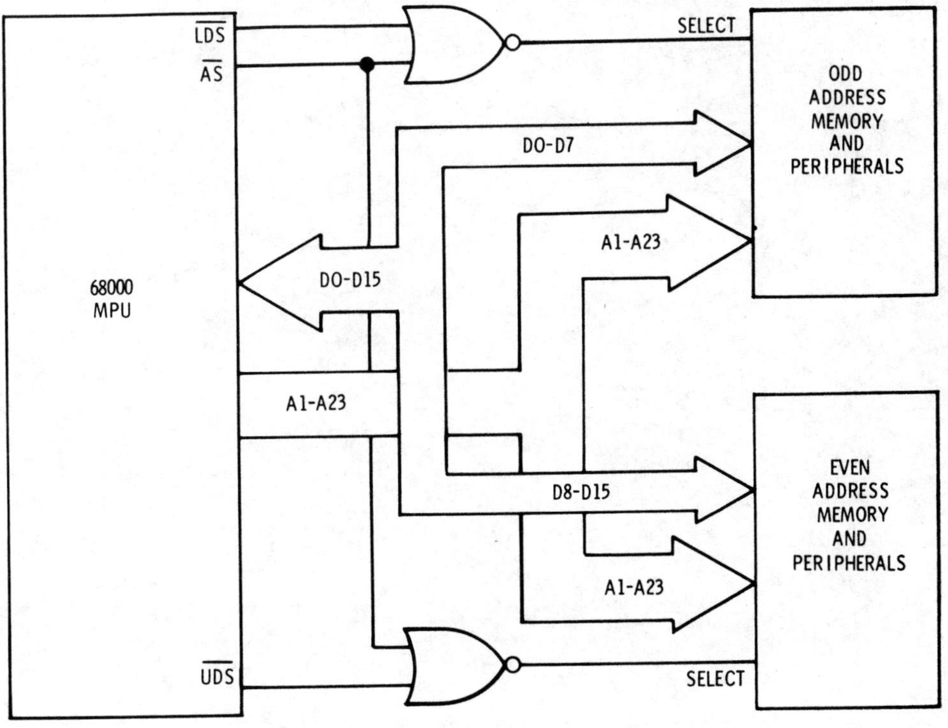

Figure 10-2
Even/odd address interfacing to the 68000.

You already know that up to 16M bytes can be interfaced to the 68000 by using its 23 address lines and odd/even address interfacing. Furthermore, the 68000 function code lines can be used with a decoder to partition the 68000 address space into **four** 16M byte blocks as shown in Figure 10-3. Notice that each of four 16M byte memory partitions can be independently enabled using the function code output signals. Consequently, an address space of up to 64M bytes can be provided for the 68000. In addition, user/supervisor program and data information can be functionally separated for more efficient programming. Recall that the 68000 function code lines provide output logic that indicates the program execution status. The function code output logic table is shown again in Figure 10-4. A simple 1-of-8 decoder is used in Figure 10-3 to decode the function code logic and enable the respective memory partition.

Now, keeping in mind how 8-bit memory and peripheral devices are mapped to the 68000 address space, let's see how several popular 6800 peripheral devices are actually interfaced to the 68000.

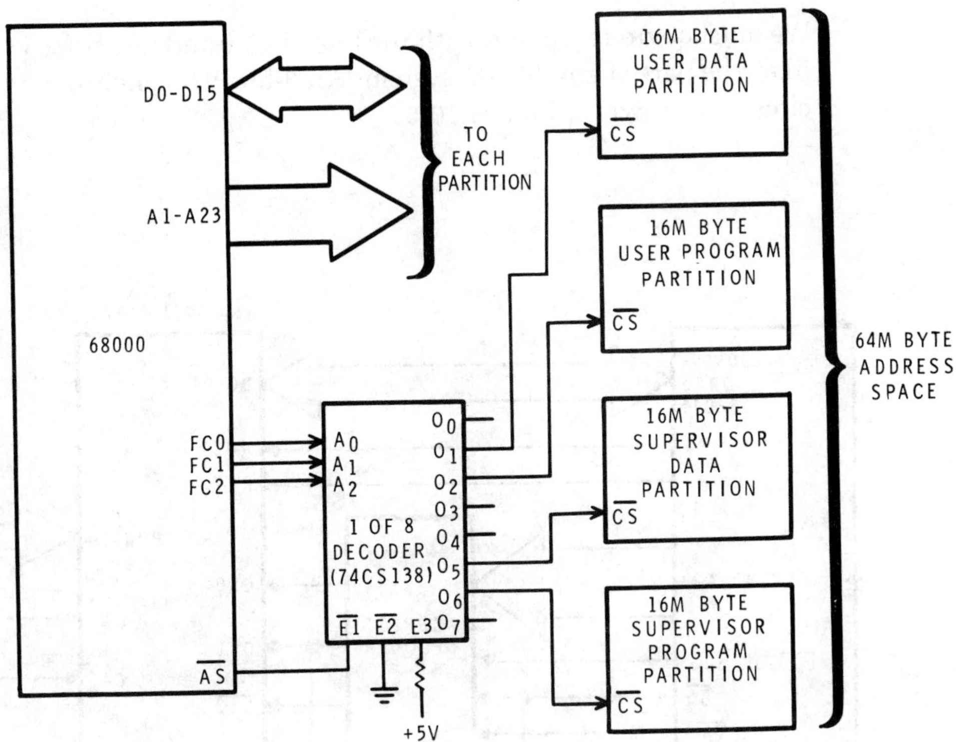

Figure 10-3
Partitioning the 68000 address space using the function code lines.

FC2	FC1	FC0	OPERATION
0	0	0	▨
0	0	1	USER DATA ACCESS
0	1	0	USER PROGRAM ACCESS
0	1	1	▨
1	0	0	▨
1	0	1	SUPERVISOR DATA ACCESS
1	1	0	SUPERVISOR PROGRAM ACCESS
1	1	1	INTERRUPT ACKNOWLEDGE

▨ = CURRENTLY UNDEFINED

Figure 10-4
Operational status indications provided by the 68000 function code lines.

THE 6821 PIA INTERFACE

We must obviously begin with the 6821 PIA interface, since it will most likely be part of any 68000 system. An 8-bit PIA synchronous interface circuit is shown in Figure 10-5.

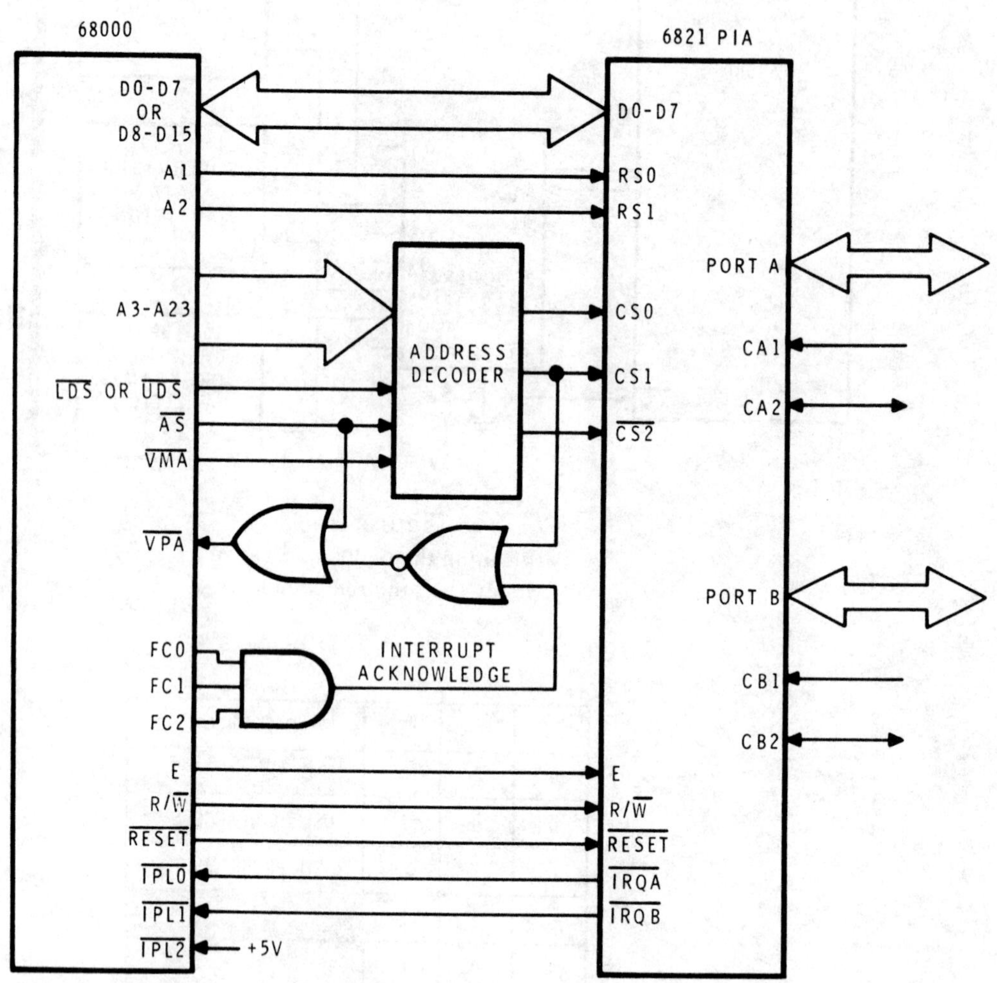

Figure 10-5
An 8-bit synchronous PIA interface to the 68000.

The address decoder is used to assign the PIA to four consecutive odd addresses **or** four consecutive even addresses. Notice that either the lower data strobe ($\overline{\text{LDS}}$) or upper data strobe ($\overline{\text{UDS}}$) must be decoded along with address lines A3-A23 to select the PIA. Since address lines A1 and A2 are connected to the PIA register select lines RS0 and RS1 respectively, the PIA registers will be located at consecutive odd or even addresses as shown in Figure 10-6. Once selected, the PIA is used to transfer 8-bit data on data lines D0-D7 or D8-D15, depending on which data strobe is decoded.

Aside from selecting the PIA, the address decoder output is used along with the 68000 address strobe, or $\overline{\text{AS}}$, line to activate the 68000 valid peripheral address, or $\overline{\text{VPA}}$, input line. Recall that this control line must be activated when synchronous data transfer is required. Consequently, when the PIA is selected, the 68000 $\overline{\text{VPA}}$ line is activated and synchronous data transfer is controlled with the 68000 enable, or E, and valid memory address, or $\overline{\text{VMA}}$, synchronous control lines.

Notice also from Figure 10-5 that the 68000 valid peripheral address, or $\overline{\text{VPA}}$, input line will be activated when a PIA interrupt is acknowledged via the 68000 function code, or FC, status lines. Recall that the 68000 $\overline{\text{VPA}}$ line must be activated when auto-interrupt vectoring is required. The PIA interrupt lines in Figure 10-5 are connected to the 68000 interrupt input lines so that $\overline{\text{IRQA}}$ will provide a level 1 interrupt and $\overline{\text{IRQB}}$ will provide a level 2 interrupt. When the 68000 accepts a level 1 or level 2 interrupt, it acknowledges the interrupt by setting all of its function code output lines. The interrupt acknowledge output activates the $\overline{\text{VPA}}$ input line and the level 1 or level 2 auto-interrupt vector is fetched, depending on which interrupt level has been accepted.

The remaining connections shown in Figure 10-5, such as $\overline{\text{VMA}}$, E, R/$\overline{\text{W}}$ and $\overline{\text{RESET}}$ should be self-explanatory at this point.

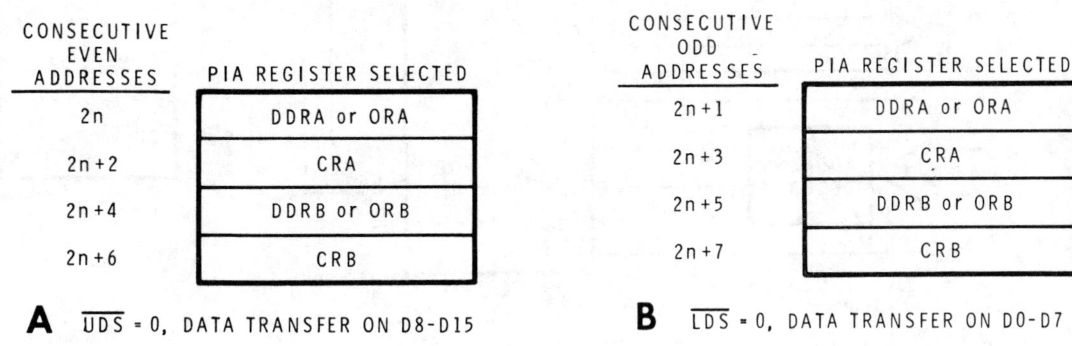

Figure 10-6
Consecutive even (A), or odd (B) address assignments provided by the PIA interface circuit in Figure 10-5.

Two PIAs can be interfaced to the 68000 as shown in Figure 10-7 and Figure 10-8 to provide 16-bit data transfers. A PIA interface for a 16-bit input peripheral is shown in Figure 10-7. A 16-bit output interface is shown in Figure 10-8. In both cases, two PIAs are required: a **high byte PIA** and a **low byte PIA**. The two PIAs are activated simultaneously by the upper and lower data strobes ($\overline{UDS}$ and $\overline{LDS}$) of the 68000. The high data byte is transferred via the high byte PIA on data lines D8-D15. The low data byte is transferred via the low byte PIA on data lines D0-D7. Address decoding, synchronous bus control, and interrupt control for each PIA must be provided as shown in Figure 10-5 and discussed previously.

Since four ports are provided by two PIAs, Figures 10-7 and 10-8 can be combined as shown in Figure 10-9 to provide both a 16-bit input interface and a 16-bit output interface. Here, the 16-bit input interface is provided by ports A of the PIAs and the 16-bit output interface is provided by ports B of the PIAs. Complete handshake control of the data transfer operation can be accomplished using any two port control lines as discussed in Unit 1 of this course. Of course, you could also configure the ports of the two PIAs in Figure 10-9 to provide two 16-bit input interfaces or two 16-bit output interfaces.

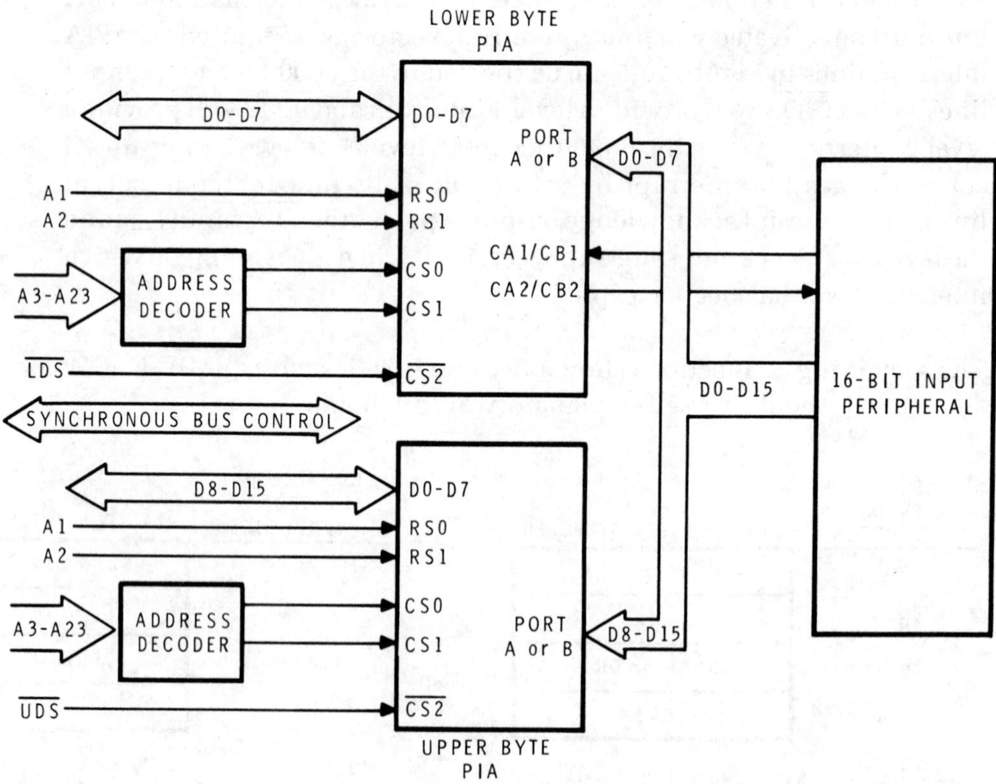

Figure 10-7
A 16-bit input interface for the 68000 using two PIAs.

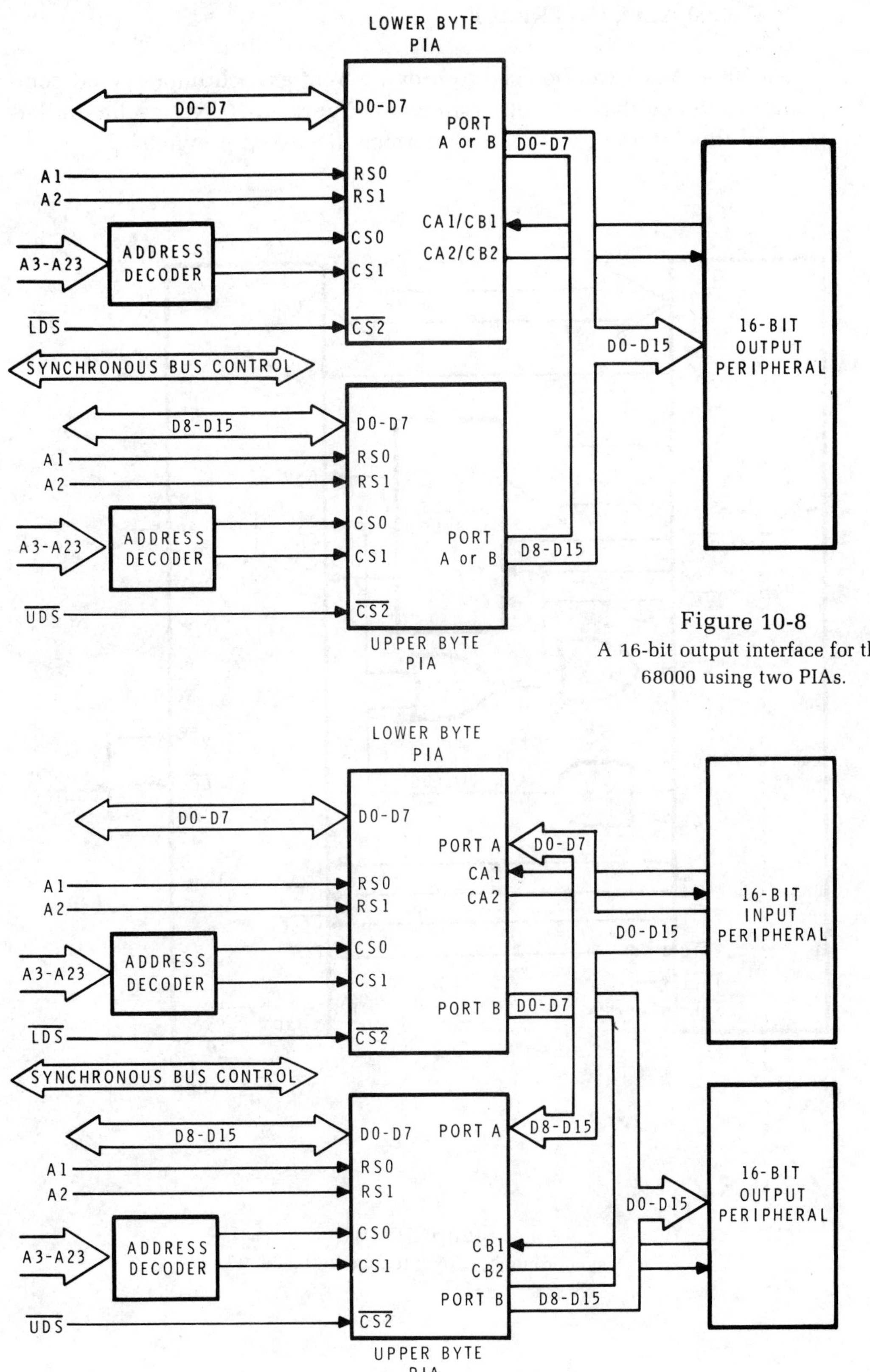

Figure 10-8
A 16-bit output interface for the 68000 using two PIAs.

Figure 10-9
A 16-bit input/output interface for the 68000 using two PIAs.

THE 6850 ACIA INTERFACE

The 6850 ACIA can be used to provide 8-bit asynchronous serial communication with the 68000 as shown in Figure 10-10. Notice the similarity of this interface to the PIA interface discussed previously.

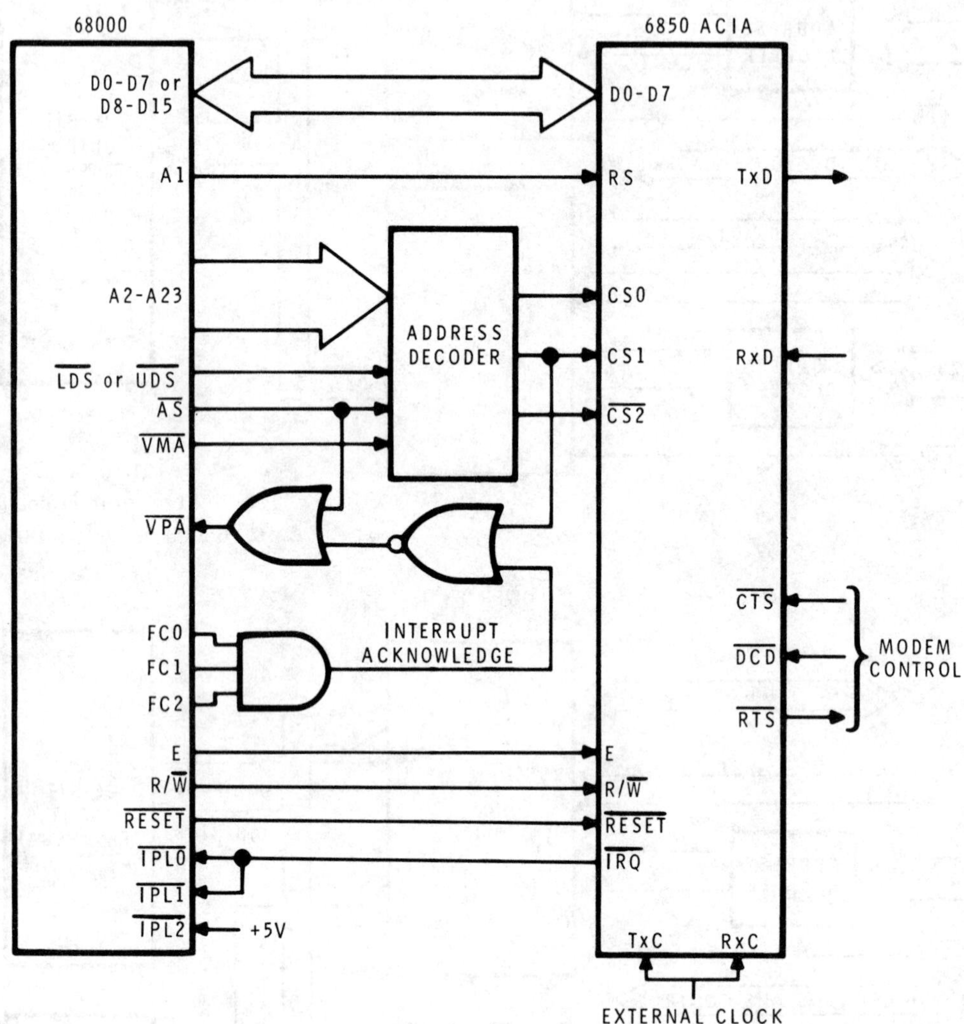

Figure 10-10
A synchronous ACIA interface to the 68000.

Address line A1 is connected directly to the ACIA register select, or RS, line. Address lines A2-A23 can be partially or completely decoded along with the 68000 $\overline{LDS}$ or $\overline{UDS}$, $\overline{AS}$, and $\overline{VMA}$ lines to select the ACIA. The lower data strobe, or $\overline{LDS}$, is decoded if 8-bit data is to be transferred on data lines D0-D7. The upper data strobe, or $\overline{UDS}$, is decoded if 8-bit data is to be transferred on data lines D8-D15. The internal ACIA registers will, therefore, be located at consecutive odd or even addresses as shown in Figure 10-11.

CONSECUTIVE EVEN ADDRESSES	ACIA REGISTER SELECTED: MPU READ	MPU WRITE
2n	STATUS REG.	CONTROL REG.
2n + 2	RECEIVE DATA REG.	TRANSMIT DATA REG.

A $\overline{UDS}$ = 0, DATA TRANSFER ON D8 - D15

CONSECUTIVE ODD ADDRESSES	ACIA REGISTER SELECTED: MPU READ	MPU WRITE
2n + 1	STATUS REG.	CONTROL REG.
2n + 3	RECEIVE DATA REG.	TRANSMIT DATA REG.

B $\overline{LDS}$ = 0, DATA TRANSFER ON D0 - D7

Figure 10-11
Consecutive even (A), or odd (B) address assignments provided by the ACIA interface circuit in Figure 10-10.

The 68000 valid peripheral address, or $\overline{VPA}$, input line is used to tell the 68000 that synchronous bus control is required as with the PIA interface. Be careful not to confuse synchronous bus control with the asynchronous serial communication provided to serial peripherals by the ACIA. They are two separate things. Synchronous bus control is provided between the 68000 and ACIA via the $\overline{VPA}$, E, and $\overline{VMA}$ lines of the 68000 as shown in Figure 10-10. On the other hand, asynchronous serial communication is provided between the ACIA and a serial peripheral via the T_xD and R_xD lines of the ACIA.

Notice that the ACIA interrupt request, or $\overline{IRQ}$, line is connected in Figure 10-10 for a level 3 interrupt. When this interrupt is acknowledged via the 68000 function code lines, the $\overline{VPA}$ input line is activated and the level 3 auto-interrupt vector is fetched. The remaining interface line connections shown in Figure 10-10 should now be self-explanatory.

It is important to note that you can only transmit or receive eight bits at a time using the 6850 ACIA. You cannot interface two ACIAs to the 68000 as you did with the PIA to provide 16-bit serial communications. Recall that the ACIA only frames 8-bit data values and no provision is made for 16-bit data framing.

THE 6840 PTM INTERFACE

A 6840 PTM is shown interfaced to the 68000 in Figure 10-12. As you can see, this interface is very similar to the PIA and ACIA interfaces discussed previously.

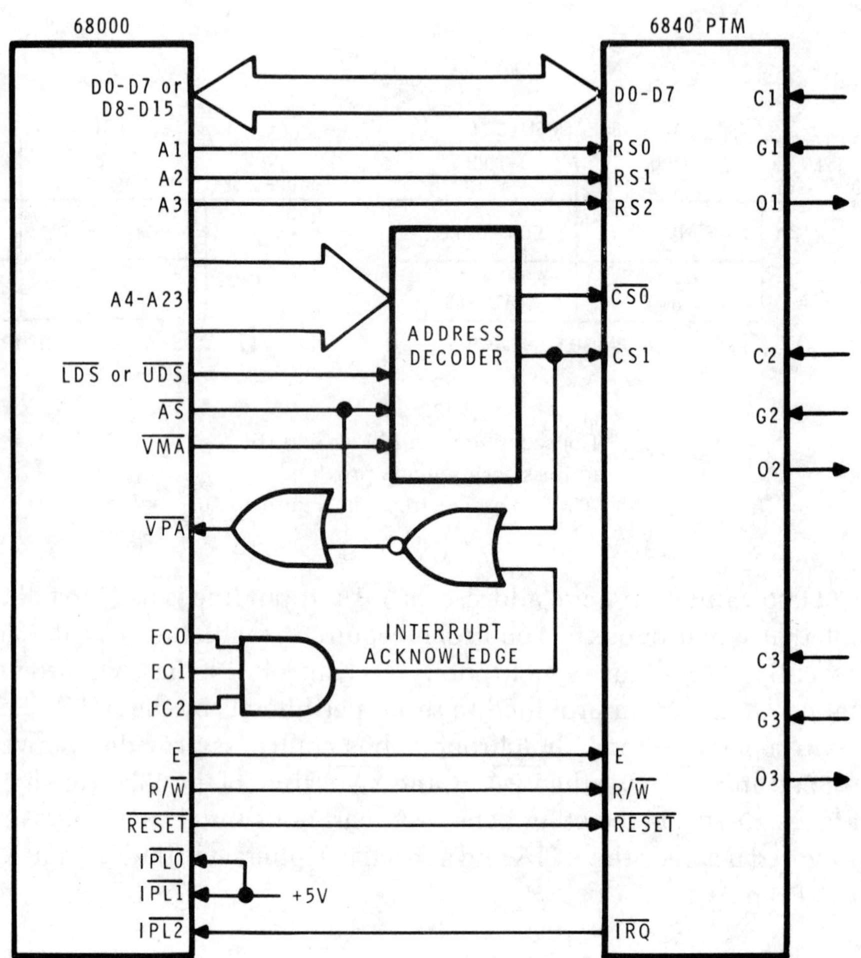

Figure 10-12
A synchronous PTM interface for the 68000.

Address lines A1, A2, and A3 are connected directly to register select lines RS0, RS1, and RS2, respectively, of the PTM. Address lines A4-A23 are then partially or completely decoded along with the 68000 $\overline{\text{LDS}}$ or $\overline{\text{UDS}}$, $\overline{\text{AS}}$, and $\overline{\text{VMA}}$ lines to select the PTM. The internal PTM registers are located at consecutive odd or even addresses as shown in Figure 10-13.

The 68000 valid peripheral address, or $\overline{\text{VPA}}$, input line is again used for synchronous bus control and auto-interrupt vectoring. The circuit in Figure 10-12 provides a level 4 interrupt for the PTM.

We do not intend to discuss the synchronous interfacing of any other 6800 family peripheral devices in this course. However, as you can see, the general synchronous interfacing concepts are the same, regardless of the 6800 family peripheral device being used.

CONSECUTIVE EVEN ADDRESSES	PTM REGISTER SELECTED MPU READ	PTM REGISTER SELECTED MPU WRITE
2n	NONE	CONTROL REG. #1 OR #3
2n+2	STATUS REG.	CONTROL REG. #2
2n+4 2n+6	TIMER #1 COUNTER	TIMER #1 LATCH
2n+8 2n+10	TIMER #2 COUNTER	TIMER #2 LATCH
2n+12 2n+14	TIMER #3 COUNTER	TIMER #3 LATCH

A $\overline{\text{UDS}}$=0, DATA TRANSFER ON D8-D15

CONSECUTIVE ODD ADDRESSES	PTM REGISTER SELECTED MPU READ	PTM REGISTER SELECTED MPU WRITE
2n+1	NONE	CONTROL REG. #1 OR #3
2n+3	STATUS REG.	CONTROL REG. #2
2n+5 2n+7	TIMER #1 COUNTER	TIMER #1 LATCH
2n+9 2n+11	TIMER #2 COUNTER	TIMER #2 LATCH
2n+13 2n+15	TIMER #3 COUNTER	TIMER #3 LATCH

B $\overline{\text{LDS}}$=0, DATA TRANSFER ON D0-D7

Figure 10-13
Consecutive even (A), or odd (B) address assignments provided by the PTM interface circuit Figure 10-12.

Asynchronous Interfacing

It is often desirable to take advantage of the asynchronous interfacing capabilities of the 68000, even when you are interfacing to synchronous devices such as the 6800 family peripheral devices. Recall that the frequency of the 68000 enable, or E, line is 10% of the internal clock frequency. Certain applications may require a different clock frequency to control data transfer. This is especially true when a peripheral device is clocked from an external clock source, other than E. With synchronous bus control, the data transfer is directly dependent on the E-clock frequency. However, with asynchronous bus control the data transfer is independent of the E-clock frequency. Another reason that asynchronous bus control might be desirable is more efficient program execution. With synchronous bus control, the 68000 must wait to receive the $\overline{\text{VPA}}$ input signal and synchronize its execution with the 90% slower E-clock frequency before an instruction can be executed. In other words, the internal synchronization required for synchronous interfacing slows down the 68000. However, with asynchronous bus control, the $\overline{\text{DTACK}}$ signal response is usually adequate to allow the 68000 to continue unimpeded instruction execution.

A functional block diagram of the circuit required to interface synchronous peripheral devices asynchronously to the 68000 is provided in Figure 10-14. This circuit performs the following major functions:

- It generates the peripheral device chip select signals.
- It latches data to satisfy the peripheral device hold time requirements.
- It provides the asynchronous data transfer acknowledge, or $\overline{\text{DTACK}}$, signal to the 68000 at the proper time to assure valid data transfer between the 68000 and the synchronous peripheral device.

Notice from Figure 10-14 that two 8-bit latches are required, a **write-only latch** and a **read-only latch**. Data to be written to the synchronous peripheral device is latched by the write-only latch. Data to be read from the peripheral device is latched by the read-only latch. Thus, during a 68000 write operation, the write-only latch is active and the read-only latch is inactive, and vice-versa for a 68000 read operation. The latches are required to assure that the hold time requirements of the synchronous peripheral device are satisfied. The **latch control** circuit in Figure 10-14 enables and disables the latches for the 68000 read/write operations.

The synchronous peripheral device is decoded as before with an address decoder. Notice that the address decoder is used to decode the address bus along with the asynchronous address strobe, or $\overline{AS}$, and the proper data strobe, $\overline{LDS}$ or $\overline{UDS}$.

A **peripheral device select and $\overline{\textbf{DTACK}}$ generation** circuit is used in Figure 10-14 to provide the final chip select signal to the peripheral device, and to supply the asynchronous $\overline{DTACK}$ input signal to the 68000.

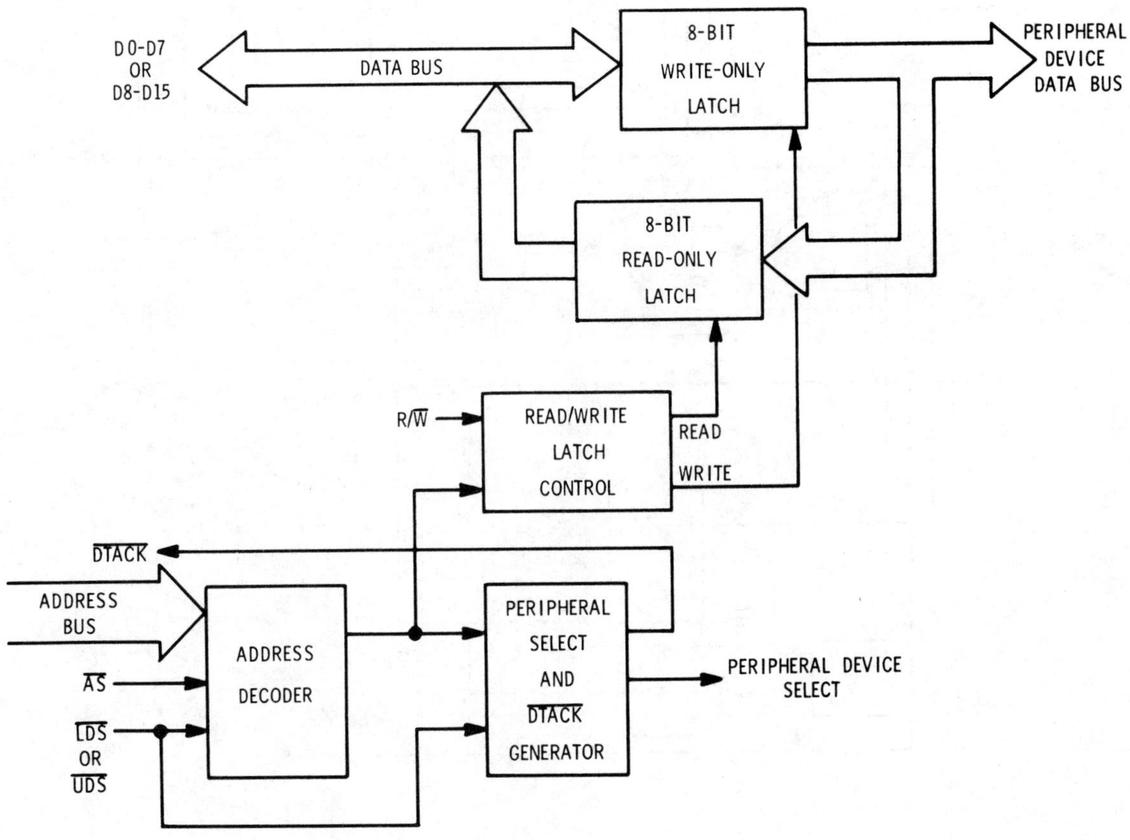

Figure 10-14
A block diagram of the circuit required to interface synchronous peripheral devices asynchronously to the 68000.

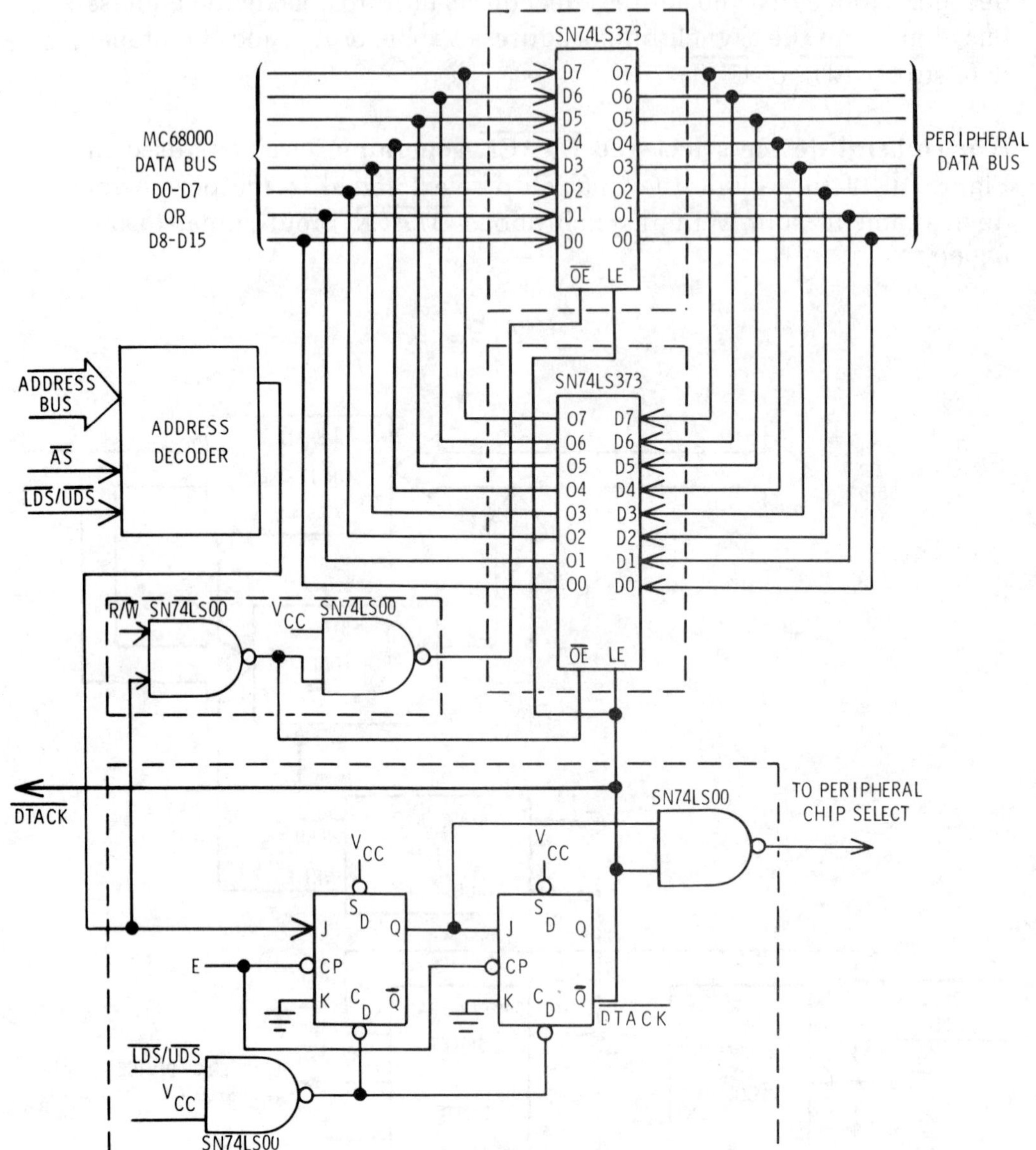

Figure 10-15
The circuit required to interface synchronous peripheral devices asynchronously to the 68000.

An actual circuit diagram of the asynchronous interface is provided in Figure 10-15. Notice that the functional blocks of the circuit are indicated by the dashed outlines in Figure 10-15. We do not intend to go through the logic of this circuit. The functional explanation provided in conjunction with the circuit block diagram in Figure 10-14 will suffice. However, you should notice from the circuit that the asynchronous interface can be constructed with as few as five TTL components: a 74LS00 NAND gate chip, two 74LS373 8-bit latches, one 74LS112 dual J-K flip-flop chip, and a decoder. Any standard decoder, such as a 74LS138 1-of-8 or 74LS154 1-of-16 decoder, can be used. Finally, a PIA is shown interfaced asynchronously to the 68000 in Figure 10-16. This type of interface will provide more efficient data transfer and program execution than the synchronous PIA interface discussed previously.

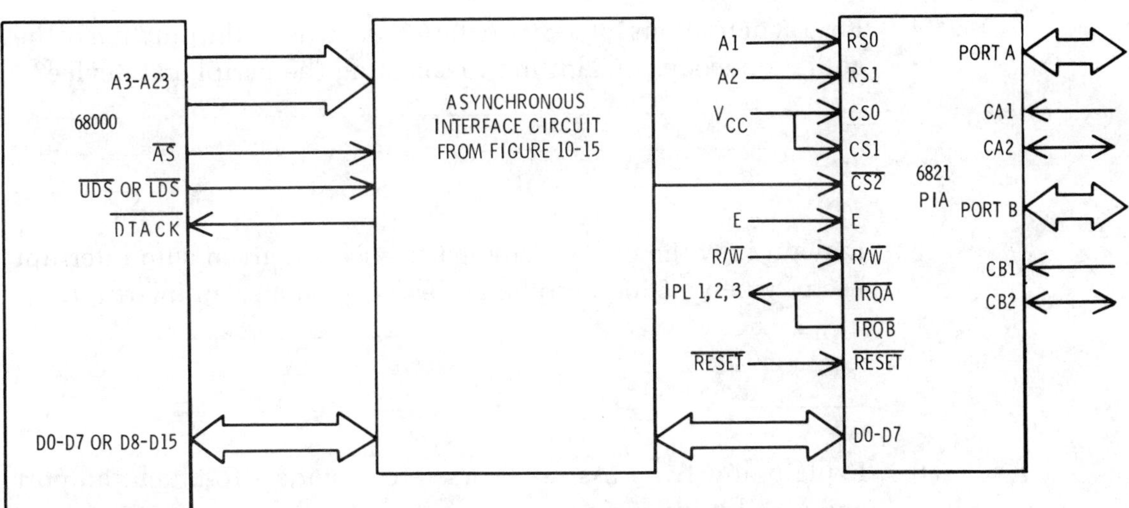

Figure 10-16
An asynchronous interface to the 68000 for the 6821 PIA.

Self-Test Review

1. What are the two ways in which a 6800 peripheral device can be interfaced to the 68000? ______

2. Explain how the 68000 address space can be expanded to 64M bytes. ______

3. State the four functional address space partitions that can be decoded with the 68000 function code lines. ______

4. For a synchronous interface to the 68000, what is the function of the address decoder in addition to selecting the peripheral device? ______

5. Explain how the 68000 is forced to access a given auto-interrupt vector when a 6800 peripheral device generates an interrupt. ______

6. Explain how two PIAs can be used to provide a 16-bit output port and a 16-bit input port. ______

7. What is the difference between synchronous bus control and asynchronous serial communication as related to the 6850 ACIA?

8. Why can't two ACIAs be interfaced to the 68000 to provide 16-bit asynchronous serial communication with a serial peripheral?

9. Why is synchronous interfacing with the 68000 generally slower than asynchronous interfacing?

10. You want to provide an asynchronous interface to the 68000 for a 6800 peripheral device. What functions must the asynchronous interface perform?

11. List the five functional regions of an asynchronous interface circuit.

12. What TTL components are required to construct an asynchronous interface circuit for a 6800 peripheral device?

Answers

1. A 6800 peripheral device can be interfaced to the 68000 by using synchronous bus control or asynchronous bus control.

2. You can expand the 68000 address space to 64M bytes by decoding the 68000 function code lines so that the address space is partitioned into four 16M byte blocks.

3. The four address space partitions that can be decoded with the 68000 function code lines are **user data, user program, supervisor data**, and **supervisor program**.

4. For a synchronous interface to the 68000, the address decoder must activate the 68000 valid peripheral address, or $\overline{VPA}$, input line in addition to selecting the peripheral device.

5. The 68000 is forced to access a given auto-interrupt vector by activating the 68000 $\overline{VPA}$ input line after a given interrupt level is accepted. The three function code output lines of the 68000 are ANDed to provide the interrupt acknowledge and required $\overline{VPA}$ input signal.

6. Two PIAs can be interfaced to the 68000 to provide 16-bit data transfers. A low byte PIA is connected to data lines D0-D7 and a high byte PIA is connected to data lines D8-D15. Both PIAs are activated simultaneously by the upper and lower data strobes ($\overline{UDS}$ and $\overline{LDS}$) of the 68000. Since four 8-bit ports are provided by the two PIAs, two of the 8-bit ports can be combined to form a 16-bit input port. The remaining two 8-bit ports are combined to form a 16-bit output port.

7. Synchronous bus control is provided between the 68000 and ACIA via the 68000 synchronous bus control lines. Asynchronous serial communication is provided between the ACIA and a serial peripheral via the T_xD and R_xD lines of the ACIA.

8. You cannot interface two ACIAs to the 68000 to provide 16-bit asynchronous serial communication since the ACIA frames 8-bit data values and no provision is provided for 16-bit data framing.

9. Synchronous interfacing with the 68000 is generally slower than asynchronous interfacing because, with a synchronous interface, the 68000 must wait to receive the $\overline{\text{VPA}}$ input signal and synchronize its program execution with the 90% slower E-clock frequency before an instruction can be executed.

10. An asynchronous interface for a 6800 peripheral device must:

    - Generate the peripheral device chip select signals.
    - Latch data to satisfy the peripheral device hold time requirements.
    - Provide the asynchronous $\overline{\text{DTACK}}$ signal to the 68000 at the proper time to assure valid data transfer.

11. The five functional regions of an asynchronous interface circuit are:

    - The address decoder.
    - The write-only latch.
    - The read-only latch.
    - The latch control.
    - The peripheral select and $\overline{\text{DTACK}}$ generator.

12. The following TTL components are required to construct an asynchronous interface circuit for a 6800 peripheral device:

    - One 74LS00 NAND gate chip.
    - Two 74LS373 8-bit latches.
    - One 74LS112 dual J-K flip-flop chip.
    - One decoder chip (74LS138, 74LS154, etc.)

THE 68000 FAMILY, SUPPORT, AND APPLICATIONS

Now that you are acquainted with the 68000 and how it is interfaced to 6800 peripheral devices, you are probably wondering what, if any, peripheral devices are available specifically for this 16-bit microprocessor. You won't be disappointed, since a complete family of peripheral devices has been designed to support the 68000. In addition, entire hardware, software, and bussing systems are available to support evaluation and system development using the 68000. Any microprocessor is only as good as the hardware and software support available for that microprocessor.

In this section, we will provide you with an overview of the emerging 68000 family. In addition, we will acquaint you with several hardware and software development tools that are available for the 68000. Finally, we will suggest possible applications for the 68000 in an effort to stimulate your thinking for the future.

The 68000 Family

The 68000 microprocessor is supported by several peripheral devices. The peripheral support devices presently available, or being developed, are listed in Figure 10-17. It is expected that this list will grow to perhaps 30 devices.

You will notice from the device descriptions in Figure 10-17 that many of the common support tasks such as timing, direct memory access, memory management, CRT control, etc. are provided for 68000-based systems by these new devices. The industry trend is to design more "intelligence" into peripheral support devices so that the system processor is free to handle data processing and system-related tasks. Consequently, you will discover more sophisticated features in the 68000 peripheral devices than those that were designed for the 6800. The peripheral device intelligence is usually derived from an 8-bit microprocessor at the heart of the device.

We do not intend to discuss each new 68000 peripheral device in detail in this course. However, let's take a look at one of the more exciting 68000 peripheral devices since you are already more or less familiar with it. Moreover, this should give you an idea of the intelligence level of the remaining 68000 peripheral support devices.

68120/68121	INTELLIGENT PERIPHERAL CONTROLLER (IPC)
68122	CLUSTER TERMINAL CONTROLLER (CTC)
68230	PARALLEL INTERFACE/TIMER (PI/T)
68340	DUAL-PORT RAM (DPR)
68341	FLOATING-POINT READ-ONLY MEMORY
68450	DIRECT MEMORY ACCESS CONTROLLER (DMAC)
68451	MEMORY MANAGEMENT UNIT (MMU)
68540	ERROR DETECTION AND CORRECTION CIRCUIT (EDCC)
68560	SERIAL DIRECT MEMORY ACCESS PROCESSOR (SDMA)
68561	MULTI-PROTOCOL COMMUNICATIONS CONTROLLER (MPCC)

Figure 10-17
The 68000 family of peripheral support devices.

The **68120/68121 Intelligent Peripheral Controller**, or **IPC**, was one of the first support devices designed for the 68000. However, it can also be used with 6800-family processors. The word "intelligent" means that the IPC can be programmed to handle many of the routine peripheral I/O control tasks. Consequently, the 68000 is free to handle the more important data processing and system related tasks. At the heart of the 68120 is a 6801. Actually, the 68120 is simply a 6801 with additional I/O lines to facilitate both synchronous and asynchronous system interfacing. Since you are familiar with the capabilities of the 6801, you should be able to predict the capabilities of the 68120.

When it is interfaced to the 68000, the 68120 provides up to 21 parallel I/O lines with handshake control, a serial communication interface, or SCI, and a 16-bit timer. The 68120 also includes 128 bytes of scratch-pad RAM, and 2K bytes of mask-programmed ROM. The 68121 is identical to the 68120 except that it doesn't have any internal ROM. You guessed it, at the heart of a 68121 is a 6803. Since both the 68120 and 68121 are 8-bit microprocessors, they can be programmed to handle routine peripheral I/O tasks. These devices are called peripheral controllers since they act as a programmable buffer between the 68000 and its peripherals.

As you are aware, the 6801 has three fundamental operating modes: single chip, expanded non-multiplexed, and expanded multiplexed. The 68120 is, therefore, capable of three fundamental operating mode configurations. A 68120 configured in its single chip mode is shown interfaced to the 68000 in Figure 10-18. Notice that the 68120 is connected to the 68000 bus structure via eight data lines and eight address lines. This permits communication to take place between the 68000 and 68120. In addition, the 68120 includes the necessary control lines for either synchronous or asynchronous interfacing. Since this device was designed specifically for the 68000, no special interface circuit is required for asynchronous interfacing. As you can see from Figure 10-18, the 68120 provides up to 21 parallel I/O lines, a serial communications interface, and a 16-bit timer when configured in its single chip operating mode.

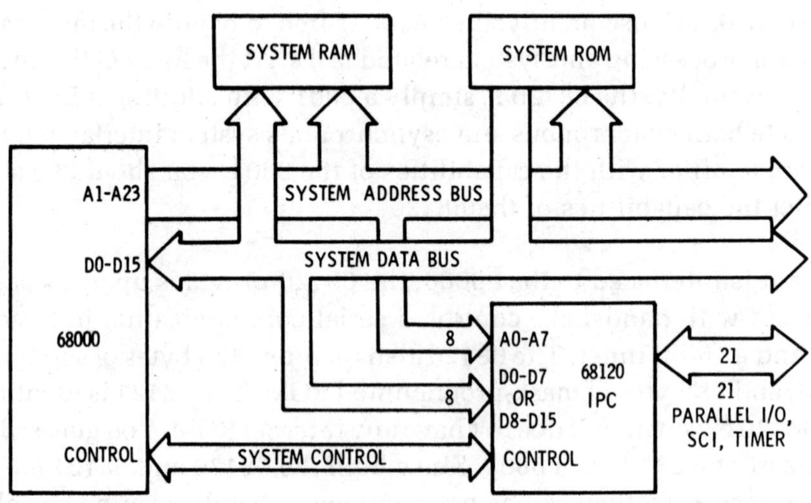

Figure 10-18
In its single-chip mode, the 68120 IPC provides up to 21 parallel I/O lines, a serial communications interface, and a 16-bit timer.

When it is configured in its non-multiplexed operating mode, the 68120 provides up to five parallel I/O lines, a serial communications interface, and a timer. In addition, the non-multiplexed mode provides eight **local address bus lines** and **eight local data bus lines** as shown in Figure 10-19. These lines provide an external 256-byte address space for interfacing to other peripheral devices. Generally, this is not enough external space to interface additional RAM and ROM to the 68120. However, other 68000 peripheral devices or 6800 peripheral devices can be interfaced to the 68120 via these local address and data lines.

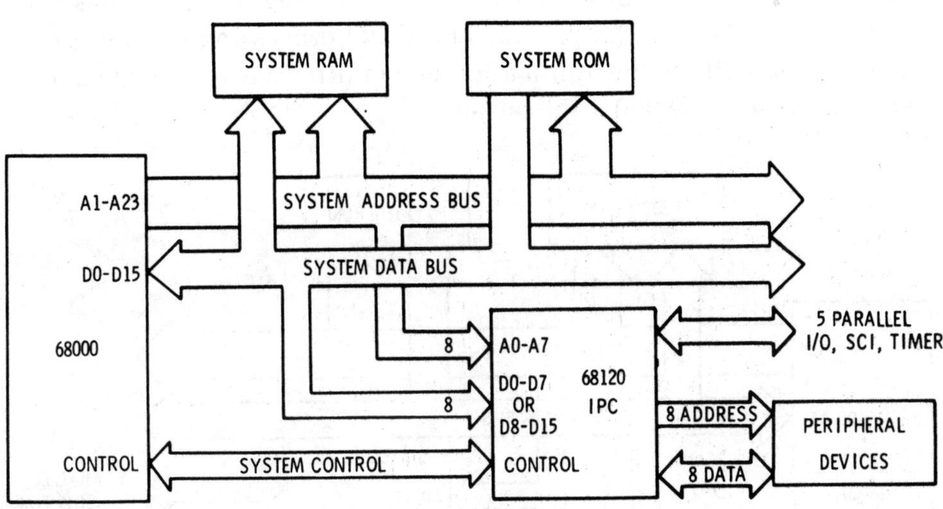

Figure 10-19
In its expanded non-multiplexed mode, the 68120 IPC provides up to five parallel I/O lines, an SCI, and a timer. In addition, eight local address and data lines provide a 256 byte local address space.

The expanded multiplexed mode of the 68120 extends the local address space to 64K bytes. Consequently, local RAM, ROM, and additional peripheral devices can be easily interfaced to the 68120 as illustrated in Figure 10-20. Notice that the 68120 still provides up to five parallel I/O lines, the serial communications interface, and 16-bit timer in this expanded mode. As you are aware from your 6801 knowledge, the local bus expansion is made possible by multiplexing the local address and data bus lines.

The various operating modes of the 68120 IPC allow the local system to be expanded according to the peripheral control task. By interfacing one or more IPCs to the 68000, you are actually creating a **multiprocessor system**. The 68000 provides system data processing and overall system control. The 68120 IPC(s) provides local I/O processing and peripheral control. You will see the application of a multiprocessor system shortly when we discuss 68000 applications.

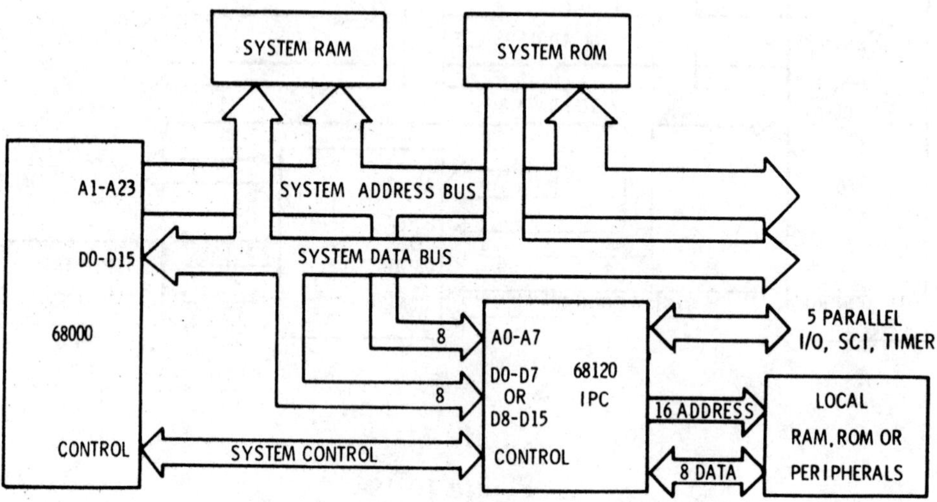

Figure 10-20
In its expanded multiplexed mode, the 68120 IPC provides up to five parallel I/O lines, an SCI, and a timer. In addition, 16 local addresses and eight local data lines provide a 64K byte local address space.

68000 Support

For any microprocessor to be successful in the marketplace it must have both hardware and software support. Hardware support ranges from single-chip peripheral devices to board level modules that perform a given I/O task. Software support must include software monitors, editors, assemblers, and cross assemblers.

To develop a microprocessor system for an industrial application, you will most likely require the use of a board level design module or a microcomputer development system. A **board level design module** is a minimum system that provides engineering evaluation and prototyping. The entire system is contained on one or two printed circuit boards. Aside from the applicable microprocessor, the system usually contains a mimimum amount of RAM, a monitor program in ROM, and various I/O features. A functional block diagram of a 68000 board level design module is provided in Figure 10-21. This particular system is the MEX68KDM 68000 design module, manufactured by Motorola. Notice that the I/O features include two RS232C serial I/O ports, two 16-bit parallel I/O ports provided by two 6821 PIAs, and a 6840 PTM. In addition, a wire wrap area and extra RAM/ROM socket area are provided on the same PC board.

You can communicate with the system in Figure 10-21 by simply connecting a CRT data terminal to the RS232C terminal port. System I/O and control are then provided by the monitor program in ROM. The monitor allows you to enter **object code** programs into RAM and execute them. Simple editing features such as breakpoints, register examine/modify, and trace are provided by the monitor ROM. You can also connect the 68000 board level system to another computer system called a **host computer system**. This connection is made via the bus edge connector or the RS232C host computer connector on the MEX68KDM board. Connecting the system to a host computer permits you to develop software using the higher level language capabilities of the host computer.

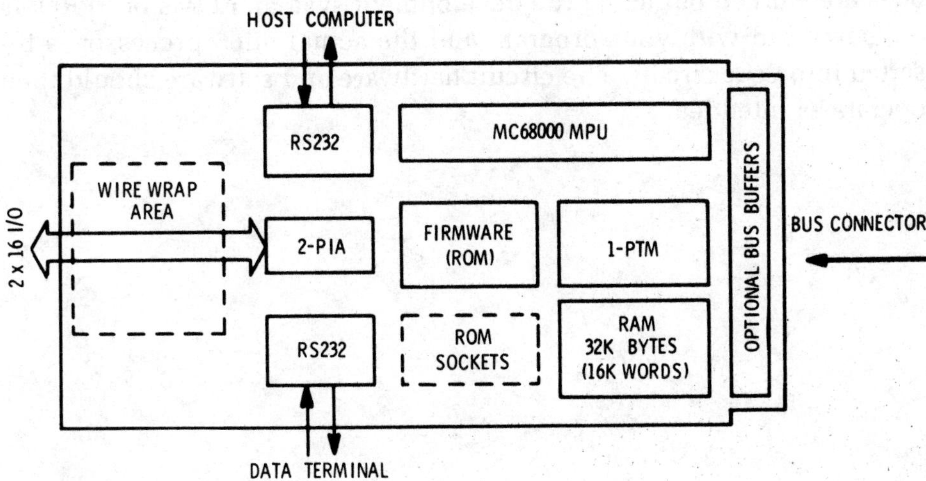

Figure 10-21
A 68000 board level design module, the MEX68KDM.

A **microcomputer development system** is a complete computer system that **emulates**, or **simulates**, the operation of the system being designed. Thus, computers are used to design computers. A 68000 development system called EXORmacs® is pictured in Figure 10-22. Notice that the basic system includes a 68000-based computer with a CRT data terminal, floppy disk system and printer. EXORmacs® is manufactured by Motorola for developing 68000-based systems. Most microprocessor chip manufacturers market similar development systems for their microprocessors. In addition, several other manufacturers market **universal development systems** that can be used to develop a wide variety of different microprocessor-based systems.

A development system uses a very powerful software package that allows you to develop software using assembler, or source code, and even higher level languages such as BASIC, FORTRAN, or PASCAL. Several powerful editing and debugging features are included in the development system software. In addition, the development system provides an umbilical cord with a connector that allows in-circuit emulation of the processor. You simply insert the connector into the microprocessor socket of your circuit. You then develop and execute your program with the development system. The action of the processor is, therefore, simulated in your circuit by the development system. If hardware or software "bugs" arise during the program execution, you have all the debugging features of the development system at your disposal. You can easily simulate real-time activities such as interrupts and interrupt response with the development system in your circuit. Once all the hardware and software bugs are worked out using the development system, ROMs or EPROMs are burned-in with your program and the actual microprocessor is inserted into your circuit. The circuit hardware and software should then operate as intended.

Obviously, development systems like EXORmacs® are not cheap. However, over 50% of the design costs for an industrial microprocessor-based system are software related. Most industrial systems, even the simplest control systems, contain several thousands of program bytes. Since completely debugged software is very costly, a good development system will rapidly pay for itself in the industrial environment.

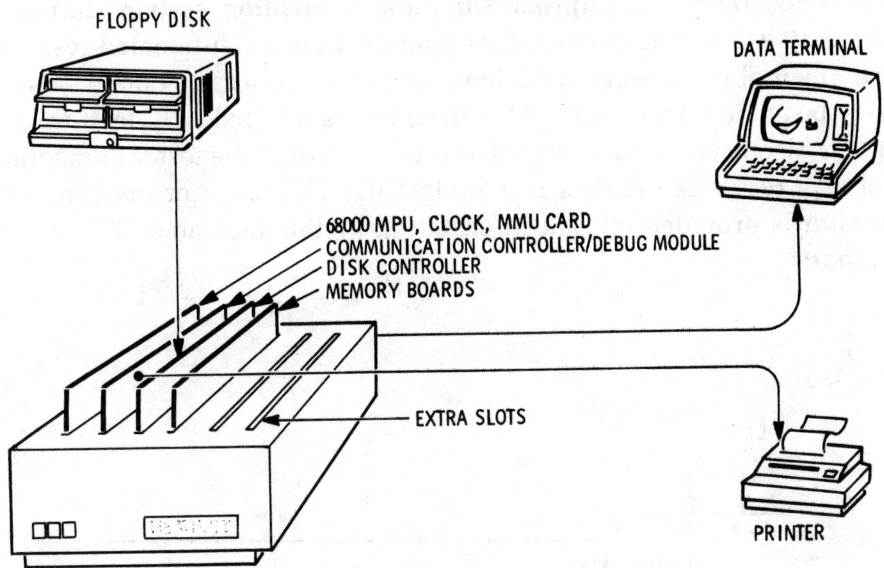

Figure 10-22
A 68000 development system called EXORmacs®.

68000 Applications

The applications of a device like the 68000 can only be limited by your imagination. A minimum 68000-based microcomputer system is shown in Figure 10-23. With your present knowledge of the 68000, you should not have any trouble understanding this circuit. This system has the basic ingredients of CPU, RAM, ROM, and parallel I/O. However, the power of the 68000 is really being wasted in a minimum system like the one shown in Figure 10-23. A more efficient use of the 68000's capabilities is demonstrated by the **multiprocessor data acquisition system** shown in Figure 10-24. In this system, data coming from an automated tester or machine tool is collected by a dedicated 6805. Since the data will most likely be analog data, a 6805R2 is used for its internal ADC feature. The 6805 is also used to provide closed loop control of the tester or machine tool as a result of the data it is collecting. The tester or machine tool operator is provided current information by the dedicated 6805 microcomputer.

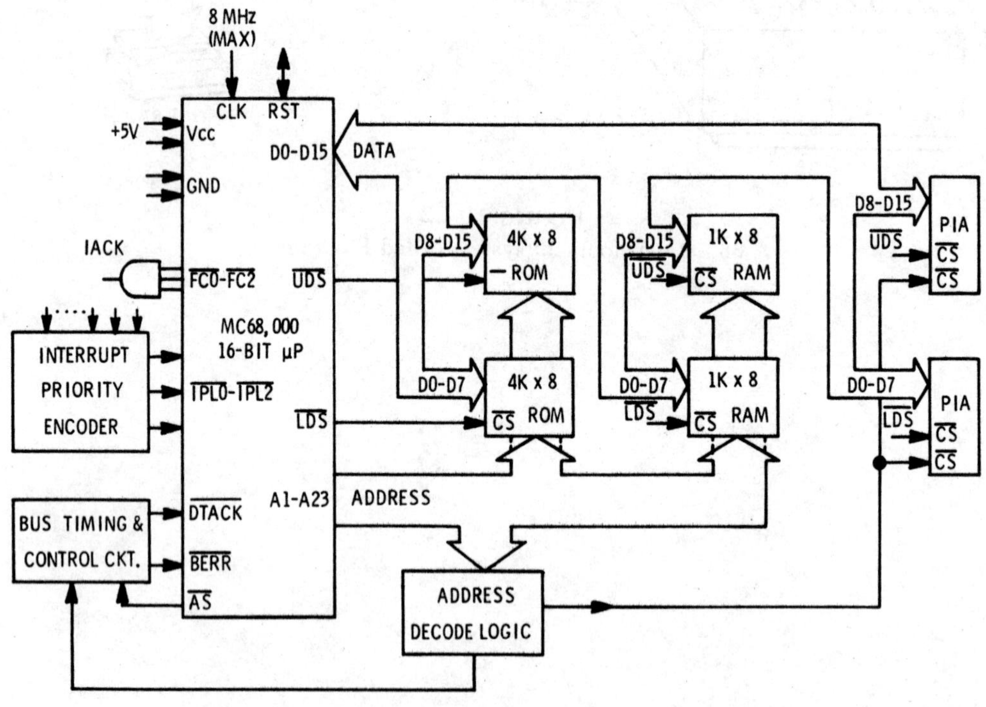

Figure 10-23
A minimum 68000 system.

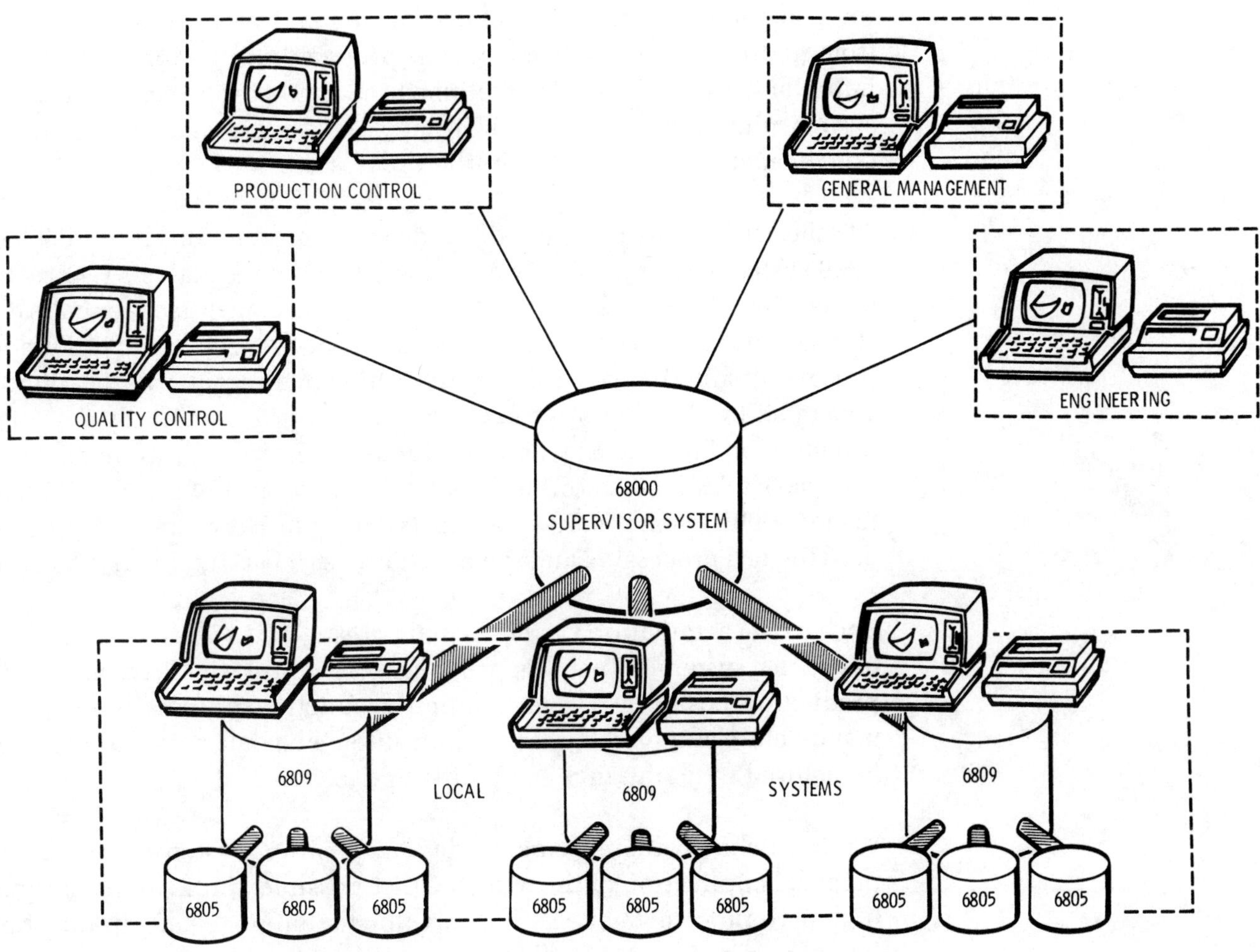

Figure 10-24
A multiprocessor industrial data acquisition system.

Periodically, the 6805 sends its data via its parallel I/O lines to a **local** 6809 based system. A local 6809 system might be available on a given production process line, collecting data from several 6805-based testers and machine tools. The local 6809 systems are used to analyze all the data from the given production process. The data analysis is used by engineering personnel to make product disposition and keep the entire process from getting out of control. Current process information is extremely important, especially in high volume production processes. A local 6809 system might include a terminal, floppy disk system, and printer to allow on-site engineering analysis of the process data.

At scheduled intervals, say at the end of each production shift, each local 6809 system will transmit its process data and data analysis reports to a larger 68000-based system. The 68000-based system is used for mass data storage and to provide a more detailed analysis of each production process. Production control, quality, and management reports might be generated by the 68000 for each production process and overall plant production. Engineering and production control departments might each have a CRT data terminal, floppy disk system, and printer all linked to the 68000 system to gain access to its data base. Here, the 68000 is being used for data processing and system control as it was intended to be used.

Such a data acquisition system is not a dream. Many industrial facilities use such a system to increase productivity, improve quality, and reduce production costs. In a high volume production process, such as the manufacture of integrated circuits, an automated data acquisition system is required to maintain a competitive edge.

We have shown the automated data acquisition system as a real and practical application of the 68000. Other possible applications of such a high performance device include artificial intelligence, computer simulation, message coding and decoding, personal and business computers, computer aided design, and games. Games? Yes, video games are becoming more and more sophisticated. The high resolution graphics needed to attract your quarters require large amounts of memory and efficient data processing. High performance 16-bit devices, like the 68000, are sure to provide some exciting games in the future. As you can see, additional applications are only limited by your imagination. Again, you are indeed in the midst of a revolution.

Now, after taking the Self-Test Review, complete the Unit Examination and check the Examination Answers. Then take the Final Exam and return it to us.

Self-Test Review

13. State the difference between the 68120 IPC and 68121 IPC.

14. What are the three operating mode configurations of the 68120 IPC?

15. Why are the 68120 and 68121 IPCs called intelligent peripheral controllers?

16. How is the 68120 connected to the 68000?

17. What is a board level design module?

18. What is a microcomputer development system?

19. What is the major difference between the EXORmacs® development system and a universal development system?

20. What is the function of the 6805R2 in the data acquisition system shown in Figure 10-24?

21. What is the function of the 6809 in the data acquisition system shown in Figure 10-24? ______

22. What is the function of the 68000 in the data acquisition system shown in Figure 10-24? ______

23. Provide at least three possible applications of a high performance 16-bit device like the 68000. ______

Answers

13. The 68120 IPC contains 2K bytes of internal mask-programmed ROM and the 68121 does not.

14. The three operating mode configurations of the 68120 IPC are: **single-chip, expanded non-multiplexed,** and **expanded multiplexed.**

15. The 68120 and 68121 IPCs are called intelligent since they are actually 8-bit microcomputers that are programmed for peripheral I/O. They are called peripheral controllers since they act as a buffer between the 68000 and its peripherals.

16. The 68120 is connected to the 68000 via eight data lines and eight address lines. In addition, the required synchronous or asynchronous bus control lines are part of the interface.

17. A board level design module is a minimum system that provides engineering evaluation and prototyping.

18. A microcomputer development system is a complete computer system that emulates, or simulates, the operation of the system being designed.

19. The EXORmacs® development system was designed to support 68000 development exclusively. Universal development systems are designed to support development of a variety of different microprocessor-based systems.

20. The function of the 6805R2 in Figure 10-24 is to collect and analyze data from an automated tester or machine tool, and possibly provide closed loop control based on the collected data. Periodically, the 6805 sends its data to a local 6809 system.

21. The function of the 6809 in Figure 10-24 is to collect and analyze production process data from the dedicated 6805-based testers and machine tools. The data analysis is used by engineering personnel to make product disposition and to keep the entire process from getting out of control.

22. The function of the 68000 in Figure 10-24 is to periodically collect product line data from the local 6809 systems. The 68000-based system is used for mass data storage and more detailed analysis of each production process. Reports are generated for the individual processes and overall plant production by the 68000 system.

23. Possible applications for a high performance 16-bit device like the 68000 include artificial intelligence, computer simulation, message coding and decoding, personal and business computers, and games. These are only a few; the possible applications of a device like the 68000 are only limited by your imagination.

Appendix A

DATA SHEETS

CONTENTS

All data sheets are reprinted courtesy of Motorola, Inc.

MC6821
(1.0 MHz)
MC68A21
(1.5 MHz)
MC68B21
(2.0 MHz)

MOS

(N-CHANNEL, SILICON-GATE, DEPLETION LOAD)

PERIPHERAL INTERFACE ADAPTER

PERIPHERAL INTERFACE ADAPTER (PIA)

The MC6821 Peripheral Interface Adapter provides the universal means of interfacing peripheral equipment to the MC6800 Microprocessing Unit (MPU). This device is capable of interfacing the MPU to peripherals through two 8-bit bidirectional peripheral data buses and four control lines. No external logic is required for interfacing to most peripheral devices.

The functional configuration of the PIA is programmed by the MPU during system initialization. Each of the peripheral data lines can be programmed to act as an input or output, and each of the four control/interrupt lines may be programmed for one of several control modes. This allows a high degree of flexibility in the over-all operation of the interface.

- 8-Bit Bidirectional Data Bus for Communication with the MPU
- Two Bidirectional 8-Bit Buses for Interface to Peripherals
- Two Programmable Control Registers
- Two Programmable Data Direction Registers
- Four Individually-Controlled Interrupt Input Lines; Two Usable as Peripheral Control Outputs
- Handshake Control Logic for Input and Output Peripheral Operation
- High-Impedance 3-State and Direct Transistor Drive Peripheral Lines
- Program Controlled Interrupt and Interrupt Disable Capability
- CMOS Drive Capability on Side A Peripheral Lines
- Two TTL Drive Capability on All A and B Side Buffers
- TTL-Compatible
- Static Operation

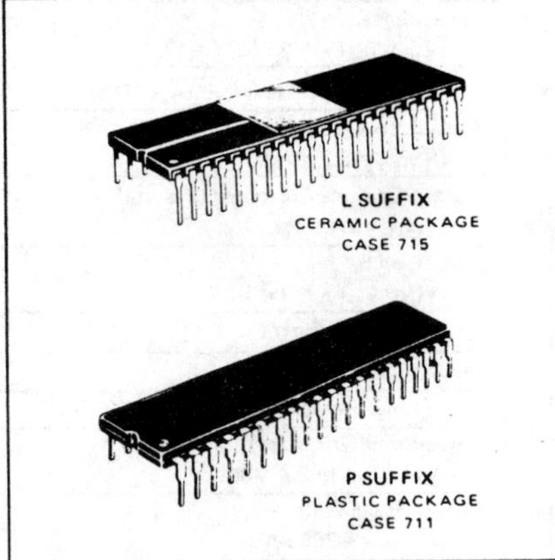

L SUFFIX
CERAMIC PACKAGE
CASE 715

P SUFFIX
PLASTIC PACKAGE
CASE 711

ORDERING INFORMATION

Speed	Device	Temperature Range
1.0 MHz	MC6821P, L	0 to +70°C
	MC6821CP, CL	-40 to +85°C
MIL-STD-883B MIL-STD-883C	MC6821BQCS MC6821CQCS	-55 to +125°C
1.5 MHz	MC68A21P, L	0 to +70°C
	MC68A21CP, CL	-40 to +85°C
2.0 MHz	MC68B21P, L	0 to +70°C

PIN ASSIGNMENT

Pin	Signal	Signal	Pin
1	V_{SS}	CA1	40
2	PA0	CA2	39
3	PA1	$\overline{IRQA}$	38
4	PA2	$\overline{IRQB}$	37
5	PA3	RS0	36
6	PA4	RS1	35
7	PA5	$\overline{Reset}$	34
8	PA6	D0	33
9	PA7	D1	32
10	PB0	D2	31
11	PB1	D3	30
12	PB2	D4	29
13	PB3	D5	28
14	PB4	D6	27
15	PB5	D7	26
16	PB6	E	25
17	PB7	CS1	24
18	CB1	$\overline{CS2}$	23
19	CB2	CS0	22
20	V_{CC}	R/$\overline{W}$	21

MC6821

MAXIMUM RATINGS

Rating	Symbol	Value	Unit
Supply Voltage	V_{CC}	−0.3 to +7.0	Vdc
Input Voltage	V_{in}	−0.3 to +7.0	Vdc
Operating Temperature Range MC6821, MC68A21, MC68B21 MC6821C, MC68A21C MC6821CQCS, MC6821BQCS	T_A	T_L to T_H 0 to 70 −40 to 85 −55 to 125	 °C °C °C
Storage Temperature Range	T_{stg}	−55 to +150	°C
Thermal Resistance	θ_{JA}	82.5	°C/W

This device contains circuitry to protect the inputs against damage due to high static voltages or electric fields; however, it is advised that normal precautions be taken to avoid application of any voltage higher than maximum rated voltages to this high impedance.

ELECTRICAL CHARACTERISTICS (V_{CC} = 5.0 V ±5%, V_{SS} = 0, T_A = T_L to T_H unless otherwise noted)

Characteristic		Symbol	Min	Typ	Max	Unit
BUS CONTROL INPUTS (R/$\overline{W}$, Enable, $\overline{Reset}$, RS0, RS1, CS0, CS1, $\overline{CS2}$)						
Input High Voltage		V_{IH}	V_{SS} + 2.0	–	V_{CC}	Vdc
Input Low Voltage		V_{IL}	V_{SS} − 0.3	–	V_{SS} + 0.8	Vdc
Input Leakage Current (V_{in} = 0 to 5.25 Vdc)		I_{in}	–	1.0	2.5	μAdc
Capacitance (V_{in} = 0, T_A = 25°C, f = 1.0 MHz)		C_{in}	–	–	7.5	pF
INTERRUPT OUTPUTS ($\overline{IRQA}$, $\overline{IRQB}$)						
Output Low Voltage (I_{Load} = 3.2 mAdc)		V_{OL}	–	–	V_{SS} + 0.4	Vdc
Output Leakage Current (Off State) (V_{OH} = 2.4 Vdc)		I_{LOH}	–	1.0	10	μAdc
Capacitance (V_{in} = 0, T_A = 25°C, f = 1.0 MHz)		C_{out}	–	–	5.0	pF
DATA BUS (D0-D7)						
Input High Voltage		V_{IH}	V_{SS} + 2.0	–	V_{CC}	Vdc
Input Low Voltage		V_{IL}	V_{SS} − 0.3	–	V_{SS} + 0.8	Vdc
Three-State (Off State) Input Current (V_{in} = 0.4 to 2.4 Vdc)		I_{TSI}	–	2.0	10	μAdc
Output High Voltage (I_{Load} = −205 μAdc)		V_{OH}	V_{SS} + 2.4	–	–	Vdc
Output Low Voltage (I_{Load} = 1.6 mAdc)		V_{OL}	–	–	V_{SS} + 0.4	Vdc
Capacitance (V_{in} = 0, T_A = 25°C, f = 1.0 MHz)		C_{in}	–	–	12.5	pF
PERIPHERAL BUS (PA0-PA7, PB0-PB7, CA1, CA2, CB1, CB2)						
Input Leakage Current (V_{in} = 0 to 5.25 Vdc)	R/$\overline{W}$, $\overline{Reset}$, RS0, RS1, CS0, CS1, $\overline{CS2}$, CA1, CB1, Enable	I_{in}	–	1.0	2.5	μAdc
Three-State (Off State) Input Current (V_{in} = 0.4 to 2.4 Vdc)	PB0-PB7, CB2	I_{TSI}	–	2.0	10	μAdc
Input High Current (V_{IH} = 2.4 Vdc)	PA0-PA7, CA2	I_{IH}	−200	−400	–	μAdc
Darlington Drive Current V_O = 1.5 Vdc	PB0-PB7,CB2	I_{OH}	−1.0	–	−10	mAdc
Input Low Current (V_{IL} = 0.4 Vdc)	PA0-PA7, CA2	I_{IL}	–	−1.3	−2.4	mAdc
Output High Voltage (I_{Load} = −200 μAdc) (I_{Load} = −10 μAdc)	 PA0-P7, PB0-PB7, CA2, CB2 PA0-PA7, CA2	V_{OH}	 V_{SS} + 2.4 V_{CC} − 1.0	 – –	 – –	Vdc
Output Low Voltage (I_{Load} = 3.2 mAdc)		V_{OL}	–	–	V_{SS} + 0.4	Vdc
Capacitance (V_{in} = 0, T_A = 25°C, f = 1.0 MHz)		C_{in}	–	–	10	pF
POWER REQUIREMENTS						
Power Dissipation		P_D	–	–	550	mW

MC6821

BUS TIMING CHARACTERISTICS (V_{CC} = 5.0 V ±5%, V_{SS} = 0, T_A = T_L to T_H unless otherwise specified.)

Characteristic	Symbol	MC6821		MC68A21		MC68B21		Unit	Ref. Fig. No.
		Min	Max	Min	Max	Min	Max		
Enable Cycle Time	t_{cycE}	1000	–	666	–	500	–	ns	1
Enable Pulse Width, High	PW_{EH}	450	–	280	–	220	–	ns	1
Enable Pulse Width, Low	PW_{EL}	430	–	280	–	210	–	ns	1
Enable Pulse Rise and Fall Times	t_{Er}, t_{Ef}	–	25	–	25	–	25	ns	1
Setup Time, Address and R/W valid to Enable positive transition	t_{AS}	160	–	140	–	70	–	ns	2, 3
Address Hold Time	t_{AH}	10	–	10	–	10	–	ns	2, 3
Data Delay Time, Read	t_{DDR}	–	320	–	220	–	180	ns	2, 4
Data Hold Time, Read	t_{DHR}	10	–	10	–	10	–	ns	2, 4
Data Setup Time, Write	t_{DSW}	195	–	80	–	60	–	ns	3, 4
Data Hold Time, Write	t_{DHW}	10	–	10	–	10	–	ns	3, 4

FIGURE 1 – ENABLE SIGNAL CHARACTERISTICS

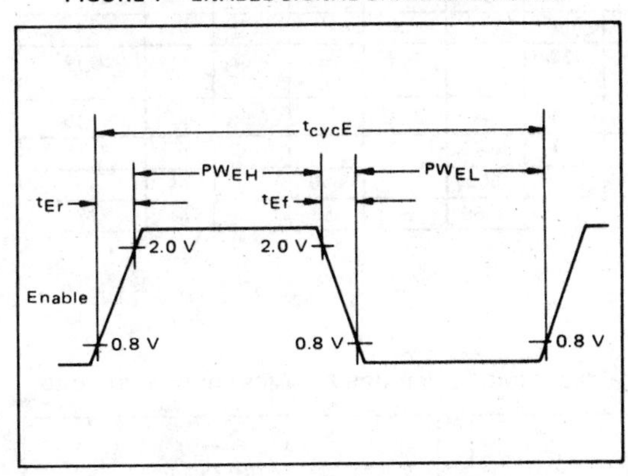

FIGURE 2 – BUS READ TIMING CHARACTERISTICS (Read Information from PIA)

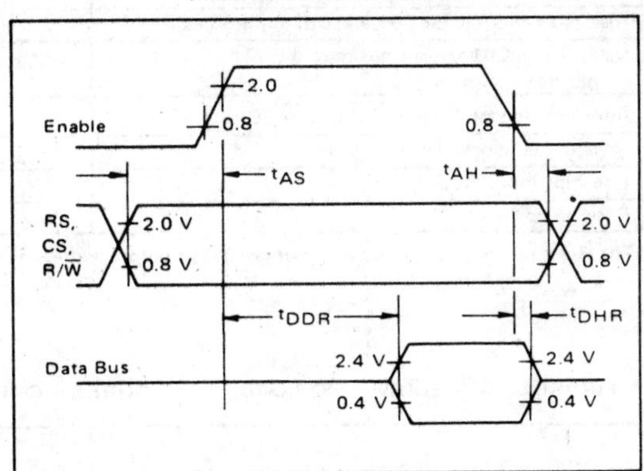

FIGURE 3 – BUS WRITE TIMING CHARACTERISTICS (Write Information into PIA)

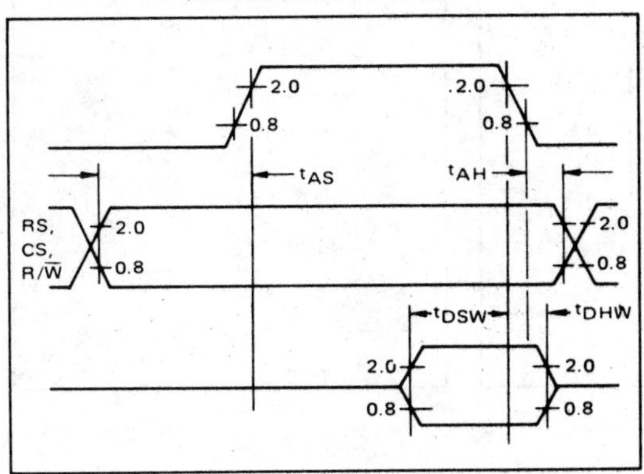

FIGURE 4 – BUS TIMING TEST LOADS

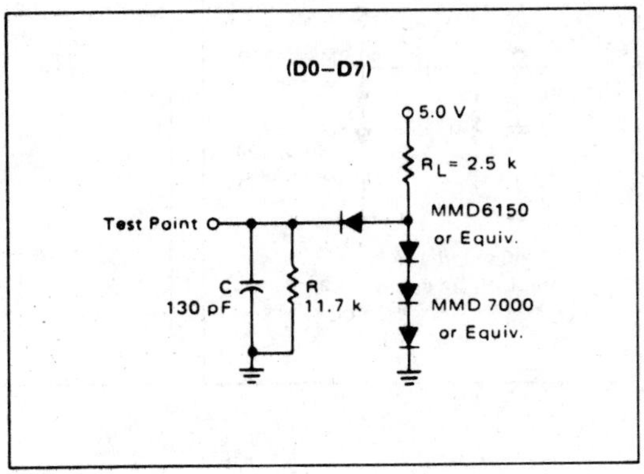

MC6821

PERIPHERAL TIMING CHARACTERISTICS (V_{CC} = 5.0 V ±5%, V_{SS} = 0 V, T_A = T_L to T_H unless otherwise specified.)

Characteristic	Symbol	MC6821 Min	MC6821 Max	MC68A21 Min	MC68A21 Max	MC68B21 Min	MC68B21 Max	Unit	Reference Fig. No.
Peripheral Data Setup Time	t_{PDSU}	200	–	135	–	100	–	ns	8
Peripheral Data Hold Time	t_{PDH}	0	–	0	–	0	–	ns	8
Delay Time, Enable negative transition to CA2 negative transition	t_{CA2}	–	1.0	–	0.670	–	0.500	μs	5, 9, 10
Delay Time, Enable negative transition to CA2 positive transition	t_{RS1}	–	1.0	–	0.670	–	0.500	μs	5, 9
Rise and Fall Times for CA1 and CA2 input signals	t_r, t_f	–	1.0	–	1.0	–	1.0	μs	5, 10
Delay Time from CA1 active transition to CA2 positive transition	t_{RS2}	–	2.0	–	1.35	–	1.0	μs	5, 10
Delay Time, Enable negative transition to Peripheral Data Valid	t_{PDW}	–	1.0	–	0.670	–	0.5	μs	5, 11, 12
Delay Time, Enable negative transition to Peripheral CMOS Data Valid PA0-PA7, CA2	t_{CMOS}	–	2.0	–	1.35	–	1.0	μs	6, 11
Delay Time, Enable positive transition to CB2 negative transition	t_{CB2}	–	1.0	–	0.670	–	0.5	μs	5, 13, 14
Delay Time, Peripheral Data Valid to CB2 negative transition	t_{DC}	20	–	20	–	20	–	ns	5, 12
Delay Time, Enable positive transition to CB2 positive transition	t_{RS1}	–	1.0	–	0.670	–	0.5	μs	5, 13
Peripheral Control Output Pulse Width, CA2/CB2	PW_{CT}	550	–	550	–	500	–	ns	5, 13
Rise and Fall Time for CB1 and CB2 input signals	t_r, t_f	–	1.0	–	1.0	–	1.0	μs	14
Delay Time, CB1 active transition to CB2 positive transition	t_{RS2}	–	2.0	–	1.35	–	1.0	μs	5, 14
Interrupt Release Time, $\overline{IRQA}$ and $\overline{IRQB}$	t_{IR}	–	1.60	–	1.10	–	0.85	μs	7, 16
Interrupt Response Time	t_{RS3}	–	1.0	–	1.0	–	1.0	μs	7, 15
Interrupt Input Pulse Width	PW_I	500	–	500	–	500	–	ns	15
Reset Low Time*	t_{RL}	1.0	–	0.66	–	0.5	–	μs	17

*The Reset line must be high a minimum of 1.0 μs before addressing the PIA.

FIGURE 5 – TTL EQUIV. TEST LOAD

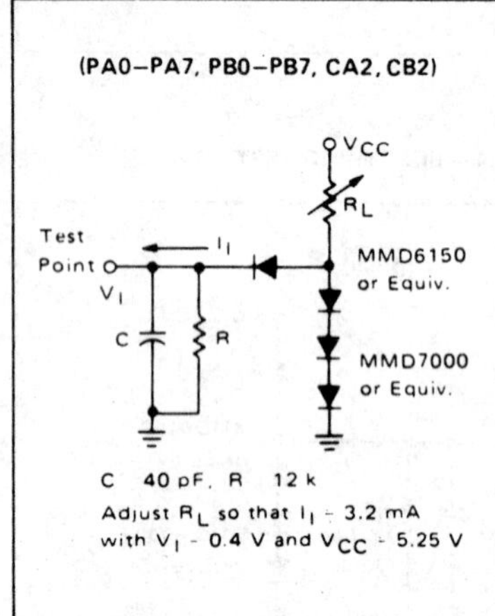

FIGURE 6 – CMOS EQUIV. TEST LOAD

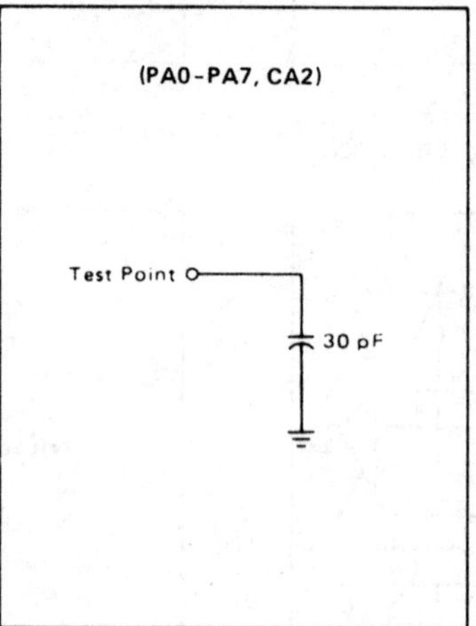

FIGURE 7 – NMOS EQUIV. TEST LOAD

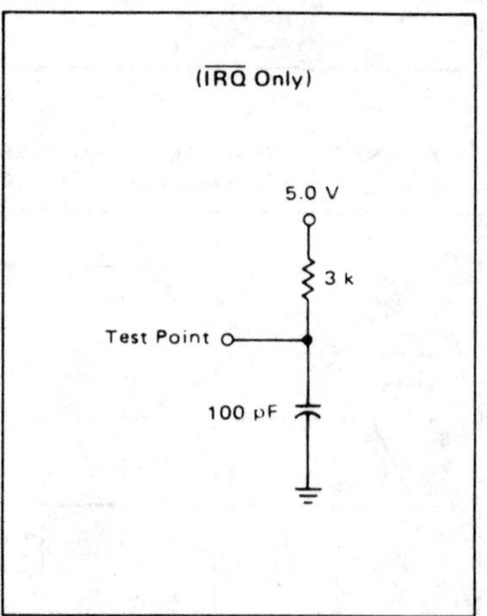

MC6821

FIGURE 8 – PERIPHERAL DATA SETUP AND HOLD TIMES
(Read Mode)

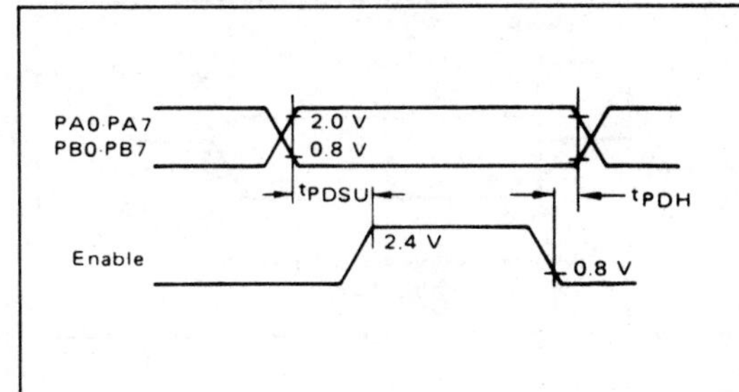

FIGURE 9 – CA2 DELAY TIME
(Read Mode; CRA-5 = CRA-3 = 1, CRA-4 = 0)

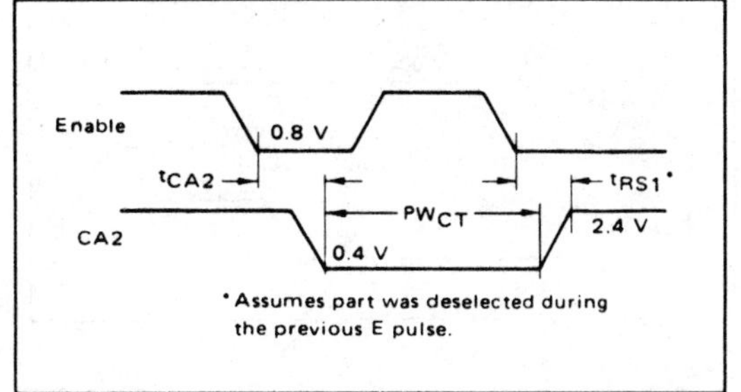

FIGURE 10 – CA2 DELAY TIME
(Read Mode; CRA-5 = 1, CRA-3 = CRA-4 = 0)

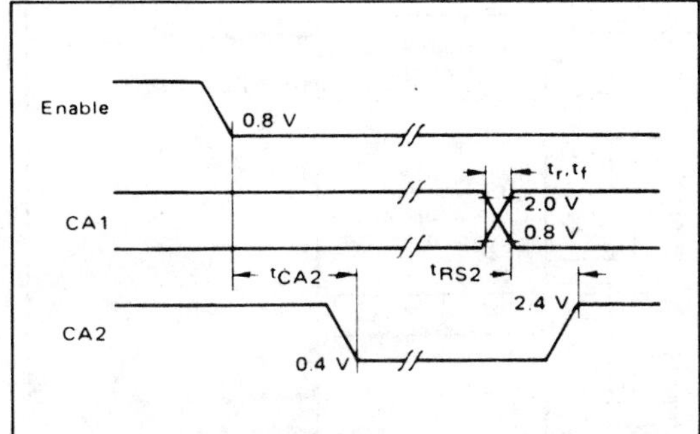

FIGURE 11 – PERIPHERAL CMOS DATA DELAY TIMES
(Write Mode; CRA-5 = CRA-3 = 1, CRA-4 = 0)

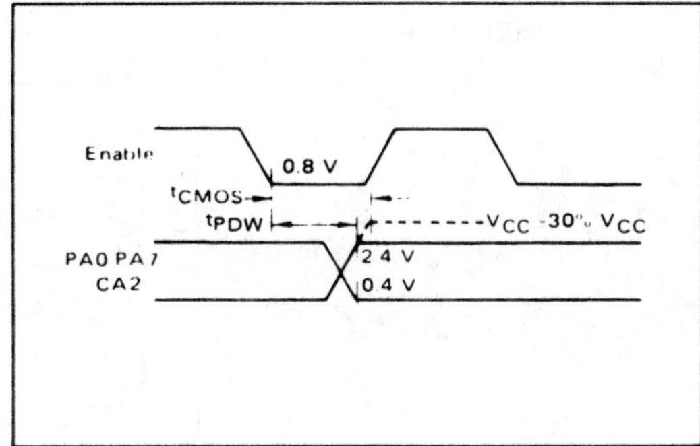

FIGURE 12 – PERIPHERAL DATA AND CB2 DELAY TIMES
(Write Mode; CRB-5 = CRB-3 = 1, CRB-4 = 0)

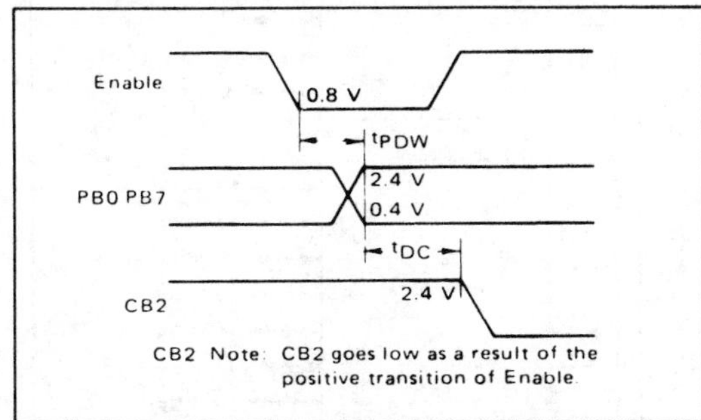

FIGURE 13 – CB2 DELAY TIME
(Write Mode; CRB-5 = CRB-3 = 1, CRB-4 = 0)

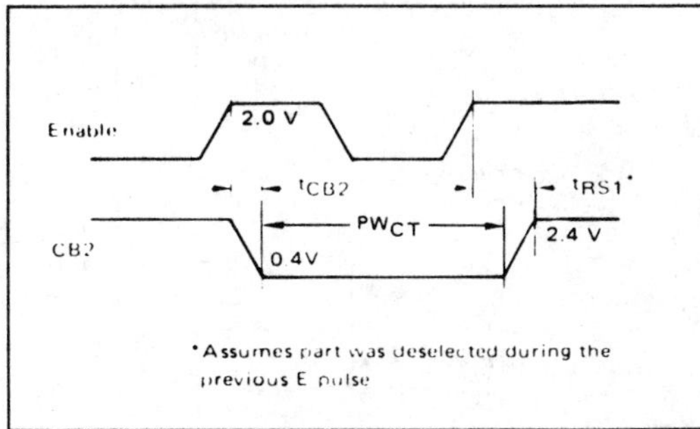

FIGURE 14 – CB2 DELAY TIME
(Write Mode; CRB-5 = 1, CRB-3 = CRB-4 = 0)

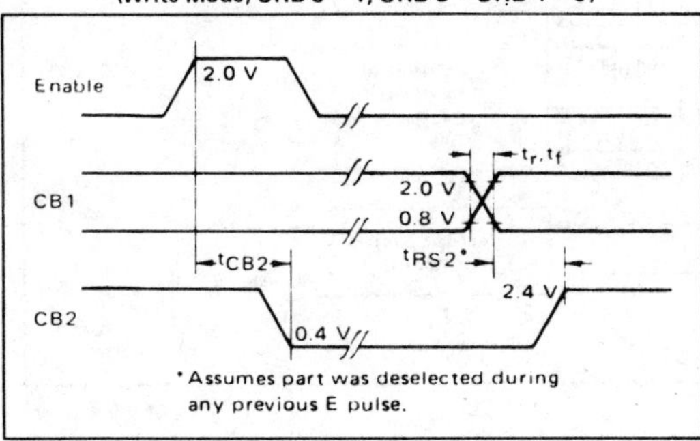

FIGURE 15 – INTERRUPT PULSE WIDTH AND $\overline{IRQ}$ RESPONSE

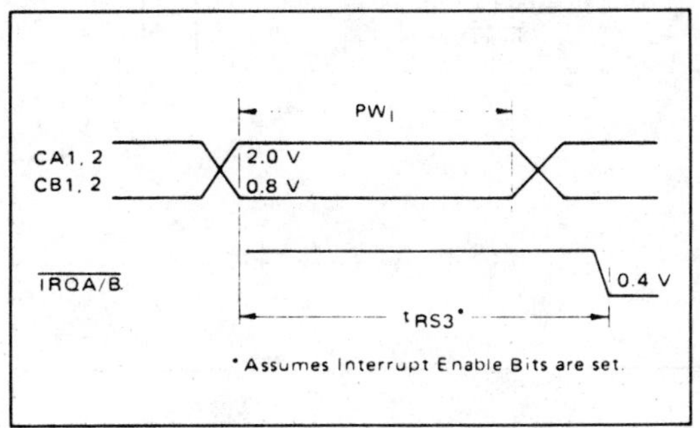

MC6821

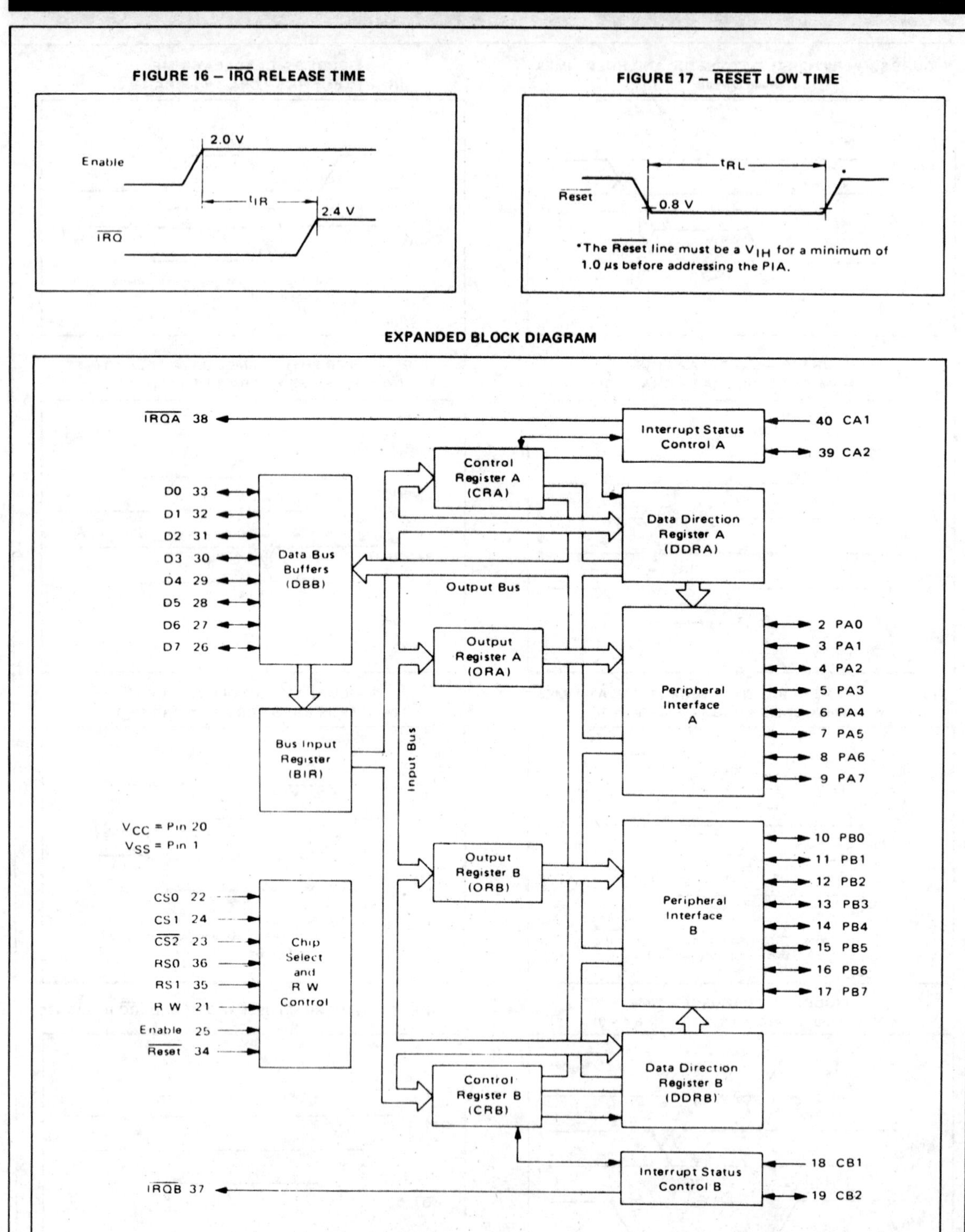
FIGURE 16 – $\overline{IRQ}$ RELEASE TIME
Enable
2.0 V
t_{IR}
2.4 V
$\overline{IRQ}$
FIGURE 17 – $\overline{RESET}$ LOW TIME
t_{RL}
$\overline{Reset}$
0.8 V
*The $\overline{Reset}$ line must be a V_{IH} for a minimum of 1.0 μs before addressing the PIA.
EXPANDED BLOCK DIAGRAM
$\overline{IRQA}$ 38
Interrupt Status Control A
40 CA1
39 CA2
Control Register A (CRA)
D0 33
D1 32
D2 31
D3 30
D4 29
D5 28
D6 27
D7 26
Data Bus Buffers (DBB)
Data Direction Register A (DDRA)
Output Bus
Output Register A (ORA)
Peripheral Interface A
2 PA0
3 PA1
4 PA2
5 PA3
6 PA4
7 PA5
8 PA6
9 PA7
Bus Input Register (BIR)
Input Bus
V_{CC} = Pin 20
V_{SS} = Pin 1
Output Register B (ORB)
Peripheral Interface B
10 PB0
11 PB1
12 PB2
13 PB3
14 PB4
15 PB5
16 PB6
17 PB7
CS0 22
CS1 24
$\overline{CS2}$ 23
RS0 36
RS1 35
R W 21
Enable 25
$\overline{Reset}$ 34
Chip Select and R W Control
Data Direction Register B (DDRB)
Control Register B (CRB)
Interrupt Status Control B
18 CB1
19 CB2
$\overline{IRQB}$ 37

MC6821

PIA INTERFACE SIGNALS FOR MPU

The PIA interfaces to the MC6800 MPU with an eight-bit bi-directional data bus, three chip select lines, two register select lines, two interrupt request lines, read/write line, enable line and reset line. These signals, in conjunction with the MC6800 VMA output, permit the MPU to have complete control over the PIA. VMA should be utilized in conjunction with an MPU address line into a chip select of the PIA.

PIA Bi-Directional Data (D0-D7) – The bi-directional data lines (D0-D7) allow the transfer of data between the MPU and the PIA. The data bus output drivers are three-state devices that remain in the high-impedance (off) state except when the MPU performs a PIA read operation. The Read/Write line is in the Read (high) state when the PIA is selected for a Read operation.

PIA Enable (E) – The enable pulse, E, is the only timing signal that is supplied to the PIA. Timing of all other signals is referenced to the leading and trailing edges of the E pulse. This signal will normally be a derivative of the MC6800 $\phi2$ Clock.

PIA Read/Write (R/W) – This signal is generated by the MPU to control the direction of data transfers on the Data Bus. A low state on the PIA Read/Write line enables the input buffers and data is transferred from the MPU to the PIA on the E signal if the device has been selected. A high on the Read/Write line sets up the PIA for a transfer of data to the bus. The PIA output buffers are enabled when the proper address and the enable pulse E are present.

$\overline{\text{Reset}}$ – The active low $\overline{\text{Reset}}$ line is used to reset all register bits in the PIA to a logical zero (low). This line can be used as a power-on reset and as a master reset during system operation.

PIA Chip Select (CS0, CS1 and $\overline{\text{CS2}}$) – These three input signals are used to select the PIA. CS0 and CS1 must be high and $\overline{\text{CS2}}$ must be low for selection of the device. Data transfers are then performed under the control of the Enable and Read/Write signals. The chip select lines must be stable for the duration of the E pulse. The device is deselected when any of the chip selects are in the inactive state.

PIA Register Select (RS0 and RS1) – The two register select lines are used to select the various registers inside the PIA. These two lines are used in conjunction with internal Control Registers to select a particular register that is to be written or read.

The register and chip select lines should be stable for the duration of the E pulse while in the read or write cycle.

$\overline{\text{Interrupt Request}}$ ($\overline{\text{IRQA}}$ and $\overline{\text{IRQB}}$) – The active low $\overline{\text{Interrupt Request}}$ lines ($\overline{\text{IRQA}}$ and $\overline{\text{IRQB}}$) act to interrupt the MPU either directly or through interrupt priority circuitry. These lines are "open drain" (no load device on the chip). This permits all interrupt request lines to be tied together in a wire-OR configuration.

Each $\overline{\text{Interrupt Request}}$ line has two internal interrupt flag bits that can cause the $\overline{\text{Interrupt Request}}$ line to go low. Each flag bit is associated with a particular peripheral interrupt line. Also four interrupt enable bits are provided in the PIA which may be used to inhibit a particular interrupt from a peripheral device.

Servicing an interrupt by the MPU may be accomplished by a software routine that, on a prioritized basis, sequentially reads and tests the two control registers in each PIA for interrupt flag bits that are set.

The interrupt flags are cleared (zeroed) as a result of an MPU Read Peripheral Data Operation of the corresponding data register. After being cleared, the interrupt flag bit cannot be enabled to be set until the PIA is deselected during an E pulse. The E pulse is used to condition the interrupt control lines (CA1, CA2, CB1, CB2). When these lines are used as interrupt inputs at least one E pulse must occur from the inactive edge to the active edge of the interrupt input signal to condition the edge sense network. If the interrupt flag has been enabled and the edge sense circuit has been properly conditioned, the interrupt flag will be set on the next active transition of the interrupt input pin.

PIA PERIPHERAL INTERFACE LINES

The PIA provides two 8-bit bi-directional data buses and four interrupt/control lines for interfacing to peripheral devices.

Section A Peripheral Data (PA0-PA7) – Each of the peripheral data lines can be programmed to act as an input or output. This is accomplished by setting a "1" in the corresponding Data Direction Register bit for those lines which are to be outputs. A "0" in a bit of the Data Direction Register causes the corresponding peripheral data line to act as an input. During an MPU Read Peripheral Data Operation, the data on peripheral lines programmed to act as inputs appears directly on the corresponding MPU Data Bus lines. In the input mode the internal pullup resistor on these lines represents a maximum of 1.5 standard TTL loads.

The data in Output Register A will appear on the data lines that are programmed to be outputs. A logical "1" written into the register will cause a "high" on the corresponding data line while a "0" results in a "low". Data in Output Register A may be read by an MPU "Read Peripheral Data A" operation when the corresponding lines are programmed as outputs. This data will be read properly if the voltage on the peripheral data lines is greater than 2.0 volts for a logic "1" output and less than 0.8 volt for a logic "0" output. Loading the output lines such that the voltage on these lines does not reach full voltage causes the data transferred into the MPU on a Read operation to differ from that contained in the respective bit of Output Register A.

Section B Peripheral Data (PB0-PB7) – The peripheral data lines in the B Section of the PIA can be programmed to act as either inputs or outputs in a similar manner to PA0-PA7. However, the output buffers driving these lines differ from those driving lines PA0-PA7. They have three-state capability, allowing them to enter a high impedance state when the peripheral data line is used as an input. In addition, data on the peripheral data lines PB0-PB7 will be read properly from those lines programmed as outputs even if the voltages are below 2.0 volts for a "high". As outputs, these lines are compatible with standard TTL and may also be used as a source of up to 1 milliampere at 1.5 volts to directly drive the base of a transistor switch.

Interrupt Input (CA1 and CB1) – Peripheral Input lines CA1 and CB1 are input only lines that set the interrupt flags of the control registers. The active transition for these signals is also programmed by the two control registers.

Peripheral Control (CA2) – The peripheral control line CA2 can be programmed to act as an interrupt input or as a peripheral control output. As an output, this line is compatible with standard TTL; as an input the internal pullup resistor on this line represents 1.5 standard TTL loads. The function of this signal line is programmed with Control Register A.

Peripheral Control (CB2) – Peripheral Control line CB2 may also be programmed to act as an interrupt input or peripheral control output. As an input, this line has high input impedance and is compatible with standard TTL. As an output it is compatible with standard TTL and may also be used as a source of up to 1 milliampere at 1.5 volts to directly drive the base of a transistor switch. This line is programmed by Control Register B.

INTERNAL CONTROLS

There are six locations within the PIA accessible to the MPU data bus: two Peripheral Registers, two Data Direction Registers, and two Control Registers. Selection of these locations is controlled by the RS0 and RS1 inputs together with bit 2 in the Control Register, as shown in Table 1.

TABLE 1 – INTERNAL ADDRESSING

RS1	RS0	Control Register Bit CRA-2	Control Register Bit CRB-2	Location Selected
0	0	1	X	Peripheral Register A
0	0	0	X	Data Direction Register A
0	1	X	X	Control Register A
1	0	X	1	Peripheral Register B
1	0	X	0	Data Direction Register B
1	1	X	X	Control Register B

X = Don't Care

INITIALIZATION

A low reset line has the effect of zeroing all PIA registers. This will set PA0-PA7, PB0-PB7, CA2 and CB2 as inputs, and all interrupts disabled. The PIA must be configured during the restart program which follows the reset.

Details of possible configurations of the Data Direction and Control Register are as follows.

DATA DIRECTION REGISTERS (DDRA and DDRB)

The two Data Direction Registers allow the MPU to control the direction of data through each corresponding peripheral data line. A Data Direction Register bit set at "0" configures the corresponding peripheral data line as an input; a "1" results in an output.

CONTROL REGISTERS (CRA and CRB)

The two Control Registers (CRA and CRB) allow the MPU to control the operation of the four peripheral control lines CA1, CA2, CB1 and CB2. In addition they allow the MPU to enable the interrupt lines and monitor the status of the interrupt flags. Bits 0 through 5 of the two registers may be written or read by the MPU when the proper chip select and register select signals are applied. Bits 6 and 7 of the two registers are read only and are modified by external interrupts occurring on control lines CA1, CA2, CB1 or CB2. The format of the control words is shown in Table 2.

TABLE 2 – CONTROL WORD FORMAT

	7	6	5	4	3	2	1	0
CRA	IRQA1	IRQA2	CA2 Control			DDRA Access	CA1 Control	

	7	6	5	4	3	2	1	0
CRB	IRQB1	IRQB2	CB2 Control			DDRB Access	CB1 Control	

Data Direction Access Control Bit (CRA-2 and CRB-2) – Bit 2 in each Control register (CRA and CRB) allows selection of either a Peripheral Interface Register or the Data Direction Register when the proper register select signals are applied to RS0 and RS1.

Interrupt Flags (CRA-6, CRA-7, CRB-6, and CRB-7) – The four interrupt flag bits are set by active transitions of signals on the four Interrupt and Peripheral Control lines when those lines are programmed to be inputs. These bits cannot be set directly from the MPU Data Bus and are reset indirectly by a Read Peripheral Data Operation on the appropriate section.

TABLE 3 – CONTROL OF INTERRUPT INPUTS CA1 AND CB1

CRA-1 (CRB-1)	CRA-0 (CRB-0)	Interrupt Input CA1 (CB1)	Interrupt Flag CRA-7 (CRB-7)	MPU Interrupt Request $\overline{IRQA}$ ($\overline{IRQB}$)
0	0	↓ Active	Set high on ↓ of CA1 (CB1)	Disabled — $\overline{IRQ}$ remains high
0	1	↓ Active	Set high on ↓ of CA1 (CB1)	Goes low when the interrupt flag bit CRA-7 (CRB-7) goes high
1	0	↑ Active	Set high on ↑ of CA1 (CB1)	Disabled — $\overline{IRQ}$ remains high
1	1	↑ Active	Set high on ↑ of CA1 (CB1)	Goes low when the interrupt flag bit CRA-7 (CRB-7) goes high

Notes:
1. ↑ indicates positive transition (low to high)
2. ↓ indicates negative transition (high to low)
3. The Interrupt flag bit CRA-7 is cleared by an MPU Read of the A Data Register, and CRB-7 is cleared by an MPU Read of the B Data Register.
4. If CRA-0 (CRB-0) is low when an interrupt occurs (Interrupt disabled) and is later brought high, $\overline{IRQA}$ ($\overline{IRQB}$) occurs after CRA-0 (CRB-0) is written to a "one"

MC6821

Control of CA1 and CB1 Interrupt Input Lines (CRA-0, CRB-0, CRA-1, and CRB-1) – The two lowest order bits of the control registers are used to control the interrupt input lines CA1 and CB1. Bits CRA-0 and CRB-0 are used to enable the MPU interrupt signals $\overline{IRQA}$ and $\overline{IRQB}$, respectively. Bits CRA-1 and CRB-1 determine the active transition of the interrupt input signals CA1 and CB1 (Table 3).

TABLE 4 – CONTROL OF CA2 AND CB2 AS INTERRUPT INPUTS
CRA5 (CRB5) is low

CRA-5 (CRB-5)	CRA-4 (CRB-4)	CRA-3 (CRB-3)	Interrupt Input CA2 (CB2)	Interrupt Flag CRA-6 (CRB-6)	MPU Interrupt Request $\overline{IRQA}$ ($\overline{IRQB}$)
0	0	0	↓ Active	Set high on ↓ of CA2 (CB2)	Disabled — $\overline{IRQ}$ remains high
0	0	1	↓ Active	Set high on ↓ of CA2 (CB2)	Goes low when the interrupt flag bit CRA-6 (CRB-6) goes high
0	1	0	↑ Active	Set high on ↑ of CA2 (CB2)	Disabled — $\overline{IRQ}$ remains high
0	1	1	↑ Active	Set high on ↑ of CA2 (CB2)	Goes low when the interrupt flag bit CRA-6 (CRB-6) goes high

Notes:
1. ↑ indicates positive transition (low to high)
2. ↓ indicates negative transition (high to low)
3. The Interrupt flag bit CRA-6 is cleared by an MPU Read of the A Data Register and CRB-6 is cleared by an MPU Read of the B Data Register.
4. If CRA-3 (CRB-3) is low when an interrupt occurs (Interrupt disabled) and is later brought high, $\overline{IRQA}$ ($\overline{IRQB}$) occurs after CRA-3 (CRB-3) is written to a "one".

TABLE 5 – CONTROL OF CB2 AS AN OUTPUT
CRB-5 is high

CRB-5	CRB-4	CRB-3	CB2 Cleared	CB2 Set
1	0	0	Low on the positive transition of the first E pulse following an MPU Write "B" Data Register operation.	High when the interrupt flag bit CRB-7 is set by an active transition of the CB1 signal.
1	0	1	Low on the positive transition of the first E pulse after an MPU Write "B" Data Register operation.	High on the positive edge of the first "E" pulse following an "E" pulse which occurred while the part was deselected.
1	1	0	Low when CRB-3 goes low as a result of an MPU Write in Control Register "B".	Always low as long as CRB-3 is low. Will go high on an MPU Write in Control Register "B" that changes CRB-3 to "one".
1	1	1	Always high as long as CRB-3 is high. Will be cleared when an MPU Write Control Register "B" results in clearing CRB-3 to "zero".	High when CRB-3 goes high as a result of an MPU Write into Control Register "B".

MC6821

Control of CA2 and CB2 Peripheral Control Lines (CRA-3, CRA-4, CRA-5, CRB-3, CRB-4, and CRB-5) – Bits 3, 4, and 5 of the two control registers are used to control the CA2 and CB2 Peripheral Control lines. These bits determine if the control lines will be an interrupt input or an output control signal. If bit CRA-5 (CRB-5) is low, CA2 (CB2) is an interrupt input line similar to CA1 (CB1) (Table 4). When CRA-5 (CRB-5) is high, CA2 (CB2) becomes an output signal that may be used to control peripheral data transfers. When in the output mode, CA2 and CB2 have slightly different characteristics (Tables 5 and 6).

TABLE 6 – CONTROL OF CA-2 AS AN OUTPUT
CRA-5 is high

CRA-5	CRA-4	CRA-3	CA2 Cleared	CA2 Set
1	0	0	Low on negative transition of E after an MPU Read "A" Data operation.	High when the interrupt flag bit CRA-7 is set by an active transition of the CA1 signal.
1	0	1	Low on negative transition of E after an MPU Read "A" Data operation.	High on the negative edge of the first "E" pulse which occurs during a deselect.
1	1	0	Low when CRA-3 goes low as a result of an MPU Write to Control Register "A".	Always low as long as CRA-3 is low. Will go high on an MPU Write to Control Register "A" that changes CRA-3 to "one".
1	1	1	Always high as long as CRA-3 is high. Will be cleared on an MPU Write to Control Register "A" that clears CRA-3 to a "zero".	High when CRA-3 goes high as a result of an MPU Write to Control Register "A".

PACKAGE DIMENSIONS

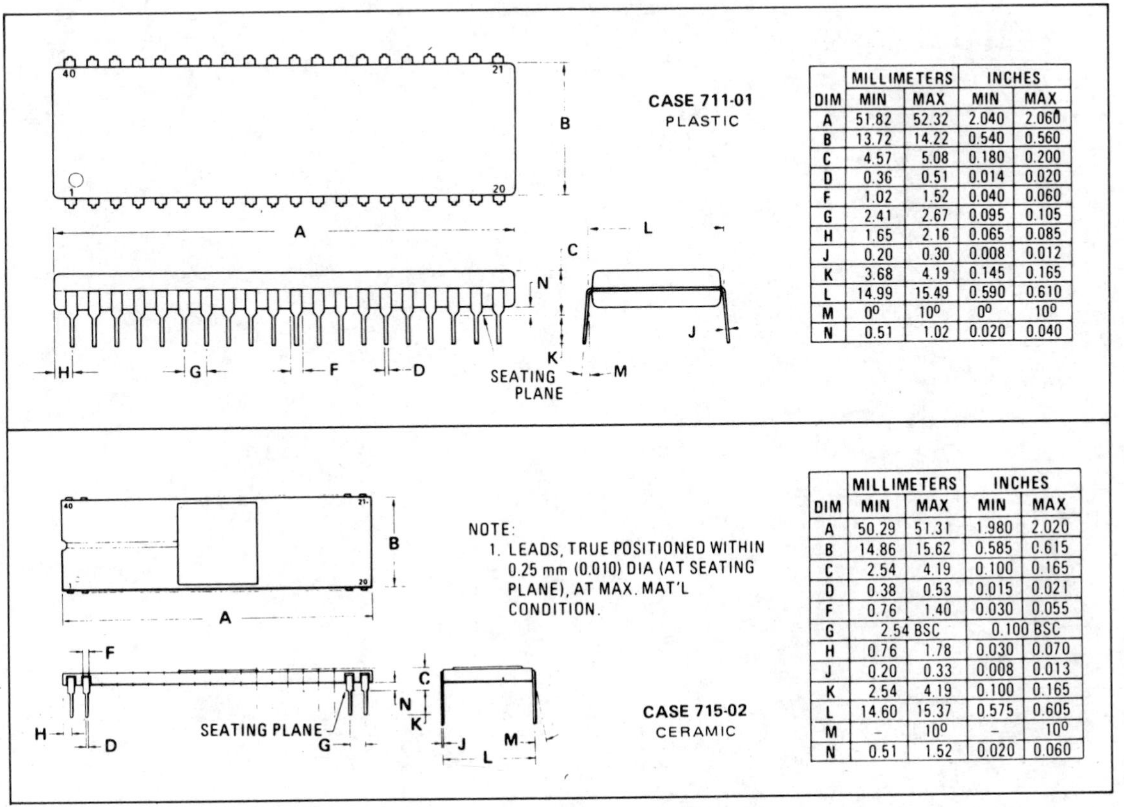

CASE 711-01 PLASTIC

DIM	MILLIMETERS MIN	MILLIMETERS MAX	INCHES MIN	INCHES MAX
A	51.82	52.32	2.040	2.060
B	13.72	14.22	0.540	0.560
C	4.57	5.08	0.180	0.200
D	0.36	0.51	0.014	0.020
F	1.02	1.52	0.040	0.060
G	2.41	2.67	0.095	0.105
H	1.65	2.16	0.065	0.085
J	0.20	0.30	0.008	0.012
K	3.68	4.19	0.145	0.165
L	14.99	15.49	0.590	0.610
M	0°	10°	0°	10°
N	0.51	1.02	0.020	0.040

CASE 715-02 CERAMIC

DIM	MILLIMETERS MIN	MILLIMETERS MAX	INCHES MIN	INCHES MAX
A	50.29	51.31	1.980	2.020
B	14.86	15.62	0.585	0.615
C	2.54	4.19	0.100	0.165
D	0.38	0.53	0.015	0.021
F	0.76	1.40	0.030	0.055
G	2.54 BSC		0.100 BSC	
H	0.76	1.78	0.030	0.070
J	0.20	0.33	0.008	0.013
K	2.54	4.19	0.100	0.165
L	14.60	15.37	0.575	0.605
M	–	10°	–	10°
N	0.51	1.52	0.020	0.060

MC1488

QUAD MDTL LINE DRIVER
RS-232C
SILICON MONOLITHIC INTEGRATED CIRCUIT

QUAD LINE DRIVER

The MC1488 is a monolithic quad line driver designed to interface data terminal equipment with data communications equipment in conformance with the specifications of EIA Standard No. RS-232C.

Features:

- Current Limited Output
  ±10 mA typ
- Power-Off Source Impedance
  300 Ohms min
- Simple Slew Rate Control with External Capacitor
- Flexible Operating Supply Range
- Compatible with All Motorola MDTL and MTTL Logic Families

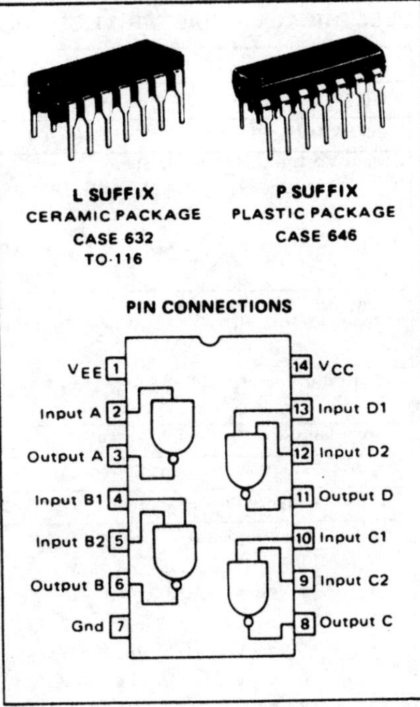

TYPICAL APPLICATION

LINE DRIVER MC1488

INTERCONNECTING CABLE

LINE RECEIVER MC1489

MDTL LOGIC INPUT — INTERCONNECTING CABLE — MDTL LOGIC OUTPUT

CIRCUIT SCHEMATIC
(1/4 OF CIRCUIT SHOWN)

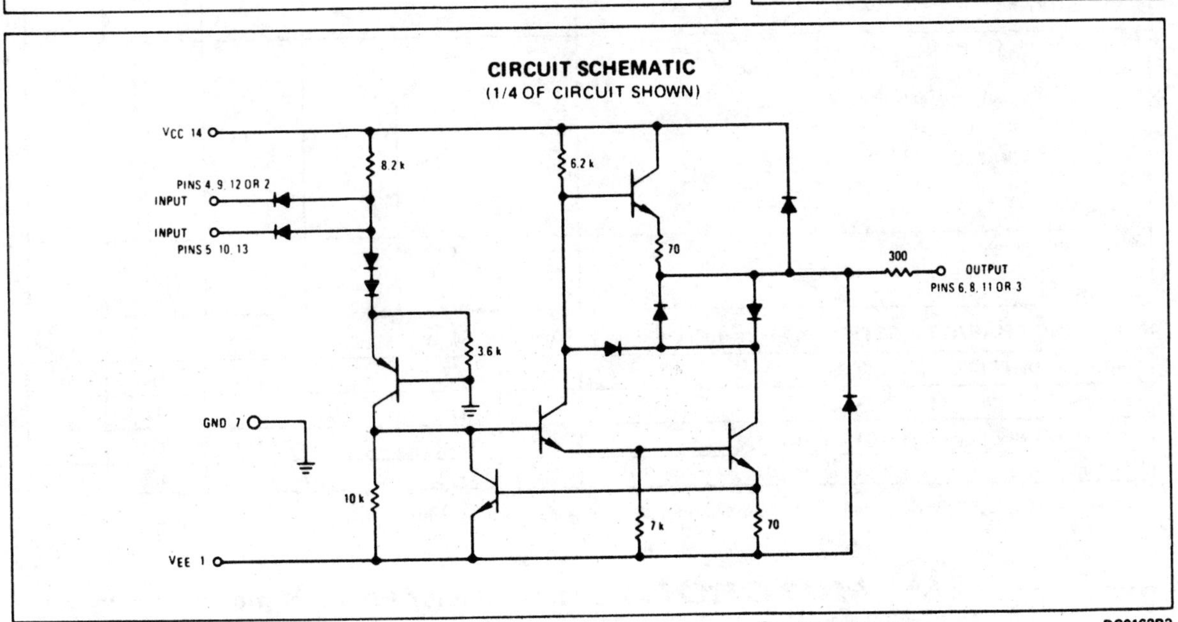

MDTL, MHTL, MRTL, MTTL are trademarks of Motorola Inc.

DS9162R2

MAXIMUM RATINGS (T_A = +25°C unless otherwise noted.)

Rating	Symbol	Value	Unit
Power Supply Voltage	V_{CC} V_{EE}	+15 -15	Vdc
Input Voltage Range	V_{IR}	$-15 \leq V_{IR} \leq 7.0$	Vdc
Output Signal Voltage	V_O	±15	Vdc
Power Derating (Package Limitation, Ceramic and Plastic Dual-In-Line Package) Derate above T_A = +25°C	P_D $1/R_{\theta JA}$	1000 6.7	mW mW/°C
Operating Ambient Temperature Range	T_A	0 to +75	°C
Storage Temperature Range	T_{stg}	-65 to +175	°C

ELECTRICAL CHARACTERISTICS (V_{CC} = +9.0 ± 1% Vdc, V_{EE} = -9.0 ± 1% Vdc, T_A = 0 to +75°C unless otherwise noted.)

Characteristic	Figure	Symbol	Min	Typ	Max	Unit
Input Current – Low Logic State (V_{IL} = 0)	1	I_{IL}		1.0	1.6	mA
Input Current – High Logic State (V_{IH} = 5.0 V)	1	I_{IH}			10	μA
Output Voltage – High Logic State (V_{IL} = 0.8 Vdc, R_L = 3.0 kΩ, V_{CC} = +9.0 Vdc, V_{EE} = -9.0 Vdc) (V_{IL} = 0.8 Vdc, R_L = 3.0 kΩ, V_{CC} = +13.2 Vdc, V_{EE} = -13.2 Vdc)	2	V_{OH}	 +6.0 +9.0	 +7.0 +10.5		Vdc
Output Voltage – Low Logic State (V_{IH} = 1.9 Vdc, R_L = 3.0 kΩ, V_{CC} = +9.0 Vdc, V_{EE} = -9.0 Vdc) (V_{IH} = 1.9 Vdc, R_L = 3.0 kΩ, V_{CC} = +13.2 Vdc, V_{EE} = -13.2 Vdc)	2	V_{OL}	 -6.0 -9.0	 -7.0 -10.5		Vdc
Positive Output Short-Circuit Current (1)	3	I_{OS+}	+6.0	+10	+12	mA
Negative Output Short-Circuit Current (1)	3	I_{OS-}	-6.0	-10	-12	mA
Output Resistance (V_{CC} V_{EE} 0, $\|V_O\|$ ±2.0 V)	4	r_o	300			Ohms
Positive Supply Current (R_L ∞) (V_{IH} = 1.9 Vdc, V_{CC} = +9.0 Vdc) (V_{IL} = 0.8 Vdc, V_{CC} = +9.0 Vdc) (V_{IH} = 1.9 Vdc, V_{CC} = +12 Vdc) (V_{IL} = 0.8 Vdc, V_{CC} = +12 Vdc) (V_{IH} = 1.9 Vdc, V_{CC} = +15 Vdc) (V_{IL} = 0.8 Vdc, V_{CC} = +15 Vdc)	5	I_{CC}		 +15 +4.5 +19 +5.5 	 +20 +6.0 +25 +7.0 +34 +12	mA
Negative Supply Current (R_L - ∞) (V_{IH} = 1.9 Vdc, V_{EE} = -9.0 Vdc) (V_{IL} = 0.8 Vdc, V_{EE} = -9.0 Vdc) (V_{IH} = 1.9 Vdc, V_{EE} = -12 Vdc) (V_{IL} = 0.8 Vdc, V_{EE} = -12 Vdc) (V_{IH} = 1.9 Vdc, V_{EE} = -15 Vdc) (V_{IL} = 0.8 Vdc, V_{EE} = -15 Vdc)	5	I_{EE}	 – – –	 -13 – -18 	 -17 -500 -23 -500 -34 -2.5	 mA μA mA μA mA mA
Power Consumption (V_{CC} = 9.0 Vdc, V_{EE} = -9.0 Vdc) (V_{CC} = 12 Vdc, V_{EE} = -12 Vdc)		P_C	 – –	 –	 333 576	mW

SWITCHING CHARACTERISTICS (V_{CC} = +9.0 ± 1% Vdc, V_{EE} = -9.0 ± 1% Vdc, T_A = +25°C.)

Characteristic	Figure	Symbol	Min	Typ	Max	Unit
Propagation Delay Time (z_l = 3.0 k and 15 pF)	6	t_{PLH}	–	275	350	ns
Fall Time (z_l = 3.0 k and 15 pF)	6	t_{THL}	–	45	75	ns
Propagation Delay Time (z_l = 3.0 k and 15 pF)	6	t_{PHL}	–	110	175	ns
Rise Time (z_l = 3.0 k and 15 pF)	6	t_{TLH}	–	55	100	ns

(1) Maximum Package Power Dissipation may be exceeded if all outputs are shorted simultaneously.

MC1488

CHARACTERISTIC DEFINITIONS

FIGURE 1 – INPUT CURRENT

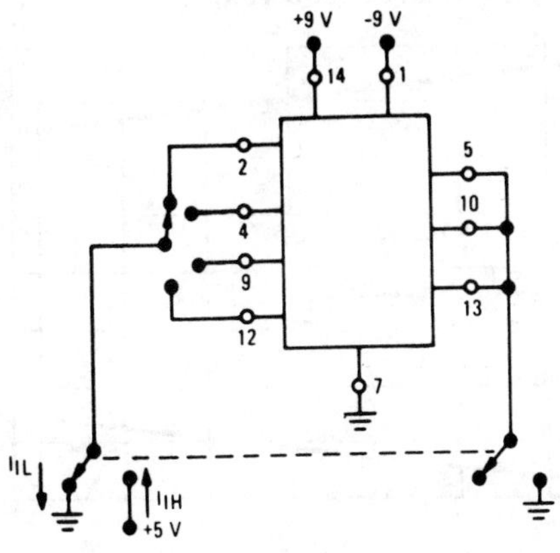

FIGURE 2 – OUTPUT VOLTAGE

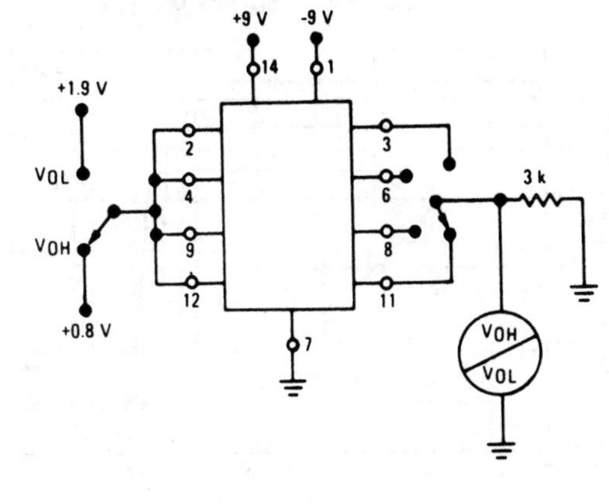

FIGURE 3 – OUTPUT SHORT-CIRCUIT CURRENT

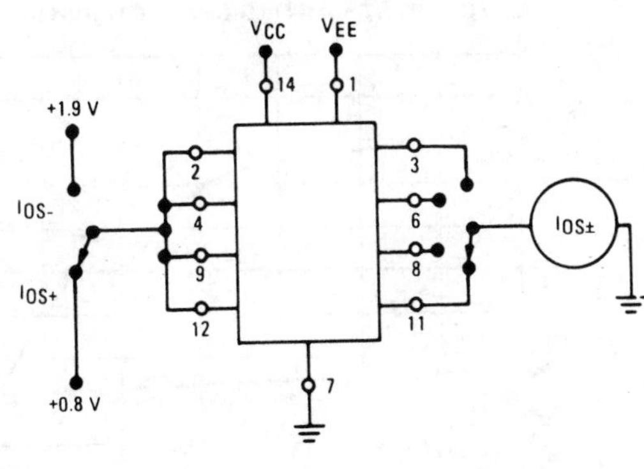

FIGURE 4 – OUTPUT RESISTANCE (POWER-OFF)

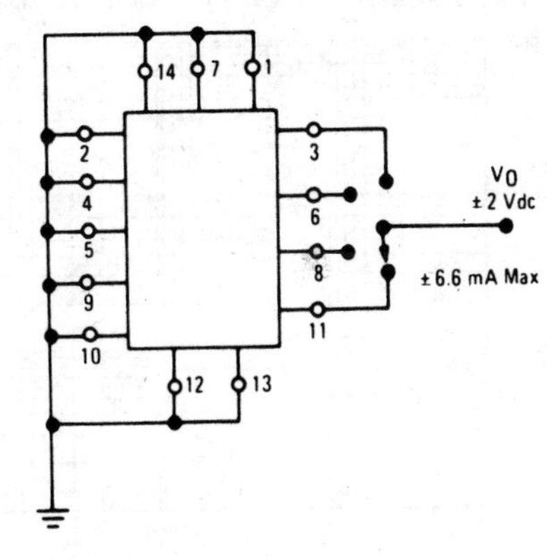

FIGURE 5 – POWER-SUPPLY CURRENTS

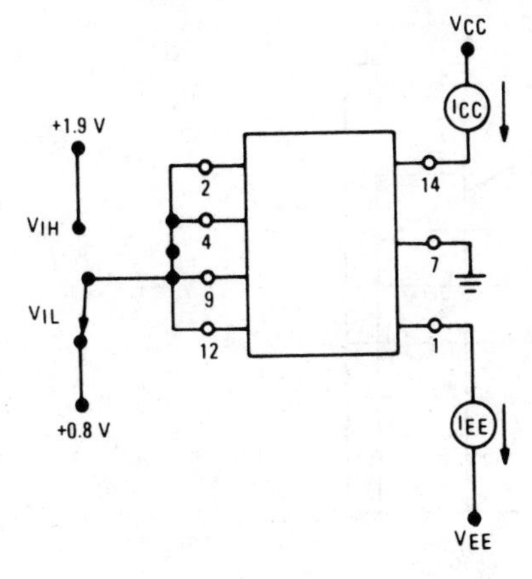

FIGURE 6 – SWITCHING RESPONSE

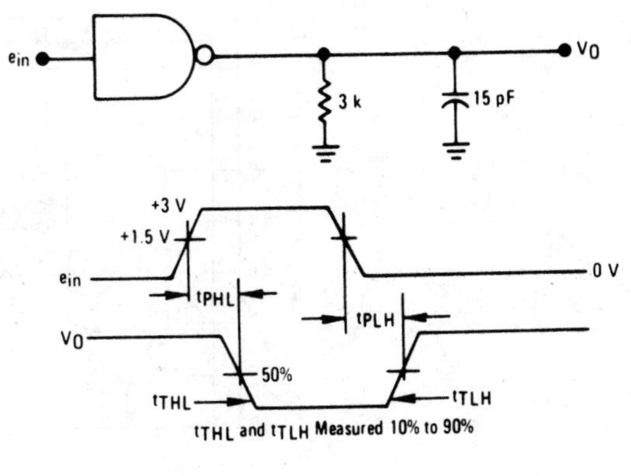

MC1488

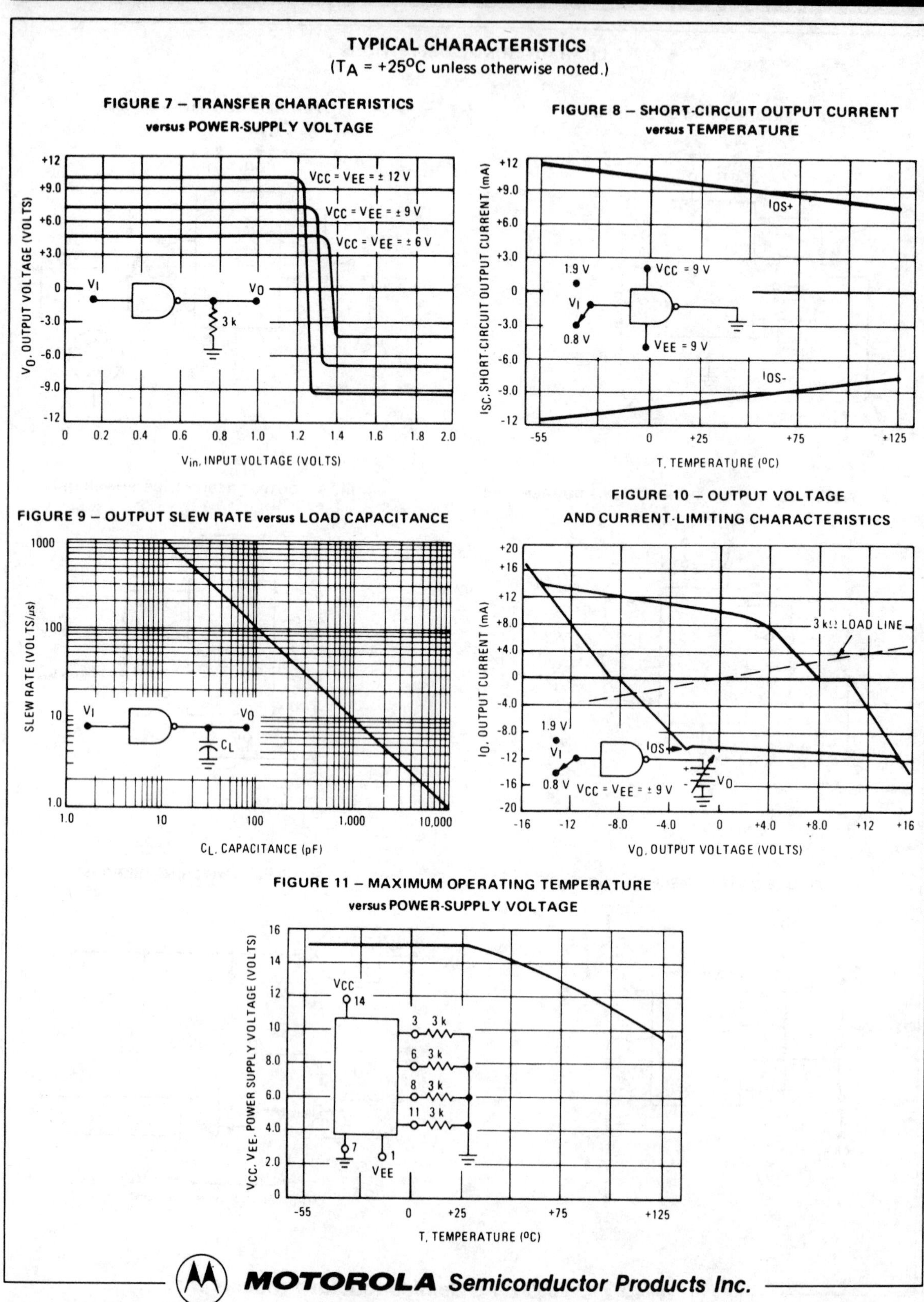
TYPICAL CHARACTERISTICS
(TA = +25°C unless otherwise noted.)
FIGURE 7 – TRANSFER CHARACTERISTICS versus POWER-SUPPLY VOLTAGE
VCC = VEE = ± 12 V
VCC = VEE = ± 9 V
VCC = VEE = ± 6 V
VI
VO
3 k
VO, OUTPUT VOLTAGE (VOLTS)
Vin, INPUT VOLTAGE (VOLTS)
FIGURE 8 – SHORT-CIRCUIT OUTPUT CURRENT versus TEMPERATURE
IOS+
IOS-
1.9 V
0.8 V
VCC = 9 V
VEE = 9 V
ISC, SHORT-CIRCUIT OUTPUT CURRENT (mA)
T, TEMPERATURE (°C)
FIGURE 9 – OUTPUT SLEW RATE versus LOAD CAPACITANCE
SLEW RATE (VOLTS/μs)
CL
CL, CAPACITANCE (pF)
FIGURE 10 – OUTPUT VOLTAGE AND CURRENT-LIMITING CHARACTERISTICS
3 kΩ LOAD LINE
IOS
VCC = VEE = ± 9 V
IO, OUTPUT CURRENT (mA)
VO, OUTPUT VOLTAGE (VOLTS)
FIGURE 11 – MAXIMUM OPERATING TEMPERATURE versus POWER-SUPPLY VOLTAGE
VCC
14
3 3 k
6 3 k
8 3 k
11 3 k
7
1
VEE
VCC, VEE, POWER SUPPLY VOLTAGE (VOLTS)
T, TEMPERATURE (°C)
MOTOROLA Semiconductor Products Inc.

MC1488

APPLICATIONS INFORMATION

The Electronic Industries Association (EIA) RS232C specification detail the requirements for the interface between data processing equipment and data communications equipment. This standard specifies not only the number and type of interface leads, but also the voltage levels to be used. The MC1488 quad driver and its companion circuit, the MC1489 quad receiver, provide a complete interface system between DTL or TTL logic levels and the RS232C defined levels. The RS232C requirements as applied to drivers are discussed herein.

The required driver voltages are defined as between 5 and 15-volts in magnitude and are positive for a logic "0" and negative for a logic "1". These voltages are so defined when the drivers are terminated with a 3000 to 7000-ohm resistor. The MC1488 meets this voltage requirement by converting a DTL/TTL logic level into RS232C levels with one stage of inversion.

The RS232C specification further requires that during transitions, the driver output slew rate must not exceed 30 volts per microsecond. The inherent slew rate of the MC1488 is much too fast for this requirement. The current limited output of the device can be used to control this slew rate by connecting a capacitor to each driver output. The required capacitor can be easily determined by using the relationship $C = I_{OS} \times \Delta T/\Delta V$ from which Figure 12 is derived. Accordingly, a 330-pF capacitor on each output will guarantee a worst case slew rate of 30 volts per microsecond.

FIGURE 12 – SLEW RATE versus CAPACITANCE FOR I_{SC} = 10 mA

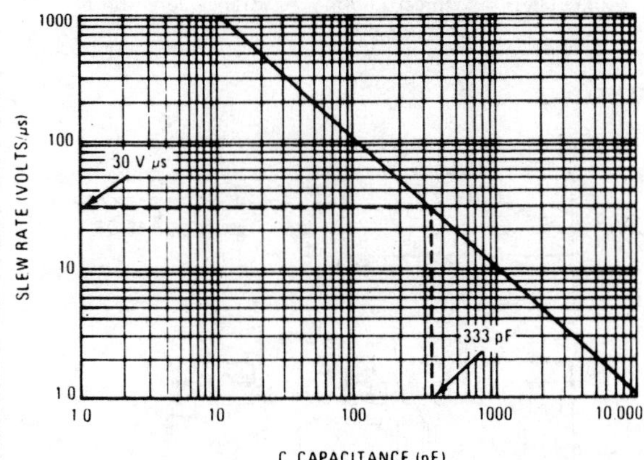

The interface driver is also required to withstand an accidental short to any other conductor in an interconnecting cable. The worst possible signal on any conductor would be another driver using a plus or minus 15-volt, 500-mA source. The MC1488 is designed to indefinitely withstand such a short to all four outputs in a package as long as the power-supply voltages are greater than 9.0 volts (i.e., $V_{CC} \geq 9.0$ V; $V_{EE} \leq -9.0$ V). In some power-supply designs, a loss of system power causes a low impedance on the power-supply outputs. When this occurs, a low impedance to ground would exist at the power inputs to the MC1488 effectively shorting the 300-ohm output resistors to ground. If all four outputs were then shorted to plus or minus 15 volts, the power dissipation in these resistors would be excessive. Therefore, if the system is designed to permit low impedances to ground at the power-supplies of the drivers, a diode should be placed in each power-supply lead to prevent overheating in this fault condition. These two diodes, as shown in Figure 13, could be used to decouple all the driver packages in a system. (These same diodes will allow the MC1488 to withstand momentary shorts to the ±25-volt limits specified in the earlier Standard RS232B.) The addition of the diodes also permits the MC1488 to withstand faults with power-supplies of less than the 9.0 volts stated above.

FIGURE 13 – POWER-SUPPLY PROTECTION TO MEET POWER-OFF FAULT CONDITIONS

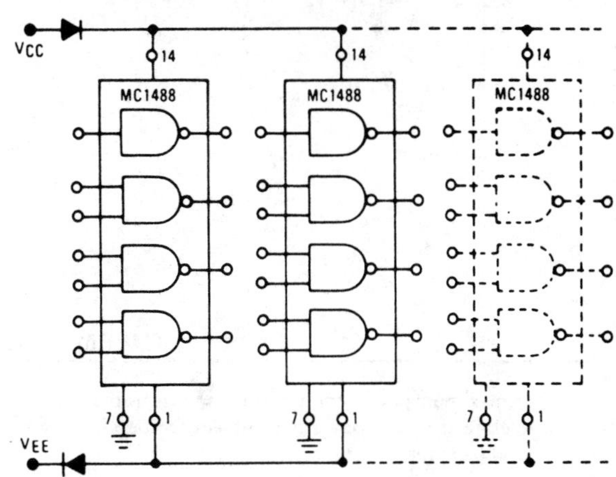

The maximum short-circuit current allowable under fault conditions is more than guaranteed by the previously mentioned 10 mA output current limiting.

Other Applications

The MC1488 is an extremely versatile line driver with a myriad of possible applications. Several features of the drivers enhance this versatility.

1. Output Current Limiting – this enables the circuit designer to define the output voltage levels independent of power-supplies and can be accomplished by diode clamping of the output pins. Figure 14 shows the MC1488 used as a DTL to MOS translator where the high-level voltage output is clamped one diode above ground. The resistor divider shown is used to reduce the output voltage below the 300 mV above ground MOS input level limit.

2. Power-Supply Range – as can be seen from the schematic drawing of the drivers, the positive and negative driving elements of the device are essentially independent and do not require matching power-supplies. In fact, the positive supply can vary from a minimum seven volts (required for driving the negative pulldown section) to the maximum specified 15 volts. The negative supply can vary from approximately -2.5 volts to the minimum specified -15 volts. The MC1488 will drive the output to within 2 volts of the positive or negative supplies as long as the current output limits are not exceeded. The combination of the current-limiting and supply-voltage features allow a wide combination of possible outputs within the same quad package. Thus if only a portion of the four drivers are used for driving RS232C lines, the remainder could be used for DTL to MOS or even DTL to DTL translation. Figure 15 shows one such combination.

FIGURE 14 – MDTL/MTTL-TO-MOS TRANSLATOR

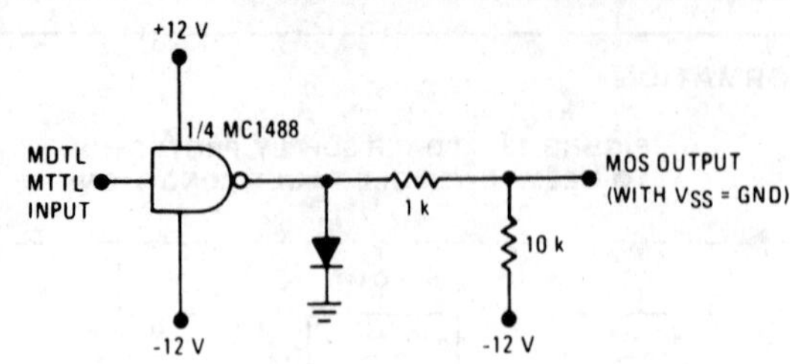

FIGURE 15 – LOGIC TRANSLATOR APPLICATIONS

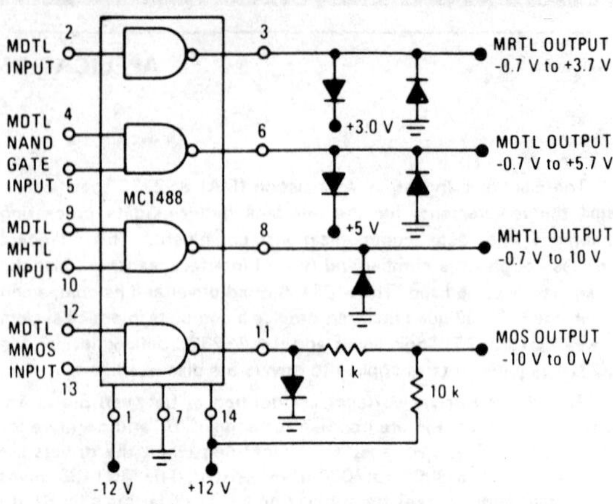

THERMAL INFORMATION

The maximum power consumption an integrated circuit can tolerate at a given operating ambient temperature, can be found from the equation:

$$P_{D(T_A)} = \frac{T_{J(max)} - T_A}{R_{\theta JA}(Typ)}$$

Where: $P_{D(T_A)}$ = Power Dissipation allowable at a given operating ambient temperature. This must be greater than the sum of the products of the supply voltages and supply currents at the worst case operating condition.

$T_{J(max)}$ = Maximum Operating Junction Temperature as listed in the Maximum Ratings Section

T_A = Maximum Desired Operating Ambient Temperature

$R_{\theta JA}(Typ)$ = Typical Thermal Resistance Junction to Ambient

OUTLINE DIMENSIONS

L SUFFIX
CERAMIC PACKAGE
CASE 632-02
TO-116

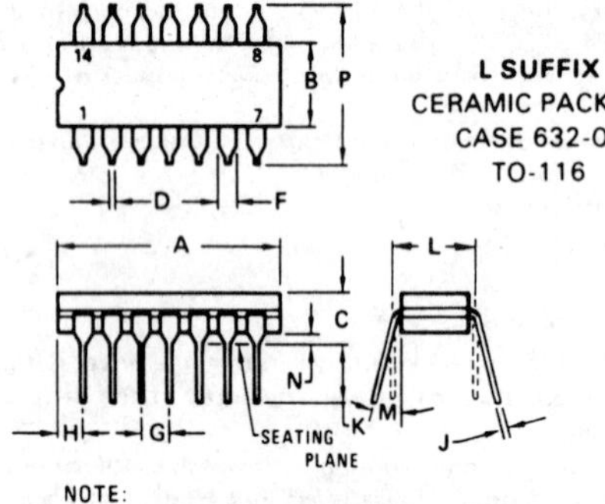

NOTE:
1. DIMENSION "L" TO CENTER OF LEADS WHEN FORMED PARALLEL.

DIM	MILLIMETERS MIN	MILLIMETERS MAX	INCHES MIN	INCHES MAX
A	19.05	19.94	0.750	0.785
B	6.22	7.11	0.245	0.280
C	3.94	5.08	0.155	0.200
D	0.38	0.51	0.015	0.020
F	0.89	1.65	0.035	0.065
G	2.54 BSC		0.100 BSC	
H	1.65	2.29	0.065	0.090
J	0.20	0.30	0.008	0.012
K	3.18	4.06	0.125	0.160
L	7.37	8.13	0.290	0.320
M	–	15°	–	15°
N	0.51	1.27	0.020	0.050

P SUFFIX
PLASTIC PACKAGE
CASE 646-05

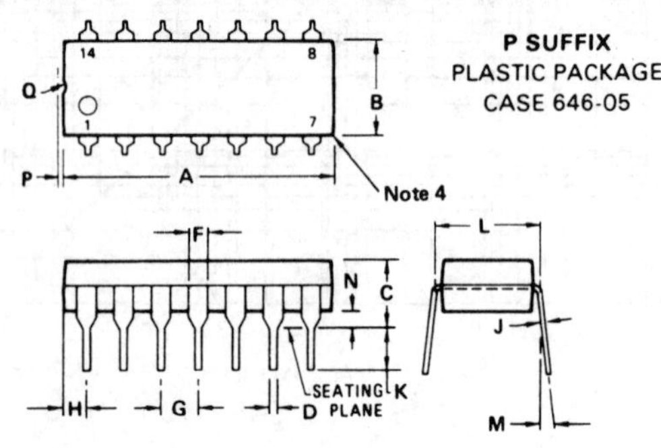

DIM	MILLIMETERS MIN	MILLIMETERS MAX	INCHES MIN	INCHES MAX
A	18.16	19.56	0.715	0.770
B	6.10	6.60	0.240	0.260
C	4.06	5.08	0.160	0.200
D	0.38	0.53	0.015	0.021
F	1.02	1.78	0.040	0.070
G	2.54 BSC		0.100 BSC	
H	1.32	2.41	0.052	0.095
J	0.20	0.38	0.008	0.015
K	2.92	3.43	0.115	0.135
L	7.62 BSC		0.300 BSC	
M	0°	10°	0°	10°
N	0.51	1.02	0.020	0.040

NOTES:
1. LEADS WITHIN 0.13 mm (0.005) RADIUS OF TRUE POSITION AT SEATING PLANE AT MAXIMUM MATERIAL CONDITION.
2. DIMENSION "L" TO CENTER OF LEADS WHEN FORMED PARALLEL.
3. DIMENSION "B" DOES NOT INCLUDE MOLD FLASH.
4. ROUNDED CORNERS OPTIONAL.

MOTOROLA *Semiconductor Products Inc.*

BOX 20912 • PHOENIX, ARIZONA 85036 • A SUBSIDIARY OF MOTOROLA INC.

5534-5 PRINTED IN USA 8-81 IMPERIAL LITHO 3B-I52 18,000 DS9162 R2

MC1489
MC1489A

QUAD LINE RECEIVERS

The MC1489 monolithic quad line receivers are designed to interface data terminal equipment with data communications equipment in conformance with the specifications of EIA Standard No. RS-232C.

- Input Resistance – 3.0 k to 7.0 kilohms
- Input Signal Range – ± 30 Volts
- Input Threshold Hysteresis Built In
- Response Control
  - a) Logic Threshold Shifting
  - b) Input Noise Filtering

QUAD MDTL LINE RECEIVERS RS-232C

SILICON MONOLITHIC INTEGRATED CIRCUIT

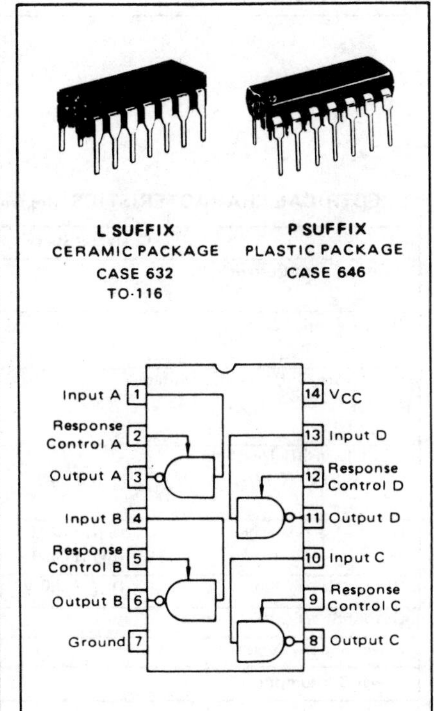

L SUFFIX CERAMIC PACKAGE CASE 632 TO-116

P SUFFIX PLASTIC PACKAGE CASE 646

TYPICAL APPLICATION

LINE DRIVER MC1488

INTERCONNECTING CABLE

LINE RECEIVER MC1489

MDTL LOGIC INPUT — INTERCONNECTING CABLE — MDTL LOGIC OUTPUT

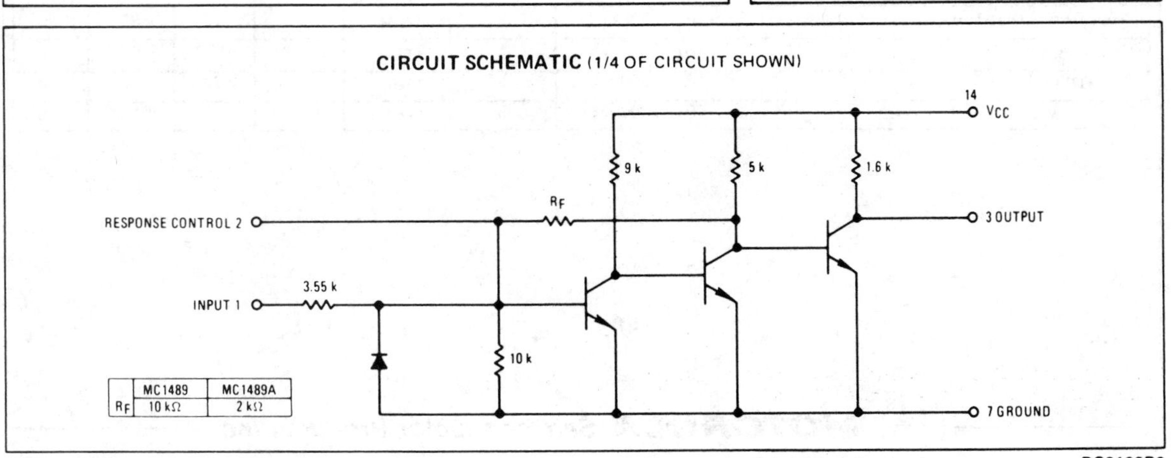

	MC1489	MC1489A
R_F	10 kΩ	2 kΩ

MDTL and MTTL are trademarks of Motorola Inc.

DS9193R2

MC1489 ● MC1489A

MAXIMUM RATINGS (T_A = +25°C unless otherwise noted)

Rating	Symbol	Value	Unit
Power Supply Voltage	V_{CC}	10	Vdc
Input Voltage Range	V_{IR}	±30	Vdc
Output Load Current	I_L	20	mA
Power Dissipation (Package Limitation, Ceramic and Plastic Dual In-Line Package) Derate above T_A = +25°C	P_D $1/\theta_{JA}$	1000 6.7	mW mW/°C
Operating Ambient Temperature Range	T_A	0 to +75	°C
Storage Temperature Range	T_{stg}	-65 to +175	°C

ELECTRICAL CHARACTERISTICS (Response control pin is open.) (V_{CC} = +5.0 Vdc ± 1%, T_A = 0 to +75°C unless otherwise noted)

Characteristics		Figure	Symbol	Min	Typ	Max	Unit
Positive Input Current	(V_{IH} = +25 Vdc) (V_{IH} = +3.0 Vdc)	1	I_{IH}	3.6 0.43		8.3	mA
Negative Input Current	(V_{IL} = -25 Vdc) (V_{IL} = -3.0 Vdc)	1	I_{IL}	-3.6 -0.43		-8.3	mA
Input Turn-On Threshold Voltage (T_A = +25°C, V_{OL} ≤ 0.45 V)	MC1489 MC1489A	2	V_{IHL}	1.0 1.75	 1.95	1.5 2.25	Vdc
Input Turn-Off Threshold Voltage (T_A = +25°C, V_{OH} ≥ 2.5 V, I_L = -0.5 mA)	MC1489 MC1489A	2	V_{ILH}	0.75 0.75	 0.8	1.25 1.25	Vdc
Output Voltage High	(V_{IH} = 0.75 V, I_L = -0.5 mA) (Input Open Circuit, I_L = -0.5 mA)	2	V_{OH}	2.6 2.6	4.0 4.0	5.0 5.0	Vdc
Output Voltage Low	(V_{IL} = 3.0 V, I_L = 10 mA)	2	V_{OL}		0.2	0.45	Vdc
Output Short-Circuit Current		3	I_{OS}		3.0		mA
Power Supply Current	(V_{IH} = +5.0 Vdc)	4	I_{CC}		20	26	mA
Power Consumption	(V_{IH} = +5.0 Vdc)	4	P_C		100	130	mW

SWITCHING CHARACTERISTICS (V_{CC} = 5.0 Vdc ± 1%, T_A = +25°C)

Characteristics		Figure	Symbol	Min	Typ	Max	Unit
Propagation Delay Time	(R_L = 3.9 kΩ)	5	t_{PLH}		25	85	ns
Rise Time	(R_L = 3.9 kΩ)	5	t_{TLH}		120	175	ns
Propagation Delay Time	(R_L = 390 Ω)	5	t_{PHL}		25	50	ns
Fall Time	(R_L = 390 Ω)	5	t_{THL}		10	20	ns

MC1489 ● MC1489A

TEST CIRCUITS

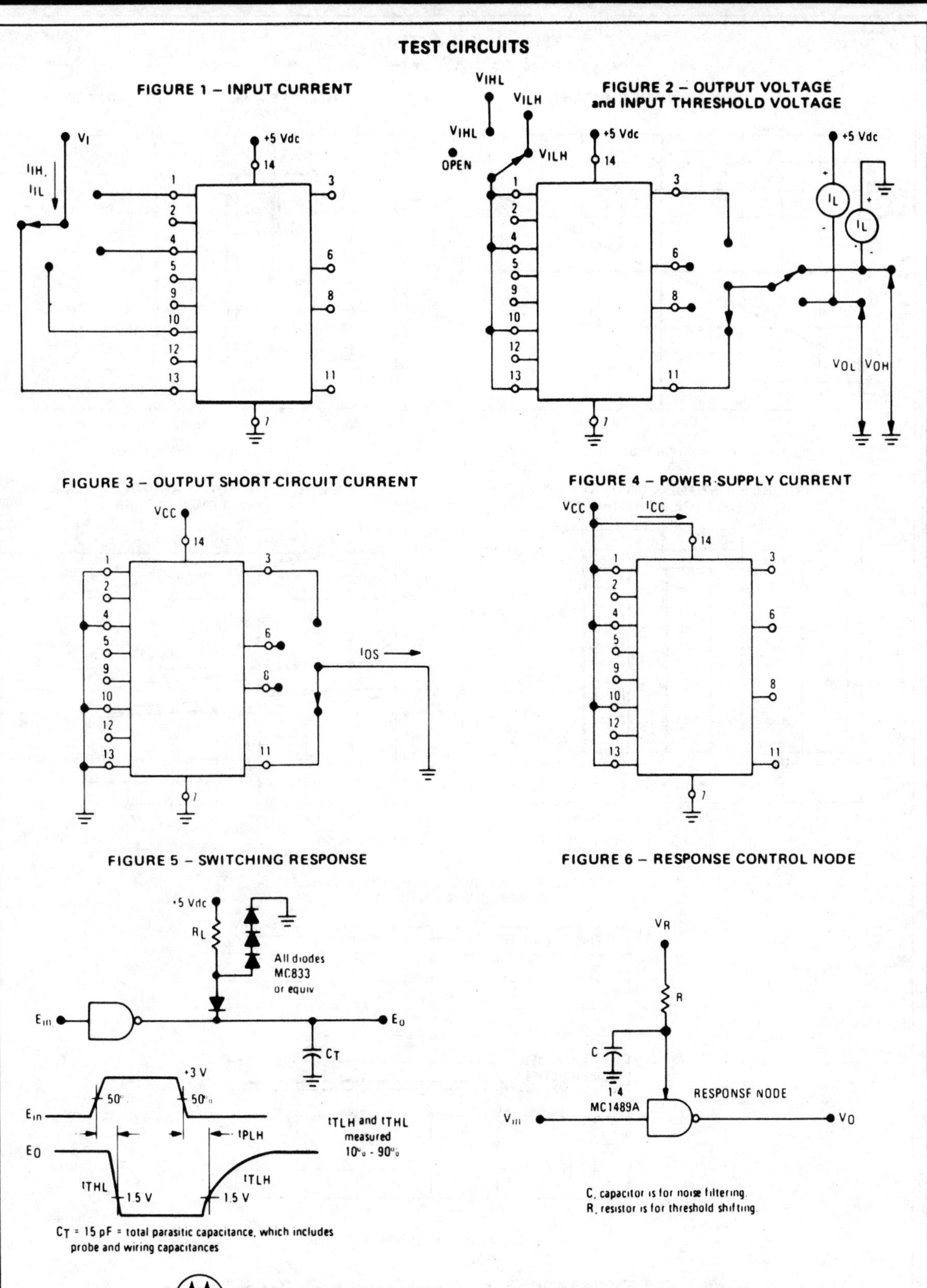

MC1489 ● MC1489A

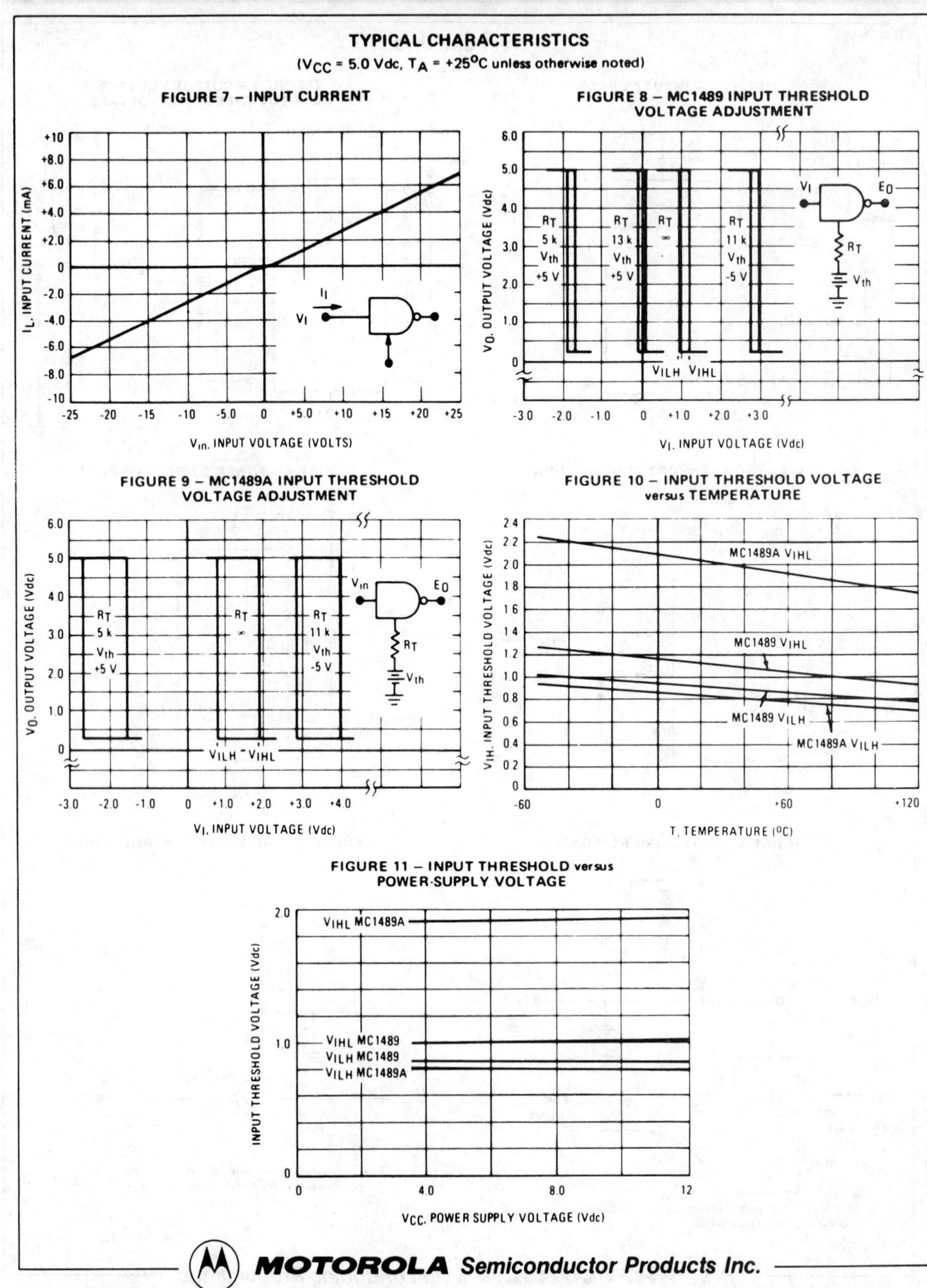

MC1489 • MC1489A

APPLICATIONS INFORMATION

General Information

The Electronic Industries Association (EIA) has released the RS-232C specification detailing the requirements for the interface between data processing equipment and data communications equipment. This standard specifies not only the number and type of interface leads, but also the voltage levels to be used. The MC1488 quad driver and its companion circuit, the MC1489 quad receiver, provide a complete interface system between DTL or TTL logic levels and the RS-232C defined levels. The RS-232C requirements as applied to receivers are discussed herein.

The required input impedance is defined as between 3000 ohms and 7000 ohms for input voltages between 3.0 and 25 volts in magnitude; and any voltage on the receiver input in an open circuit condition must be less than 2.0 volts in magnitude. The MC1489 circuits meet these requirements with a maximum open circuit voltage of one V_{BE} (Ref. Sect. 2.4).

The receiver shall detect a voltage between -3.0 and -25 volts as a logic "1" and inputs between +3.0 and +25 volts as a logic "0" (Ref. Sect. 2.3). On some interchange leads, an open circuit or power "OFF" condition (300 ohms or more to ground) shall be decoded as an "OFF" condition or logic "1" (Ref. Sect. 2.5). For this reason, the input hysteresis thresholds of the MC1489 circuits are all above ground. Thus an open or grounded input will cause the same output as a negative or logic "1" input.

Device Characteristics

The MC1489 interface receivers have internal feedback from the second stage to the input stage providing input hysteresis for noise rejection. The MC1489 input has typical turn-on voltage of 1.25 volts and turn-off of 1.0 volt for a typical hysteresis of 250 mV. The MC1489A has typical turn-on of 1.95 volts and turn-off of 0.8 volt for typically 1.15 volts of hysteresis.

Each receiver section has an external response control node in addition to the input and output pins, thereby allowing the designer to vary the input threshold voltage levels. A resistor can be connected between this node and an external power-supply. Figures 6, 8 and 9 illustrate the input threshold voltage shift possible through this technique.

This response node can also be used for the filtering of high-frequency, high-energy noise pulses. Figures 12 and 13 show typical noise-pulse rejection for external capacitors of various sizes.

These two operations on the response node can be combined or used individually for many combinations of interfacing applications. The MC1489 circuits are particularly useful for interfacing between MOS circuits and MDTL/MTTL logic systems. In this application, the input threshold voltages are adjusted (with the appropriate supply and resistor values) to fall in the center of the MOS voltage logic levels. (See Figure 14)

The response node may also be used as the receiver input as long as the designer realizes that he may not drive this node with a low impedance source to a voltage greater than one diode above ground or less than one diode below ground. This feature is demonstrated in Figure 15 where two receivers are slaved to the same line that must still meet the RS-232C impedance requirement.

FIGURE 12 – TURN-ON THRESHOLD versus CAPACITANCE FROM RESPONSE CONTROL PIN TO GND

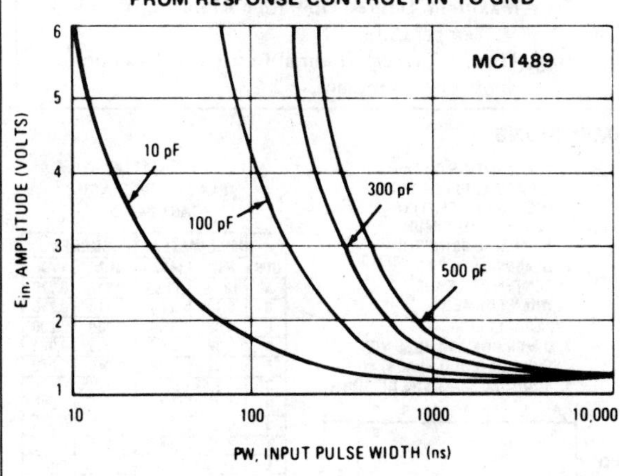

FIGURE 13 – TURN-ON THRESHOLD versus CAPACITANCE FROM RESPONSE CONTROL PIN TO GND

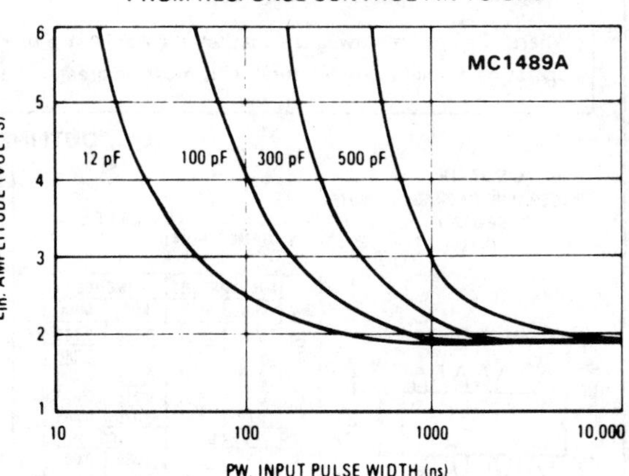

FIGURE 14 – TYPICAL TRANSLATOR APPLICATION – MOS TO DTL OR TTL

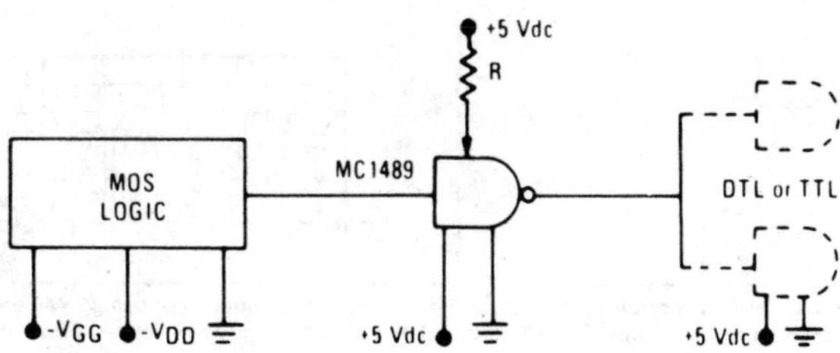

APPLICATIONS INFORMATION (continued)

FIGURE 15 – TYPICAL PARALLELING OF TWO MC1489,A RECEIVERS TO MEET RS-232C

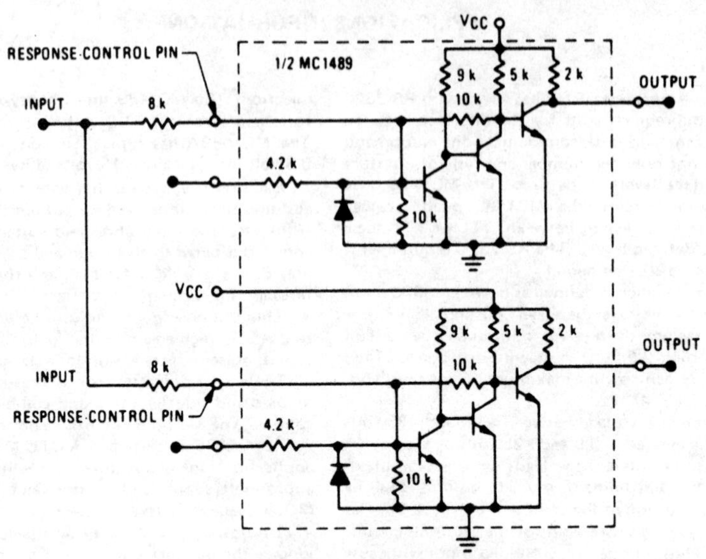

THERMAL INFORMATION

The maximum power consumption an integrated circuit can tolerate at a given operating ambient temperature, can be found from the equation:

$$P_{D(T_A)} = \frac{T_{J(max)} - T_A}{R_{\theta JA}(Typ)}$$

Where: $P_{D(T_A)}$ = Power Dissipation allowable at a given operating ambient temperature. This must be greater than the sum of the products of the supply voltages and supply currents at the worst case operating condition.

$T_{J(max)}$ = Maximum Operating Junction Temperature as listed in the Maximum Ratings Section

T_A = Maximum Desired Operating Ambient Temperature

$R_{\theta JA}(Typ)$ = Typical Thermal Resistance Junction to Ambient

OUTLINE DIMENSIONS

L SUFFIX
CERAMIC PACKAGE
CASE 632-05
TO-116

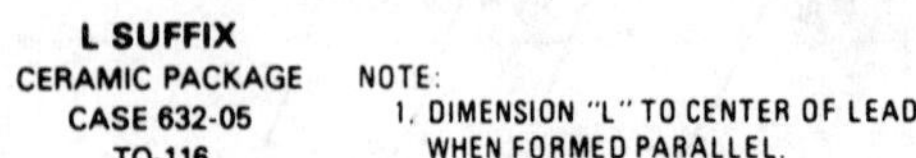

NOTE:
1. DIMENSION "L" TO CENTER OF LEADS WHEN FORMED PARALLEL.

DIM	MILLIMETERS MIN	MILLIMETERS MAX	INCHES MIN	INCHES MAX
A	19.05	19.94	0.750	0.785
B	6.22	7.11	0.245	0.280
C	3.94	5.08	0.155	0.200
D	0.38	0.51	0.015	0.020
F	0.89	1.65	0.035	0.065
G	2.54 BSC		0.100 BSC	
H	1.65	2.29	0.065	0.090
J	0.20	0.30	0.008	0.012
K	3.18	4.06	0.125	0.160
L	7.37	8.13	0.290	0.320
M	–	15°	–	15°
N	0.51	1.27	0.020	0.050

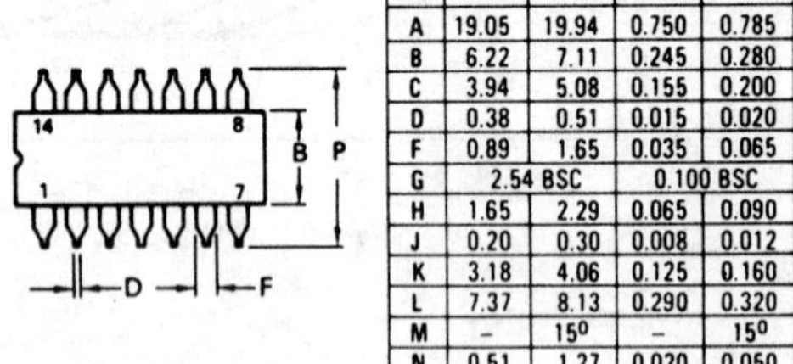

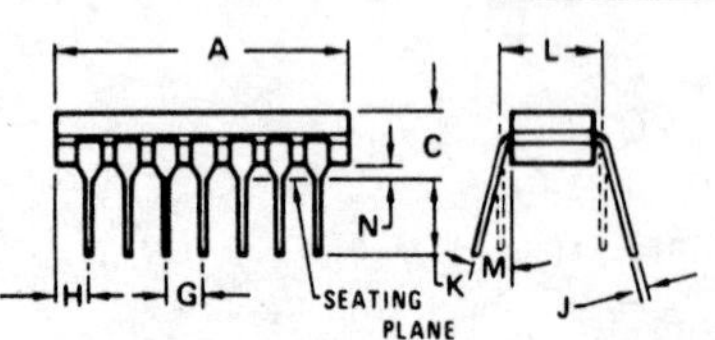

NOTES:
1. LEADS WITHIN 0.13 mm (0.005) RADIUS OF TRUE POSITION AT SEATING PLANE AT MAXIMUM MATERIAL CONDITION.
2. DIMENSION "L" TO CENTER OF LEADS WHEN FORMED PARALLEL.
3. DIMENSION "B" DOES NOT INCLUDE MOLD FLASH.
4. ROUNDED CORNERS OPTIONAL.

P SUFFIX
PLASTIC PACKAGE
CASE 646-05

DIM	MILLIMETERS MIN	MILLIMETERS MAX	INCHES MIN	INCHES MAX
A	18.16	19.56	0.715	0.770
B	6.10	6.60	0.240	0.260
C	4.06	5.08	0.160	0.200
D	0.38	0.53	0.015	0.021
F	1.02	1.78	0.040	0.070
G	2.54 BSC		0.100 BSC	
H	1.32	2.41	0.052	0.095
J	0.20	0.38	0.008	0.015
K	2.92	3.43	0.115	0.135
L	7.62 BSC		0.300 BSC	
M	0°	10°	0°	10°
N	0.51	1.02	0.020	0.040

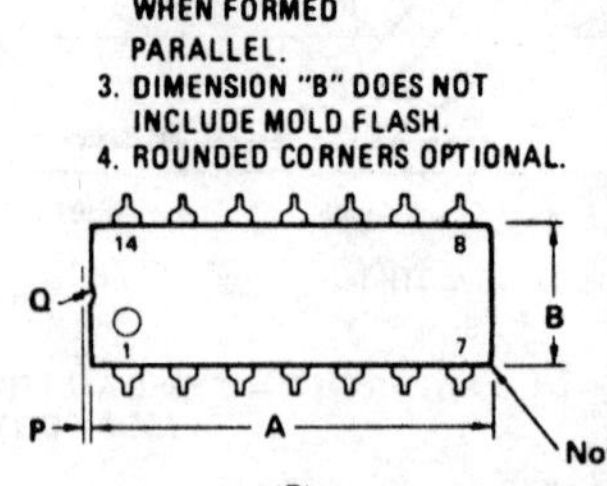

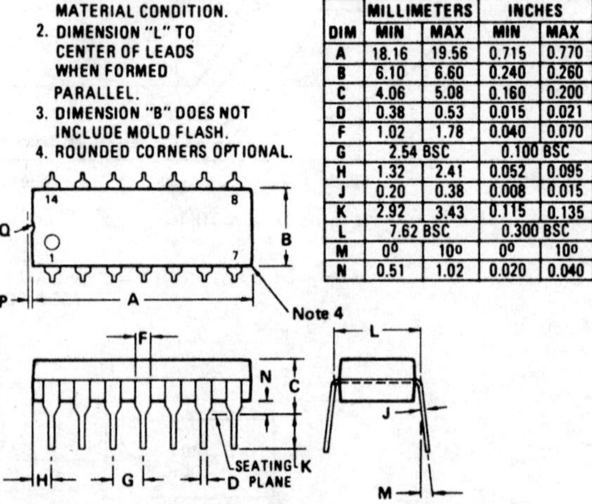

MOTOROLA *Semiconductor Products Inc.*

BOX 20912 • PHOENIX, ARIZONA 85036 • A SUBSIDIARY OF MOTOROLA INC.

5535-4 PRINTED IN USA 8-81 IMPERIAL LITHO 98052 18,000

DS9193 R2

MCM2708
MCM27A08

1024 X 8 ERASABLE PROM

The MCM2708/27A08 is an 8192-bit Erasable and Electrically Reprogrammable PROM designed for system debug usage and similar applications requiring nonvolatile memory that could be reprogrammed periodically. The transparent window on the package allows the memory content to be erased with ultraviolet light. Pin-for-pin mask-programmable ROMs are available for large volume production runs of systems initially using the MCM2708/27A08.

- Organized as 1024 Bytes of 8 Bits
- Static Operation
- Standard Power Supplies of +12 V, +5 V and −5 V
- Maximum Access Time = 300 ns – MCM27A08
  450 ns – MCM2708
- Low Power Dissipation
- Chip-Select Input for Memory Expansion
- TTL Compatible
- Three-State Outputs
- Pin Equivalent to the 2708
- Pin-for-Pin Compatible to MCM65308, MCM68308 or 2308 Mask-Programmable ROMs

MOS

(N-CHANNEL, SILICON-GATE)

1024 X 8-BIT UV ERASABLE PROM

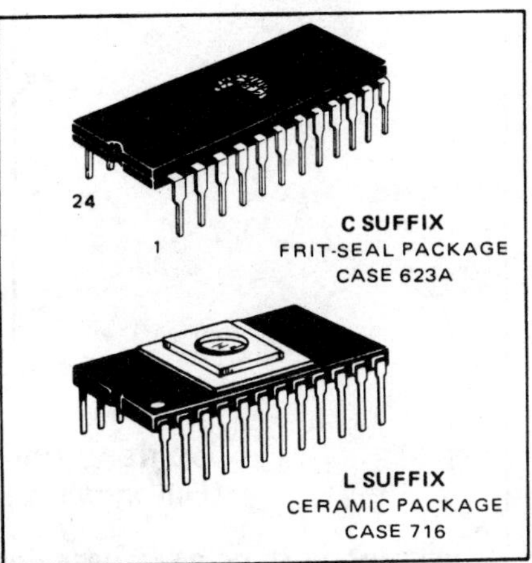

C SUFFIX
FRIT-SEAL PACKAGE
CASE 623A

L SUFFIX
CERAMIC PACKAGE
CASE 716

PIN CONNECTION DURING READ OR PROGRAM

Mode	Pin Number						
	9-11, 13-17	12	18	19	20	21	24
Read	D_{out}	V_{SS}	V_{SS}	V_{DD}	V_{IL}	V_{BB}	V_{CC}
Program	Din	V_{SS}	Pulsed V_{IHP}	V_{DD}	V_{IHW}	V_{BB}	V_{CC}

ABSOLUTE MAXIMUM RATINGS (1)

Rating	Value	Unit
Operating Temperature	0 to +70	°C
Storage Temperature	-65 to +125	°C
V_{DD} with Respect to V_{BB}	+20 to -0.3	Vdc
V_{CC} and V_{SS} with Respect to V_{BB}	+15 to -0.3	Vdc
All Input or Output Voltages with Respect to V_{BB} during Read	+15 to -0.3	Vdc
$\overline{CS}$/WE Input with Respect to V_{BB} during Programming	+20 to -0.3	Vdc
Program Input with Respect to V_{BB}	+35 to -0.3	Vdc
Power Dissipation	1.8	Watts

Note 1:
Permanent device damage may occur if ABSOLUTE MAXIMUM RATINGS are exceeded. Functional operation should be restricted to RECOMMENDED OPERATING CONDITIONS. Exposure to higher than recommended voltages for extended periods of time could affect device reliability.

PIN ASSIGNMENT

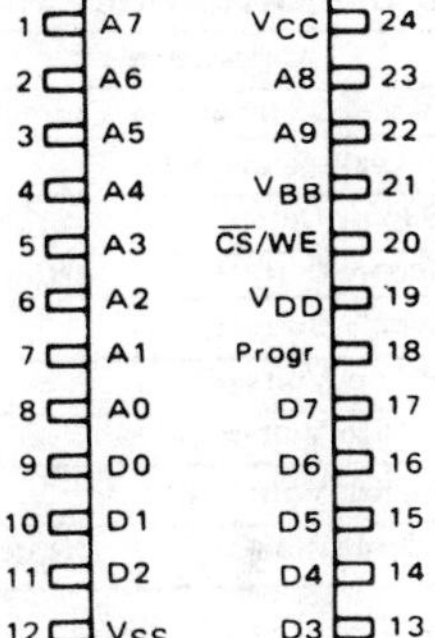

MCM2708 • MCM27A08

BLOCK DIAGRAM

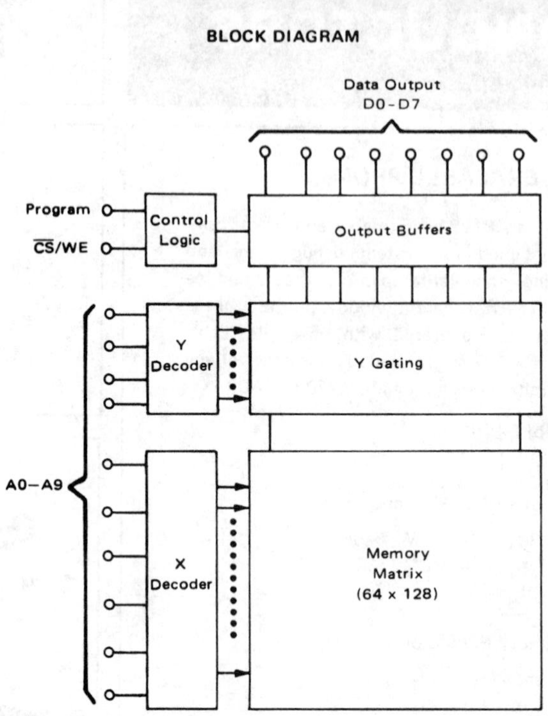

DC READ OPERATING CONDITIONS AND CHARACTERISTICS
(Full operating voltage and temperature range unless otherwise noted.)

RECOMMENDED DC READ OPERATING CONDITIONS

Parameter	Symbol	Min	Nom	Max	Unit
Supply Voltage	V_{CC}	4.75	5.0	5.25	Vdc
	V_{DD}	11.4	12	12.6	Vdc
	V_{BB}	-5.25	-5.0	-4.75	Vdc
Input High Voltage	V_{IH}	3.0	–	V_{CC} + 1.0	Vdc
Input Low Voltage	V_{IL}	V_{SS}	–	0.65	Vdc

READ OPERATION DC CHARACTERISTICS

Characteristic		Condition	Symbol	Min	Typ	Max	Unit
Address and CS Input Sink Current		V_{in} = 5.25 V or V_{in} = V_{IL}	I_{in}	–	1	10	μA
Output Leakage Current		V_{out} = 5.25 V, $\overline{CS}$/WE = 5 V	I_{LO}	–	1	10	μA
V_{DD} Supply Current	(Note 2)	Worst-Case Supply Currents	I_{DD}	–	50	65	mA
V_{CC} Supply Current	(Note 2)	All Inputs High	I_{CC}	–	6	10	mA
V_{BB} Supply Current	(Note 2)	$\overline{CS}$/WE = 5.0 V, T_A = 0°C	I_{BB}	–	30	45	mA
Output Low Voltage		I_{OL} = 1.6 mA	V_{OL}	–	–	0.45	V
Output High Voltage		I_{OH} = -100 μA	V_{OH1}	3.7	–	–	V
Output High Voltage		I_{OH} = -1.0 mA	V_{OH2}	2.4	–	–	V
Power Dissipation	(Note 2)	T_A = 70°C	P_D	–	–	800	mW

Note 2:
The total power dissipation is specified at 800 mW. It is not calculable by summing the various current (I_{DD}, I_{CC}, and I_{BB}) multiplied by their respective voltages, since current paths exist between the various power supplies and V_{SS}. The I_{DD}, I_{CC}, and I_{BB} currents should be used to determine power supply capacity only.

V_{BB} must be applied prior to V_{CC} and V_{DD}. V_{BB} must also be the last power supply switched off.

MCM2708 • MCM27A08

AC READ OPERATING CONDITIONS AND CHARACTERISTICS
(Full operating voltage and temperature range unless otherwise noted.)
(All timing with $t_r = t_f = 20$ ns, Load per Note 3)

Characteristic	Symbol	MCM27A08			MCM2708			Unit
		Min	Typ	Max	Min	Typ	Max	
Address to Output Delay	t_{AO}	–	220	300	–	280	450	ns
Chip Select to Output Delay	t_{CO}	–	60	120	–	60	120	ns
Data Hold from Address	t_{DHA}	0	–	–	0	–	–	ns
Data Hold from Deselection	t_{DHD}	0	–	120	0	–	120	ns

CAPACITANCE (periodically sampled rather than 100% tested.)

Characteristic	Condition	Symbol	Typ	Max	Unit
Input Capacitance (f = 1.0 MHz)	$V_{in} = 0$ V, $T_A = 25°C$	C_{in}	4.0	6.0	pF
Output Capacitance (f = 1.0 MHz)	$V_{out} = 0$ V, $T_A = 25°C$	C_{out}	8.0	12	pF

Note 3:
Output Load = 1 TTL Gate and C_L = 100 pF (Includes Jig Capacitance)
Timing Measurement Reference Levels: Inputs: 0.8 V and 2.8 V
Outputs: 0.8 V and 2.4 V

AC TEST LOAD

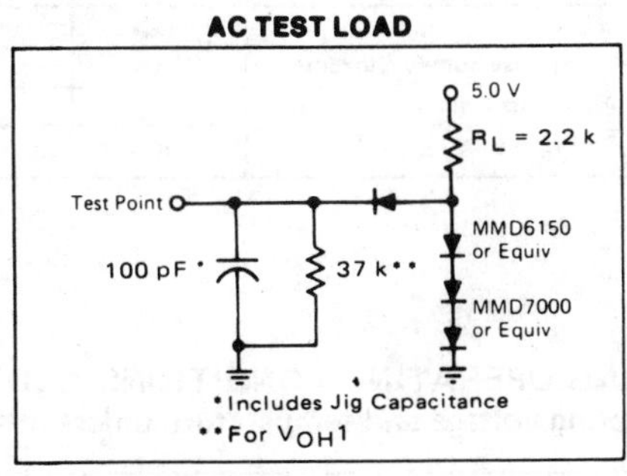

READ OPERATION TIMING DIAGRAM

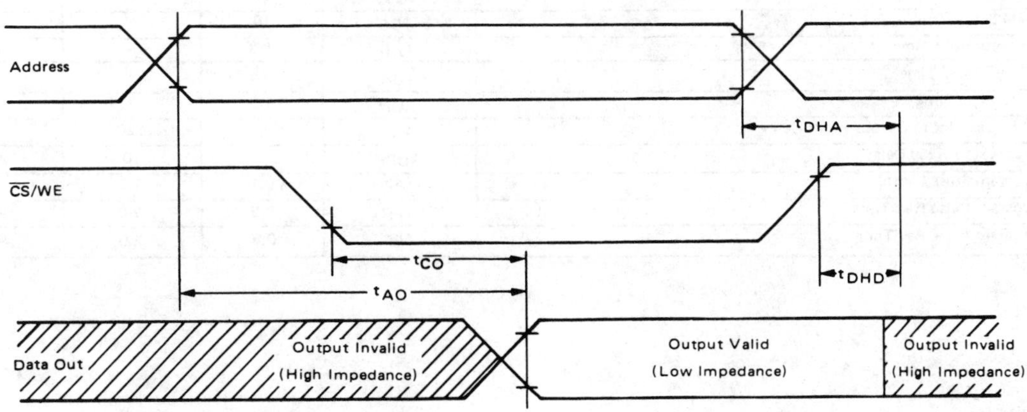

MCM2708 • MCM27A08

DC PROGRAMMING CONDITIONS AND CHARACTERISTICS
(Full operating voltage and temperature range unless otherwise noted.)

RECOMMENDED PROGRAMMING OPERATING CONDITIONS

Parameter	Symbol	Min	Nom	Max	Unit
Supply Voltage	V_{CC}	4.75	5.0	5.25	Vdc
	V_{DD}	11.4	12	12.6	Vdc
	V_{BB}	-5.25	-5.0	-4.75	Vdc
Input High Voltage for All Addresses and Data	V_{IH}	3.0	–	V_{CC} + 1.0	Vdc
Input Low Voltage (except Program)	V_{IL}	V_{SS}	–	0.65	Vdc
$\overline{CS}$/WE Input High Voltage (Note 4)	V_{IHW}	11.4	12	12.6	Vdc
Program Pulse Input High Voltage (Note 4)	V_{IHP}	25	–	27	Vdc
Program Pulse Input Low Voltage (Note 5)	V_{ILP}	V_{SS}	–	1.0	Vdc

Note 4: Referenced to V_{SS}.
Note 5: $V_{IHP} - V_{ILP}$ = 25 V min.

PROGRAMMING OPERATION DC CHARACTERISTICS

Characteristic	Condition	Symbol	Min	Typ	Max	Unit
Address and $\overline{CS}$/WE Input Sink Current	V_{in} = 5.25 V	I_{LI}	–	–	10	μAdc
Program Pulse Source Current		I_{IPL}	–	–	3.0	mAdc
Program Pulse Sink Current		I_{IPH}	–	–	20	mAdc
V_{DD} Supply Current	Worst-Case Supply Currents	I_{DD}	–	50	65	mAdc
V_{CC} Supply Current	All Inputs High	I_{CC}	–	6	10	mAdc
V_{BB} Supply current	$\overline{CS}$/WE = 5 V, T_A = 0°C	I_{BB}	–	30	45	mAdc

AC PROGRAMMING OPERATING CONDITIONS AND CHARACTERISTICS
(Full operating voltage and temperature unless otherwise noted.)

Characteristic	Symbol	Min	Max	Unit
Address Setup Time	t_{AS}	10	–	μs
$\overline{CS}$/WE Setup Time	t_{CSS}	10	–	μs
Data Setup Time	t_{DS}	10	–	μs
Address Hold Time	t_{AH}	1.0	–	μs
$\overline{CS}$/WE Hold Time	t_{CH}	0.5	–	μs
Data Hold Time	t_{DH}	1.0	–	μs
Chip Deselect to Output Float Delay	t_{DF}	0	120	ns
Program to Read Delay	t_{DPR}	–	10	μs
Program Pulse Width	t_{PW}	0.1	1.0	ms
Program Pulse Rise Time	t_{PR}	0.5	2.0	μs
Program Pulse Fall Time	t_{PF}	0.5	2.0	μs

MCM2708 • MCM27A08

PROGRAMMING OPERATION TIMING DIAGRAM

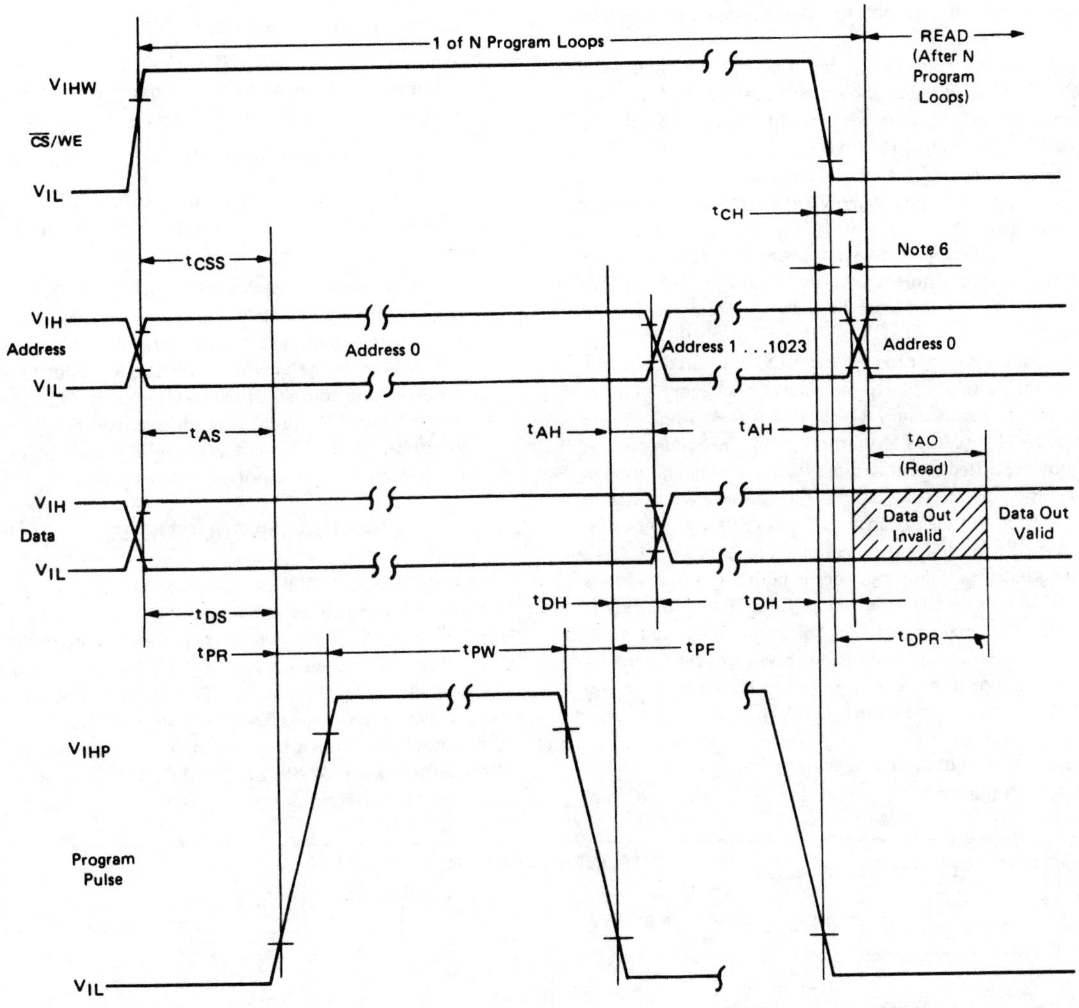

Note 6: The $\overline{CS}$/WE transition must occur after the Program Pulse transition and before the Address Transition.

MCM2708 • MCM27A08

PROGRAMMING INSTRUCTIONS

After the completion of an ERASE operation, every bit in the device is in the "1" state (represented by Output High). Data are entered by programming zeros (Output Low) into the required bits. The words are addressed the same way as in the READ operation. A programmed "0" can only be changed to a "1" by ultraviolet light erasure.

To set the memory up for programming mode, the $\overline{CS}$/WE input (Pin 20) should be raised to +12 V. Programming data is entered in 8-bit words through the data output terminals (D0 to D7).

Logic levels for the data lines and addresses and the supply voltages (V_{CC}, V_{DD}, V_{BB}) are the same as for the READ operation.

After address and data setup one program pulse per address is applied to the program input (Pin 18). A program loop is a full pass through all addresses. Total programming time, $T_{Ptotal} = N \times t_{PW} \geq 100$ ms. The required number of program loops (N) is a function of the program pulse width (t_{PW}), where: 0.1 ms $\leq t_{PW} \leq$ 1.0 ms; correspondingly N is: $100 \leq N \leq 1000$. There must be N successive loops through all 1024 addresses. It is not permitted to apply more than one program pulse in succession to the same address (i.e., N program pulses to an address and then change to the next address to be programmed). At the end of a program sequence the $\overline{CS}$/WE falling edge transition must occur before the first address transition, when changing from a PROGRAM to a READ cycle. The program pin (Pin 18) should be pulled down to V_{ILP} with an active device, because this pin sources a small amount of current (I_{IPL}) when $\overline{CS}$/WE is at V_{IHW} (12 V) and the program pulse is at V_{ILP}.

EXAMPLES FOR PROGRAMMING

Always use the $T_{Ptotal} = N \times t_{PW} \geq 100$ ms relationship.

1. All 8192 bits should be programmed with a 0.2 ms program pulse width.

   The minimum number of program loops:

   $$N = \frac{T_{Ptotal}}{t_{PW}} = \frac{100 \text{ ms}}{0.2 \text{ ms}} = 500.$$ One program loop consists of words 0 to 1023.

2. Words 0 to 200 and 300 to 700 are to be programmed. All other bits are "don't care". The program pulse width is 0.5 ms. The minimum number of program loops, $N = \frac{100}{0.5} = 200$. One program loop consists of words 0 to 1023. The data entered into the "don't care" bits should be all 1s.

3. Same requirements as example 2, but the EPROM is now to be updated to include data for words 850 to 880. The minimum number of program loops is the same as in the previous example, N = 200. One program loop consists of words 0 to 1023. The data entered into the "don't care" bits should be all 1s. Addresses 0 to 200 and 300 to 700 must be reprogrammed with their original data pattern.

ERASING INSTRUCTIONS

The MCM2708/27A08 can be erased by exposure to high intensity shortwave ultraviolet light, with a wavelength of 2537 Å. The recommended integrated dose (i.e., UV-intensity x exposure time) is 12.5 Ws/cm^2. As an example, using the "Model 30-000" UV-Eraser (Turner Designs, Mountain View, CA94043) the ERASE-time is 30 minutes. The lamps should be used without shortwave filters and the MCM2708/27A08 should be positioned about one inch away from the UV-tubes.

OUTLINE DIMENSIONS

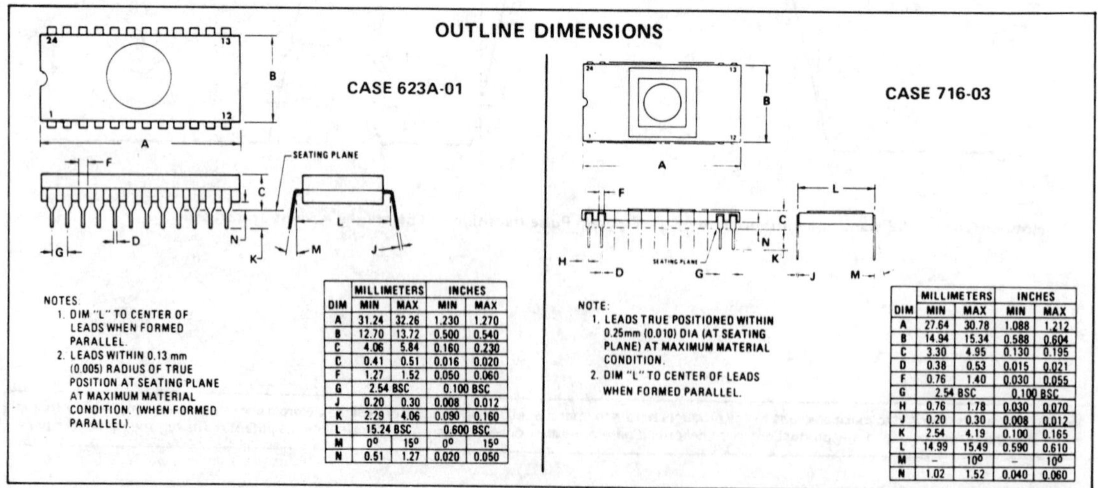

CASE 623A-01

DIM	MILLIMETERS		INCHES	
	MIN	MAX	MIN	MAX
A	31.24	32.26	1.230	1.270
B	12.70	13.72	0.500	0.540
C	4.06	5.84	0.160	0.230
C	0.41	0.51	0.016	0.020
F	1.27	1.52	0.050	0.060
G	2.54 BSC		0.100 BSC	
J	0.20	0.30	0.008	0.012
K	2.29	4.06	0.090	0.160
L	15.24 BSC		0.600 BSC	
M	0°	15°	0°	15°
N	0.51	1.27	0.020	0.050

CASE 716-03

DIM	MILLIMETERS		INCHES	
	MIN	MAX	MIN	MAX
A	27.64	30.78	1.088	1.212
B	14.94	15.34	0.588	0.604
C	3.30	4.95	0.130	0.195
D	0.38	0.53	0.015	0.021
F	0.76	1.40	0.030	0.055
G	2.54 BSC		0.100 BSC	
H	0.76	1.78	0.030	0.070
J	0.20	0.30	0.008	0.012
K	2.54	4.19	0.100	0.165
L	14.99	15.49	0.590	0.610
M	–	10°	–	10°
N	1.02	1.52	0.040	0.060

MOTOROLA Semiconductor Products Inc.

3501 ED BLUESTEIN BLVD., AUSTIN, TEXAS 78721 • A SUBSIDIARY OF MOTOROLA INC.

11133-2 PRINTED IN USA 1-79 IMPERIAL LITHO B76308 15M DS-9440-R2

MCM4116A

MOS

(N-CHANNEL)

16,384-BIT DYNAMIC RANDOM ACCESS MEMORY

16,384-BIT DYNAMIC RANDOM ACCESS MEMORY

The MCM4116A is a 16,384-bit, high-speed dynamic Random Access Memory designed for high-performance, low-cost applications in mainframe and buffer memories and peripheral storage. Organized as 16,384 one-bit words and fabricated using Motorola's highly reliable N-channel double-polysilicon technology, this device optimizes speed, power, and density tradeoffs.

By muliplexing row and column address inputs, the MCM4116A requires only seven address lines and permits packaging in Motorola's standard 16-pin dual in-line packages. This packaging technique allows high system density and is compatible with widely available automated test and insertion equipment. Complete address decoding is done on chip with address latches incorporated.

All inputs are TTL compatible, and the output is 3-state TTL compatible. The data output of the MCM4116A is controlled by the column address strobe and remains valid from access time until the column address strobe returns to the high state. This output scheme allows higher degrees of system design flexibility such as common input/output operation and two dimensional memory selection by decoding both row address and column address strobes.

The MCM4116A incorporates a one-transistor cell design and dynamic storage techniques, with each of the 128 row addresses requiring a refresh cycle every 2 milliseconds.

- Flexible Timing with Read-Modify-Write, RAS-Only Refresh, and Page-Mode Capability
- Industry Standard 16-Pin Package
- 16,384 × 1 Organization
- ±10% Tolerance on All Power Supplies
- All Inputs are Fully TTL Compatible
- Three-State Fully TTL-Compatible Output
- Common I/O Capability When Using "Early Write" Mode
- On-Chip Latches for Addresses and Data In
- Low Power Dissipation – 462 mW Active, 20 mW Standby (Max)
- Fast Access Time Options: 150 ns – MCM4116AL-15, AC-15
  200 ns – MCM4116AL-20, AC-20
  250 ns – MCM4116AL-25, AC-25
  300 ns – MCM4116AL-30, AC-30
- Easy Upgrade from 16-Pin 4K RAMs
- Pin Compatible with 2117, 2116, 6616, µPD416, and 4116

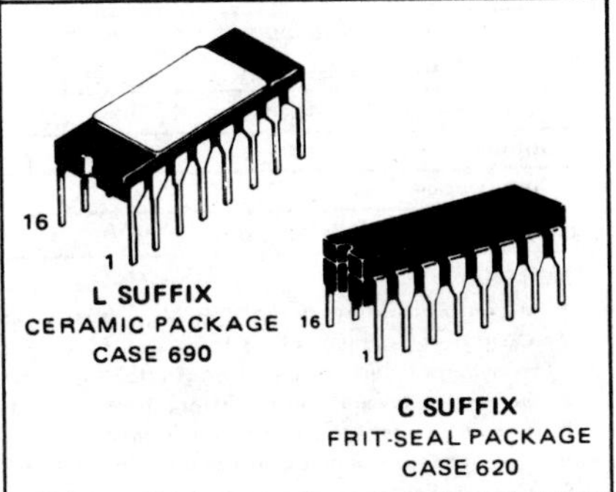

PIN ASSIGNMENT

Name	Pin	Pin	Name
V_{BB}	1	16	V_{SS}
D_{in}	2	15	$\overline{CAS}$
$\overline{WRITE}$	3	14	D_{out}
$\overline{RAS}$	4	13	A6
A0	5	12	A3
A2	6	11	A4
A1	7	10	A5
V_{DD}	8	9	V_{CC}

PIN NAMES

A0–A6	Address Inputs
$\overline{CAS}$	Column Address Strobe
D_{in}	Data In
D_{out}	Data Out
$\overline{RAS}$	Row Address Strobe
$\overline{WRITE}$	Read/Write Input
V_{BB}	Power (-5 V)
V_{CC}	Power (+5 V)
V_{DD}	Power (+12 V)
V_{SS}	Ground

ABSOLUTE MAXIMUM RATINGS (See Note 1)

Rating	Symbol	Value	Unit
Voltage on Any Pin Relative to V_{BB}	V_{in}, V_{out}	-0.5 to +20	Vdc
Operating Temperature Range	T_A	0 to +70	°C
Storage Temperature Range	T_{stg}	–65 to +150	°C
Power Dissipation	P_D	1.0	W
Data Out Current	I_{out}	50	mA

NOTE 1: Permanent device damage may occur if ABSOLUTE MAXIMUM RATINGS are exceeded. Functional operation should be restricted to RECOMMENDED OPERATING CONDITIONS. Exposure to higher than recommended voltages for extended periods of time could affect device reliability.

This device contains circuitry to protect the inputs against damage due to high static voltages or electric fields; however, it is advised that normal precautions be taken to avoid application of any voltage higher than maximum rated voltages to this high impedance circuit.

DC OPERATING CONDITIONS AND CHARACTERISTICS

(Full operating voltage and temperature range unless otherwise noted.)

RECOMMENDED OPERATING CONDITIONS

Parameter	Symbol	Min	Typ	Max	Unit	Notes
Supply Voltage	V_{DD}	10.8	12.0	13.2	Vdc	1
	V_{CC}	4.5	5.0	5.5	Vdc	1, 2
	V_{SS}	0	0	0	Vdc	1
	V_{BB}	-4.5	-5.0	-5.5	Vdc	1
Logic 1 Voltage, $\overline{RAS}$, $\overline{CAS}$, $\overline{WRITE}$	V_{IHC}	2.7	–	7.0	Vdc	1
Logic 1 Voltage, all inputs except $\overline{RAS}$, $\overline{CAS}$, $\overline{WRITE}$	V_{IH}	2.4	–	7.0	Vdc	1
Logic 0 Voltage, all inputs	V_{IL}	-1.0	–	0.8	Vdc	1

DC CHARACTERISTICS (V_{DD} = 12 V ± 10%, V_{CC} = 5.0 V ± 10%, V_{BB} = -5.0 V ± 10%, V_{SS} = 0 V, T_A = 0 to 70°C.)

Characteristic	Symbol	Min	Max	Units	Notes
Average V_{DD} Power Supply Current	I_{DD1}	–	35	mA	4
V_{CC} Power Supply Current	I_{CC}	–	–	mA	5
Average V_{BB} Power Supply Current	$I_{BB1,3}$	–	200	μA	
Standby V_{BB} Power Supply Current	I_{BB2}	–	100	μA	
Standby V_{DD} Power Supply Current	I_{DD2}	–	1.5	mA	6
Average V_{DD} Power Supply Current during "$\overline{RAS}$ only" cycles	I_{DD3}	–	27	mA	4
Input Leakage Current (any input)	$I_{I(L)}$	–	10	μA	
Output Leakage Current	$I_{O(L)}$	–	10	μA	6, 7
Output Logic 1 Voltage @ I_{out} = -5 mA	V_{OH}	2.4	–	Vdc	2
Output Logic 0 Voltage @ I_{out} = 4.2 mA	V_{OL}	–	0.4	Vdc	

NOTES:

1. All voltages referenced to V_{SS}. V_{BB} must be applied before and removed after other supply voltages.
2. Output voltage will swing from V_{SS} to V_{CC} under open circuit conditions. For purposes of maintaining data in power-down mode, V_{CC} may be reduced to V_{SS} without affecting refresh operations. V_{OH}(min) specification is not guaranteed in this mode.
3. Several cycles are required after power-up before proper device operation is achieved. Any 8 cycles which perform refresh are adequate.
4. Current is proportional to cycle rate; maximum current is measured at the fastest cycle rate.
5. I_{CC} depends upon output loading. The V_{CC} supply is connected to the output buffer only.
6. Output is disabled (open-circuit) and $\overline{RAS}$ and $\overline{CAS}$ are both at a logic 1.
7. 0 V ≤ V_{out} ≤ +5.5 V.
8. Capacitance measured with a Boonton Meter or effective capacitance calculated from the equation: $C = \frac{I\Delta_t}{\Delta V}$

BLOCK DIAGRAM

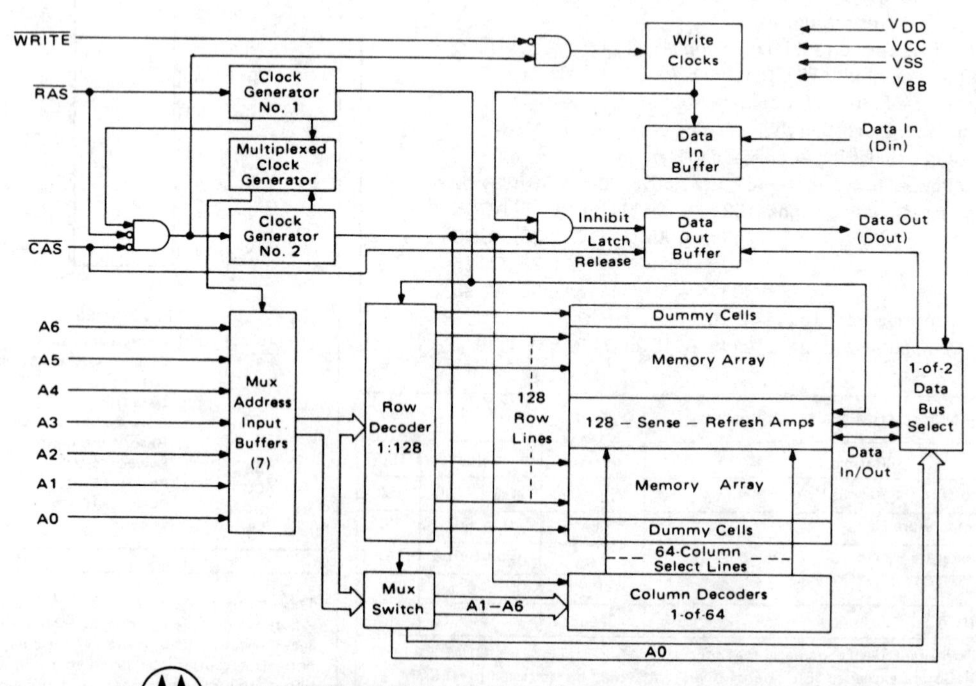

AC OPERATING CONDITIONS AND CHARACTERISTICS (See Notes 3, 9, 14)
(Read, Write, and Read-Modify-Write Cycles)

RECOMMENDED AC OPERATING CONDITIONS
(V_{DD} = 12 V ± 10%, V_{CC} = 5.0 V ± 10%, V_{BB} = −5.0 V ± 10%, V_{SS} = 0 V, T_A = 0 to 70°C.)

Parameter	Symbol	MCM4116A-15		MCM4116A-20		MCM4116A-25		MCM4116A-30		Units	Notes
		Min	Max	Min	Max	Min	Max	Min	Max		
Random Read or Write Cycle Time	t_{RC}	375	–	375	–	410	–	480	–	ns	
Read Write Cycle Time	t_{RWC}	375	–	375	–	515	–	660	–	ns	
Access Time from Row Address Strobe	t_{RAC}	–	150	–	200	–	250	–	300	ns	10, 12
Access Time from Column Address Strobe	t_{CAC}	–	90	–	135	–	165	–	200	ns	11, 12
Output Buffer and Turn-off Delay	t_{OFF}	0	50	0	50	0	60	0	60	ns	17
Row Address Strobe Precharge Time	t_{RP}	100	–	120	–	150	–	180	–	ns	
Row Address Strobe Pulse Width	t_{RAS}	150	10,000	200	10,000	250	10,000	300	10,000	ns	
Column Address Strobe Pulse Width	t_{CAS}	90	10,000	135	10,000	165	10,000	200	10,000	ns	
Row to Column Strobe Lead Time	t_{RCD}	20	60	25	65	35	85	60	100	ns	13
Row Address Setup Time	t_{ASR}	0	–	0	–	0	–	0	–	ns	
Row Address Hold Time	t_{RAH}	20	–	25	–	35	–	60	–	ns	
Column Address Setup Time	t_{ASC}	−10	–	−10	–	−10	–	−10	–	ns	
Column Address Hold Time	t_{CAH}	45	–	55	–	75	–	100	–	ns	
Column Address Hold Time Referenced to $\overline{RAS}$	t_{AR}	105	–	120	–	160	–	200	–	ns	
Transition Time (Rise and Fall)	t_T	3.0	35	3.0	50	3.0	50	3.0	50	ns	14
Read Command Setup Time	t_{RCS}	0	–	0	–	0	–	0	–	ns	
Read Command Hold Time	t_{RCH}	0	–	0	–	0	–	0	–	ns	
Write Command Hold Time	t_{WCH}	45	–	55	–	75	–	100	–	ns	
Write Command Hold Time Referenced to $\overline{RAS}$	t_{WCR}	105	–	120	–	160	–	200	–	ns	
Write Command Pulse Width	t_{WP}	45	–	55	–	75	–	100	–	ns	
Write Command to Row Strobe Lead Time	t_{RWL}	60	–	80	–	100	–	180	–	ns	
Write Command to Column Strobe Lead Time	t_{CWL}	60	–	80	–	100	–	180	–	ns	
Data in Setup Time	t_{DS}	0	–	0	–	0	–	0	–	ns	15
Data in Hold Time	t_{DH}	45	–	55	–	75	–	100	–	ns	15
Data in Hold Time Referenced to $\overline{RAS}$	t_{DHR}	105	–	120	–	160	–	200	–	ns	
Column to Row Strobe Precharge Time	t_{CRP}	−20	–	−20	–	−20	–	−20	–	ns	
$\overline{RAS}$ Hold Time	t_{RSH}	100	–	135	–	165	–	200	–	ns	
Refresh Period	t_{RFSH}	–	2.0	–	2.0	–	2.0	–	2.0	ms	
$\overline{WRITE}$ Command Setup Time	t_{WCS}	−20	–	−20	–	−20	–	−20	–	ns	
$\overline{CAS}$ to $\overline{WRITE}$ Delay	t_{CWD}	70	–	95	–	125	–	180	–	ns	16
$\overline{RAS}$ to $\overline{WRITE}$ Delay	t_{RWD}	120	–	160	–	210	–	280	–	ns	16
$\overline{CAS}$ Precharge Time (Page mode cycle only)	t_{CP}	60	–	80	–	100	–	100	–	ns	
Page Mode Cycle Time	t_{PC}	170	–	225	–	275	–	325	–	ns	
$\overline{CAS}$ Hold Time	t_{CSH}	150	–	200	–	250	–	300	–	ns	

Parameter	Symbol	Typ	Max	Units	Notes
Input Capacitance (A0–A5), D_{in}	C_{I1}	4.0	5.0	pF	9
Input Capacitance $\overline{RAS}$, $\overline{CAS}$, $\overline{WRITE}$	C_{I2}	8.0	10	pF	9
Output Capacitance (D_{out})	C_o	5.0	7.0	pF	7, 9

NOTES: (continued)

9. AC measurements assume t_T = 5.0 ns.
10. Assumes that $t_{RCD} + t_T \leq t_{RCD}$ (max).
11. Assumes that $t_{RCD} + t_T \geq t_{RCD}$ (max).
12. Measured with a load circuit equivalent to 2 TTL loads and 100 pF.
13. Operation within the t_{RCD} (max) limit ensures that t_{RAC} (max) can be met. t_{RCD} (max) is specified as a reference point only; if t_{RCD} is greater than the specified t_{RCD} (max) limit, then access time is controlled exclusively by t_{CAC}.
14. V_{IHC} (min) or V_{IH} (min) and V_{IL} (max) are reference levels for measuring timing of input signals. Also, transistion times are measured between V_{IHC} or V_{IH} and V_{IL}.
15. These parameters are referenced to $\overline{CAS}$ leading edge in random write cycles and to $\overline{WRITE}$ leading edge in delayed write or read-modify-write cycles.
16. t_{WCS}, t_{CWD} and t_{RWD} are not restrictive operating parameters. They are included in the data sheet as electrical characteristics only: If $t_{WCS} \geq t_{WCS}$ (min), the cycle is an early write cycle and the data out pin will remain open circuit (high impedance) throughout the entire cycle; If $t_{CWD} \geq t_{CWD}$ (min) and $t_{RWD} \geq t_{RWD}$ (min), the cycle is a read-write cycle and the data out will contain data read from the selected cell; If neither of the above sets of conditions is satisfied the condition of the data out (at access time) is indeterminate.
17. Assumes that t_{CRP} > 50 ns.

MCM4116A

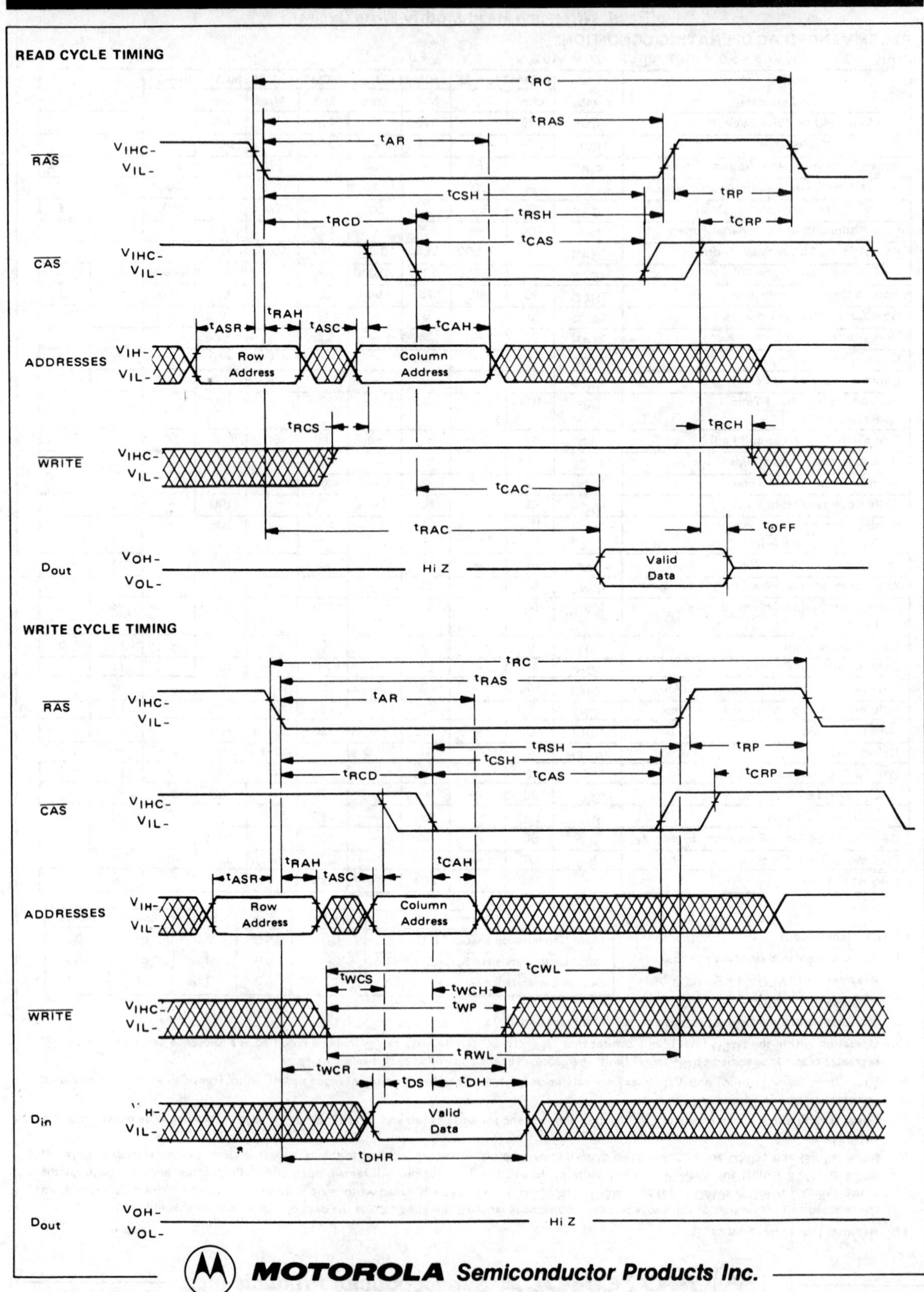
READ CYCLE TIMING
tRC
tRAS
tAR
RAS
VIHC-
VIL-
tCSH
tRP
tRSH
tRCD
tCRP
tCAS
CAS
tASR
tRAH
tASC
tCAH
ADDRESSES
VIH-
VIL-
Row Address
Column Address
tRCS
tRCH
WRITE
tCAC
tRAC
tOFF
Dout
VOH-
VOL-
Hi Z
Valid Data
WRITE CYCLE TIMING
tCWL
tWCS
tWCH
tWP
tRWL
tWCR
tDS
tDH
Din
tDHR

MCM4116A

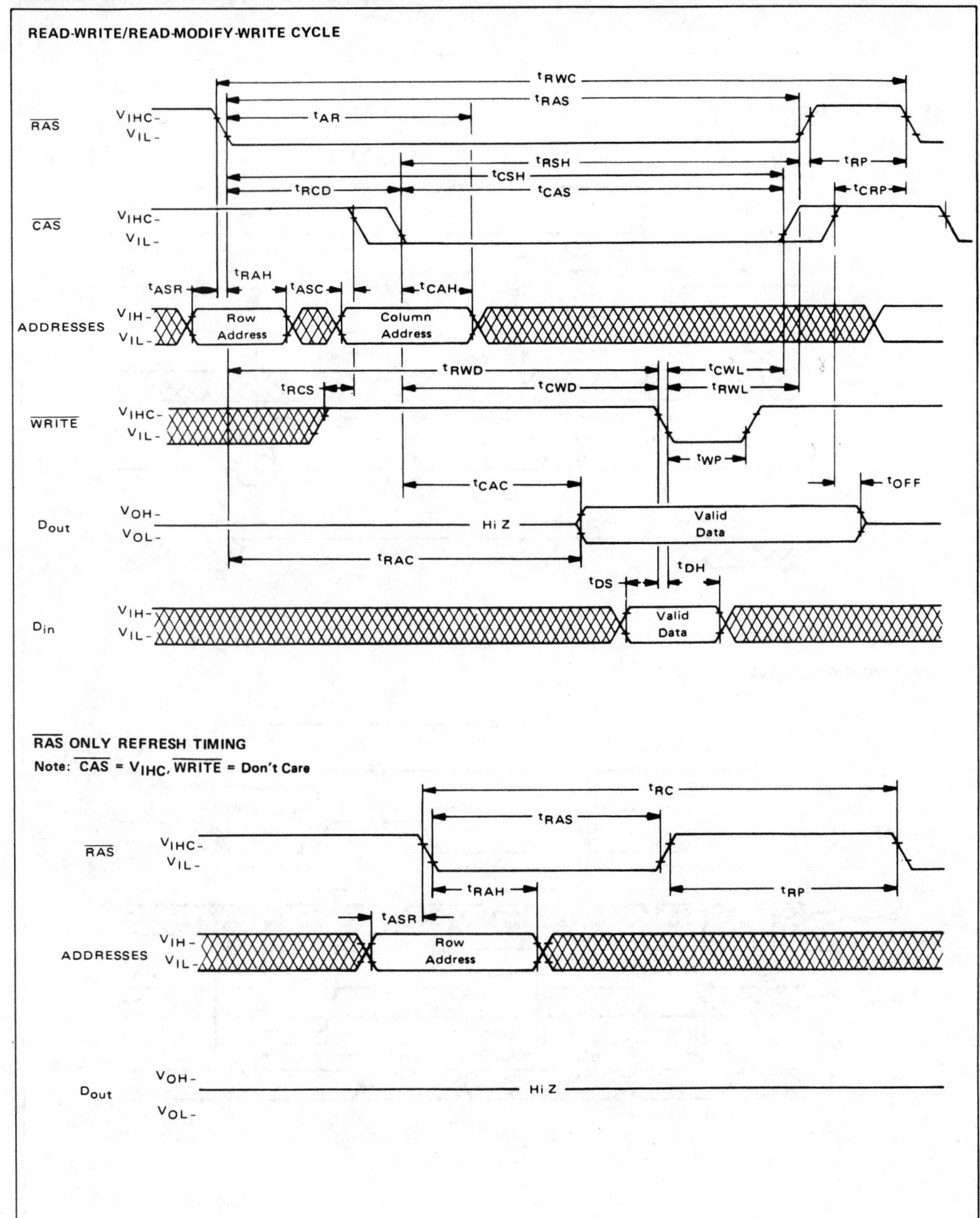
READ-WRITE/READ-MODIFY-WRITE CYCLE
tRWC
tRAS
tAR
RAS
VIHC-
VIL-
tRSH
tCSH
tRCD
tCAS
tRP
tCRP
CAS
VIHC-
VIL-
tASR
tRAH
tASC
tCAH
ADDRESSES
VIH-
VIL-
Row Address
Column Address
tRWD
tCWD
tRCS
tCWL
tRWL
WRITE
VIHC-
VIL-
tWP
tCAC
tOFF
Dout
VOH-
VOL-
Hi Z
Valid Data
tRAC
tDS
tDH
Din
VIH-
VIL-
Valid Data
RAS ONLY REFRESH TIMING
Note: CAS = VIHC, WRITE = Don't Care
tRC
tRAS
RAS
VIHC-
VIL-
tRAH
tRP
tASR
ADDRESSES
VIH-
VIL-
Row Address
Dout
VOH-
VOL-
Hi Z

MCM4116A

PAGE MODE READ CYCLE

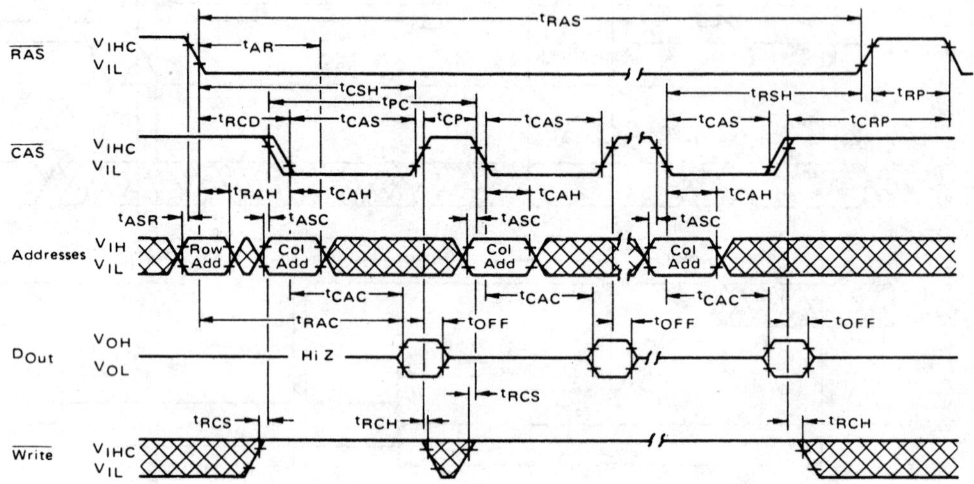

PAGE MODE WRITE CYCLE

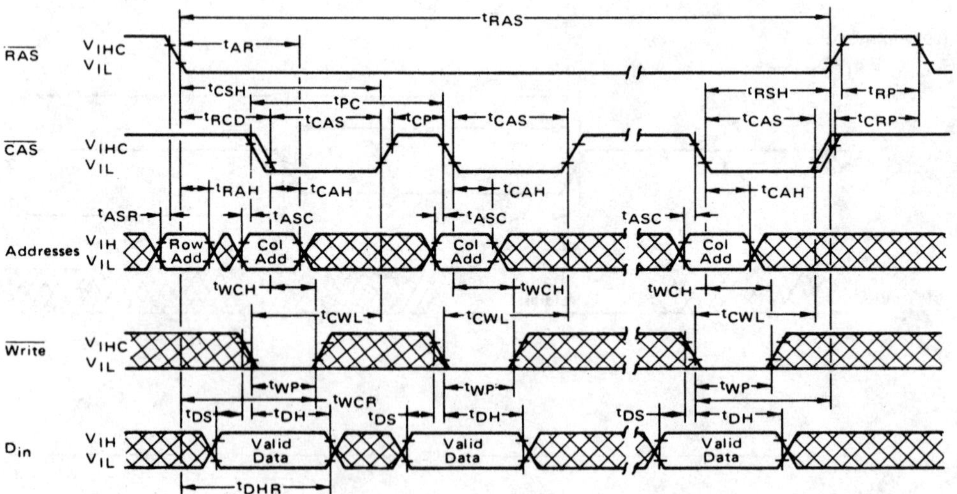

MCM4116A

OUTLINE DRAWINGS

CASE 620-06

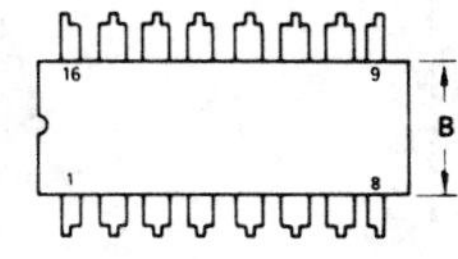

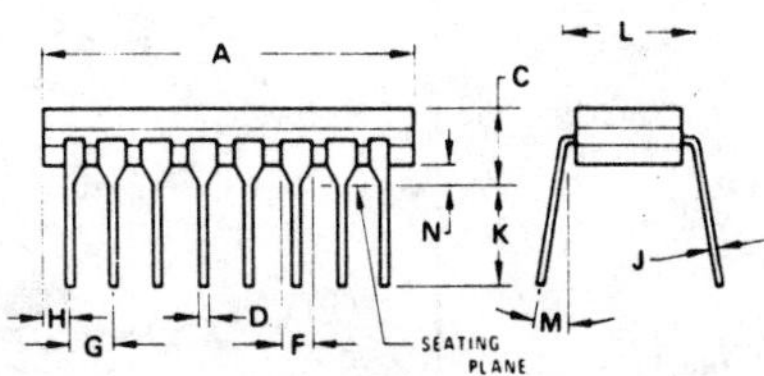

DIM	MILLIMETERS MIN	MILLIMETERS MAX	INCHES MIN	INCHES MAX
A	19.05	19.94	0.750	0.785
B	6.22	7.11	0.245	0.280
C	3.94	5.08	0.155	0.200
D	0.38	0.51	0.015	0.020
F	0.89	1.65	0.035	0.065
G	2.54 BSC		0.100 BSC	
H	0.38	1.52	0.015	0.060
J	0.20	0.30	0.008	0.012
K	3.18	5.08	0.125	0.200
L	7.37	8.13	0.290	0.320
M	–	15°	–	15°
N	0.51	1.27	0.020	0.050

1. LEADS WITHIN 0.13 mm (0.005) RADIUS OF TRUE POSITION AT SEATING PLANE AT MAXIMUM MATERIAL CONDITION.
2. PACKAGE INDEX: NOTCH IN LEAD NOTCH IN CERAMIC OR INK DOT.
3. DIM "A" AND "B" (620-06) DO NOT INCLUDE GLASS RUN-OUT.
4. DIM "L" TO INSIDE OF LEADS (MEASURED 0.51 mm (0.020) BELOW BODY).

CASE 690-09

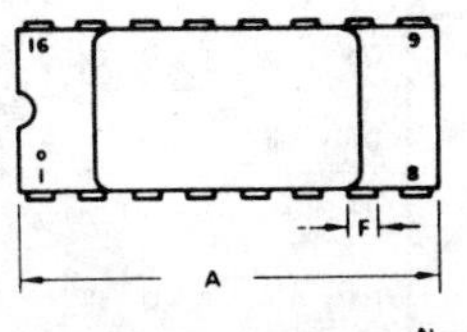

NOTE:
1. LEADS WITHIN 0.13 mm (0.005) RADIUS OF TRUE POSITION AT SEATING PLANE AT MAXIMUM MATERIAL CONDITION.

DIM	MILLIMETERS MIN	MILLIMETERS MAX	INCHES MIN	INCHES MAX
A	20.07	20.57	0.790	0.810
C	2.67	3.94	0.105	0.155
D	0.38	0.53	0.015	0.021
F	1.22	1.52	0.048	0.060
G	2.54 BSC		0.100 BSC	
H	0.76	1.78	0.030	0.070
J	0.20	0.31	0.008	0.012
K	3.05	4.83	0.120	0.190
L	7.62 BSC		0.300 BSC	
M	–	10°	–	10°
N	0.64	1.52	0.025	0.060

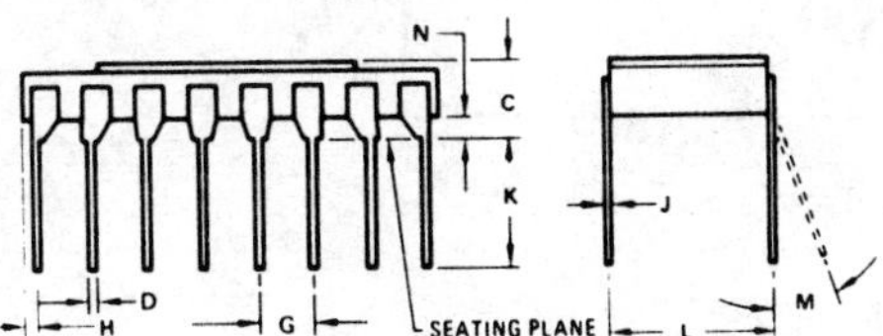

MCM4116A

MCM4116A BIT ADDRESS MAP

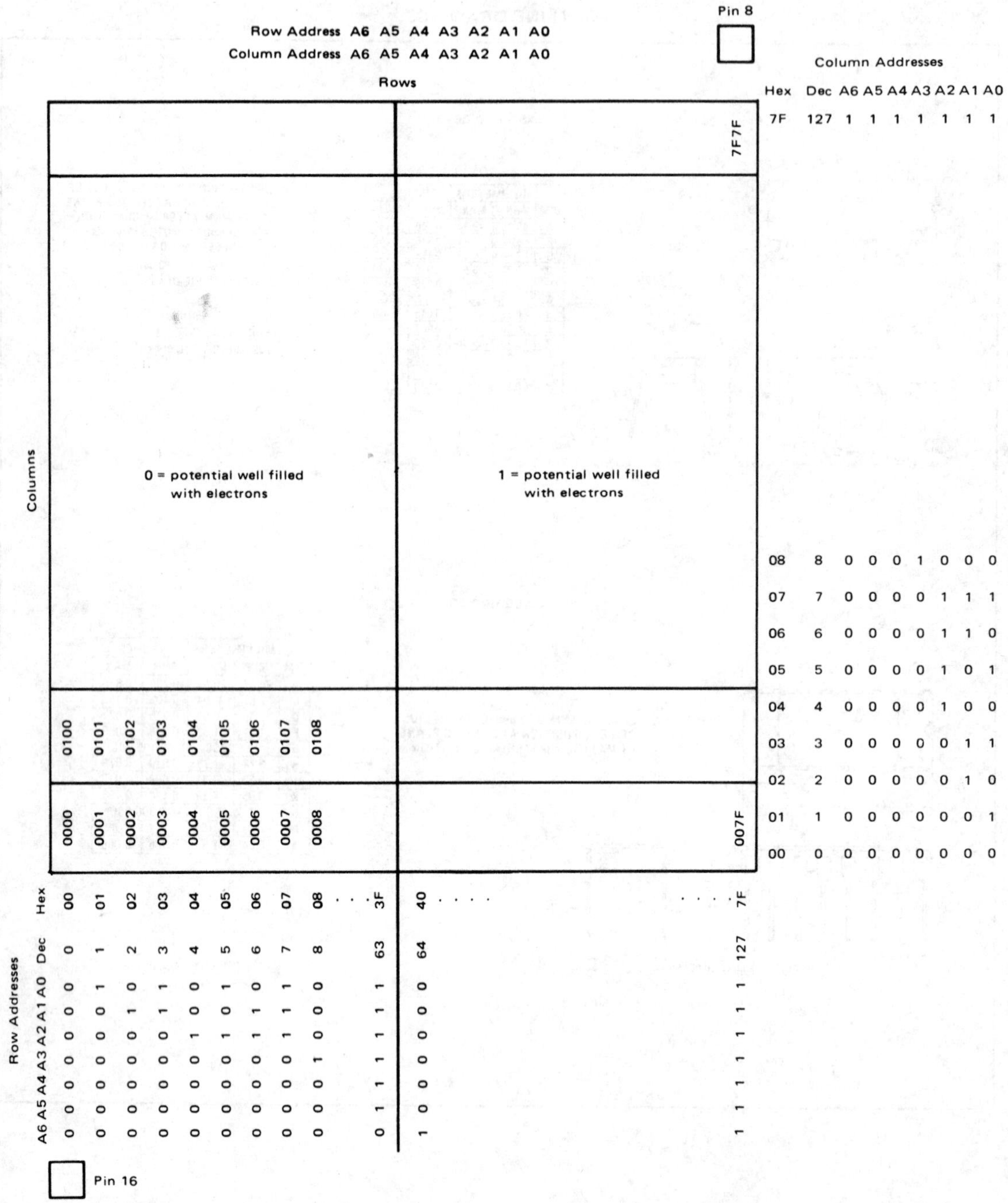

Row Address A6 A5 A4 A3 A2 A1 A0
Column Address A6 A5 A4 A3 A2 A1 A0

Pin 8

Rows

Columns

7F7F

0 = potential well filled with electrons

1 = potential well filled with electrons

0100 0101 0102 0103 0104 0105 0106 0107 0108

0000 0001 0002 0003 0004 0005 0006 0007 0008 007F

Column Addresses

Hex	Dec	A6	A5	A4	A3	A2	A1	A0
7F	127	1	1	1	1	1	1	1
08	8	0	0	0	1	0	0	0
07	7	0	0	0	0	1	1	1
06	6	0	0	0	0	1	1	0
05	5	0	0	0	0	1	0	1
04	4	0	0	0	0	1	0	0
03	3	0	0	0	0	0	1	1
02	2	0	0	0	0	0	1	0
01	1	0	0	0	0	0	0	1
00	0	0	0	0	0	0	0	0

Row Addresses

Hex	Dec	A0	A1	A2	A3	A4	A5	A6
00	0	0	0	0	0	0	0	0
01	1	1	0	0	0	0	0	0
02	2	0	1	0	0	0	0	0
03	3	1	1	0	0	0	0	0
04	4	0	0	1	0	0	0	0
05	5	1	0	1	0	0	0	0
06	6	0	1	1	0	0	0	0
07	7	1	1	1	0	0	0	0
08	8	0	0	0	1	0	0	0
3F	63	1	1	1	1	1	1	0
40	64	0	0	0	0	0	0	1
7F	127	1	1	1	1	1	1	1

Pin 16

MOTOROLA Semiconductor Products Inc.
3501 ED BLUESTEIN BLVD., AUSTIN, TEXAS 78721 • A SUBSIDIARY OF MOTOROLA INC.

11500-3 PRINTED IN USA 11-78 IMPERIAL LITHO B74929 15M DS-9513-R1

MCM68A30A
MCM68B30A

1024 X 8-BIT READ ONLY MEMORY

The MCM68A30A/MCM68B30A are mask-programmable byte-organized memories designed for use in bus-organized systems. They are fabricated with N-channel silicon-gate technology. For ease of use, the device operates from a single power supply, has compatibility with TTL and DTL, and needs no clocks or refreshing because of static operation.

The memory is compatible with the M6800 Microcomputer Family, providing read only storage in byte increments. Memory expansion is provided through multiple Chip Select inputs. The active level of the Chip Select inputs and the memory content are defined by the customer.

- Organized as 1024 Bytes of 8 Bits
- Static Operation
- Three-State Data Output
- Four Chip Select Inputs (Programmable)
- Single ±10% 5-Volt Power Supply
- TTL Compatible
- Maximum Access Time = 350 ns – MCM68A30A
  250 ns – MCM68B30A

MOS

(N-CHANNEL, SILICON-GATE)

1024 X 8-BIT
READ ONLY MEMORY

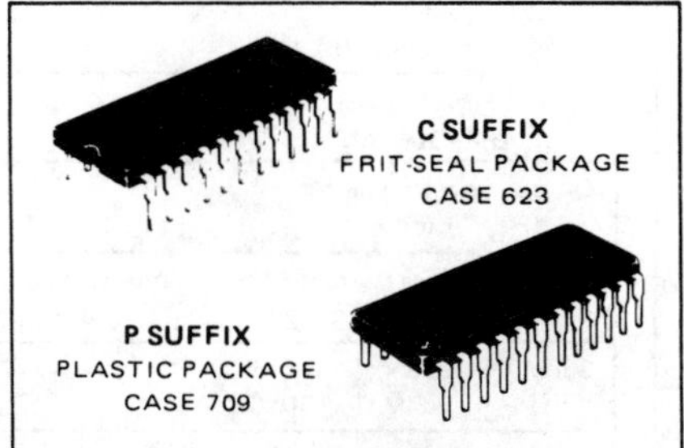

ABSOLUTE MAXIMUM RATINGS (See Note 1)

Rating	Symbol	Value	Unit
Supply Voltage	V_{CC}	-0.3 to +7.0	Vdc
Input Voltage	V_{in}	-0.3 to +7.0	Vdc
Operating Temperature Range	T_A	0 to +70	°C
Storage Temperature Range	T_{stg}	-65 to +150	°C

NOTE 1: Permanent device damage may occur if ABSOLUTE MAXIMUM RATINGS are exceeded. Functional operation should be restricted to RECOMMENDED OPERATING CONDITIONS. Exposure to higher than recommended voltages for extended periods of time could affect device reliability.

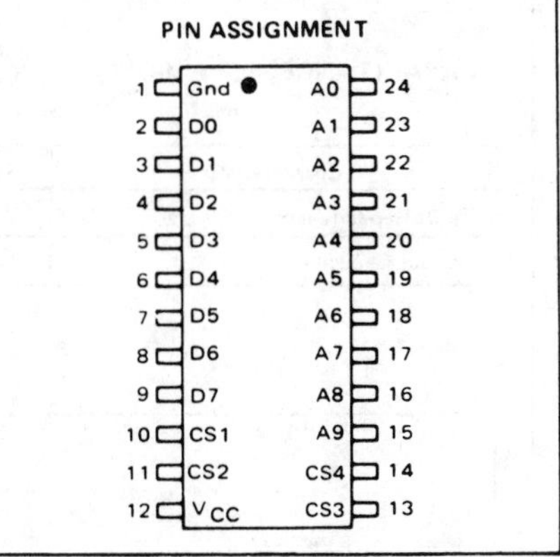

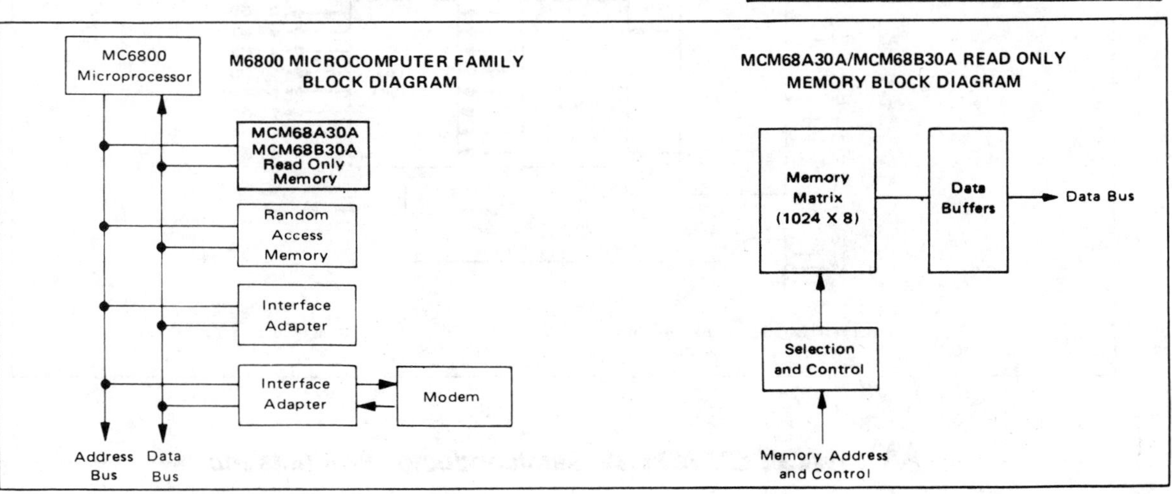

 DS9456 R1

DC OPERATING CONDITIONS AND CHARACTERISTICS

(Full operating voltage and temperature range unless otherwise noted.)

RECOMMENDED DC OPERATING CONDITIONS

Parameter	Symbol	Min	Nom	Max	Unit
Supply Voltage	V_{CC}	4.5	5.0	5.5	Vdc
Input High Voltage	V_{IH}	2.0	–	5.5	Vdc
Input Low Voltage	V_{IL}	-0.3	–	0.8	Vdc

DC CHARACTERISTICS

Characteristic	Symbol	Min	Typ	Max	Unit
Input Current (V_{in} = 0 to 5.5 V)	I_{in}	–	–	2.5	μAdc
Output High Voltage (I_{OH} = −205μA)	V_{OH}	2.4	–	–	Vdc
Output Low Voltage (I_{OL} = 1.6 mA)	V_{OL}	–	–	0.4	Vdc
Output Leakage Current (Three State) (CS = 0.8 V or $\overline{CS}$ = 2.0 V, V_{out} = 0.4 V to 2.4 V)	I_{LO}	–	–	10	μAdc
Supply Current (V_{CC} = 5.5 V, T_A = 0°C)	I_{CC}	–	–	130	mAdc

CAPACITANCE (f = 1.0 MHz, T_A = 25°C, periodically sampled rather than 100% tested.)

Characteristic	Symbol	Max	Unit
Input Capacitance	C_{in}	7.5	pF
Output Capacitance	C_{out}	12.5	pF

This device contains circuitry to protect the inputs against damage due to high static voltages or electric fields; however, it is advised that normal precautions be taken to avoid application of any voltage higher than maximum rated voltages to this high-impedance circuit.

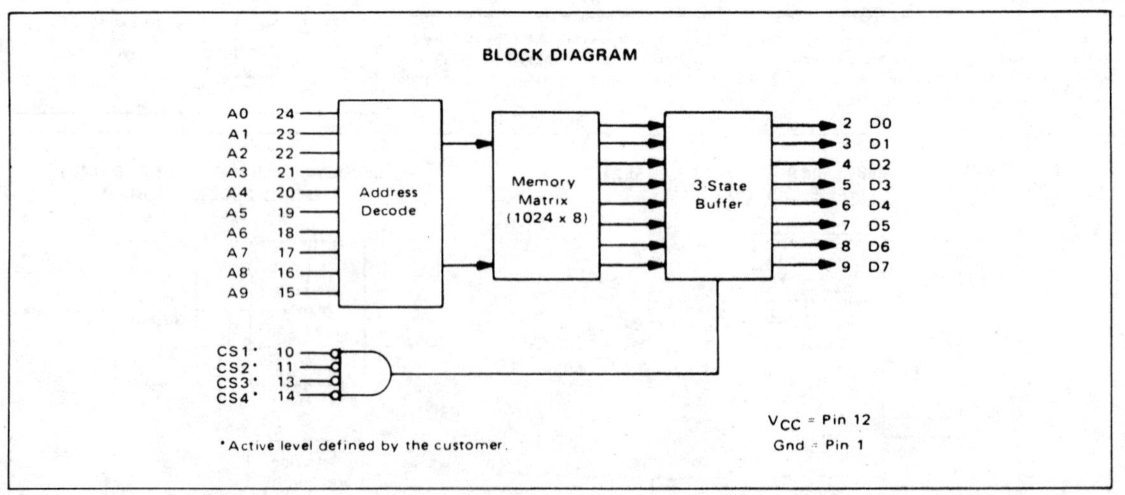

MCM68A30A • MCM68B30A

AC OPERATING CONDITIONS AND CHARACTERISTICS

(Full operating voltage and temperature unless otherwise noted.)

(All timing with $t_r = t_f = 20$ ns, Load of Figure 1)

Characteristic	Symbol	MCM68A30AL		MCM68B30AL		Unit
		Min	Max	Min	Max	
Cycle Time	t_{cyc}	350	–	250	–	ns
Access Time	t_{acc}	–	350	–	250	ns
Chip Select to Output Delay	t_{CO}	–	150	–	125	ns
Data Hold from Address	t_{DHA}	10	–	10	–	ns
Data Hold from Deselection	t_{DHD}	10	150	10	125	ns

FIGURE 1 – AC TEST LOAD

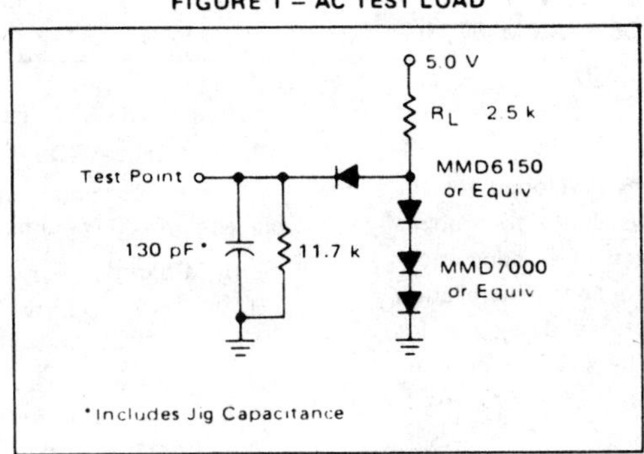

TIMING DIAGRAM

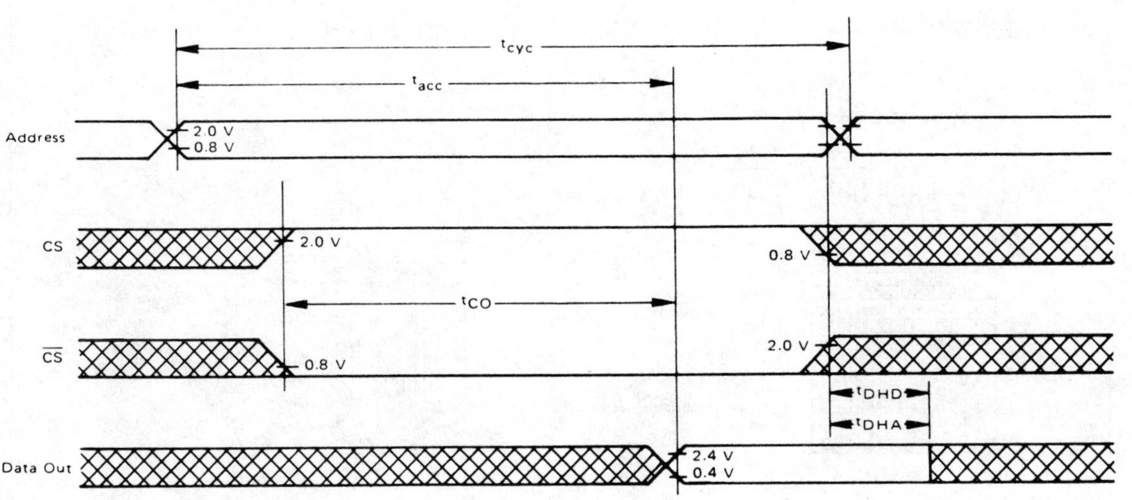

MCM68A30A • MCM68B30A

CUSTOM PROGRAMMING

By the programming of a single photomask for the MCM68A30A/MCM68B30A, the customer may specify the content of the memory and the method of enabling the outputs.

Information on the general options of the MCM68A30A/MCM68B30A should be submitted on an Organizational Data form such as that shown in Figure 3. ("No Connect" must always be the highest order Chip Select pin(s).)

Information for custom memory content may be sent to Motorola in one of four forms (shown in order of preference):

1. Paper tape output of the Motorola M6800 Software.
2. Hexadecimal coding using IBM Punch Cards.
3. EPROM (MCM2708, MCM27A08, or MCM68708).
4. Hand-punched paper tape (Figure 3).

PAPER TAPE

Included in the software packages developed for the M6800 Microcomputer Family is the ability to produce a paper tape output for computerized mask generation. The assembler directives are used to control allocation of memory, to assign values for stored data, and for controlling the assembly process. The paper tape must specify the full 1024 bytes.

FIGURE 2 – BINARY TO HEXADECIMAL CONVERSION

Binary Data				Hexadecimal Character
0	0	0	0	0
0	0	0	1	1
0	0	1	0	2
0	0	1	1	3
0	1	0	0	4
0	1	0	1	5
0	1	1	0	6
0	1	1	1	7
1	0	0	0	8
1	0	0	1	9
1	0	1	0	A
1	0	1	1	B
1	1	0	0	C
1	1	0	1	D
1	1	1	0	E
1	1	1	1	F

IBM PUNCH CARDS

The hexadecimal equivalent (from Figure 2) may be placed on 80 column IBM punch cards as follows:

Step	Column	
1	12	Byte "0" Hexadecimal equivalent for outputs D7 thru D4 (D7 = M.S.B.)
2	13	Byte "0" Hexadecimal equivalent for outputs D3 thru D0 (D3 = M.S.B.)
3	14-75	Alternate steps 1 and 2 for consecutive bytes.
4	77-80	Card number (starting 0001)

PACKAGE DIMENSIONS

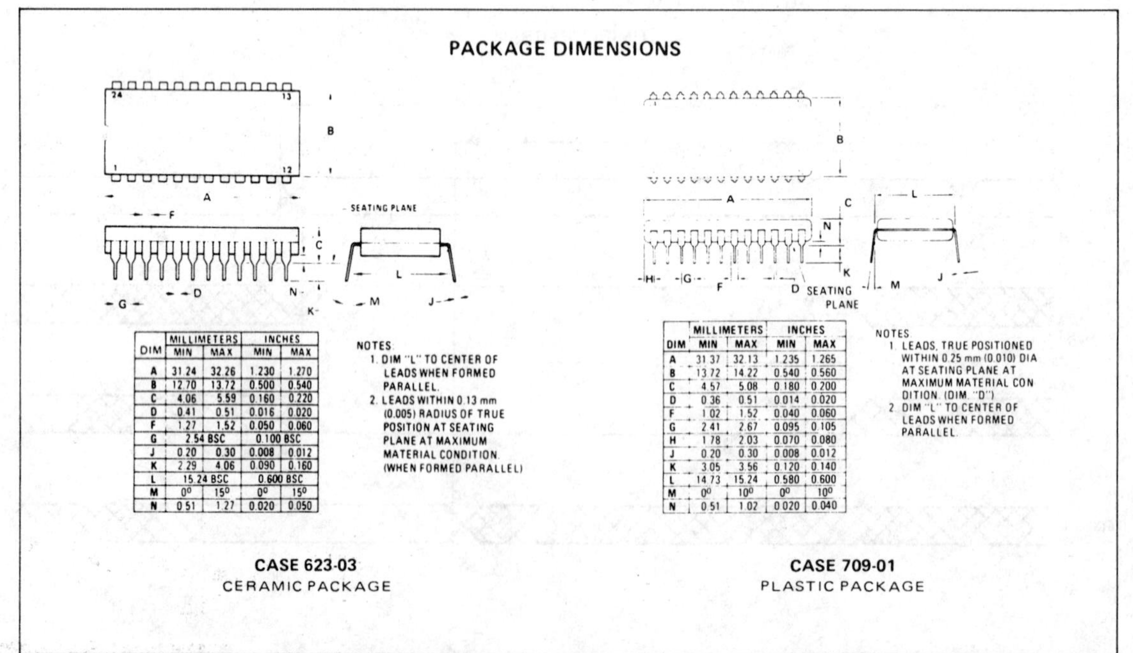

DIM	MILLIMETERS MIN	MILLIMETERS MAX	INCHES MIN	INCHES MAX
A	31.24	32.26	1.230	1.270
B	12.70	13.72	0.500	0.540
C	4.06	5.59	0.160	0.220
D	0.41	0.51	0.016	0.020
F	1.27	1.52	0.050	0.060
G	2.54 BSC		0.100 BSC	
J	0.20	0.30	0.008	0.012
K	2.29	4.06	0.090	0.160
L	15.24 BSC		0.600 BSC	
M	0°	15°	0°	15°
N	0.51	1.27	0.020	0.050

NOTES:
1. DIM "L" TO CENTER OF LEADS WHEN FORMED PARALLEL.
2. LEADS WITHIN 0.13 mm (0.005) RADIUS OF TRUE POSITION AT SEATING PLANE AT MAXIMUM MATERIAL CONDITION. (WHEN FORMED PARALLEL)

CASE 623-03
CERAMIC PACKAGE

DIM	MILLIMETERS MIN	MILLIMETERS MAX	INCHES MIN	INCHES MAX
A	31.37	32.13	1.235	1.265
B	13.72	14.22	0.540	0.560
C	4.57	5.08	0.180	0.200
D	0.36	0.51	0.014	0.020
F	1.02	1.52	0.040	0.060
G	2.41	2.67	0.095	0.105
H	1.78	2.03	0.070	0.080
J	0.20	0.30	0.008	0.012
K	3.05	3.56	0.120	0.140
L	14.73	15.24	0.580	0.600
M	0°	10°	0°	10°
N	0.51	1.02	0.020	0.040

NOTES:
1. LEADS, TRUE POSITIONED WITHIN 0.25 mm (0.010) DIA AT SEATING PLANE AT MAXIMUM MATERIAL CONDITION. (DIM. "D")
2. DIM "L" TO CENTER OF LEADS WHEN FORMED PARALLEL.

CASE 709-01
PLASTIC PACKAGE

FIGURE 3 – HAND-PUNCHED PAPER TAPE FORMAT

Frames	
Leader	Blank Tape
1 to M	Allowed for customer use (M ≤ 64)
M + 1, M + 2	CR; LF (Carriage Return; Line Feed)
M + 3 to M + 66	First line of pattern information (64 hex figures per line)
M + 67, M + 68	CR; LF
M + 69 to M + 2112	Remaining 31 lines of hex figures, each line followed by a Carriage Return and Line Feed
Blank Tape	

Frames 1 to M are left to the customer for internal identification, where M ≤ 64. Any combination of alphanumerics may be used. This information is terminated with a Carriage Return and Line Feed, delineating the start of data entry. (Note that the tape cannot begin with a CR and/or LF, or the customer identification will be assumed to be programming data.)

Option A (1024 x 8)

Frame M + 3 contains the hexadecimal equivalent of bits D7 thru D4 of byte 0. Frame M + 4 contains bits D3 thru D0. These two hex figures together program byte 0. Likewise, frames M + 5 and M + 6 program byte 1, while M + 7 and M + 8 program byte 2. Frames M + 3 to M + 66 comprise the first line of the printout and program, in sequence, the first 32 bytes of storage. The line is terminated with a CR and LF.

Option B (2048 x 4)

Frame M + 3 contains the hexadecimal equivalent of byte 0, bits D3 thru D0. Frame M + 4 contains byte 1, frame M + 5 byte 2, and so on. Frames M + 3 to M + 66 sequentially program bytes 0 to 31 (the first 32 bytes). The line is terminated with a CR and LF.

Both Options

The remaining 31 lines of data are punched in sequence using the same format, each line terminated with a CR and LF. The total 32 lines of data contain 32 x 64 or 2048 characters. Since each character programs 4 bits of information, a full 8192 bits are programmed.

As an example, a printout of the punched tape for Figure 13 would read as shown in Figure 10 (a CR and LF is implicit at the end of each line).

FIGURE 4 – FORMAT FOR PROGRAMMING GENERAL OPTIONS

ORGANIZATIONAL DATA
MCM68A30A/68B30A MOS READ ONLY MEMORY

Customer:

Company ______________________

Part No. ______________________

Originator ______________________

Phone No. ______________________

Motorola Use Only:

Quote: ______________________

Part No.: ______________________

Specif. No.: ______________________

Chip Select Options:

	Active High	Active Low	No Connect "Don't Care"
CS1	☐	☐	☐
CS2	☐	☐	☐
CS3	☐	☐	☐
CS4	☐	☐	☐

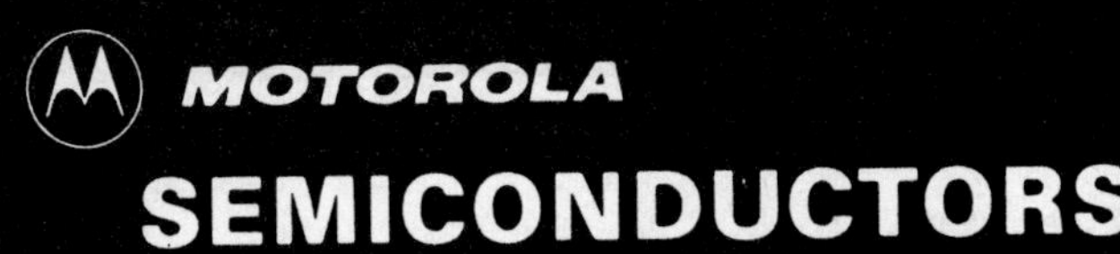

MC6840
(1.0 MHz)
MC68A40
(1.5 MHz)
MC68B40
(2.0 MHz)

PROGRAMMABLE TIMER MODULE (PTM)

The MC6840 is a programmable subsystem component of the M6800 family designed to provide variable system time intervals.

The MC6840 has three 16-bit binary counters, three corresponding control registers, and a status register. These counters are under software control and may be used to cause system interrupts and/or generate output signals. The MC6840 may be utilized for such tasks as frequency measurements, event counting, interval measuring, and similar tasks. The device may be used for square wave generation, gated delay signals, single pulses of controlled duration, and pulse width modulation as well as system interrupts.

- Operates from a Single 5 Volt Power Supply
- Fully TTL Compatible
- Single System Clock Required (Enable)
- Selectable Prescaler on Timer 3 Capable of 4 MHz for the MC6840, 6 MHz for the MC68A40 and 8 MHz for the MC68B40
- Programmable Interrupts ($\overline{\text{IRQ}}$) Output to MPU
- Readable Down Counter Indicates Counts to Go Until Time-Out
- Selectable Gating for Frequency or Pulse-Width Comparison
- $\overline{\text{RESET}}$ Input
- Three Asynchronous External Clock and Gate/Trigger Inputs Internally Synchronized
- Three Maskable Outputs

MOS

(N-CHANNEL, SILICON-GATE DEPLETION LOAD)

PROGRAMMABLE TIMER

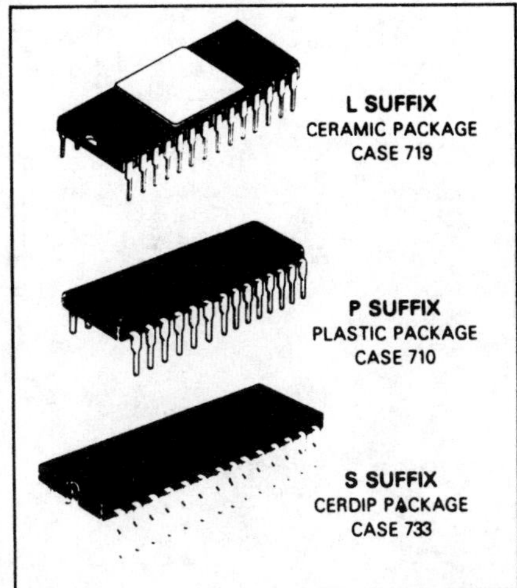

MAXIMUM RATINGS

Rating	Symbol	Value	Unit
Supply Voltage	V_{CC}	−0.3 to +7.0	V
Input Voltage	V_{in}	−0.3 to +7.0	V
Operating Temperature Range − T_L to T_h MC6840, MC68A40, MC68B40 MC6840C, MC68A40C	T_A	0 to +70 −40 to +85	°C
Storage Temperature Range	T_{stg}	−55 to +150	°C

THERMAL CHARACTERISTICS

Characteristic	Symbol	Value	Unit
Thermal Resistance Cerdip Plastic Ceramic	θ_{JA}	 65 115 60	°C/W

This device contains circuitry to protect the inputs against damage due to high static voltages or electric fields; however, it is advised that normal precautions be taken to avoid application of any voltage higher than maximum rated voltages to this high-impedance circuit. Reliability of operation is enhanced if unused inputs are tied to an appropriate logic voltage level (e.g., either V_{SS} or V_{CC}).

FIGURE 1 — PIN ASSIGNMENT

Signal	Pin	Pin	Signal
V_{SS}	1	28	C1
G2	2	27	O1
O2	3	26	G1
C2	4	25	D0
G3	5	24	D1
O3	6	23	D2
C3	7	22	D3
RESET	8	21	D4
IRQ	9	20	D5
RS0	10	19	D6
RS1	11	18	D7
RS2	12	17	E
R/W	13	16	CS1
V_{CC}	14	15	CS0

FIGURE 2 — BLOCK DIAGRAM

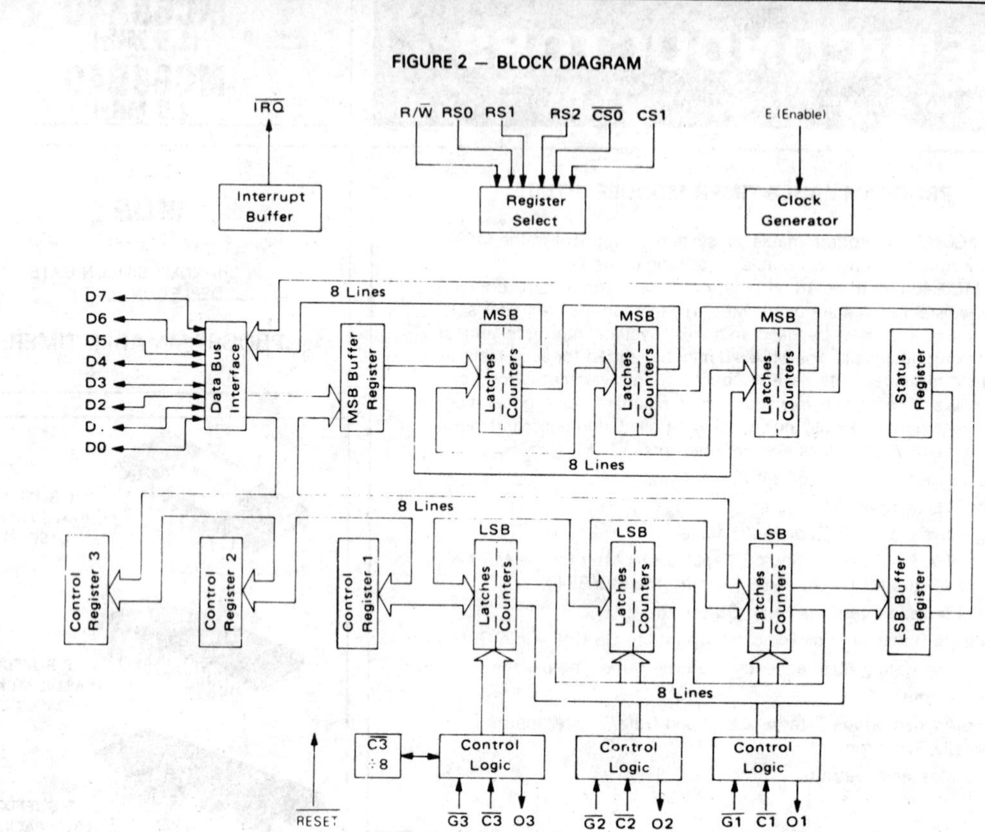

POWER CONSIDERATIONS

The average chip-junction temperature, T_J, in °C can be obtained from:

$$T_J = T_A + (P_D \bullet \theta_{JA}) \tag{1}$$

Where:

$T_A \equiv$ Ambient Temperature, °C

$\theta_{JA} \equiv$ Package Thermal Resistance, Junction-to-Ambient, °C/W

$P_D \equiv P_{INT} + P_{PORT}$

$P_{INT} \equiv I_{CC} \times V_{CC}$, Watts — Chip Internal Power

$P_{PORT} \equiv$ Port Power Dissipation, Watts — User Determined

For most applications $P_{PORT} \ll P_{INT}$ and can be neglected. P_{PORT} may become significant if the device is configured to drive Darlington bases or sink LED loads.

An approximate relationship between P_D and T_J (if P_{PORT} is neglected) is:

$$P_D = K \div (T_J + 273°C) \tag{2}$$

Solving equations 1 and 2 for K gives:

$$K = P_D \bullet (T_A + 273°C) + \theta_{JA} \bullet P_D^2 \tag{3}$$

Where K is a constant pertaining to the particular part. K can be determined from equation 3 by measuring P_D (at equilibrium) for a known T_A. Using this value of K the values of P_D and T_J can be obtained by solving equations (1) and (2) iteratively for any value of T_A.

MC6840•MC68A40•MC68B40

DC ELECTRICAL CHARACTERISTICS (V_{CC} = 5.0 Vdc ±5%, V_{SS} = 0, T_A = T_L to T_H unless otherwise noted)

Characteristic		Symbol	Min	Typ	Max	Unit
Input High Voltage		V_{IH}	V_{SS} + 2.0	–	V_{CC}	V
Input Low Voltage		V_{IL}	V_{SS} − 0.3	–	V_{SS} + 0.8	V
Input Leakage Current (V_{in} = 0 to 5.25 V)		I_{in}	–	1.0	2.5	μA
Three-State (Off State) Input Current (V_{in} = 0.5 to 2.4 V)	D0-D7	I_{TSI}	–	2.0	10	μA
Output High Voltage (I_{Load} = −205 μA) (I_{Load} = −200 μA)	D0-D7 Other Outputs	V_{OH}	V_{SS} + 2.4 V_{SS} + 2.4	– –	– –	V
Output Low Voltage (I_{Load} = 1.6 mA) (I_{Load} = 3.2 mA)	D0-D7 O1-O3, $\overline{IRQ}$	V_{OL}	– –	– –	V_{SS} + 0.4 V_{SS} + 0.4	V
Output Leakage Current (Off State) (V_{OH} = 2.4 V)	$\overline{IRQ}$	I_{LOH}	–	1.0	10	μA
Internal Power Dissipation (Measured at T_A = T_L)		P_{INT}	–	470	700	mW
Input Capacitance (V_{in} = 0, T_A = 25°C, f = 1.0 MHz)	D0-D7 All Others	C_{in}	– –	– –	12.5 7.5	pF
Output Capacitance (V_{in} = 0, T_A = 25°C, f = 1.0 MHz)	$\overline{IRQ}$ O1, O2, O3	C_{out}	– –	– –	5.0 10	pF

AC OPERATING CHARACTERISTICS (See Figures 4-9)

Characteristic		Symbol	MC6840		MC68A40		MC68B40		Unit
			Min	Max	Min	Max	Min	Max	
Input Rise and Fall Times (Figures 4 and 5) $\overline{C}$, $\overline{G}$ and $\overline{RESET}$		t_r, t_f	–	1.0*	–	0.666*	–	0.500*	μs
Input Pulse Width Low (Figure 4) (Asynchronous Input) $\overline{C}$, $\overline{G}$ and $\overline{RESET}$		PW_L	$t_{cycE} + t_{su} + t_{hd}$	–	$t_{cycE} + t_{su} + t_{hd}$	–	$t_{cycE} + t_{su} + t_{hd}$	–	ns
Input Pulse Width High (Figure 5) (Asynchronous Input) $\overline{C}$, $\overline{G}$		PW_H	$t_{cycE} + t_{su} + t_{hd}$	–	$t_{cycE} + t_{su} + t_{hd}$	–	$t_{cycE} + t_{su} + t_{hd}$	–	ns
Input Setup Time (Figure 6) (Synchronous Input) $\overline{C}$, $\overline{G}$ and $\overline{RESET}$		t_{su}	200	–	120	–	75	–	ns
Input Hold Time (Figure 6) (Synchronous Input) $\overline{C}$, $\overline{G}$ and $\overline{RESET}$		t_{hd}	50	–	50	–	50	–	ns
Input Synchronization Time (Figure 9) $\overline{C3}$ (÷8 Prescaler Mode Only)		t_{sync}	250	–	200	–	175	–	ns
Input Pulse Width $\overline{C3}$ (÷8 Prescaler Mode Only)		PW_L, PW_H	120	–	80	–	60	–	ns
Output Delay, O1-O3 (Figure 7) (V_{OH} = 2.4 V, Load B) (V_{OH} = 2.4 V, Load D) (V_{OH} = 0.7 V_{DD}, Load D) Interrupt Release Time	 TTL MOS CMOS	 t_{co} t_{cm} t_{cmos} t_{IR}	 – – – –	 700 450 2.0 1.2	 – – – –	 460 450 1.35 0.9	 – – – –	 340 340 1.0 0.7	 ns ns μs μs

*t_r and $t_f \le t_{cycE}$

BUS TIMING CHARACTERISTICS (See Notes 1, 2, and 3)

Ident. Number	Characteristic	Symbol	MC6840 Min	MC6840 Max	MC68A40 Min	MC68A40 Max	MC68B40 Min	MC68B40 Max	Unit
1	Cycle Time	t_{cyc}	1.0	10	0.67	10	0.5	10	μs
2	Pulse Width, E Low	PW_{EL}	430	9500	280	9500	210	9500	ns
3	Pulse Width, E High	PW_{EH}	450	9500	280	9500	220	9500	ns
4	Clock Rise and Fall Time	t_r, t_f	–	25	–	25	–	20	ns
9	Address Hold Time	t_{AH}	10	–	10	–	10	–	ns
13	Address Setup Time Before E	t_{AS}	80	–	60	–	40	–	ns
14	Chip Select Setup Time Before E	t_{CS}	80	–	60	–	40	–	ns
15	Chip Select Hold Time	t_{CH}	10	–	10	–	10	–	ns
18	Read Data Hold Time	t_{DHR}	20	50*	20	50*	20	50*	ns
21	Write Data Hold Time	t_{DHW}	10	–	10	–	10	–	ns
30	Peripheral Output Data Delay Time	t_{DDR}	–	290	–	180	–	150	ns
31	Peripheral Input Data Setup Time	t_{DSW}	165	–	80	–	60	–	ns

*The data bus output buffers are no longer sourcing or sinking current by t_{DHR} max (High Impedance).

FIGURE 3 — BUS TIMING

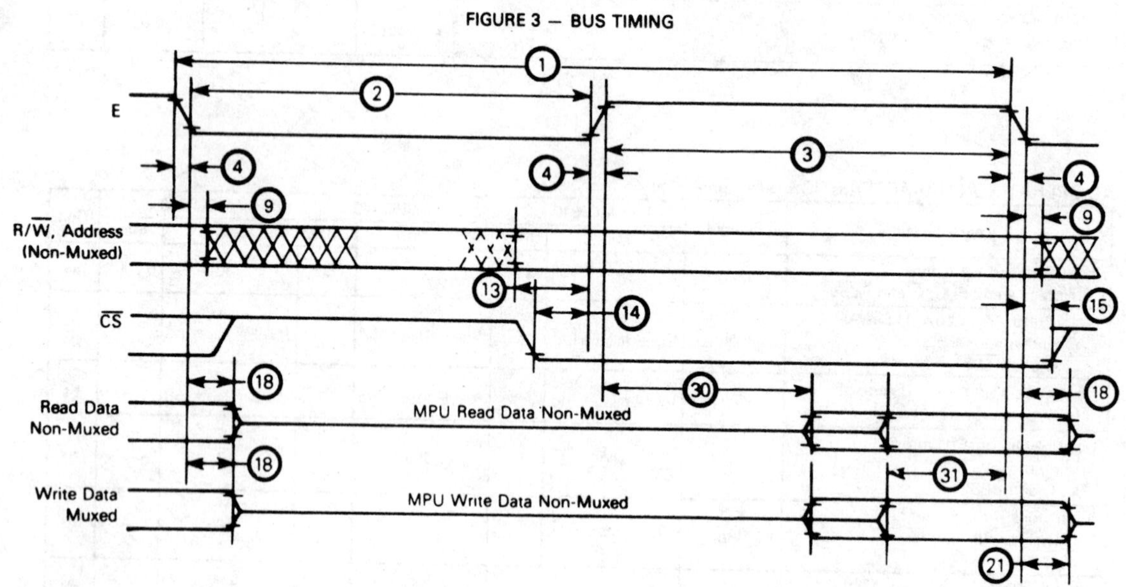

FIGURE 4 — INPUT PULSE WIDTH LOW

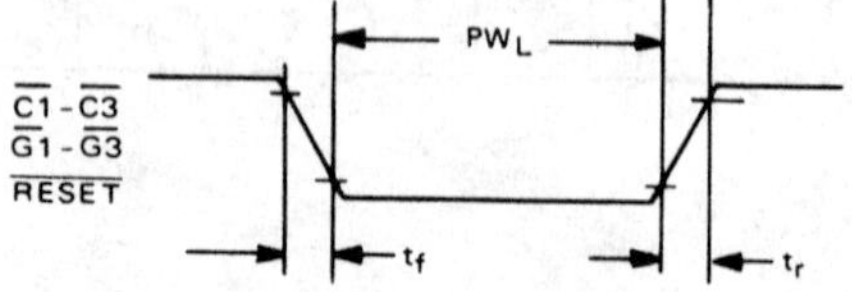

FIGURE 5 — INPUT PULSE WIDTH HIGH

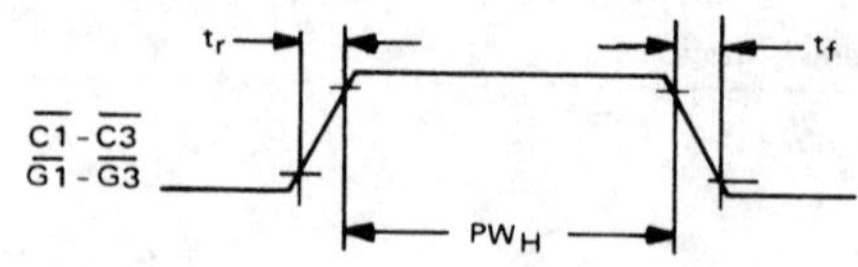

NOTES:

1. Not all signals are applicable to every part.
2. Voltage levels shown are $V_L \leq 0.4$ V, $V_H \geq 2.4$ V, unless otherwise specified.
3. Measurement points shown are 0.8 V and 2.0 V, unless otherwise specified.

FIGURE 6 – INPUT SETUP AND HOLD TIMES

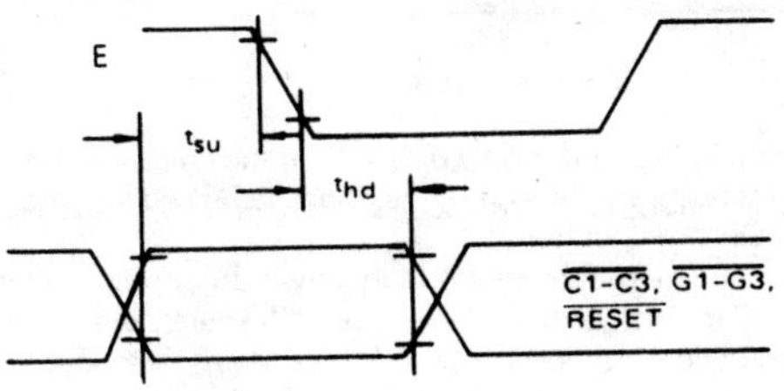

E

t_{su}

t_{hd}

$\overline{C1-C3}$, $\overline{G1-G3}$, $\overline{RESET}$

FIGURE 7 – OUTPUT DELAY

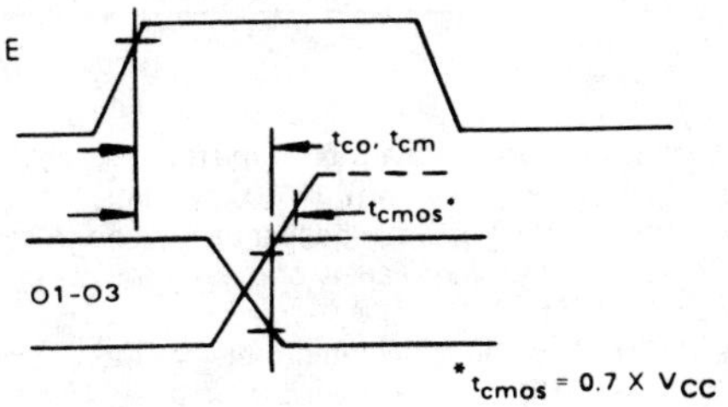

E

t_{co}, t_{cm}

t_{cmos}*

O1-O3

*t_{cmos} = 0.7 X V_{CC}

FIGURE 8 – $\overline{IRQ}$ RELEASE TIME

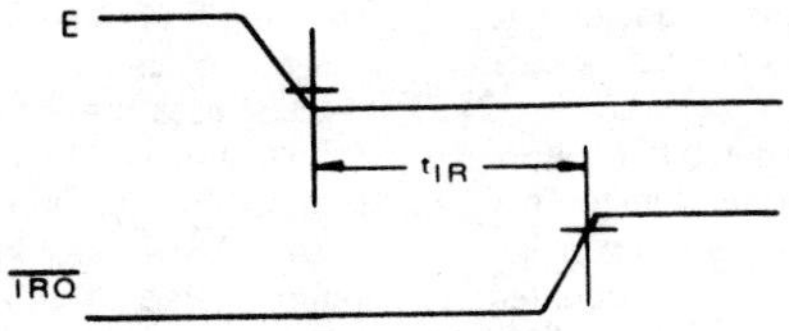

E

t_{IR}

$\overline{IRQ}$

FIGURE 9 – $\overline{C3}$ INPUT SYNCHRONIZATION TIME (÷8 PRESCALER MODE ONLY)

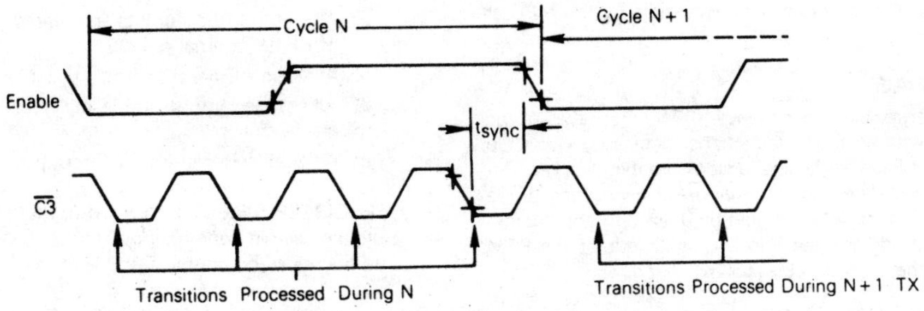

Cycle N

Cycle N+1

Enable

t_{sync}

$\overline{C3}$

Transitions Processed During N

Transitions Processed During N+1 TX

FIGURE 10 – BUS TIMING TEST LOADS

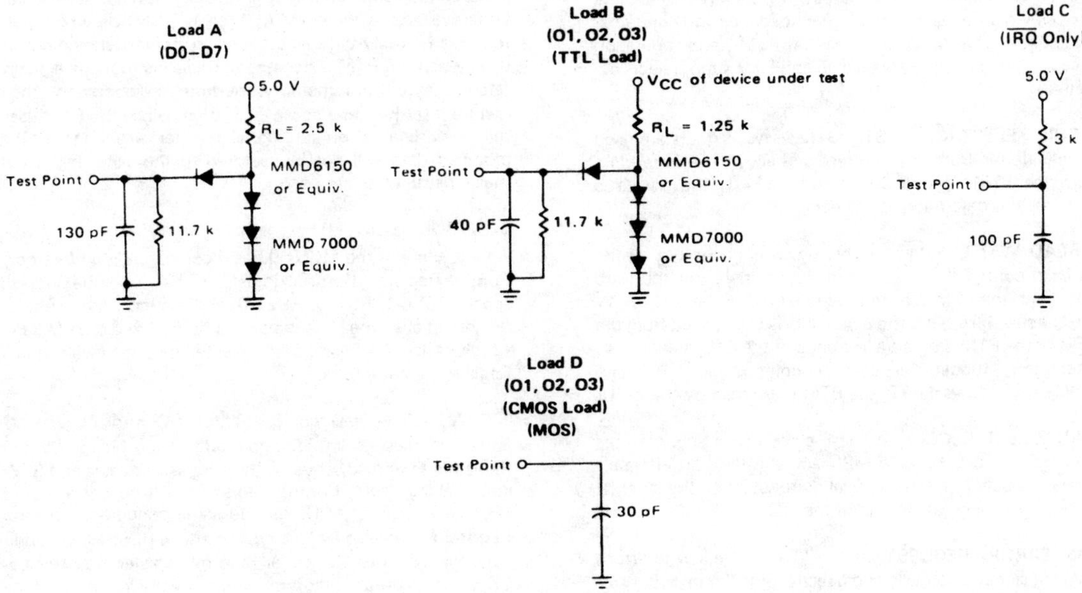

Load A
(D0–D7)

5.0 V
R_L = 2.5 k
MMD6150 or Equiv.
Test Point
130 pF
11.7 k
MMD 7000 or Equiv.

Load B
(O1, O2, O3)
(TTL Load)

V_{CC} of device under test
R_L = 1.25 k
MMD6150 or Equiv.
Test Point
40 pF
11.7 k
MMD7000 or Equiv.

Load C
($\overline{IRQ}$ Only)

5.0 V
3 k
Test Point
100 pF

Load D
(O1, O2, O3)
(CMOS Load)
(MOS)

Test Point
30 pF

NOTE: Timing measurements are referenced to and from a low voltage of 0.8 volts and a high voltage of 2.0 volts, unless otherwise noted.

DEVICE OPERATION

The MC6840 is part of the M6800 microprocessor family and is fully bus compatible with M6800 systems. The three timers in the MC6840 operate independently and in several distinct modes to fit a wide variety of measurement and synthesis applications.

The MC6840 is an integrated set of three distinct counter/timers (Figure 1). It consists of three 16-bit data latches, three 16-bit counters (clocked independently), and the comparison and enable circuitry necessary to implement various measurement and synthesis functions. In addition, it contains interrupt drivers to alert the processor that a particular function has been completed.

In a typical application, a timer will be loaded by first storing two bytes of data into an associated Counter Latch. This data is then transferred into the counter via a Counter Initialization cycle. If the counter is enabled, the counter decrements on each subsequent clock period which may be an external clock, or Enable (E) until one of several predetermined conditions causes it to halt or recycle. The timers are thus programmable, cyclic in nature, controllable by external inputs or the MPU program, and accessible by the MPU at any time.

BUS INTERFACE

The Programmable Timer Module (PTM) interfaces to the M6800 Bus with an 8-bit bidirectional data bus, two Chip Select lines, a Read/Write line, a clock (Enable) line, and Interrupt Request line, an external Reset line, and three Register select lines. VMA should be utilized in conjunction with an MPU address line into a Chip Select of the PTM when using the MC6800/6802/6808.

BIDIRECTIONAL DATA (D0-D7) – The bidirectional data lines (D0-D7) allow the transfer of data between the MPU and PTM. The data bus output drivers are three-state devices which remain in the high-impedance (off) state except when the MPU performs a PTM read operation (Read/Write and Enable lines high and PTM Chip Selects activated).

CHIP SELECT ($\overline{\text{CS0}}$, CS1) – These two signals are used to activate the Data Bus interface and allow transfer of data from the PTM. With $\overline{\text{CS0}}=0$ and $\text{CS1}=1$, the device is selected and data transfer will occur.

READ/WRITE (R/$\overline{\text{W}}$) – This signal is generated by the MPU to control the direction of data transfer on the Data Bus. With the PTM selected, a low state on the PTM R/$\overline{\text{W}}$ line enables the input buffers and data is transferred from the MPU to the PTM on the trailing edge of the E (Enable) clock. Alternately, (under the same conditions) R/$\overline{\text{W}}=1$ and Enable high allows data in the PTM to be read by the MPU.

ENABLE (E CLOCK) – The E clock signal synchronizes data transfer between the MPU and the PTM. It also performs an equivalent synchronization function on the external clock, reset, and gate inputs of the PTM.

INTERRUPT REQUEST ($\overline{\text{IRQ}}$) – The active low Interrupt Request signal is normally tied directly (or through priority interrupt circuitry) to the $\overline{\text{IRQ}}$ input of the MPU. This is an "open drain" output (no load device on the chip) which permits other similar interrupt request lines to be tied together in a wire-$\overline{\text{OR}}$ configuration.

The $\overline{\text{IRQ}}$ line is activated if, and only if, the Composite Interrupt Flag (Bit 7 of the Internal Status Register) is asserted. The conditions under which the $\overline{\text{IRQ}}$ line is activated are discussed in conjunction with the Status Register.

$\overline{\text{RESET}}$ – A low level at this input is clocked into the PTM by the E (Enable) input. Two Enable pulses are required to synchronize and process the signal. The PTM then recognizes the active "low" or inactive "high" on the third Enable pulse. If the $\overline{\text{RESET}}$ signal is asynchronous, an additional Enable period is required if setup times are not met. The $\overline{\text{RESET}}$ input must be stable High/Low for the minimum time stated in the AC Operating Characteristics.

Recognition of a low level at this input by the PTM causes the following action to occur:

a. All counter latches are preset to their maximum count values.
b. All Control Register bits are cleared with the exception of CR10 (internal reset bit) which is set.
c. All counters are preset to the contents of the latches.
d. All counter outputs are reset and all counter clocks are disabled.
e. All Status Register bits (interrupt flags) are cleared.

REGISTER SELECT LINES (RS0, RS1, RS2) – These inputs are used in conjunction with the R/$\overline{\text{W}}$ line to select the internal registers, counters and latches as shown in Table 1.

NOTE:

The PTM is accessed via MPU Load and Store operations in much the same manner as a memory device. The instructions available with the M6800 family of MPUs which perform read-modify-write operations on memory should not be used when the PTM is accessed. These instructions actually fetch a byte from memory, perform an operation, then restore it to the same address location. Since the PTM uses the R/$\overline{\text{W}}$ line as an additional register select input, the modified data will not be restored to the same register if these instructions are used.

CONTROL REGISTER

Each timer in the MC6840 has a corresponding write-only Control Register. Control Register #2 has a unique address space (RS0 = 1, RS = 0, RS2 = 0) and therefore may be written into at any time. The remaining Control Registers (#1 and #3) share the Address Space selected by a logic zero on all Register Select inputs.

CR20 – The least-significant bit of Control Register #2 (CR20) is used as an additional addressing bit for Control Registers #1 and #3. Thus, with all Register selects and R/W inputs at logic zero, Control Register #1 will be written into if CR20 is a logic one. Under the same conditions, Control Register #3 can also be written into after a $\overline{\text{RESET}}$ low condition has occurred, since all control register bits (except CR10) are cleared. Therefore, one may write in the sequence CR3, CR2, CR1.

TABLE 1 – REGISTER SELECTION

Register Select Inputs			Operations	
RS2	RS1	RS0	R/$\overline{W}$ = 0	R/$\overline{W}$ = 1
0	0	0	CR20 = 0 Write Control Register #3 CR20 = 1 Write Control Register #1	No Operation
0	0	1	Write Control Register #2	Read Status Register
0	1	0	Write MSB Buffer Register	Read Timer #1 Counter
0	1	1	Write Timer #1 Latches	Read LSB Buffer Register
1	0	0	Write MSB Buffer Register	Read Timer #2 Counter
1	0	1	Write Timer #2 Latches	Read LSB Buffer Register
1	1	0	Write MSB Buffer Register	Read Timer #3 Counter
1	1	1	Write Timer #3 Latches	Read LSB Buffer Register

CR10 – The least-significant bit of Control Register #1 is used as an Internal Reset bit. When this bit is a logic zero, all timers are allowed to operate in the modes prescribed by the remaining bits of the control registers. Writing a "one" into CR10 causes all counters to be preset with the contents of the corresponding counter latches, all counter clocks to be disabled, and the timer outputs and interrupt flags (Status Register) to be reset. Counter Latches and Control Registers are undisturbed by an Internal Reset and may be written into regardless of the state of CR10.

The least-signifcant bit of Control Register #3 is used as a selector for a ÷8 prescaler which is available with Timer #3 only. The prescaler, if selected, is effectively placed between the clock input circuitry and the input to Counter #3. It can therefore be used with either the internal clock (Enable) or an external clock source.

CR30 – The functions depicted in the foregoing discussions are tabulated in Table 2 for ease of reference.

TABLE 2 – CONTROL REGISTER BITS

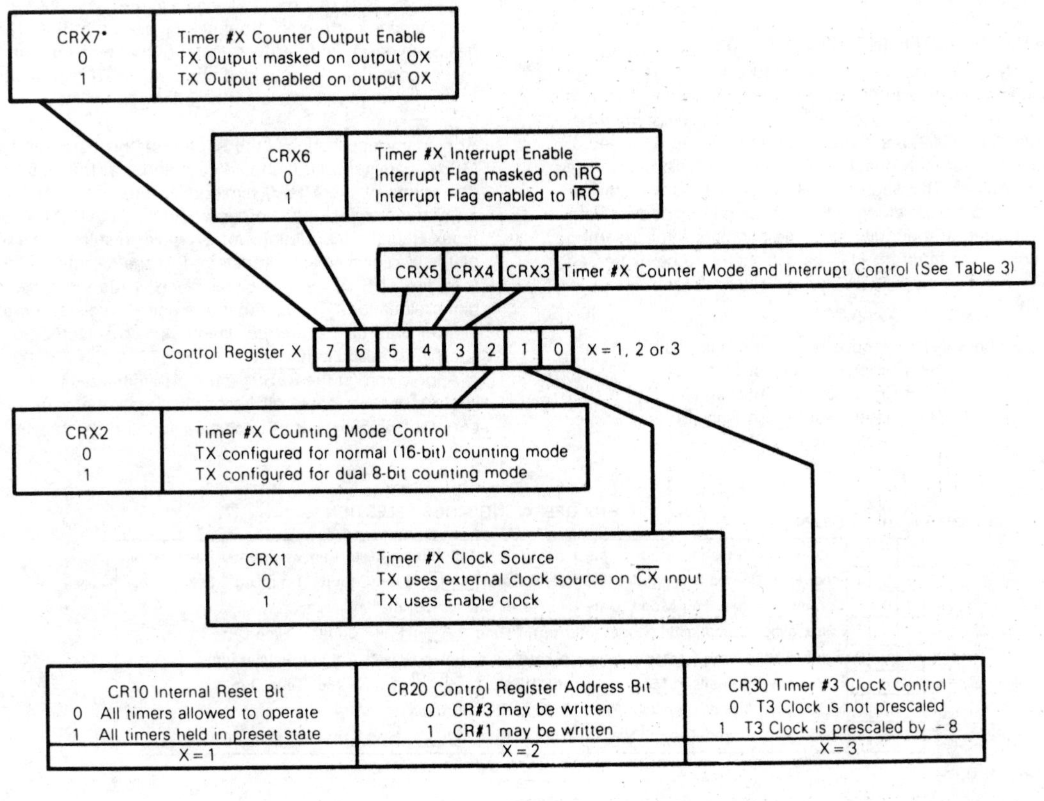

Control Register Bits CR10, CR20, and CR30 are unique in that each selects a different function. The remaining bits (1 through 7) of each Control Register select common functions, with a particular Control Register affecting only its corresponding timer.

CRX1 – Bit 1 of Control Register #1 (CR11) selects whether an internal or external clock source is to be used with Timer #1. Similarly, CR21 selects the clock source for Timer #2, and CR31 performs this function for Timer #3. The function of each bit of Control Register "X" can therefore be defined as shown in the remaining section of Table 2.

CRX2 – Control Register Bit 2 selects whether the binary information contained in the Counter Latches (and subsequently loaded into the counter) is to be treated as a single 16-bit word or two 8-bit bytes. In the single 16-bit Counter Mode (CRX2 = 0) the counter will decrement to zero after N + 1 enabled (G = 0) clock periods, where N is defined as the 16-bit number in the Counter Latches. With CRX2 = 1, a similar Time Out will occur after (L + 1)•(M + 1) enabled clock periods, where L and M, respectively, refer to the LSB and MSB bytes in the Counter Latches.

CRX3-CRX7 – Control Register Bits 3, 4, and 5 are explained in detail in the Timer Operating Mode section. Bit 6 is an interrupt mask bit which will be explained more fully in conjunction with the Status Register, and bit 7 is used to enable the corresponding Timer Output. A summary of the control register programming modes is shown in Table 3.

STATUS REGISTER/INTERRUPT FLAGS

The MC6840 has an internal Read-Only Status Register which contains four Interrupt Flags. (The remaining four bits of the register are not used, and defaults to zeros when being read.) Bits 0, 1, and 2 are assigned to Timers 1, 2, and 3, respectively, as individual flag bits, while Bit 7 is a Composite Interrupt Flag. This flag bit will be asserted if any of the individual flag bits is set while Bit 6 of the corresponding Control Register is at a logic one. The conditions for asserting the composite Interrupt Flag bit can therefore be expressed as:

$$INT = I1 \cdot CR16 + I2 \cdot CR26 + I3 \cdot CR36$$

where INT = Composite Interrupt Flag (Bit 7)
I1 = Timer #1 Interrupt Flag (Bit 0)
I2 = Timer #2 Interrupt Flag (Bit 1)
I3 = Timer #3 Interrupt Flag (Bit 2)

An interrupt flag is cleared by a Timer Reset condition, i.e., External $\overline{RESET}$ = 0 or Internal Reset Bit (CR10) = 1. It will also be cleared by a Read Timer Counter Command provided that the Status Register has previously been read while the interrupt flag was set. This condition on the Read Status Register-Read Timer Counter (RS-RT) sequence is designed to prevent missing interrupts which might occur after the status register is read, but prior to reading the Timer Counter.

An Individual Interrupt Flag is also cleared by a Write Timer Latches (W) command or a Counter Initialization (CI) sequence, provided that W or CI affects the Timer corresponding to the individual Interrupt Flag.

COUNTER LATCH INITIALIZATION

Each of the three independent timers consists of a 16-bit addressable counter and a 16-bit addressable latch. The counters are preset to the binary numbers stored in the latches. Counter initialization results in the transfer of the latch contents to the counter. See notes in Table 4 regarding the binary number N, L, or M placed into the Latches and their relationship to the output waveforms and counter Time-Outs.

Since the PTM data bus is 8-bits wide and the counters are 16-bits wide, a temporary register (MSB Buffer Register) is provided. This "write only" register is for the Most-Significant Byte of the desired latch data. Three addresses are provided for the MSB Buffer Register (as indicated in Table 1), but they all lead to the same Buffer. Data from the MSB Buffer will automatically be transferred into the Most-Significant Byte of Timer #X when a Write Timer #X Latches Command is performed. So it can be seen that the MC6840 has been designed to allow transfer of two bytes of data into the counter latches provided that the MSB is transferred first. The storage order must be observed to ensure proper latch operation.

In many applications, the source of the data will be an M6800 Family MPU. It should be noted that the 16-bit store operations of the M6800 family microprocessors (STS and STX) transfer data in the order required by the PTM. A Store Index Register Instruction, for example, results in the MSB of the X register being transferred to the selected address, then the LSB of the X register being written into the next higher location. Thus, either the index register or stack pointer may be transferred directly into a selected counter latch with a single instruction.

A logic zero at the $\overline{RESET}$ input also initializes the counter latches. In this case, all latches will assume a maximum count of $65{,}535_{10}$. It is important to note that an Internal

TABLE 3 – PTM OPERATING MODE SELECTION

CRX3	CRX4	CRX5	
0	0	0	Continuous Operating Mode: Gate ↓ or Write to Latches or Reset Causes Counter Initialization
0	0	1	Frequency Comparison Mode: Interrupt If Gate ↑__‾‾↓ is < Counter Time Out
0	1	0	Continuous Operating Mode: Gate ↓ or Reset Causes Counter Initialization
0	1	1	Pulse Width Comparison Mode: Interrupt if Gate ↑___↑ is < Counter Time Out
1	0	0	Single Shot Mode: Gate ↓ or Write to Latches or Reset Causes Counter Initialization
1	0	1	Frequency Comparison Mode: Interrupt If Gate ↑__‾‾↓ is > Counter Time Out
1	1	0	Single Shot Mode: Gate ↓ or Reset Causes Counter Initialization
1	1	1	Pulse Width Comparison Mode: Interrupt If Gate ↑___↑ is > Counter Time Out

MC6840•MC68A40•MC68B40

Reset (Bit zero of Control Register 1 Set) has no effect on the counter latches.

COUNTER INITIALIZATION

Counter Initialization is defined as the transfer of data from the latches to the counter with subsequent clearing of the Individual Interrupt Flag associated with the counter. Counter Initialization always occurs when a reset condition ($\overline{RESET}$ = 0 or CR10 = 1) is recognized. It can also occur – depending on Timer Mode – with a Write Timer Latches command or recognition of a negative transition of the Gate input.

Counter recycling or re-initialization occurs when a negative transition of the clock input is recognized after the counter has reached an all-zero state. In this case, data is transferred from the Latches to the Counter.

ASYNCHRONOUS INPUT/OUTPUT LINES

Each of the three timers within the PTM has external clock and gate inputs as well as a counter output line. The inputs are high-impedance, TTL-compatible lines and ouputs are capable of driving two standard TTL loads.

CLOCK INPUTS ($\overline{C1}$, $\overline{C2}$, and $\overline{C3}$) – Input pins $\overline{C1}$, $\overline{C2}$, and $\overline{C3}$ will accept asynchronous TTL voltage level signals to decrement Timers 1, 2, and 3, respectively. The high and low levels of the external clocks must each be stable for at least one system clock period plus the sum of the setup and hold times for the clock inputs. The asynchronous clock rate can vary from dc to the limit imposed by the Enable Clock Setup, and Hold times.

The external clock inputs are clocked in by Enable pulses. Three Enable periods are used to synchronize and process the external clock. The fourth Enable pulse decrements the internal counter. This does not affect the input frequency, it merely creates a delay between a clock input transition and internal recognition of that transition by the PTM. All references to C inputs in this document relate to internal recognition of the input transition. Note that a clock high or low level which does not meet setup and hold time specifications may require an additional Enable pulse for recognition. When observing recurring events, a lack of synchronization will result in "jitter" being observed on the output of the PTM when using asynchronous clocks and gate input signals. There are two types of jitter. "System jitter" is the result of the input signals being out of synchronization with Enable, permitting signals with marginal setup and hold time to be recognized by either the bit time nearest the input transition or the subsequent bit time.

"Input jitter" can be as great as the time between input signal negative going transitions plus the system jitter, if the first transition is recognized during one system cycle, and not recognized the next cycle, or vice versa. See Figure 11.

FIGURE 11 – INPUT JITTER

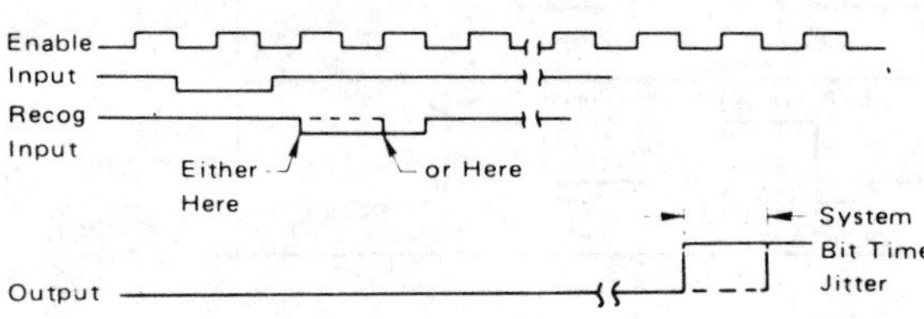

CLOCK INPUT $\overline{C3}$ (÷8 PRESCALER MODE) – External clock input $\overline{C3}$ represents a special case when Timer #3 is programmed to utilize its optional ÷8 prescaler mode.

The divide-by-8 prescaler contains an asynchronous ripple counter; thus, input setup (t_{su}) and hold times (t_{hd}) do not apply. As long as minimum input pulse widths are maintained, the counter will recognize and process all input clock ($\overline{C3}$) transitions. However, in order to guarantee that a clock transition is processed during the current E cycle, a certain amount of synchronization time (t_{sync}) is required between the $\overline{C3}$ transition and the falling edge of Enable (see Figure 9). If the synchronization time requirement is not met, it is possible that the $\overline{C3}$ transition will not be processed until the following E cycle.

The maximum input frequency and allowable duty cycles for the ÷8 prescaler mode are specified under the AC Operating Characteristics. Internally, the ÷8 prescaler output is treated in the same manner as the previously discussed clock inputs.

GATE INPUTS ($\overline{G1}$, $\overline{G2}$, $\overline{G3}$) – Input pins $\overline{G1}$, $\overline{G2}$, and $\overline{G3}$ accept asynchronous TTL-compatible signals which are used as triggers or clock gating functions to Timers 1, 2, and 3, respectively. The gating inputs are clocked into the PTM by the E (enable) clock in the same manner as the previously discussed clock inputs. That is, a Gate transition is recognized by the PTM on the fourth Enable pulse (provided setup and hold time requirements are met), and the high or low levels of the Gate input must be stable for at least one system clock period plus the sum of setup and hold times. All references to G transition in this document relate to internal recognition of the input transition.

The Gate inputs of all timers directly affect the internal 16-bit counter. The operation of $\overline{G3}$ is therefore independent of the ÷8 prescaler selection.

TIMER OUTPUTS (O1, O2, O3) – Timer outputs O1, O2, and O3 are capable of driving up to two TTL loads and produce a defined output waveform for either Continuous or Single-Shot Timer modes. Output waveform definition is accomplished by selecting either Single 16-bit or Dual 8-bit operating modes. The Single 16-bit mode will produce a square-wave output in the continuous mode and a single pulse in the single-shot mode. The Dual 8-bit mode will produce a variable duty cycle pulse in both the continuous and single-shot timer modes. One bit of each Control Register (CRX7) is used to enable the corresponding output. If this bit is cleared, the output will remain low (V_{OL}) regardless of the operating mode. If it is cleared while the output is high the output will go low during the first enable cycle following a write to the Control Register.

The Continuous and Single-Shot Timer Modes are the only ones for which output response is defined in this data sheet. Refer to the Programmable Timer Fundamentals and Applications manual for a discussion of the output signals in other modes. Signals appear at the outputs (unless CRX7 = 0) during Frequency and Pulse Width comparison modes, but the actual waveform is not predictable in typical applications.

TIMER OPERATING MODES

The MC6840 has been designed to operate effectively in a wide variety of applications. This is accomplished by using three bits of each control register (CRX3, CRX4, and CRX5) to define different operating modes of the Timers. These modes are divided into WAVE SYNTHESIS and WAVE MEASUREMENT modes, and are outlined in Table 4.

TABLE 4 – OPERATING MODES

Control Register			Timer Operating Mode	
CRX3	CRX4	CRX5		
0	•	0	Continuous	Synthesizer
0	•	1	Single-Shot	
1	0	•	Frequency Comparison	Measurement
1	1	•	Pulse Width Comparison	

•Defines Additional Timer Function Selection.

One of the WAVE SYNTHESIS modes is the Continuous Operating mode, which is useful for cyclic wave generation. Either symmetrical or variable duty-cycle waves can be generated in this mode. The other wave synthesis mode, the Single-Shot mode, is similar in use to the Continuous operating mode, however, a single pulse is generated, with a programmable preset width.

The WAVE MEASUREMENT modes include the Frequency Comparison and Pulse Width Comparison modes which are used to measure cyclic and singular pulse widths, respectively.

In addition to the four timer modes in Table 4, the remaining control register bit is used to modify counter initialization and enabling or interrupt conditions.

WAVE SYNTHESIS MODES

CONTINUOUS OPERATING MODE (TABLE 5) – The continuous mode will synthesize a continuous wave with a period proportional to the preset number in the particular timer latches. Any of the timers in the PTM may be programmed to operate in a continuous mode by writing zeroes into bits 3 and 5 of the corresponding control register. Assuming that the timer output is enabled (CRX7 = 1), either a square wave or a variable duty cycle waveform will be generated at the Timer Output, OX. The type of output is selected via Control Register Bit 2.

Either a Timer Reset (CR10 = 1 or External Reset = 0) condition or internal recognition of a negative transition of the Gate input results in Counter Initialization. A Write Timer latches command can be selected as a Counter Initialization signal by clearing CRX4.

The counter is enabled by an absence of a Timer Reset condition and a logic zero at the Gate input. In the 16-bit mode, the counter will decrement on the first clock cycle during or after the counter initialization cycle. It continues to decrement on each clock signal so long as G remains low and no reset condition exists. A Counter Time Out (the first clock after all counter bits = 0) results in the Individual Interrupt Flag being set and reinitialization of the counter.

In the Dual 8-bit mode (CRX2 = 1) [refer to the example in Figure 12 and Tables 5 and 6] the MSB decrements once for every full countdown of the LSB + 1. When the LSB = 0, the MSB is unchanged; on the next clock pulse the LSB is reset to the count in the LSB Latches, and the MSB is decremented by 1 (one). The output, if enabled, remains low during and after initialization and will remain low until the counter MSB is all zeroes. The output will go high at the beginning of the next clock pulse. The output remains high until both the LSB and MSB of the counter are all zeroes. At the beginning of the next clock pulse the defined Time Out (TO) will occur and the output will go low. In the Dual 8-bit mode the period of the output of the example in Figure 12 would span 20 clock pulses as opposed to 1546 clock pulses using the normal 16-bit mode.

A special time-out condition exists for the dual 8-bit mode (CRX2 = 1) if L = 0. In this case, the counter will revert to a mode similar to the single 16-bit mode, except Time Out occurs after M + 1* clock pulses. The output, if enabled, goes low during the Counter Initialization cycle and reverses state at each Time Out. The counter remains cyclical (is re-initialized at each Time Out) and the Individual Interrupt Flag is set when Time Out occurs. If M = L = 0, the internal counters do not change, but the output toggles at a rate of ½ the clock frequency.

TABLE 5 – CONTINUOUS OPERATING MODES

Synthesis Modes			CONTINUOUS MODE (CRX3 = 0, CRX5 = 0)
Control Register		Initialization/Output Waveforms	
CRX2	CRX4	Counter Initialization	*Timer Output (OX) (CRX7 = 1)
0	0	$\overline{G}\downarrow$+W+R	(N+1)(T) (N+1)(T) (N+1)(T) — V_{OH} — V_{OL}; t_o TO TO TO
0	1	$\overline{G}\downarrow$+R	
1	0	$\overline{G}\downarrow$+W+R	(L+1)(M+1)(T) (L+1)(M+1)(T) — V_{OH}; (L)(T) (L)(T) — V_{OL}; t_o TO TO
1	1	$\overline{G}\downarrow$+R	

FIGURE 12 — TIMER OUTPUT WAVEFORM EXAMPLE
(Continuous Dual 8-Bit Mode Using Internal Enable)

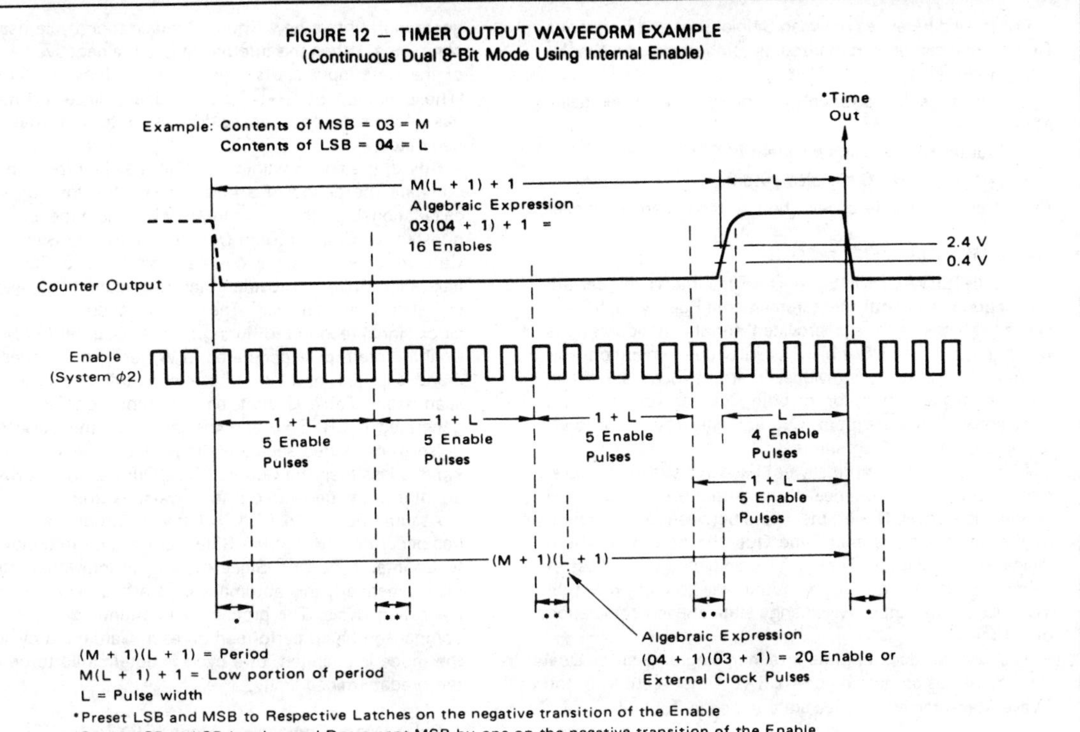

The discussion of the Continuous Mode has assumed that the application requires an output signal. It should be noted that the Timer operates in the same manner with the output disabled (CRX7 = 0). A Read Timer Counter command is valid regardless of the state of CRX7.

SINGLE-SHOT TIMER MODE — This mode is identical to the Continuous Mode with three exceptions. The first of these is obvious from the name — the output returns to a low level after the initial Time Out and remains low until another Counter Initialization cycle occurs.

As indicated in Table 6, the internal counting mechanism remains cyclical in the Single-Shot Mode. Each Time Out of the counter results in the setting of an Individual Interrupt Flag and re-initialization of the counter.

The second major difference between the Single-Shot and Continuous modes is that the internal counter enable is not dependent on the Gate input level reamining in the low state for the Single-Shot mode.

Another special condition is introduced in the Single-Shot mode. If L = M = 0 (Dual 8-bit) or N = 0 (Single 16-bit), the output goes low on the first clock received during or after Counter Initialization. The output remains low until the Operating Mode is changed or nonzero data is written into the Counter Latches. Time Outs continue to occur at the end of each clock period.

TABLE 6 — SINGLE-SHOT OPERATING MODES

Synthesis Modes		SINGLE-SHOT MODE (CRX3 = 0, CRX7 = 1, CRX5 = 1)	
Control Register		Initialization/Output Waveforms	
CRX2	CRX4	Counter Initialization	Timer Output (OX)
0	0	G̅↓+W+R	(N+1)(T) — (N)(T) — (N+1)(T); t_0, TO, TO
0	1	G̅↓+R	
1	0	G̅↓+W+R	(L+1)(M+1)(T) — (L)(T) — (L+1)(M+1)(T); t_0, TO, TO
1	1	G̅↓+R	

Symbols are as defined in Table 5.

The three differences between Single-Shot and Continous Timer Mode can be summarized as attributes of the Single-Shot mode:

1. Output is enabled for only one pulse until it is reinitialized.
2. Counter Enable is independent of Gate.
3. L = M = 0 or N = 0 disables output.

Aside from these differences, the two modes are identical.

WAVE MEASUREMENT MODES

TIME INTERVAL MODES – The Time Interval Modes are the Frequency (period) Measurement and Pulse Width Comparison Modes, and are provided for those applications which require more flexibility of interrupt generation and Counter Initialization. Individual Interrupt Flags are set in these modes as a function of both Counter Time Out and transitions of the $\overline{\text{Gate}}$ input. Counter Initialization is also affected by Interrupt Flag status.

A timer's output is normally not used in a Wave Measurement mode, but it is defined. If the output is enabled, it will operate as follows. During the period between reinitialization of the timer and the first Time Out, the output will be a logical zero. If the first Time Out is completed (regardless of its method of generation), the output will go high. If further TO's occur, the output will change state at each completion of a Time-Out.

The counter does operate in either Single 16-bit or Dual 8-bit modes as programmed by CRX2. Other features of the Wave Measurement Modes are outlined in Table 7.

Frequency Comparison Or Period Measurement Mode (CRX3 = 1, CRX4 = 0) – The Frequency Comparison Mode with CRX5 = 1 is straightforward. If Time Out occurs prior to the first negative transition of the $\overline{\text{Gate}}$ input after a Counter Initialization cycle, and Individual Interrupt Flag is set. The counter is disabled, and a Counter Initialization cycle cannot begin until the interrupt flag is cleared and a negative transition on $\overline{\text{G}}$ is detected.

If CRX5 = 0, as shown in Tables 7 and 8, an interrupt is generated if $\overline{\text{Gate}}$ input returns low prior to a Time Out. If a Counter Time Out occurs first, the counter is recycled and continues to decrement. A bit is set within the timer on the initial Time Out which precludes further individual interrupt generation until a new Counter Initialization cycle has been completed. When this internal bit is set, a negative transition of the $\overline{\text{Gate}}$ input starts a new Counter Initialization cycle. (The condition of $\overline{\text{G}}\downarrow \cdot \overline{\text{I}} \cdot \text{TO}$ is satisfied, since a Time Out has occurred and no individual Interrupt has been generated.)

Any of the timers within the PTM may be programmed to compare the period of a pulse (giving the frequency after calculations) at the $\overline{\text{Gate}}$ input with the time period requested for Counter Time Out. A negative transition of the $\overline{\text{Gate}}$ Input enables the counter and starts a Counter Initialization cycle – provided that other conditions, as noted in Table 8, are satisfied. The counter decrements on each clock signal recognized during or after Counter Initialization until an Interrupt is generated, a Write Timer Latches command is issued, or a Timer Reset condition occurs. It can be seen from Table 8 that an interrupt condition will be generated if CRX5 = 0 and the period of the pulse (single pulse or measured separately repetitive pulses) at the Gate input is less than the Counter Time Out period. If CRX5 = 1, an interrupt is generated if the reverse is true.

Assume now with CRX5 = 1 that a Counter Initialization has occurred and that the Gate input has returned low prior to Counter Time Out. Since there is no Individual Interrupt Flag generated, this automatically starts a new Counter Initialization Cycle. The process will continue with frequency comparison being performed on each Gate input cycle until the mode is changed, or a cycle is determined to be above the predetermined limit.

Pulse Width Comparison Mode (CRX3 = 1, CRX4 = 1) – This mode is similar to the Frequency Comparison Mode except for a positive, rather than negative, transition of the Gate input termintes the count. With CRX5 = 0, an Individual Interrupt Flag will be generated if the zero level pulse applied to the Gate input is less than the time period required for Counter Time Out. With CRX5 = 1, the interrupt is generated when the reverse condition is true.

As can be seen in Table 8, a positive transition of the Gate input disables the counter. With CRX5 = 0, it is therefore possible to directly obtain the width of any pulse causing an interrupt. Similar data for other Time Interval Modes and conditions can be obtained, if two sections of the PTM are dedicated to the purpose.

FIGURE 7 — OUTPUT DELAY

CRX3 = 1			
CRX4	**CRX5**	**Application**	**Condition for Setting Individual Interrupt Flag**
0	0	Frequency Comparison	Interrupt Generated if $\overline{\text{Gate}}$ Input Period (1/F) is less than Counter Time Out (TO)
0	1	Frequency Comparison	Interrupt Generated if $\overline{\text{Gate}}$ Input Period (1/F) is greater than Counter Time Out (TO)
1	0	Pulse Width Comparison	Interrupt Generated if $\overline{\text{Gate}}$ Input "Down Time" is less than Counter Time Out (TO)
1	1	Pulse Width Comparison	Interrupt Generated if $\overline{\text{Gate}}$ Input "Down Time" is greater than Counter Time Out (TO)

MC6840•MC68A40•MC68B40

TABLE 8 — FREQUENCY COMPARISON MODE

Mode	Bit 3	Bit 4	Control Reg. Bit 5	Counter Initialization	Counter Enable Flip-Flop Set (CE)	Counter Enable Flip-Flop Reset (CE)	Interrupt Flag Set (I)
Frequency	1	0	0	$\overline{G\downarrow}\cdot I \pm (\overline{CE}+TO)+R$	$\overline{G\downarrow}\cdot\overline{W}\cdot\overline{R}\cdot\overline{I}$	$W+R+I$	$\overline{G}\downarrow$ Before TO
Comparison	1	0	1	$\overline{G\downarrow}\cdot\overline{I}+R$	$\overline{G\downarrow}\cdot\overline{W}\cdot\overline{R}\cdot\overline{I}$	$W+R+I$	TO Before $\overline{G}\downarrow$
Pulse Width	1	1	0	$\overline{G\downarrow}\cdot\overline{I}+\overline{R}$	$\overline{G\downarrow}\overline{W}\cdot\overline{R}\cdot\overline{I}$	$W+R+I+G$	$\overline{G}\uparrow$ Before TO
Comparison	1	1	1	$\overline{G\downarrow}\cdot\overline{I}+\overline{R}$	$\overline{G\downarrow}\cdot\overline{W}\cdot\overline{R}\cdot\overline{I}$	$W+R+I+G$	$\overline{G}\uparrow$ Before TO

$\overline{G}\downarrow$ = Negative transition of $\overline{\text{Gate}}$ input.
W = Write Timer Latches Command.
R = Timer Reset (CR10 = 1 or External $\overline{\text{RESET}}$ = 0)
N = 16-Bit Number in Counter Latch.
TO = Counter Time Out (All Zero Condition)
I = Interrupt for a given timer.

*All time intervals shown above assume the Gate ($\overline{G}$) and Clock ($\overline{C}$) signals are sycnhronized to the system clock (E) with the specified setup and hold time requirements.

ORDERING INFORMATION

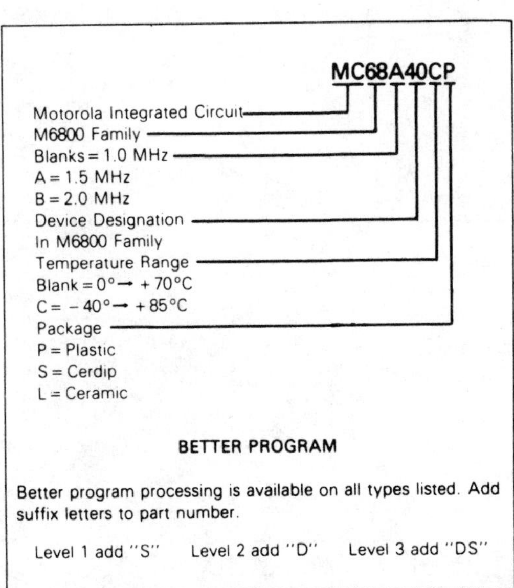

BETTER PROGRAM

Better program processing is available on all types listed. Add suffix letters to part number.

Level 1 add "S"   Level 2 add "D"   Level 3 add "DS"

S = Level 1 — 10 temp cycles — (−25 to 150°C); high temp. testing at t_{AMAX}
D = Level 2 — 168-Hour burn-in at 125°C
DS = Level 3 — combination of Level I and Level II.

MOTOROLA *Semiconductor Products Inc.*

MC6840•MC68A40•MC68B40

PACKAGE DIMENSIONS

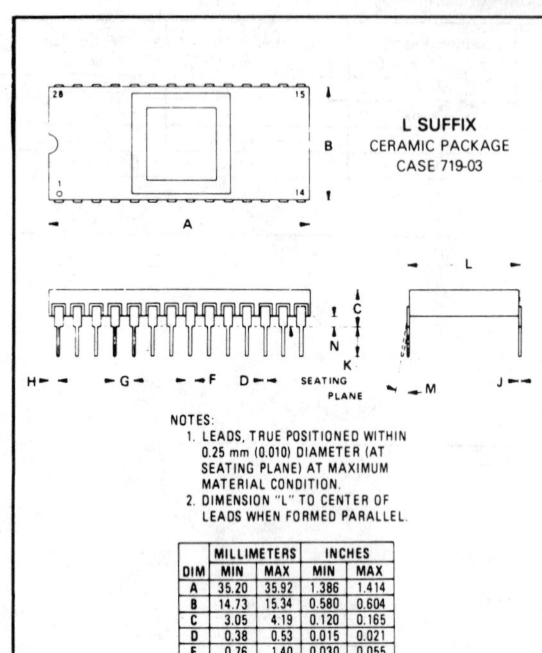

L SUFFIX
CERAMIC PACKAGE
CASE 719-03

NOTES:
1. LEADS, TRUE POSITIONED WITHIN 0.25 mm (0.010) DIAMETER (AT SEATING PLANE) AT MAXIMUM MATERIAL CONDITION.
2. DIMENSION "L" TO CENTER OF LEADS WHEN FORMED PARALLEL.

DIM	MILLIMETERS		INCHES	
	MIN	MAX	MIN	MAX
A	35.20	35.92	1.386	1.414
B	14.73	15.34	0.580	0.604
C	3.05	4.19	0.120	0.165
D	0.38	0.53	0.015	0.021
F	0.76	1.40	0.030	0.055
G	2.54 BSC		0.100 BSC	
H	0.76	1.78	0.030	0.070
J	0.20	0.30	0.008	0.012
K	2.54	4.19	0.100	0.165
L	14.99	15.49	0.590	0.610
M	–	10°	–	10°
N	0.51	1.52	0.020	0.060

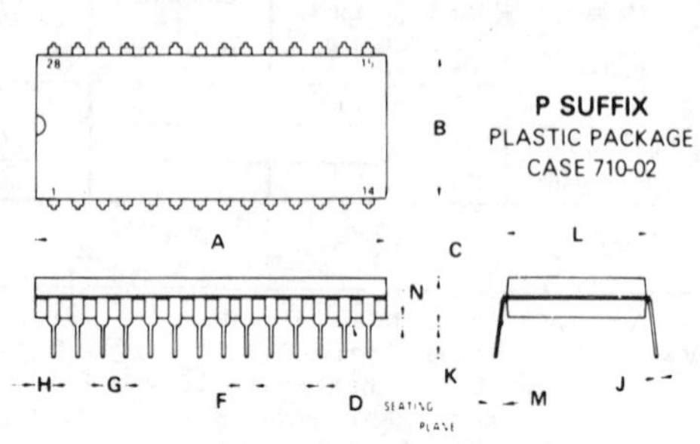

P SUFFIX
PLASTIC PACKAGE
CASE 710-02

NOTES:
1. POSITIONAL TOLERANCE OF LEADS (D), SHALL BE WITHIN 0.25mm(0.010) AT MAXIMUM MATERIAL CONDITION, IN RELATION TO SEATING PLANE AND EACH OTHER.
2. DIMENSION L TO CENTER OF LEADS WHEN FORMED PARALLEL.
3. DIMENSION B DOES NOT INCLUDE MOLD FLASH.

DIM	MILLIMETERS		INCHES	
	MIN	MAX	MIN	MAX
A	36.45	37.21	1.435	1.465
B	13.72	14.22	0.540	0.560
C	3.94	5.08	0.155	0.200
D	0.36	0.56	0.014	0.022
F	1.02	1.52	0.040	0.060
G	2.54 BSC		0.100 BSC	
H	1.65	2.16	0.065	0.085
J	0.20	0.38	0.008	0.015
K	2.92	3.43	0.115	0.135
L	15.24 BSC		0.600 BSC	
M	0°	15°	0°	15°
N	0.51	1.02	0.020	0.040

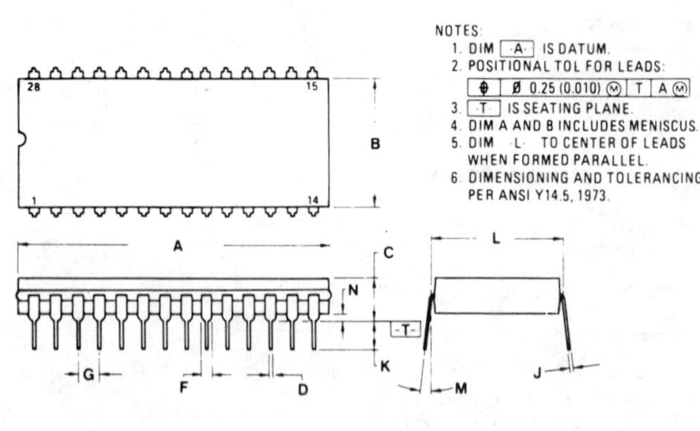

NOTES:
1. DIM -A- IS DATUM.
2. POSITIONAL TOL FOR LEADS:
   ⊕ Ø 0.25 (0.010) Ⓜ T A Ⓜ
3. -T- IS SEATING PLANE.
4. DIM A AND B INCLUDES MENISCUS.
5. DIM -L- TO CENTER OF LEADS WHEN FORMED PARALLEL.
6. DIMENSIONING AND TOLERANCING PER ANSI Y14.5, 1973.

S SUFFIX
CERDIP PACKAGE
CASE 733-01

DIM	MILLIMETERS		INCHES	
	MIN	MAX	MIN	MAX
A	36.45	37.85	1.435	1.490
B	12.70	15.37	0.500	0.605
C	4.06	5.84	0.160	0.230
D	0.38	0.56	0.015	0.022
F	1.27	1.65	0.050	0.065
G	2.54 BSC		0.100 BSC	
J	0.20	0.30	0.008	0.012
K	2.54	4.06	0.100	0.160
L	15.24 BSC		0.600 BSC	
M	5°	15°	5°	15°
N	0.51	1.27	0.020	0.050

MC6850
1.0 MHz
MC68A50
1.5 MHz
MC68B50
2.0 MHz

ASYNCHRONOUS COMMUNICATIONS INTERFACE ADAPTER (ACIA)

The MC6850 Asynchronous Communications Interface Adapter provides the data formatting and control to interface serial asynchronous data communications information to bus organized systems such as the MC6800 Microprocessing Unit.

The bus interface of the MC6850 includes select, enable, read/write, interrupt and bus interface logic to allow data transfer over an 8-bit bi-directional data bus. The parallel data of the bus system is serially transmitted and received by the asynchronous data interface, with proper formatting and error checking. The functional configuration of the ACIA is programmed via the data bus during system initialization. A programmable Control Register provides variable word lengths, clock division ratios, transmit control, receive control, and interrupt control. For peripheral or modem operation three control lines are provided. These lines allow the ACIA to interface directly with the MC6860L 0-600 bps digital modem.

- Eight and Nine-Bit Transmission
- Optional Even and Odd Parity
- Parity, Overrun and Framing Error Checking
- Programmable Control Register
- Optional ÷1, ÷16, and ÷64 Clock Modes
- Up to 500 kbps Transmission
- False Start Bit Deletion
- Peripheral/Modem Control Functions
- Double Buffered
- One or Two Stop Bit Operation

MOS

(N-CHANNEL, SILICON-GATE)

ASYNCHRONOUS COMMUNICATIONS INTERFACE ADAPTER

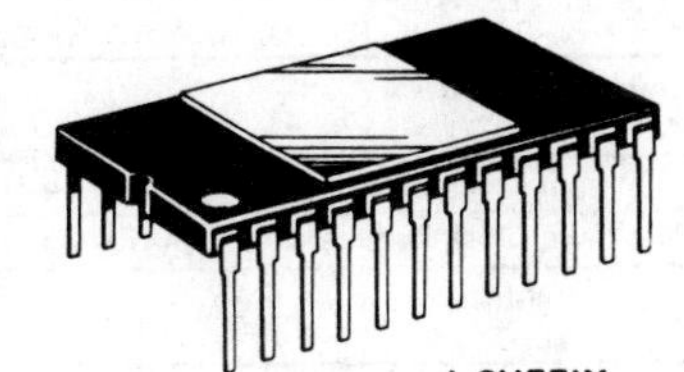

L SUFFIX
CERAMIC PACKAGE
CASE 716

NOT SHOWN: P SUFFIX
PLASTIC PACKAGE
CASE 709

MC6850 ASYNCHRONOUS COMMUNICATIONS INTERFACE ADAPTER BLOCK DIAGRAM

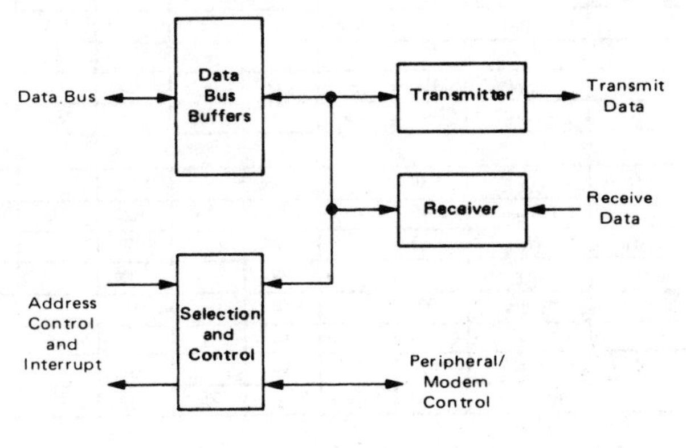

ORDERING INFORMATION

Speed	Device	Temperature Range
1.0 MHz	MC6850P,L	0 to +70°C
	MC6850CP,CL	-40 to +85°C
MIL-STD-883B	MC6850BJCS	-55 to +125°C
MIL-STD-883C	MC6850CJCS	
1.5 MHz	MC68A50P,L	0 to +70°C
	MC68A50CP,CL	-40 to +85°C
2.0 MHz	MC68B50P,L	0 to +70°C

DS 9493 R1

MAXIMUM RATINGS

Rating		Symbol	Value	Unit
Supply Voltage		V_{CC}	-0.3 to +7.0	Vdc
Input Voltage		V_{in}	-0.3 to +7.0	Vdc
Operating Temperature Range		T_A	0 to +70	°C
Storage Temperature Range		T_{stg}	-55 to +150	°C
Thermal Resistance	Plastic Ceramic	θ_{JA}	120 60	°C/W

This device contains circuitry to protect the inputs against damage due to high static voltages or electric fields; however, it is advised that normal precautions be taken to avoid application of any voltage higher than maximum rated voltages to this high-impedance circuit.

ELECTRICAL CHARACTERISTICS (V_{CC} = 5.0 V ±5%, V_{SS} = 0, T_A = 0 to 70°C unless otherwise noted.)

Characteristic		Symbol	Min	Typ	Max	Unit
Input High Voltage		V_{IH}	V_{SS} + 2.0	–	V_{CC}	Vdc
Input Low Voltage		V_{IL}	V_{SS} -0.3	–	V_{SS} + 0.8	Vdc
Input Leakage Current (V_{in} = 0 to 5.25 Vdc)	R/$\overline{W}$,CS0,CS1,$\overline{CS2}$,Enable RS, Rx D, Rx C, $\overline{CTS}$, $\overline{DCD}$	I_{in}	–	1.0	2.5	μAdc
Three-State (Off State) Input Current (V_{in} = 0.4 to 2.4 Vdc)	D0-D7	I_{TSI}	–	2.0	10	μAdc
Output High Voltage	D0-D7	V_{OH}				Vdc
(I_{Load} = -205 μAdc, Enable Pulse Width <25 μs)			V_{SS} + 2.4	–	–	
(I_{Load} = -100 μAdc, Enable Pulse Width <25 μs)	Tx Data, $\overline{RTS}$		V_{SS} + 2.4	–	–	
Output Low Voltage (I_{Load} = 1.6 mAdc, Enable Pulse Width <25 μs)		V_{OL}	–	–	V_{SS} + 0.4	Vdc
Output Leakage Current (Off State) (V_{OH} = 2.4 Vdc)	$\overline{IRQ}$	I_{LOH}	–	1.0	10	μAdc
Power Dissipation		P_D	–	300	525	mW
Input Capacitance		C_{in}				pF
(V_{in} = 0, T_A = 25°C, f = 1.0 MHz)	D0-D7		–	10	12.5	
	E, Tx Clk, Rx Clk, R/$\overline{W}$, RS, Rx Data, CS0, CS1, $\overline{CS2}$, $\overline{CTS}$, $\overline{DCD}$		–	7.0	7.5	
Output Capacitance (V_{in} = 0, T_A = 25°C, f = 1.0 MHz)	$\overline{RTS}$, Tx Data $\overline{IRQ}$	C_{out}	– –	– –	10 5.0	pF
Minimum Clock Pulse Width, Low (Figure 1)	÷16, ÷64 Modes	PW_{CL}	600	–	–	ns
Minimum Clock Pulse Width, High (Figure 2)	÷16, ÷64 Modes	PW_{CH}	600	–	–	ns
Clock Frequency	÷1 Mode ÷16, ÷64 Modes	f_C	– –	– –	500 800	kHz
Clock-to-Data Delay for Transmitter (Figure 3)		t_{TDD}	–	–	1.0	μs
Receive Data Setup Time (Figure 4)	÷1 Mode	t_{RDSU}	500	–	–	ns
Receive Data Hold Time (Figure 5)	÷1 Mode	t_{RDH}	500	–	–	ns
$\overline{\text{Interrupt Request}}$ Release Time (Figure 6)		t_{IR}	–	–	1.2	μs
$\overline{\text{Request-to-Send}}$ Delay Time (Figure 6)		t_{RTS}	–	–	1.0	μs
Input Transition Times (Except Enable)		t_r, t_f	–	–	1.0*	μs

*1.0 μs or 10% of the pulse width, whichever is smaller.

BUS TIMING CHARACTERISTICS

Characteristic	Symbol	MC6850		MC68A50		MC68B50		Unit
		Min	Max	Min	Max	Min	Max	
READ (Figures 7 and 9)								
Enable Cycle Time	t_{cycE}	1.0	–	0.666	–	0.500	–	μs
Enable Pulse Width, High	PW_{EH}	0.45	25	0.28	25	0.22	25	μs
Enable Pulse Width, Low	PW_{EL}	0.43	–	0.28	–	0.21	–	μs
Setup Time, Address and R/$\overline{W}$ valid to Enable positive transistion	t_{AS}	160	–	140	–	70	–	ns
Data Delay Time	t_{DDR}	–	320	–	220	–	180	ns
Data Hold Time	t_H	10	–	10	–	10	–	ns
Address Hold Time	t_{AH}	10	–	10	–	10	–	ns
Rise and Fall Time for Enable input	t_{Er}, t_{Ef}	–	25	–	25	–	25	ns
WRITE (Figures 8 and 9)								
Enable Cycle Time	t_{cycE}	1.0	–	0.666	–	500	–	μs
Enable Pulse Width, High	PW_{EH}	0.45	25	0.28	25	0.22	25	μs
Enable Pulse Width, Low	PW_{EL}	0.43	–	0.28	–	0.21	–	μs
Setup Time, Address and R/$\overline{W}$ valid to Enable positive transition	t_{AS}	160	–	140	–	70	–	ns
Data Setup Time	t_{DSW}	195	–	80	–	60	–	ns
Data Hold Time	t_H	10	–	10	–	10	–	ns
Address Hold Time	t_{AH}	10	–	10	–	10	–	ns
Rise and Fall Time for Enable input	t_{Er}, t_{Ef}	–	25	–	25	–	25	ns

FIGURE 1 – CLOCK PULSE WIDTH, LOW-STATE

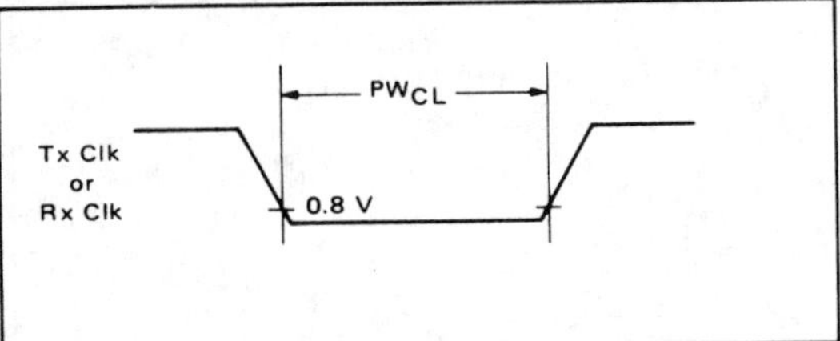

FIGURE 2 – CLOCK PULSE WIDTH, HIGH-STATE

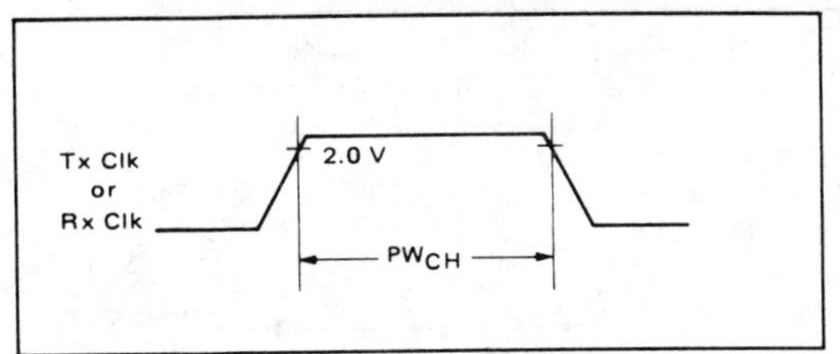

FIGURE 3 – TRANSMIT DATA OUTPUT DELAY

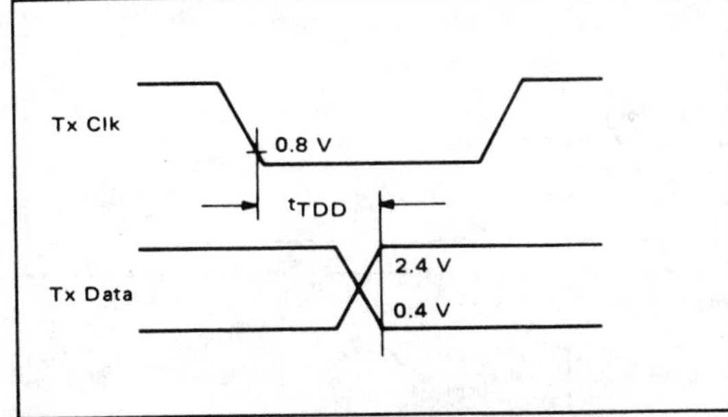

FIGURE 4 – RECEIVE DATA SETUP TIME
(÷1 Mode)

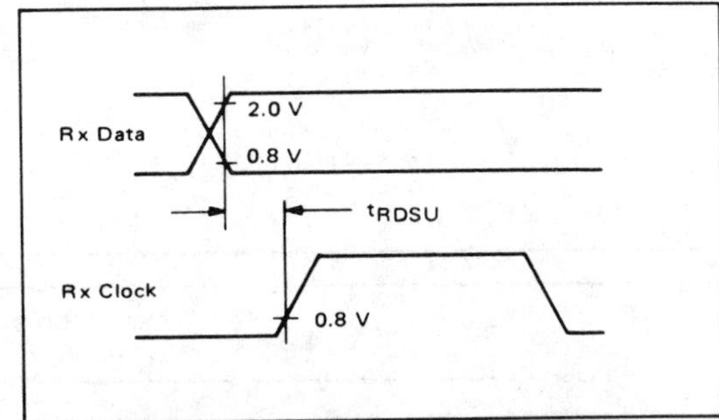

FIGURE 5 – RECEIVE DATA HOLD TIME
(÷1 Mode)

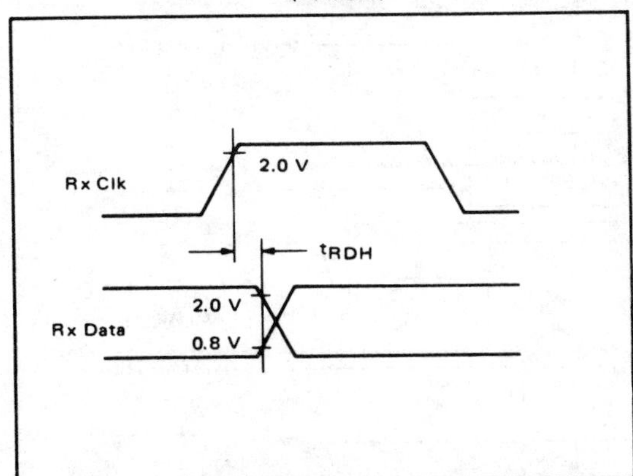

FIGURE 6 – $\overline{\text{REQUEST-TO-SEND}}$ DELAY AND $\overline{\text{INTERRUPT-REQUEST}}$ RELEASE TIMES

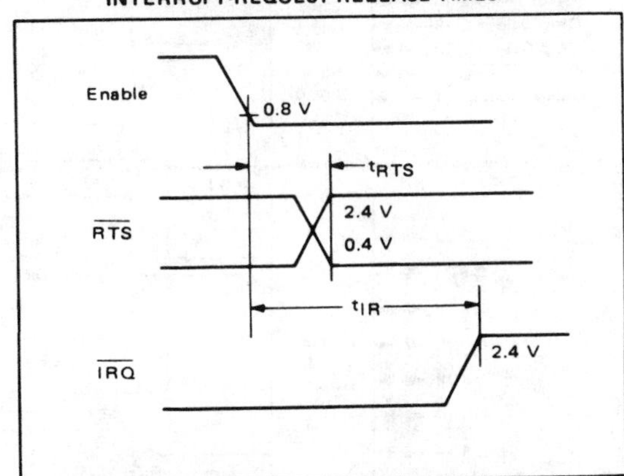

FIGURE 7 – BUS READ TIMING CHARACTERISTICS
(Read information from ACIA)

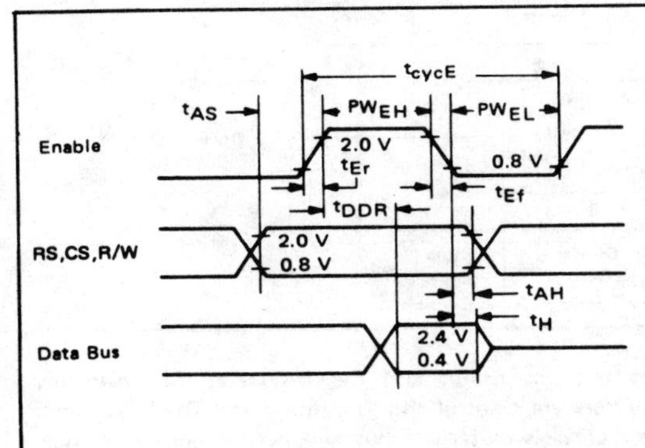

FIGURE 8 – BUS WRITE TIMING CHARACTERISTICS
(Write information into ACIA)

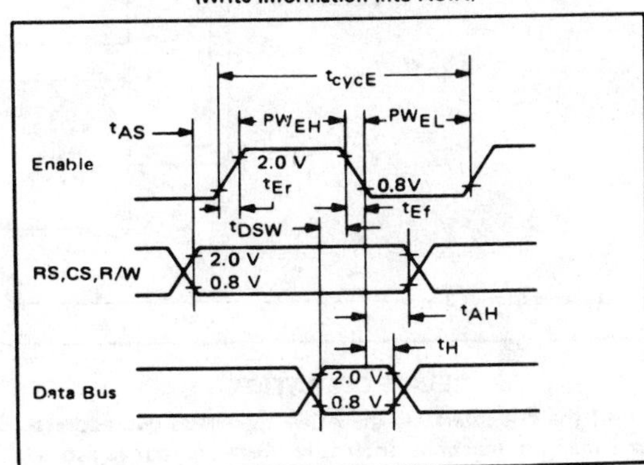

FIGURE 9 – BUS TIMING TEST LOADS

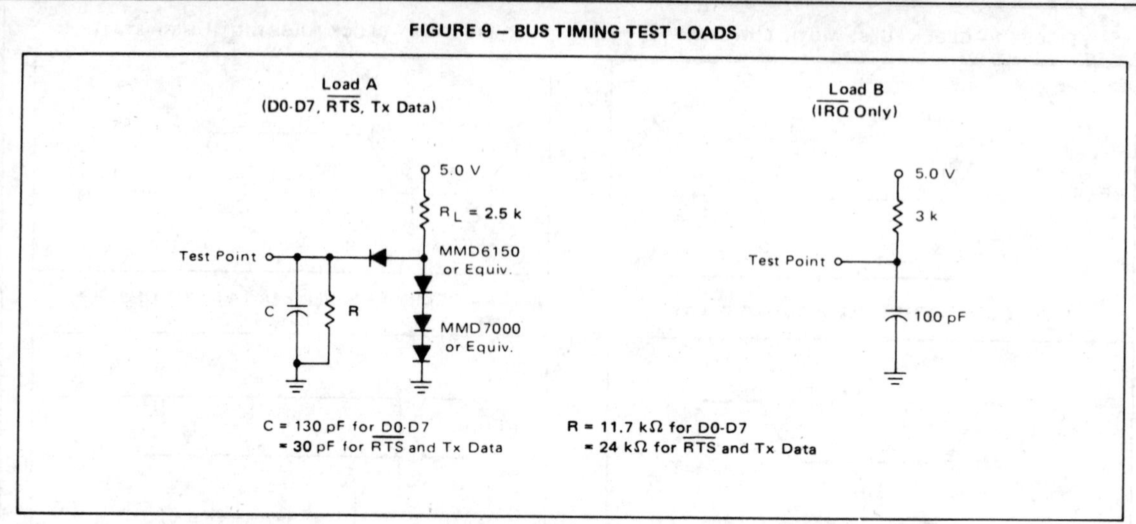

EXPANDED BLOCK DIAGRAM

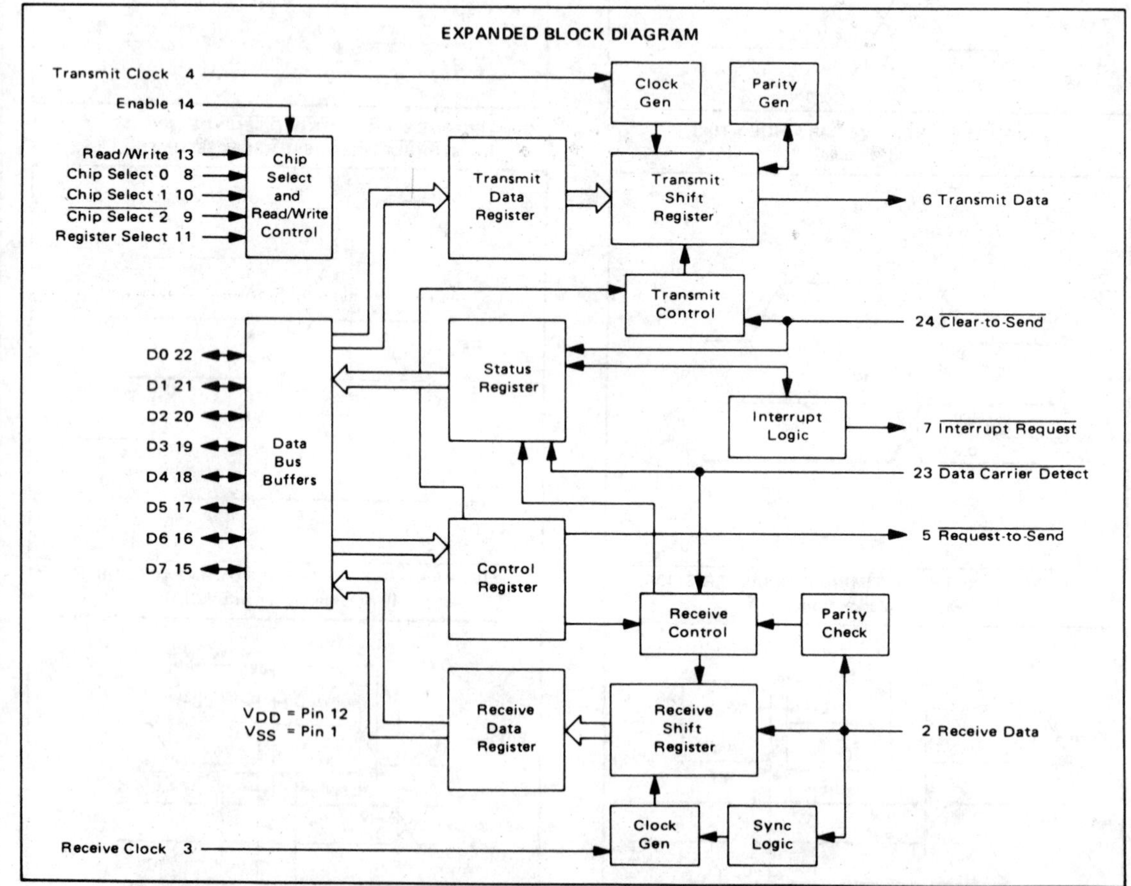

DEVICE OPERATION

At the bus interface, the ACIA appears as two addressable memory locations. Internally, there are four registers: two read-only and two write-only registers. The read-only registers are Status and Receive Data; the write-only registers are Control and Transmit Data. The serial interface consists of serial input and output lines with independent clocks, and three peripheral/modem control lines.

MC6850

POWER ON/MASTER RESET

The master reset (CR0, CR1) should be set during system initialization to insure the reset condition and prepare for programming the ACIA functional configuration when the communications channel is required. Control bits CR5 and CR6 should also be programmed to define the state of $\overline{RTS}$ whenever master reset is utilized. The ACIA also contains internal power-on reset logic to detect the power line turn-on transition and hold the chip in a reset state to prevent erroneous output transitions prior to initialization. This circuitry depends on clean power turn-on transitions. The power-on reset is released by means of the bus-programmed master reset which must be applied prior to operating the ACIA. After master resetting the ACIA, the programmable Control Register can be set for a number of options such as variable clock divider ratios, variable word length, one or two stop bits, parity (even, odd, or none), etc.

TRANSMIT

A typical transmitting sequence consists of reading the ACIA Status Register either as a result of an interrupt or in the ACIA's turn in a polling sequence. A character may be written into the Transmit Data Register if the status read operation has indicated that the Transmit Data Register is empty. This character is transferred to a Shift Register where it is serialized and transmitted from the Transmit Data output preceded by a start bit and followed by one or two stop bits. Internal parity (odd or even) can be optionally added to the character and will occur between the last data bit and the first stop bit. After the first character is written in the Data Register, the Status Register can be read again to check for a Transmit Data Register Empty condition and current peripheral status. If the register is empty, another character can be loaded for transmission even though the first character is in the process of being transmitted (because of double buffering). The second character will be automatically transferred into the Shift Register when the first character transmission is completed. This sequence continues until all the characters have been transmitted.

RECEIVE

Data is received from a peripheral by means of the Receive Data input. A divide-by-one clock ratio is provided for an externally synchronized clock (to its data) while the divide-by-16 and 64 ratios are provided for internal synchronization. Bit synchronization in the divide-by-16 and 64 modes is initiated by the detection of the leading mark-to-space transition of the start bit. False start bit deletion capability insures that a full half bit of a start bit has been received before the internal clock is synchronized to the bit time. As a character is being received, parity (odd or even) will be checked and the error indication will be available in the Status Register along with framing error, overrun error, and Receive Data Register full. In a typical receiving sequence, the Status Register is read to determine if a character has been received from a peripheral. If the Receiver Data Register is full, the character is placed on the 8-bit ACIA bus when a Read Data command is received from the MPU. When parity has been selected for an 8-bit word (7 bits plus parity), the receiver strips the parity bit (D7 = 0) so that data alone is transferred to the MPU. This feature reduces MPU programming. The Status Register can continue to be read again to determine when another character is available in the Receive Data Register. The receiver is also double buffered so that a character can be read from the data register as another character is being received in the shift register. The above sequence continues until all characters have been received.

INPUT/OUTPUT FUNCTIONS

ACIA INTERFACE SIGNALS FOR MPU

The ACIA interfaces to the MC6800 MPU with an 8-bit bi-directional data bus, three chip select lines, a register select line, an interrupt request line, read/write line, and enable line. These signals, in conjunction with the MC6800 VMA output, permit the MPU to have complete control over the ACIA.

ACIA Bi-Directional Data (D0-D7) – The bi-directional data lines (D0-D7) allow for data transfer between the ACIA and the MPU. The data bus output drivers are three-state devices that remain in the high-impedance (off) state except when the MPU performs an ACIA read operation.

ACIA Enable (E) – The Enable signal, E, is a high impedance TTL compatible input that enables the bus input/output data buffers and clocks data to and from the ACIA. This signal will normally be a derivative of the MC6800 $\phi 2$ Clock.

Read/Write (R/W) – The Read/Write line is a high impedance input that is TTL compatible and is used to control the direction of data flow through the ACIA's input/output data bus interface. When Read/Write is high (MPU Read cycle), ACIA output drivers are turned on and a selected register is read. When it is low, the ACIA output drivers are turned off and the MPU writes into a selected register. Therefore, the Read/Write signal is used to select read-only or write-only registers within the ACIA.

Chip Select (CS0, CS1, $\overline{CS2}$) – These three high impedance TTL compatible input lines are used to address the ACIA. The ACIA is selected when CS0 and CS1 are high and $\overline{CS2}$ is low. Transfers of data to and from the ACIA are then performed under the control of the Enable signal, Read/Write, and Register Select.

Register Select (RS) – The Register Select line is a high impedance input that is TTL compatible. A high level is used to select the Transmit/Receive Data Registers and a low level the Control/Status Registers. The Read/Write signal line is used in conjunction with Register Select to select the read-only or write-only register in each register pair.

$\overline{\text{Interrupt Request}}$ ($\overline{IRQ}$) – $\overline{\text{Interrupt Request}}$ is a TTL compatible, open-drain (no internal pullup), active low output that is used to interrupt the MPU. The $\overline{IRQ}$ output remains low as long as the cause of the interrupt is present and the appropriate interrupt enable within the ACIA is set. The IRQ status bit, when high, indicates the $\overline{IRQ}$ output is in the active state.

Interrupts result from conditions in both the transmitter and receiver sections of the ACIA. The transmitter section causes an interrupt when the Transmitter Interrupt Enabled condition is selected (CR5 · $\overline{CR6}$), and the Transmit Data Register Empty (TDRE) status bit is high. The TDRE status bit indicates the current status of the Transmitter Data Register except when inhibited by Clear-to-Send ($\overline{CTS}$) being high or the ACIA being maintained in the Reset condition. The interrupt is cleared by writing data into the Transmit Data Register. The interrupt is masked by disabling the Transmitter Interrupt via CR5 or CR6 or by the loss of $\overline{CTS}$ which inhibits the TDRE status bit. The Receiver section causes an interrupt when the Receiver Interrupt Enable is set and the Receive Data Register Full (RDRF) status bit is high, an Overrun has occurred, or Data Carrier Detect ($\overline{DCD}$) has gone high. An interrupt resulting from the RDRF status bit can be cleared by reading data or resetting the ACIA. Interrupts caused by Overrun or loss of $\overline{DCD}$ are cleared by reading the status register after the error condition has occurred and then reading the Receive Data Register or resetting the ACIA. The receiver interrupt is masked by resetting the Receiver Interrupt Enable.

CLOCK INPUTS

Separate high impedance TTL compatible inputs are provided for clocking of transmitted and received data. Clock frequencies of 1, 16 or 64 times the data rate may be selected.

Transmit Clock (Tx Clk) – The Transmit Clock input is used for the clocking of transmitted data. The transmitter initiates data on the negative transition of the clock.

Receive Clock (Rx Clk) – The Receive Clock input is used for synchronization of received data. (In the ÷ 1 mode, the clock and data must be synchronized externally.) The receiver samples the data on the positive transiton of the clock.

SERIAL INPUT/OUTPUT LINES

Receive Data (Rx Data) – The Receive Data line is a high impedance TTL compatible input through which data is received in a serial format. Synchronization with a clock for detection of data is accomplished internally when clock rates of 16 or 64 times the bit rate are used. Data rates are in the range of 0 to 500 kbps when external synchronization is utilized.

Transmit Data (Tx Data) – The Transmit Data output line transfers serial data to a modem or other peripheral. Data rates are in the range of 0 to 500 kbps when external synchronization is utilized.

PERIPHERAL/MODEM CONTROL

The ACIA includes several functions that permit limited control of a peripheral or modem. The functions included are Clear-to-Send, Request-to-Send and Data Carrier Detect.

Clear-to-Send ($\overline{CTS}$) – This high impedance TTL compatible input provides automatic control of the transmitting end of a communications link via the modem Clear-to-Send active low output by inhibiting the Transmit Data Register Empty (TDRE) status bit.

Request-to-Send ($\overline{RTS}$) – The Request-to-Send output enables the MPU to control a peripheral or modem via the data bus. The $\overline{RTS}$ output corresponds to the state of the Control Register bits CR5 and CR6. When CR6 = 0 or both CR5 and CR6 = 1, the $\overline{RTS}$ output is low (the active state). This output can also be used for Data Terminal Ready ($\overline{DTR}$).

Data Carrier Detect ($\overline{DCD}$) – This high impedance TTL compatible input provides automatic control, such as in the receiving end of a communications link by means of a modem Data Carrier Detect output. The $\overline{DCD}$ input inhibits and initializes the receiver section of the ACIA when high. A low to high transition of the Data Carrier Detect initiates an interrupt to the MPU to indicate the occurrence of a loss of carrier when the Receive Interrupt Enable bit is set.

ACIA REGISTERS

The expanded block diagram for the ACIA indicates the internal registers on the chip that are used for the status, control, receiving, and transmitting of data. The content of each of the registers is summarized in Table 1.

TRANSMIT DATA REGISTER (TDR)

Data is written in the Transmit Data Register during the negative transition of the enable (E) when the ACIA has been addressed and RS · $\overline{R/W}$ is selected. Writing data into the register causes the Transmit Data Register Empty bit in the Status Register to go low. Data can then be transmitted. If the transmitter is idling and no character is being transmitted, then the transfer will take place within one bit time of the trailing edge of the Write command. If a character is being transmitted, the new data character will commence as soon as the previous character is complete. The transfer of data causes the Transmit Data Register Empty (TDRE) bit to indicate empty.

RECEIVE DATA REGISTER (RDR)

Data is automatically transferred to the empty Receive Data Register (RDR) from the receiver deserializer (a shift register) upon receiving a complete character. This event causes the Receive Data Register Full bit (RDRF) in the status buffer to go high (full). Data may then be read through the bus by addressing the ACIA and selecting the Receive Data Register with RS and R/W high when the ACIA is enabled. The non-destructive read cycle causes the RDRF bit to be cleared to empty although

TABLE 1 – DEFINITION OF ACIA REGISTER CONTENTS

Data Bus Line Number	Buffer Address RS • $\overline{R/W}$ Transmit Data Register (Write Only)	RS • R/W Receive Data Register (Read Only)	$\overline{RS}$ • $\overline{R/W}$ Control Register (Write Only)	$\overline{RS}$ • R/W Status Register (Read Only)
0	Data Bit 0*	Data Bit 0	Counter Divide Select 1 (CR0)	Receive Data Register Full (RDRF)
1	Data Bit 1	Data Bit 1	Counter Divide Select 2 (CR1)	Transmit Data Register Empty (TDRE)
2	Data Bit 2	Data Bit 2	Word Select 1 (CR2)	Data Carrier Detect ($\overline{DCD}$)
3	Data Bit 3	Data Bit 3	Word Select 2 (CR3)	Clear to Send ($\overline{CTS}$)
4	Data Bit 4	Data Bit 4	Word Select 3 (CR4)	Framing Error (FE)
5	Data Bit 5	Data Bit 5	Transmit Control 1 (CR5)	Receiver Overrun (OVRN)
6	Data Bit 6	Data Bit 6	Transmit Control 2 (CR6)	Parity Error (PE)
7	Data Bit 7***	Data Bit 7**	Receive Interrupt Enable (CR7)	Interrupt Request (IRQ)

* Leading bit = LSB = Bit 0
** Data bit will be zero in 7-bit plus parity modes.
*** Data bit is "don't care" in 7-bit plus parity modes.

the data is retained in the RDR. The status is maintained by RDRF as to whether or not the data is current. When the Receive Data Register is full, the automatic transfer of data from the Receiver Shift Register to the Data Register is inhibited and the RDR contents remain valid with its current status stored in the Status Register.

CONTROL REGISTER

The ACIA Control Register consists of eight bits of write-only buffer that are selected when RS and R/W are low. This register controls the function of the receiver, transmitter, interrupt enables, and the $\overline{\text{Request-to-Send}}$ peripheral/modem control output.

Counter Divide Select Bits (CR0 and CR1) – The Counter Divide Select Bits (CR0 and CR1) determine the divide ratios utilized in both the transmitter and receiver sections of the ACIA. Additionally, these bits are used to provide a master reset for the ACIA which clears the Status Register (except for external conditions on $\overline{CTS}$ and $\overline{DCD}$) and initializes both the receiver and transmitter. Master reset does not affect other Control Register bits. Note that after power-on or a power fail/restart, these bits must be set high to reset the ACIA. After reseting, the clock divide ratio may be selected. These counter select bits provide for the following clock divide ratios:

CR1	CR0	Function
0	0	÷ 1
0	1	÷ 16
1	0	÷ 64
1	1	Master Reset

Word Select Bits (CR2, CR3, and CR4) – The Word Select bits are used to select word length, parity, and the number of stop bits. The encoding format is as follows:

CR4	CR3	CR2	Function
0	0	0	7 Bits + Even Parity + 2 Stop Bits
0	0	1	7 Bits + Odd Parity + 2 Stop Bits
0	1	0	7 Bits + Even Parity + 1 Stop Bit
0	1	1	7 Bits + Odd Parity + 1 Stop Bit
1	0	0	8 Bits + 2 Stop Bits
1	0	1	8 Bits + 1 Stop Bit
1	1	0	8 Bits + Even Parity + 1 Stop Bit
1	1	1	8 Bits + Odd Parity + 1 Stop Bit

Word length, Parity Select, and Stop Bit changes are not buffered and therefore become effective immediately.

Transmitter Control Bits (CR5 and CR6) – Two Transmitter Control bits provide for the control of the interrupt from the Transmit Data Register Empty condition, the $\overline{\text{Request-to-Send}}$ ($\overline{RTS}$) output, and the transmission of a Break level (space). The following encoding format is used:

CR6	CR5	Function
0	0	$\overline{RTS}$ = low, Transmitting Interrupt Disabled.
0	1	$\overline{RTS}$ = low, Transmitting Interrupt Enabled.
1	0	$\overline{RTS}$ = high, Transmitting Interrupt Disabled.
1	1	$\overline{RTS}$ = low, Transmits a Break level on the Transmit Data Output. Transmitting Interrupt Disabled.

Receive Interrupt Enable Bit (CR7) – The following interrupts will be enabled by a high level in bit position 7 of the Control Register (CR7): Receive Data Register Full, Overrun, or a low to high transistion on the $\overline{\text{Data Carrier Detect}}$ ($\overline{DCD}$) signal line.

STATUS REGISTER

Information on the status of the ACIA is available to the MPU by reading the ACIA Status Register. This read-only register is selected when RS is low and R/W is high. Information stored in this register indicates the status of the Transmit Data Register, the Receive Data Register and error logic, and the peripheral/modem status inputs of the ACIA.

Receive Data Register Full (RDRF), Bit 0 – Receive Data Register Full indicates that received data has been transferred to the Receive Data Register. RDRF is cleared after an MPU read of the Receive Data Register or by a master reset. The cleared or empty state indicates that the contents of the Receive Data Register are not current. $\overline{\text{Data Carrier Detect}}$ being high also causes RDRF to indicate empty.

Transmit Data Register Empty (TDRE), Bit 1 – The Transmit Data Register Empty bit being set high indicates that the Transmit Data Register contents have been transferred and that new data may be entered. The low state indicates that the register is full and that transmission of a new character has not begun since the last write data command.

$\overline{\text{Data Carrier Detect}}$ ($\overline{\text{DCD}}$), Bit 2 – The $\overline{\text{Data Carrier Detect}}$ bit will be high when the $\overline{\text{DCD}}$ input from a modem has gone high to indicate that a carrier is not present. This bit going high causes an Interrupt Request to be generated when the Receive Interrupt Enable is set. It remains high after the $\overline{\text{DCD}}$ input is returned low until cleared by first reading the Status Register and then the Data Register or until a master reset occurs. If the $\overline{\text{DCD}}$ input remains high after read status and read data or master reset has occurred, the interrupt is cleared, the $\overline{\text{DCD}}$ status bit remains high and will follow the $\overline{\text{DCD}}$ input.

$\overline{\text{Clear-to-Send}}$ ($\overline{\text{CTS}}$), Bit 3 – The $\overline{\text{Clear-to-Send}}$ bit indicates the state of the $\overline{\text{Clear-to-Send}}$ input from a modem. A low $\overline{\text{CTS}}$ indicates that there is a $\overline{\text{Clear-to-Send}}$ from the modem. In the high state, the Transmit Data Register Empty bit is inhibited and the $\overline{\text{Clear-to-Send}}$ status bit will be high. Master reset does not affect the $\overline{\text{Clear-to-Send}}$ Status bit.

Framing Error (FE), Bit 4 – Framing error indicates that the received character is improperly framed by a start and a stop bit and is detected by the absence of the 1st stop bit. This error indicates a synchronization error, faulty transmission, or a break condition. The framing error flag is set or reset during the receive data transfer time. Therefore, this error indicator is present throughout the time that the associated character is available.

Receiver Overrun (OVRN), Bit 5 – Overrun is an error flag that indicates that one or more characters in the data stream were lost. That is, a character or a number of characters were received but not read from the Receive Data Register (RDR) prior to subsequent characters being received. The overrun condition begins at the midpoint of the last bit of the second character received in succession without a read of the RDR having occurred. The Overrun does not occur in the Status Register until the valid character prior to Overrun has been read. The RDRF bit remains set until the Overrun is reset. Character synchronization is maintained during the Overrun condition. The Overrun indication is reset after the reading of data from the Receive Data Register or by a Master Reset.

Parity Error (PE), Bit 6 – The parity error flag indicates that the number of highs (ones) in the character does not agree with the preselected odd or even parity. Odd parity is defined to be when the total number of ones is odd. The parity error indication will be present as long as the data character is in the RDR. If no parity is selected, then both the transmitter parity generator output and the receiver parity check results are inhibited.

Interrupt Request (IRQ), Bit 7 – The IRQ bit indicates the state of the $\overline{\text{IRQ}}$ output. Any interrupt condition with its applicable enable will be indicated in this status bit. Anytime the $\overline{\text{IRQ}}$ output is low the IRQ bit will be high to indicate the interrupt or service request status. IRQ is cleared by a read operation to the Receive Data Register or a write operation to the Transmit Data Register.

PIN ASSIGNMENT

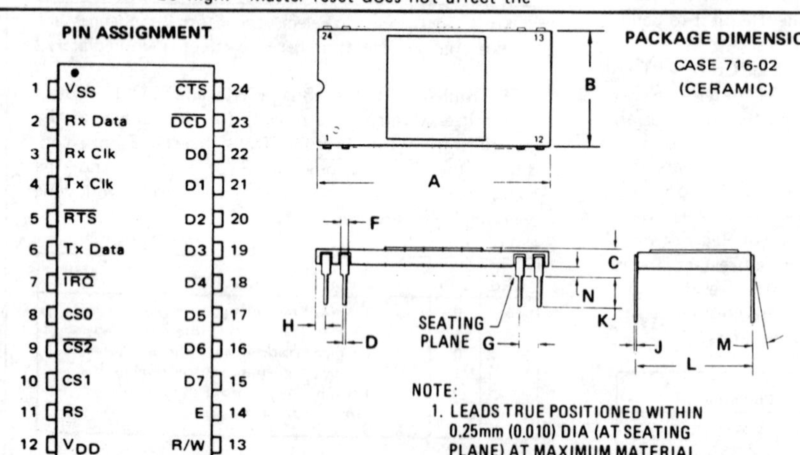

NOTE:
1. LEADS TRUE POSITIONED WITHIN 0.25mm (0.010) DIA (AT SEATING PLANE) AT MAXIMUM MATERIAL CONDITION.

PACKAGE DIMENSIONS

CASE 716-02
(CERAMIC)

DIM	MILLIMETERS		INCHES	
	MIN	MAX	MIN	MAX
A	29.97	30.99	1.180	1.220
B	14.88	15.62	0.585	0.615
C	3.05	4.19	0.120	0.165
D	0.38	0.53	0.015	0.021
F	0.76	1.40	0.030	0.055
G	2.54 BSC		0.100 BSC	
H	0.76	1.78	0.030	0.070
J	0.20	0.30	0.008	0.012
K	2.54	4.19	0.100	0.165
L	14.88	15.37	0.585	0.605
M	–	10°	–	10°
N	0.51	1.52	0.020	0.060

MOTOROLA Semiconductor Products Inc.

3501 ED BLUESTEIN BLVD., AUSTIN, TEXAS 78721 • A SUBSIDIARY OF MOTOROLA INC.

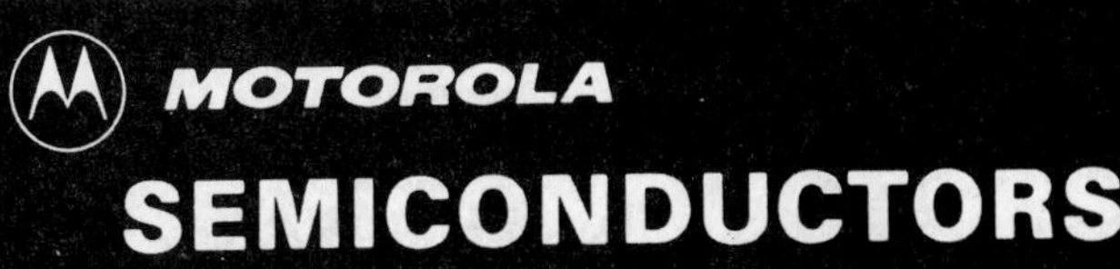

MC6843

MOS

(N-CHANNEL, SILICON-GATE)

FLOPPY DISK CONTROLLER

FLOPPY DISK CONTROLLER (FDC)

The MC6843 Floppy Disk Controller performs the complex MPU/Floppy interface function. The FDC was designed to optimize the balance between Hardware and Software in order to achieve integration of all key functions and maintain flexibility.

The FDC can interface a wide range of drives with a minimum of external hardware. Multiple drives can be controlled with the addition of external multiplexing rather than additional FDCs.

- Format Compatible with IBM 3740
- User Programmable Read/Write Format
- Ten Powerful Macro Commands
- Macro-End Interrupt Allows Parallel Processing of MPU and FDC
- Controls Multiple Floppies with External Multiplexing
- Direct Interface with M6800 Bus
- Programmable Step and Settling Times Enable Operation with a Wide Range of Floppy Drives
- Offers Both Program Controlled I/O (PCIO) and DMA Data Transfer Mode
- Free-Format Read or Write
- Single 5-Volt Power Supply
- All Registers Directly Accessible

P SUFFIX
PLASTIC PACKAGE
CASE 711

FIGURE 1 — SYSTEM BLOCK DIAGRAM

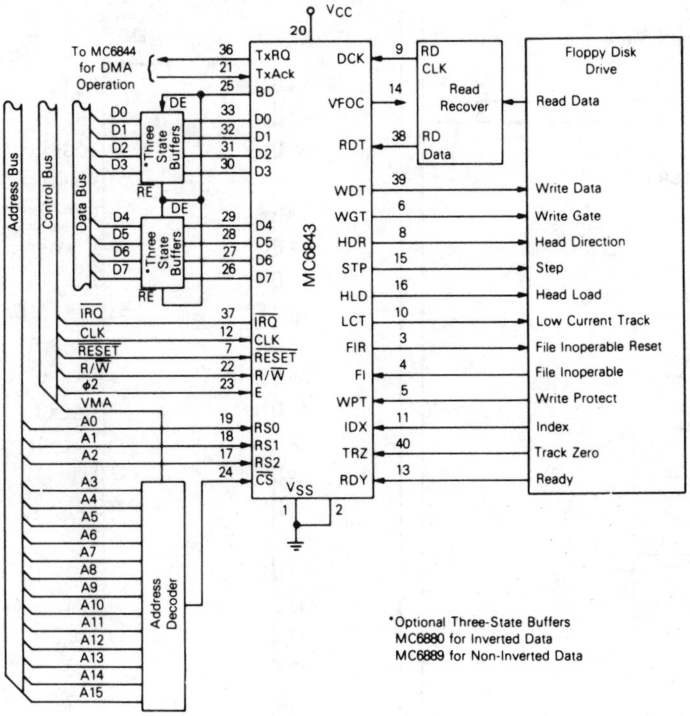

*Optional Three-State Buffers
MC6880 for Inverted Data
MC6889 for Non-Inverted Data

FIGURE 2 — PIN ASSIGNMENT

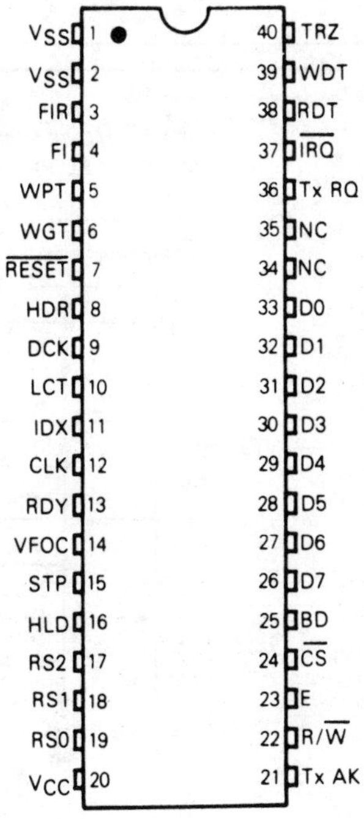

Signal	Pin	Pin	Signal
V_{SS}	1	40	TRZ
V_{SS}	2	39	WDT
FIR	3	38	RDT
FI	4	37	$\overline{IRQ}$
WPT	5	36	Tx RQ
WGT	6	35	NC
$\overline{RESET}$	7	34	NC
HDR	8	33	D0
DCK	9	32	D1
LCT	10	31	D2
IDX	11	30	D3
CLK	12	29	D4
RDY	13	28	D5
VFOC	14	27	D6
STP	15	26	D7
HLD	16	25	BD
RS2	17	24	$\overline{CS}$
RS1	18	23	E
RS0	19	22	R/$\overline{W}$
V_{CC}	20	21	Tx AK

DS9837
(Replaces ADI-477)

MC6844 (1.0 MHz)
MC68A44 (1.5 MHz)
MC68B44 (2.0 MHz)

MOS

(N-CHANNEL, SILICON-GATE)

DIRECT MEMORY ACCESS CONTROLLER (DMAC)

DIRECT MEMORY ACCESS CONTROLLER (DMAC)

The MC6844 Direct Memory Access Controller (DMAC) performs the function of transferring data directly between memory and peripheral device controllers. It directly transfers the data by controlling the address and data bus in place of an MPU in a bus organized system.

The bus interface of the MC6844 includes select, read/write, interrupt, transfer request/grant, a data port, and an address port which allow data transfer over an 8-bit bidirectional data bus. The funtional configuration of the DMAC is programmed via the data bus. The internal structure provides for control and handling of four individual channels, each of which is separately configured. Programmable control registers provide control for data transfer location and data block length, individual channel control and transfer mode configuration, priority of channel servicing, data chaining, and interrupt control. Status and control lines provide control to peripheral controllers.

The mode of transfer for each channel can be programmed as one of two single-byte transfer modes or a burst transfer mode.

Typical MC6844 applications are a Floppy Disk Controller (FDC) and an Advanced Data Link Controller (ADLC) DMA interface.

MC6844 features include:

- Four DMA Channels, Each Having a 16-Bit Address Register and a 16-Bit Byte Count Register
- 2 M Byte/Sec Maximum Data Transfer Rate
- Selection of Fixed or Rotating Priority Service Control
- Separate Control Bits for Each Channel
- Data Chain Function
- Address Increment or Decrement Update
- Programmable Interrupts and DMA End to Peripheral Controllers

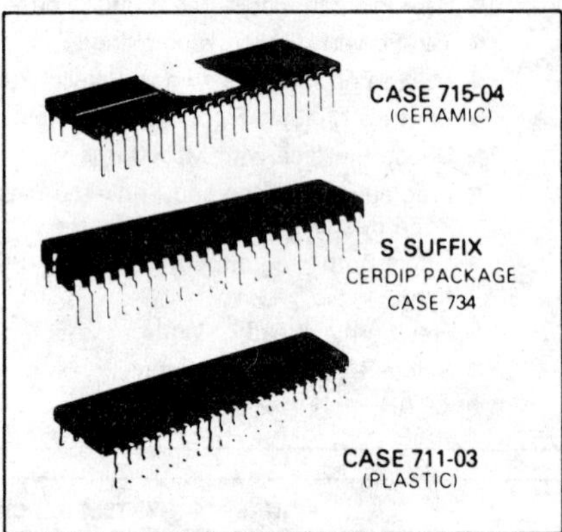

FIGURE 1 – M6800 MICROCOMPUTER FAMILY BLOCK DIAGRAM

Microprocessor
Read Only Memory
Random Access Memory
Peripheral Controller
MC6844 Direct Memory Access
Address Bus
Data Bus

PIN ASSIGNMENT

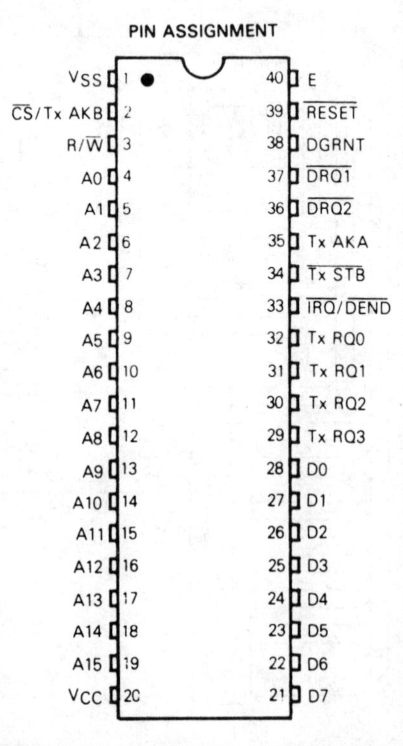

3501 ED BLUESTEIN BLVD., AUSTIN, TEXAS 78721

MC6845 (1.0 MHz) **MC6845☆1** (1.0 MHz)
MC68A45 (1.5 MHz) **MC68A45☆1** (1.5 MHz)
MC68B45 (2.0 MHz) **MC68B45☆1** (2.0 MHz)

MOS

(N-CHANNEL, SILICON-GATE)

CRT CONTROLLER (CRTC)

CRT CONTROLLER (CRTC)

The MC6845 CRT Controller performs the interface between an MPU and a raster-scan CRT display. It is intended for use in MPU-based controllers for CRT terminals in stand-alone or cluster configurations.

The CRTC is optimized for the hardware/software balance required for maximum flexibility. All keyboard functions, reads, writes, cursor movements, and editing are under processor control. The CRTC provides video timing and refresh memory addressing.

- Useful in Monochrome or Color CRT Applications
- Applications Include "Glass-Teletype," Smart, Programmable, Intelligent CRT Terminals; Video Games; Information Displays
- Alphanumeric, Semi-Graphic, and Full-Graphic Capability
- Fully Programmable Via Processor Data Bus. Timing May Be Generated for Almost Any Alphanumeric Screen Format, e.g., 80 × 24, 72 × 64, 132 × 20
- Single +5 V Supply
- M6800 Compatible Bus Interface
- TTL-Compatible Inputs and Outputs
- Start Address Register Provides Hardware Scroll (by Page, Line, or Character)
- Programmable Cursor Register Allows Control of Cursor Format and Blink Rate
- Light Pen Register
- Refresh (Screen) Memory May be Multiplexed Between the CRTC and the MPU Thus Removing the Requirements for Line Buffers or External DMA Devices
- Programmable Interlace or Non-Interlace Scan Modes
- 14-Bit Refresh Address Allows Up to 16K of Refresh Memory for Use in Character or Semi-Graphic Displays
- 5-Bit Row Address Allows Up to 32 Scan-Line Character Blocks
- By Utilizing Both the Refresh Addresses and the Row Addresses, a 512K Address Space is Available for Use in Graphics Systems
- Refresh Addresses are Provided During Retrace, Allowing the CRTC to Provide Row Addresses to Refresh Dynamic RAMs
- Programmable Skew for Cursor and Display Enable (DE)
- Pin Compatible with the MC6835

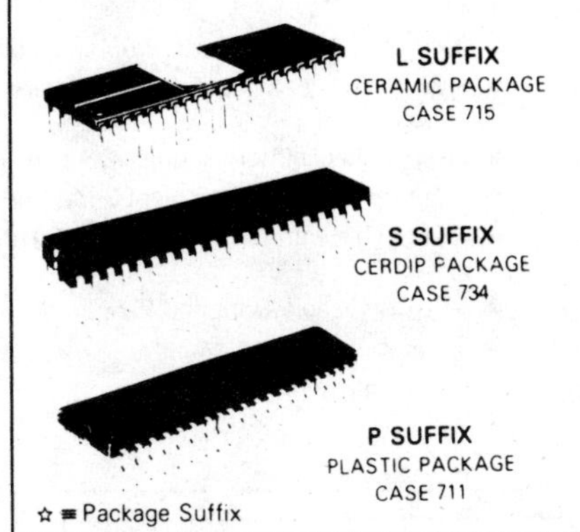

☆ ≡ Package Suffix

MAXIMUM RATINGS

Rating	Symbol	Value	Unit
Supply Voltage	V_{CC}*	−0.3 to +7.0	V
Input Voltage	V_{in}*	−0.3 to +7.0	V
Operating Temperature Range MC6845, MC68A45, MC68B45 MC6845C, MC68A45C, MC68B45C	T_A	T_L to T_H 0 to 70 −40 to +85	°C
Storage Temperature Range	T_{stg}	−55 to +150	°C

THERMAL CHARACTERISTICS

Characteristic	Symbol	Value	Rating
Thermal Resistance Plastic Package Cerdip Package Ceramic Package	θ_{JA}	 100 60 50	°C/W

*This device contains circuitry to protect the inputs against damage due to high static voltages or electric fields; however, it is advised that normal precautions be taken to avoid application of any voltage higher than maximum rated voltages to this high-impedance circuit. For proper operation it is recommended that V_{in} and V_{out} be constrained to the range $V_{SS} \le (V_{in}$ or $V_{out}) \le V_{CC}$.

FIGURE 1 — PIN ASSIGNMENTS

Signal	Pin	Pin	Signal
GND	1	40	VS
$\overline{RESET}$	2	39	HS
LPSTB	3	38	RA0
MA0	4	37	RA1
MA1	5	36	RA2
MA2	6	35	RA3
MA3	7	34	RA4
MA4	8	33	D0
MA5	9	32	D1
MA6	10	31	D2
MA7	11	30	D3
MA8	12	29	D4
MA9	13	28	D5
MA10	14	27	D6
MA11	15	26	D7
MA12	16	25	$\overline{CS}$
MA13	17	24	RS
DE	18	23	E
CURSOR	19	22	R/$\overline{W}$
V_{CC}	20	21	CLK

DS9838

MC6846 (1.0 MHz)
MC68A46 (1.5 MHz)

MOS

(N-CHANNEL, SILICON-GATE, DEPLETION LOAD)

ROM—I/O—TIMER

ROM — I/O — TIMER

The MC6846 combination chip provides the means, in conjunction with the MC6802, to develop a basic 2-chip microcomputer system. The MC6846 consists of 2048 bytes of mask-programmable ROM, an 8-bit bidirectional data port with control lines, and a 16-bit programmable timer-counter.

This device is capable of interfacing with the MC6802 (basic MC6800, clock, and 128 bytes of RAM) as well as the entire M6800 family if desired. No external logic is required to interface with most peripheral devices.

- 2048 8-Bit Bytes of Mask-Programmable ROM
- 8-Bit Bidirectional Data Port for Parallel Interface plus Two Control Lines
- Programmable Interval Timer-Counter Functions
- Programmable I/O Peripheral Data, Control, and Direction Registers
- Compatible with the Complete M6800 Microcomputer Product Family
- TTL-Compatible Data and Peripheral Lines
- Single 5-Volt Power Supply

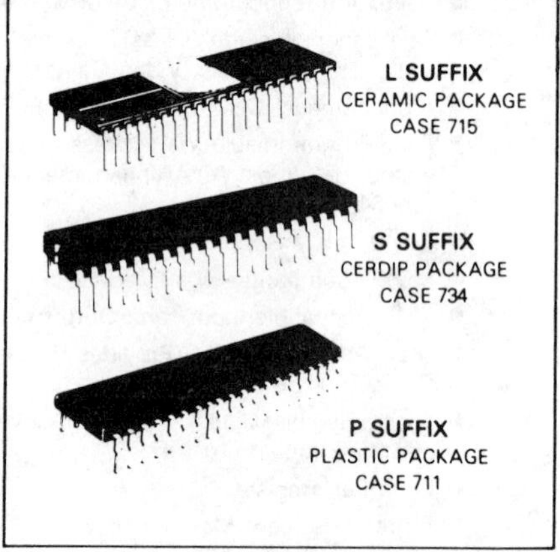

FIGURE 1 — MC6846 BLOCK DIAGRAM

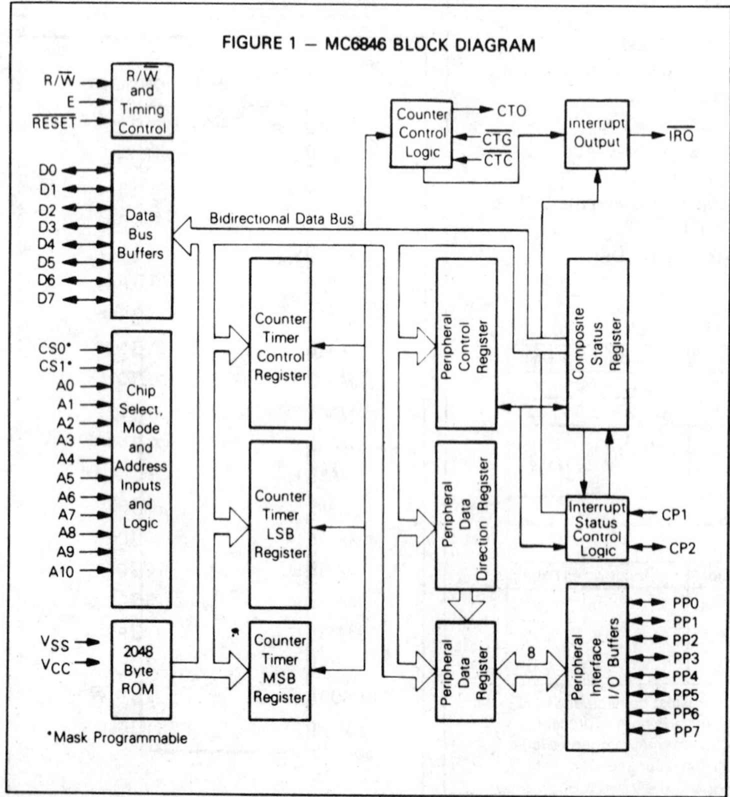

*Mask Programmable

FIGURE 2 — PIN ASSIGNMENTS

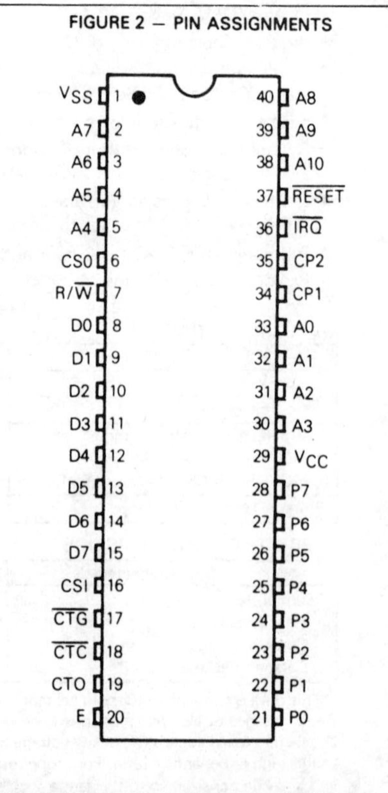

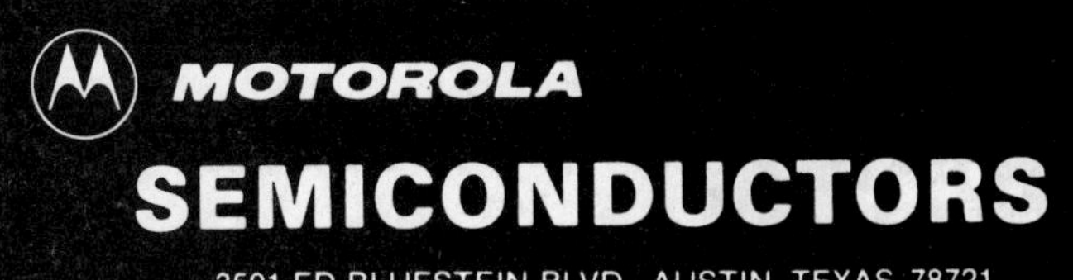

MC6847 Non-Interlace MC6847Y Interlace

MOS
(N-CHANNEL, SILICON-GATE)

VIDEO DISPLAY GENERATOR

MC6847/MC6847Y VIDEO DISPLAY GENERATOR (VDG)

The video display generator (VDG) provides a means of interfacing the M6800 microprocessor family (or similar products) to a standard color or black and white NTSC television receiver. Applications of the VDG include video games, process control displays, home computers, education, communications, and graphics applications.

The VDG reads data from memory and produces a video signal which will allow the generation of alphanumeric or graphic displays. The generated video signal may be modulated to either channel 3 or 4 by using the compatible MC1372 (TV chroma and video modulator). This modulated signal is suitable for reception by a standard unmodified television receiver.

- Compatible with the M6800 Family, the M68000 Family, and Other Microprocessor Families
- Generates Four Different Alphanumeric Display Modes, Two Semigraphic Modes, and Eight Graphic Display Modes
- The Alphanumeric Modes Display 32 Characters Per Line by 16 Lines Using Either the Internal ROM or an External Character Generator
- Alphanumeric and Semigraphic Modes May Be Mixed on a Character-by-Character Basis
- Alphanumeric Modes Support Selectable Inverse on a Character-by-Character Basis
- Internal ROM May Be Mask Programmed with a Custom Pattern
- Full Graphic Modes Offer 64×64, 128×64, 128×96, 128×192, or 256×192 Densities
- Full Graphic Modes Use One of Two 4-Color Sets or One of Two 2-Color Sets
- Compatible with the MC1372 and MC1373 Modulators Via Y, R-Y (ϕA), and B-Y (ϕB) Interface
- Compatible with the MC6883 (74LS783) Synchronous-Address Multiplexer
- Available in Either an Interlace (NTSC Standard) or Non-interlace Version

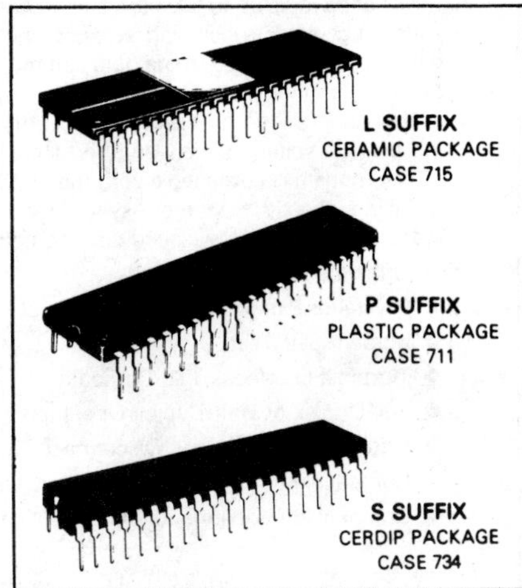

PIN ASSIGNMENT

Signal	Pin	Pin	Signal
V_{SS}	1	40	DD7
DD6	2	39	CSS
DD0	3	38	$\overline{HS}$
DD1	4	37	$\overline{FS}$
DD2	5	36	$\overline{RP}$
DD3	6	35	$\overline{A}$/G
DD4	7	34	$\overline{A}$/S
DD5	8	33	CLK
CHB	9	32	INV
ϕB	10	31	$\overline{INT}$/EXT
ϕA	11	30	GM0
$\overline{MS}$	12	29	GM1
DA5	13	28	Y
DA6	14	27	GM2
DA7	15	26	DA4
DA8	16	25	DA3
V_{CC}	17	24	DA2
DA9	18	23	DA1
DA10	19	22	DA0
DA11	20	21	DA12

MOTOROLA
SEMICONDUCTORS
3501 ED BLUESTEIN BLVD., AUSTIN, TEXAS 78721

MC6860

MOS

(N-CHANNEL, SILICON-GATE)

0-600 bps DIGITAL MODEM

0-600 bps DIGITAL MODEM

The MC6860 is a MOS subsystem designed to be integrated into a wide range of equipment utilizing serial data communications.

The modem provides the necessary modulation, demodulation and supervisory control functions to implement a serial data communications link, over a voice grade channel, utilizing frequency shift keying (FSK) at bit rates up to 600 bps. The MC6860 can be implemented into a wide range of data handling systems, including stand alone modems, data storage devices, remote data communication terminals and I/O interfaces for minicomputers.

N-channel silicon-gate technology permits the MC6860 to operate using a single-voltage supply and be fully TTL compatible.

The modem is compatible with the M6800 microcomputer family, interfacing directly with the Asynchronous Communications Interface Adapter to provide low-speed data communications capability.

- Originate and Answer Mode
- Crystal or External Reference Control
- Modem Self Test
- Terminal Interfaces TTL-Compatible
- Full-Duplex or Half-Duplex Operation
- Automatic Answer and Disconnect
- Compatible Functions for 100 Series Data Sets
- Compatible Functions for 1001A/B Data Couplers

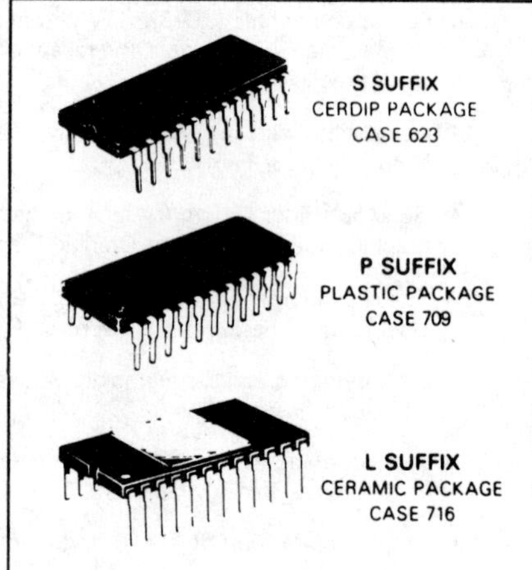

FIGURE 1 — TYPICAL MC6860 SYSTEM CONFIGURATION

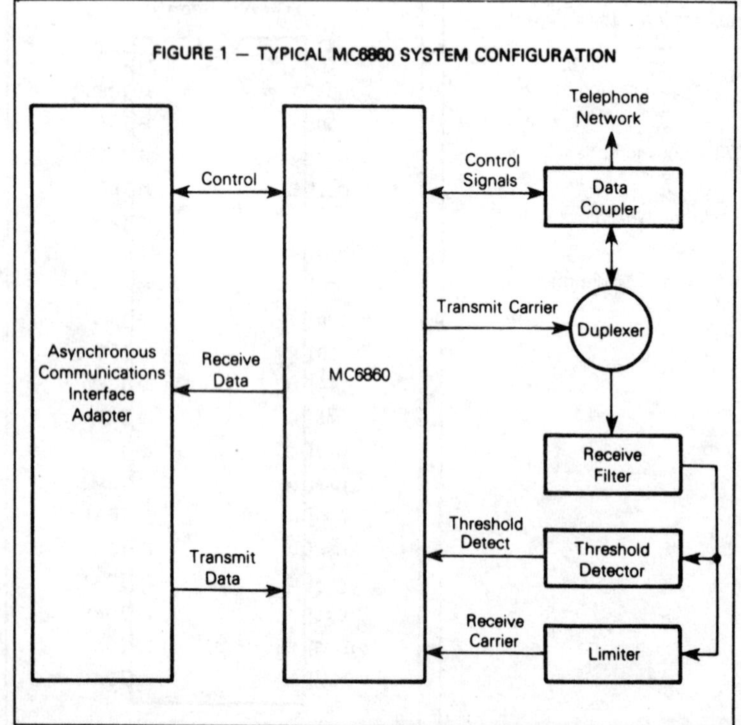

PIN ASSIGNMENT

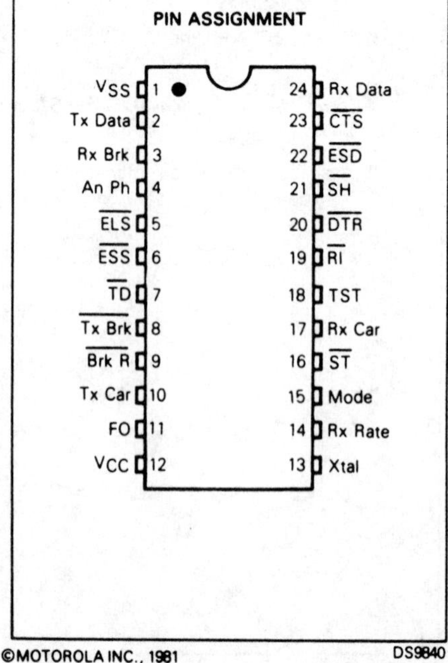

This is advance information and specifications are subject to change without notice.

DS9840
(Replaces ADI-300)

Appendix B

6800 FAMILY SUMMARY

CONTENTS

All data sheets are reprinted courtesy of Motorola, Inc.

MC6800 (1.0 MHz)
MC68A00 (1.5 MHz)
MC68B00 (2.0 MHz)

MOS

(N-CHANNEL, SILICON-GATE, DEPLETION LOAD)

MICROPROCESSOR

8-BIT MICROPROCESSING UNIT (MPU)

The MC6800 is a monolithic 8-bit microprocessor forming the central control function for Motorola's M6800 family. Compatible with TTL, the MC6800, as with all M6800 system parts, requires only one +5.0-volt power supply, and no external TTL devices for bus interface.

The MC6800 is capable of addressing 64K bytes of memory with its 16-bit address lines. The 8-bit data bus is bidirectional as well as three-state, making direct memory addressing and multiprocessing applications realizable.

- 8-Bit Parallel Processing
- Bidirectional Data Bus
- 16-Bit Address Bus – 64K Bytes of Addressing
- 72 Instructions – Variable Length
- Seven Addressing Modes – Direct, Relative, Immediate, Indexed, Extended, Implied and Accumulator
- Variable Length Stack
- Vectored Restart
- Maskable Interrupt Vector
- Separate Non-Maskable Interrupt – Internal Registers Saved in Stack
- Six Internal Registers – Two Accumulators, Index Register, Program Counter, Stack Pointer and Condition Code Register
- Direct Memory Addressing (DMA) and Multiple Processor Capability
- Simplified Clocking Characteristics
- Clock Rates as High as 2.0 MHz
- Simple Bus Interface Without TTL
- Halt and Single Instruction Execution Capability

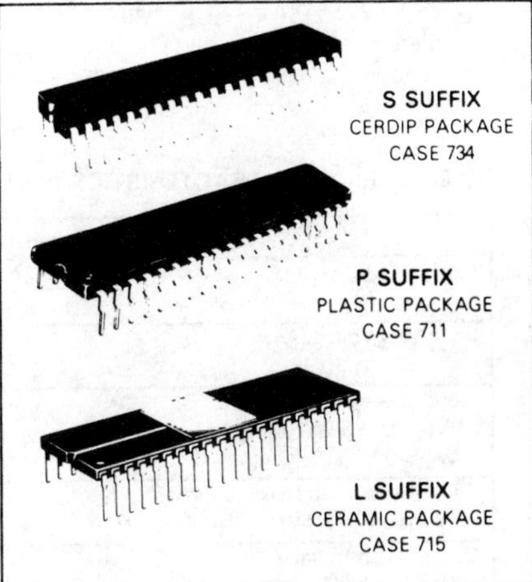

S SUFFIX
CERDIP PACKAGE
CASE 734

P SUFFIX
PLASTIC PACKAGE
CASE 711

L SUFFIX
CERAMIC PACKAGE
CASE 715

MAXIMUM RATINGS

Rating	Symbol	Value	Unit
Supply Voltage	V_{CC}	−0.3 to +7.0	V
Input Voltage	V_{in}	−0.3 to +7.0	V
Operating Temperature Range MC6800, MC68A00, MC68B00 MC6800C, MC68A00C	T_A	T_L to T_H 0 to +70 −40 to +85	°C
Storage Temperature Range	T_{stg}	−55 to +150	°C

THERMAL RESISTANCE

Rating	Symbol	Value	Unit
Plastic Package Cerdip Package Ceramic Package	θ_{JA}	100 60 50	°C/W

This device contains circuitry to protect the inputs against damage due to high static voltages or electrical fields; however, it is advised that normal precautions be taken to avoid application of any voltage higher than maximum-rated voltages to this high-impedance circuit. Reliability of operation is enhanced if unused inputs are tied to an appropriate logic voltage (e.g., either V_{SS} or V_{CC}).

PIN ASSIGNMENT

Signal	Pin	Pin	Signal
V_{SS}	1	40	$\overline{RESET}$
$\overline{HALT}$	2	39	TSC
$\phi 1$	3	38	N.C.
$\overline{IRQ}$	4	37	$\phi 2$
VMA	5	36	DBE
$\overline{NMI}$	6	35	N.C.
BA	7	34	R/$\overline{W}$
V_{CC}	8	33	D0
A0	9	32	D1
A1	10	31	D2
A2	11	30	D3
A3	12	29	D4
A4	13	28	D5
A5	14	27	D6
A6	15	26	D7
A7	16	25	A15
A8	17	24	A14
A9	18	23	A13
A10	19	22	A12
A11	20	21	V_{SS}

 DS9471-R1

POWER CONSIDERATIONS

The average chip-junction temperature, T_J, in °C can be obtained from:

$$T_J = T_A + (P_D \bullet \theta_{JA}) \qquad (1)$$

Where:

$T_A \equiv$ Ambient Temperature, °C

$\theta_{JA} \equiv$ Package Thermal Resistance, Junction-to-Ambient, °C/W

$P_D \equiv P_{INT} + P_{PORT}$

$P_{INT} \equiv I_{CC} \times V_{CC}$, Watts – Chip Internal Power

$P_{PORT} \equiv$ Port Power Dissipation, Watts – User Determined

For most applications $P_{PORT} \ll P_{INT}$ and can be neglected. P_{PORT} may become significant if the device is configured to drive Darlington bases or sink LED loads.

An approximate relationship between P_D and T_J (if P_{PORT} is neglected) is:

$$P_D = K \div (T_J + 273°C) \qquad (2)$$

Solving equations 1 and 2 for K gives:

$$K = P_D \bullet (T_A + 273°C) + \theta_{JA} \bullet P_D^2 \qquad (3)$$

Where K is a constant pertaining to the particular part. K can be determined from equation 3 by measuring P_D (at equilibrium) for a known T_A. Using this value of K the values of P_D and T_J can be obtained by solving equations (1) and (2) iteratively for any value of T_A.

DC ELECTRICAL CHARACTERISTICS (V_{CC} = 5.0 Vdc, ±5%, V_{SS} = 0, $T_A = T_L$ to T_H unless otherwise noted)

Characteristic		Symbol	Min	Typ	Max	Unit
Input High Voltage	Logic	V_{IH}	$V_{SS}+2.0$	–	V_{CC}	V
	φ1, φ2	V_{IHC}	$V_{CC}-0.6$	–	$V_{CC}+0.3$	
Input Low Voltage	Logic	V_{IL}	$V_{SS}-0.3$	–	$V_{SS}+0.8$	V
	φ1, φ2	V_{ILC}	$V_{SS}-0.3$	–	$V_{SS}+0.4$	
Input Leakage Current (V_{in} = 0 to 5.25 V, V_{CC} = Max)	Logic	I_{in}	–	1.0	2.5	μA
(V_{in} = 0 to 5.25 V, V_{CC} = 0 V to 5.25 V)	φ1, φ2		–	–	100	
Three-State Input Leakage Current (V_{in} = 0.4 to 2.4 V, V_{CC} = Max)	D0-D7	I_{IZ}	–	2.0	10	μA
	A0-A15, R/$\overline{W}$		–	–	100	
Output High Voltage (I_{Load} = −205 μA, V_{CC} = Min)	D0-D7	V_{OH}	$V_{SS}+2.4$	–	–	V
(I_{Load} = −145 μA, V_{CC} = Min)	A0-A15, R/$\overline{W}$, VMA		$V_{SS}+2.4$	–	–	
(I_{Load} = −100 μA, V_{CC} = Min)	BA		$V_{SS}+2.4$	–	–	
Output Low Voltage (I_{Load} = 1.6 mA, V_{CC} = Min)		V_{OL}	–	–	$V_{SS}+0.4$	V
Internal Power Dissipation (Measured at $T_A = T_L$)		P_{INT}	–	0.5	1.0	W
Capacitance (V_{in} = 0, T_A = 25°C, f = 1.0 MHz)	φ1	C_{in}	–	25	35	pF
	φ2		–	45	70	
	D0-D7		–	10	12.5	
	Logic Inputs		–	6.5	10	
	A0-A15, R/$\overline{W}$, VMA	C_{out}	–	–	12	pF

CLOCK TIMING (V_{CC} = 5.0 V, ±5%, V_{SS} = 0, $T_A = T_L$ to T_H unless otherwise noted)

Characteristic		Symbol	Min	Typ	Max	Unit
Frequency of Operation	MC6800	f	0.1	–	1.0	MHz
	MC68A00		0.1	–	1.5	
	MC68B00		0.1	–	2.0	
Cycle Time (Figure 1)	MC6800	t_{cyc}	1.000	–	10	μs
	MC68A00		0.666	–	10	
	MC68B00		0.500	–	10	
Clock Pulse Width (Measured at $V_{CC}-0.6$ V)	φ1, φ2 – MC6800	$PW_{\phi H}$	400	–	9500	ns
	φ1, φ2 – MC68A00		230	–	9500	
	φ1, φ2 – MC68B00		180	–	9500	
Total φ1 and φ2 Up Time	MC6800	t_{ut}	900	–	–	ns
	MC68A00		600	–	–	
	MC68B00		440	–	–	
Rise and Fall Time (Measured between $V_{SS}+0.4$ and $V_{CC}-0.6$)		t_r, t_f	–	–	100	ns
Delay Time or Clock Separation (Figure 1) (Measured at $V_{OV} = V_{SS}+0.6$ V @ $t_r = t_f \le 100$ ns)		t_d	0	–	9100	ns
(Measured at $V_{OV} = V_{SS}+1.0$ V @ $t_r = t_f \le 35$ ns)			0	–	9100	

MC6800

FIGURE 1 — CLOCK TIMING WAVEFORM

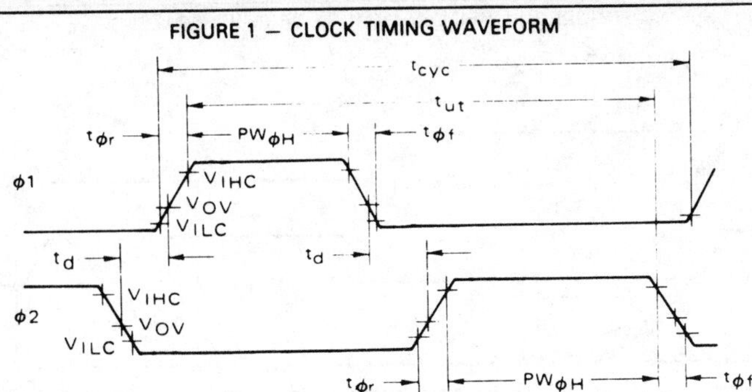

READ/WRITE TIMING (Reference Figures 2 through 6, 8, 9, 11, 12 and 13)

Characteristic	Symbol	MC6800			MC68A00			MC68B00			Unit
		Min	Typ	Max	Min	Typ	Max	Min	Typ	Max	
Address Delay C = 90 pF	t_{AD}	–	–	270	–	–	180	–	–	150	ns
C = 30 pF		–	–	250	–	–	165	–	–	135	
Peripheral Read Access Time $t_{acc} = t_{ut} - (t_{AD} + t_{DSR})$	t_{acc}	605	–	—	400	–	—	290	–	—	ns
Data Setup Time (Read)	t_{DSR}	100	–	–	60	–	–	40	–	–	ns
Input Data Hold Time	t_H	10	–	–	10	–	–	10	–	–	ns
Output Data Hold Time	t_H	10	25	–	10	25	–	10	25	–	ns
Address Hold Time (Address, R/$\overline{W}$, VMA)	t_{AH}	30	50	–	30	50	–	30	50	–	ns
Enable High Time for DBE Input	t_{EH}	450	–	–	280	–	–	220	–	–	ns
Data Delay Time (Write)	t_{DDW}	–	–	225	–	–	200	–	–	160	ns
Processor Controls											ns
Processor Control Setup Time	t_{PCS}	200	–	–	140	–	–	110	–	–	
Processor Control Rise and Fall Time	t_{PCr}, t_{PCf}	–	–	100	–	–	100	–	–	100	
Bus Available Delay	t_{BA}	–	–	250	–	–	165	–	–	135	
Three-State Enable	t_{TSE}	–	–	40	–	–	40	–	–	40	
Three-State Delay	t_{TSD}	–	–	270	–	–	270	–	–	220	
Data Bus Enable Down Time During φ1 Up Time	t_{DBE}	150	–	–	120	–	–	75	–	–	
Data Bus Enable Rise and Fall Times	t_{DBEr}, t_{DBEf}	–	–	25	–	–	25	–	–	25	

FIGURE 2 — READ DATA FROM MEMORY OR PERIPHERALS

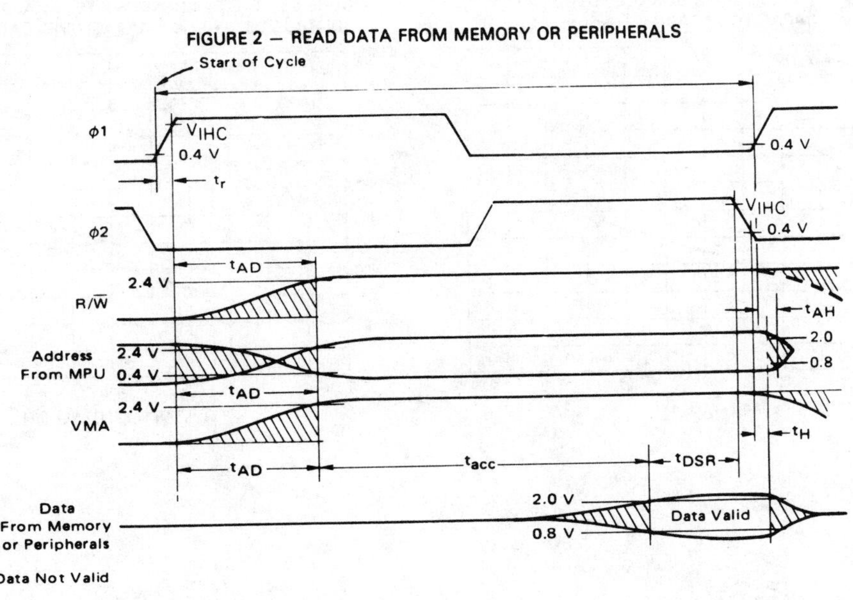

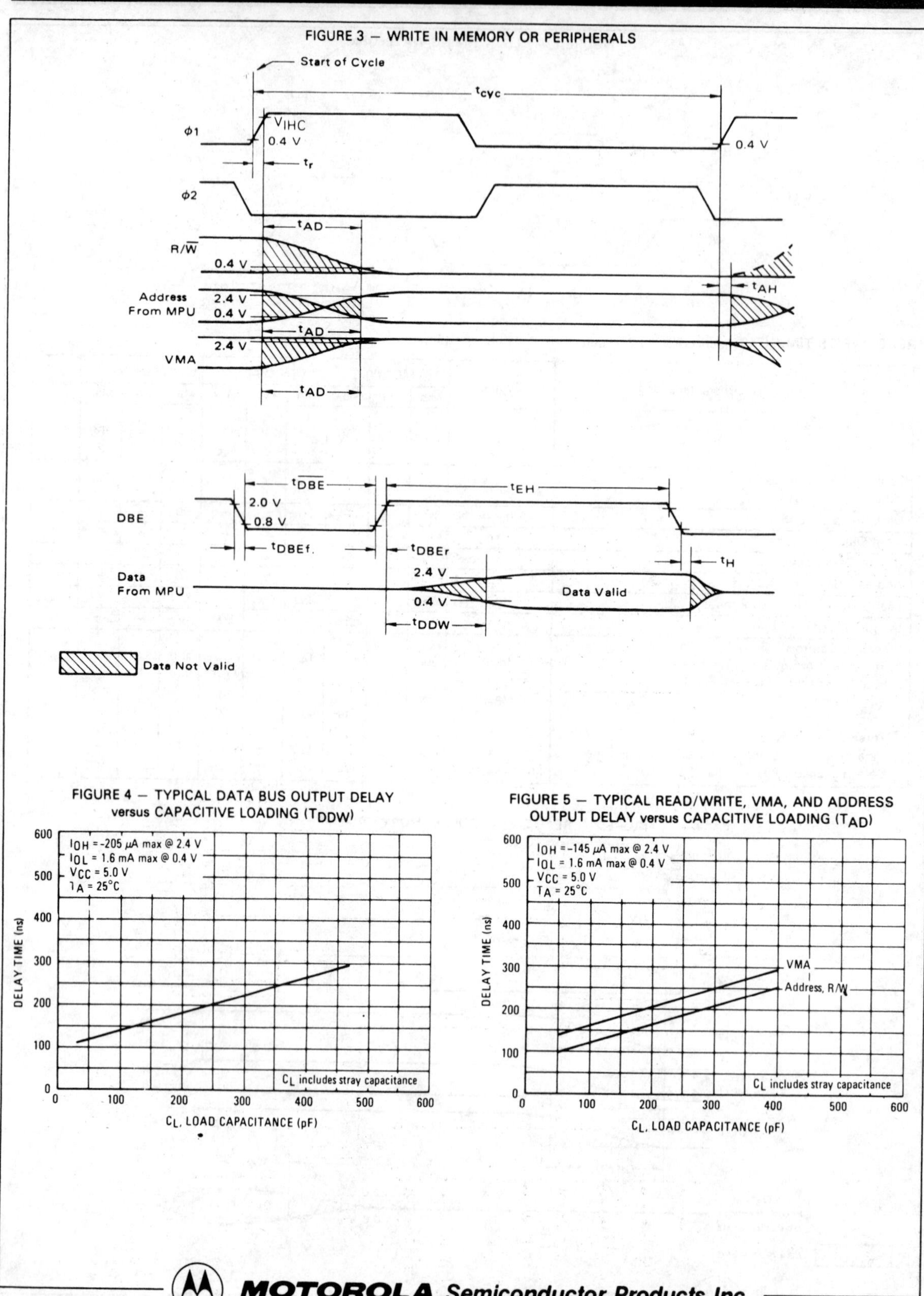

FIGURE 3 — WRITE IN MEMORY OR PERIPHERALS

FIGURE 4 — TYPICAL DATA BUS OUTPUT DELAY versus CAPACITIVE LOADING (T_{DDW})

FIGURE 5 — TYPICAL READ/WRITE, VMA, AND ADDRESS OUTPUT DELAY versus CAPACITIVE LOADING (T_{AD})

MC6800

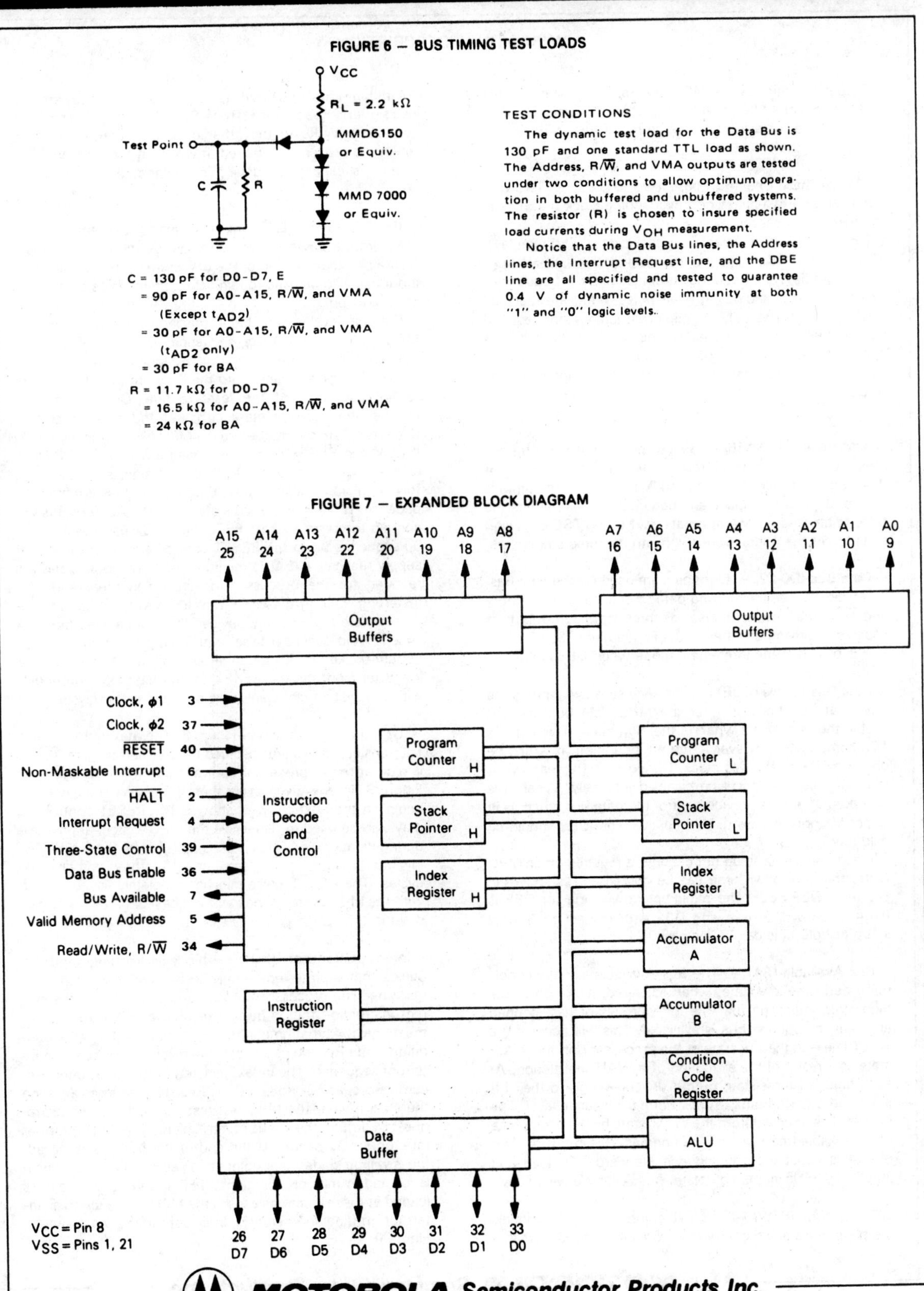

FIGURE 6 — BUS TIMING TEST LOADS

C = 130 pF for D0-D7, E
= 90 pF for A0-A15, R/$\overline{W}$, and VMA
(Except t_{AD2})
= 30 pF for A0-A15, R/$\overline{W}$, and VMA
(t_{AD2} only)
= 30 pF for BA
R = 11.7 kΩ for D0-D7
= 16.5 kΩ for A0-A15, R/$\overline{W}$, and VMA
= 24 kΩ for BA

TEST CONDITIONS

The dynamic test load for the Data Bus is 130 pF and one standard TTL load as shown. The Address, R/$\overline{W}$, and VMA outputs are tested under two conditions to allow optimum operation in both buffered and unbuffered systems. The resistor (R) is chosen to insure specified load currents during V_{OH} measurement.

Notice that the Data Bus lines, the Address lines, the Interrupt Request line, and the DBE line are all specified and tested to guarantee 0.4 V of dynamic noise immunity at both "1" and "0" logic levels.

FIGURE 7 — EXPANDED BLOCK DIAGRAM

MC6800

MPU SIGNAL DESCRIPTION

Proper operation of the MPU requires that certain control and timing signals be provided to accomplish specific functions and that other signal lines be monitored to determine the state of the processor.

Clocks Phase One and Phase Two (ϕ1, ϕ2) – Two pins are used for a two-phase non-overlapping clock that runs at the V_{CC} voltage level.

Figure 1 shows the microprocessor clocks. The high level is specified at V_{IHC} and the low level is specified at V_{ILC}. The allowable clock frequency is specified by f (frequency). The minimum ϕ1 and ϕ2 high level pulse widths are specified by $PW_{\phi H}$ (pulse width high time). To guarantee the required access time for the peripherals, the clock up time, t_{ut}, is specified. Clock separation, t_d, is measured at a maximum voltage of V_{OV} (overlap voltage). This allows for a multitude of clock variations at the system frequency rate.

Address Bus (A0-A15) – Sixteen pins are used for the address bus. The outputs are three-state bus drivers capable of driving one standard TTL load and 90 pF. When the output is turned off, it is essentially an open circuit. This permits the MPU to be used in DMA applications. Putting TSC in its high state forces the Address bus to go into the three-state mode.

Data Bus (D0-D7) – Eight pins are used for the data bus. It is bidirectional, transferring data to and from the memory and peripheral devices. It also has three-state output buffers capable of driving one standard TTL load and 130 pF. Data Bus is placed in the three-state mode when DBE is low.

Data Bus Enable (DBE) – This level sensitive input is the three-state control signal for the MPU data bus and will enable the bus drivers when in the high state. This input is TTL compatible; however in normal operation, it would be driven by the phase two clock. During an MPU read cycle, the data bus drivers will be disabled internally. When it is desired that another device control the data bus, such as in Direct Memory Access (DMA) applications, DBE should be held low.

If additional data setup or hold time is required on an MPU write, the DBE down time can be decreased, as shown in Figure 3 (DBE≠ϕ2). The minimum down time for DBE is t_{DBE} as shown. By skewing DBE with respect to E, data setup or hold time can be increased.

Bus Available (BA) – The Bus Available signal will normally be in the low state; when activated, it will go to the high state indicating that the microprocessor has stopped and that the address bus is available. This will occur if the $\overline{HALT}$ line is in the low state or the processor is in the WAIT state as a result of the execution of a WAIT instruction. At such time, all three-state output drivers will go to their off state and other outputs to their normally inactive level. The processor is removed from the WAIT state by the occurrence of a maskable (mask bit I = 0) or nonmaskable interrupt. This output is capable of driving one standard TTL load and 30 pF. If TSC is in the high state, Bus Available will be low.

Read/Write (R/$\overline{W}$) – This TTL compatible output signals the peripherals and memory devices wether the MPU is in a Read (high) or Write (low) state. The normal standby state of this signal is Read (high). Three-State Control going high will turn Read/Write to the off (high impedance) state. Also, when the processor is halted, it will be in the off state. This output is capable of driving one standard TTL load and 90 pF.

$\overline{RESET}$ – The $\overline{RESET}$ input is used to reset and start the MPU from a power down condition resulting from a power failure or initial start-up of the processor. This level sensitive input can also be used to reinitialize the machine at any time after start-up.

If a high level is detected in this input, this will signal the MPU to begin the reset sequence. During the reset sequence, the contents of the last two locations (FFFE, FFFF) in memory will be loaded into the Program Counter to point to the beginning of the reset routine. During the reset routine, the interrupt mask bit is set and must be cleared under program control before the MPU can be interrupted by $\overline{IRQ}$. While $\overline{RESET}$ is low (assuming a minimum of 8 clock cycles have occurred) the MPU output signals will be in the following states: VMA = low, BA = low, Data Bus = high impedance, R/$\overline{W}$ = high (read state), and the Address Bus will contain the reset address FFFE. Figure 8 illustrates a power up sequence using the $\overline{RESET}$ control line. After the power supply reaches 4.75 V, a minimum of eight clock cycles are required for the processor to stabilize in preparation for restarting. During these eight cycles, VMA will be in an indeterminate state so any devices that are enabled by VMA which could accept a false write during this time (such as battery-backed RAM) must be disabled until VMA is forced low after eight cycles. $\overline{RESET}$ can go high asynchronously with the system clock any time after the eighth cycle.

$\overline{RESET}$ timing is shown in Figure 8. The maximum rise and fall transition times are specified by t_{PCr} and t_{PCf}. If $\overline{RESET}$ is high at t_{PCS} (processor control setup time), as shown in Figure 8, in any given cycle then the restart sequence will begin on the next cycle as shown. The $\overline{RESET}$ control line may also be used to reinitialize the MPU system at any time during its operation. This is accomplished by pulsing RESET low for the duration of a minimum of three complete ϕ2 cycles. The $\overline{RESET}$ pulse can be completely asynchronous with the MPU system clock and will be recognized during ϕ2 if setup time t_{PCS} is met.

Interrupt Request ($\overline{IRQ}$) – This level sensitive input requests that an interrupt sequence be generated within the machine. The processor will wait until it completes the current instruction that is being executed before it recognizes the request. At that time, if the interrupt mask bit in the Condition Code Register is not set, the machine will begin an interrupt sequence. The Index Register, Program Counter, Accumulators, and Condition Code Register are stored away on the stack. Next, the MPU will respond to the interrupt request by setting the interrupt mask bit high so that no further interrupts may occur. At the end of the cycle, a 16-bit address will be loaded that points to a vectoring address which is located in memory locations FFF8 and FFF9. An address loaded at these locations causes the MPU to branch to an interrupt routine in memory. Interrupt timing is shown in Figure 9.

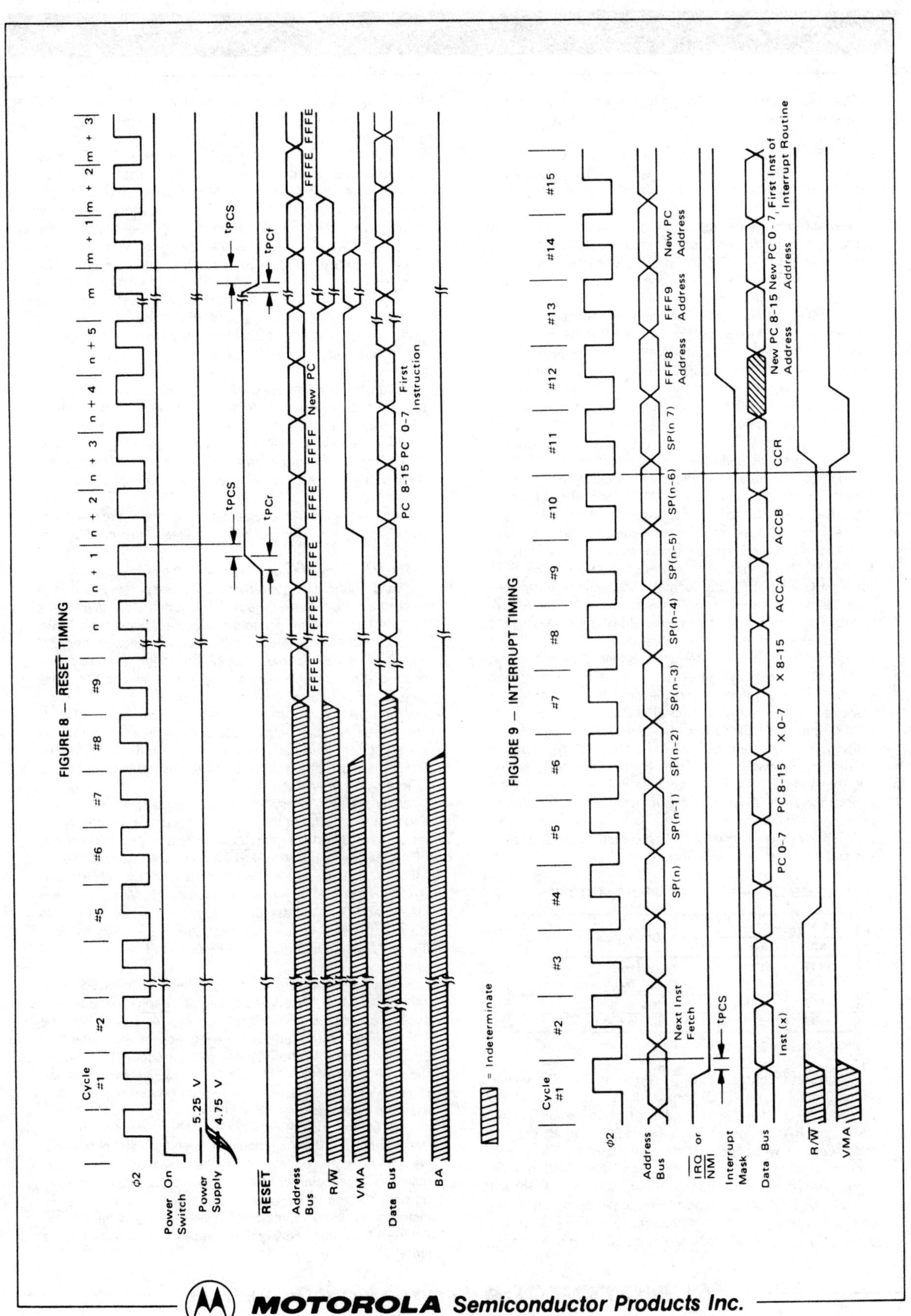

FIGURE 8 — RESET TIMING

FIGURE 9 — INTERRUPT TIMING

MC6800

The HALT line must be in the high state for interrupts to be serviced. Interrupts will be latched internally while HALT is low.

The IRQ has a high-impedance pullup device internal to the chip; however, a 3 kΩ external resistor to V_{CC} should be used for wire-OR and optimum control of interrupts.

Non-Maskable Interrupt (NMI) and Wait for Interrupt (WAI) – The MC6800 is capable of handling two types of interrupts: maskable (IRQ) as described earlier, and non-maskable (NMI) which is an edge sensitive input. IRQ is maskable by the interrupt mask in the condition code register while NMI is not maskable. The handling of these interrupts by the MPU is the same except that each has its own vector address. The behavior of the MPU when interrupted is shown in Figure 9 which details the MPU response to an interrupt while the MPU is executing the control program. The interrupt shown could be either IRQ or NMI and can be asynchronous with respect to $\phi 2$. The interrupt is shown going low at time t_{PCS} in cycle #1 which precedes the first cycle of an instruction (OP code fetch). This instruction is not executed but instead the Program Counter (PC), Index Register (IX), Accumulators (ACCX), and the Condition Code Register (CCR) are pushed onto the stack.

The Interrupt Mask bit is set to prevent further interrupts. The address of the interrupt service routine is then fetched from FFFC, FFFD for an NMI interrupt and from FFF8, FFF9 for an IRQ interrupt. Upon completion of the interrupt service routine, the execution of RTI will pull the PC, IX, ACCX, and CCR off the stack; the Interrupt Mask bit is restored to its condition prior to Interrupts (see Figure 10).

Figure 11 is a similar interrupt sequence, except in this case, a WAIT instruction has been executed in preparation for the interrupt. This technique speeds up the MPU's response to the interrupt because the stacking of the PC, IX, ACCX, and the CCR is already done. While the MPU is waiting for the interrupt, Bus Available will go high indicating the following states of the control lines: VMA is low, and the Address Bus, R/W and Data Bus are all in the high impedance state. After the interrupt occurs, it is serviced as previously described.

A 3-10 kΩ external resistor to V_{CC} should be used for wire-OR and optimum control of interrupts.

MEMORY MAP FOR INTERRUPT VECTORS

Vector MS	Vector LS	Description
FFFE	FFFF	Reset
FFFC	FFFD	Non-Maskable Interrupt
FFFA	FFFB	Software Interrupt
FFF8	FFF9	Interrupt Request

Refer to Figure 10 for program flow for Interrupts.

Three-State Control (TSC) – When the level sensitive Three-State Control (TSC) line is a logic "1", the Address Bus and the R/W line are placed in a high-impedance state. VMA and BA are forced low when TSC="1" to prevent false reads or writes on any device enabled by VMA. It is necessary to delay program execution while TSC is held high. This is done by insuring that no transitions of $\phi 1$ (or $\phi 2$) occur during this period. (Logic levels of the clocks are irrelevant so long as they do not change). Since the MPU is a dynamic device, the $\phi 1$ clock can be stopped for a maximum time $PW_{\phi H}$ without destroying data within the MPU. TSC then can be used in a short Direct Memory Access (DMA) application.

Figure 12 shows the effect of TSC on the MPU. TSC must have its transitions at t_{TSE} (three-state enable) while holding $\phi 1$ high and $\phi 2$ low as shown. The Address Bus and R/W line will reach the high-impedance state at t_{TSD} (three-state delay), with VMA being forced low. In this example, the Data Bus is also in the high-impedance state while $\phi 2$ is being held low since DBE=$\phi 2$. At this point in time, a DMA transfer could occur on cycles #3 and #4. When TSC is returned low, the MPU Address and R/W lines return to the bus. Because it is too late in cycle #5 to access memory, this cycle is dead and used for synchronization. Program execution resumes in cycle #6.

Valid Memory Address (VMA) – This output indicates to peripheral devices that there is a valid address on the address bus. In normal operation, this signal should be utilized for enabling peripheral interfaces such as the PIA and ACIA. This signal is not three-state. One standard TTL load and 90 pF may be directly driven by this active high signal.

HALT – When this level sensitive input is in the low state, all activity in the machine will be halted. This input is level sensitive.

The HALT line provides an input to the MPU to allow control of program execution by an outside source. If HALT is high, the MPU will execute the instructions; if it is low, the MPU will go to a halted or idle mode. A response signal, Bus Available (BA) provides an indication of the current MPU status. When BA is low, the MPU is in the process of executing the control program; if BA is high, the MPU has halted and all internal activity has stopped.

When BA is high, the Address Bus, Data Bus, and R/W line will be in a high-impedance state, effectively removing the MPU from the system bus. VMA is forced low so that the floating system bus will not activate any device on the bus that is enabled by VMA.

While the MPU is halted, all program activity is stopped, and if either an NMI or IRQ interrupt occurs, it will be latched into the MPU and acted on as soon as the MPU is taken out of the halted mode. If a RESET command occurs while the MPU is halted, the following states occur: VMA=low, BA=low, Data Bus=high impedance, R/W=high (read state), and the Address Bus will contain address FFFE as long as RESET is low. As soon as the RESET line goes high, the MPU will go to locations FFFE and FFFF for the address of the reset routine.

Figure 13 shows the timing relationships involved when halting the MPU. The instruction illustrated is a one byte, 2 cycle instruction such as CLRA. When HALT goes low, the MPU will halt after completing execution of the current instruction. The transition of HALT must occur t_{PCS} before the trailing edge of $\phi 1$ of the last cycle of an instruction (point A of Figure 13). HALT must not go low any time later than the minmum t_{PCS} specified.

The fetch of the OP code by the MPU is the first cycle of the instruction. If HALT had not been low at Point A but went low during $\phi 2$ of that cycle, the MPU would have halted after completion of the following instruction. BA will go high by time t_{BA} (bus available delay time) after the last instruction cycle. At this point in time, VMA is low and R/W, Address Bus, and the Data Bus are in the high-impedance state.

MC6800

To debug programs it is advantageous to step through programs instruction by instruction. To do this, HALT must be brought high for one MPU cycle and then returned low as shown at point B of Figure 13. Again, the transitions of $\overline{\text{HALT}}$ must occur t_{PCS} before the trailing edge of $\phi 1$. BA will go low at t_{BA} after the leading edge of the next $\phi 1$, indicating that the Address Bus, Data Bus, VMA and R/$\overline{\text{W}}$ lines are back on the bus. A single byte, 2 cycle instruction such as LSR is used for this example also. During the first cycle, the instruction Y is fetched from address M+1. BA returns high at t_{BA} on the last cycle of the instruction indicating the MPU is off the bus. If instruction Y had been three cycles, the width of the BA low time would have been increased by one cycle.

FIGURE 10 — MPU FLOW CHART

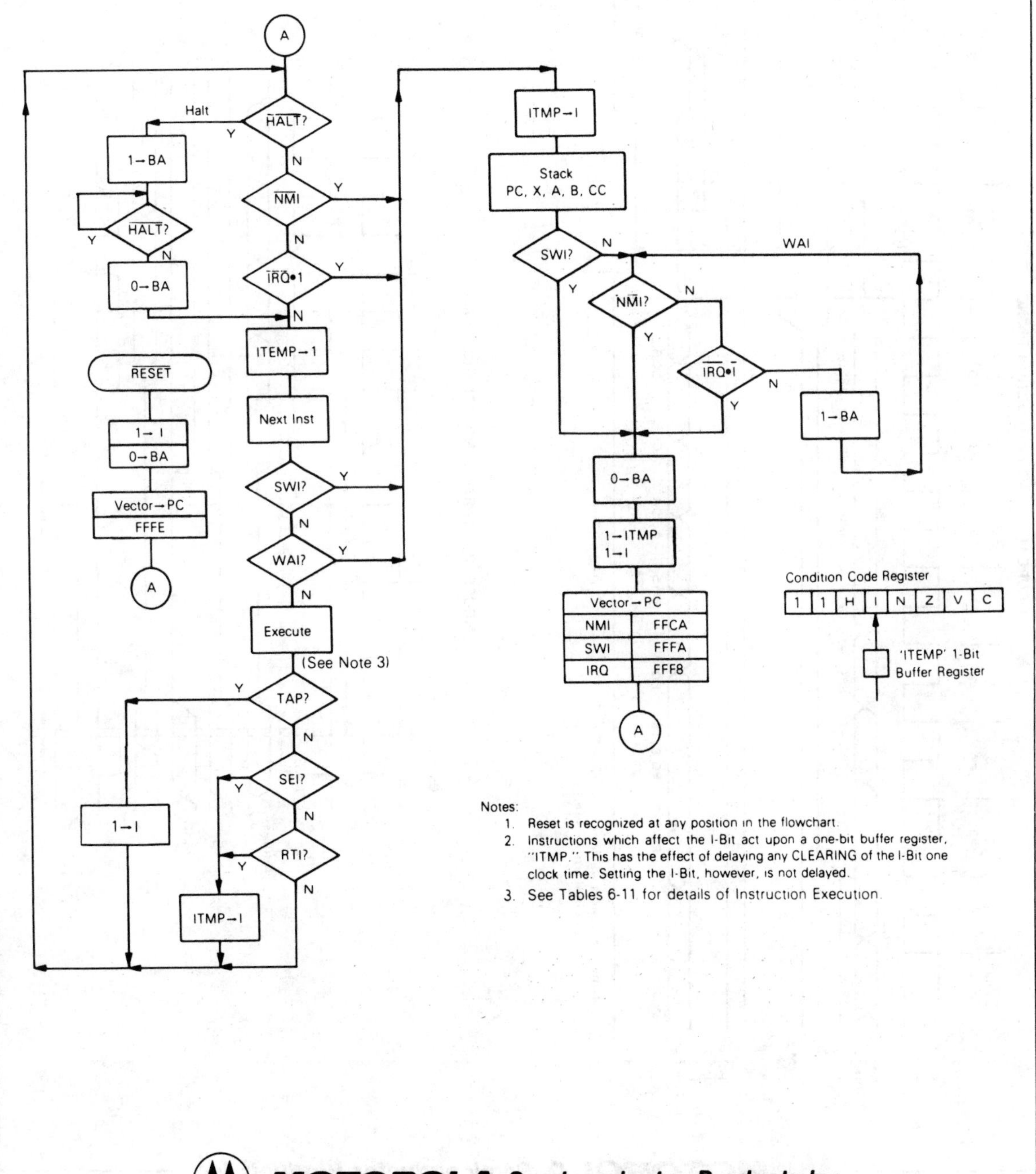

Notes:
1. Reset is recognized at any position in the flowchart.
2. Instructions which affect the I-Bit act upon a one-bit buffer register, "ITMP." This has the effect of delaying any CLEARING of the I-Bit one clock time. Setting the I-Bit, however, is not delayed.
3. See Tables 6-11 for details of Instruction Execution.

FIGURE 11 — WAIT INSTRUCTION TIMING

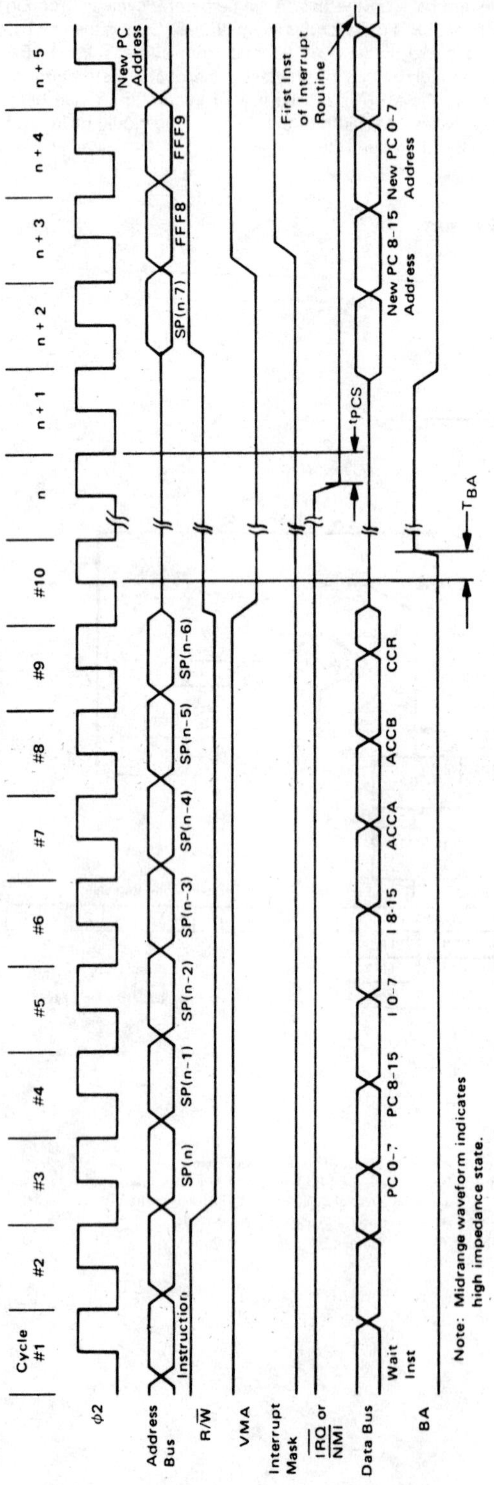

Note: Midrange waveform indicates high impedance state.

FIGURE 12 — THREE-STATE CONTROL TIMING

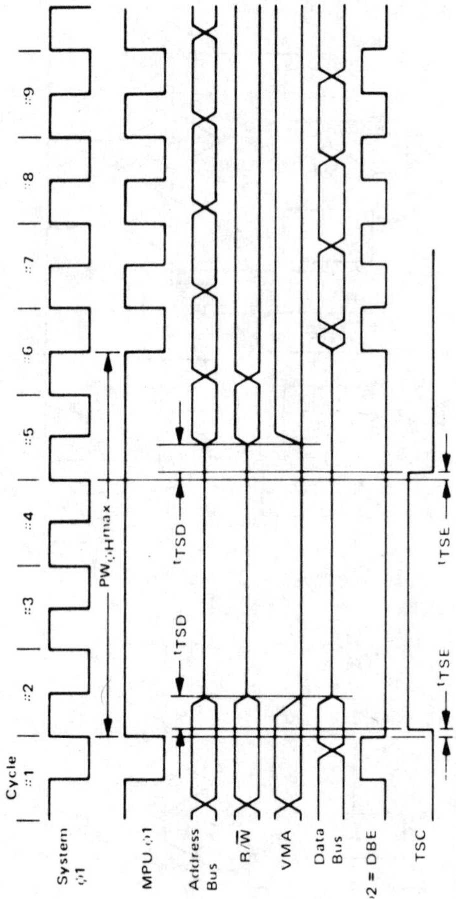

FIGURE 13 – $\overline{HALT}$ AND SINGLE INSTRUCTION EXECUTION FOR SYSTEM DEBUG

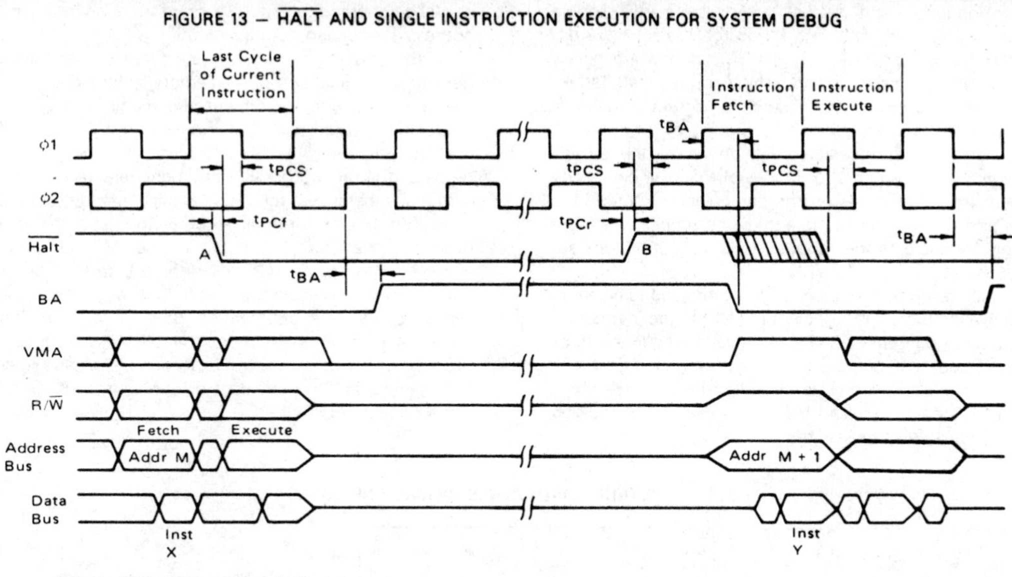

Note: Midrange waveform indicates high impedance state.

MPU REGISTERS

The MPU has three 16-bit registers and three 8-bit registers available for use by the programmer (Figure 14).

FIGURE 14 – PROGRAMMING MODEL OF THE MICROPROCESSING UNIT

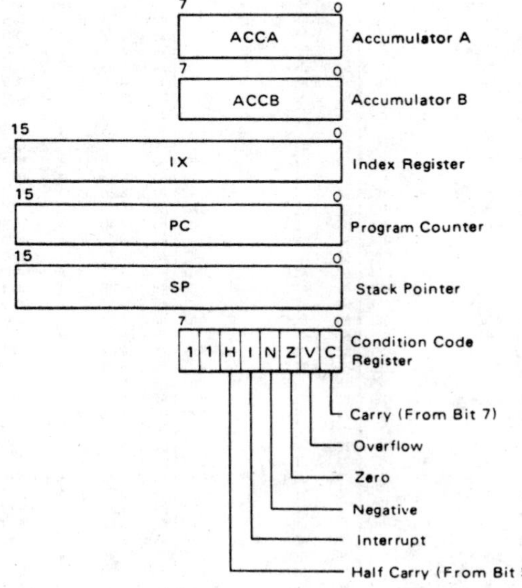

Program Counter – The program counter is a two byte (16 bits) register that points to the current program address.

Stack Pointer – The stack ponter is a two byte register that contains the address of the next available location in an external push-down/pop-up stack. This stack is normally a random access Read/Write memory that may have any location (address) that is convenient. In those applications that require storage of information in the stack when power is lost, the stack must be nonvolatile.

Index Register – The index register is a two byte register that is used to store data or a sixteen bit memory address for the Indexed mode of memory addressing.

Accumulators – The MPU contains two 8-bit accumulators that are used to hold operands and results from an arithmetic logic unit (ALU).

Condition Code Register – The condition code register indicates the results of an Arithmetic Logic Unit operation: Negative (N), Zero (Z), Overflow (V), Carry from bit 7 (C), and half carry from bit 3 (H). These bits of the Condition Code Register are used as testable conditions for the conditional branch instructions. Bit 4 is the interrupt mask bit (I). The unused bits of the Condition Code Register (b6 and b7) are ones.

MPU INSTRUCTION SET

The MC6800 instructions are described in detail in the M6800 Programming Manual. This Section will provide a brief introduction and discuss their use in developing MC6800 control programs. The MC6800 has a set of 72 different executable source instructions. Included are binary and decimal arithmetic, logical, shift, rotate, load, store, conditional or unconditional branch, interrupt and stack manipulation instructions.

Each of the 72 executable instructions of the source language assembles into 1 to 3 bytes of machine code. The number of bytes depends on the particular instruction and on the addressing mode. (The addressing modes which are available for use with the various executive instructions are discussed later.)

The coding of the first (or only) byte corresponding to an executable instruction is sufficient to identify the instruction and the addressing mode. The hexadecimal equivalents of the binary codes, which result from the translation of the 72 instructions in all valid modes of addressing, are shown in Table 1. There are 197 valid machine codes, 59 of the 256 possible codes being unassigned.

When an instruction translates into two or three bytes of code, the second byte, or the second and third bytes contain(s) an operand, an address, or information from which an address is obtained during execution.

Microprocessor instructions are often divided into three general classifications: (1) memory reference, so called because they operate on specific memory locations; (2) operating instructions that function without needing a memory reference; (3) I/O instructions for transferring data between the microprocessor and peripheral devices.

In many instances, the MC6800 performs the same operation on both its internal accumulators and the external memory locations. In addition, the MC6800 interface adapters (PIA and ACIA) allow the MPU to treat peripheral devices exactly like other memory locations, hence, no I/O instructions as such are required. Because of these features, other classifications are more suitable for introducing the MC6800's instruction set: (1) Accumulator and memory operations; (2) Program control operations; (3) Condition Code Register operations.

TABLE 1 — HEXADECIMAL VALUES OF MACHINE CODES

00	*			40	NEG	A		80	SUB	A	IMM	C0	SUB	B	IMM
01	NOP			41	*			81	CMP	A	IMM	C1	CMP	B	IMM
02	*			42	*			82	SBC	A	IMM	C2	SBC	B	IMM
03	*			43	COM	A		83	*			C3	*		
04	*			44	LSR	A		84	AND	A	IMM	C4	AND	B	IMM
05	*			45	*			85	BIT	A	IMM	C5	BIT	B	IMM
06	TAP			46	ROR	A		86	LDA	A	IMM	C6	LDA	B	IMM
07	TPA			47	ASR	A		87	*			C7	*		
08	INX			48	ASL	A		88	EOR	A	IMM	C8	EOR	B	IMM
09	DEX			49	ROL	A		89	ADC	A	IMM	C9	ADC	B	IMM
0A	CLV			4A	DEC	A		8A	ORA	A	IMM	CA	ORA	B	IMM
0B	SEV			4B	*			8B	ADD	A	IMM	CB	ADD	B	IMM
0C	CLC			4C	INC	A		8C	CPX	A	IMM	CC	*		
0D	SEC			4D	TST	A		8D	BSR		REL	CD	*		
0E	CLI			4E	*			8E	LDS		IMM	CE	LDX		IMM
0F	SEI			4F	CLR	A		8F	*			CF	*		
10	SBA			50	NEG	B		90	SUB	A	DIR	D0	SUB	B	DIR
11	CBA			51	*			91	CMP	A	DIR	D1	CMP	B	DIR
12	*			52	*			92	SBC	A	DIR	D2	SBC	B	DIR
13	*			53	COM	B		93	*			D3	*		
14	*			54	LSR	B		94	AND	A	DIR	D4	AND	B	DIR
15	*			55	*			95	BIT	A	DIR	D5	BIT	B	DIR
16	TAB			56	ROR	B		96	LDA	A	DIR	D6	LDA	B	DIR
17	TBA			57	ASR	B		97	STA	A	DIR	D7	STA	B	DIR
18	*			58	ASL	B		98	EOR	A	DIR	D8	EOR	B	DIR
19	DAA			59	ROL	B		99	ADC	A	DIR	D9	ADC	B	DIR
1A	*			5A	DEC	B		9A	ORA	A	DIR	DA	ORA	B	DIR
1B	ABA			5B	*			9B	ADD	A	DIR	DB	ADD	B	DIR
1C	*			5C	INC	B		9C	CPX		DIR	DC	*		
1D	*			5D	TST	B		9D	*			DD	*		
1E	*			5E	*			9E	LDS		DIR	DE	LDX		DIR
1F	*			5F	CLR	B		9F	STS		DIR	DF	STX		DIR
20	BRA		REL	60	NEG		IND	A0	SUB	A	IND	E0	SUB	B	IND
21	*			61	*			A1	CMP	A	IND	E1	CMP	B	IND
22	BHI		REL	62	*			A2	SBC	A	IND	E2	SBC	B	IND
23	BLS		REL	63	COM		IND	A3	*			E3	*		
24	BCC		REL	64	LSR		IND	A4	AND	A	IND	E4	AND	B	IND
25	BCS		REL	65	*			A5	BIT	A	IND	E5	BIT	B	IND
26	BNE		REL	66	ROR		IND	A6	LDA	A	IND	E6	LDA	B	IND
27	BEQ		REL	67	ASR		IND	A7	STA	A	IND	E7	STA	B	IND
28	BVC		REL	68	ASL		IND	A8	EOR	A	IND	E8	EOR	B	IND
29	BVS		REL	69	ROL		IND	A9	ADC	A	IND	E9	ADC	B	IND
2A	BPL		REL	6A	DEC		IND	AA	ORA	A	IND	EA	ORA	B	IND
2B	BMI		REL	6B	*			AB	ADD	A	IND	EB	ADD	B	IND
2C	BGE		REL	6C	INC		IND	AC	CPX		IND	EC	*		
2D	BLT		REL	6D	TST		IND	AD	JSR		IND	ED	*		
2E	BGT		REL	6E	JMP		IND	AE	LDS		IND	EE	LDX		IND
2F	BLE		REL	6F	CLR		IND	AF	STS		IND	EF	STX		IND
30	TSX			70	NEG		EXT	B0	SUB	A	EXT	F0	SUB	B	EXT
31	INS			71	*			B1	CMP	A	EXT	F1	CMP	B	EXT
32	PUL	A		72	*			B2	SBC	A	EXT	F2	SBC	B	EXT
33	PUL	B		73	COM		EXT	B3	*			F3	*		
34	DES			74	LSR		EXT	B4	AND	A	EXT	F4	AND	B	EXT
35	TXS			75	*			B5	BIT	A	EXT	F5	BIT	B	EXT
36	PSH	A		76	ROR		EXT	B6	LDA	A	EXT	F6	LDA	B	EXT
37	PSH	B		77	ASR		EXT	B7	STA	A	EXT	F7	STA	B	EXT
38	*			78	ASL		EXT	B8	EOR	A	EXT	F8	EOR	B	EXT
39	RTS			79	ROL		EXT	B9	ADC	A	EXT	F9	ADC	B	EXT
3A	*			7A	DEC		EXT	BA	ORA	A	EXT	FA	ORA	B	EXT
3B	RTI			7B	*			BB	ADD	A	EXT	FB	ADD	B	EXT
3C	*			7C	INC		EXT	BC	CPX		EXT	FC	*		
3D	*			7D	TST		EXT	BD	JSR		EXT	FD	*		
3E	WAI			7E	JMP		EXT	BE	LDS		EXT	FE	LDX		EXT
3F	SWI			7F	CLR		EXT	BF	STS		EXT	FF	STX		EXT

Notes: 1. Addressing Modes:

A	Accumulator A
B	Accumulator B
REL	Relative
IND	Indexed
IMM	Immediate
DIR	Direct

2. Unassigned code indicated by "*".

TABLE 2 — ACCUMULATOR AND MEMORY OPERATIONS

OPERATIONS	MNEMONIC	IMMED OP	~	#	DIRECT OP	~	#	INDEX OP	~	#	EXTND OP	~	#	IMPLIED OP	~	#	BOOLEAN/ARITHMETIC OPERATION (All register labels refer to contents)	5 H	4 I	3 N	2 Z	1 V	0 C
Add	ADDA	8B	2	2	9B	3	2	AB	5	2	BB	4	3				A + M → A	↕	•	↕	↕	↕	↕
	ADDB	CB	2	2	DB	3	2	EB	5	2	FB	4	3				B + M → B	↕	•	↕	↕	↕	↕
Add Acmltrs	ABA													1B	2	1	A + B → A	↕	•	↕	↕	↕	↕
Add with Carry	ADCA	89	2	2	99	3	2	A9	5	2	B9	4	3				A + M + C → A	↕	•	↕	↕	↕	↕
	ADCB	C9	2	2	D9	3	2	E9	5	2	F9	4	3				B + M + C → B	↕	•	↕	↕	↕	↕
And	ANDA	84	2	2	94	3	2	A4	5	2	B4	4	3				A · M → A	•	•	↕	↕	R	•
	ANDB	C4	2	2	D4	3	2	E4	5	2	F4	4	3				B · M → B	•	•	↕	↕	R	•
Bit Test	BITA	85	2	2	95	3	2	A5	5	2	B5	4	3				A · M	•	•	↕	↕	R	•
	BITB	C5	2	2	D5	3	2	E5	5	2	F5	4	3				B · M	•	•	↕	↕	R	•
Clear	CLR							6F	7	2	7F	6	3				00 → M	•	•	R	S	R	R
	CLRA													4F	2	1	00 → A	•	•	R	S	R	R
	CLRB													5F	2	1	00 → B	•	•	R	S	R	R
Compare	CMPA	81	2	2	91	3	2	A1	5	2	B1	4	3				A − M	•	•	↕	↕	↕	↕
	CMPB	C1	2	2	D1	3	2	E1	5	2	F1	4	3				B − M	•	•	↕	↕	↕	↕
Compare Acmltrs	CBA													11	2	1	A − B	•	•	↕	↕	↕	↕
Complement, 1's	COM							63	7	2	73	6	3				$\overline{M}$ → M	•	•	↕	↕	R	S
	COMA													43	2	1	$\overline{A}$ → A	•	•	↕	↕	R	S
	COMB													53	2	1	$\overline{B}$ → B	•	•	↕	↕	R	S
Complement, 2's	NEG							60	7	2	70	6	3				00 − M → M	•	•	↕	↕	①	②
(Negate)	NEGA													40	2	1	00 − A → A	•	•	↕	↕	①	②
	NEGB													50	2	1	00 − B → B	•	•	↕	↕	①	②
Decimal Adjust, A	DAA													19	2	1	Converts Binary Add. of BCD Characters into BCD Format	•	•	↕	↕	↕	③
Decrement	DEC							6A	7	2	7A	6	3				M − 1 → M	•	•	↕	↕	4	•
	DECA													4A	2	1	A − 1 → A	•	•	↕	↕	4	•
	DECB													5A	2	1	B − 1 → B	•	•	↕	↕	4	•
Exclusive OR	EORA	88	2	2	98	3	2	A8	5	2	B8	4	3				A⊕M → A	•	•	↕	↕	R	•
	EORB	C8	2	2	D8	3	2	E8	5	2	F8	4	3				B⊕M → B	•	•	↕	↕	R	•
Increment	INC							6C	7	2	7C	6	3				M + 1 → M	•	•	↕	↕	⑤	•
	INCA													4C	2	1	A + 1 → A	•	•	↕	↕	⑤	•
	INCB													5C	2	1	B + 1 → B	•	•	↕	↕	⑤	•
Load Acmltr	LDAA	86	2	2	96	3	2	A6	5	2	B6	4	3				M → A	•	•	↕	↕	R	•
	LDAB	C6	2	2	D6	3	2	E6	5	2	F6	4	3				M → B	•	•	↕	↕	R	•
Or, Inclusive	ORAA	8A	2	2	9A	3	2	AA	5	2	BA	4	3				A + M → A	•	•	↕	↕	R	•
	ORAB	CA	2	2	DA	3	2	EA	5	2	FA	4	3				B + M → B	•	•	↕	↕	R	•
Push Data	PSHA													36	4	1	A → M_{SP}, SP − 1 → SP	•	•	•	•	•	•
	PSHB													37	4	1	B → M_{SP}, SP − 1 → SP	•	•	•	•	•	•
Pull Data	PULA													32	4	1	SP + 1 → SP, M_{SP} → A	•	•	•	•	•	•
	PULB													33	4	1	SP + 1 → SP, M_{SP} → B	•	•	•	•	•	•
Rotate Left	ROL							69	7	2	79	6	3				M	•	•	↕	↕	⑥	↕
	ROLA													49	2	1	A } □ ← ▭▭▭▭▭▭▭▭ (C ← b7 ← b0)	•	•	↕	↕	⑥	↕
	ROLB													59	2	1	B	•	•	↕	↕	⑥	↕
Rotate Right	ROR							66	7	2	76	6	3				M	•	•	↕	↕	⑥	↕
	RORA													46	2	1	A } □ → ▭▭▭▭▭▭▭▭ (C, b7 → b0)	•	•	↕	↕	⑥	↕
	RORB													56	2	1	B	•	•	↕	↕	⑥	↕
Shift Left, Arithmetic	ASL							68	7	2	78	6	3				M	•	•	↕	↕	⑥	↕
	ASLA													48	2	1	A } □ ← ▭▭▭▭▭▭▭▭ ← 0 (C, b7, b0)	•	•	↕	↕	⑥	↕
	ASLB													58	2	1	B	•	•	↕	↕	⑥	↕
Shift Right, Arithmetic	ASR							67	7	2	77	6	3				M	•	•	↕	↕	⑥	↕
	ASRA													47	2	1	A } ▭▭▭▭▭▭▭▭ → □ (b7, b0, C)	•	•	↕	↕	⑥	↕
	ASRB													57	2	1	B	•	•	↕	↕	⑥	↕
Shift Right, Logic	LSR							64	7	2	74	6	3				M	•	•	R	↕	⑥	↕
	LSRA													44	2	1	A } 0 → ▭▭▭▭▭▭▭▭ → □ (b7, b0, C)	•	•	R	↕	⑥	↕
	LSRB													54	2	1	B	•	•	R	↕	⑥	↕
Store Acmltr.	STAA				97	4	2	A7	6	2	B7	5	3				A → M	•	•	↕	↕	R	•
	STAB				D7	4	2	E7	6	2	F7	5	3				B → M	•	•	↕	↕	R	•
Subtract	SUBA	80	2	2	90	3	2	A0	5	2	B0	4	3				A − M → A	•	•	↕	↕	↕	↕
	SUBB	C0	2	2	D0	3	2	E0	5	2	F0	4	3				B − M → B	•	•	↕	↕	↕	↕
Subtract Acmltrs.	SBA													10	2	1	A − B → A	•	•	↕	↕	↕	↕
Subtr. with Carry	SBCA	82	2	2	92	3	2	A2	5	2	B2	4	3				A − M − C → A	•	•	↕	↕	↕	↕
	SBCB	C2	2	2	D2	3	2	E2	5	2	F2	4	3				B − M − C → B	•	•	↕	↕	↕	↕
Transfer Acmltrs	TAB													16	2	1	A → B	•	•	↕	↕	R	•
	TBA													17	2	1	B → A	•	•	↕	↕	R	•
Test, Zero or Minus	TST							6D	7	2	7D	6	3				M − 00	•	•	↕	↕	R	R
	TSTA													4D	2	1	A − 00	•	•	↕	↕	R	R
	TSTB													5D	2	1	B − 00	•	•	↕	↕	R	R
																		H	I	N	Z	V	C

LEGEND:

OP Operation Code (Hexadecimal);
~ Number of MPU Cycles;
# Number of Program Bytes;
+ Arithmetic Plus;
− Arithmetic Minus;
· Boolean AND;
M_{SP} Contents of memory location pointed to be Stack Pointer;
+ Boolean Inclusive OR;
⊕ Boolean Exclusive OR;
$\overline{M}$ Complement of M;
→ Transfer Into;
0 Bit = Zero;
00 Byte = Zero;

CONDITION CODE SYMBOLS:

H Half-carry from bit 3;
I Interrupt mask
N Negative (sign bit)
Z Zero (byte)
V Overflow, 2's complement
C Carry from bit 7
R Reset Always
S Set Always
↕ Test and set if true, cleared otherwise
• Not Affected

CONDITION CODE REGISTER NOTES:
(Bit set if test is true and cleared otherwise)

1 (Bit V) Test: Result = 10000000?
2 (Bit C) Test: Result = 00000000?
3 (Bit C) Test: Decimal value of most significant BCD Character greater than nine? (Not cleared if previously set.)
4 (Bit V) Test: Operand = 10000000 prior to execution?
5 (Bit V) Test: Operand = 01111111 prior to execution?
6 (Bit V) Test: Set equal to result of N⊕C after shift has occurred.

Note – Accumulator addressing mode instructions are included in the column for IMPLIED addressing

PROGRAM CONTROL OPERATIONS

Program Control operation can be subdivided into two categories: (1) Index Register/Stack Pointer instructions; (2) Jump and Branch operations.

Index Register/Stack Pointer Operations

The instructions for direct operation on the MPU's Index Register and Stack Pointer are summarized in Table 3. Decrement (DEX, DES), increment (INX, INS), load (LDX, LDS), and store (STX, STS) instructions are provided for both. The Compare instruction, CPX, can be used to compare the Index Register to a 16-bit value and update the Condition Code Register accordingly.

The TSX instruction causes the Index Register to be loaded with the address of the last data byte put onto the "stack." The TXS instruction loads the Stack Pointer with a value equal to one less than the current contents of the Index Register. This causes the next byte to be pulled from the "stack" to come from the location indicated by the Index Register. The utility of these two instructions can be clarified by describing the "stack" concept relative to the M6800 system.

The "stack" can be thought of as a sequential list of data stored in the MPU's read/write memory. The Stack Pointer contains a 16-bit memory address that is used to access the list from one end on a last-in-first-out (LIFO) basis in contrast to the random access mode used by the MPU's other addressing modes.

The MC6800 instruction set and interrupt structure allow extensive use of the stack concept for efficient handling of data movement, subroutines and interrupts. The instructions can be used to establish one or more "stacks" anywhere in read/write memory. Stack length is limited only by the amount of memory that is made available.

Operation of the Stack Pointer with the Push and Pull instructions is illustrated in Figures 15 and 16. The Push instruction (PSHA) causes the contents of the indicated accumulator (A in this example) to be stored in memory at the location indicated by the Stack Pointer. The Stack Pointer is automatically decremented by one following the storage operation and is "pointing" to the next empty stack location. The Pull instruction (PULA or PULB) causes the last byte stacked to be loaded into the appropriate accumulator. The Stack Pointer is automatically incremented by one just prior to the data transfer so that it will point to the last byte stacked rather than the next empty location. Note that the PULL instruction does not "remove" the data from memory; in the example, 1A is still in location (m + 1) following execution of PULA. A subsequent PUSH instruction would overwrite that location with the new "pushed" data.

Execution of the Branch to Subroutine (BSR) and Jump to Subroutine (JSR) instructions cause a return address to be saved on the stack as shown in Figures 18 through 20. The stack is decremented after each byte of the return address is pushed onto the stack. For both of these instructions, the return address is the memory location following the bytes of code that correspond to the BSR and JSR instruction. The code required for BSR or JSR may be either two or three bytes, depending on whether the JSR is in the indexed (two bytes) or the extended (three bytes) addressing mode. Before it is stacked, the Program Counter is automatically incremented the correct number of times to be pointing at the location of the next instruction. The Return from Subroutine Instruction, RTS, causes the return address to be retrieved and loaded into the Program Counter as shown in Figure 21.

There are several operations that cause the status of the MPU to be saved on the stack. The Software Interrupt (SWI) and Wait for Interrupt (WAI) instructions as well as the maskable ($\overline{IRQ}$) and non-maskable ($\overline{NMI}$) hardware interrupts all cause the MPU's internal registers (except for the Stack Pointer itself) to be stacked as shown in Figure 23. MPU status is restored by the Return from Interrupt, RTI, as shown in Figure 22.

Jump and Branch Operation

The Jump and Branch instructions are summarized in Table 4. These instructions are used to control the transfer or operation from one point to another in the control program.

The No Operation instruction, NOP, while included here, is a jump operation in a very limited sense. Its only effect is to increment the Program Counter by one. It is useful during program development as a "stand-in" for some other instruction that is to be determined during debug. It is also used for equalizing the execution time through alternate paths in a control program.

TABLE 3 — INDEX REGISTER AND STACK POINTER INSTRUCTIONS

		IMMED			DIRECT			INDEX			EXTND			IMPLIED				COND. CODE REG. 5	4	3	2	1	0
POINTER OPERATIONS	MNEMONIC	OP	~	=	OP	~	=	OP	~	=	OP	~	=	OP	~	=	BOOLEAN/ARITHMETIC OPERATION	H	I	N	Z	V	C
Compare Index Reg	CPX	8C	3	3	9C	4	2	AC	6	2	BC	5	3				$X_H - M, X_L - (M+1)$	•	•	①	↕	②	•
Decrement Index Reg	DEX													09	4	1	$X - 1 \rightarrow X$	•	•	•	↕	•	•
Decrement Stack Pntr	DES													34	4	1	$SP - 1 \rightarrow SP$	•	•	•	•	•	•
Increment Index Reg	INX													08	4	1	$X + 1 \rightarrow X$	•	•	•	↕	•	•
Increment Stack Pntr	INS													31	4	1	$SP + 1 \rightarrow SP$	•	•	•	•	•	•
Load Index Reg	LDX	CE	3	3	DE	4	2	EE	6	2	FE	5	3				$M \rightarrow X_H, (M+1) \rightarrow X_L$	•	•	③	↕	R	•
Load Stack Pntr	LDS	8E	3	3	9E	4	2	AE	6	2	BE	5	3				$M \rightarrow SP_H, (M+1) \rightarrow SP_L$	•	•	③	↕	R	•
Store Index Reg	STX				DF	5	2	EF	7	2	FF	6	3				$X_H \rightarrow M, X_L \rightarrow (M+1)$	•	•	③	↕	R	•
Store Stack Pntr	STS				9F	5	2	AF	7	2	BF	6	3				$SP_H \rightarrow M, SP_L \rightarrow (M+1)$	•	•	③	↕	R	•
Indx Reg → Stack Pntr	TXS													35	4	1	$X - 1 \rightarrow SP$	•	•	•	•	•	•
Stack Pntr → Indx Reg	TSX													30	4	1	$SP + 1 \rightarrow X$	•	•	•	•	•	•

① (Bit N) Test: Sign bit of most significant (MS) byte of result = 1?
② (Bit V) Test: 2's complement overflow from subtraction of ms bytes?
③ (Bit N) Test: Result less than zero? (Bit 15 = 1)

FIGURE 15 — STACK OPERATION, PUSH INSTRUCTION

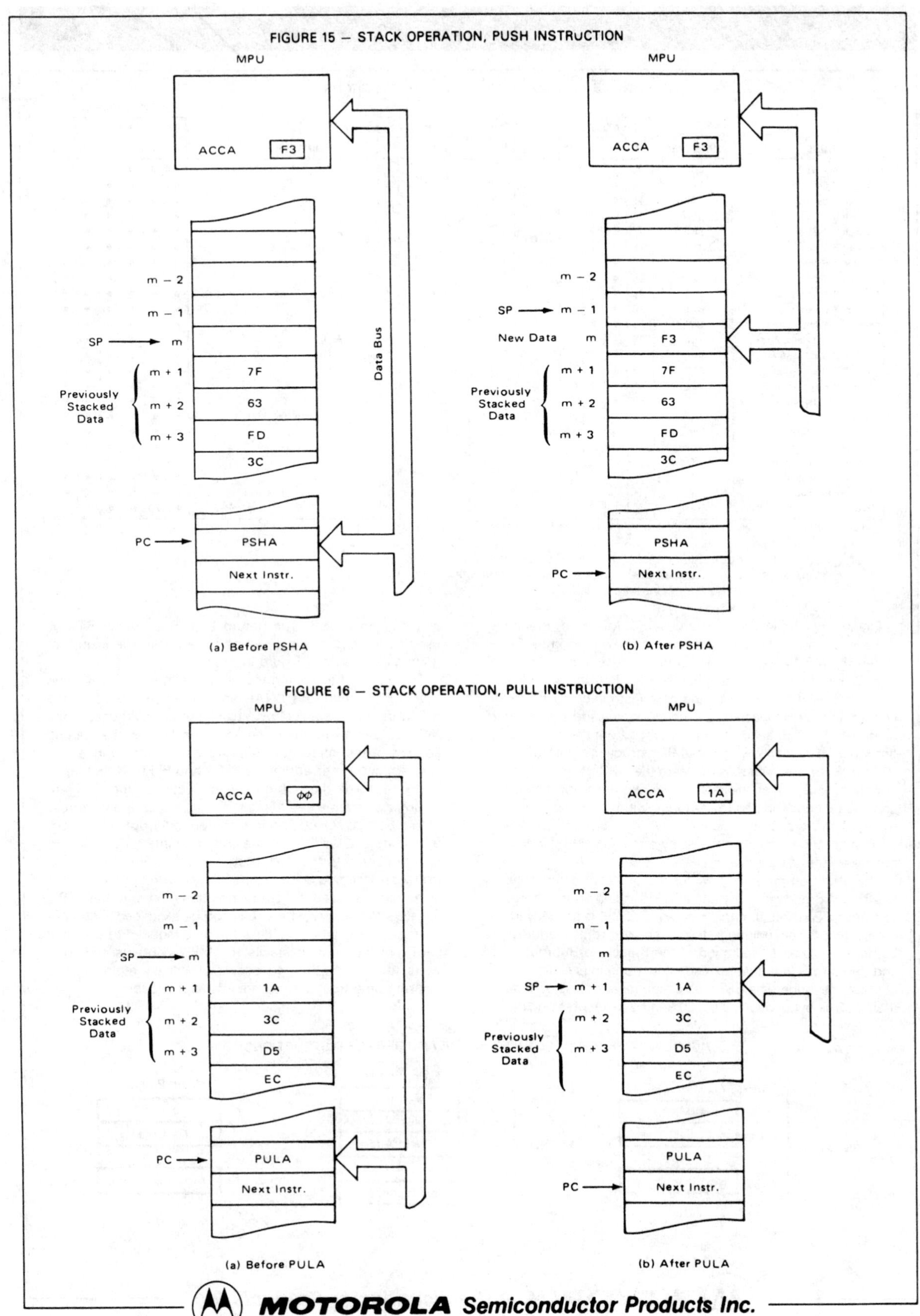

MC6800

TABLE 4 — JUMP AND BRANCH INSTRUCTIONS

OPERATIONS	MNEMONIC	RELATIVE OP	~	=	INDEX OP	~	=	EXTND OP	~	=	IMPLIED OP	~	=	BRANCH TEST	COND. CODE REG. 5 H	4 I	3 N	2 Z	1 V	0 C
Branch Always	BRA	20	4	2										None	•	•	•	•	•	•
Branch If Carry Clear	BCC	24	4	2										C = 0	•	•	•	•	•	•
Branch If Carry Set	BCS	25	4	2										C = 1	•	•	•	•	•	•
Branch If = Zero	BEQ	27	4	2										Z = 1	•	•	•	•	•	•
Branch If ≥ Zero	BGE	2C	4	2										$N \oplus V = 0$	•	•	•	•	•	•
Branch If > Zero	BGT	2E	4	2										$Z + (N \oplus V) = 0$	•	•	•	•	•	•
Branch If Higher	BHI	22	4	2										C + Z = 0	•	•	•	•	•	•
Branch If ≤ Zero	BLE	2F	4	2										$Z + (N \oplus V) = 1$	•	•	•	•	•	•
Branch If Lower Or Same	BLS	23	4	2										C + Z = 1	•	•	•	•	•	•
Branch If < Zero	BLT	2D	4	2										$N \oplus V = 1$	•	•	•	•	•	•
Branch If Minus	BMI	2B	4	2										N = 1	•	•	•	•	•	•
Branch If Not Equal Zero	BNE	26	4	2										Z = 0	•	•	•	•	•	•
Branch If Overflow Clear	BVC	28	4	2										V = 0	•	•	•	•	•	•
Branch If Overflow Set	BVS	29	4	2										V = 1	•	•	•	•	•	•
Branch If Plus	BPL	2A	4	2										N = 0	•	•	•	•	•	•
Branch To Subroutine	BSR	8D	8	2										See Special Operations	•	•	•	•	•	•
Jump	JMP				6E	4	2	7E	3	3				See Special Operations	•	•	•	•	•	•
Jump To Subroutine	JSR				AD	8	2	BD	9	3				See Special Operations	•	•	•	•	•	•
No Operation	NOP										01	2	1	Advances Prog. Cntr. Only	•	•	•	•	•	•
Return From Interrupt	RTI										3B	10	1		①					
Return From Subroutine	RTS										39	5	1	See Special Operations	•	•	•	•	•	•
Software Interrupt	SWI										3F	12	1	See Special Operations	•	•	•	•	•	•
Wait for Interrupt*	WAI										3E	9	1	See Special Operations	•	②	•	•	•	•

*WAI puts Address Bus, R/W, and Data Bus in the three-state mode while VMA is held low.

① (All) Load Condition Code Register from Stack. (See Special Operations)
② (Bit 1) Set when interrupt occurs. If previously set, a Non-Maskable Interrupt is required to exit the wait state.

Execution of the Jump Instruction, JMP, and Branch Always, BRA, affects program flow as shown in Figure 17. When the MPU encounters the Jump (Indexed) instruction, it adds the offset to the value in the Index Register and uses the result as the address of the next instruction to be executed. In the extended addressing mode, the address of the next instruction to be executed is fetched from the two locations immediately following the JMP instruction. The Branch Always (BRA) instruction is similar to the JMP (extended) instruction except that the relative addressing mode applies and the branch is limited to the range within −125 or +127 bytes of the branch instruction itself. The opcode for the BRA instruction requires one less byte than JMP (extended) but takes one more cycle to execute.

The effect on program flow for the Jump to Subroutine (JSR) and Branch to Subroutine (BSR) is shown in Figures 18 through 20. Note that the Program Counter is properly incremented to be pointing at the correct return address before it is stacked. Operation of the Branch to Subroutine and Jump to Subroutine (extended) instruction is similar except for the range. The BSR instruction requires less opcode than JSR (2 bytes versus 3 bytes) and also executes one cycle faster than JSR. The Return from Subroutine, RTS, is used as the end of a subroutine to return to the main program as indicated in Figure 21.

The effect of executing the Software Interrupt, SWI, and the Wait for Interrupt, WAI, and their relationship to the hardware interrupts is shown in Figure 22. SWI causes the MPU contents to be stacked and then fetches the starting address of the interrupt routine from the memory locations that respond to the addresses FFFA and FFFB. Note that as in the case of the subroutine instructions, the Program Counter is incremented to point at the correct return address before being stacked. The Return from Interrupt instruction, RTI, (Figure 22) is used at the end of an interrupt routine to restore control to the main program. The SWI instruction is useful for inserting break points in the control program, that is, it can be used to stop operation and put the MPU registers in memory where they can be examined. The WAI instruction is used to decrease the time required to service a hardware interrupt; it stacks the MPU contents and then waits for the interrupt to occur, effectively removing the stacking time from a hardware interrupt sequence.

FIGURE 17 — PROGRAM FLOW FOR JUMP AND BRANCH INSTRUCTIONS

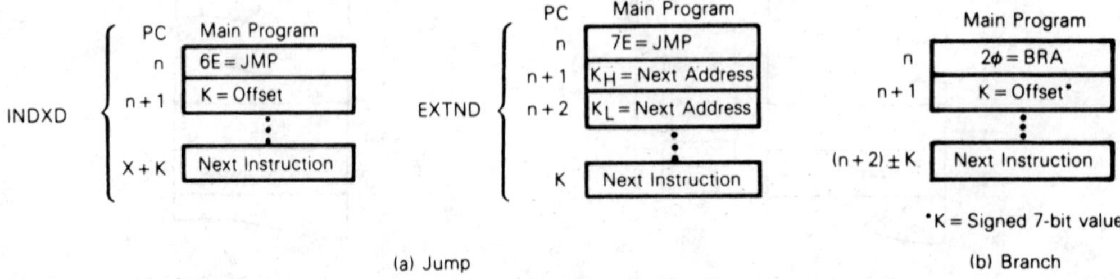

(a) Jump (b) Branch

MC6800

FIGURE 18 — PROGRAM FLOW FOR BSR

FIGURE 19 — PROGRAM FLOW FOR JSR (EXTENDED)

FIGURE 20 — PROGRAM FLOW FOR JSR (INDEXED)

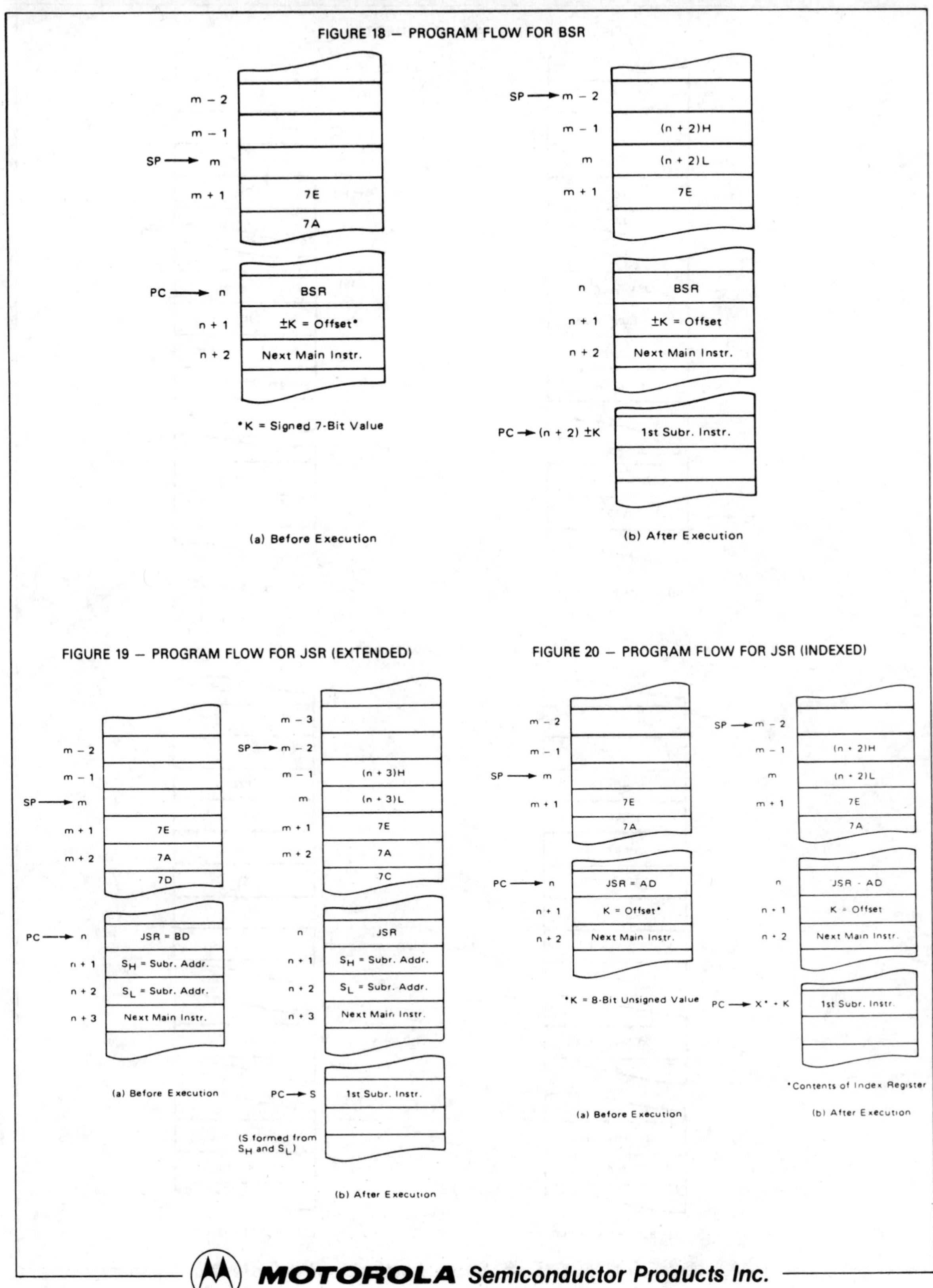

MC6800

FIGURE 21 — PROGRAM FLOW FOR RTS

FIGURE 22 — PROGRAM FLOW FOR RTI

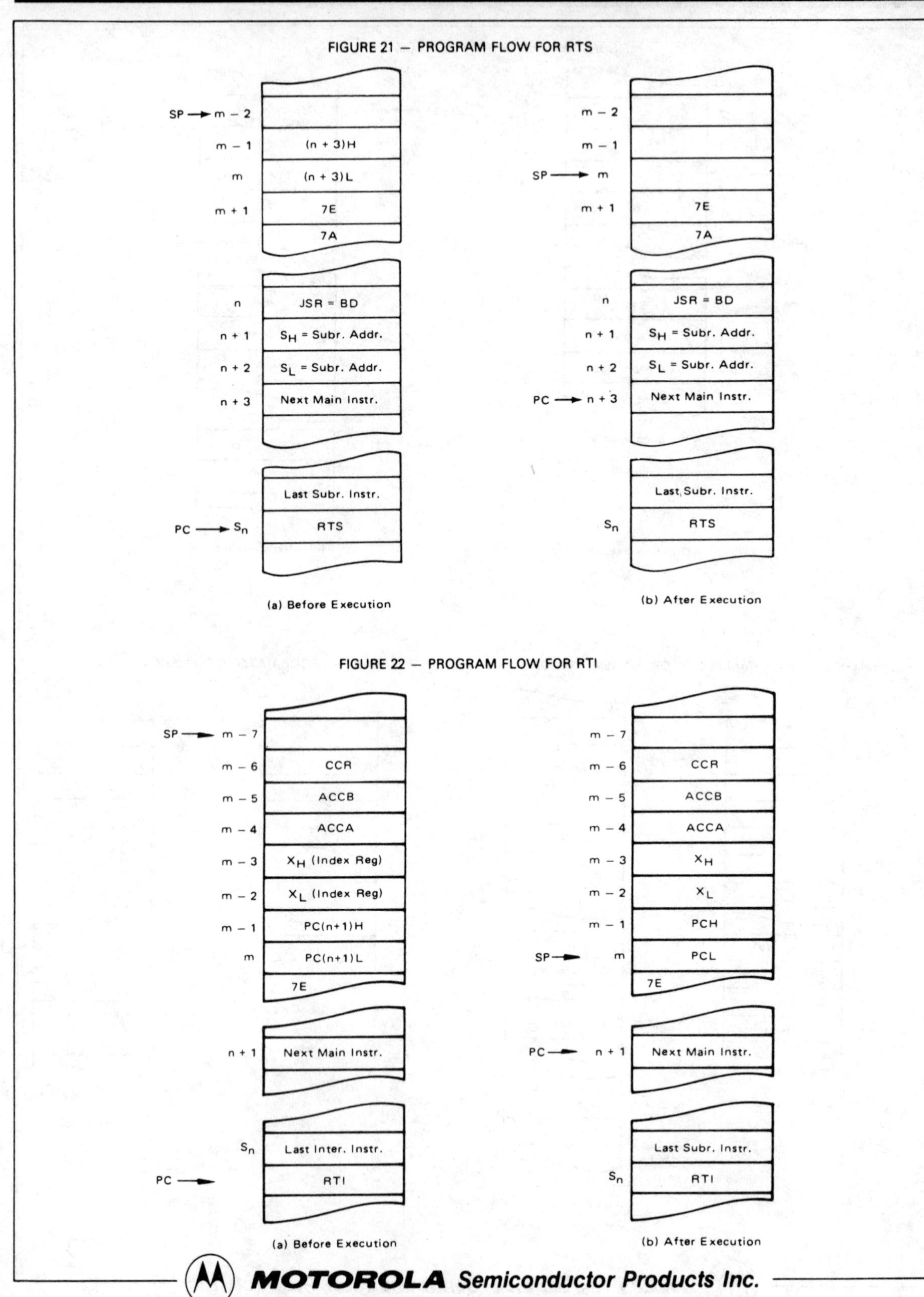

(a) Before Execution

(b) After Execution

MC6800

FIGURE 23 — PROGRAM FLOW FOR INTERRUPTS

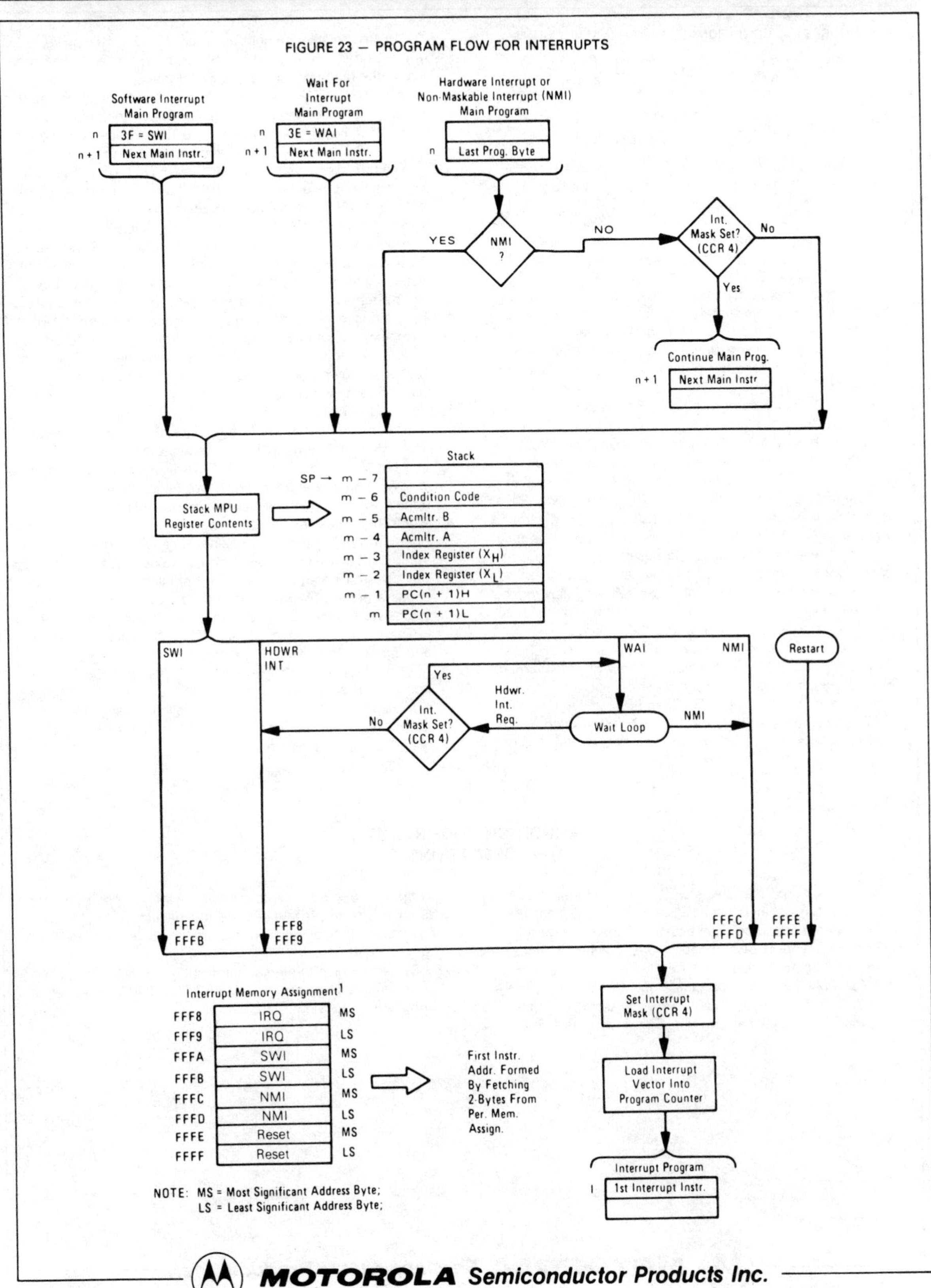

FIGURE 24 — CONDITIONAL BRANCH INSTRUCTIONS

BMI :	N = 1 ;	BEQ :	Z = 1 ;
BPL :	N = ϕ ;	BNE :	Z = ϕ ;
BVC :	V = ϕ ;	BCC :	C = ϕ ;
BVS :	V = 1 ;	BCS :	C = 1 ;
BHI :	C + Z = ϕ ;	BLT :	N⊕V = 1 ;
BLS :	C + Z = 1 ;	BGE :	N⊕V = ϕ ;
BLE :	Z + (N⊕V) = 1 ;		
BGT :	Z + (N⊕V) = ϕ ;		

The conditional branch instructions, Figure 24, consists of seven pairs of complementary instructions. They are used to test the results of the preceding operation and either continue with the next instruction in sequence (test fails) or cause a branch to another point in the program (test succeeds).

Four of the pairs are used for simple tests of status bits N, Z, V, and C:

1. Branch on Minus (BMI) and Branch On Plus (BPL) tests the sign bit, N, to determine if the previous result was negative or positive, respectively.

2. Branch On Equal (BEQ) and Branch On Not Equal (BNE) are used to test the zero status bit, Z, to determine whether or not the result of the previous operation was equal to zero. These two instructions are useful following a Compare (CMP) instruction to test for equality between an accumulator and the operand. They are also used following the Bit Test (BIT) to determine whether or not the same bit positions are set in an accumulator and the operand.

3. Branch On Overflow Clear (BVC) and Branch On Overflow Set (BVS) tests the state of the V bit to determine if the previous operation caused an arithmetic overflow.

4. Branch On Carry Clear (BCC) and Branch On Carry Set (BCS) tests the state of the C bit to determine if the previous operation caused a carry to occur. BCC and BCS are useful for testing relative magnitude when the values being tested are regarded as unsigned binary numbers, that is, the values are in the range 00 (lowest) to FF (highest). BCC following a comparison (CMP) will cause a branch if the (unsigned) value in the accumulator is higher than or the same as the value of the operand. Conversely, BCS will cause a branch if the accumulator value is lower than the operand.

The fifth complementary pair, Branch On Higher (BHI) and Branch On Lower or Same (BLS) are, in a sense, complements to BCC and BCS. BHI tests for both C and Z = 0; if used following a CMP, it will cause a branch if the value in the accumulator is higher than the operand. Conversely, BLS will cause a branch if the unsigned binary value in the accumulator is lower than or the same as the operand.

The remaining two pairs are useful in testing results of operations in which the values are regarded as signed two's complement numbers. This differs from the unsigned binary case in the following sense: in unsigned, the orientation is higher or lower; in signed two's complement, the comparison is between larger or smaller where the range of values is between −128 and +127.

Branch On Less Than Zero (BLT) and Branch On Greater Than Or Equal Zero (BGE) test the status bits for N ⊕ V = 1 and N ⊕ V = 0, respectively. BLT will always cause a branch following an operation in which two negative numbers were added. In addition, it will cause a branch following a CMP in which the value in the accumulator was negative and the operand was positive. BLT will never cause a branch following a CMP in which the accumulator value was positive and the operand negative. BGE, the complement to BLT, will cause a branch following operations in which two positive values were added or in which the result was zero.

The last pair, Branch On Less Than Or Equal Zero (BLE) and Branch On Greater Than Zero (BGT) test the status bits for Z ⊕ (N + V) = 1 and Z ⊕ (N + V) = 0, respectively. The action of BLE is identical to that for BLT except that a branch will also occur if the result of the previous result was zero. Conversely, BGT is similar to BGE except that no branch will occur following a zero result.

CONDITION CODE REGISTER OPERATIONS

The Condition Code Register (CCR) is a 6-bit register within the MPU that is useful in controlling program flow during system operation. The bits are defined in Figure 25.

The instructions shown in Table 5 are available to the user for direct manipulation of the CCR.

A CLI-WAI instruction sequence operated properly, with early MC6800 processors, only if the preceding instruction was odd (Least Significant Bit = 1). Similarly it was advisable to precede any SEI instruction with an odd opcode — such as NOP. These precautions are not necessary for MC6800 processors indicating manufacture in November 1977 or later.

Systems which require an interrupt window to be opened under program control should use a CLI-NOP-SEI sequence rather than CLI-SEI.

FIGURE 25 — CONDITION CODE REGISTER BIT DEFINITION

b_5	b_4	b_3	b_2	b_1	b_0
H	I	N	Z	V	C

H = Half-carry; set whenever a carry from b_3 to b_4 of the result is generated by ADD, ABA, ADC; cleared if no b_3 to b_4 carry; not affected by other instructions.

I = Interrupt Mask; set by hardware or software interrupt or SEI instruction; cleared by CLI instruction. (Normally not used in arithmetic operations.) Restored to a zero as a result of an RT1 instruction if I_m stored on the stacked is low.

N = Negative; set if high order bit (b_7) of result is set; cleared otherwise.

Z = Zero; set if result = 0; cleared otherwise.

V = Overlow; set if there was arithmetic overflow as a result of the operation; cleared otherwise.

C = Carry; set if there was a carry from the most significant bit (b_7) of the result; cleared otherwise.

TABLE 5 — CONDITION CODE REGISTER INSTRUCTIONS

		IMPLIED				COND. CODE REG.					
						5	4	3	2	1	0
OPERATIONS	MNEMONIC	OP	~	=	BOOLEAN OPERATION	H	I	N	Z	V	C
Clear Carry	CLC	0C	2	1	0 · C	•	•	•	•	•	R
Clear Interrupt Mask	CLI	0E	2	1	0 · I	•	R	•	•	•	•
Clear Overflow	CLV	0A	2	1	0 → V	•	•	•	•	R	•
Set Carry	SEC	0D	2	1	1 · C	•	•	•	•	•	S
Set Interrupt Mask	SEI	0F	2	1	1 · I	•	S	•	•	•	•
Set Overflow	SEV	0B	2	1	1 · V	•	•	•	•	S	•
Acmltr A → CCR	TAP	06	2	1	A · CCR	(1)					
CCR → Acmltr A	TPA	07	2	1	CCR · A	•	•	•	•	•	•

R = Reset
S = Set
• = Not affected

(1) (ALL) Set according to the contents of Accumulator A.

ADDRESSING MODES

The MPU operates on 8-bit binary numbers presented to it via the Data Bus. A given number (byte) may represent either data or an instruction to be executed, depending on where it is encountered in the control program. The M6800 has 72 unique instructions, however, it recognizes and takes action on 197 of the 256 possibilitis that can occur using an 8-bit word length. This larger number of instructions results from the fact that many of the executive instructions have more than one addressing mode.

These addressing modes refer to the manner in which the program causes the MPU to obtain its instructions and data. The programmer must have a method for addressing the MPU's internal registers and all of the external memory locations.

Selection of the desired addressing mode is made by the user as the source statements are written. Translation into appropriate opcode then depends on the method used. If manual translation is used, the addressing mode is inherent in the opcode. For example, the Immediate, Direct, Indexed, and Extended modes may all be used with the ADD instruction. The proper mode is determined by selecting (hexadecimal notation) 8B, 9B, AB, or BB, respectively.

The source statement format includes adequate information for the selection if an assembler program is used to generate the opcode. For instance, the Immediate mode is selected by the Assembler whenever it encounters the "#" symbol in the operand field. Similarly, an "X" in the operand field causes the Indexed mode to be selected. Only the Relative mode applies to the branch instructions, therefore, the mnemonic instruction itself is enough for the Assembler to determine addressing mode.

MC6800

For the instructions that use both Direct and Extended modes, the Assembler selects the Direct mode if the operand value is in the range 0-255 and Extended otherwise. There are a number of instructions for which the Extended mode is valid but the Direct is not. For these instructions, the Assembler automatically selects the Extended mode even if the operand is in the 0-255 range. The addressing modes are summarized in Figure 26.

Inherent (Includes "Accumulator Addressing" Mode)

The successive fields in a statement are normally separated by one or more spaces. An exception to this rule occurs for instructions that use dual addressing in the operand field and for instructions that must distinguish between the two accumulators. In these cases, A and B are "operands" but the space between them and the operator may be omitted. This is commonly done, resulting in apparent four character mnemonics for those instructions.

The addition instruction, ADD, provides an example of dual addressing in the operand field:

Operator	Operand	Comment
ADDA	MEM12	ADD CONTENTS OF MEM12 TO ACCA
or		
ADDB	MEM12	ADD CONTENTS OF MEM12 TO ACCB

The example used earlier for the test instruction, TST, also applies to the accumulators and uses the "accumulator addressing mode" to designate which of the two accumulators is being tested:

FIGURE 26 — ADDRESSING MODE SUMMARY

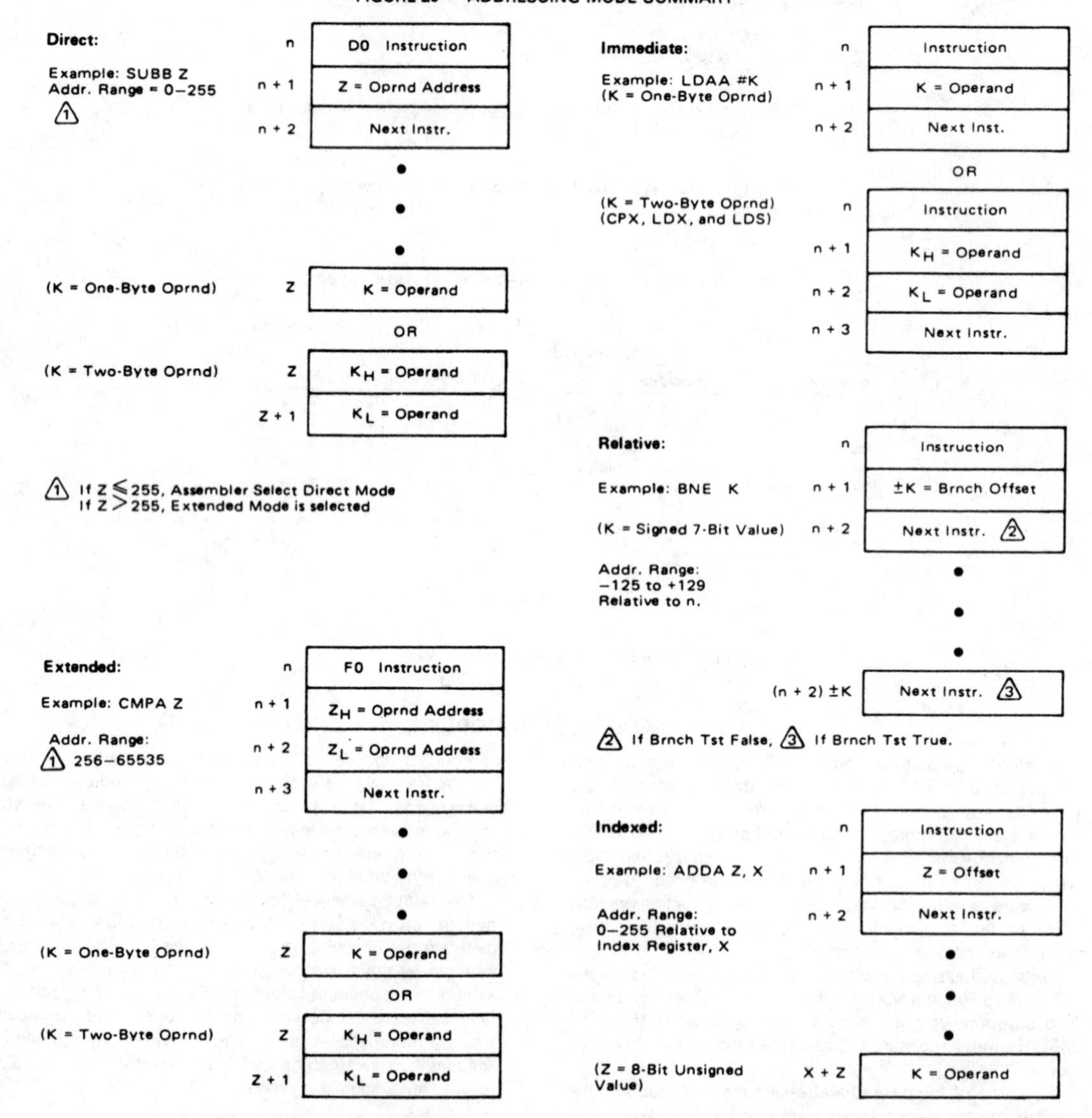

Operator	Comment
TSTB	TEST CONTENTS OF ACCB

or

TSTA	TEST CONTENTS OF ACCA

A number of the instructions either alone or together with an accumulator operand contain all of the address information that is required, that is, "inherent" in the instruction itself. For instance, the instruction ABA causes the MPU to add the contents of accmulators A and B together and place the result in accumulator A. The instruction INCB, another example of "accumulator addressing," causes the contents of accumulator B to be increased by one. Similarly, INX, increment the Index Register, causes the contents of the Index Register to be increased by one.

Program flow for instructions of this type is illustrated in Figures 27 and 28. In these figures, the general case is shown on the left and a specific example is shown on the right. Numerical examples are in decimal notation. Instructions of this type require only one byte of opcode. Cycle-by-cycle operation of the inherent mode is shown in Table 6.

Immediate Addressing Mode – In the Immediate addressing mode, the operand is the value that is to be operated on. For instance, the instruction

Operator	Operand	Comment
LDAA	#25	LOAD 25 INTO ACCA

causes the MPU to "immediately load accumulator A with the value 25"; no further address reference is required. The Immediate mode is selected by preceding the operand value with the "#" symbol. Program flow for this addressing mode is illustrated in Figure 29.

The operand format allows either properly defined symbols or numerical values. Except for the instructions CPX, LDX, and LDS, the operand may be any value in the range 0 to 255. Since Compare Index Register (CPX), Load Index Register (LDX), and Load Stack Pointer (LDS), require 16-bit values, the immediate mode for these three instructions require two-byte operands. In the Immediate addressing mode, the "address" of the operand is effectively the memory location immediately following the instruction itself. Table 7 shows the cycle-by-cycle operation for the immediate addressing mode.

Direct and Extended Addressing Modes – In the Direct and Extended modes of addressing, the operand field of the source statement is the *address* of the value that is to be operated on. The Direct and Extended modes differ only in the range of memory locations to which they can direct the MPU. Direct addressing generates a single 8-bit operand and, hence, can address only memory locations 0 through 255; a two byte operand is generated for Extended addressing, enabling the MPU to reach the remaining memory locations, 256 through 65535. An example of Direct addressing and its effect on program flow is illustrated in Figure 30.

The MPU, after encountering the opcode for the instruction LDAA (Direct) at memory location 5004 (Program Counter = 5004), looks in the next location, 5005, for the address of the operand. It then sets the program counter equal to the value found there (100 in the example) and fetches the operand, in this case a value to be loaded into accumulator A, from that location. For instructions requiring a two-byte operand such as LDX (Load the Index Register), the operand bytes would be retrieved from locations 100 and 101. Table 8 shows the cycle-by-cycle operation for the direct mode of addressing.

Extended addressing, Figure 31, is similar except that a two-byte address is obtained from locations 5007 and 5008 after the LDAB (Extended) opcode shows up in location 5006. Extended addressing can be thought of as the "standard" addressing mode, that is, it is a method of reaching any place in memory. Direct addressing, since only one address byte is required, provides a faster method of processing data and generates fewer bytes of control code. In most applications, the direct addressing range, memory locations 0-255, are reserved for RAM. They are used for data buffering and temporary storage of system variables, the area in which faster addressing is of most value. Cycle-by-cycle operation is shown in Table 9 for Extended Addressing.

FIGURE 27 – INHERENT ADDRESSING

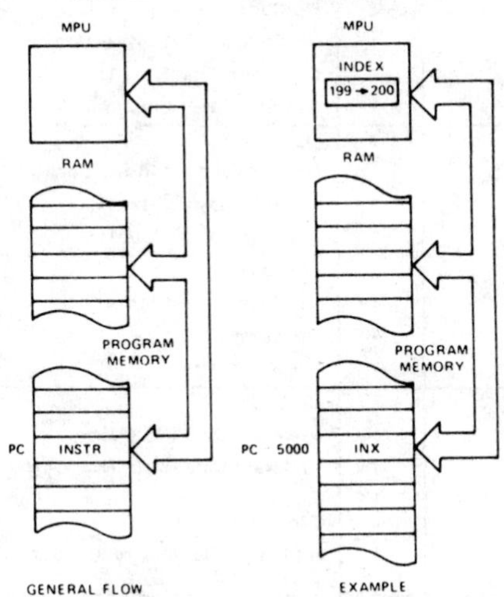

FIGURE 28 – ACCUMULATOR ADDRESSING

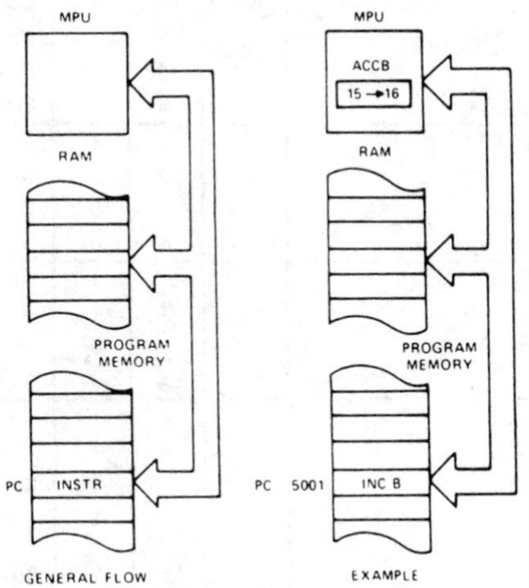

Relative Address Mode – In both the Direct and Extended modes, the address obtained by the MPU is an absolute numerical address. The Relative addressing mode, implemented for the MPU's branch instructions, specifies a memory location relative to the Program Counter's current location. Branch instructions generate two bytes of machine code, one for the instruction opcode and one for the "relative" address (see Figure 32). Since it is desirable to be able to branch in either direction, the 8-bit address byte is interpreted as a signed 7-bit value; the 8th bit of the operand is treated as a sign bit, "0" = plus and "1" = minus. The remaining seven bits represent the numerical value. This results in a relative addressing range of ± 127 with respect to the location of the branch instruction itself. However, the branch range is computed with respect to the next instruction that would be executed if the branch conditions are not satisfied. Since two bytes are generated, the next instruction is located at PC + 2. If D is defined as the address of the branch destination, the range is then:

$$(PC + 2) - 127 \leq D \leq (PC + 2) + 127$$

or

$$PC - 125 \leq D \leq PC + 129$$

that is, the destination of the branch instruction must be within −125 to +129 memory locations of the branch instruction itself. For transferring control beyond this range, the unconditional jump (JMP), jump to subroutine (JSR), and return from subroutine (RTS) are used.

In Figure 32, when the MPU encounters the opcode for BEQ (Branch if result of last instruction was zero), it tests the Zero bit in the Condition Code Register. If that bit is "0," indicating a non-zero result, the MPU continues execution with the next instruction (in location 5010 in Figure 32). If the previous result was zero, the branch condition is satisfied and the MPU adds the offset, 15 in this case, to PC + 2 and branches to location 5025 for the next instruction.

The branch instructions allow the programmer to efficiently direct the MPU to one point or another in the control program depending on the outcome of test results. Since the control program is normally in read-only memory and cannot be changed, the relative address used in execution of branch instructions is a constant numerical value. Cycle-by-cycle operation is shown in Table 10 for relative addressing.

Indexed Addressing Mode – With Indexed addressing, the numerical address is variable and depends on the current contents of the Index Register. A source statement such as

Operator	**Operand**	**Comment**
STAA	X	PUT A IN INDEXED LOCATION

causes the MPU to store the contents of accumulator A in

TABLE 6 – INHERENT MODE CYCLE-BY-CYCLE OPERATION

Address Mode and Instructions	Cycles	Cycle #	VMA Line	Address Bus	R/$\overline{W}$ Line	Data Bus
ABA DAA SEC ASL DEC SEI ASR INC SEV CBA LSR TAB CLC NEG TAP CLI NOP TBA CLR ROL TPA CLV ROR TST COM SBA	2	1	1	Op Code Address	1	Op Code
		2	1	Op Code Address + 1	1	Op Code of Next Instruction
DES DEX INS INX	4	1	1	Op Code Address	1	Op Code
		2	1	Op Code Address + 1	1	Op Code of Next Instruction
		3	0	Previous Register Contents	1	Irrelevant Data (Note 1)
		4	0	New Register Contents	1	Irrelevant Data (Note 1)
PSH	4	1	1	Op Code Address	1	Op Code
		2	1	Op Code Address + 1	1	Op Code of Next Instruction
		3	1	Stack Pointer	0	Accumulator Data
		4	0	Stack Pointer – 1	1	Accumulator Data
PUL	4	1	1	Op Code Address	1	Op Code
		2	1	Op Code Address + 1	1	Op Code of Next Instruction
		3	0	Stack Pointer	1	Irrelevant Data (Note 1)
		4	1	Stack Pointer + 1	1	Operand Data from Stack
TSX	4	1	1	Op Code Address	1	Op Code
		2	1	Op Code Address + 1	1	Op Code of Next Instruction
		3	0	Stack Pointer	1	Irrelevant Data (Note 1)
		4	0	New Index Register	1	Irrelevant Data (Note 1)
TXS	4	1	1	Op Code Address	1	Op Code
		2	1	Op Code Address + 1	1	Op Code of Next Instruction
		3	0	Index Register	1	Irrelevant Data
		4	0	New Stack Pointer	1	Irrelevant Data
RTS	5	1	1	Op Code Address	1	Op Code
		2	1	Op Code Address + 1	1	Irrelevant Data (Note 2)
		3	0	Stack Pointer	1	Irrelevant Data (Note 1)
		4	1	Stack Pointer + 1	1	Address of Next Instruction (High Order Byte)
		5	1	Stack Pointer + 2	1	Address of Next Instruction (Low Order Byte)

MC6800

TABLE 6 — INHERENT MODE CYCLE-BY-CYCLE OPERATION (CONTINUED)

Address Mode and Instructions	Cycles	Cycle #	VMA Line	Address Bus	R/$\overline{W}$ Line	Data Bus
WAI	9	1	1	Op Code Address	1	Op Code
		2	1	Op Code Address + 1	1	Op Code of Next Instruction
		3	1	Stack Pointer	0	Return Address (Low Order Byte)
		4	1	Stack Pointer – 1	0	Return Address (High Order Byte)
		5	1	Stack Pointer – 2	0	Index Register (Low Order Byte)
		6	1	Stack Pointer – 3	0	Index Register (High Order Byte)
		7	1	Stack Pointer – 4	0	Contents of Accumulator A
		8	1	Stack Pointer – 5	0	Contents of Accumulator B
		9	1	Stack Pointer – 6 (Note 3)	1	Contents of Cond. Code Register
RTI	10	1	1	Op Code Address	1	Op Code
		2	1	Op Code Address + 1	1	Irrelevant Data (Note 2)
		3	0	Stack Pointer	1	Irrelevant Data (Note 1)
		4	1	Stack Pointer + 1	1	Contents of Cond. Code Register from Stack
		5	1	Stack Pointer + 2	1	Contents of Accumulator B from Stack
		6	1	Stack Pointer + 3	1	Contents of Accumulator A from Stack
		7	1	Stack Pointer + 4	1	Index Register from Stack (High Order Byte)
		8	1	Stack Pointer + 5	1	Index Register from Stack (Low Order Byte)
		9	1	Stack Pointer + 6	1	Next Instruction Address from Stack (High Order Byte)
		10	1	Stack Pointer + 7	1	Next Instruction Address from Stack (Low Order Byte)
SWI	12	1	1	Op Code Address	1	Op Code
		2	1	Op Code Address + 1	1	Irrelevant Data (Note 1)
		3	1	Stack Pointer	0	Return Address (Low Order Byte)
		4	1	Stack Pointer – 1	0	Return Address (High Order Byte)
		5	1	Stack Pointer – 2	0	Index Register (Low Order Byte)
		6	1	Stack Pointer – 3	0	Index Register (High Order Byte)
		7	1	Stack Pointer – 4	0	Contents of Accumulator A
		8	1	Stack Pointer – 5	0	Contents of Accumulator B
		9	1	Stack Pointer – 6	0	Contents of Cond. Code Register
		10	0	Stack Pointer – 7	1	Irrelevant Data (Note 1)
		11	1	Vector Address FFFA (Hex)	1	Address of Subroutine (High Order Byte)
		12	1	Vector Address FFFB (Hex)	1	Address of Subroutine (Low Order Byte)

Note 1. If device which is addressed during this cycle uses VMA, then the Data Bus will go to the high impedance three-state condition. Depending on bus capacitance, data from the previous cycle may be retained on the Data Bus.
Note 2. Data is ignored by the MPU.
Note 3. While the MPU is waiting for the interrupt, Bus Available will go high indicating the following states of the control lines: VMA is low; Address Bus, R/$\overline{W}$, and Data Bus are all in the high impedance state.

the memory location specified by the contents of the Index Register (recall that the label "X" is reserved to designate the Index Register). Since there are instructions for manipulating X during program execution (LDX, INX, DEC, etc.), the Indexed addressing mode provides a dynamic "on the fly" way to modify program activity.

The operand field can also contain a numerical value that will be automatically added to X during execution. This format is illustrated in Figure 33.

When the MPU encounters the LDAB (Indexed) opcode in location 5006, it looks in the next memory location for the value to be added to X (5 in the example) and calculates the required address by adding 5 to the present Index Register value of 400. In the operand format, the offset may be represented by a label or a numerical value in the range 0-255 as in the example. In the earlier example, STAA X, the operand is equivalent to 0, X, that is, the 0 may be omitted when the desired address is equal to X. Table 11 shows the cycle-by-cycle operation for the Indexed Mode of Addressing.

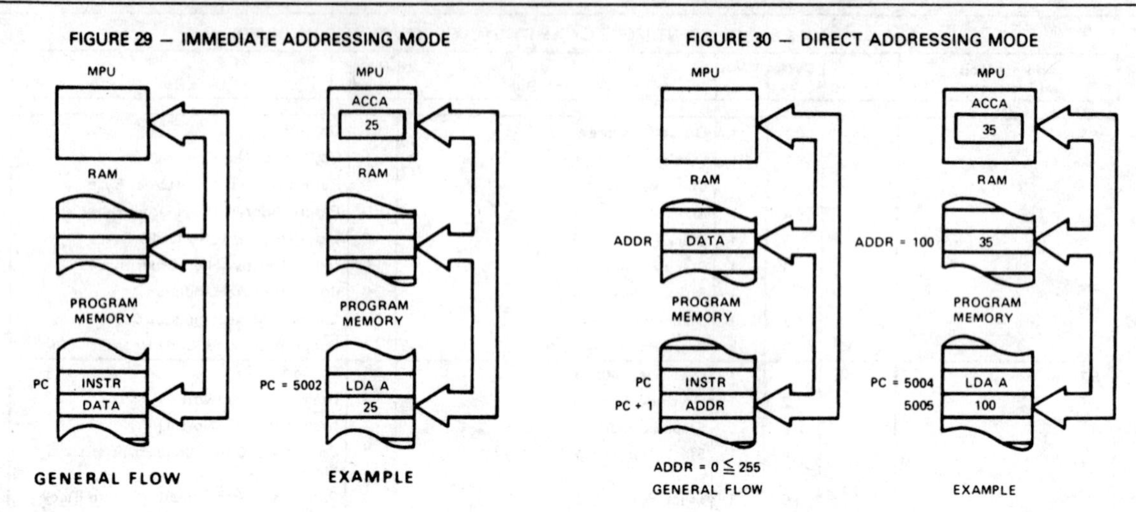

FIGURE 29 — IMMEDIATE ADDRESSING MODE

FIGURE 30 — DIRECT ADDRESSING MODE

TABLE 7 — IMMEDIATE MODE CYCLE-BY-CYCLE OPERATION

Address Mode and Instructions	Cycles	Cycle #	VMA Line	Address Bus	R/$\overline{W}$ Line	Data Bus
ADC EOR ADD LDA AND ORA BIT SBC CMP SUB	2	1	1	Op Code Address	1	Op Code
		2	1	Op Code Address + 1	1	Operand Data
CPX LDS LDX	3	1	1	Op Code Address	1	Op Code
		2	1	Op Code Address + 1	1	Operand Data (High Order Byte)
		3	1	Op Code Address + 2	1	Operand Data (Low Order Byte)

TABLE 8 — DIRECT MODE CYCLE-BY-CYCLE OPERATION

Address Mode and Instructions	Cycles	Cycle #	VMA Line	Address Bus	R/$\overline{W}$ Line	Data Bus
ADC EOR ADD LDA AND ORA BIT SBC CMP SUB	3	1	1	Op Code Address	1	Op Code
		2	1	Op Code Address + 1	1	Address of Operand
		3	1	Address of Operand	1	Operand Data
CPX LDS LDX	4	1	1	Op Code Address	1	Op Code
		2	1	Op Code Address + 1	1	Address of Operand
		3	1	Address of Operand	1	Operand Data (High Order Byte)
		4	1	Operand Address + 1	1	Operand Data (Low Order Byte)
STA	4	1	1	Op Code Address	1	Op Code
		2	1	Op Code Address + 1	1	Destination Address
		3	0	Destination Address	1	Irrelevant Data (Note 1)
		4	1	Destination Address	0	Data from Accumulator
STS STX	5	1	1	Op Code Address	1	Op Code
		2	1	Op Code Address + 1	1	Address of Operand
		3	0	Address of Operand	1	Irrelevant Data (Note 1)
		4	1	Address of Operand	0	Register Data (High Order Byte)
		5	1	Address of Operand + 1	0	Register Data (Low Order Byte)

Note 1. If device which is address during this cycle uses VMA, then the Data Bus will go to the high impedance three-state condition. Depending on bus capacitance, data from the previous cycle may be retained on the Data Bus.

FIGURE 31 — EXTENDED ADDRESSING MODE

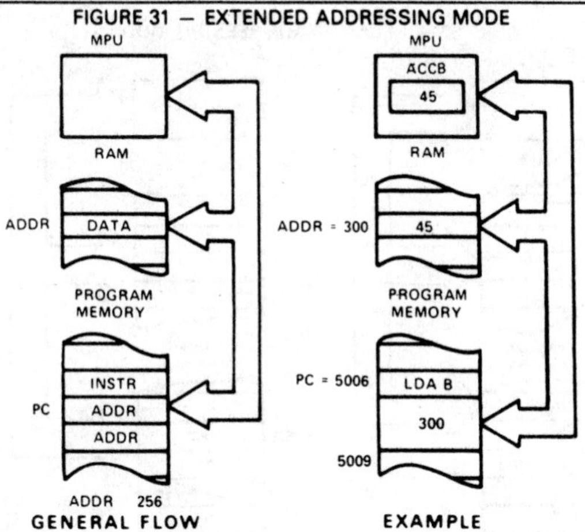

TABLE 9 — EXTENDED MODE CYCLE-BY-CYCLE

Address Mode and Instructions	Cycles	Cycle #	VMA Line	Address Bus	R/W̄ Line	Data Bus
STS STX	6	1	1	Op Code Address	1	Op Code
		2	1	Op Code Address + 1	1	Address of Operand (High Order Byte)
		3	1	Op Code Address + 2	1	Address of Operand (Low Order Byte)
		4	0	Address of Operand	1	Irrelevant Data (Note 1)
		5	1	Address of Operand	0	Operand Data (High Order Byte)
		6	1	Address of Operand + 1	0	Operand Data (Low Order Byte)
JSR	9	1	1	Op Code Address	1	Op Code
		2	1	Op Code Address + 1	1	Address of Subroutine (High Order Byte)
		3	1	Op Code Address + 2	1	Address of Subroutine (Low Order Byte)
		4	1	Subroutine Starting Address	1	Op Code of Next Instruction
		5	1	Stack Pointer	0	Return Address (Low Order Byte)
		6	1	Stack Pointer – 1	0	Return Address (High Order Byte)
		7	0	Stack Pointer – 2	1	Irrelevant Data (Note 1)
		8	0	Op Code Address + 2	1	Irrelevant Data (Note 1)
		9	1	Op Code Address + 2	1	Address of Subroutine (Low Order Byte)
JMP	3	1	1	Op Code Address	1	Op Code
		2	1	Op Code Address + 1	1	Jump Address (High Order Byte)
		3	1	Op Code Address + 2	1	Jump Address (Low Order Byte)
ADC EOR ADD LDA AND ORA BIT SBC CMP SUB	4	1	1	Op Code Address	1	Op Code
		2	1	Op Code Address + 1	1	Address of Operand (High Order Byte)
		3	1	Op Code Address + 2	1	Address of Operand (Low Order Byte)
		4	1	Address of Operand	1	Operand Data
CPX LDS LDX	5	1	1	Op Code Address	1	Op Code
		2	1	Op Code Address + 1	1	Address of Operand (High Order Byte)
		3	1	Op Code Address + 2	1	Address of Operand (Low Order Byte)
		4	1	Address of Operand	1	Operand Data (High Order Byte)
		5	1	Address of Operand + 1	1	Operand Data (Low Order Byte)
STA A STA B	5	1	1	Op Code Address	1	Op Code
		2	1	Op Code Address + 1	1	Destination Address (High Order Byte)
		3	1	Op Code Address + 2	1	Destination Address (Low Order Byte)
		4	0	Operand Destination Address	1	Irrelevant Data (Note 1)
		5	1	Operand Destination Address	0	Data from Accumulator
ASL LSR ASR NEG CLR ROL COM ROR DEC TST INC	6	1	1	Op Code Address	1	Op Code
		2	1	Op Code Address + 1	1	Address of Operand (High Order Byte)
		3	1	Op Code Address + 2	1	Address of Operand (Low Order Byte)
		4	1	Address of Operand	1	Current Operand Data
		5	0	Address of Operand	1	Irrelevant Data (Note 1)
		6	1/0 (Note 2)	Address of Operand	0	New Operand Data (Note 2)

Note 1. If device which is addressed during this cycle uses VMA, then the Data Bus will go to the high impedance three-state condition. Depending on bus capacitance, data from the previous cycle may be retained on the Data Bus.

Note 2. For TST, VMA = 0 and Operand data does not change.

FIGURE 32 — RELATIVE ADDRESSING MODE

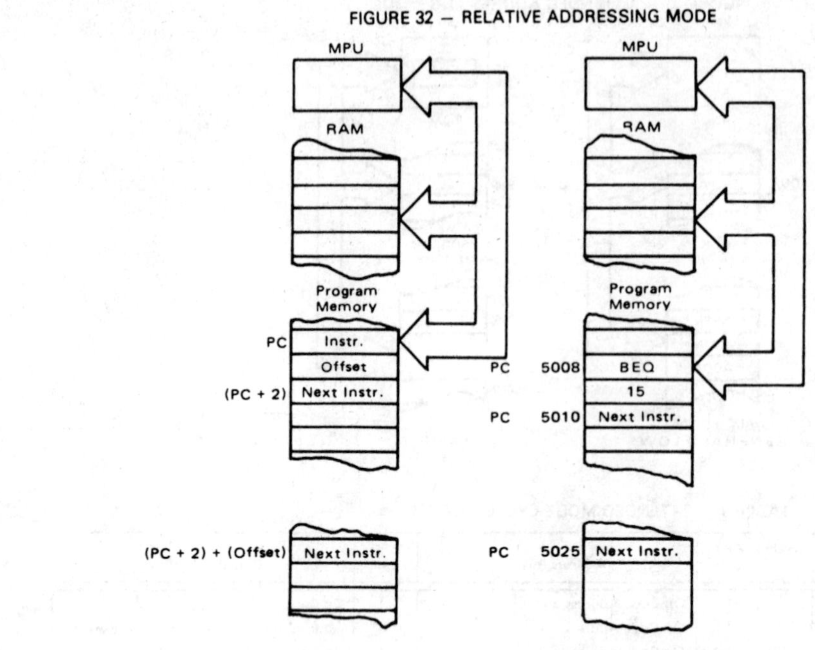

FIGURE 33 — INDEXED ADDRESSING MODE

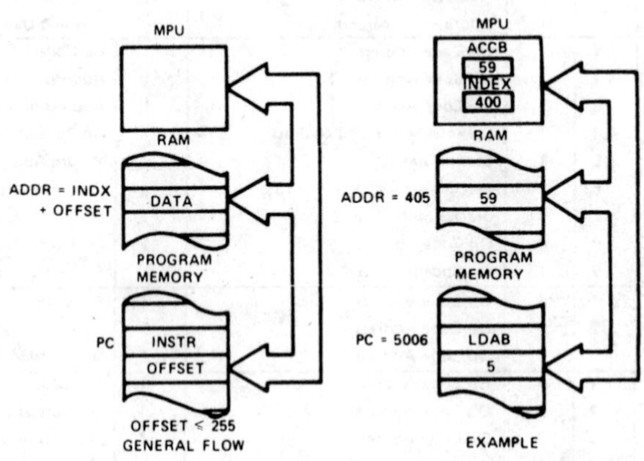

TABLE 10 — RELATIVE MODE CYCLE-BY-CYCLE OPERATION

Address Mode and Instructions	Cycles	Cycle #	VMA Line	Address Bus	R/$\overline{W}$ Line	Data Bus
BCC BHI BNE BCS BLE BPL BEQ BLS BRA BGE BLT BVC BGT BMI BVS	4	1	1	Op Code Address	1	Op Code
		2	1	Op Code Address + 1	1	Branch Offset
		3	0	Op Code Address + 2	1	Irrelevant Data (Note 1)
		4	0	Branch Address	1	Irrelevant Data (Note 1)
BSR	8	1	1	Op Code Address	1	Op Code
		2	1	Op Code Address + 1	1	Branch Offset
		3	0	Return Address of Main Program	1	Irrelevant Data (Note 1)
		4	1	Stack Pointer	0	Return Address (Low Order Byte)
		5	1	Stack Pointer – 1	0	Return Address (High Order Byte)
		6	0	Stack Pointer – 2	1	Irrelevant Data (Note 1)
		7	0	Return Address of Main Program	1	Irrelevant Data (Note 1)
		8	0	Subroutine Address	1	Irrelevant Data (Note 1)

Note 1. If device which is addressed during this cycle uses VMA, then the Data Bus will go to the high impedance three-state condition. Depending on bus capacitance, data from the previous cycle may be retained on the Data Bus.

MC6800

TABLE 11 – INDEXED MODE CYCLE-BY-CYCLE

Address Mode and Instructions	Cycles	Cycle #	VMA Line	Address Bus	R/W̄ Line	Data Bus
INDEXED						
JMP	4	1	1	Op Code Address	1	Op Code
		2	1	Op Code Address + 1	1	Offset
		3	0	Index Register	1	Irrelevant Data (Note 1)
		4	0	Index Register Plus Offset (w/o Carry)	1	Irrelevant Data (Note 1)
ADC EOR ADD LDA AND ORA BIT SBC CMP SUB	5	1	1	Op Code Address	1	Op Code
		2	1	Op Code Address + 1	1	Offset
		3	0	Index Register	1	Irrelevant Data (Note 1)
		4	0	Index Register Plus Offset (w/o Carry)	1	Irrelevant Data (Note 1)
		5	1	Index Register Plus Offset	1	Operand Data
CPX LDS LDX	6	1	1	Op Code Address	1	Op Code
		2	1	Op Code Address + 1	1	Offset
		3	0	Index Register	1	Irrelevant Data (Note 1)
		4	0	Index Register Plus Offset (w/o Carry)	1	Irrelevant Data (Note 1)
		5	1	Index Register Plus Offset	1	Operand Data (High Order Byte)
		6	1	Index Register Plus Offset + 1	1	Operand Data (Low Order Byte)
STA	6	1	1	Op Code Address	1	Op Code
		2	1	Op Code Address + 1	1	Offset
		3	0	Index Register	1	Irrelevant Data (Note 1)
		4	0	Index Register Plus Offset (w/o Carry)	1	Irrelevant Data (Note 1)
		5	0	Index Register Plus Offset	1	Irrelevant Data (Note 1)
		6	1	Index Register Plus Offset	0	Operand Data
ASL LSR ASR NEG CLR ROL COM ROR DEC TST INC	7	1	1	Op Code Address	1	Op Code
		2	1	Op Code Address + 1	1	Offset
		3	0	Index Register	1	Irrelevant Data (Note 1)
		4	0	Index Register Plus Offset (w/o Carry)	1	Irrelevant Data (Note 1)
		5	1	Index Register Plus Offset	1	Current Operand Data
		6	0	Index Register Plus Offset	1	Irrelevant Data (Note 1)
		7	1/0 (Note 2)	Index Register Plus Offset	0	New Operand Data (Note 2)
STS STX	7	1	1	Op Code Address	1	Op Code
		2	1	Op Code Address + 1	1	Offset
		3	0	Index Register	1	Irrelevant Data (Note 1)
		4	0	Index Register Plus Offset (w/o Carry)	1	Irrelevant Data (Note 1)
		5	0	Index Register Plus Offset	1	Irrelevant Data (Note 1)
		6	1	Index Register Plus Offset	0	Operand Data (High Order Byte)
		7	1	Index Register Plus Offset + 1	0	Operand Data (Low Order Byte)
JSR	8	1	1	Op Code Address	1	Op Code
		2	1	Op Code Address + 1	1	Offset
		3	0	Index Register	1	Irrelevant Data (Note 1)
		4	1	Stack Pointer	0	Return Address (Low Order Byte)
		5	1	Stack Pointer – 1	0	Return Address (High Order Byte)
		6	0	Stack Pointer – 2	1	Irrelevant Data (Note 1)
		7	0	Index Register	1	Irrelevant Data (Note 1)
		8	0	Index Register Plus Offset (w/o Carry)	1	Irrelevant Data (Note 1)

Note 1. If device which is addressed during this cycle uses VMA, then the Data Bus will go to the high impedance three-state condition. Depending on bus capacitance, data from the previous cycle may be retained on the Data Bus.

Note 2. For TST, VMA = 0 and Operand data does not change.

ORDERING INFORMATION

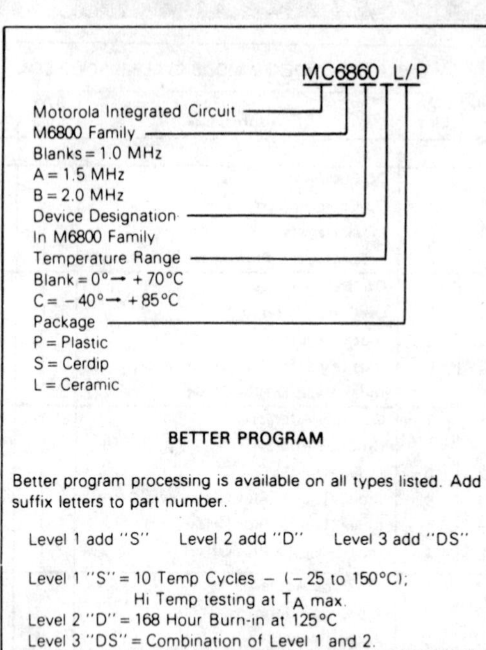

MC6860 L/P

Motorola Integrated Circuit
M6800 Family
Blanks = 1.0 MHz
A = 1.5 MHz
B = 2.0 MHz
Device Designation
In M6800 Family
Temperature Range
Blank = 0° → +70°C
C = −40° → +85°C
Package
P = Plastic
S = Cerdip
L = Ceramic

BETTER PROGRAM

Better program processing is available on all types listed. Add suffix letters to part number.

Level 1 add "S" Level 2 add "D" Level 3 add "DS"

Level 1 "S" = 10 Temp Cycles − (−25 to 150°C);
Hi Temp testing at T_A max.
Level 2 "D" = 168 Hour Burn-in at 125°C
Level 3 "DS" = Combination of Level 1 and 2.

Speed	Device	Temperature Range
1.0 MHz	MC6800P,L,S MC6800CP,CL,CS	0 to 70°C −40 to +85°C
1.5 MHz	MC68A00P,L,S MC68A00CP,CL,CS	0 to +70°C −40 to +85°C
2.0 MHz	MC68B00P,L,S	0 to +70°C

PACKAGE DIMENSIONS

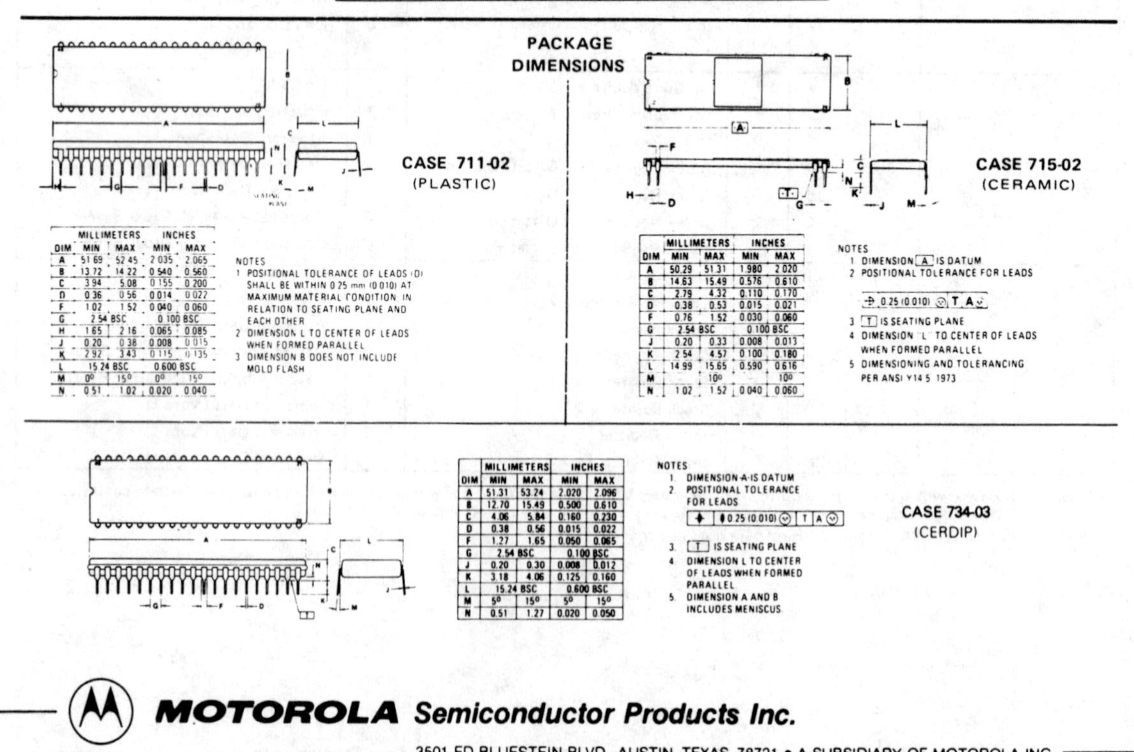

CASE 711-02
(PLASTIC)

DIM	MILLIMETERS MIN	MILLIMETERS MAX	INCHES MIN	INCHES MAX
A	51.69	52.45	2.035	2.065
B	13.72	14.22	0.540	0.560
C	3.94	5.08	0.155	0.200
D	0.36	0.56	0.014	0.022
F	1.02	1.52	0.040	0.060
G	2.54 BSC		0.100 BSC	
H	1.65	2.16	0.065	0.085
J	0.20	0.38	0.008	0.015
K	2.92	3.43	0.115	0.135
L	15.24 BSC		0.600 BSC	
M	0°	15°	0°	15°
N	0.51	1.02	0.020	0.040

NOTES
1. POSITIONAL TOLERANCE OF LEADS (D) SHALL BE WITHIN 0.25 mm (0.010) AT MAXIMUM MATERIAL CONDITION, IN RELATION TO SEATING PLANE AND EACH OTHER
2. DIMENSION L TO CENTER OF LEADS WHEN FORMED PARALLEL
3. DIMENSION B DOES NOT INCLUDE MOLD FLASH

CASE 715-02
(CERAMIC)

DIM	MILLIMETERS MIN	MILLIMETERS MAX	INCHES MIN	INCHES MAX
A	50.29	51.31	1.980	2.020
B	14.63	15.49	0.576	0.610
C	2.79	4.32	0.110	0.170
D	0.38	0.53	0.015	0.021
F	0.76	1.52	0.030	0.060
G	2.54 BSC		0.100 BSC	
J	0.20	0.33	0.008	0.013
K	2.54	4.57	0.100	0.180
L	14.99	15.65	0.590	0.616
M	–	10°	–	10°
N	1.02	1.52	0.040	0.060

NOTES
1. DIMENSION A IS DATUM
2. POSITIONAL TOLERANCE FOR LEADS
   0.25 (0.010) Ⓜ T A Ⓜ
3. T IS SEATING PLANE
4. DIMENSION "L" TO CENTER OF LEADS WHEN FORMED PARALLEL
5. DIMENSIONING AND TOLERANCING PER ANSI Y14.5, 1973

CASE 734-03
(CERDIP)

DIM	MILLIMETERS MIN	MILLIMETERS MAX	INCHES MIN	INCHES MAX
A	51.31	53.24	2.020	2.096
B	12.70	15.49	0.500	0.610
C	4.06	5.84	0.160	0.230
D	0.38	0.56	0.015	0.022
F	1.27	1.65	0.050	0.065
G	2.54 BSC		0.100 BSC	
J	0.20	0.30	0.008	0.012
K	3.18	4.06	0.125	0.160
L	15.24 BSC		0.600 BSC	
M	5°	15°	5°	15°
N	0.51	1.27	0.020	0.050

NOTES
1. DIMENSION -A- IS DATUM
2. POSITIONAL TOLERANCE FOR LEADS
   0.25 (0.010) Ⓜ T A Ⓜ
3. T IS SEATING PLANE
4. DIMENSION L TO CENTER OF LEADS WHEN FORMED PARALLEL
5. DIMENSION A AND B INCLUDES MENISCUS

MC6808

Advance Information

MOS

(N-CHANNEL, SILICON-GATE, DEPLETION LOAD)

MICROPROCESSOR WITH CLOCK

MICROPROCESSOR WITH CLOCK

The MC6808 is a monolithic 8-bit microprocessor that contains all the registers and accumulators of the present MC6800 plus an internal clock oscillator and driver on the same chip.

The MC6808 is completely software-compatible with the MC6800 as well as the entire M6800 family of parts. Hence the MC6808 is expandable to 65K words.

This very cost-effective MPU allows the designer to use the MC6808 in consumer as well as industrial applications without sacrificing industrial specifications.

- On-Chip Clock Circuit
- Software-Compatible with the MC6800
- Expandable to 65K words
- Standard TTL-Compatible Inputs and Outputs
- 8-Bit Word Size
- 16-Bit Memory Addressing
- Interrupt Capability

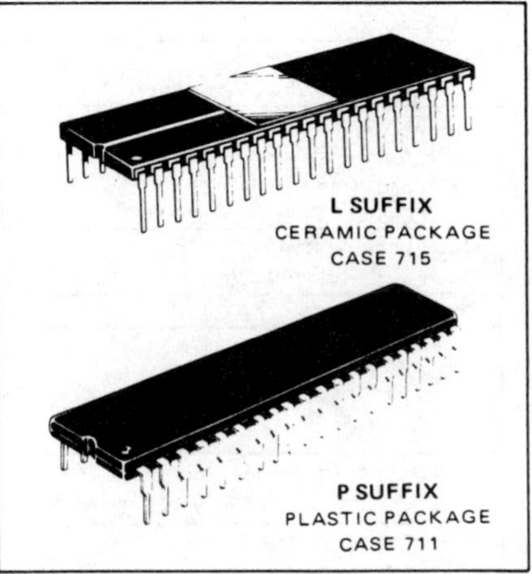

L SUFFIX
CERAMIC PACKAGE
CASE 715

P SUFFIX
PLASTIC PACKAGE
CASE 711

FIGURE 1 – TYPICAL MICROPROCESSOR INTERFACE

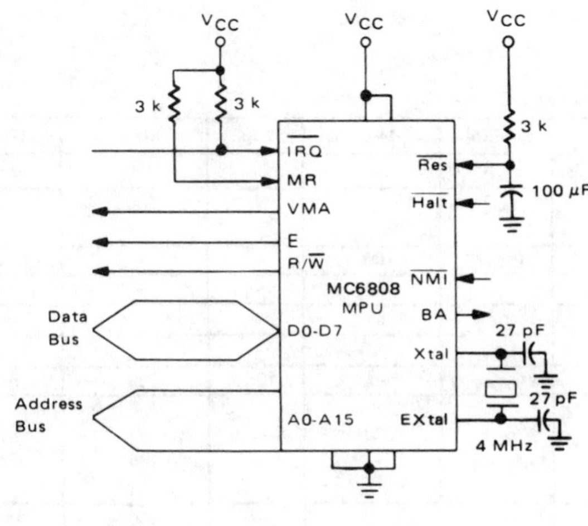

PIN ASSIGNMENT

Pin	Signal	Signal	Pin
1	V_{SS}	$\overline{Reset}$	40
2	$\overline{Halt}$	EXtal	39
3	MR	Xtal	38
4	$\overline{IRQ}$	E	37
5	VMA	V_{SS}	36
6	$\overline{NMI}$	V_{CC}	35
7	BA	R/$\overline{W}$	34
8	V_{CC}	D0	33
9	A0	D1	32
10	A1	D2	31
11	A2	D3	30
12	A3	D4	29
13	A4	D5	28
14	A5	D6	27
15	A6	D7	26
16	A7	A15	25
17	A8	A14	24
18	A9	A13	23
19	A10	A12	22
20	A11	V_{SS}	21

This is advance information and specifications are subject to change without notice.

MC6808

MAXIMUM RATINGS

Rating	Symbol	Value	Unit
Supply Voltage	V_{CC}	-0.3 to +7.0	Vdc
Input Voltage	V_{in}	-0.3 to +7.0	Vdc
Operating Temperature Range	T_A	0 to +70	°C
Storage Temperature Range	T_{stg}	-55 to +150	°C
Thermal Resistance	θ_{JA}		°C/W
Plastic		100	
Ceramic		50	

This device contains circuitry to protect the inputs against damage due to high static voltages or electric fields; however, it is advised that normal precautions be taken to avoid application of any voltage higher than maximum rated voltages to this high impedance circuit.

ELECTRICAL CHARACTERISTICS (V_{CC} = 5.0 V ± 5%, V_{SS} = 0, T_A = 0 to 70°C unles otherwise noted.)

Characteristic		Symbol	Min	Typ	Max	Unit
Input High Voltage	Logic, EXtal Reset	V_{IH}	V_{SS} + 2.0 V_{SS} + 4.0	– –	V_{CC} V_{CC}	Vdc
Input Low Voltage	Logic, EXtal Reset	V_{IL}	V_{SS} – 0.3 V_{SS} – 0.3	–	V_{SS} + 0.8 V_{SS} + 2.3	Vdc
Input Leakage Current (V_{in} = 0 to 5.25 V, V_{CC} = max)	Logic*	I_{in}	–	1.0	2.5	μAdc
Output High Voltage		V_{OH}				Vdc
(I_{Load} = -205 μAdc, V_{CC} = min)	D0-D7		V_{SS} + 2.4	–	–	
(I_{Load} = -145 μAdc, V_{CC} = min)	A0-A15, R/W, VMA, E		V_{SS} + 2.4	–	–	
(I_{Load} = -100 μAdc, V_{CC} = min)	BA		V_{SS} + 2.4	–	–	
Output Low Voltage (I_{Load} = 1.6 mAdc, V_{CC} = min)		V_{OL}	–	–	V_{SS} + 0.4	Vdc
Power Dissipation		P_D**	–	0.600	1.2	W
Capacitance # (V_{in} = 0, T_A = 25°C, f = 1.0 MHz)		C_{in}				pF
	D0-D7		–	10	12.5	
	Logic Inputs, EXtal		–	6.5	10	
	A0-A15, R/W, VMA	C_{out}	–	–	12	pF
Frequency of Operation (Input Clock ÷4)		f	0.1	–	1.0	MHz
(Crystal Frequency)		f_{Xtal}	1.0	–	4.0	
Clock Timing						
Cycle Time		t_{cyc}	1.0	–	10	μs
Clock Pulse Width (measured at 2.4V) (measured at 0.4V)		$PW_{\phi Hs}$ $PW_{\phi L}$	450 450	–	4500 4500	ns
Fall Time (Measured between V_{SS} + 0.4 V and V_{SS} + 2.4 V)		t_ϕ	–	–	25	ns

*Except IRQ and NMI, which require 3 kΩ pullup load resistors for wire-OR capability at optimum operation. Does not include EXtal and Xtal, which are crystal inputs.

#Capacitances are periodically sampled rather than 100% tested.

READ/WRITE TIMING (Figures 2 through 6; Load Circuit of Figure 4.)

Characteristic	Symbol	Min	Typ	Max	Unit
Address Delay	t_{AD}	–	–	270	ns
Peripheral Read Access Time $t_{acc} = t_{ut} - (t_{AD} + t_{DSR})$; $t_{ut} = t_{cyc} - t_\phi$	t_{acc}	–	–	530	ns
Data Setup Time (Read)	t_{DSR}	100	–	–	ns
Input Data Hold Time	t_H	10	–	–	ns
Output Data Hold Time	t_H	30	–	–	ns
Address Hold Time (Address, R/W, VMA)	t_{AH}	20	–	–	ns
Data Delay Time (Write)	t_{DDW}	–	165	225	ns
Processor Controls					
Processor Control Setup Time	t_{PCS}	200	–	–	ns
Processor Control Rise and Fall Time (Measured between 0.8 V and 2.0 V)	t_{PCr}, t_{PCf}	–	–	100	ns
Bus Available Delay Time	t_{BA}	–	–	250	ns

FIGURE 2 – READ DATA FROM MEMORY OR PERIPHERALS

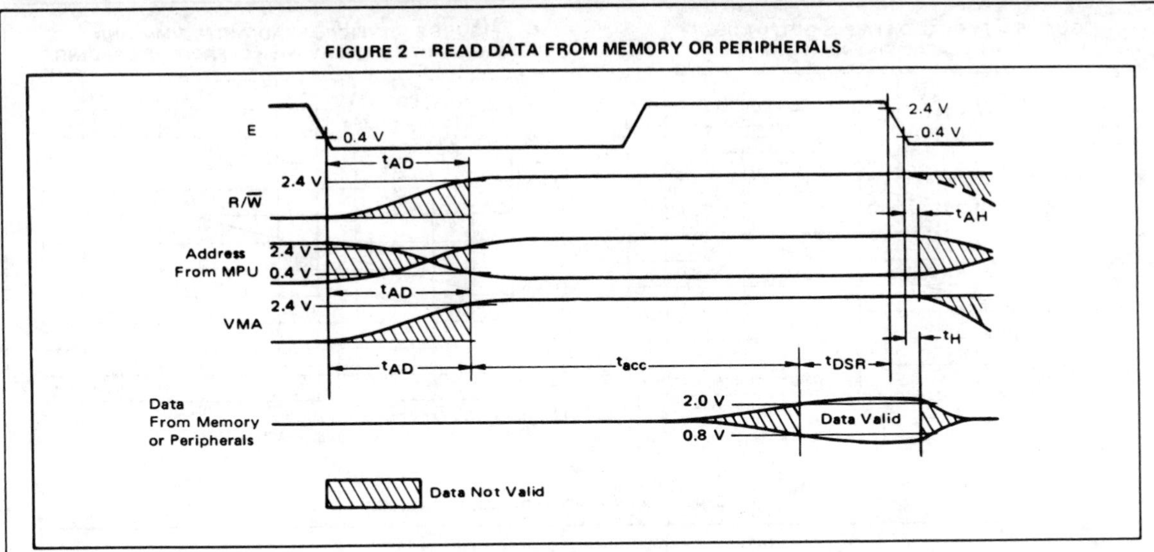

FIGURE 3 – WRITE DATA IN MEMORY OR PERIPHERALS

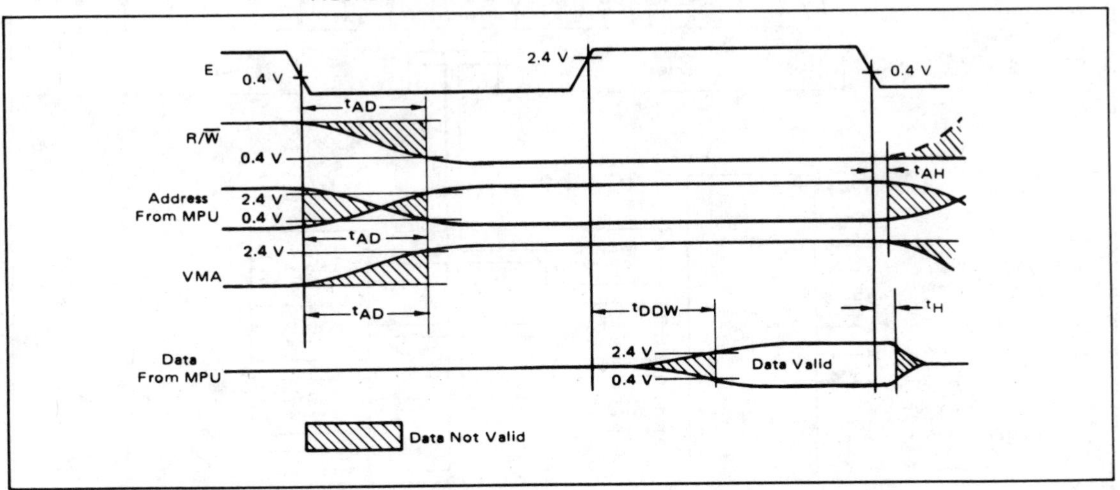

FIGURE 4 – BUS TIMING TEST LOAD

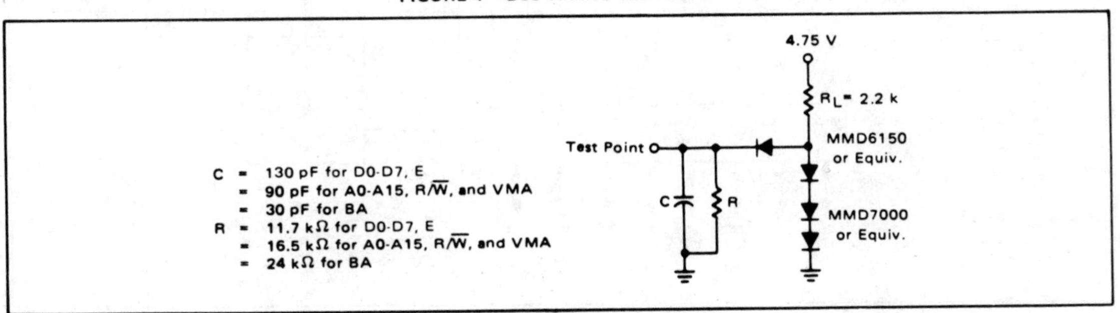

MC6808

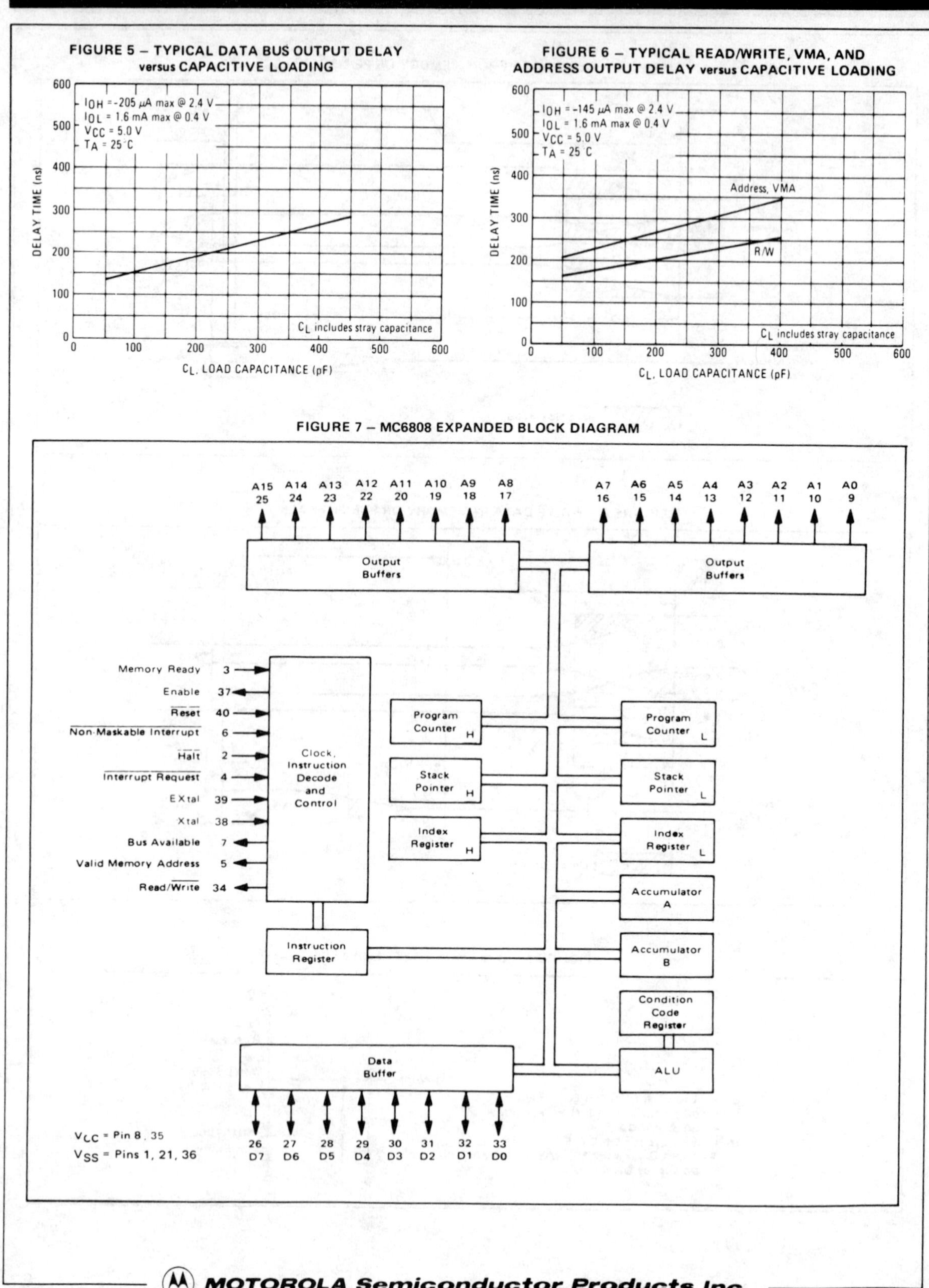
FIGURE 5 – TYPICAL DATA BUS OUTPUT DELAY versus CAPACITIVE LOADING
IOH = -205 μA max @ 2.4 V
IOL = 1.6 mA max @ 0.4 V
VCC = 5.0 V
TA = 25°C
DELAY TIME (ns)
CL includes stray capacitance
CL, LOAD CAPACITANCE (pF)
FIGURE 6 – TYPICAL READ/WRITE, VMA, AND ADDRESS OUTPUT DELAY versus CAPACITIVE LOADING
IOH = -145 μA max @ 2.4 V
IOL = 1.6 mA max @ 0.4 V
VCC = 5.0 V
TA = 25°C
Address, VMA
R/W
DELAY TIME (ns)
CL includes stray capacitance
CL, LOAD CAPACITANCE (pF)
FIGURE 7 – MC6808 EXPANDED BLOCK DIAGRAM
Output Buffers
Output Buffers
Memory Ready
Enable
Reset
Non-Maskable Interrupt
Halt
Interrupt Request
EXtal
Xtal
Bus Available
Valid Memory Address
Read/Write
Clock, Instruction Decode and Control
Program Counter H
Stack Pointer H
Index Register H
Program Counter L
Stack Pointer L
Index Register L
Accumulator A
Accumulator B
Condition Code Register
Instruction Register
Data Buffer
ALU
VCC = Pin 8, 35
VSS = Pins 1, 21, 36

MC6808

MPU REGISTERS

A general block diagram of the MC6808 is shown in Figure 7. As shown, the number and configuration of the registers are the same as for the MC6800.

The MPU has three 16-bit registers and three 8-bit registers available for use by the programmer (Figure 8).

Program Counter – The program counter is a two byte (16-bits) register that points to the current program address.

Stack Pointer – The stack pointer is a two byte register that contains the address of the next available location in an external push-down/pop-up stack. This stack is normally a random access Read/Write memory that may have any location (address) that is convenient. In those applications that require storage of information in the stack when power is lost, the stack must be non-volatile.

Index Register – The index register is a two byte register that is used to store data or a sixteen bit memory address for the Indexed mode of memory addressing.

Accumulators – The MPU contains two 8-bit accumulators that are used to hold operands and results from an arithmetic logic unit (ALU).

Condition Code Register – The condition code register indicates the results of an Arithmetic Logic Unit operation: Negative (N), Zero (Z), Overflow (V), Carry from bit 7 (C), and half carry from bit 3 (H). These bits of the Condition Code Register are used as testable conditions for the conditional branch instructions. Bit 4 is the interrupt mask bit (I). The used bits of the Condition Code Register (b6 and b7) are ones.

Figure 9 shows the order of saving the microprocessor status within the stack.

FIGURE 8 – PROGRAMMING MODEL OF THE MICROPROCESSING UNIT

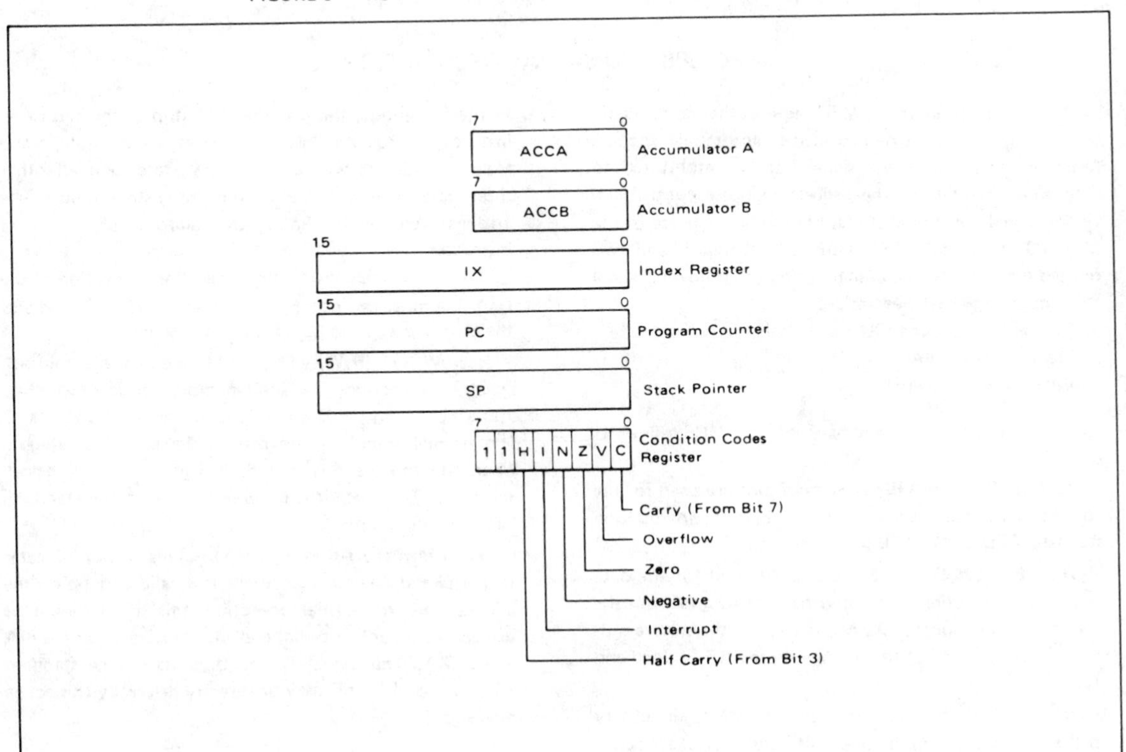

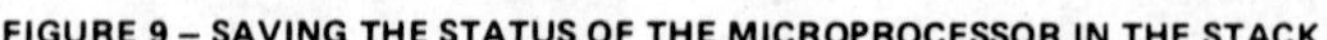

MC6808

FIGURE 9 – SAVING THE STATUS OF THE MICROPROCESSOR IN THE STACK

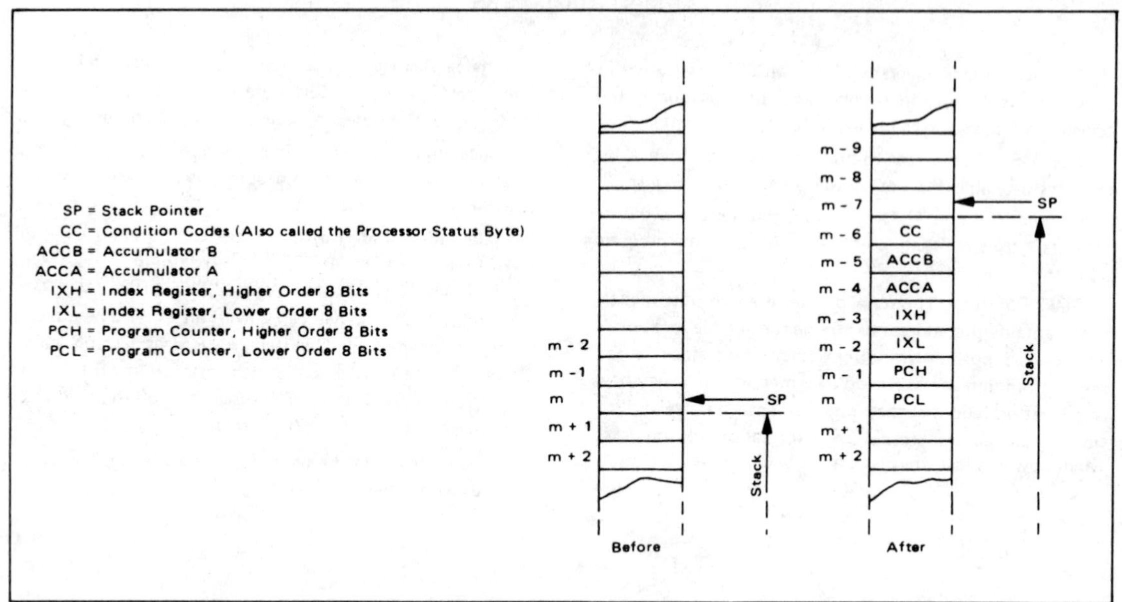

MC6808 MPU SIGNAL DESCRIPTION

Proper operation of the MPU requires that certain control and timing signals be provided to accomplish specific functions and that other signal lines be monitored to determine the state of the processor. These control and timing signals for the MC6808 are similar to those of the MC6800 except that TSC, DBE, $\phi1$, $\phi2$ input, and two unused pins have been eliminated, and the following signal and timing lines have been added:

Crystal Connections EXtal and Xtal
Memory Ready (MR)
Enable $\phi2$ Output (E)

The following is a summary of the MC6808 MPU signals:

Address Bus (A0-A15) – Sixteen pins are used for the address bus. The outputs are capable of driving one standard TTL load and 90 pF.

Data Bus (D0-D7) – Eight pins are used for the data bus. It is bidirectional, transferring data to and from the memory and peripheral devices. It also has three-state output buffers capable of driving one standard TTL load and 130 pF.

$\overline{\text{Halt}}$ – When this input is in the low state, all activity in the machine will be halted. This input is level sensitive. In the halt mode, the machine will stop at the end of an instruction, Bus Available will be at a high state, Valid Memory Address will be at a low state, and all other three-state lines will be in the three-state mode. The address bus will display the address of the next instruction.

To insure single instruction operation, transition of the $\overline{\text{Halt}}$ line must not occur during the last 200 ns of E and the $\overline{\text{Halt}}$ line must go high for one Clock cycle.

Read/$\overline{\text{Write}}$ (R/$\overline{\text{W}}$) – This TTL compatible output signals the peripherals and memory devices whether the MPU is in a Read (high) or Write (low) state. The normal standby state of this signal is Read (high). When the processor is halted, it will be in the logical one state. This output is capable of driving one standard TTL load and 90 pF.

Valid Memory Address (VMA) – This output indicates to peripheral devices that there is a valid address on the address bus. In normal operation, this signal should be utilized for enabling peripheral interfaces such as the PIA and ACIA. This signal is not three-state. One standard TTL load and 90 pF may be directly driven by this active high signal.

MC6808

Bus Available (BA) – The Bus Available signal will normally be in the low state; when activated, it will go to the high state indicating that the microprocessor has stopped and that the address bus is available but not in three-state. This will occur if the $\overline{\text{Halt}}$ line is in the low state or the processor is in the WAIT state as a result of the execution of a WAIT instruction. At such time, all three-state output drivers will go to their off state and other outputs to their normally inactive level. The processor is removed from the WAIT state by the occurrence of a maskable (mask bit I = 0) or nonmaskable interrupt. This output is capable of driving one standard TTL load and 30 pF.

$\overline{\text{Interrupt Request}}$ ($\overline{\text{IRQ}}$) – This level sensitive input requests that an interrupt sequence be generated within the machine. The processor will wait until it completes the current instruction that is being executed before it recognizes the request. At that time, if the interrupt mask bit in the Condition Code Register is not set, the machine will begin an interrupt sequence. The Index Register, Program Counter, Accumulators, and Condition Code Register are stored away on the stack. Next the MPU will respond to the interrupt request by setting the interrupt mask bit high so that no further interrupts may occur. At the end of the cycle, a 16-bit address will be loaded that points to a vectoring address which is located in memory locations FFF8 and FFF9. An address loaded at these locations causes the MPU to branch to an interrupt routine in memory.

The $\overline{\text{Halt}}$ line must be in the high state for interrupts to be serviced. Interrupts will be latched internally while $\overline{\text{Halt}}$ is low.

The $\overline{\text{IRQ}}$ has a high impedance pullup device internal to the chip; however a 3 kΩ external resistor to V_{CC} should be used for wire-OR and optimum control of interrupts.

$\overline{\text{Reset}}$ – This input is used to reset and start the MPU from a power down condition, resulting from a power failure or an initial start-up of the processor. When this line is low, the MPU is inactive and the information in the registers will be lost. If a high level is detected on the input, this will signal the MPU to begin the restart sequence. This will start execution of a routine to initialize the processor from its reset condition. All the higher order address lines will be forced high. For the restart, the last two (FFFE, FFFF) locations in memory will be used to load the program that is addressed by the program counter. During the restart routine, the interrupt mask bit is set and must be reset before the MPU can be interrupted by $\overline{\text{IRQ}}$. Power-up and reset timing sequences are shown in Figure 10.

FIGURE 10 – POWER-UP AND RESET TIMING

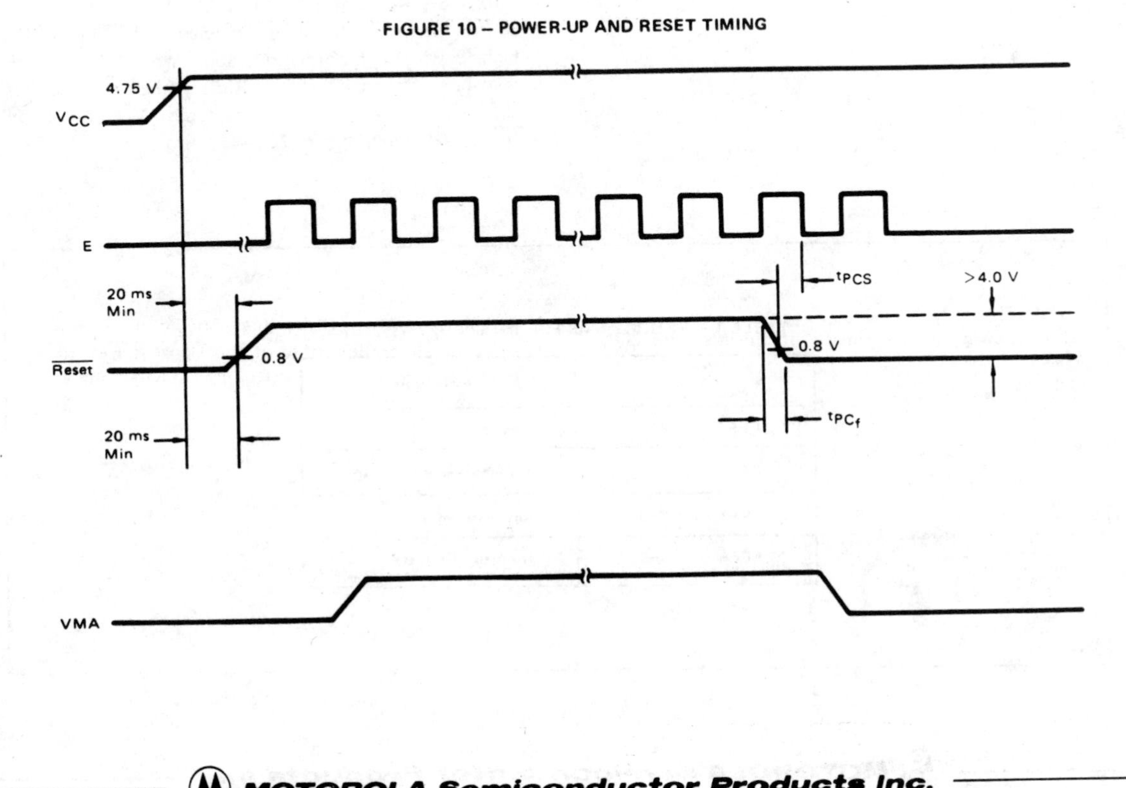

MC6808

EXtal and Xtal – The MC 6808 has an internal oscillator that may be crystal controlled. These connections are for a parallel resonant fundamental crystal. (AT cut.) A divide-by-four circuit has been added to the MC6808 so that a 4 MHz crystal may be used in lieu of a 1 MHz crystal for a more cost-effective system. Pin 39 of the MC6808 may be driven externally by a TTL input signal if a separate clock is required. Pin 38 is to be left open in this mode. Crystal parameters to be specified are in Figure 11.

FIGURE 11–CRYSTAL PARAMETERS

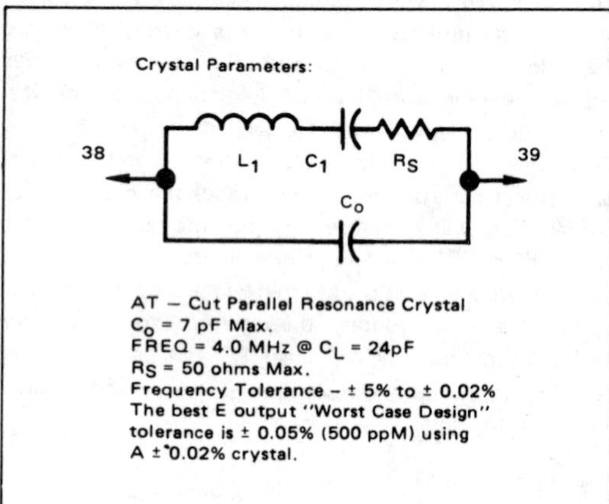

Non-Maskable Interrupt (NMI) – A low-going edge on this input requests that a non-mask-interrupt sequence be generated within the processor. As with the $\overline{\text{Interrupt Request}}$ signal, the processor will complete the current instruction that is being executed before it recognizes the $\overline{\text{NMI}}$ signal. The interrupt mask bit in the Condition Code Register has no effect on $\overline{\text{NMI}}$.

The index Register, Program Counter, Accumulators, and Condition Code Register are stored away on the stack. At the end of the cycle, a 16-bit address will be loaded that points to a vectoring address which is located in memory locations FFFC and FFFD. An address loaded at these locations caused the MPU to branch to a non-maskable interrupt routine in memory.

$\overline{\text{NMI}}$ has a high impedance pullup resistor internal to the chip; however a 3 kΩ external resistor to V_{CC} should be used for wire-OR and optimum control of interrupts.

Inputs $\overline{\text{IRQ}}$ and $\overline{\text{NMI}}$ are hardware interrupt lines that are sampled when E is high and will start the interrupt routine on a low E following the completion of an instruction.

Figure 12 is a flow chart describing the major decision paths and interrupt vectors of the microprocessor. Table 1 gives the memory map for interrupt vectors.

Memory Ready (MR) – MR is a TTL compatible input control signal which allows stretching of E. When MR is high, E will be in normal operation. When MR is low, E may be stretched integral multiples of half periods, thus allowing interface to slow memories. Memory Ready timing is shown in Figure 13.

TABLE 1 – MEMORY MAP FOR INTERRUPT VECTORS

Vector MS	Vector LS	Description
FFFE	FFFF	Restart
FFFC	FFFD	Non-maskable Interrupt
FFFA	FFFB	Software Interrupt
FFF8	FFF9	Interrupt Request

MC6808

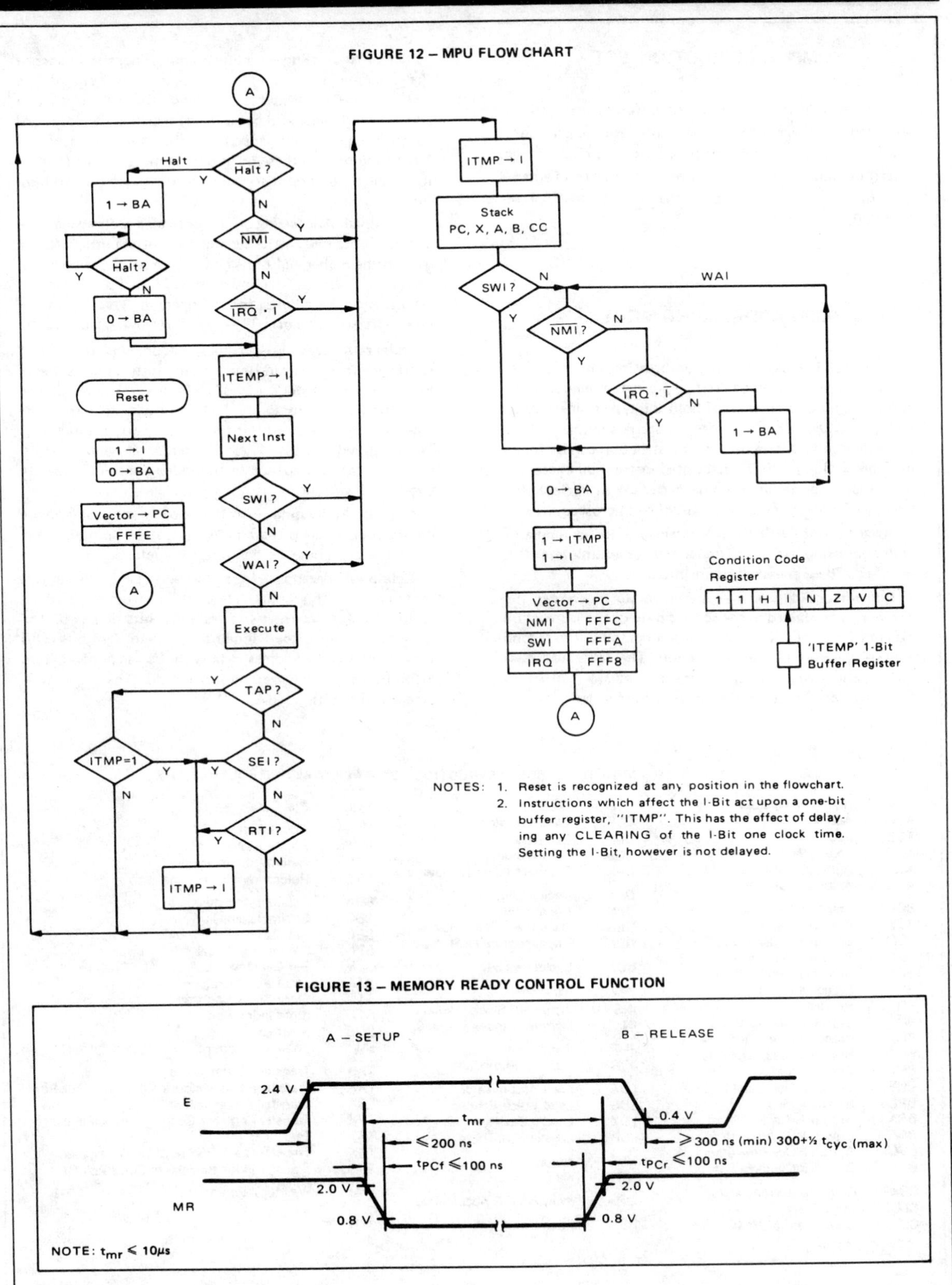

FIGURE 12 – MPU FLOW CHART

NOTES: 1. Reset is recognized at any position in the flowchart.
2. Instructions which affect the I-Bit act upon a one-bit buffer register, "ITMP". This has the effect of delaying any CLEARING of the I-Bit one clock time. Setting the I-Bit, however is not delayed.

FIGURE 13 – MEMORY READY CONTROL FUNCTION

MPU INSTRUCTION SET

The MC6808 has a set of 72 different instructions. Included are binary and decimal arithmetic, logical, shift, rotate, load, store, conditional or unconditional branch, interrupt and stack manipulation instructions (Tables 2 thru 6). This instruction set is the same as that for the MC6800.

MPU ADDRESSING MODES

The MC6808 eight-bit microprocessing unit has seven address modes that can be used by a programmer, with the addressing mode a function of both the type of instruction and the coding within the instruction. A summary of the addressing modes for a particular instruction can be found in Table 7 along with the associated instruction execution time that is given in machine cycles. With a clock frequency of 1 MHz, these times would be microseconds.

Accumulator (ACCX) Addressing – In accumulator only addressing, either accumulator A or accumulator B is specified. These are one-byte instructions.

Immediate Addressing – In immediate addressing, the operand is contained in the second byte of the instruction except LDS and LDX which have the operand in the second and third bytes of the instruction. The MPU addresses this location when it fetches the immediate instruction for execution. These are two or three-byte instructions.

Direct Addressing – In direct addressing, the address of the operand is contained in the second byte of the instruction. Direct addressing allows the user to directly address the lowest 256 bytes in the machine i.e., locations zero through 255. Enhanced execution times are achieved by storing data in these locations. In most configurations, it should be a random access memory. These are two-byte instructions.

Extended Addressing – In extended addressing, the address contained in the second byte of the instruction is used as the higher eight-bits of the address of the operand. The third byte of the instruction is used as the lower eight-bits of the address for the operand. This is an absolute address in memory. These are three-byte instructions.

Indexed Addressing – In indexed addressing, the address contained in the second byte of the instruction is added to the index register's lowest eight bits in the MPU. The carry is then added to the higher order eight bits of the index register. This result is then used to address memory. The modified address is held in a temporary address register so there is no change to the index register. These are two-byte instructions.

Implied Addressing – In the implied addressing mode the instruction gives the address (i.e., stack pointer, index register, etc.). These are one-byte instructions.

Relative Addressing – In relative addressing, the address contained in the second byte of the instruction is added to the program counter's lowest eight bits plus two. The carry or borrow is then added to the high eight bits. This allows the user to address data within a range of -125 to +129 bytes of the present instruction. These are two-byte instructions.

TABLE 2 – MICROPROCESSOR INSTRUCTION SET – ALPHABETIC SEQUENCE

Mnemonic	Instruction
ABA	Add Accumulators
ADC	Add with Carry
ADD	Add
AND	Logical And
ASL	Arithmetic Shift Left
ASR	Arithmetic Shift Right
BCC	Branch if Carry Clear
BCS	Branch if Carry Set
BEQ	Branch if Equal to Zero
BGE	Branch if Greater or Equal Zero
BGT	Branch if Greater than Zero
BHI	Branch if Higher
BIT	Bit Test
BLE	Branch if Less or Equal
BLS	Branch if Lower or Same
BLT	Branch if Less than Zero
BMI	Branch if Minus
BNE	Branch if Not Equal to Zero
BPL	Branch if Plus
BRA	Branch Always
BSR	Branch to Subroutine
BVC	Branch if Overflow Clear
BVS	Branch if Overflow Set
CBA	Compare Accumulators
CLC	Clear Carry
CLI	Clear Interrupt Mask
CLR	Clear
CLV	Clear Overflow
CMP	Compare
COM	Complement
CPX	Compare Index Register
DAA	Decimal Adjust
DEC	Decrement
DES	Decrement Stack Pointer
DEX	Decrement Index Register
EOR	Exclusive OR
INC	Increment
INS	Increment Stack Pointer
INX	Increment Index Register
JMP	Jump
JSR	Jump to Subroutine
LDA	Load Accumulator
LDS	Load Stack Pointer
LDX	Load Index Register
LSR	Logical Shift Right
NEG	Negate
NOP	No Operation
ORA	Inclusive OR Accumulator
PSH	Push Data
PUL	Pull Data
ROL	Rotate Left
ROR	Rotate Right
RTI	Return from Interrupt
RTS	Return from Subroutine
SBA	Subtract Accumulators
SBC	Subtract with Carry
SEC	Set Carry
SEI	Set Interrupt Mask
SEV	Set Overflow
STA	Store Accumulator
STS	Store Stack Register
STX	Store Index Register
SUB	Subtract
SWI	Software Interrupt
TAB	Transfer Accumulators
TAP	Transfer Accumulators to Condition Code Reg.
TBA	Transfer Accumulators
TPA	Transfer Condition Code Reg. to Accumulator
TST	Test
TSX	Transfer Stack Pointer to Index Register
TXS	Transfer Index Register to Stack Pointer
WAI	Wait for Interrupt

MC6808

TABLE 3 – ACCUMULATOR AND MEMORY INSTRUCTIONS

OPERATIONS	MNEMONIC	IMMED OP	IMMED ~	IMMED =	DIRECT OP	DIRECT ~	DIRECT =	INDEX OP	INDEX ~	INDEX =	EXTND OP	EXTND ~	EXTND =	IMPLIED OP	IMPLIED ~	IMPLIED =	BOOLEAN/ARITHMETIC OPERATION (All register labels refer to contents)	5 H	4 I	3 N	2 Z	1 V	0 C
Add	ADDA	8B	2	2	9B	3	2	AB	5	2	BB	4	3				A + M → A	:	●	:	:	:	:
	ADDB	CB	2	2	DB	3	2	EB	5	2	FB	4	3				B + M → B	:	●	:	:	:	:
Add Acmltrs	ABA													1B	2	1	A + B → A	:	●	:	:	:	:
Add with Carry	ADCA	89	2	2	99	3	2	A9	5	2	B9	4	3				A + M + C → A	:	●	:	:	:	:
	ADCB	C9	2	2	D9	3	2	E9	5	2	F9	4	3				B + M + C → B	:	●	:	:	:	:
And	ANDA	84	2	2	94	3	2	A4	5	2	B4	4	3				A · M → A	●	●	:	:	R	●
	ANDB	C4	2	2	D4	3	2	E4	5	2	F4	4	3				B · M → B	●	●	:	:	R	●
Bit Test	BITA	85	2	2	95	3	2	A5	5	2	B5	4	3				A · M	●	●	:	:	R	●
	BITB	C5	2	2	D5	3	2	E5	5	2	F5	4	3				B · M	●	●	:	:	R	●
Clear	CLR							6F	7	2	7F	6	3				00 → M	●	●	R	S	R	R
	CLRA													4F	2	1	00 → A	●	●	R	S	R	R
	CLRB													5F	2	1	00 → B	●	●	R	S	R	R
Compare	CMPA	81	2	2	91	3	2	A1	5	2	B1	4	3				A – M	●	●	:	:	:	:
	CMPB	C1	2	2	D1	3	2	E1	5	2	F1	4	3				B – M	●	●	:	:	:	:
Compare Acmltrs	CBA													11	2	1	A – B	●	●	:	:	:	:
Complement, 1's	COM							63	7	2	73	6	3				M̄ → M	●	●	:	:	R	S
	COMA													43	2	1	Ā → A	●	●	:	:	R	S
	COMB													53	2	1	B̄ → B	●	●	:	:	R	S
Complement, 2's	NEG							60	7	2	70	6	3				00 – M → M	●	●	:	:	①	②
(Negate)	NEGA													40	2	1	00 – A → A	●	●	:	:	①	②
	NEGB													50	2	1	00 – B → B	●	●	:	:	①	②
Decimal Adjust, A	DAA													19	2	1	Converts Binary Add. of BCD Characters into BCD Format	●	●	:	:	:	③
Decrement	DEC							6A	7	2	7A	6	3				M – 1 → M	●	●	:	:	4	●
	DECA													4A	2	1	A – 1 → A	●	●	:	:	4	●
	DECB													5A	2	1	B – 1 → B	●	●	:	:	4	●
Exclusive OR	EORA	88	2	2	98	3	2	A8	5	2	B8	4	3				A⊕M → A	●	●	:	:	R	●
	EORB	C8	2	2	D8	3	2	E8	5	2	F8	4	3				B⊕M → B	●	●	:	:	R	●
Increment	INC							6C	7	2	7C	6	3				M + 1 → M	●	●	:	:	⑤	●
	INCA													4C	2	1	A + 1 → A	●	●	:	:	⑤	●
	INCB													5C	2	1	B + 1 → B	●	●	:	:	⑤	●
Load Acmltr	LDAA	86	2	2	96	3	2	A6	5	2	B6	4	3				M → A	●	●	:	:	R	●
	LDAB	C6	2	2	D6	3	2	E6	5	2	F6	4	3				M → B	●	●	:	:	R	●
Or, Inclusive	ORAA	8A	2	2	9A	3	2	AA	5	2	BA	4	3				A + M → A	●	●	:	:	R	●
	ORAB	CA	2	2	DA	3	2	EA	5	2	FA	4	3				B + M → B	●	●	:	:	R	●
Push Data	PSHA													36	4	1	A → M_{SP}, SP – 1 → SP	●	●	●	●	●	●
	PSHB													37	4	1	B → M_{SP}, SP – 1 → SP	●	●	●	●	●	●
Pull Data	PULA													32	4	1	SP + 1 → SP, M_{SP} → A	●	●	●	●	●	●
	PULB													33	4	1	SP + 1 → SP, M_{SP} → B	●	●	●	●	●	●
Rotate Left	ROL							69	7	2	79	6	3				M	●	●	:	:	⑥	:
	ROLA													49	2	1	A	●	●	:	:	⑥	:
	ROLB													59	2	1	B (C ← b7 ← b0)	●	●	:	:	⑥	:
Rotate Right	ROR							66	7	2	76	6	3				M	●	●	:	:	⑥	:
	RORA													46	2	1	A	●	●	:	:	⑥	:
	RORB													56	2	1	B (C ← b7 → b0)	●	●	:	:	⑥	:
Shift Left, Arithmetic	ASL							68	7	2	78	6	3				M	●	●	:	:	⑥	:
	ASLA													48	2	1	A (C ← b7 … b0 ← 0)	●	●	:	:	⑥	:
	ASLB													58	2	1	B	●	●	:	:	⑥	:
Shift Right, Arithmetic	ASR							67	7	2	77	6	3				M	●	●	:	:	⑥	:
	ASRA													47	2	1	A (b7 … b0 → C)	●	●	:	:	⑥	:
	ASRB													57	2	1	B	●	●	:	:	⑥	:
Shift Right, Logic	LSR							64	7	2	74	6	3				M	●	●	R	:	⑥	:
	LSRA													44	2	1	A (0 → b7 … b0 → C)	●	●	R	:	⑥	:
	LSRB													54	2	1	B	●	●	R	:	⑥	:
Store Acmltr.	STAA				97	4	2	A7	6	2	B7	5	3				A → M	●	●	:	:	R	●
	STAB				D7	4	2	E7	6	2	F7	5	3				B → M	●	●	:	:	R	●
Subtract	SUBA	80	2	2	90	3	2	A0	5	2	B0	4	3				A – M → A	●	●	:	:	:	:
	SUBB	C0	2	2	D0	3	2	E0	5	2	F0	4	3				B – M → B	●	●	:	:	:	:
Subtract Acmltrs.	SBA													10	2	1	A – B → A	●	●	:	:	:	:
Subtr. with Carry	SBCA	82	2	2	92	3	2	A2	5	2	B2	4	3				A – M – C → A	●	●	:	:	:	:
	SBCB	C2	2	2	D2	3	2	E2	5	2	F2	4	3				B – M – C → B	●	●	:	:	:	:
Transfer Acmltrs	TAB													16	2	1	A → B	●	●	:	:	R	●
	TBA													17	2	1	B → A	●	●	:	:	R	●
Test, Zero or Minus	TST							6D	7	2	7D	6	3				M – 00	●	●	:	:	R	R
	TSTA													4D	2	1	A – 00	●	●	:	:	R	R
	TSTB													5D	2	1	B – 00	●	●	:	:	R	R
																		H	I	N	Z	V	C

LEGEND:

- OP Operation Code (Hexadecimal);
- ~ Number of MPU Cycles;
- = Number of Program Bytes;
- \+ Arithmetic Plus;
- – Arithmetic Minus;
- · Boolean AND;
- M_{SP} Contents of memory location pointed to be Stack Pointer;
- \+ Boolean Inclusive OR;
- ⊙ Boolean Exclusive OR;
- ■ Complement of M;
- → Transfer Into;
- 0 Bit = Zero;
- 00 Byte = Zero;

Note – Accumulator addressing mode instructions are included in the column for IMPLIED addressing

CONDITION CODE SYMBOLS:

- H Half-carry from bit 3;
- I Interrupt mask
- N Negative (sign bit)
- Z Zero (byte)
- V Overflow, 2's complement
- C Carry from bit 7
- R Reset Always
- S Set Always
- : Test and set if true, cleared otherwise
- ● Not Affected

TABLE 4 – INDEX REGISTER AND STACK MANIPULATION INSTRUCTIONS

		IMMED			DIRECT			INDEX			EXTND			IMPLIED				COND. CODE REG.					
																		5	4	3	2	1	0
POINTER OPERATIONS	MNEMONIC	OP	~	#	OP	~	#	OP	~	#	OP	~	#	OP	~	#	BOOLEAN/ARITHMETIC OPERATION	H	I	N	Z	V	C
Compare Index Reg	CPX	8C	3	3	9C	4	2	AC	6	2	BC	5	3				$X_H - M, X_L - (M + 1)$	•	•	⑦	↕	⑧	•
Decrement Index Reg	DEX													09	4	1	$X - 1 \rightarrow X$	•	•	•	↕	•	•
Decrement Stack Pntr	DES													34	4	1	$SP - 1 \rightarrow SP$	•	•	•	•	•	•
Increment Index Reg	INX													08	4	1	$X + 1 \rightarrow X$	•	•	•	↕	•	•
Increment Stack Pntr	INS													31	4	1	$SP + 1 \rightarrow SP$	•	•	•	•	•	•
Load Index Reg	LDX	CE	3	3	DE	4	2	EE	6	2	FE	5	3				$M \rightarrow X_H, (M + 1) \rightarrow X_L$	•	•	⑨	↕	R	•
Load Stack Pntr	LDS	8E	3	3	9E	4	2	AE	6	2	BE	5	3				$M \rightarrow SP_H, (M + 1) \rightarrow SP_L$	•	•	⑨	↕	R	•
Store Index Reg	STX				DF	5	2	EF	7	2	FF	6	3				$X_H \rightarrow M, X_L \rightarrow (M + 1)$	•	•	⑨	↕	R	•
Store Stack Pntr	STS				9F	5	2	AF	7	2	BF	6	3				$SP_H \rightarrow M, SP_L \rightarrow (M + 1)$	•	•	⑨	↕	R	•
Indx Reg → Stack Pntr	TXS													35	4	1	$X - 1 \rightarrow SP$	•	•	•	•	•	•
Stack Pntr → Indx Reg	TSX													30	4	1	$SP + 1 \rightarrow X$	•	•	•	•	•	•

TABLE 5 – JUMP AND BRANCH INSTRUCTIONS

		RELATIVE			INDEX			EXTND			IMPLIED				COND. CODE REG.					
															5	4	3	2	1	0
OPERATIONS	MNEMONIC	OP	~	#	OP	~	#	OP	~	#	OP	~	#	BRANCH TEST	H	I	N	Z	V	C
Branch Always	BRA	20	4	2										None	•	•	•	•	•	•
Branch If Carry Clear	BCC	24	4	2										$C = 0$	•	•	•	•	•	•
Branch If Carry Set	BCS	25	4	2										$C = 1$	•	•	•	•	•	•
Branch If = Zero	BEQ	27	4	2										$Z = 1$	•	•	•	•	•	•
Branch If ≥ Zero	BGE	2C	4	2										$N \oplus V = 0$	•	•	•	•	•	•
Branch If > Zero	BGT	2E	4	2										$Z + (N \oplus V) = 0$	•	•	•	•	•	•
Branch If Higher	BHI	22	4	2										$C + Z = 0$	•	•	•	•	•	•
Branch If ≤ Zero	BLE	2F	4	2										$Z + (N \oplus V) = 1$	•	•	•	•	•	•
Branch If Lower Or Same	BLS	23	4	2										$C + Z = 1$	•	•	•	•	•	•
Branch If < Zero	BLT	2D	4	2										$N \oplus V = 1$	•	•	•	•	•	•
Branch If Minus	BMI	2B	4	2										$N = 1$	•	•	•	•	•	•
Branch If Not Equal Zero	BNE	26	4	2										$Z = 0$	•	•	•	•	•	•
Branch If Overflow Clear	BVC	28	4	2										$V = 0$	•	•	•	•	•	•
Branch If Overflow Set	BVS	29	4	2										$V = 1$	•	•	•	•	•	•
Branch If Plus	BPL	2A	4	2										$N = 0$	•	•	•	•	•	•
Branch To Subroutine	BSR	8D	8	2										} See Special Operations	•	•	•	•	•	•
Jump	JMP				6E	4	2	7E	3	3					•	•	•	•	•	•
Jump To Subroutine	JSR				AD	8	2	BD	9	3					•	•	•	•	•	•
No Operation	NOP										01	2	1	Advances Prog. Cntr. Only	•	•	•	•	•	•
Return From Interrupt	RTI										3B	10	1		⑩					
Return From Subroutine	RTS										39	5	1	} See Special Operations	•	•	•	•	•	•
Software Interrupt	SWI										3F	12	1		•	•	•	•	•	•
Wait for Interrupt*	WAI										3E	9	1		•	⑪	•	•	•	•

*WAI puts Address Bus, R/W, and Data Bus in the three-state mode while VMA is held low.

MC6808

SPECIAL OPERATIONS

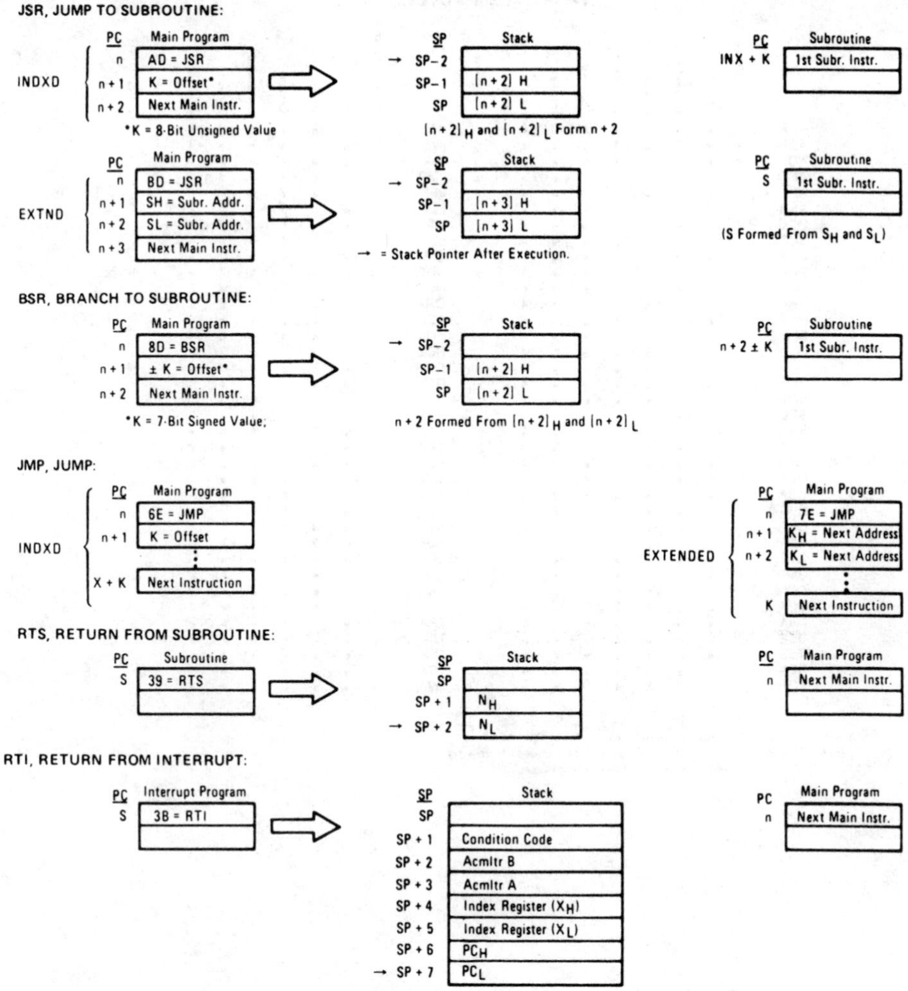

JSR, JUMP TO SUBROUTINE:

INDXD

PC	Main Program
n	AD = JSR
n + 1	K = Offset*
n + 2	Next Main Instr.

*K = 8-Bit Unsigned Value

⇨

SP	Stack
→ SP − 2	
SP − 1	[n + 2] H
SP	[n + 2] L

[n + 2] $_H$ and [n + 2] $_L$ Form n + 2

PC	Subroutine
INX + K	1st Subr. Instr.

EXTND

PC	Main Program
n	BD = JSR
n + 1	SH = Subr. Addr.
n + 2	SL = Subr. Addr.
n + 3	Next Main Instr.

⇨

SP	Stack
→ SP − 2	
SP − 1	[n + 3] H
SP	[n + 3] L

→ = Stack Pointer After Execution.

PC	Subroutine
S	1st Subr. Instr.

(S Formed From S_H and S_L)

BSR, BRANCH TO SUBROUTINE:

PC	Main Program
n	8D = BSR
n + 1	± K = Offset*
n + 2	Next Main Instr.

*K = 7-Bit Signed Value;

⇨

SP	Stack
→ SP − 2	
SP − 1	[n + 2] H
SP	[n + 2] L

n + 2 Formed From [n + 2] $_H$ and [n + 2] $_L$

PC	Subroutine
n + 2 ± K	1st Subr. Instr.

JMP, JUMP:

INDXD

PC	Main Program
n	6E = JMP
n + 1	K = Offset
⋮	⋮
X + K	Next Instruction

EXTENDED

PC	Main Program
n	7E = JMP
n + 1	K_H = Next Address
n + 2	K_L = Next Address
⋮	⋮
K	Next Instruction

RTS, RETURN FROM SUBROUTINE:

PC	Subroutine
S	39 = RTS

⇨

SP	Stack
SP	
SP + 1	N_H
→ SP + 2	N_L

PC	Main Program
n	Next Main Instr.

RTI, RETURN FROM INTERRUPT:

PC	Interrupt Program
S	3B = RTI

⇨

SP	Stack
SP	
SP + 1	Condition Code
SP + 2	Acmltr B
SP + 3	Acmltr A
SP + 4	Index Register (X_H)
SP + 5	Index Register (X_L)
SP + 6	PC_H
→ SP + 7	PC_L

PC	Main Program
n	Next Main Instr.

TABLE 6 – CONDITION CODE REGISTER MANIPULATION INSTRUCTIONS

		IMPLIED				COND. CODE REG. 5	4	3	2	1	0
OPERATIONS	MNEMONIC	OP	~	=	BOOLEAN OPERATION	H	I	N	Z	V	C
Clear Carry	CLC	0C	2	1	0 → C	•	•	•	•	•	R
Clear Interrupt Mask	CLI	0E	2	1	0 → I	•	R	•	•	•	•
Clear Overflow	CLV	0A	2	1	0 → V	•	•	•	•	R	•
Set Carry	SEC	0D	2	1	1 → C	•	•	•	•	•	S
Set Interrupt Mask	SEI	0F	2	1	1 → I	•	S	•	•	•	•
Set Overflow	SEV	0B	2	1	1 → V	•	•	•	•	S	•
Acmltr A → CCR	TAP	06	2	1	A → CCR				(12)		
CCR → Acmltr A	TPA	07	2	1	CCR → A	•	•	•	•	•	•

CONDITION CODE REGISTER NOTES: (Bit set if test is true and cleared otherwise)

1 (Bit V) Test: Result = 10000000?
2 (Bit C) Test: Result ≠ 00000000?
3 (Bit C) Test: Decimal value of most significant BCD Character greater than nine? (Not cleared if previously set.)
4 (Bit V) Test: Operand = 10000000 prior to execution?
5 (Bit V) Test: Operand = 01111111 prior to execution?
6 (Bit V) Test: Set equal to result of N⊕C after shift has occurred.
7 (Bit N) Test: Sign bit of most significant (MS) byte = 1?
8 (Bit V) Test: 2's complement overflow from subtraction of MS bytes?
9 (Bit N) Test: Result less than zero? (Bit 15 = 1)
10 (All) Load Condition Code Register from Stack. (See Special Operations)
11 (Bit I) Set when interrupt occurs. If previously set, a Non-Maskable Interrupt is required to exit the wait state.
12 (All) Set according to the contents of Accumulator A.

MC6808

TABLE 7 – INSTRUCTION ADDRESSING MODES AND ASSOCIATED EXECUTION TIMES
(Times in Machine Cycles)

	(Dual Operand)	ACCX	Immediate	Direct	Extended	Indexed	Implied	Relative
ABA		•	•	•	•	•	2	•
ADC	x	•	2	3	4	5	•	•
ADD	x	•	2	3	4	5	•	•
AND	x	•	2	3	4	5	•	•
ASL		2	•	•	6	7	•	•
ASR		2	•	•	6	7	•	•
BCC		•	•	•	•	•	•	4
BCS		•	•	•	•	•	•	4
BEA		•	•	•	•	•	•	4
BGE		•	•	•	•	•	•	4
BGT		•	•	•	•	•	•	4
BHI		•	•	•	•	•	•	4
BIT	x	•	2	3	4	5	•	•
BLE		•	•	•	•	•	•	4
BLS		•	•	•	•	•	•	4
BLT		•	•	•	•	•	•	4
BMI		•	•	•	•	•	•	4
BNE		•	•	•	•	•	•	4
BPL		•	•	•	•	•	•	4
BRA		•	•	•	•	•	•	4
BSR		•	•	•	•	•	•	8
BVC		•	•	•	•	•	•	4
BVS		•	•	•	•	•	•	4
CBA		•	•	•	•	•	2	•
CLC		•	•	•	•	•	2	•
CLI		•	•	•	•	•	2	•
CLR		2	•	•	6	7	•	•
CLV		•	•	•	•	•	2	•
CMP	x	•	2	3	4	5	•	•
COM		2	•	•	6	7	•	•
CPX		•	3	4	5	6	•	•
DAA		•	•	•	•	•	2	•
DEC		2	•	•	6	7	•	•
DES		•	•	•	•	•	4	•
DEX		•	•	•	•	•	4	•
EOR	x	•	2	3	4	5	•	•

	(Dual Operand)	ACCX	Immediate	Direct	Extended	Indexed	Implied
INC		2	•	•	6	7	•
INS		•	•	•	•	•	4
INX		•	•	•	•	•	4
JMP		•	•	•	3	4	•
JSR		•	•	•	9	8	•
LDA	x	•	2	3	4	5	•
LDS		•	3	4	5	6	•
LDX		•	3	4	5	6	•
LSR		2	•	•	6	7	•
NEG		2	•	•	6	7	•
NOP		•	•	•	•	•	2
ORA	x	•	2	3	4	5	•
PSH		•	•	•	•	•	4
PUL		•	•	•	•	•	4
ROL		2	•	•	6	7	•
ROR		2	•	•	6	7	•
RTI		•	•	•	•	•	10
RTS		•	•	•	•	•	5
SBA		•	•	•	•	•	2
SBC	x	•	2	3	4	5	•
SEC		•	•	•	•	•	2
SEI		•	•	•	•	•	2
SEV		•	•	•	•	•	2
STA	x	•	•	4	5	6	•
STS		•	•	5	6	7	•
STX		•	•	5	6	7	•
SUB	x	•	2	3	4	5	•
SWI		•	•	•	•	•	12
TAB		•	•	•	•	•	2
TAP		•	•	•	•	•	2
TBA		•	•	•	•	•	2
TPA		•	•	•	•	•	2
TST		2	•	•	6	7	•
TSX		•	•	•	•	•	4
TSX		•	•	•	•	•	4
WAI		•	•	•	•	•	9

NOTE: Interrupt time is 12 cycles from the end of the instruction being executed, except following a WAI instruction. Then it is 4 cycles.

MC6808

SUMMARY OF CYCLE BY CYCLE OPERATION

Table 8 provides a detailed description of the information present on the Address Bus, Data Bus, Valid Memory Address line (VMA), and the Read/Write line (R/W) during each cycle for each instruction.

This information is useful in comparing actual with expected results during debug of both software and hardware as the control program is executed. The information is categorized in groups according to Addressing Mode and Number of Cycles per instruction. (In general, instructions with the same Addressing Mode and Number of Cycles execute in the same manner; exceptions are indicated in the table.)

TABLE 8 – OPERATION SUMMARY

Address Mode and Instructions	Cycles	Cycle #	VMA Line	Address Bus	R/W Line	Data Bus
IMMEDIATE						
ADC EOR ADD LDA AND ORA BIT SBC CMP SUB	2	1	1	Op Code Address	1	Op Code
		2	1	Op Code Address + 1	1	Operand Data
CPX LDS LDX	3	1	1	Op Code Address	1	Op Code
		2	1	Op Code Address + 1	1	Operand Data (High Order Byte)
		3	1	Op Code Address + 2	1	Operand Data (Low Order Byte)
DIRECT						
ADC EOR ADD LDA AND ORA BIT SBC CMP SUB	3	1	1	Op Code Address	1	Op Code
		2	1	Op Code Address + 1	1	Address of Operand
		3	1	Address of Operand	1	Operand Data
CPX LDS LDX	4	1	1	Op Code Address	1	Op Code
		2	1	Op Code Address + 1	1	Address of Operand
		3	1	Address of Operand	1	Operand Data (High Order Byte)
		4	1	Operand Address + 1	1	Operand Data (Low Order Byte)
STA	4	1	1	Op Code Address	1	Op Code
		2	1	Op Code Address + 1	1	Destination Address
		3	0	Destination Address	1	Irrelevant Data (Note 1)
		4	1	Destination Address	0	Data from Accumulator
STS STX	5	1	1	Op Code Address	1	Op Code
		2	1	Op Code Address + 1	1	Address of Operand
		3	0	Address of Operand	1	Irrelevant Data (Note 1)
		4	1	Address of Operand	0	Register Data (High Order Byte)
		5	1	Address of Operand + 1	0	Register Data (Low Order Byte)
INDEXED						
JMP	4	1	1	Op Code Address	1	Op Code
		2	1	Op Code Address + 1	1	Offset
		3	0	Index Register	1	Irrelevant Data (Note 1)
		4	0	Index Register Plus Offset (w/o Carry)	1	Irrelevant Data (Note 1)
ADC EOR ADD LDA AND ORA BIT SBC CMP SUB	5	1	1	Op Code Address	1	Op Code
		2	1	Op Code Address + 1	1	Offset
		3	0	Index Register	1	Irrelevant Data (Note 1)
		4	0	Index Register Plus Offset (w/o Carry)	1	Irrelevant Data (Note 1)
		5	1	Index Register Plus Offset	1	Operand Data
CPX LDS LDX	6	1	1	Op Code Address	1	Op Code
		2	1	Op Code Address + 1	1	Offset
		3	0	Index Register	1	Irrelevant Data (Note 1)
		4	0	Index Register Plus Offset (w/o Carry)	1	Irrelevant Data (Note 1)
		5	1	Index Register Plus Offset	1	Operand Data (High Order Byte)
		6	1	Index Register Plus Offset + 1	1	Operand Data (Low Order Byte)

MC6808

TABLE 8 – OPERATION SUMMARY (Continued)

Address Mode and Instructions	Cycles	Cycle #	VMA Line	Address Bus	R/W Line	Data Bus
INDEXED (Continued)						
STA	6	1	1	Op Code Address	1	Op Code
		2	1	Op Code Address + 1	1	Offset
		3	0	Index Register	1	Irrelevant Data (Note 1)
		4	0	Index Register Plus Offset (w/o Carry)	1	Irrelevant Data (Note 1)
		5	0	Index Register Plus Offset	1	Irrelevant Data (Note 1)
		6	1	Index Register Plus Offset	0	Operand Data
ASL LSR ASR NEG CLR ROL COM ROR DEC TST INC	7	1	1	Op Code Address	1	Op Code
		2	1	Op Code Address + 1	1	Offset
		3	0	Index Register	1	Irrelevant Data (Note 1)
		4	0	Index Register Plus Offset (w/o Carry)	1	Irrelevant Data (Note 1)
		5	1	Index Register Plus Offset	1	Current Operand Data
		6	0	Index Register Plus Offset	1	Irrelevant Data (Note 1)
		7	1/0 (Note 3)	Index Register Plus Offset	0	New Operand Data (Note 3)
STS STX	7	1	1	Op Code Address	1	Op Code
		2	1	Op Code Address + 1	1	Offset
		3	0	Index Register	1	Irrelevant Data (Note 1)
		4	0	Index Register Plus Offset (w/o Carry)	1	Irrelevant Data (Note 1)
		5	0	Index Register Plus Offset	1	Irrelevant Data (Note 1)
		6	1	Index Register Plus Offset	0	Operand Data (High Order Byte)
		7	1	Index Register Plus Offset + 1	0	Operand Data (Low Order Byte)
JSR	8	1	1	Op Code Address	1	Op Code
		2	1	Op Code Address + 1	1	Offset
		3	0	Index Register	1	Irrelevant Data (Note 1)
		4	1	Stack Pointer	0	Return Address (Low Order Byte)
		5	1	Stack Pointer – 1	0	Return Address (High Order Byte)
		6	0	Stack Pointer – 2	1	Irrelevant Data (Note 1)
		7	0	Index Register	1	Irrelevant Data (Note 1)
		8	0	Index Register Plus Offset (w/o Carry)	1	Irrelevant Data (Note 1)
EXTENDED						
JMP	3	1	1	Op Code Address	1	Op Code
		2	1	Op Code Address + 1	1	Jump Address (High Order Byte)
		3	1	Op Code Address + 2	1	Jump Address (Low Order Byte)
ADC EOR ADD LDA AND ORA BIT SBC CMP SUB	4	1	1	Op Code Address	1	Op Code
		2	1	Op Code Address + 1	1	Address of Operand (High Order Byte)
		3	1	Op Code Address + 2	1	Address of Operand (Low Order Byte)
		4	1	Address of Operand	1	Operand Data
CPX LDS LDX	5	1	1	Op Code Address	1	Op Code
		2	1	Op Code Address + 1	1	Address of Operand (High Order Byte)
		3	1	Op Code Address + 2	1	Address of Operand (Low Order Byte)
		4	1	Address of Operand	1	Operand Data (High Order Byte)
		5	1	Address of Operand + 1	1	Operand Data (Low Order Byte)
STA A STA B	5	1	1	Op Code Address	1	Op Code
		2	1	Op Code Address + 1	1	Destination Address (High Order Byte)
		3	1	Op Code Address + 2	1	Destination Address (Low Order Byte)
		4	0	Operand Destination Address	1	Irrelevant Data (Note 1)
		5	1	Operand Destination Address	0	Data from Accumulator
ASL LSR ASR NEG CLR ROL COM ROR DEC TST INC	6	1	1	Op Code Address	1	Op Code
		2	1	Op Code Address + 1	1	Address of Operand (High Order Byte)
		3	1	Op Code Address + 2	1	Address of Operand (Low Order Byte)
		4	1	Address of Operand	1	Current Operand Data
		5	0	Address of Operand	1	Irrelevant Data (Note 1)
		6	1/0 (Note 3)	Address of Operand	0	New Operand Data (Note 3)

MC6808

TABLE 8 – OPERATION SUMMARY (Continued)

Address Mode and Instructions	Cycles	Cycle #	VMA Line	Address Bus	R/W Line	Data Bus
EXTENDED (Continued)						
STS STX	6	1	1	Op Code Address	1	Op Code
		2	1	Op Code Address + 1	1	Address of Operand (High Order Byte)
		3	1	Op Code Address + 2	1	Address of Operand (Low Order Byte)
		4	0	Address of Operand	1	Irrelevant Data (Note 1)
		5	1	Address of Operand	0	Operand Data (High Order Byte)
		6	1	Address of Operand + 1	0	Operand Data (Low Order Byte)
JSR	9	1	1	Op Code Address	1	Op Code
		2	1	Op Code Address + 1	1	Address of Subroutine (High Order Byte)
		3	1	Op Code Address + 2	1	Address of Subroutine (Low Order Byte)
		4	1	Subroutine Starting Address	1	Op Code of Next Instruction
		5	1	Stack Pointer	0	Return Address (Low Order Byte)
		6	1	Stack Pointer – 1	0	Return Address (High Order Byte)
		7	0	Stack Pointer – 2	1	Irrelevant Data (Note 1)
		8	0	Op Code Address + 2	1	Irrelevant Data (Note 1)
		9	1	Op Code Address + 2	1	Address of Subroutine (Low Order Byte)
INHERENT						
ABA DAA SEC ASL DEC SEI ASR INC SEV CBA LSR TAB CLC NEG TAP CLI NOP TBA CLR ROL TPA CLV ROR TST COM SBA	2	1	1	Op Code Address	1	Op Code
		2	1	Op Code Address + 1	1	Op Code of Next Instruction
DES DEX INS INX	4	1	1	Op Code Address	1	Op Code
		2	1	Op Code Address + 1	1	Op Code of Next Instruction
		3	0	Previous Register Contents	1	Irrelevant Data (Note 1)
		4	0	New Register Contents	1	Irrelevant Data (Note 1)
PSH	4	1	1	Op Code Address	1	Op Code
		2	1	Op Code Address + 1	1	Op Code of Next Instruction
		3	1	Stack Pointer	0	Accumulator Data
		4	0	Stack Pointer – 1	1	Accumulator Data
PUL	4	1	1	Op Code Address	1	Op Code
		2	1	Op Code Address + 1	1	Op Code of Next Instruction
		3	0	Stack Pointer	1	Irrelevant Data (Note 1)
		4	1	Stack Pointer + 1	1	Operand Data from Stack
TSX	4	1	1	Op Code Address	1	Op Code
		2	1	Op Code Address + 1	1	Op Code of Next Instruction
		3	0	Stack Pointer	1	Irrelevant Data (Note 1)
		4	0	New Index Register	1	Irrelevant Data (Note 1)
TXS	4	1	1	Op Code Address	1	Op Code
		2	1	Op Code Address + 1	1	Op Code of Next Instruction
		3	0	Index Register	1	Irrelevant Data
		4	0	New Stack Pointer	1	Irrelevant Data
RTS	5	1	1	Op Code Address	1	Op Code
		2	1	Op Code Address + 1	1	Irrelevant Data (Note 2)
		3	0	Stack Pointer	1	Irrelevant Data (Note 1)
		4	1	Stack Pointer + 1	1	Address of Next Instruction (High Order Byte)
		5	1	Stack Pointer + 2	1	Address of Next Instruction (Low Order Byte)

TABLE 8 – OPERATION SUMMARY (Continued)

Address Mode and Instructions	Cycles	Cycle #	VMA Line	Address Bus	R/W Line	Data Bus
INHERENT (Continued)						
WAI	9	1	1	Op Code Address	1	Op Code
		2	1	Op Code Address + 1	1	Op Code of Next Instruction
		3	1	Stack Pointer	0	Return Address (Low Order Byte)
		4	1	Stack Pointer – 1	0	Return Address (High Order Byte)
		5	1	Stack Pointer – 2	0	Index Register (Low Order Byte)
		6	1	Stack Pointer – 3	0	Index Register (High Order Byte)
		7	1	Stack Pointer – 4	0	Contents of Accumulator A
		8	1	Stack Pointer – 5	0	Contents of Accumulator B
		9	1	Stack Pointer – 6 (Note 4)	1	Contents of Cond. Code Register
RTI	10	1	1	Op Code Address	1	Op Code
		2	1	Op Code Address + 1	1	Irrelevant Data (Note 2)
		3	0	Stack Pointer	1	Irrelevant Data (Note 1)
		4	1	Stack Pointer + 1	1	Contents of Cond. Code Register from Stack
		5	1	Stack Pointer + 2	1	Contents of Accumulator B from Stack
		6	1	Stack Pointer + 3	1	Contents of Accumulator A from Stack
		7	1	Stack Pointer + 4	1	Index Register from Stack (High Order Byte)
		8	1	Stack Pointer + 5	1	Index Register from Stack (Low Order Byte)
		9	1	Stack Pointer + 6	1	Next Instruction Address from Stack (High Order Byte)
		10	1	Stack Pointer + 7	1	Next Instruction Address from Stack (Low Order Byte)
SWI	12	1	1	Op Code Address	1	Op Code
		2	1	Op Code Address + 1	1	Irrelevant Data (Note 1)
		3	1	Stack Pointer	0	Return Address (Low Order Byte)
		4	1	Stack Pointer – 1	0	Return Address (High Order Byte)
		5	1	Stack Pointer – 2	0	Index Register (Low Order Byte)
		6	1	Stack Pointer – 3	0	Index Register (High Order Byte)
		7	1	Stack Pointer – 4	0	Contents of Accumulator A
		8	1	Stack Pointer – 5	0	Contents of Accumulator B
		9	1	Stack Pointer – 6	0	Contents of Cond. Code Register
		10	0	Stack Pointer – 7	1	Irrelevant Data (Note 1)
		11	1	Vector Address FFFA (Hex)	1	Address of Subroutine (High Order Byte)
		12	1	Vector Address FFFB (Hex)	1	Address of Subroutine (Low Order Byte)
RELATIVE						
BCC BHI BNE BCS BLE BPL BEQ BLS BRA BGE BLT BVC BGT BMI BVS	4	1	1	Op Code Address	1	Op Code
		2	1	Op Code Address + 1	1	Branch Offset
		3	0	Op Code Address + 2	1	Irrelevant Data (Note 1)
		4	0	Branch Address	1	Irrelevant Data (Note 1)
BSR	8	1	1	Op Code Address	1	Op Code
		2	1	Op Code Address + 1	1	Branch Offset
		3	0	Return Address of Main Program	1	Irrelevant Data (Note 1)
		4	1	Stack Pointer	0	Return Address (Low Order Byte)
		5	1	Stack Pointer – 1	0	Return Address (High Order Byte)
		6	0	Stack Pointer – 2	1	Irrelevant Data (Note 1)
		7	0	Return Address of Main Program	1	Irrelevant Data (Note 1)
		8	0	Subroutine Address	1	Irrelevant Data (Note 1, Note 5)

Note 1. If device which is addressed during this cycle uses VMA, then the Data Bus will go to the high impedance three-state condition. Depending on bus capacitance, data from the previous cycle may be retained on the Data Bus.
Note 2. Data is ignored by the MPU.
Note 3. For TST, VMA = 0 and Operand data does not change.
Note 4. While the MPU is waiting for the interrupt, Bus Available will go high, VMA is low.
Note 5. MS Byte = MS Byte of BSR instruction address, LS Byte = LS Byte of subroutine address.

MC6808

P SUFFIX
PLASTIC PACKAGE
CASE 711-03

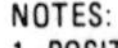

NOTES:
1. POSITIONAL TOLERANCE OF LEADS (D), SHALL BE WITHIN 0.25 mm (0.010) AT MAXIMUM MATERIAL CONDITION, IN RELATION TO SEATING PLANE AND EACH OTHER.
2. DIMENSION L TO CENTER OF LEADS WHEN FORMED PARALLEL.
3. DIMENSION B DOES NOT INCLUDE MOLD FLASH.
4. 711-02 OBSOLETE, NEW STANDARD 711-03.

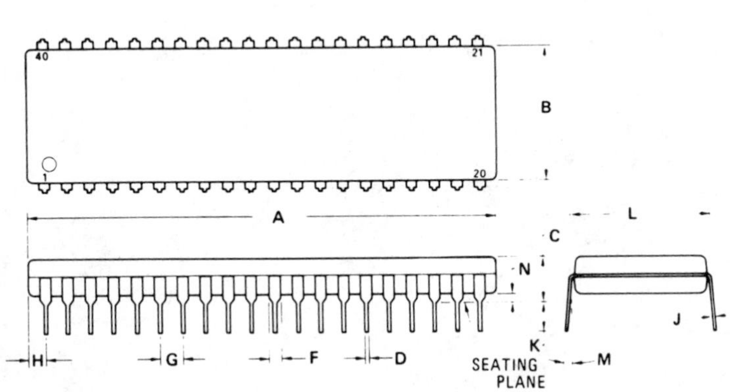

DIM	MILLIMETERS		INCHES	
	MIN	MAX	MIN	MAX
A	51.69	52.45	2.035	2.065
B	13.72	14.22	0.540	0.560
C	3.94	5.08	0.155	0.200
D	0.36	0.56	0.014	0.022
F	1.02	1.52	0.040	0.060
G	2.54 BSC		0.100 BSC	
H	1.65	2.16	0.065	0.085
J	0.20	0.38	0.008	0.015
K	2.92	3.43	0.115	0.135
L	15.24 BSC		0.600 BSC	
M	0°	15°	0°	15°
N	0.51	1.02	0.020	0.040

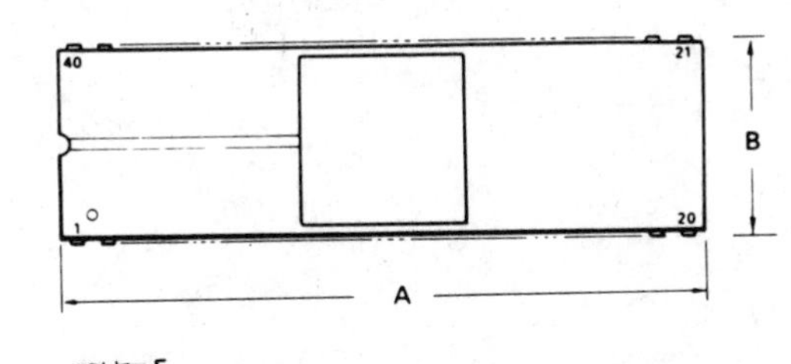

L SUFFIX
CERAMIC PACKAGE
CASE 715-02

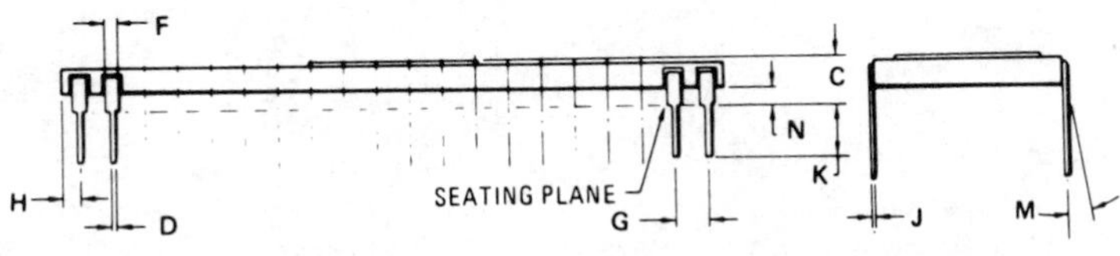

DIM	MILLIMETERS		INCHES	
	MIN	MAX	MIN	MAX
A	50.29	51.31	1.980	2.020
B	14.86	15.62	0.585	0.615
C	2.54	4.19	0.100	0.165
D	0.38	0.53	0.015	0.021
F	0.76	1.40	0.030	0.055
G	2.54 BSC		0.100 BSC	
H	0.76	1.78	0.030	0.070
J	0.20	0.33	0.008	0.013
K	2.54	4.19	0.100	0.165
M	0°	10°	0°	10°
N	0.51	1.52	0.020	0.060

NOTE:
1. LEADS, TRUE POSITIONED WITHIN 0.25 mm (0.010) DIA (AT SEATING PLANE), AT MAX. MAT'L CONDITION.

MC6801 (1.0 MHz)
MC6801-1 (1.25 MHz)

Advance Information

MOS

(N-CHANNEL, SILICON-GATE, DEPLETION LOAD)

MICROCOMPUTER

MC6801 MICROCOMPUTER UNIT (MCU)

The MC6801 is an 8-bit single chip microcomputer unit (MCU) which significantly enhances the capabilities of the M6800 family of parts. It includes an upgraded M6800 microprocessor unit (MPU) while retaining upward source and object code compatibility. Execution times of key instructions have been improved and several new instructions have been added including an unsigned multiply. The MCU can function as a monolithic microcomputer or is expandable to a 64K byte address space. It is TTL compatible and requires one +5 volt power supply. On-chip resources include 2048 bytes of ROM, 128 bytes of RAM, Serial Communications Interface (SCI), parallel I/O, and a three function Programmable Timer. A summary of MCU features includes:

- Enhanced MC6800 Instruction Set
- 8×8 Multiply Instruction
- Serial Communications Interface (SCI)
- Upward Source and Object Code Compatible with MC6800
- 16-Bit Three-Function Programmable Timer
- Single-Chip or Expandable to 64K-Byte Address Space
- Bus Compatible with M6800 Family
- 2048 Bytes of ROM
- 128 Bytes of RAM (64 Bytes Retainable on Powerdown)
- 29 Parallel I/O and Two Handshake Control Lines
- Internal Clock Generator with Divide-by-Four Output

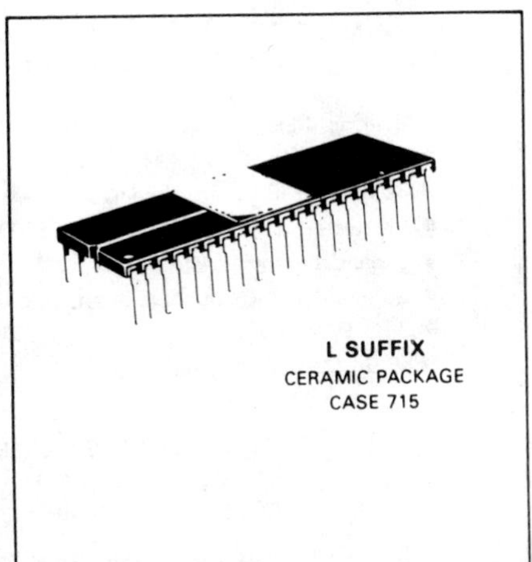

L SUFFIX
CERAMIC PACKAGE
CASE 715

FIGURE 2 — MC6801 MICROCOMPUTER BLOCK DIAGRAM

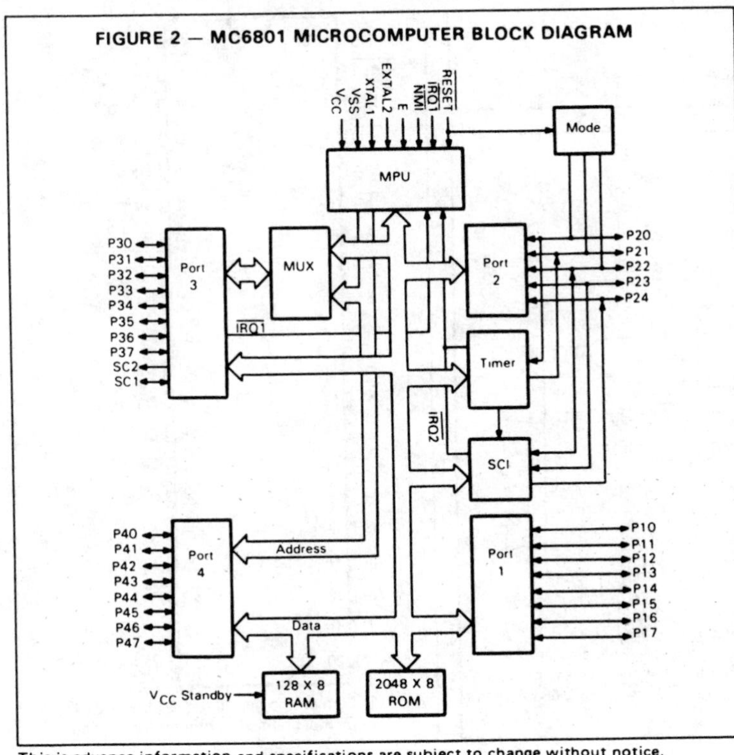

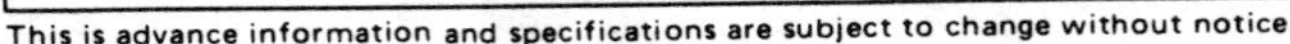
This is advance information and specifications are subject to change without notice.

FIGURE 1 — PIN ASSIGNMENT

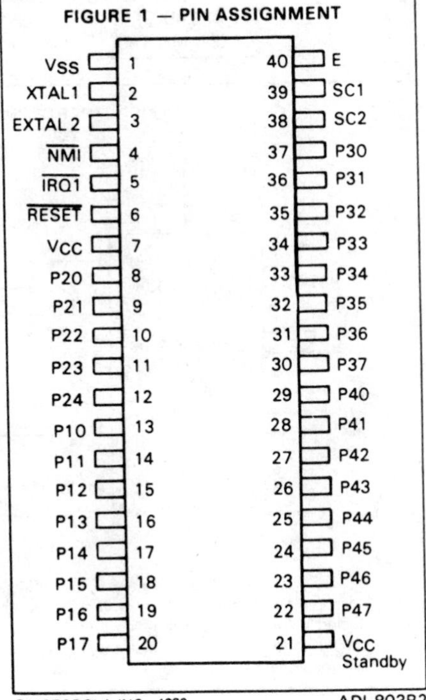

ADI-803R2

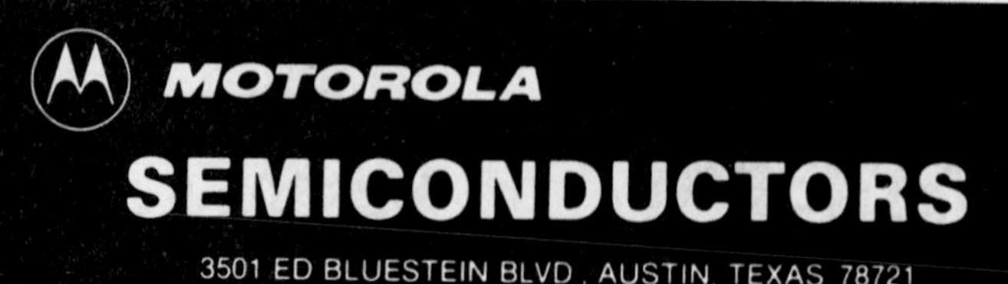

MC6802
MC6808
MC6802NS

MOS

(N-CHANNEL, SILICON-GATE, DEPLETION LOAD)

MICROPROCESSOR WITH CLOCK AND OPTIONAL RAM

MICROPROCESSOR WITH CLOCK AND OPTIONAL RAM

The MC6802 is a monolithic 8-bit microprocessor that contains all the registers and accumulators of the present MC6800 plus an internal clock oscillator and driver on the same chip. In addition, the MC6802 has 128 bytes of on-board RAM located at hex addresses \$0000 to \$007F. The first 32 bytes of RAM, at hex addresses \$0000 to \$001F, may be retained in a low power mode by utilizing V_{CC} standby; thus, facilitating memory retention during a power-down situation.

The MC6802 is completely software compatible with the MC6800 as well as the entire M6800 family of parts. Hence, the MC6802 is expandable to 64K words.

The MC6802NS is identical to the MC6802 without standby RAM feature. The MC6808 is identical to the MC6802 without on-board RAM.

- On-Chip Clock Circuit
- 128 × 8 Bit On-Chip RAM
- 32 Bytes of RAM are Retainable
- Software-Compatible with the MC6800
- Expandable to 64K Words
- Standard TTL-Compatible Inputs and Outputs
- 8-Bit Word Size
- 16-Bit Memory Addressing
- Interrupt Capability

PART NUMBER DESIGNATION BY SPEED

MC6802 (1.0 MHz)	MC6808 (1.0 MHz)	MC6802NS (1.0 MHz)
MC68A02 (1.5 MHz)	MC68A08 (1.5 MHz)	
MC68B02 (2.0 MHz)	MC68B08 (2.0 MHz)	

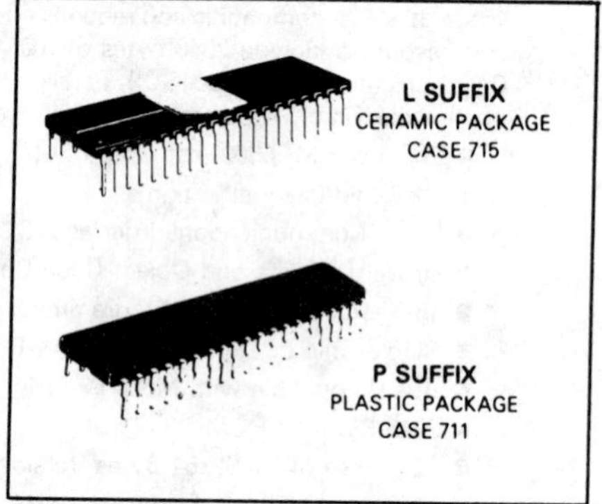

TYPICAL MICROCOMPUTER

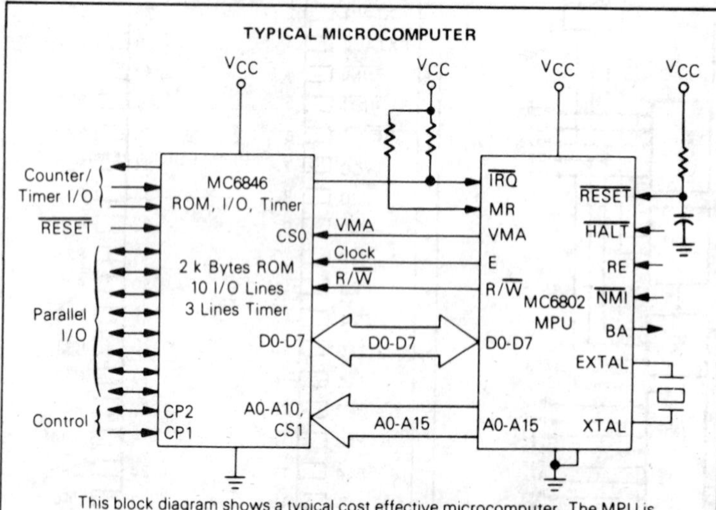

This block diagram shows a typical cost effective microcomputer. The MPU is the center of the microcoputer system and is shown in a minimum system interfacing with a ROM combination chip. It is not intended that this system be limited to this function but that it be expandable with other parts in the M6800 Microcomputer family.

PIN ASSIGNMENT

Signal	Pin	Pin	Signal
V_{SS}	1	40	$\overline{RESET}$
$\overline{HALT}$	2	39	EXTAL
MR	3	38	XTAL
$\overline{IRQ}$	4	37	E
VMA	5	36	RE**
$\overline{NMI}$	6	35	V_{CC} Standby*
BA	7	34	R/$\overline{W}$
V_{CC}	8	33	D0
A0	9	32	D1
A1	10	31	D2
A2	11	30	D3
A3	12	29	D4
A4	13	28	D5
A5	14	27	D6
A6	15	26	D7
A7	16	25	A15
A8	17	24	A14
A9	18	23	A13
A10	19	22	A12
A11	20	21	V_{SS}

*Pin 35 must be tied to 5 V on the 6802NS
**Pin 36 must be tied to ground for the 6808

DS9818-R1

MC6805P2

Advance Information

HMOS

(HIGH DENSITY N-CHANNEL, SILICON-GATE DEPLETION LOAD)

8-BIT MICROCOMPUTER

8-BIT MICROCOMPUTER UNIT

The MC6805P2 Microcomputer Unit (MCU) is a member of the M6805 Family of microcomputers. This 8-bit microcomputer contains a CPU, on-chip clock, ROM, RAM, I/O and timer. It is designed for the user who needs an economical microcomputer with the proven capabilities of the M6800-based instruction set. Table 9 compares the key features of the M6805 Family of microcomputers. The following are some of the hardware and software highlights of the MCU.

HARDWARE FEATURES:

- 8-Bit Architecture
- 64 Bytes of RAM
- Memory Mapped I/O
- 1100 Bytes of User ROM
- Internal 8-Bit Timer with 7-Bit Prescaler
- Vectored Interrupts — External and Timer
- 20 TTL/CMOS Compatible I/O Lines; 8 Lines LED Compatible
- On-Chip Clock Circuit
- Self-Check Mode
- Master Reset
- Low Voltage Inhibit
- Complete Development System Support on EXORciser
- 5 Vdc Single Supply

SOFTWARE FEATURES:

- Similar to M6800
- Byte Efficient Instruction Set
- Easy to Program
- True Bit Manipulation
- Bit Test and Branch Instructions
- Versatile Interrupt Handling
- Powerful Indexed Addressing for Tables
- Full Set of Conditional Branches
- Memory Usable as Registers/Flags
- Single Instruction Memory Examine/Change
- 10 Powerful Addressing Modes
- All Addressing Modes Apply to ROM, RAM and I/O

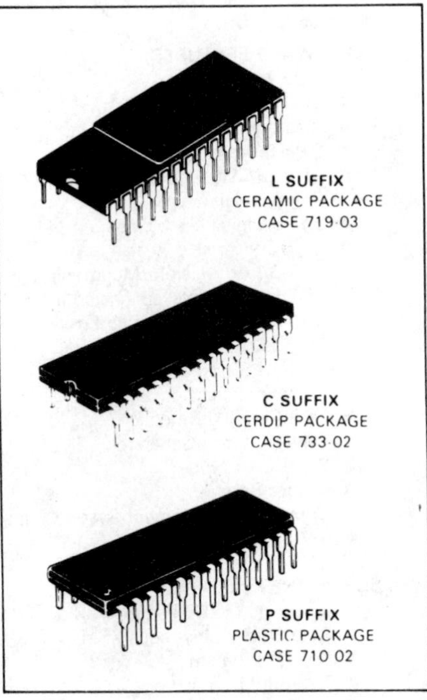

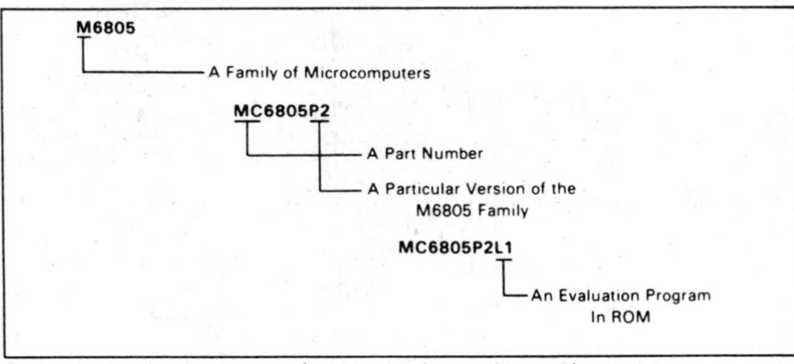

FIGURE 1 — PIN ASSIGNMENTS

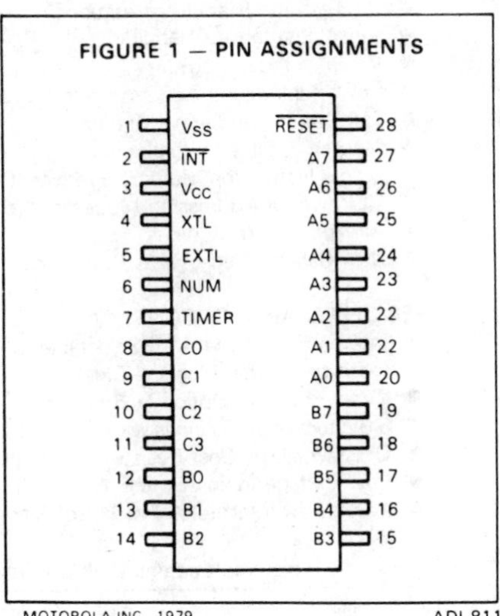

This is advance information and specifications are subject to change without notice

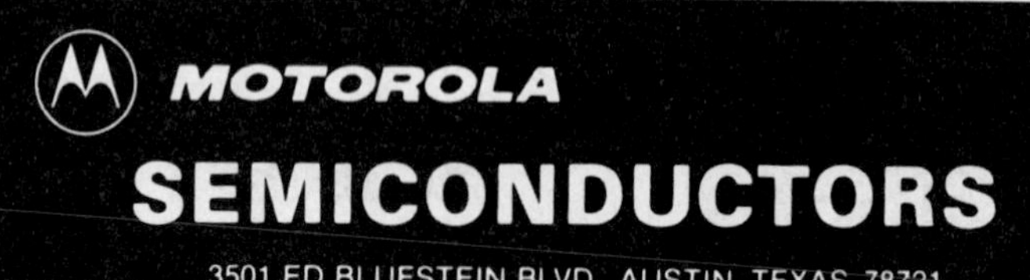

MC6805R2

Advance Information

HMOS

(HIGH DENSITY N-CHANNEL, SILICON-GATE DEPLETION LOAD)

8-BIT MICROCOMPUTER WITH A/D

8-BIT MICROCOMPUTER UNIT WITH A/D

The MC6805R2 Microcomputer Unit (MCU) is a member of the M6805 Family of low-cost single-chip Microcomputers. The 8-bit microcomputer contains a CPU, on-chip CLOCK, ROM, RAM, I/O, 4-channel 8-bit A/D, and TIMER. It is designed for the user who needs an economical microcomputer with the proven capabilities of the M6800-based instruction set. A comparison of the key features of several members of the M6805 Family of microcomputers is shown on the last page of this data sheet. The following are some of the hardware and software highlights of the MC6805R2 MCU.

HARDWARE FEATURES:

- 8-Bit Architecture
- 64 Bytes of RAM
- Memory Mapped I/O
- 2048 Bytes of User ROM
- 24 TTL/CMOS Compatible Bidirectional I/O Lines (8 lines are LED Compatible)
- 2 to 5 Digital Input Lines
- A/D Converter
  - 8-Bit Conversion, Monotonic
  - 1 to 4 Multiplexed Analog Inputs
  - ± 1/2 LSB Quantizing Error
  - ± 1/2 LSB All Other Errors
  - ± 1 LSB Total Error (max)
  - Ratiometric Conversion
- Zero-Crossing Detection
- On-Chip Clock Generator
- Self-Check Mode
- Master Reset
- Complete Development System Support On EXORciser®
- 5 V Single Supply

SOFTWARE FEATURES:

- Similar to M6800 Family
- Byte Efficient Instruction Set
- Easy to Program
- True Bit Manipulation
- Bit Test and Branch Instructions
- Versatile Interrupt Handling
- Versatile Index Register
- Powerful Indexed Addressing for Tables
- Full Set of Conditional Branches
- Memory Usable as Register/Flags
- Single Instruction Memory Examine/Change
- 10 Powerful Addressing Modes
- All Addressing Modes
- User Callable Self-Check Subroutines

USER SELECTABLE OPTIONS:

- Internal 8-Bit Timer with Selectable Clock Source (External Timer Input or Internal Machine Clock)
- Timer Prescaler Option (7 Bits 2^N)
- 8 Bidirectional I/O Lines with TTL or TTL/CMOS Interface Option
- Crystal or Low-Cost Resistor Oscillator Option
- Low Voltage Inhibit Option
- 4 Vectored Interrupts; Timer, Software, and 2 External

® EXORciser is a registered trademark of Motorola Inc.

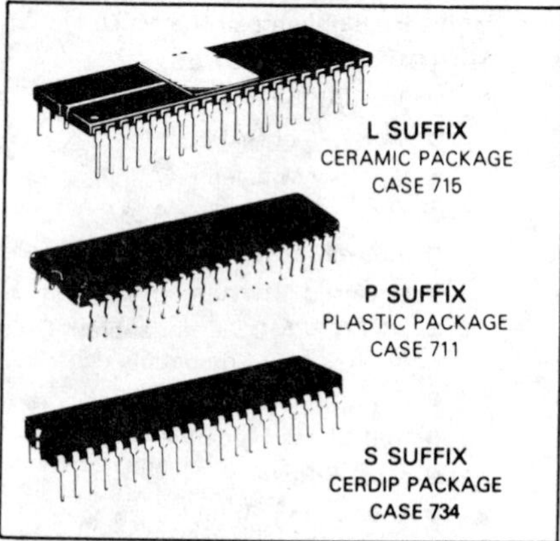

L SUFFIX
CERAMIC PACKAGE
CASE 715

P SUFFIX
PLASTIC PACKAGE
CASE 711

S SUFFIX
CERDIP PACKAGE
CASE 734

FIGURE 1 — PIN ASSIGNMENTS

Signal	Pin	Pin	Signal
V_{SS}	1	40	PA7
$\overline{RESET}$	2	39	PA6
$\overline{INT}$	3	38	PA5
V_{CC}	4	37	PA4
EXTAL	5	36	PA3
XTAL	6	35	PA2
NUM	7	34	PA1
TIMER	8	33	PA0
PC0	9	32	PB7
PC1	10	31	PB6
PC2	11	30	PB5
PC3	12	29	PB4
PC4	13	28	PB3
PC5	14	27	PB2
PC6	15	26	PB1
PC7	16	25	PB0
PD7	17	24	PD0/AN0
PD6/$\overline{INT2}$	18	23	PD1/AN1
V_{RH}	19	22	PD2/AN2
V_{RL}	20	21	PD3/AN3

This document contains information on a new product. Specifications and information herein are subject to change without notice.

ADI-845-R1

MC6805U2

Advance Information

8-BIT MICROCOMPUTER UNIT WITH A/D

The MC6805R2 Microcomputer Unit (MCU) is a member of the M6805 Family of low-cost single-chip Microcomputers. The 8-bit microcomputer contains a CPU, on-chip CLOCK, ROM, RAM, I/O, 4-channel 8-bit A/D, and TIMER. It is designed for the user who needs an economical microcomputer with the proven capabilities of the M6800-based instruction set. A comparison of the key features of several members of the M6805 Family of microcomputers is shown on the last page of this data sheet. The following are some of the hardware and software highlights of the MC6805R2 MCU.

HARDWARE FEATURES:

- 8-Bit Architecture
- 64 Bytes of RAM
- Memory Mapped I/O
- 2048 Bytes of User ROM
- 24 TTL/CMOS Compatible Bidirectional I/O Lines (8 lines are LED Compatible)
- 2 to 5 Digital Input Lines
- A/D Converter
  - 8-Bit Conversion, Monotonic
  - 1 to 4 Multiplexed Analog Inputs
  - ± 1/2 LSB Quantizing Error
  - ± 1/2 LSB All Other Errors
  - ± 1 LSB Total Error (max)
  - Ratiometric Conversion
- Zero-Crossing Detection
- On-Chip Clock Generator
- Self-Check Mode
- Master Reset
- Complete Development System Support On EXORciser®
- 5 V Single Supply

SOFTWARE FEATURES:

- Similar to M6800 Family
- Byte Efficient Instruction Set
- Easy to Program
- True Bit Manipulation
- Bit Test and Branch Instructions
- Versatile Interrup Handling
- Versatile Index Register
- Powerful Indexed Addressing for Tables
- Full Set of Conditional Branches
- Memory Usable as Register/Flags
- Single Instruction Memory Examine/Change
- 10 Powerful Addressing Modes
- All Addressing Modes
- User Callable Self-Check Subroutines

USER SELECTABLE OPTIONS:

- Internal 8-Bit Timer with Selectable Clock Source (External Timer Input or Internal Machine Clock)
- Timer Prescaler Option (7 Bits 2^N)
- 8 Bidirectional I/O Lines with TTL or TTL/CMOS Interface Option
- Crystal or Low-Cost Resistor Oscillator Option
- Low Voltage Inhibit Option
- 4 Vectored Interrupts; Timer, Software, and 2 External

® EXORciser is a registered trademark of Motorola Inc.

HMOS

(HIGH DENSITY N-CHANNEL, SILICON-GATE DEPLETION LOAD)

8-BIT MICROCOMPUTER

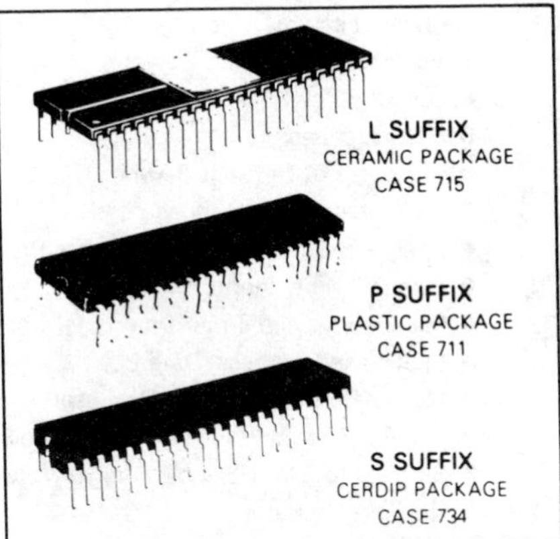

FIGURE 1 — PIN ASSIGNMENTS

Pin name	Pin	Pin	Pin name
V_{SS}	1	40	PA7
$\overline{RESET}$	2	39	PA6
$\overline{INT}$	3	38	PA5
V_{CC}	4	37	PA4
EXTAL	5	36	PA3
XTAL	6	35	PA2
NUM	7	34	PA1
TIMER	8	33	PA0
PC0	9	32	PB7
PC1	10	31	PB6
PC2	11	30	PB5
PC3	12	29	PB4
PC4	13	28	PB3
PC5	14	27	PB2
PC6	15	26	PB1
PC7	16	25	PB0
PD7	17	24	PD0
PD6/$\overline{INT2}$	18	23	PD1
PD5	19	22	PD2
PD4	20	21	PD3

This document contains information on a new product. Specifications and information herein are subject to change without notice.

ADI-853-R1

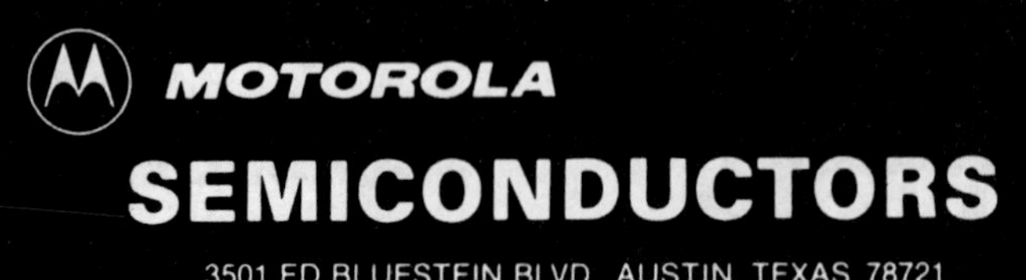

MC146805E2

Advance Information

CMOS

(HIGH PERFORMANCE SILICON GATE)

8-BIT MICROPROCESSOR

8-BIT MICROPROCESSOR UNIT

The MC146805E2 Microprocessor Unit (MPU) belongs to the M6805 Family of microcomputers. This 8-bit fully static and expandable microprocessor contains a CPU, on-chip RAM, I/O and timer. It is a low-power, low cost processor designed for low-end to mid-range applications in the consumer, automotive, industrial, and communications markets where very low power consumption constitutes an important factor. The following are the major features of the MC146805E2 MPU:

Hardware Features

- Full Speed Operating Power of 20 mW
- Standby Power Less than 1 mW
- 8-Bit Architecture
- 112 Bytes of On-Chip RAM
- 16 Bidirectional I/O Lines
- Internal 8-Bit Timer with Software Programmable 7-Bit Prescaler
- External Timer Input
- Full External and Timer Interrupts
- Multiplexed Address/Data Bus
- Master Reset and Power-On Reset
- Capable of Addressing Up to 8k Bytes of External Memory
- Single 3 to 6 Volt Supply, Higher Voltage Version Soon
- On-Chip Oscillator
- 40-Pin Dual-In-Line Package
- Chip Carrier Also Available

Software Features

- Similar to the MC6800
- Efficient Use of Program Space
- Versatile Interrupt Handling
- True Bit Manipulation
- Addressing Modes With Indexed Addressing for Tables
- Efficient Instruction Set
- Memory Mapped I/O
- Two Power Saving Standby Modes

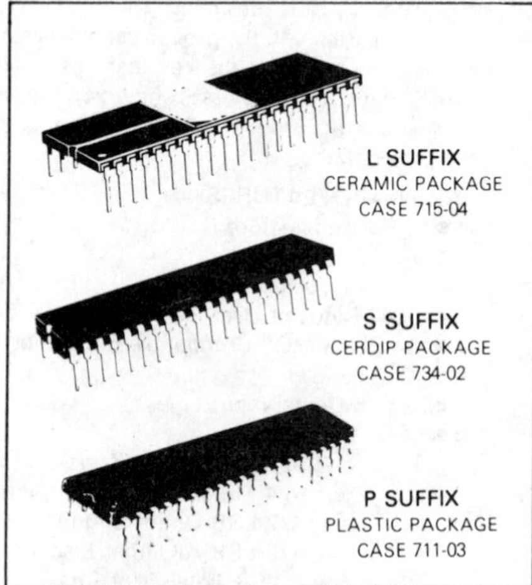

L SUFFIX
CERAMIC PACKAGE
CASE 715-04

S SUFFIX
CERDIP PACKAGE
CASE 734-02

P SUFFIX
PLASTIC PACKAGE
CASE 711-03

M6805 — A Family of Microcomputers

MC6805P2 — A Part Number; A Particular M6805 Family Version

MC68705P3 — EPROM Version

MC146805E2 — A CMOS M6805 Family Member

MC6805P2L1 — An Evaluation Program Stored in ROM

PIN ASSIGNMENTS

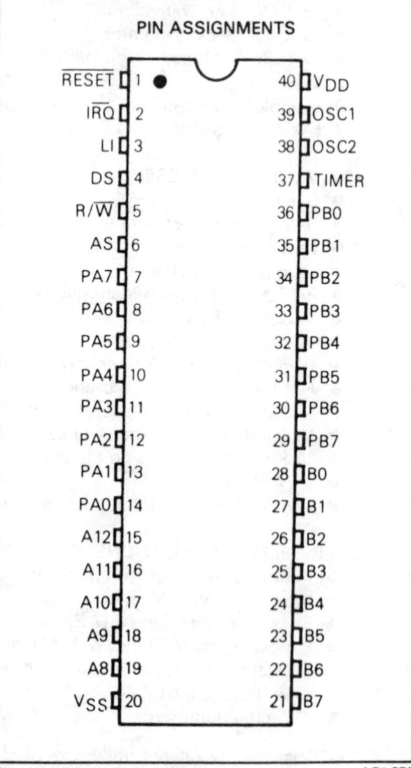

This is advance information and specifications are subject to change without notice.

ADI-850

SEMICONDUCTORS

3501 ED BLUESTEIN BLVD., AUSTIN, TEXAS 78721

MC68701 (1.0 MHz)
MC68701-1 (1.25 MHz)

Advance Information

MOS

(N-CHANNEL, SILICON-GATE, DEPLETION LOAD)

MICROCOMPUTER WITH EPROM

MC68701 MICROCOMPUTER UNIT (MCU)

The MC68701 is an 8-bit single chip microcomputer unit (MCU) which significantly enhances the capabilities of the M6800 family of parts. It can be used in production systems to allow for easy firmware changes with minimum delay or it can be used to emulate the MC6801/03 for software development. It includes an upgraded M6800 microprocessor unit (MPU) while retaining upward source and object code compatibility. Execution times of key instructions have been improved and several new instructions have been added including an unsigned multiply. The MCU can function as a monolithic microcomputer or can be expanded to a 64K byte address space. It is TTL compatible and requires one +5 volt power supply for nonprogramming operation. An additional V_{PP} power supply is needed for EPROM programming. On-chip resources include 2048 bytes of EPROM, 128 bytes of RAM, Serial Communications Interface (SCI), parallel I/O, and a three function Programmable Timer. A summary of MCU features includes:

- Enhanced MC6800 Instruction Set
- 8×8 Multiply Instruction
- Serial Communications Interface (SCI)
- Upward Source and Object Code Compatible with MC6800
- 16-Bit Three-Function Programmable Timer
- Single-Chip or Expandable to 64K-Byte Address Space
- Bus Compatible with M6800 Family
- 2048 Bytes of UV Erasable, User Programmable ROM
- 128 Bytes of RAM (64 Bytes Retainable on Powerdown)
- 29 Parallel I/O and Two Handshake Control Lines
- Internal Clock Generator with Divide-by-Four Output

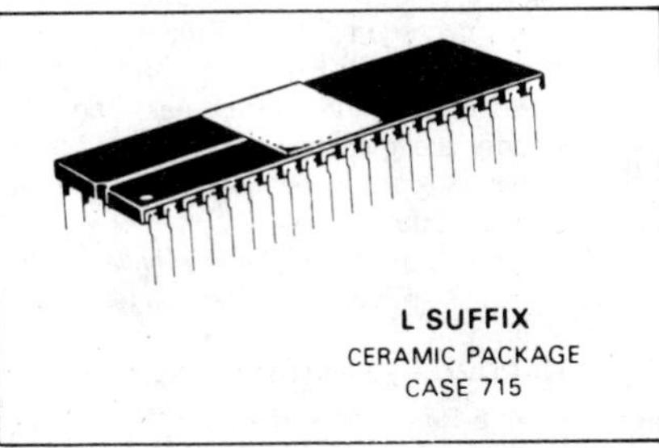

L SUFFIX
CERAMIC PACKAGE
CASE 715

FIGURE 2 — MC68701 MICROCOMPUTER BLOCK DIAGRAM

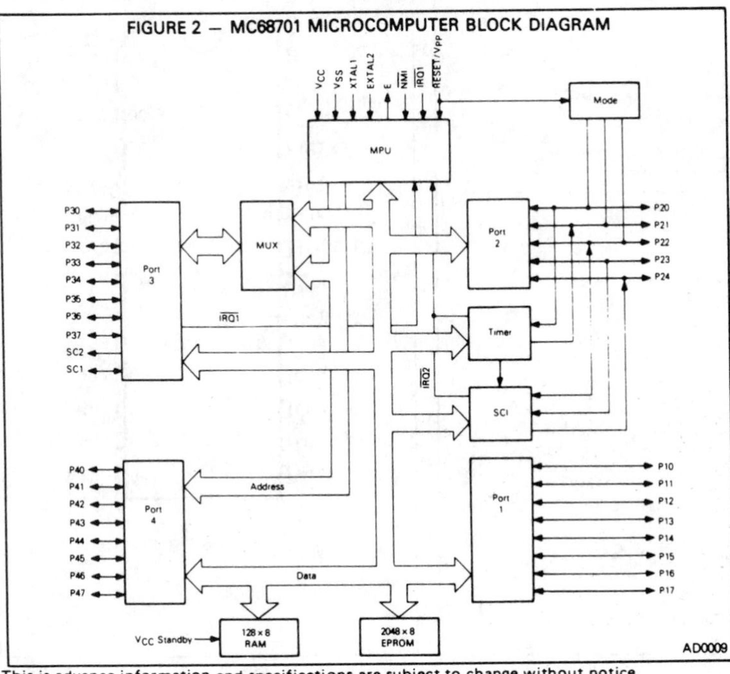

FIGURE 1 — PIN ASSIGNMENT

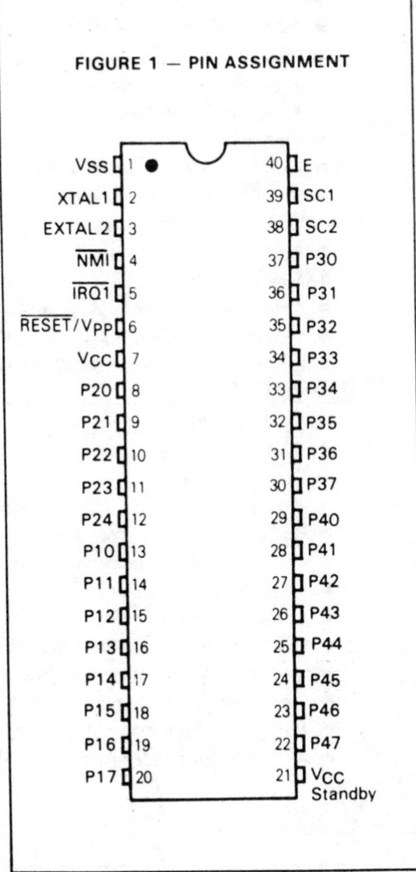

This is advance information and specifications are subject to change without notice.

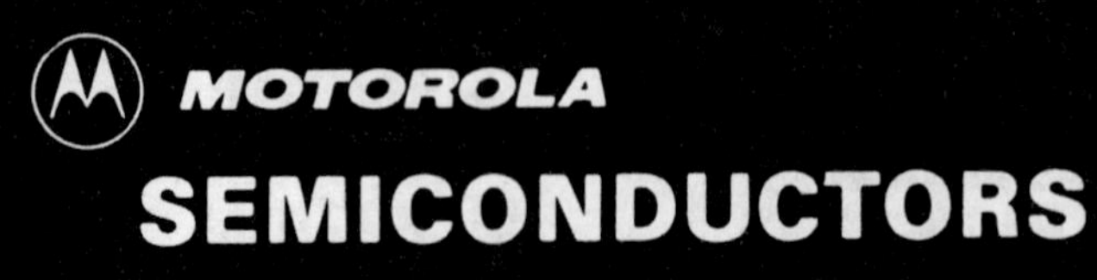

MC68705P3

Advance Information

HMOS

(HIGH-DENSITY, N-CHANNEL DEPLETION LOAD, 5 V EPROM PROCESS)

8-BIT EPROM MICROCOMPUTER

8-BIT EPROM MICROCOMPUTER UNIT

The MC68705P3 Microcomputer Unit (MCU) is an EPROM member of the M6805 Family of low-cost single-chip microcomputers. The user programmable EPROM allows program changes and lower volume applications in comparison to the factory mask programmable versions. The EPROM versions also reduce the development costs and turn-around time for prototype evaluation of the mask ROM versions. This 8-bit microcomputer contains a CPU, on-chip CLOCK, EPROM, bootstrap ROM, RAM, I/O, and a TIMER.

Because of these features, the MC68705P3 offers the user an economical means of designing an M6805 Family MCU into his system, either as a prototype evaluation, as a low-volume production run, or a pilot production run.

A comparison table of key features for several members of the M6805 Family is shown on the last page of this data sheet.

HARDWARE FEATURES:

- 8-Bit Architecture
- 112 bytes of RAM
- Memory Mapped I/O
- 1804 Bytes of User EPROM
- Internal 8-Bit Timer with 7-Bit Prescaler
  - Programmable Prescaler
  - Programmable Timer Input Modes
- Vectored Interrupts – External, Timer, and Software
- Zero-Cross Detection on $\overline{INT}$ Input
- 20 TTL/CMOS Compatible Bidirectional I/O Lines (8 Lines are LED Compatible)
- On-Chip Clock Generator
- Master Reset
- Complete Development System Support on EXORciser®
- Emulates the MC6805P2 and MC6805P4
- Bootstrap Program in ROM Simplifies EPROM Programming

SOFTWARE

- Similar to M6800 Family
- Byte Efficient Instruction Set
- Easy to Program
- True Bit Manipulation
- Bit Test and Branch Instructions
- Versatile Interrupt Handling
- Versatile Index Register
- Powerful Indexed Addressing for Tables
- Full Set of Conditional Branches
- Memory Usable as Registers/Flags
- Single Instruction Memory Examine/Change
- 10 Powerful Addressing Modes
- All Addressing Modes Apply to EPROM, RAM, and I/O

® EXORciser is a registered trademark of Motorola Inc.

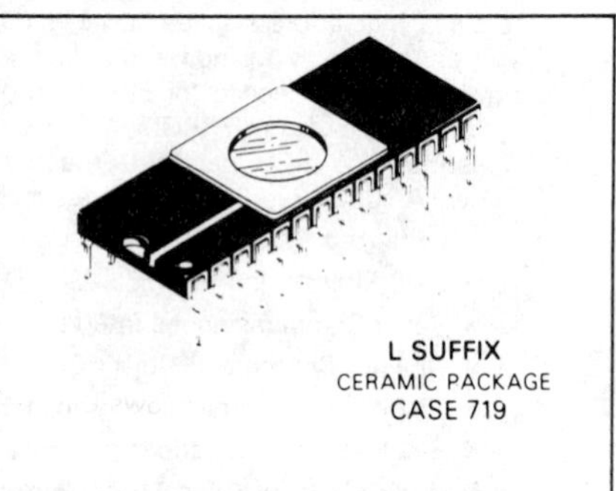

L SUFFIX
CERAMIC PACKAGE
CASE 719

FIGURE 1 – PIN ASSIGNMENTS

Pin	Name	Pin	Name
1	V_{SS}	28	$\overline{RESET}$
2	$\overline{INT}$	27	PA7
3	V_{CC}	26	PA6
4	EXTAL	25	PA5
5	XTAL	24	PA4
6	V_{PP}	23	PA3
7	TIMER/BOOT	22	PA2
8	PC0	21	PA1
9	PC1	20	PA0
10	PC2	19	PB7
11	PC3	18	PB6
12	PB0	17	PB5
13	PB1	16	PB4
14	PB2	15	PB3

This document contains information on a new product. Specifications and information herein are subject to change without notice.

ADI-848 R1

MC6809
(1.0 MHz)
MC68A09
(1.5 MHz)
MC68B09
(2.0 MHz)

HMOS

(HIGH DENSITY N-CHANNEL, SILICON-GATE)

8-BIT MICROPROCESSING UNIT

8-BIT MICROPROCESSING UNIT

The MC6809 is a revolutionary high-performance 8-bit microprocessor which supports modern programming techniques such as position independence, reentrancy, and modular programming.

This third-generation addition to the M6800 family has major architectural improvements which include additional registers, instructions, and addressing modes.

The basic instructions of any computer are greatly enhanced by the presence of powerful addressing modes. The MC6809 has the most complete set of addressing modes available on any 8-bit microprocessor today.

The MC6809 has hardware and software features which make it an ideal processor for higher level language execution or standard controller applications.

MC6800 COMPATIBLE

- Hardware – Interfaces with All M6800 Peripherals
- Software – Upward Source Code Compatible Instruction Set and Addressing Modes

ARCHITECTURAL FEATURES

- Two 16-bit Index Registers
- Two 16-bit Indexable Stack Pointers
- Two 8-bit Accumulators can be Concatenated to Form One 16-Bit Accumulator
- Direct Page Register Allows Direct Addressing Throughout Memory

HARDWARE FEATURES

- On-Chip Oscillator (Crystal Frequency = 4XE)
- $\overline{DMA/BREQ}$ Allows DMA Operation on Memory Refresh
- Fast Interrupt Request Input Stacks Only Condition Code Register and Program Counter
- MRDY Input Extends Data Access Times for Use with Slow Memory
- Interrupt Acknowledge Output Allows Vectoring By Devices
- SYNC Acknowledge Output Allows for Synchronization to External Event
- Single Bus-Cycle $\overline{RESET}$
- Single 5-Volt Supply Operation
- $\overline{NMI}$ Inhibited After $\overline{RESET}$ Until After First Load of Stack Pointer
- Early Address Valid Allows Use With Slower Memories
- Early Write-Data for Dynamic Memories

SOFTWARE FEATURES

- 10 Addressing Modes
  - 6800 Upward Compatible Addressing Modes
  - Direct Addressing Anywhere in Memory Map
  - Long Relative Branches
  - Program Counter Relative
  - True Indirect Addressing
  - Expanded Indexed Addressing:
    0-, 5-, 8-, or 16-bit Constant Offsets
    8-, or 16-bit Accumulator Offsets
    Auto-Increment/Decrement by 1 or 2
- Improved Stack Manipulation
- 1464 Instructions with Unique Addressing Modes
- 8 × 8 Unsigned Multiply
- 16-bit Arithmetic
- Transfer/Exchange All Registers
- Push/Pull Any Registers or Any Set of Registers
- Load Effective Address

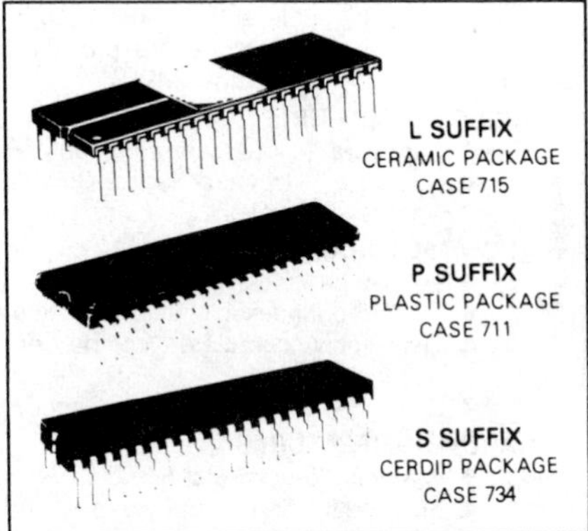

L SUFFIX
CERAMIC PACKAGE
CASE 715

P SUFFIX
PLASTIC PACKAGE
CASE 711

S SUFFIX
CERDIP PACKAGE
CASE 734

FIGURE 1 — PIN ASSIGNMENT

Signal	Pin	Pin	Signal
V_{SS}	1	40	$\overline{HALT}$
$\overline{NMI}$	2	39	XTAL
$\overline{IRQ}$	3	38	EXTAL
$\overline{FIRQ}$	4	37	$\overline{RESET}$
BS	5	36	MRDY
BA	6	35	Q
V_{CC}	7	34	E
A0	8	33	$\overline{DMA/BREQ}$
A1	9	32	R/$\overline{W}$
A2	10	31	D0
A3	11	30	D1
A4	12	29	D2
A5	13	28	D3
A6	14	27	D4
A7	15	26	D5
A8	16	25	D6
A9	17	24	D7
A10	18	23	A15
A11	19	22	A14
A12	20	21	A13

DS9845
(Replaces ADI-804 R1)

MC6809E
(1.0 MHz)
MC68A09E
(1.5 MHz)
MC68B09E
(2.0 MHz)

HMOS
(HIGH-DENSITY N-CHANNEL, SILICON-GATE)

8-BIT MICROPROCESSING UNIT

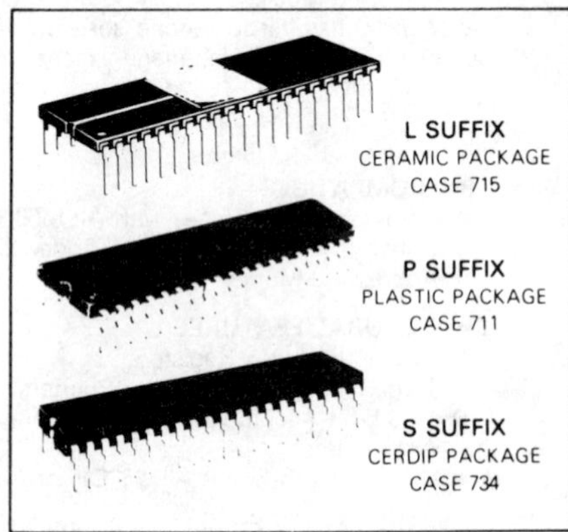

L SUFFIX
CERAMIC PACKAGE
CASE 715

P SUFFIX
PLASTIC PACKAGE
CASE 711

S SUFFIX
CERDIP PACKAGE
CASE 734

8-BIT MICROPROCESSING UNIT

The MC6809E is a revolutionary high performance 8-bit microprocessor which supports modern programming techniques such as position independence, reentrancy, and modular programming.

This third-generation addition to the M6800 family has major architectural improvements which include additional registers, instructions and addressing modes.

The basic instructions of any computer are greatly enhanced by the presence of powerful addressing modes. The MC6809E has the most complete set of addressing modes available on any 8-bit microprocessor today.

The MC6809E has hardware and software features which make it an ideal processor for higher level language execution or standard controller applications. External clock inputs are provided to allow synchronization with peripherals, systems or other MPUs.

MC6800 COMPATIBLE
- Hardware – Interfaces with All M6800 Peripherals
- Software – Upward Source Code Compatible Instruction Set and Addressing Modes

ARCHITECTURAL FEATURES
- Two 16-bit Index Registers
- Two 16-bit Indexable Stack Pointers
- Two 8-bit Accumulators can be Concatenated to Form One 16-Bit Accumulator
- Direct Page Register Allows Direct Addressing Throughout Memory

HARDWARE FEATURES
- External Clock Inputs, E and Q, Allow Synchronization
- TSC Input Controls Internal Bus Buffers
- LIC Indicates Opcode Fetch
- AVMA Allows Efficient Use of Common Resources in A Multiprocessor System
- BUSY is a Status Line for Multiprocessing
- Fast Interrupt Request Input Stacks Only Condition Code Register and Program Counter
- Interrupt Acknowledge Output Allows Vectoring By Devices
- SYNC Acknowledge Output Allows for Synchronization to External Event
- Single Bus-Cycle $\overline{\text{RESET}}$
- Single 5-Volt Supply Operation
- $\overline{\text{NMI}}$ Inhibited After $\overline{\text{RESET}}$ Until After First Load of Stack Pointer
- Early Address Valid Allows Use With Slower Memories
- Early Write-Data for Dynamic Memories

SOFTWARE FEATURES
- 10 Addressing Modes
  - M6800 Upward Compatible Addressing Modes
  - Direct Addressing Anywhere in Memory Map
  - Long Relative Branches
  - Program Counter Relative
  - True Indirect Addressing
  - Expanded Indexed Addressing:
    0, 5, 8, or 16-bit Constant Offsets
    8, or 16-bit Accumulator Offsets
    Auto-Increment/Decrement by 1 or 2
- Improved Stack Manipulation
- 1464 Instruction with Unique Addressing Modes
- 8 × 8 Unsigned Multiply
- 16-bit Arithmetic
- Transfer/Exchange All Registers
- Push/Pull Any Registers or Any Set of Registers
- Load Effective Address

FIGURE 1 — PIN ASSIGNMENT

Signal	Pin	Pin	Signal
V_{SS}	1	40	$\overline{\text{HALT}}$
$\overline{\text{NMI}}$	2	39	TSC
$\overline{\text{IRQ}}$	3	38	LIC
$\overline{\text{FIRQ}}$	4	37	$\overline{\text{RESET}}$
BS	5	36	AVMA
BA	6	35	Q
V_{CC}	7	34	E
A0	8	33	BUSY
A1	9	32	R/$\overline{\text{W}}$
A2	10	31	D0
A3	11	30	D1
A4	12	29	D2
A5	13	28	D3
A6	14	27	D4
A7	15	26	D5
A8	16	25	D6
A9	17	24	D7
A10	18	23	A15
A11	19	22	A14
A12	20	21	A13

DS9846
(Replaces ADI-847)

Advance Information

MC68000L4 (4 MHz) MC68000L6 (6 MHz) MC68000L8 (8 MHz) MC68000L10 (10 MHz)

16-BIT MICROPROCESSING UNIT

Advances in semiconductor technology have provided the capability to place on a single silicon chip a microprocessor at least an order of magnitude higher in performance and circuit complexity than has been previously available. The MC68000 is the first of a family of such VLSI microprocessors from Motorola. It combines state-of-the-art technology and advanced circuit design techniques with computer sciences to achieve an architecturally advanced 16-bit microprocessor.

The resources available to the MC68000 user consist of the following:

- 32-Bit Data and Address Registers
- 16 Megabyte Direct Addressing Range
- 56 Powerful Instruction Types
- Operations on Five Main Data Types
- Memory Mapped I/O
- 14 Addressing Modes

As shown in the programming model, the MC68000 offers seventeen 32-bit registers in addition to the 32-bit program counter and a 16-bit status register. The first eight registers (D0-D7) are used as data registers for byte (8-bit), word (16-bit), and long word (32-bit) data operations. The second set of seven registers (A0-A6) and the system stack pointer may be used as software stack pointers and base address registers. In addition, these registers may be used for word and long word address operations. All seventeen registers may be used as index registers.

HMOS
(HIGH-DENSITY, N-CHANNEL, SILICON-GATE DEPLETION LOAD)

16-BIT MICROPROCESSOR

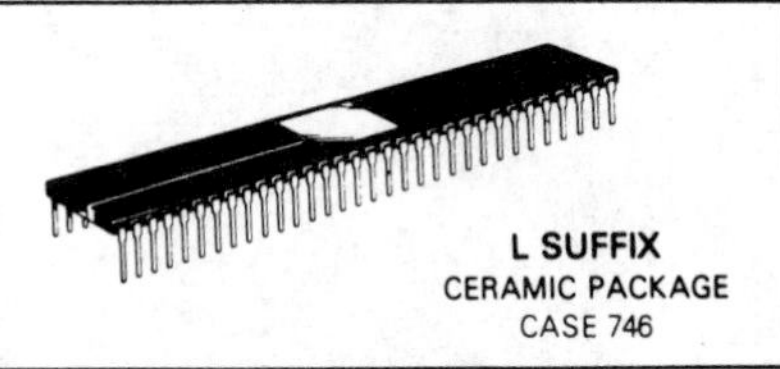

L SUFFIX
CERAMIC PACKAGE
CASE 746

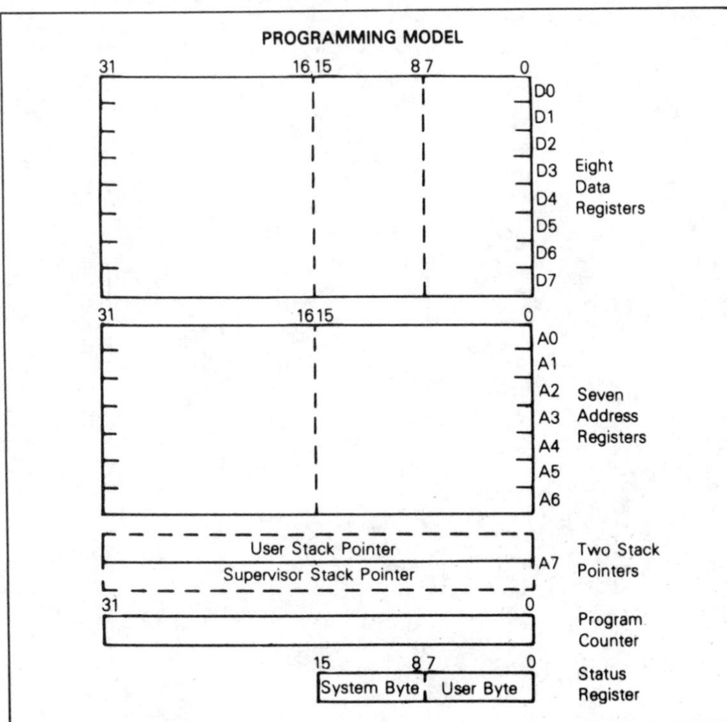

PIN ASSIGNMENT

Signal	Pin	Pin	Signal
D4	1	64	D5
D3	2	63	D6
D2	3	62	D7
D1	4	61	D8
D0	5	60	D9
$\overline{AS}$	6	59	D10
$\overline{UDS}$	7	58	D11
$\overline{LDS}$	8	57	D12
R/$\overline{W}$	9	56	D13
$\overline{DTACK}$	10	55	D14
$\overline{BG}$	11	54	D15
$\overline{BGACK}$	12	53	GND
$\overline{BR}$	13	52	A23
V_{CC}	14	51	A22
CLK	15	50	A21
GND	16	49	V_{CC}
$\overline{HALT}$	17	48	A20
$\overline{RESET}$	18	47	A19
$\overline{VMA}$	19	46	A18
E	20	45	A17
$\overline{VPA}$	21	44	A16
$\overline{BERR}$	22	43	A15
$\overline{IPL2}$	23	42	A14
$\overline{IPL1}$	24	41	A13
$\overline{IPL0}$	25	40	A12
FC2	26	39	A11
FC1	27	38	A10
FC0	28	37	A9
A1	29	36	A8
A2	30	35	A7
A3	31	34	A6
A4	32	33	A5

This document contains information on a new product. Specifications and information herein are subject to change without notice.

ADI-814R2

INDEX

A

B

C

D

E

F

H

I

J

K

M

N

O

P

Q

R

S